FULL-LENGTH PORTRAIT OF BURNS
by Alexander Nasmyth, painted in 1828
by courtesy of the National Galleries of Scotland, Edinburgh

The Complete Works of Robert Burns

The
Complete Works
of
ROBERT
BURNS

Edited and Introduced by
JAMES A. MACKAY

The Official Bicentenary Edition
authorised by
THE BURNS FEDERATION

Alloway Publishing Ltd., Ayrshire.

First Published, July 1986
Reprinted, October 1986
Reprinted, October 1987

ISBN 0-907526-23-3

Alloway Publishing
AYR

Printed and bound in Scotland
Design and Printing
Walker & Connell Ltd., Darvel, Ayrshire.
Bell & Bain Ltd., Thornliebank, Glasgow.

Binding
Hunter & Foulis Ltd., Edinburgh.

Paper
Inveresk Paper Mills, Fife.

CONTENTS

The cover and title page reproduce the Silhouette of Burns by John Miers, 1787.

To
Katie Elizabeth

PREFACE

This edition of the poems of Robert Burns is intended as a tribute to Scotland's national bard, the poet of humanity and all mankind, in celebration of the bicentenary of *Poems, Chiefly in the Scottish Dialect* published at Kilmarnock in July 1786. This, in itself, was a major landmark in Scottish literary history. In the two hundred years since then the poems of Burns have been produced in countless editions in almost forty different languages. Burns ranks not only as one of the world's greatest poets of all time, but as probably the only major British poet whose appeal is universal down to the present day. No one else has conveyed the full gamut of human feeling so tenderly or movingly in poetry as Burns, so that his work has an immediate appeal to people in all classes of society, in every part of the world.

It has been estimated that ten new editions of Burns have appeared for every year since 1786, so why should we add to that number? For some time now the Burns Federation has felt the want of an authoritative and comprehensive single-volume edition which fully meets the requirements of the present day. The initial proposal that the Federation undertake such a publication was made by Charles Kennedy of the Bowhill People's Burns Club, and I am indebted to Archie MacArthur of Kelso Burns Club for the invaluable suggestion that we emulate Burns himself and adopt the advance subscription method of raising the money to finance such an undertaking. I owe a very great deal of encouragement to D. Wilson Ogilvie, Convener of the Literature Committee of the Burns Federation. Above all else, however, this book owes everything to the enthusiasm, drive and energy of John Inglis, President of the Burns Federation (1984-85) who has done so much to ensure its success at a practical level.

Of all the editions of Burns which I have consulted in the compilation of this work, one towers head and shoulders above all the others. I refer, of course, to the magnificent three-volume work by the late Professor James Kinsley (Oxford, 1968). He and his predecessor, Professor Dewar, laboured for more than forty years to produce what will be for all time *the* definitive edition of the *Poems*. Like every other labourer in this field in the past seventeen years, my debt to James Kinsley is enormous. I must also express my indebtedness to Maurice Lindsay, whose *Burns Encyclopedia* (3rd Edition 1980) has been my constant companion and *vade mecum* ever since it was published. I have also had a great deal of help and advice from Professor G. Ross Roy of Columbia University, South Carolina, whose own contribution to Burns literature, the revised edition of *The Letters of Robert Burns,* was published in two volumes at Oxford in 1985. Nearer home, I owe a great debt to Alistair Cowper and the staff of the Ewart Library, Dumfries, to William Anderson and the staff of the Dick Institute, Kilmarnock, and to the personnel of the Mitchell Library, Glasgow and the British Library, London. Rita Turner of the Burns Federation has given me constant support at a practical level. Last, but by no means least, I must express my heart-felt thanks to my wife Joyce, who not only has been an immense help to me throughout this project, but also assisted with the proof-reading and compiled the alphabetical listing of Subscribers — no mean feat in itself.

The poems and songs have been arranged in broadly chronological order, and therefore follow to a very large extent the order used by Professor Kinsley. I have had the temerity to differ from him in certain respects, however, and have placed some of the undated works in what I felt was more proper chronological sequence, rather than relegate them to the end as Kinsley has done. Brief head-notes have been provided in the majority of cases to explain the circumstances or events alluded to in the poems, while a marginal gloss of archaic or dialect words has been inserted so that the meaning of the poems will be immediately apparent, without the problem of constantly consulting the glossary at the end of the volume.

Robert Burns, arguably one of the ten greatest poets of the world, was born in 1759 in the hamlet of Alloway, near Ayr, in 'an auld clay biggin', a cottage which had been built by his father's own hand. William Burnes, a descendant of the Campbells of Burnhouse who had been displaced in the aftermath of the 1715 rebellion, was born at Dunnottar, Kincardineshire, in 1721. Poverty forced him to leave his native district and move south, first to Edinburgh (1748) and then across country to Ayrshire two years later. He found employment as a gardener, but subsequently took a lease on seven acres in Alloway where he married a local girl, Agnes Broun. Robert, the future poet, was the eldest of the seven children — four boys and three girls — born between 1759 and 1771. Remarkably for that time, John, who died in his sixteenth year, was the only member of the family who did not reach maturity.

For the first few years of Robert's life his father continued to work as head gardener at Doonholm, the estate of Dr William Ferguson, Provost of Ayr, while trying to make a go of his seven acres as a nurseryman. By 1765, however, the cottage at Alloway was becoming too cramped for the growing family and Burnes obtained a lease on the farm of Mount Oliphant two miles away. Provost Ferguson granted him a twelve-year lease and even lent him £100 to buy stock; but the farm turned out to be unproductive despite unremitting toil. Burnes laboured at Mount Oliphant for more than a decade before giving up the struggle and moving to Lochlie, near Tarbolton. Here he fared no better; he fell into arrears with his rent and incurred the worry of prolonged litigation. Although Burnes eventually won his appeal to the Court of Session in January 1784, and paid in the balance of the rent which had been set against his own expenses in improvements, he died on 13th February 1784 of 'a phthisical consumption', worn out by physical hardship.

Burnes seems to have been not untypical of his class and his time. His overriding ambition was to ensure that this children fared better in life than he had done, and he regarded their education as top priority. He combined with some neighbours to hire John Murdoch as a teacher. The formal education which Robert and his brother Gilbert received may not have been as long as could have been wished, but one cannot over-estimate its quality. Given the small number of pupils he had to teach, Murdoch seems to have been just the man to recognise an exceptionally high level of intelligence. 'I was a good deal noted for a retentive memory', wrote Burns to Dr Moore years later, 'Though I cost the schoolmaster some thrashings, I made an excellent English scholar; and against the years of ten or eleven, I was absolutely a Critic in substantives, verbs and particles.'

Burns also acknowledged the immense debt he owed to 'an old Maid of my Mother's, remarkable for her ignorance, credulity and superstition', from whom he derived his life-long interest in folklore and traditional ballads. Indeed, his pre-eminence as a poet has tended to overshadow his importance as a folklorist and song-collector. Later, William Burnes undertook to complete his sons' education personally. Another mark of the poet's high intelligence was his voracious appetite for books. The quantity and diversity of his reading matter would be outstanding in any age, but against the harsh background of an agricultural labourer in the late eighteenth century it seems well-nigh incredible. He devoured Shakespeare, Pope and Smollett, he studied world geography, theology, philosophy, political economy, biblical history and, above all, read contemporary novels and volumes of poetry: 'I pored over them, driving my cart or walking to labor, song by song, verse by verse; carefully noting the true tender or sublime from affectation and fustian. I am convinced I owe much to this for my critic-craft such as it is.' He became fluent in French and acquired a smattering of Latin. In his sixteenth summer he studied mensuration, surveying, geometry and trigonometry under Hugh Rodger. Later he would study physics, astronomy, botany and anthropology, heraldry and music. Far from being the 'Heaven-taught ploughman' as Edinburgh society lionised him, he was something of a polymath in the best Renaissance tradition.

Scottish society, both in the rural areas and in the 'lands' (tenements) of Edinburgh, was far more egalitarian in the eighteenth century than it is today — at least in so far as it brought old and young of all classes of society into close proximity. 'My social disposition', he wrote to Moore, 'when not checked by some modification of spited pride . . . . was without bounds or limits.' He formed close associations with many youngsters drawn from the ranks of the nobility and gentry. 'It takes a few dashes into the world to give the young Great man that proper, decent, unnoticing disregard for the poor, insignificant, stupid devils, the mechanics and peasantry around him; who were perhaps born in the same village.' Though they might outrank him, according to their inherited station in life, Burns seems to have been conscious of his own innate superiority to them, intellectually. It is not surprising that the young Robert should resentfully question the nature of things which doomed him to penury and hardship, while others, by virtue of rank, wealth and privilege, enjoyed a far better life than they deserved.

This inculcated a highly developed introspection on the one hand, and on the other, constant questioning, criticism and appraisal of society, religion and moral values. While William Burnes lived, he managed to curb the restlessness and soaring ambition of his exceptionally gifted son. Inevitably there were frequent clashes of personality; as, for example, when Robert attended a country dancing school 'to give my manners a brush'. To Moore he later confided, 'My father . . . . was the sport of strong passions: from that instance of rebellion he took a kind of dislike to me, which, I believe, was one cause of that dissipation which marked my future years.'

He hastened to add, however, that he used the term dissipation only in a sense relative to the strictness and sobriety of Presbyterian country life. His early ambitions were blind and aimless. He perceived that his father's situation condemned him to a life of perpetual drudgery. Only 'the most niggardly economy, or the little chicaning art of bargain-making' offered any escape to fortune, and neither alternative appealed to him. He confessed that a strong appetite for sociability 'as well from native hilarity as from a pride of observation and remark, a reputation for bookish knowledge, a certain wild, logical talent, and a strength of thought something like the rudiments of good sense, made me generally a welcome guest.'

In addition to this restlessness and as yet ill-defined ambition to make something of himself, and his pleasure in congenial company, there was an intensely passionate nature which remained with him to his dying day. 'My heart was completely tinder, and was eternally lighted up by some Goddess or other; and like every warfare in this world, I was sometimes crowned with success, and sometimes mortified with defeat.' Gilbert Burns later wrote that his brother frequently turned to *The Rudiments of the Latin Tongue* 'on any little chagrin or disappointment, particularly in his love affairs; but the Latin seldom predominated more than a day or two at a time, or a week at most.' We must suppose that the disappointments in affairs of the heart were of similarly short duration.

Gilbert, who, presumably, knew his brother better than most, and was his equal in intelligence if not in those indefinable qualities that compose genius, has left us a most perceptive description of him:

'The seven years we lived in Tarbolton parish (1777-85) were not marked by much literary improvement; but, during this time, the foundation was laid of certain habits in my brother's character, which afterwards became but too prominent, and which malice and envy have taken delight to enlarge on. Though when young he was bashful and awkward in his intercourse with women, yet when he approached manhood, his attachment to their society became very strong, and he was constantly the victim of some fair enslaver . . . I never indeed knew that he fainted, sunk and died away: but the agitation of his mind and body exceeded anything of the kind I ever knew in real life. He had always a particular jealousy over people who were richer than himself, or who had more consequence in life. His love, therefore, rarely settled on persons of this description. When he selected any one out of the sovereignty of his good pleasure to whom he should pay his particular attention, she was instantly invested with a sufficient stock of charms, out of the plentiful stores of his own imagination; and there was often a great disparity between his fair captivator, and her attributes.' Robert himself endorsed this view, in his description of Richard Brown: 'the only man I ever saw who was a greater fool than myself when woman was the presiding star'.

Interestingly, Gilbert continues to elaborate that this was largely an intellectual passion, governed by the strictest rules of virtue and modesty from which he never deviated till his 23rd year. The change was undoubtedly brought by the death of William Burnes in February 1784. The death of his much respected, but strict father, freed Robert in more ways than one. Whatever caution may have existed in his amorous adventures previously was now thrown to the winds. By the autumn of that year Elizabeth Paton, a servant who had helped at Lochlie while William Burnes was dying, was pregnant by Robert. A year later she was supplanted in his affections by Jean Armour, daughter of a master mason in Mauchline, and she, too, succumbed to his charms. Burns was hailed before the Kirk Session and his reaction to the humiliation and degradation of kirk penitence expressed itself in those brilliant but savage satires on Auld Licht Calvinism 'The Holy Fair' and 'Holy Willie's Prayer'.

There was, however, a very strong Calvinistic streak in Robert himself, which balanced each bout of dissipation with severe pangs of remorse, bordering on mental and physical distress. These phenomena are by no means uncommon in puritanical or repressive societies, inducing in many either fits of conscience or morbid religiosity, while others seek consolation in alcohol. In Robert's case consolation and alleviation of symptoms were to be found in poetical composition. He had first discovered a facility for poetry in his sixteenth year, emboldened by the example of 'a small country laird's son' who had composed a song on one of his father's maids, and inspired by Nellie Kilpatrick, his fourteen-year-old partner in the harvest. 'Thus with me began Love and Poesy; which at times have been my only, and till this last twelve month [1786-7] have been my highest enjoyment.' Writing poetry became for him both an escape from the mundane world and, in a sense, an expiation of his shortcomings. Versifying provided the safety-valve which a person of his temperament sorely needed. The years 1784-85 were tumultuous ones for Burns, and his poetic output reflects this.

At the same time, he discovered the poetry of Robert Fergusson, who had died ten years earlier in an Edinburgh mad-house at the tragically early age of 24. Burns immediately identified with Fergusson.

'. . . my elder brother in misfortune,
By far my elder brother in the muse'

Fergusson was, in turn, the direct poetic descendant of Allan Ramsay. Both poets played a major part in shaping Burns's outlook and their poems served as models in the perfection of his own craft. The verse epistle, which Ramsay had considerably developed, and above all, the six-line stanza known as Standart Habby, invented by Sempill but used to great effect by both Ramsay and Fergusson, left their indelible mark on Burns's earlier work. When he came to select poems for his first published volume, Burns included no fewer than seven verse epistles and fifteen poems in Standart Habby. In the ensuing decade he was to experiment with other verse forms, but always returned to the six-line stanza. He gave to it an incredible degree of fluency and spontaneity that ever afterwards marked it out as Burnsian metre. The deceptive artlessness of this verse form, however, has duped generations of poetasters and doggerel-rhymers into thinking that they could emulate the Master; but it was a peculiar mark of Burns's genius that he could take what is essentially a difficult and tricky verse-form and make it seem so simple.

Poetry became for Burns a diversion, a recreation, an opiate from a harsh world, an intellectual exercise and eventually a natural medium of expression that permeated his whole being. In his autobiographical letter to Dr Moore he wrote: 'I now began to be known in the neighbourhood as a maker of rhymes. The first of my poetic offspring that saw the light was a burlesque lamentation on a quarrel between two revd Calvinists both of them dramatis person in my Holy Fair. I had an idea myself that the piece had some merit; but to prevent the worst, I gave a copy of it to a friend who was very fond of these things, and told him I could not guess who was the Author of it, but that I thought it pretty clever.'

He then went on to allude to 'my idle wanderings' which drew down upon his head the wrath of the Kirk. 'Twas a shocking affair, which I cannot yet bear to recollect' is how he refers (less than two years later) to his courtship of Jean Armour in 1785 and her consequent pregnancy. The reaction of her family was nothing if not dramatic. Once James Armour had recovered his composure he mutilated the document which constituted a marriage contract, banished his wayward daughter to her relatives in Paisley, and took out a writ against the luckless Robert. 'I gave up my part of the farm Mossgiel to my brother, as in truth it was only nominally mine; and made what little preparation was in my power for Jamaica. Before leaving my native country for ever, I resolved to publish my Poems. I weighed my productions as impartially as in my power; I thought they had merit; and 'twas a delicious idea that I would be called a clever fellow, even though it should never reach my ears a poor Negro-driver, or perhaps a victim to that inhospitable clime gone to the world of Spirits.'

This light, somewhat self-deprecatory, account conceals the anguish and mortification which Burns must have felt when Jean repudiated him and he was hounded by her father. Inevitably he turned elsewhere for consolation, hence the curious episode with Mary Campbell, terminated abruptly by her death in the autumn of 1786. On a more constructive note, however, Robert was advised by his friend Gavin Hamilton to publish his poems as a means of raising the money for his passage to the West Indies. The idea of seeing his words in 'guid black prent' appealed to Burns, as a gesture of defiance against a world that had treated him harshly. *Poems, Chiefly in the Scottish Dialect* was published by John Wilson at Kilmarnock at the end of July 1786 in an edition of 612 copies, priced three shillings.

It is difficult for us, at this remove in time, to appreciate what a landmark this must have been in Scottish literature, or its impact at the time, although Robert Heron's memoir of Burns describes it vividly:

'Old and young, high and low, grave and gay, learned or ignorant, all were alike delighted, agitated, transported. I was at that time resident in Galloway contiguous to Ayrshire, and I can well remember, how that even the plough-boys and maid-servants would have gladly bestowed their wages which they earned the most hardly, and which they wanted to purchase the necessary clothing . . . '

15

By this venture Burns made a modest profit of £20. Soon ideas of emigration vanished, and he began planning a second edition. Wilson declined, possibly on the grounds that there might be only limited further sales in the southwest of Scotland, but Burns had the bit between his teeth and, nothing daunted, set out for Edinburgh, armed only with a good conceit of himself and a few introductions which, as he had hoped, soon opened the doors of Scotland's polite society to him. Burns's change of plans was in large measure dictated by the very favourable response to his poems in a letter written by Dr Blacklock to the Rev. Dr George Lawrie who had sent him a copy. Lawrie sent this letter to Gavin Hamilton, who showed it to Burns. As he put it in his letter to Moore:

'I had taken the last farewell of my new friends; my chest was on the road to Greenock; I had composed my last song I should ever measure in Caledonia, "The gloomy night is gathering fast", when a letter from Dr Blacklock to a friend of mine overthrew all my schemes by rousing my poetic ambition. The Doctor belonged to a set of Critics for whose applause I had not even dared to hope. His idea that I would meet with every encouragement for a second edition fired me so much that away I posted to Edinburgh without a single acquaintance in town, or a single letter of introduction in my pocket.'

The Ploughman Poet was lionised and patronised by Edinburgh society, and Burns was astute enough to play up to the role which the Establishment had created for him. His sojourn in Edinburgh paid handsome dividends. The immediate result was the first Edinburgh Edition, a greatly expanded volume containing some new works and several earlier pieces which he had deemed it prudent to omit from the Kilmarnock Edition. It has been estimated that he netted over £850 from this venture, including the sale of his copyright to Creech. As a consequence of this unwise act, however, Burns received no more than a few complimentary copies of the second Edinburgh Edition, published in February 1793 in two volumes and including for the first time the mock epic 'Tam o Shanter'. This edition was re-issued in 1794, the last edition made in the poet's own life-time.

The fame (if not the fortune) which the publication of his poems brought him unsettled Burns. At last his restless ambition found a focus; he would live up to the toast of Caledonia's Bard which had greeted him at the Grand Lodge of Scotland. He embarked on a series of tours to the Borders, Argyll, the Highlands and Stirlingshire, where he developed his interest in collecting old ballads, and considerably extended his network of useful contacts. Through one of these, Patrick Miller, he was to secure the lease of Ellisland near Dumfries; through another, Robert Graham of Fintry, he won *entrée* to the Excise service which was eventually to give him a measure of security which farming, from the bitter experience of his father, was unlikely to provide.

After several adventures of the amatory kind, interspersed by a renewal of his affair with Jean Armour — resulting in a second set of twins — he finally decided to make amends for his cavalier treatment. Later he was to describe this change of heart, in a letter of September 1788 to Peggy Chalmers. His marriage, he confessed 'was not in consequence of the attachment of romance perhaps; but I had a long and much-loved fellow creature's happiness or misery in my determination, and I durst not trifle with so important a deposit. Nor have I any cause to repent it.' At any rate Jean and Robert were privately married in the office of Gavin Hamilton, by John Gilminscroft, J.P. and set up house together, first at Mauchline and later at Ellisland.

Jean was inevitably much inferior to her husband in intellect. 'She scarcely ever in her life, except the Scriptures of the Old and New Testament and the Psalms of David in metre, spent five minutes together on either prose or verse', wrote Burns, adding 'I must except also from this last a certain late publication of Scots poems, which she has perused very devoutly.' Any intellectual shortcomings, however, were more than balanced by her sweet, generous nature. She recognised the extraordinary qualities of her temperamental husband, and willingly tolerated his quixotic nature, even to the extent of rearing his bastard daughter by Anne Park, with the comment 'Our Robbie should have had twa wives.'

Farming Ellisland was no more rewarding than his father's ventures at Mount Oliphant and Lochlie, but the Excise offered a more promising career. He began work as an exciseman in September 1789 and secured transfer to the more lucrative and less demanding Dumfries Third Division the following July. The demands of the Excise were incompatible with the labour of running a farm, though it was not until September 1791 that he finally gave up the latter and moved his family to the town of Dumfries. In February 1792 he was promoted to the Dumfries Port Division, with a substantial increase in salary and perquisites. Much has been made lately of Burns's rapid advancement in the Excise and charges of string-pulling have even been made; but whatever pressure Burns may have been able to exert in his own behalf, with Graham of Fintry, was no more and a great deal less than the common practice of the time. It is perhaps worth noting that, only a generation later, William Wordsworth was rewarded with the Distributorship of Stamps for Westmorland, a virtual sinecure that netted him ten times the money for which Burns had to work long and hard.

The other side of the coin is the immense debt which succeeding generations owe to Burns, not only in respect of his own poetry, for which he earned remarkably little in his lifetime, but for his Herculean labours as a collector, preserver and mender of old ballads. The last five years of his life were largely devoted to this work which he regarded as a service to his native land and resolutely refused to accept any payment from either James Johnson or George Thomson. There were song-collectors before his time and there have been many since; but no one else possessed Burns's unique flair for combining the antiquarian element with his own creative genius. Many of the songs he salvaged were little more than fragments, sometimes no more than a title and a chorus; others survived only as bawdy ballads which he sanitized or clothed in entirely new words. Over 300 songs were mended, revised, transformed or wholly re-written by Burns during this period. At the same time he expanded his poetic range, experimenting with sonnets and elegiac pieces composed in the Augustan English which was then so fashionable; but his power is seen at its best in that great mock epic 'Tam o Shanter', based on a folk legend and drawing upon Burns's immense storehouse of country lore.

The image of Burns best known to the world at large is the bust painted by Alexander Nasmyth in 1787, later engraved by John Beugo and much reproduced and copied in the past two centuries. Like the poet's reputation in the same period, it has tended to become a stereotype — instantly recognisable, but is it true to life? The same may be said of the chalk drawing which Archibald Skirving produced some time after the poet's death — a much-loved image but a heavily romanticised one. Truer to life are Nasmyth's full-length portrait, showing a hatted Burns, and the profile miniature painted by Alexander Reid in the early summer of 1795. Probably the best likeness of all is the bust by an unknown painter, the so-called Swinton portrait which belonged to Agnes Burnes, the poet's mother. This is the strongest and most rustic of the contemporary likenesses — poles apart from the delicacy — refined almost to the point of effeminacy — of the Beugo engraving and its later derivatives.

Fortunately there is an abundance of contemporary eye-witness accounts of Burns to augment the pictorial likenesses. Dugald Stewart first met Burns on 23rd October 1786. ' . . . His manners were then, as they continued ever afterwards, simple, manly, and independent; strongly expressive of conscious genius and worth; but without any thing that indicated forwardness, arrogance or vanity . . . If there had been a little more of gentleness and accommodation in his temper, he would, I think, have been still more interesting; but he had been accustomed to give law in the circle of his ordinary acquaintance, and his dread of any thing approaching to meanness or servility, rendered his manner somewhat decided and hard. Nothing perhaps was more remarkable among his various attainments, than the fluency, and precision, and originality of his language, when he spoke in company; more particularly as he aimed at purity in his turn of expression, and avoided more successfully than most Scotchmen, the peculiarities of Scottish phraseology . . . All the faculties of Burns' mind were, as far as I could judge, equally vigorous; and his predilection for poetry, was rather the result of his own enthusiastic and impassioned temper, than of a genius exclusively adapted to that species of composition . . . ' Stewart later added that if Burns had an affection in anything it was in his habit of peppering his conversation with French words and phrases!

Robert Anderson, who first met Burns in the house of David Ramsay, printer of the Edinburgh *Courant,* wrote to Dr Currie in 1799: 'I was struck with his appearance, so different from what I had expected in an uneducated rustic. His person, though neither robust nor elegant, was manly and pleasing; and his countenance, though dark and coarse, uncommonly expressive and interesting . . . He wore his hair, which was black and thin, in a queue, without powder. Such was Burns, as he stood before me on the floor when I entered the drawing-room. His behaviour was suitable to his appearance; neither awkward, arrogant, nor affected, but decent, dignified and simple. In the midst of a large company of ladies and gentlemen assembled to see him, and attentive to his every look, word and motion, he was no way disconcerted, but seemed perfectly easy, unembarrassed, and unassuming . . . No words can do justice to the captivating charms of his conversation. It was even more fascinating than his poetry. He was truly a great orator . . . he conversed on every subject in a manner that evinced the strongest marks of genius, sagacity, and acuteness, combined with the most powerful sallies of wit, sarcasm, and satire . . . In his intercourse with persons in high stations he was no sycophant; but he was always the slave of his own passions, which were powerful, ardent, and irritable in such an excessive degree as to unfit him for the commerce of life. Pride was most frequently predominant, appearing sometimes in the form of insolence and sometimes in that of resentment . . . The pride of genius or the affectation of singularity often led him wantonly to oppose received opinions, and pertinaciously to maintain the most unreasonable positions. His prejudices, personal, and religious, were strong, and misguided the rectitude of his judgment; and his temper was uncertain and capricious, being influenced by the impulse of passion or the whim of the moment . . . His morality with regard to women was lax; he transgressed the rules of sobriety openly; he was accused of ingratitude — perhaps justly, for he could not bear to conceive himself under an obligation; but his integrity was never questioned. Though proud and revengeful, he was naturally generous and compassionate; zealous in serving those he loved, and always ready to perform offices of kindness and humanity.'

All of the assessments of Burns, the majority composed shortly after his death, are tainted to some extent by the subjectivity of their writers, none more so than Henry Mackenzie, author of *The Man of Feeling* and editor of some periodicals that Burns greatly admired. Mackenzie's portrait of Burns, as published in *Anecdotes and Egotisms,* comes into the category of 'damning with faint praise' at the best of times, but at worst is a vicious exercise in character assassination. The late Dr Robert S. Gilchrist has argued very plausibly for a political motive, and detected the influence if not actually the hand of none other than Henry Dundas, the most powerful man in Scotland at the time. To Mackenzie we owe the canard about the poet's hard drinking, although even this was only a matter of hearsay which Mackenzie, while mentioning it, tended to discount: 'Dugald Stewart told me latterly, that his Conduct and Manners had become so degraded that decent persons could hardly take any notice of him. I suspect my excellent friend had been deceived by exaggerated accounts of his irregularities; and certainly his genius had not sunk with his Condition, nor lost by the taint of his manners; for it appears by the Account given of him by Mr Thomson, and his last letters to that gentleman, that the vigor of his fancy and power of Composition still remained.'

Other contemporary accounts make some reference to Burns's drinking habits. Anderson wrote ' . . . though addicted to convivial excesses, yet I never heard that he violated the rules of sobriety in private families.' There was, of course, the celebrated 'Rape of the Sabines' incident at Friars' Carse which caused a breach with the Riddell family. Less forgivable than any drunken lapse of the moment, however, was the manner in which Burns took his revenge, prostituting his poetic skills to produce such tasteless verses as 'Monody on a Lady Famed for her Caprice', the lines 'Pinned to Mrs Walter Riddell's Carriage' and that mean pastiche of Pope, 'Epistle from Esopus to Maria'. The letter to Clarinda which accompanied the 'Monody' and 'Carriage' lines also reflects more adversely on the writer than the subject, and bears out Anderson's comment about Burns's 'proud and revengeful' nature.

Gilbert Burns tried to set the record straight regarding his brother's reputation as a drinker. He was of the opinion that Robert's poems praising Scotch drink had misled his biographers. 'I do not recollect', he wrote, 'during these seven years [1779-86], nor till towards the end of his commencing author (when his growing celebrity occasioned his being often in company) to have ever seen him intoxicated; nor was he at all given to drinking.' He goes on to demonstrate quite conclusively that, in the period up to the end of 1786 at any rate, Burns never had the money to indulge such a habit. 'His temperance and frugality were everything that could be wished.'

So, too, in the last few years of his short life, when the demands of his career, in which he showed immense promise and was rewarded by accelerated promotion, and the sheer volume of his poetic output give the lie to the charges of alcoholism. As well as Henry Mackenzie, the chief architects of this canard were reformed reprobates like Robert Heron and James Currie, both of whom dwelt on this aspect to serve their own ends. Apart from the 'Sabine Women' incident, the facts tend to support the opposite view. Burns was a witness to, but certainly no participant in, the drinking contest at Friars' Carse on 16th October 1789, immortalised in his poem 'The Whistle'; and his revulsion at the drunken behaviour of the farmers who gathered for the roup of his crops at Ellisland comes across most vividly in his description of that scene. Hard drinking, then as now, is Scotland's curse. Burns was no worse than most of his contemporaries, and far better than many in this respect.

Burns was a man of startling contrasts, who could be both Jacobite and Arminian at the same time. His Jacobitism, however, was of the romantic and sentimental variety, though held no less passionately for all that, and was derived from the hardships suffered by his paternal grandfather for his support of the Earl Marischal in 1715. His Arminianism, or religious radicalism, was derived from his maternal great-grandfather, one of the Covenanters shot in the skirmish at Airds Moss. So also in politics Burns could write against or for the Whigs by turn, although his 'Election Ballad for Westerha' was really aimed against the Duke of Queensberry (whom he disliked intensely) rather than taking a particular stance; and though he supported Patrick Heron's Whig candidature in 1795 he felt uneasy at the propriety of this, as reflected in his long, self-justifying letter to Heron in March 1795. A passionate supporter of the Rights of Man and fellow exciseman, Tom Paine, he was rash enough to make a quixotic gesture of support towards the Jacobins in the early stages of the French Revolution — as witnessed by his purchase of the *Rosamond* carronades (which he could ill afford) to send to the revolutionaries; but he quickly backtracked when his Excise career might be jeopardised, and went to considerable lengths to conceal letters, poems and even an inscription on the fly-leaf of a book, which might betray his radical sentiments. For this, Burns has been accused of moral cowardice, but it is easy to criticize such recantation from the standpoint of a more liberal and enlightened age, and not so easy to comprehend the very real dangers faced by men who dared speak their minds in those repressive times.

Ramsay of Ochtertyre wrote of Burns 'I have been in the company of many men of genius, some of them poets, but never witnessed such flashes of intellectual brightness as from him, the impulse of the moment, sparks of celestial fire.' Josiah Walker described Burns's countenance as 'not of that elegant cast which is most frequent among the upper ranks, but it was manly and intelligent, and marked by a thoughtful gravity which shaded at times into sternness. In his large dark eye the most striking index of his genius resided. It was full of mind, and would have been singularly expressive, under the management of one who could employ it with more art, for the purpose of expression.'

This is confirmed in the famous description given by Sir Walter Scott, who met Burns at Sciennes House in the winter of 1786-7, when Scott was a lad of fifteen: 'There was a strong expression of sense and shrewdness in all his lineaments; the eye alone, I think, indicated the poetical character and temperament. It was large, and of a dark cast, and glowed (I say literally glowed) when he spoke with feeling or interest. I never saw such another eye in a human head, though I have seen the most distinguished men in my time.'

Burns's intensity of expression is the characteristic which seems to have impressed most of those who met him; often it was a first and lasting impression. Sir Samuel Brydges wrote: 'His dark eye had at first a character of sternness; but as he became warmed, though this did not entirely melt away, it was mingled with changes of extreme softness.' The same critic observed, 'His great beauty was his manly strength, and his energy and elevation of thought and feeling. He had always a full mind, and all flowed from a genuine spring. I never conversed with a man who appeared to be more warmly impressed with the beauties of nature; and visions of female beauty and tenderness seemed to transport him. He did not merely appear to be a poet at casual intervals; but at every moment a poetical enthusiasm seemed to beat in his veins, and he lived all his days the inward if not the outward life of a poet.'

The last word, however, should fittingly rest with Maria Riddell. She and Burns became reconciled in the last few months of his life, when paroxysmal tachycardia and deep depression daily took their toll on his weakened condition. To Maria fell the responsibility of composing the obituary notice published in the Dumfries *Journal*, and unanimously regarded as the best contemporary comment on Burns:

'It will be an injustice done to Burns's reputation in the records of literature, not only as respects future generations and foreign countries, but even with his native Scotland and some of his contemporaries, that he is generally talked of and considered with reference to his poetical talents only. In regarding Burns as something more than a Poet, it must not be supposed that I consider that title as a trivial one. . . Nevertheless I hesitate not to affirm . . . that Poetry was actually not his forte. If others have climbed more successfully the heights of Parnassus, none certainly ever outshone Burns in the charms — the sorcery I would almost call it — of fascinating conversation; the spontaneous eloquence of social argument, or the unstudied poignancy of brilliant repartee . . .

'Much indeed has been said of his inconsistency and caprice; but I am inclined to believe they originated less in a levity of sentiment, than from an extreme impetuosity of feeling which rendered him prompt to take umbrage . . . He was candid and manly in the avowal of his errors, and his *avowal* was a *reparation*. His native *fierte* never forsaking him for a moment, the value of frank acknowledgment was enhanced tenfold towards a generous mind from its never being attended with servility . . . '

This man of high intellect, great and varied talents, of genius, and of contrasts and complexities of character, has probably been more written about — and certainly more talked about — than any other literary figure, past or present. A superb narrative poet, profound delineator of human emotions, whose soaring powers to convey the full range of feelings have touched a deeply responsive chord in the heart of all mankind, Burns was also a belletrist of outstanding range and quality, evinced in the latest edition of his correspondence, recently revised by Ross Roy. It is, of course, idle to speculate what might have been, had he not died in his 38th year, at an age when most men have not yet attained their peak. He might have risen to high office in government service, perhaps even entered the political arena for which he was so well equipped, or diversified into prose and drama as well as continuing to develop his poetic skills. What we have, however, is a legacy of outstanding importance to world literature, transcending both the time and place of their creation. Truly is Robert Burns a great poet for all time.

ROBERT BURNS
1759-1796

1757	William Burnes (1721-84) tenant-farmer of Alloway, marries Agnes Broun (1732-1820) of Craigenton, Maybole.
1759	25th January. Robert Burns born at Alloway.
1760	28th September. Gilbert Burns born. Later children: Agnes (1762-1834), Annabella (1764-1832, William (1767-90), John (1769-85) and Isabella (1771-1858).
1765	Robert and Gilbert taught by John Murdoch (1747-1824), engaged by William Burnes and four neighbours; a three-year period of formal and intensive education.
1766	William Burnes moves to Mount Oliphant, a 70-acre farm (£40 annual rent) near Alloway.
1768	Murdoch leaves Alloway; William Burnes continues his sons' education himself.
1772	Robert and Gilbert attend Dalrymple school, week about, during the summer quarter.
1773	Murdoch now at Ayr. Robert has three weeks' tuition in English grammar, French and some Latin, and is introduced to the poetry of Alexander Pope.
1774	Despite hard times at Mount Oliphant, Burns writes his first song, 'Handsome Nell', for Nellie Kilpatrick.
1775	Burns studies mathematics under Hugh Rodger at Kirkoswald.
1777	Whitsun. The Burnes family move to Lochlie, Tarbolton, 130 acres at an annual rent of £130. Burns now a voracious reader and student of all manner of subjects. Burns attends a dancing class in Tarbolton 'to give my manners a brush' — the beginning of a period of antipathy between father and son, ' . . . one cause of the dissipation which marked my future years'.
1780	The Tarbolton Bachelors' Club formed by Burns and six others.
1781	Burns courts Alison Begbie. Dispute between Burnes and his landlord, David MacLure, begins. Spring. Burns goes to Irvine to learn the trade of flax-dressing. 4th July. Burns inducted into St David's Lodge, No. 174, Tarbolton; passed and raised in the same lodge on 1st October.
1782	1st January. The flax shop in the Glasgow Vennel, Irvine 'burnt to ashes and left me, like a true poet, not worth a sixpence'. Burns returns to Lochlie. *Tristram Shandy* and *The Man of Feeling* his favourite reading matter. Interest in poetic composition developing. 24th September. Dispute between Burnes and MacLure referred to arbiters.
1783	16th January. Burns awarded £3 prize for linseed growing. April. Burns begins his first Commonplace Book (1CPB). 17th May. Burnes's financial difficulties culminate in a writ of sequestration. 18th August. The 'Oversman' reports in favour of Burnes. 25th August. Burnes makes his first appeal to the Court of Session.

	Autumn. Robert and Gilbert secretly arrange to lease Mossgiel, 118 acres at £90 a year, from Gavin Hamilton 'as an asylum for the family in case of the worst.'
1784	27th January. Court of Session upholds William Burnes.
	13th February. William Burnes dies.
	March. Burns and his family move into Mossgiel, about three miles from Lochlie, in Mauchline parish.
	27th July. Burns elected Depute Master of St James's Lodge Kilwinning, Tarbolton.
1785	April. Race Week. Burns first meets Jean Armour at a dance in Mauchline.
	22nd May. Birth of Elizabeth, the poet's daughter by Elizabeth Paton.
	September. Burns 'attests' his marriage to Jean Armour.
	October. John, the poet's youngest brother, dies. Burns finishes his first Commonplace Book.
1786	March. James Armour, master-mason of Mauchline, faints on learning of his daughter's pregnancy. Burns repudiated by the Armour family and marriage attestation mutilated. Burns contemplates emigration to Jamaica, but plans to publish his poems first.
	3rd April. Proposals for the Kilmarnock Edition sent to the printer; published eleven days later.
	23rd April. James Armour repudiates Burns as a son-in-law; Jean sent off to relatives in Paisley. Burns takes up with Mary Campbell, dairymaid at Coilsfield.
	14th May. Burns and Mary meet for the last time at Failford, exchange 'matrimonial vows' and part to make their respective arrangements to emigrate.
	June. Copy for the Kilmarnock Edition sent to John Wilson.
	10th June. Jean Armour confesses by letter to the Kirk Session, that she is pregnant by Robert Burns.
	25th June. Burns appears before the Kirk Session. In July and August he makes the requisite three appearances before the congregation and gets his certificate from 'Daddy' Auld.
	22nd July. Robert transfers his share of Mossgiel to Gilbert.
	30th July. Burns goes into hiding, after Jean Armour gets a writ 'to throw me in jail till I find security for an enormous sum . . . and I am wandering from one friend's house to another.'
	31st July. *Poems, Chiefly in the Scottish Dialect* published at Kilmarnock, price 3s.
	6th August. Last penitential appearance before the Mauchline congregation.
	1st September. Voyage to Jamaica first postponed.
	3rd September. Jean Armour gives birth to twins, christened Robert and Jean.
	27th September. Voyage to Jamaica again postponed; Burns planning a second edition.

October. Mary Campbell dies at Greenock, possibly in premature childbirth induced by typhus. Burns now abandons all plans to emigrate, and first considers the Excise as a career.

15th November. Correspondence with Mrs Dunlop of Dunlop begins.

27th November. Burns sets out for Edinburgh, arriving there two days later.

1st December. Elizabeth Paton accepts Burns's settlement of her claim.

9th December. Henry Mackenzie praises the Kilmarnock *Poems*, reviewed in *The Lounger*.

14th December. William Creech issues proposals for the second (first Edinburgh) edition of the *Poems*.

1787   7th January. Burns forms an association 'with a very pretty girl, a Lothian farmer's daughter, whom I have almost persuaded to accompany me to the west country.'

13th January. The Grand Lodge of Scotland toasts Burns as 'Caledonia's Bard'.

14th January. Patrick Miller of Dalswinton discusses with Burns the possible lease of a farm near Dumfries.

6th February. Burns writes to the Bailies of the Canongate seeking permission to erect a memorial to Robert Fergusson 'my elder brother in misfortune'.

22nd March. Burns completes the proof-reading of the first Edinburgh Edition and plans 'to make leisurely pilgrimages through Caledonia'.

9th April. Second Commonplace Book (2 CPB) begun.

17th April. First Edinburgh Edition published.

23rd April. Burns sells his copyright to Creech for 100 guineas.

5th May — 1st June. Burns tours the Borders with Robert Ainslie.

22nd May. First volume of *Scots Musical Museum* (SMM) published by James Johnson.

2nd June. Burns receives May Cameron's letter of 26th May advising him of her giving birth to his child. Burns writes to Ainslie: 'send for the wench and give her ten or twelve shillings . . . and advise her out to some country friends'.

4th June. Burns made an Honorary Burgess of Dumfries.

8th June. Burns returns *éclatant* to Mauchline.

late June. Burns makes a tour of the West Highlands, as far as Inveraray.

2nd August. Autobiographical letter to Dr John Moore.

8th August. Burns returns to Edinburgh.

15th August. Burns freed of writ *in meditatione fugae* brought by May Cameron.

25th August. Burns begins his Highland tour with William Nicol.

16th September. Burns returns to Edinburgh, via Queensferry at the end of his tour.

4th October. Burns begins a tour of Stirlingshire with Dr Adair.
20th October. Burns again in Edinburgh. The poet's infant daughter Jean dies. Burns takes up residence with William Cruickshank in St James's Square. First London edition of the *Poems* published.
November. Burns begins serious collaboration with Johnson in *The Scots Musical Museum*. Burns meets Patrick Miller at Dalswinton to discuss the lease of a farm, before returning to Edinburgh.
4th December. Burns meets Mrs Agnes McLehose ('Clarinda').
7th December. Burns dislocates his knee in a carriage accident.
28th December. Correspondence between Sylvander and Clarinda begins.

1788   4th January. Burns's first visit to Clarinda at home.
7th January. Burns seeks the patronage of Graham of Fintry in the Excise.
14th February. Second volume of *Scots Musical Museum* published. Sylvander-Clarinda correspondence peaks, with four letters in two days.
18th February. Burns leaves Edinburgh for Ayrshire.
23rd February. Burns returns to Mauchline, buys Jean 'a mahogany bed' and sets up house with her. 'Farthing taper' letter to Clarinda.
27th (?) February. Burns visits Ellisland with John Tennant of Glenconner as his adviser.
3rd March. Jean Armour gives birth to twin girls who die on 10th and 22nd March. 'Horse litter' letter to Ainslie.
13th March (?). Burns returns to Edinburgh.
18th March. Burns signs the lease of Ellisland.
20th March. Burns leaves Edinburgh, and makes preparations to settle down at Ellisland (annual rent of £50).
April-May. Burns receives a course of Excise instruction at Mauchline and Tarbolton.
11th June. Burns settles at Ellisland.
14th July. Excise commission issued to Burns.
5th August. Authenticity of the marriage between Burns and Jean Armour recognised by the Rev. William Auld and Mauchline Kirk Session.
August. Friendship established between Burns and the Millers of Dalswinton and the Riddells of Friars' Carse.
September. Burns commuting between Nithsdale and Mauchline.
November. Jenny Clow, with whom Burns had had an affair in Edinburgh during his platonic friendship with Clarinda, bears him a son.
December. Jean Armour moves to Nithsdale and joins Burns in rented accommodation at the Isle.

1789   16th February. Burns in Edinburgh to settle accounts with Creech and the writ taken out against him by Jenny Clow.

27th February. Legal process with Jenny Clow settled.

28th February. Burns returns to Ellisland.

April. Burns orders a dictionary and the works of Shakespeare; plans the Monkland Friendly Society with Robert Riddell in Dunscore parish, Nithsdale.

May. Reading Adam Smith's *Wealth of Nations*. Hopes for an Excise appointment promising.

June or July. Burns meets Captain Francis Grose at Friars' Carse.

18th August. Francis Wallace Burns born.

1st September. Burns commences work as an Excise officer at a salary of £50 per annum.

October. Election for the Dumfries Burghs; Burns composes 'The Five Carlins'.

November. Burns ill with 'malignant squinancy and low fever.'

23rd December. Burns, influenced by reading Shakespeare, plans 'some thoughts of the Drama', but dreams of becoming a playwright are never realised.

1790.

January. Burns riding up to 200 miles a week on Excise duties and attempting to run a farm at the same time, but complains of 'An incessant headache, depression of spirits, and all the truly miserable consequences of a deranged nervous system . .'

27th January. Burns listed as eligible for promotion to Examiner or Supervisor or Excise.

February. Third volume of *Scots Musical Museum* published.

18th February. Inaugural meeting of subscribers of the Dumfries Theatre, of which Burns and Robert Riddell were among the chief instigators.

July. Burns transferred to the Dumfries Third Division of Excise. Burns introduces Francis Grose to Dugald Stewart.

24th July. William Burns (the poet's younger brother) dies in London.

November. Burns composes 'Tam o Shanter'; manuscript sent to Grose on 1st December.

1791

January. Burns crippled by a fall 'not from my horse, but with my horse.'

30th January. Death of the Earl of Glencairn at Falmouth, on return from Portugal.

31st March. Anne Park, barmaid of the Globe Inn, gives birth to a daughter, Elizabeth, fathered by Burns.

9th April. William Nicol Burns born.

April. 'Tam o Shanter' published in the second volume of Grose's *Antiquities of Scotland*.

27th April. Glenriddell Manuscript collection formed.

11th June. Burns intervenes on behalf of James Clark of Moffat.

17th June. The Earl of Buchan invites Burns to the coronation of Thomson's bust.

19th — 22nd June. Burns in Ayrshire, attending Gilbert's wedding.

25th August. Burns's crops auctioned at Ellisland. Over thirty people engaged in a drunken riot for three hours after the roup; 'Such a scene of drunkenness was hardly ever seen in this country.'

August — September. Burns sends an account of the Monkland Friendly Society to Sir John Sinclair for inclusion in the *Statistical Account.*

10th September. Formal renunciation of the Ellisland lease.

11th November. The Burns family moves to Dumfries, and takes up residence in a three-room apartment in the Wee Vennel (now Bank Street), above John Syme's office.

29th November — 11th December. Burns in Edinburgh.

6th December. Burns and Mrs McLehose meet for the last time, at Lamont's Land.

27th December. Burns sends Clarinda 'Ae Fond Kiss' as a parting gift.

1792   February. Burns promoted to the Dumfries Port Division 'worth twenty pounds a year more than any other Division, besides as much rum and brandy as will easily supply an ordinary family.' His salary was now £70 a year, with £15-£20 extra in perquisites.

29th February. Capture of the brig *Rosamond* at Gretna.

10th April. Burns made an honorary member of the Royal Company of Archers.

16th April. Burns offers Creech 'about fifty pages of new material' for a fresh edition of his *Poems.*

19th April. Sale of the *Rosamond's* carronades, which Burns tried to send to the French revolutionaries.

August. Fourth volume of *Scots Musical Museum,* including 60 songs contributed by Burns.

September. Burns visits Ayrshire.

16th September. Burns undertakes to contribute to George Thomson's *Select Collection of Scottish Airs.*

29th September. The Theatre Royal, Dumfries opens in Shakespeare Street.

October. Burns begins work on contributions to a fifth volume of *Scots Musical Museum.*

13th November. Burns subscribes to the Edinburgh *Gazetteer.*

21st November. Birth of Elizabeth Riddell Burns.

December. Four-day visit to Dunlop House with Dr Adair, Burns's last. First General Convention of the Friends of the People at Edinburgh;, much political commotion in Dumfries.

31st December. John Mitchell, Collector of Excise, ordered by his Board to investigate Burns's political conduct 'as a person disaffected to Government'.

1793   5th January. Burns defends himself to Robert Graham of Fintry, Excise Commissioner.

18th February. Second Edinburgh edition of the *Poems* published by Creech.

BURNS AND THE VISION
by James Christie
by courtesy of Irvine Burns Club

PORTRAIT OF BURNS
by Alexander Nasmyth, painted in 1787
by courtesy of the National Galleries of Scotland, Edinburgh

March. Burns asks for, and receives burgess privileges in the Dumfries School for his children.

19th May. Burns family move to a house in Millbrae Vennel (now Burns Street).

May. First set of Thomson's *Select Collection* published. Over twenty letters, many with songs enclosed, from Burns to Thomson in the ensuing seven months alone.

30th July (?) — 2nd August. Burns and John Syme tour Galloway.

1st August. Burns meets Pietro Urbani at the home of Lord Selkirk, St Mary's Isle.

October. Meeting between Burns and Nathaniel Gow, the celebrated fiddler and son of Neil Gow.

December. Burns lends his collection of bawdy ballads to John McMurdo of Drumlanrig: 'I have for some years been making . . . There is not another copy of the collection in the world.'

9th December. Isabella Burns married at Mossgiel.

Late December. 'Rape of the Sabines' incident at Friars' Carse; rift between Burns and the Riddells.

1794   7th January. Burns proposes the reorganization of the Dumfries excise service.

12th January. Maria Riddell breaks with Burns.

20th April. Robert Riddell dies.

1st May (?) Burns declines a post with the *Morning Chronicle*, London.

June. Friars' Carse put up for sale.

25th — 28th June. Burns and Syme make their second tour of Galloway.

12th August. Birth of James Glencairn Burns.

November. Burns commences his notes on songs for Thomson, and seeks out English ballads for the *Select Collection*.

22nd December. Burns promoted to Acting Supervisor of Excise, Dumfries. Correspondence with Maria Riddell resumed.

1795   January. Burns working harder than ever for the Excise, but income much reduced: 'These accursed times, by stopping up Importation, have for this year at least lopt off a full third of my income.'

12th January. Burns writes the letter which estranges Mrs Dunlop.

31st. January. Burns a founder member of the Dumfries Volunteers.

February — March. Burns and Maria Riddell fully reconciled.

March. Patrick Heron declares his candidacy for the Election in the Stewarty.

April. Alexander Reid paints a miniature portrait of Burns. Alexander Findlater resumes his duties as Excise Supervisor at Dumfries.

24th June. Death of William Smellie, Burns's Edinburgh printer.

September. Death of Elizabeth Riddell Burns.

December — January. Burns ill with 'a most severe Rheumatic fever'.

1796   31st January. Burns 'beginning to crawl across my room'.

January — March. Famine in Dumfries. 'Many days my family, and hundreds of other families, are absolutely without one grain of meal; as money cannot purchase it.'

12th — 14th March. Food riots in Dumfries.

June. Burns's last letter to Johnson.

3rd — 16th July. Burns at the Brow Well.

12th July. Last letter to Thomson, begging for five pounds in order to pay off 'A cruel scoundrel of a Haberdasher to whom I owe an account . . .'

18th July. Burns writes his last letter: to his father-in-law James Armour.

21st July. Burns dies in Dumfries.

25th July. Funeral of Burns, and birth of his son Maxwell.

December. Fifth volume of *Scots Musical Museum* published.

NOTE ON THE KILMARNOCK EDITION

Burns's first essay in 'guid black prent' was produced by John Wilson (1759-1821), a Kilmarnock printer and co-founder (with his brother Peter) of the earliest Ayrshire newspaper, the Ayr *Advertiser*. No record has been preserved of the manner and circumstances surrounding Burns's choice of printer, although Burns and Wilson were possibly introduced by John Goldie, the Kilmarnock cabinetmaker and wine-merchant turned author on scientific, philosophical and theological treatises, who stood surety for Burns with the printer for the publication of the *Poems*.

On 17th April 1786 there appeared

'Proposals for publishing by subscription,
Scottish Poems, by Robert Burns.
The work to be elegantly printed, in
one volume, octavo. Price, stitched, three
shillings. As the author has not the most
distant mercenary view in publishing, as
soon as so many subscribers appear as will
defray the necessary expense, the work will
be sent to the press.'

This was followed by a quotation from Allan Ramsay and then the statement: 'We, the underscribers, engage to take the above-mentioned work on the conditions specified.' Robert Aiken (to whom 'The Cotter's Saturday Night' was dedicated) took no fewer than 145 copies of the total edition of 612. Gilbert Burns, John Wilson himself, and Robert Muir of Kilmarnock took seventy copies each, Gavin Hamilton took forty, and Ayr lawyer McWhinnie, John Kennedy of Dumfries House and John Logan of Knockshinnoch took twenty apiece. By the end of May approximately half of the edition had been subscribed for, and the poems went to the printer in June. The actual work of printing began on 13th July and on the last day of that month the entire edition was ready for distribution. By 28th August Wilson had only thirteen copies left and a few weeks later, when the entire edition was exhausted, he offered to print a second edition of a thousand copies, but demanded that Burns pay the costs of materials and printing in advance — about £43 in all which Burns was unable to meet.

There appears to be some discrepancy in the estimated accounts for the Kilmarnock Edition. Total receipts from the edition amounted to about £90. Wilson's note of the costs of production shows an outlay of £35.17s which should have left Burns with a profit of about £54 — almost three times the 'twenty pounds' which he later said the venture had brought him. Doubtless Wilson's canniness regarding the second edition, and perhaps Burns's disappointment that his efforts had actually yielded so little, played a part in deciding Burns to try for a national edition, published in Edinburgh.

Three shillings for a volume of 240 pages was no small sum in 1786. It represented a good week's wages for a coal-miner or farm labourer. As for the plough-boys and maid-servants, whom Robert Heron recalled 'would have gladly bestowed the wages which they earned most hardly', this sum probably represented two or three weeks' earnings. In terms of our modern, rather depreciated currency, therefore, the Kilmarnock Edition cost £150 — £200, which would be a colossal sum to pay for a book nowadays.

After the publication of the various Edinburgh editions, more expensive but also more voluminous, the market for second-hand copies of the Kilmarnock *Poems* sagged. As late as 1850 copies could still be picked up for as little as a shilling. Antiquarian interest, however, developed from 1859, the year of the poet's centenary, and rapidly gathered momentum. J.C. Ewing (*Burns Chronicle,* 1930) makes the point that the Kilmarnock Edition is not a rare book in the true bibliophilic sense, although booksellers and auctioneers might be forgiven for thus describing a book confined to 612 copies from an obscure provincial press in the late eighteenth century. In mint condition, with full margins and original paper wrappers, it is a scarce work, much sought after by bibliophiles. Most of the known surviving copies have been sumptuously rebound.

The earliest auction records show that a copy sold in Edinburgh in 1860 fetched £3.10s. In 1869 two copies made £10 and £14 respectively and twenty years later the first price to reach the £100 level was recorded. In 1898 a copy in the original blue paper covers was sold for £590. Ten years later the Trustees of the Burns Monument and Cottage at Alloway paid £1,000 for another mint copy. By that time interest in Burns as an author of bibliophilic interest was well-established. In 1923 the Carysfort copy fetched £1,600 and two years later the same purchaser paid £1,750 for another copy. The record price seemed to be attained in 1929 when a copy was sold for £2,450 at Sotheby's.

Thereafter the market in Kilmarnock Editions, as in so much else of antiquarian interest, dipped sharply. After the Second World War prices began to recover slowly, but the Bute copy made only £880 at auction in 1950 and as recently as 1957 a copy was sold for a mere £600.

The market began to recover at the time of the poet's bicentenary and has gone from strength to strength ever since. Sotheby Parke Bernet sold a copy in New York for $9,000 in 1974, while Christie auctioned a copy in the same city seven years later for $8,000. Maggs of London sold a copy in 1979 for £3,800, while the copy in the possession of the Irvine Burns Club cost them £4,000. Even higher prices are believed to have been paid in recent private treaty sales. It has been estimated that there are about fifteen copies in institutional collections in Britain and America and about a dozen in private hands — an astonishingly low survival rate (about 4 per cent) for a work which was so highly prized from the outset.

The Preface to the Kilmarnock Edition, in which Burns showed his desire to communicate with his readers, is an extraordinary example of the prose affectations of the late-eighteenth century. With its studied literary phraseology and liberal use of circumlocution and personification, its style seems somewhat artificial and contrived. As for its actual contents, it cannot be denied that there is a certain tendency to pose, a tendency to which Burns was prone to give way, both in his life and in his letters. Note how he emphasises the shortcomings of his education compared with that of poets who 'look down for a rural theme, with an eye to Theocrites or Virgil', belying the truth of his actual educational attainments. He speaks of 'the obscure, nameless Bard, who appears with fear and trembling in the public character of an Author', cowering at the prospect of adverse criticism; and he constantly reminds his readers that he, a mere peasant, is 'unacquainted with the necessary requisites for commencing Poet by rule.' On the other hand his conscious pride as the lineal descendant of Ramsay and Fergusson, in his own poetic genius and the realization of his peculiar literary position, shows through very clearly. While acknowledging his debt to his predecessors, he is in no doubt that poetry has been transformed by his own forceful personality: it is his own life, his own outlook, his own experiences and convictions that have inspired his verse.

The first Edinburgh Edition, published in April 1787, replaced the original Preface with a Dedication to the noblemen and gentlemen of the Caledonian Hunt. If anything, this Dedication was couched in even more high-flown language, acknowledging the Bard's great indebtedness while, at the same time, restating his rustic background and sturdy independence of character as well as the originality of his art. The most striking aspect of his Dedication is is the forceful image, suggested to Burns by I Kings, xix, 19, of the Muse finding him as Elijah did Elisha, at the plough, and throwing her mantle over him. The Dedication concludes with a blessing upon his patrons, in some of the the most florid language to be found anywhere in Burns's prose writings.

PREFACE TO THE KILMARNOCK EDITION, 1786

The following trifles are not the production of the Poet, who, with all the advantages of learned art, and perhaps amid the elegancies and idlenesses of upper life, looks down for a rural theme, with an eye to Theocrites or Virgil. To the Author of this, these and other celebrated names their countrymen are, in their original languages, 'A fountain shut up, and a book sealed'. Unacquainted with the necessary requisites for commencing Poet by rule, he sings the sentiments and manners, he felt and saw in himself and his rustic compeers around him, in his and their native language. Though a Rhymer from his earliest years, at least from the earliest impulses of the softer passions, it was not till very lately, that the applause, perhaps the partiality, of Friendship, wakened his vanity so far as to make him think any thing of his was worth showing; and none of the following works were ever composed with a view to the press. To amuse himself with the little creations of his own fancy, amid the toil and fatigues of a labouring life; to transcribe the various feelings, the loves, the griefs, the hopes, the fears, in his own breast; to find some kind of counterpoise to the struggles of a world, always an alien scene, a task uncouth to the poetical mind; these were his motives for courting the Muses, and in these he found Poetry to be its own reward.

Now that he appears in the public character of an Author, he does it with fear and trembling. So dear is fame to the rhyming tribe, that even he, an obscure, nameless Bard, shrinks aghast, at the thought of being branded as 'An impertinent blockhead, obtruding his nonsense on the world; and because he can make a shift to jingle a few doggerel, Scotch rhymes together, looks upon himself as a Poet of no small consequence forsooth.'

It is an observation of that celebrated Poet*, whose divine Elegies do honor to our language, our nation, and our species, that 'Humility has depressed many a genius to a hermit, but never raised one to fame.' If any Critic catches at the word genius, the Author tells him, once for all, that he certainly looks upon himself as possest of some poetic abilities, otherwise his publishing in the manner he has done, would be a manoeuvre below the worst character, which, he hopes, his worst enemy will ever give him: but to the genius of a Ramsay, or the glorious dawnings of the poor, unfortunate Fergusson, he, with equal unaffected sincerity, declares, that, even in his highest pulse of vanity, he has not the most distant pretensions. These two justly admired Scotch Poets he has often had in his eye in the following pieces; but rather with a view to kindle at their flame, than for servile imitation.

To his Subscribers, the Author returns his most sincere thanks. Not the mercenary bow over a counter, but the heart-throbbing gratitude of the Bard, conscious how much he is indebted to

Benevolence and Friendship, for gratifying him, if he deserves it, in that dearest wish of every poetic bosom — to be distinguished. He begs his readers, particularly the Learned and the Polite, who may honor him with a perusal, that they will make every allowance for Education and Circumstances of Life: but, if after a fair, candid, and impartial criticism, he shall stand convicted of Dulness and Nonsense, let him be done by, as he would in that case do by others — let him be condemned, without mercy, to contempt and oblivion.

* William Shenstone (1714-63), one of the best-known minor poets of the 18th century, much of whose fame now rests on the fact that his sentiments, rather than his expression, were so much admired by Burns.

DEDICATION TO THE NOBLEMEN AND GENTLEMEN
OF THE CALEDONIAN HUNT

My Lords and Gentlemen,

A Scotch Bard, proud of the name, and whose highest ambition is to sing in his Country's service, where shall he so properly look for patronage as to the illustrious names of his native Land; those who bear the honours and inherit the virtues of their Ancestors? The Poetic Genius of my Country found me, as the prophetic bard Elijah did Elisha — at the Plough; and threw her inspiring mantle over me. She bade me sing the loves, the joys, the rural scenes and rural pleasures of my natal Soil, in my native tongue: I tuned my wild, artless notes, as she inspired. — She whispered me to come to this ancient Metropolis of Caledonia, and lay my Songs under your honoured protection: I now obey her dictates.

Though much indebted to your goodness, I do not approach you, my Lords and Gentlemen, in the usual style of dedication, to thank you for past favours: that path is so hackneyed by prostituted Learning, that honest Rusticity is ashamed of it' — Nor do I present this Address with the venal soul of a servile Author, looking for a continuation of those favours: I was bred to the Plough, and am independent. I come to claim the common Scottish name with you, my illustrious Countrymen; and to tell the world that I glory in the title. — I come to congratulate my country, that the blood of her ancient heroes still runs uncontaminated; and that, from your courage, knowledge, and public spirit, she may expect protection, wealth, and liberty. — In the last place, I come to proffer my warmest wishes to the Great Fountain of honour, the Monarch of the Universe, for your welfare and happiness.

When you go forth to waken the Echoes, in the ancient and favourite amusement of your Forefathers, may Pleasure ever be of your party; and may Social Joy await your return! When harassed in courts or camps with the justlings of bad men and bad measures, may the honest consciousness of injured worth attend your return to your native seats; and may domestic Happiness, with a smiling welcome, meet you at your gates! May corruption shrink at your kindling indignant glance; and may tyranny in the Ruler, and licentiousness in the people, equally find you an inexorable foe!

    I have the honour to be,
      With the sincerest gratitude and highest respect,
      MY LORDS AND GENTLEMEN,
        Your most devoted humble servant,
        ROBERT BURNS

Edinburgh
April 4, 1787

*Badge of the Burns Federation, based on the heraldic
device which Robert Burns himself composed, and
which it is hoped to matriculate at the Court of the
Lord Lyon, King of Arms, as the result of generous
funding by the Burns Howff Club, Dumfries.*

HANDSOME NELL

TUNE: I am a man unmarried

In the autumn of 1774 Burns 'first committed the sin of RHYME' as he later wrote Dr Moore: 'You know our country custom of coupling a man and woman together as Partners in the labors of Harvest. In my fifteenth autumn, my Partner was a bewitching creature who just counted an autumn less . . . a bonie, sweet, sonsie lass.' She was Nelly Kilpatrick, daughter of a farmer at Parclewan, Dalrymple. She married William Bone and died about 1820. She is referred to in the third stanza of the poem 'To the Guidwife of Wauchope House'.

O once I lov'd a bonie lass,
  Ay, and I love her still!
And whilst that virtue warms my breast,
  I'll love my handsome Nell.

As bonie lasses I hae seen,
  And monie full as braw,   handsome
But for a modest gracefu mien
  The like I never saw.

A bonie lass, I will confess,
  Is pleasant to the e'e;
But without some better qualities
  She's no a lass for me.

But Nelly's looks are blythe and sweet,
  And what is best of a',
Her reputation is complete,
  And fair without a flaw.

She dresses ay sae clean and neat,
  Both decent and genteel;
And then there's something in her gait
  Gars onie dress look weel.   makes

A gaudy dress and gentle air
  May slightly touch the heart;
But it's innocence and modesty
  That polishes the dart.

'Tis this in Nelly pleases me,
  'Tis this enchants my soul;
For absolutely in my breast
  She reigns without controul.

NOW WESTLIN WINDS

TUNE: Port Gordon

Composed in the summer of 1775, while studying
mathematics at Hugh Rodger's school in Kirkoswald.
Peggy (fourth stanza) was Margaret Thompson, 'a
charming Fillette who lived next door to the school
overset my Trigonometry, and set me off at a tangent
from the sphere of my studies'.

western
    Now westlin winds and slaught'ring guns
      Bring Autumn's pleasant weather;
    The moorcock springs on whirring wings
      Amang the blooming heather:
    Now waving grain, wide o'er the plain,
      Delights the weary farmer;
    And the moon shines bright, as I rove by night,
      To muse upon my charmer.

partridge
    The paitrick lo'es the fruitfu fells,
      The plover lo'es the mountains;
    The woodcock haunts the lonely dells,
heron
      The soaring hern the fountains:
pigeon
    Thro lofty groves the cushat roves,
      The path o man to shun it;
    The hazel bush o'erhangs the thrush,
      The spreading thorn the linnet.

    Thus ev'ry kind their pleasure find,
      The savage and the tender;
    Some social join, and leagues combine,
      Some solitary wander:
    Avaunt, away, the cruel sway!
      Tyrannic man's dominion!
    The sportsman's joy, the murd'ring cry,
      The flutt'ring, gory pinion!

    But, Peggy dear, the ev'ning's clear,
      Thick flies the skimming swallow;
    The sky is blue, the fields in view,
      All fading-green and yellow:
    Come let us stray our gladsome way,
      And view the charms of Nature;
    The rustling corn, the fruited thorn,
every
      And ilka happy creature.

    We'll gently walk, and sweetly talk,
      While the silent moon shines clearly;
    I'll clasp thy waist, and, fondly prest,
      Swear how I lo'e thee dearly:
    Not vernal show'rs to budding flow'rs,
      Not Autumn to the farmer,
    So dear can be as thou to me,
      My fair, my lovely charmer!

I DREAM'D I LAY

TUNE: *The Young Man's Dream*

'These two stanzas I composed when I was seventeen and are among the eldest of my printed pieces' — Burns.

I dream'd I lay where flowers were springing
    Gaily in the sunny beam,
List'ning to the wild birds singing,
    By a falling crystal stream;
Straight the sky grew black and daring,
    Thro the woods the whirlwinds rave,
Trees with aged arms were warring
    O'er the swelling, drumlie wave.   *turbid*

Such was my life's deceitful morning,
    Such the pleasures I enjoy'd!
But lang or noon, loud tempests storming,   *ere*
    A' my flowery bliss destroy'd.
Tho fickle Fortune has deceiv'd me
    (She promis'd fair, and perform'd but ill),
Of monie a joy and hope bereav'd me,   *many*
    I bear a heart shall support me still.

MY NANIE, O

The date of composition is unknown but Burns described it as 'done at a very early period of life, and consequently . . . . incorrect'. Nanie, according to Gilbert Burns, was probably Agnes Fleming, daughter of a Tarbolton farmer. In the original version the river in line 1 was the Stinchar, which Burns thought 'horridly prosaic'. Afton, Girvan and Lugar were later alternatives.

Behind yon hills where Lugar flows,
    'Mang moors an mosses many, O,   *bogs*
The wintry sun the day has clos'd,
    And I'll awa to Nanie, O.

The westlin wind blaws loud an shill;   *western, shrill*
    The night's baith mirk and rainy, O;   *murky*
But I'll get my plaid an out I'll steal,
    An owre the hill to Nanie, O.

My Nanie's charming, sweet, an young;
    Nae artfu wiles to win ye, O:
May ill befa' the flattering tongue
    That wad beguile my Nanie, O.

45

My Nanie, O

Her face is fair, her heart is true;
   As spotless as she's bonie, O;
daisy   The op'ning gowan, wat wi dew,
   Nae purer is than Nanie, O.

A country lad is my degree,
   An few there be that ken me, O;
But what care I how few they be?
   I'm welcome ay to Nanie, O.

My riches a's my penny-fee,
manage carefully   An I maun guide it cannie, O;
wordly goods   But warl's gear ne'er troubles me,
   My thoughts are a'—my Nanie, O.

Our auld guidman delights to view
cattle   His sheep an kye thrive bonie, O;
holds, plough   But I'm as blythe that hauds his pleugh,
   An has nae care but Nanie, O.

do not care   Come weel, come woe, I care na by;
   I'll tak what Heav'n will send me, O:
Nae ither care in life have I,
   But live, an love my Nanie, O.

TRAGIC FRAGMENT

These lines are thought to have been written in 1777 at Mount Oliphant and reflect the misery of the Burnes family at this time, before William Burnes was able to throw off the burden of this lease and move to Lochlie at Whitsun that year.

All villain as I am—a damned wretch,
A hardened, stubborn, unrepenting sinner—
Still my heart melts at human wretchedness,
And with sincere, tho unavailing sighs
I view the helpless children of distress.
With tears indignant I behold the oppressor
Rejoicing in the honest man's destruction,
Whose unsubmitting heart was all his crime.
Ev'n you, ye hapless crew! I pity you;
Ye, whom the seeming good think sin to pity:
Ye poor, despised, abandoned vagabonds,
Whom Vice, as usual, has turn'd o'er to ruin.

46

Oh! but for friends and interposing Heaven,
I had been driven forth, like you forlorn,
The most detested, worthless wretch among you!
O injured God! Thy goodness has endow'd me
With talents passing most of my compeers,
Which I in just proportion have abused,
As far as surpassing other common villains
As Thou in natural parts has given me more.

O TIBBIE, I HAE SEEN THE DAY

TUNE: Invercauld's Reel

Composed when Burns was about seventeen years
old. Tibbie was Isabella Steven of Littlehill, near
Lochlie which the poet's father farmed from
Whitsun 1777.

CHORUS

O Tibbie, I hae seen the day,
Ye wadna been sae shy!   would not have been
For laik o gear ye lightly me,   lack of wealth
But, trowth, I care na by.   I care not in return

Yestreen I met you on the moor,   Last night
Ye spak na, but gaed by like stoure!   went by like dust
Ye geck at me because I'm poor—   toss your head
    But fient a hair care I!   not

When comin hame on Sunday last,
Upon the road as I cam past,
Ye snufft an gae your head a cast—   sniffed
    But, trowth, I care't na by!   cared

I doubt na, lass, but ye may think,
Because ye hae the name o clink,   money
That ye can please me at a wink,
    When'er ye like to try.

But sorrow tak him that's sae mean,
Altho his pouch o coin were clean,
Wha follows onie saucy quean,   girl
    That looks sae proud and high!

O Tibbie, I hae seen the day

Altho a lad were e'er sae smart,
If that he want the yellow dirt,
direction   Ye'll cast your head anither airt,
    And answer him fu dry.

But if he hae the name o gear,
Ye'll fasten to him like a brier,
learning   Tho hardly he for sense or lear,
cows   Be better than the kye.

But, Tibbie, lass, tak my advice:
Your daddie's gear maks you sae nice,
ask   The Deil a ane wad spier your price,
    Were ye as poor as I.

There lives a lass beside yon park,
shift   I'd rather hae her in her sark
Than you wi a' your thousand mark,
makes   That gars you look sae high.

ONE NIGHT AS I DID WANDER

A FRAGMENT

Date unknown, but probably early.

One night as I did wander,
    When corn begins to shoot,
I sat me down to ponder
    Upon an auld tree-root
Auld Ayr ran by before me,
    And bicker'd to the seas;
pigeon   A cushat crooded o'er me,
    That echoed through the trees.

THE RIGS O BARLEY

TUNE: *Corn Rigs*

Burns composed this version of a well-known old song about 1782. Previous versions of Corn Rigs are recorded in published form from 1681 onwards, and also provided the basis for Allan Ramsay's My Patie is a Lover Gay (1725).

CHORUS

Corn rigs, an barley rigs,
An corn rigs are bonie:
I'll ne'er forget that happy night,
Amang the rigs wi Annie.

It was upon a Lammas night,
  When corn rigs are bonie,   ridges
Beneath the moon's unclouded light,
  I held awa to Annie;
The time flew by, wi tentless heed;   careless
  Till, 'tween the late and early,
Wi sma' persuasion she agreed
  To see me thro the barley.

The sky was blue, the wind was still,
  The moon was shining clearly;
I set her down, wi right good will,
  Amang the rigs o barley:
I ken't her heart was a' my ain;   knew
  I lov'd her most sincerely;
I kiss'd her owre and owre again,
  Amang the rigs o barley.

I lock'd her in my fond embrace;
  Her heart was beating rarely:
My blessings on that happy place,
  Amang the rigs o barley!
But by the moon and stars so bright,
  That shone that hour so clearly!
She ay shall bless that happy night
  Amang the rigs o barley.

I hae been blythe wi comrades dear;
  I hae been merry drinking;
I hae been joyfu gath'rin gear;   making money
  I hae been happy thinking:
But a' the pleasures e'er I saw,
  Tho three times doubl'd fairly—
That happy night was worth them a',
  Amang the rigs o barley.

FAREWELL TO ELIZA

TUNE: *Gilderoy*

Eliza has been identified as Elizabeth Barbour, to
whom Burns turned 'when rejected of Jean Armour',
or Elizabeth Miller of Mauchline, also in 1786, but
Burns told Dr Moore that he composed this song
before 1782.

From thee, Eliza, I must go,
    And from my native shore:
The cruel fates between us throw
    A boundless ocean's roar;
But boundless oceans, roaring wide
    Between my love and me,
They never, never can divide
    My heart and soul from thee.

Farewell, farewell, Eliza dear,
    The maid that I adore!
A boding voice is in mine ear,
    We part to meet no more!
But the latest throb that leaves my heart,
    While Death stand victor by,
That throb, Eliza, is thy part,
    And thine that latest sigh!

WINTER: A DIRGE

TUNE: *MacPherson's Rant*

Burns (1CPB) metioned Winter as his favourite season
which 'may be partly owing to my misfortunes giving
my mind a melancholy cast'. Elsewhere he wrote 'In
one of these seasons, just after a tract of misfortunes I
composed the following song.'

The wintry west extends his blast,
    And hail and rain does blaw;
Or the stormy north sends driving forth
    The blinding sleet and snaw:
Wild-tumbling brown, the burn comes down,
slope   And roars frae bank to brae:
And bird and beast in covert rest,
    And pass the heartless day.

'The sweeping blast, the sky o'ercast,'
    The joyless winter day
Let others fear, to me more dear
    Than all the pride of May:
The tempest's howl, it soothes my soul,
    My griefs it seems to join;
The leafless trees my fancy please,
    Their fate resembles mine!

Thou Pow'r Supreme, whose mighty scheme
    These woes of mine fulfil,
Here, firm I rest, they must be best,
    Because they are Thy will!
Then all I want (O do Thou grant
    This one request of mine!):
Since to enjoy Thou dost deny,
    Assist me to resign.

THE LASS OF CESSNOCK BANKS

TUNE: *The Butcher Boy*

The subject of this song has been identified as Alison Begbie, daughter of a Galston farmer, who rejected his proposal of marriage in 1781-2 'with peculiar circumstances of mortification'. She was also the Peggy Alison of 'Ilk care and fear, when thou art near.'

On Cessnock banks a lassie dwells,
    Could I describe her shape and mien!
Our lasses a' she far excels—
    An she has twa sparkling, rogueish een!   *eyes*

She's sweeter than the morning dawn,
    When rising Phœbus first is seen,
And dew-drops twinkle o'er the lawn—
    An she has twa sparkling, rogueish een!

She's stately like yon youthful ash,   *yonder*
    That grows the cowslip braes between,   *hillsides*
And drinks the stream with vigour fresh—
    An she has twa sparkling, rogueish een!

She's spotless like the flow'ring thorn,
    With flow'rs so white and leaves so green,
When purest in the dewy morn—
    An she has twa sparkling, rogueish een!

The Lass of Cessnock Banks

Her looks are like the vernal May,
    When ev'ning Phœbus shines serene,
While birds rejoice on every spray—
    An she has twa sparkling, rogueish een!

Her hair is like the curling mist,
    That climbs the mountain-sides at e'en,
When flow'r-reviving rains are past—
    An she has twa sparkling, rogueish een!

Her forehead's like the show'ry bow,
    When gleaming sunbeams intervene,
And gild the distant mountain's brow—
    An she has twa sparkling, rogueish een!

Her cheeks are like yon crimson gem,
    The pride of all the flowery scene,
Just opening on its thorny stem—
    An she has twa sparkling, rogueish een!

Her bosom's like the nightly snow,
    When pale the morning rises keen,
While hid the murm'ring streamlets flow—
    An she has twa sparkling, rogueish een!

Her lips are like yon cherries ripe,
    That sunny walls from Boreas screen:
They tempt the taste and charm the sight—
    An she has twa sparkling, rogueish een!

Her teeth are like a flock of sheep,
    With fleeces newly washen clean,
That slowly mount the rising steep—
    An she has twa sparkling, rogueish een!

Her breath is like the fragrant breeze,
    That gently stirs the blossom'd bean,
When Phœbus sinks behind the seas—
    An she has twa sparkling, rogueish een!

Her voice is like the ev'ning thrush,
    That sings on Cessnock banks unseen,
While his mate sits nestling in the bush—
    An she has twa sparkling, rogueish een!

But it's not her air, her form, her face,
    Tho matching Beauty's fabled Queen:
'Tis the mind that shines in ev'ry grace—
    An chiefly in her rogueish een!

TO RUIN

Written in the winter of 1781-2, a melancholy period when his rejection by Alison Begbie, his father's business misfortunes and poor health left Burns in a very sombre mood.

All hail, inexorable lord!
At whose destruction-breathing word,
   The mightiest empires fall!
Thy cruel, woe-delighted train,
The ministers of grief and pain,
   A sullen welcome, all!
With stern-resolv'd, despairing eye,
   I see each aimed dart;
For one has cut my dearest tie,
   And quivers in my heart.
     Then low'ring and pouring,
      The storm no more I dread;
     Tho thick'ning, and black'ning,
      Round my devoted head.

And thou grim Pow'r, by Life abhorr'd,
While Life a pleasure can afford,
   Oh! hear a wretch's pray'r!
No more I shrink appall'd, afraid;
I court, I beg thy friendly aid,
   To close this scene of care!
When shall my soul, in silent peace,
   Resign Life's joyless day?
My weary heart its throbbings cease,
   Cold-mould'ring in the clay?
     No fear more, no tear more
      To stain my lifeless face,
     Enclasped and grasped,
      Within thy cold embrace!

A PRAYER IN THE PROSPECT OF DEATH

Though usually assigned to 1784, this poem was probably composed in December 1781, at a time when Burns was writing from Irvine to his father '. . . . my only pleasurable employment is looking backwards and forwards in a moral and religious way - I am quite transported at the thought that ere long, perhaps very soon, I shall bid an eternal adiew to all the pains, and uneasiness and disquietudes of this weary life.'

O Thou unknown, Almighty Cause
   Of all my hope and fear!
In whose dread presence, ere an hour,
   Perhaps I must appear!

A Prayer in the Prospect of Death

If I have wander'd in those paths
  Of life I ought to shun—
As something, loudly, in my breast,
  Remonstrates I have done—

Thou know'st that Thou hast formed me
  With passions wild and strong;
And list'ning to their witching voice
  Has often led me wrong.

Where human weakness has come short,
  Or frailty stept aside,
Do Thou, All-Good—for such Thou art—
  In shades of darkness hide.

Where with intention I have err'd,
  No other plea I have,
But, Thou art good; and Goodness still
  Delighteth to forgive.

STANZAS, ON THE SAME OCCASION

Why am I loth to leave this earthly scene?
  Have I so found it full of pleasing charms?
Some drops of joy with draughts of ill between;
  Some gleams of sunshine 'mid renewing storms?
Is it departing pangs my soul alarms?
  Or death's unlovely, dreary, dark abode?
For guilt, for guilt, my terrors are in arms:
  I tremble to approach an angry God,
And justly smart beneath His sin-avenging rod.

Fain would I say: 'Forgive my foul offence,'
  Fain promise never more to disobey;
But, should my Author health again dispense,
  Again I might desert fair virtue's way;
Again in folly's path might go astray;
  Again exalt the brute and sink the man;
Then how should I for heavenly mercy pray,
  Who act so counter heavenly mercy's plan?
Who sin so oft have mourn'd, yet to temptation ran?

Stanzas, on the same Occasion

O Thou great Governor of all below!
    If I may dare a lifted eye to Thee—
Thy nod can make the tempest cease to blow,
    Or still the tumult of the raging sea:
With that controlling pow'r assist ev'n me,
    Those headlong furious passions to confine,
For all unfit I feel my pow'rs to be,
    To rule their torrent in th' allowed line;
    O, aid me with Thy help, Omnipotence Divine!

PRAYER UNDER THE PRESSURE
OF VIOLENT ANGUISH

Burns annotated this poem in 1CPB (March 1784):
'There was a certain period of my life that my spirit
was broke by repeated losses and disasters, which
threatened, and indeed effected the utter ruin of my
fortune. My body too was attacked by that most
dreadful distemper, a Hypochondria, or confirmed
Melancholy: in this wretched state, the recollection of
which makes me yet shudder, I hung my harp on the
Willow tree, except in some lucid intervals, in which I
composed the following.'

O Thou Great Being! what Thou art,
    Surpasses me to know;
Yet sure I am, that known to Thee
    Are all Thy works below.

Thy creature here before Thee stands,
    All wretched and distrest;
Yet sure those ills that wring my soul
    Obey Thy high behest.

Sure Thou, Almighty, canst not act
    From cruelty or wrath!
O, free my weary eyes from tears,
    Or close them fast in death!

But, if I must afflicted be
    To suit some wise design,
Then man my soul with firm resolves
    To bear and not repine!

FICKLE FORTUNE

TUNE: *I dream'd I lay*

'An extempore under the pressure of a heavy train of Misfortunes' (1CPB)

Tho fickle Fortune has deceived me,
   (She promis'd fair and perform'd but ill);
Of mistress, friends, and wealth bereav'd me,
   Yet I bear a heart shall support me still.

I'll act with prudence as far as I'm able,
   But if success I must never find,
Then come, Misfortune, I bid thee welcome—
   I'll meet thee with an undaunted mind!

RAGING FORTUNE

Like the previous poem, written during the sombre winter of 1781-2

O, raging Fortune's withering blast
   Has laid my leaf full low!
O, raging Fortune's withering blast
   Has laid my leaf full low!

My stem was fair, my bud was green,
   My blossom sweet did blow;
The dew fell fresh, the sun rose mild,
   And made my branches grow.

But luckless Fortune's northern storms
   Laid a' my blossoms low!
But luckless Fortune's northern storms
   Laid a' my blossoms low!

I'LL GO AND BE A SODGER

Allegedly a reference to the sudden collapse of the poet's business as a flax-dresser at Irvine in the winter of 1781. 'My partner was a scoundrel of the first water who made money by the mystery of thieving; and to finish the whole, while we were giving a welcome carousel to the New Year, our shop burnt to ashes and left me, like a true poet, not worth a sixpence.'

O, why the deuce should I repine,
   And be an ill foreboder?
I'm twenty-three, and five feet nine,
soldier   I'll go and be a sodger!

I'll go and be a Sodger

I gat some gear wi meikle care,   wealth, much
    I held it weel thegither;   together
But now it's gane—and something mair: gone, more
    I'll go and be a sodger!

PARAPHRASE OF THE FIRST PSALM

This and the next poem provide interesting evidence
of the poet's recourse to religion at a time of deep
crisis in his life. Burns clearly felt that the lines of the
1st and 90th Psalms contained much that was relevant
to his condition and he derived great comfort from
them. These exercises in versification were for him the
natural outcome.

The man, in life wherever plac'd,
    Hath happiness in store,
Who walks not in the wicked's way
    Nor learns their guilty lore!

Nor from the seat of scornful pride
    Casts forth his eyes abroad,
But with humility and awe
    Still walks before his God!

That man shall flourish like the trees,
    Which by the streamlets grow:
The fruitful top is spread on high,
    And firm the root below.

But he, whose blossom buds in guilt,
    Shall to the ground be cast,
And, like the rootless stubble, tost
    Before the sweeping blast.

For why? that God the good adore,
    Hath giv'n them peace and rest,
But hath decreed that wicked men
    Shall ne'er be truly blest.

THE NINETIETH PSALM VERSIFIED

O Thou, the first, the greatest friend
    Of all the human race!
Whose strong right hand has ever been
    Their stay and dwelling place!

Before the mountains heav'd their heads
    Beneath Thy forming hand,
Before this ponderous globe itself
    Arose at Thy command.

That Pow'r, which rais'd and still upholds
    This universal frame,
From countless, unbeginning time
    Was ever still the same.

Those mighty periods of years
    Which seem to us so vast,
Appear no more before Thy sight
    Than yesterday that's past.

Thou giv'st the word: Thy creature, man,
    Is to existence brought;
Again Thou say'st: 'Ye sons of men,
    Return ye into nought!'

Thou layest them, with all their cares,
    In everlasting sleep;
As with a flood Thou tak'st them off
    With overwhelming sweep.

They flourish like the morning flower,
    In beauty's pride array'd,
But long ere night, cut down, it lies
    All wither'd and decay'd.

MY FATHER WAS A FARMER

TUNE: *The Weaver and his Shuttle, O*

Probably composed early in 1782.

My father was a farmer upon the Carrick border, O,
And carefully he bred me in decency and order, O.
He bade me act a manly part, though I had ne'er a farthing, O,
For without an honest manly heart, no man was worth regard-
    ing, O.

My Father was a Farmer

Then out into the world my course I did determine, O,
Tho to be rich was not my wish, yet to be great was charming, O.
My talents they were not the worst, nor yet my education, O,
Resolv'd was I, at least to try, to mend my situation. O.

In many a way, and vain essay, I courted Fortune's favour, O:
Some cause unseen still stept between, to frustrate each endeavour, O.
Sometimes by foes I was o'erpower'd, sometimes by friends forsaken, O,
And when my hope was at the top, I still was worst mistaken, O.

Then sore harass'd, and tir'd at last, with Fortune's vain delusion,O,
I dropt my schemes, like idle dreams, and came to this conclusion, O—
The past was bad, and the future hid, its good or ill untried, O,
But the present hour was in my pow'r, and so I would enjoy it, O.

No help, nor hope, nor view had I, not person to befriend me, O,
So I must toil, and sweat, and moil, and labour to sustain me, O.
To plough and sow, to reap and mow, my father bred me early, O;
For one, he said, to labour bred, was a match for Fortune fairly, O.

Thus all obscure, unknown, and poor, thro life I'm doom'd to wander, O,
Till down my weary bones I lay in everlasting slumber, O.
No view nor care, but shun whate'er might breed me pain or sorrow, O,
I live to-day as well's I may, regardless of to-morrow, O.

But cheerful still, I am as well as a monarch in his palace, O,
Tho Fortune's frown still hunts me down, with all her wonted malice, O:
I make indeed my daily bread, but ne'er can make it farther, O,
But, as daily bread is all I need, I do not much regard her, O.

When sometimes by my labour, I earn a little money, O,
Some unforeseen misfortune comes gen'rally upon me, O;
Mischance, mistake, or by neglect, or my good-natur'd folly, O:
But, come what will, I've sworn it still, I'll ne'er be melancholy, O.

All you who follow wealth and power with unremitting ardour, O,
The more in this you look for bliss, you leave your view the farther, O,
Had you the wealth Potosi boasts, or nations to adore you, O,   Latin American
A cheerful honest-hearted clown I will prefer before you, O.   silvermine

59

MONTGOMERIE'S PEGGY

TUNE: *Galla Water*

Written in imitation of an old song 'McMillan's Peggy',
it immortalises the housekeeper at Coilsfield House.
The least-known of the poet's heroines '. . . . Peggy
was my Deity for six, or eight months. She had been
bred . . . . in a style of life rather elegant . . . . A vanity
of showing my parts in Courtship . . . . made me lay
siege to her; and when, as I always do in my foolish
gallantries, I had battered myself into a very warm
affection for her, she told me that her fortress had
been for some time before the rightful property of
another; but with the greatest friendship and
politeness, she offered me every alliance, except actual
possession.'

that   Altho my bed were in yon muir,
             Amang the heather, in my plaidie,
       Yet happy, happy I would be,
             Had I my dear Montgomerie's Peggy.

       When o'er the hill beat surly storms,
             And winter nights were dark and rainy,
       I'd seek some dell, and in my arms
             I'd shelter dear Montgomerie's Peggy.

       Were I a Baron proud and high,
             And horse and servants waiting ready,
'twould give   Then a' 'twad gie o joy to me
sharing it   The sharin's with Montgomerie's Peggy.

JOHN BARLEYCORN: A BALLAD

TUNE: *Lull me beyond thee*

Numerous variants of an ancient folk ballad are
extant, dealing with the legend of the corn spirit and
allegorising the treatment of barley from the threshing
and winnowing of the harvest to the brewing of ale.
Burns (1CPB) recalled the first three stanzas and 'some
scraps' of one such version and developed this poem
out of these fragments.

       There was three kings into the east,
             Three kings both great and high,
       And they hae sworn a solemn oath
             John Barleycorn should die.

       They took a plough and plough'd him down,
             Put clods upon his head,
       And they hae sworn a solemn oath
             John Barleycorn was dead.

John Barleycorn: A Ballad

But the cheerful Spring came kindly on,
    And show'rs began to fall;
John Barleycorn got up again,
    And sore surpris'd them all.

The sultry suns of Summer came,
    And he grew thick and strong:
His head weel arm'd wi pointed spears,
    That no one should him wrong.

The sober Autumn enter'd mild,
    When he grew wan and pale;
His bending joints and drooping head
    Show'd he began to fail.

His colour sicken'd more and more,
    He faded into age;
And then his enemies began
    To show their deadly rage.

They've taen a weapon, long and sharp,
    And cut him by the knee;
They ty'd him fast upon a cart,
    Like a rogue for forgerie.

They laid him down upon his back,
    And cudgell'd him full sore.
They hung him up before the storm,
    And turn'd him o'er and o'er.

They filled up a darksome pit
    With water to the brim,
They heav'd in John Barleycorn—
    There, let him sink or swim!

They laid him upon the floor,
    To work him farther woe;
And still, as signs of life appear'd,
    They toss'd him to and fro.

They wasted o'er a scorching flame
    The marrow of his bones;
But a miller us'd him worst of all,
    For he crush'd him between two stones.

And they hae taen his very heart's blood,
    And drank it round and round;
And still the more and more they drank,
    Their joy did more abound.

John Barleycorn: A Ballad

John Barleycorn was a hero bold,
 Of noble enterprise;
For if you do but taste his blood,
 'Twill make your courage rise.

'Twill make a man forget his woe;
 'Twill heighten all his joy:
'Twill make the widow's heart to sing,
 Tho the tear were in her eye.

Then let us toast John Barleycorn,
 Each man a glass in hand;
And may his great posterity
 Ne'er fail in old Scotland!

THE DEATH AND DYING WORDS
OF POOR MAILIE

THE AUTHOR'S ONLY PET YOWE:
AN UNCO MOURNFU TALE

Mollie

ewe
uncommonly

Gilbert Burns, writing to Dr Currie in April 1798, said that the events were pretty much as described. Robert had 'partly by way of frolic, bought a ewe and two lambs from a neighbour, and she was tethered in a field adjoining the house at Lochlie . . . Poor Mailie was set to rights, and when we returned from the plough in the evening, he repeated to me her *Death and Dying Words* pretty much in the way they now stand.'

together

hoof, looped
floundered

staggering

As Mailie, an her lambs thegither,
Was ae day nibblin on the tether,
Upon her cloot she coost a hitch,
An owre she warsl'd in the ditch:
There, groanin, dying, she did lie,
When Hughoc he cam doytin by.

staring

woe

 Wi glowrin een, and lifted han's
Poor Hughoc like a statue stan's;
He saw her days were near-hand ended,
But, wae's my heart! he could na mend it!
He gaped wide, but naething spak,
At length poor Mailie silence brak:—

62

The Death and Dying Words of Poor Mailie

'O thou, whase lamentable face
Appears to mourn my woefu case!
My dying words attentive hear,
An bear them to my Master dear.

'Tell him, if e'er again he keep   own
As muckle gear as buy a sheep—   much money
O, bid him never tie them mair,
Wi wicked strings o hemp or hair!
But ca' them out to park or hill,   drive
An let them wander at their will:
So may his flock increase, an grow
To scores o lambs, and packs o woo'!

'Tell him, he was a Master kin',
An ay was guid to me an mine;
An now my dying charge I gie him,
My helpless lambs, I trust them wi him.

'O bid him save their harmless lives,
Frae dogs, an tods, and butcher's knives!   foxes
But gie them guid cow-milk their fill,
Till they be fit to fend themsel;   look after
An tent them duly, e'en an morn,   tend, evening
Wi teats o hay an ripps o corn.   morsels, handfuls

'An may they never learn the gaets,   ways
Of ither vile, wanrestfu pets—   restless
To slink thro slaps, an reave an steal,   broken fences
At stacks o pease, or stocks o kail!
So may they, like their great forbears,
For monie a year come thro the sheers:
So wives will gie them bits o bread,
An bairns greet for them when they're dead.   children weep

'My poor toop-lamb, my son an heir,   tup
O, bid him breed him up wi care!
An if he live to be a beast,
To pit some havins in his breast!   conduct

'An warn him—what I winna name—   will not
To stay content wi yowes at hame;   ewes
An no to rin an wear his cloots,
Like ither menseless, graceless brutes.   unmannerly

The Death and Dying Words of Poor Mailie

next   'An niest, my yowie, silly thing,

Gude keep thee frae a tether string!

make friends   O, may thou ne'er forgather up,

Wi onie blastit, moorland toop;

nibble and meddle   But ay keep mind to moop an mell,

Wi sheep o credit like thysel!

                         'And now, my bairns, wi my last breath,

I lea'e my blessin wi you baith:

An when you think upo your mither,

Mind to be kind to ane anither.

                         'Now, honest Hughoc, dinna fail,

To tell my master a' my tale;

An bid him burn this cursed tether,

bladder   An for thy pains thou'se get my blether.'

                         This said, poor Mailie turn'd her head,

eyes   An clos'd her een amang the dead!

POOR MAILIE'S ELEGY

This sequel to the previous poem was written in 1785-86 to accompany it in the Kilmarnock Edition.

                         Lament in rhyme, lament in prose,

salt   Wi saut tears trickling down your nose;

Our Bardie's fate is at a close,

                               Past a' remead!

keystone   The last, sad cape-stane of his woes;

                               Poor Mailie's dead!

world's   It's no the loss o warl's gear,

That could sae bitter draw the tear

Or make our bardie, dowie, wear

                               The mourning weed:

neighbour   He's lost a friend and neebor dear,

                               In Mailie dead.

                         Thro a' the town she trotted by him;

A lang half-mile she could descry him;

Wi kindly bleat, when she did spy him,

                               She ran wi speed:

A friend mair faithfu ne'er came nigh him,

                               Than Mailie dead.

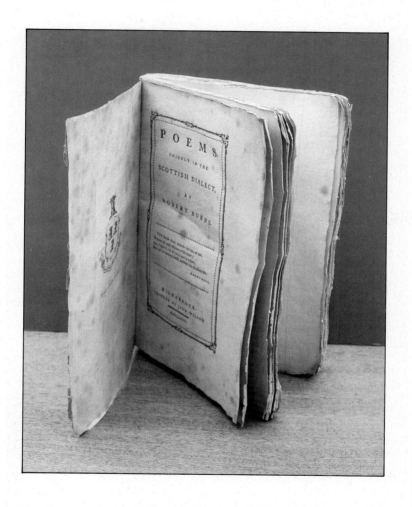

**THE KILMARNOCK EDITION OF BURNS'S POEMS
IN ITS ORIGINAL BINDING**

courtesy of the Trustees of the Burns Monument, Burns Cottage, Alloway.

BURNS IN EDINBURGH by C.M. Hardie

courtesy of Irvine Burns Club

Poor Mailie's Elegy

I wat she was a sheep o sense,   wot
An could behave hersel wi mense: grace
I'll say't, she never brak a fence,
     Thro thievish greed.
Our Bardie, lanely, keeps the spence   parlour
     Sin' Mailie's dead.

Or, if he wanders up the howe,   glen
Her living image in her yowe,   ewe
Comes bleating to him, owre the knowe, knoll
     For bits o bread;
An down the briny pearls rowe   roll
     For Mailie dead.

She was nae get o moorlan tips,   issue, tups
Wi tauted ket, an hairy hips;   matted coat
For her forbears were brought in ships,
     Frae 'yont the Tweed:
A bonier fleesh ne'er cross'd the clips fleece, clippers
     Than Mailie's dead.

Wae worth that man wha first did shape, woe betide
That vile, wanchancie thing—a rape!   dangerous, rope
It maks guid fellows girn an gape,   grin
     Wi chokin dread;
An Robin's bonnet wave wi crape
     For Mailie dead.

O, a' ye Bards on bonie Doon!
An wha on Aire your chanters tune!
Come, join the melancholious croon
     O Robin's reed!
His heart will never get aboon!
     His Mailie's dead!

REMORSE

This poem was inspired by Adam Smith's Theory of
Moral Sentiments (1759). The poet's copy of this
philosophical work is now preserved in the library of
Glasgow University.

Of all the numerous ills that hurt our peace,
That press the soul, or wring the mind with anguish,
Beyond comparison the worst are those
By our own folly, or our guilt brought on:
In ev'ry other circumstance, the mind
Has this to say:— 'It was no deed of mine.'
But, when to all the evil of misfortune
This sting is added:— 'Blame thy foolish self!'
Or, worser far, the pangs of keen remorse,
The torturing, gnawing consciousness of guilt,
Of guilt, perhaps, where we've involved others,
The young, the innocent, who fondly lov'd us;
Nay, more, that very love their cause of ruin!
O burning Hell! in all thy store of torments
There's not a keener lash!

Lives there a man so firm, who, while his heart
Feels all the bitter horrors of his crime,
Can reason down its agonizing throbs,
And, after proper purpose of amendment,
Can firmly force his jarring thoughts to peace?
O happy, happy, enviable man!
O glorious magnanimity of soul!

NO CHURCHMAN AM I

TUNE: *Prepare, my dear Brethren*

Earlier editors assigned this work to 1781-2 and
associated it with the Bachelors' Club and the
Masonic Lodge at Tarbolton, but Kinsley has
demonstrated (from a verse cut out in 1787) that it
must date from 1783, when the parliamentary
enquiry into Warren Hastings' administration of India
was under way and Pitt became Chancellor of the
Exchequer in December 1783.

No churchman am I for to rail and to write,
No statesman nor soldier to plot or to fight,
No sly man of business contriving a snare,
For a big-belly'd bottle's the whole of my care.

The peer I don't envy, I give him his bow;
I scorn not the peasant, tho ever so low;
But a club of good fellows, like those that are here,
And a bottle like this, are my glory and care.

Here passes the squire on his brother—his horse,
There centum per centum, the cit with his purse,
But see you *The Crown* how it waves in the air?
There a big-belly'd·bottle still eases my care.

The wife of my bosom, alas! she did die;
For sweet consolation to church I did fly;
I found that old Solomon proved it fair,
That a big-belly'd bottle's a cure for all care.

I once was persuaded a venture to make;
A letter inform'd me that all was to wreck;
But the pursy old landlord just waddled upstairs,
With a glorious bottle that ended my cares.

'Life's cares they are comforts' — a maxim laid down
By the Bard, what d'ye call him? that wore the black gown;
And faith I agree with th' old prig to a hair:
For a big-belly'd bottle's a heav'n of a care.

A STANZA ADDED IN A MASON LODGE

Then fill up a bumper and make it o'erflow,
And honours Masonic prepare for to throw:
May ev'ry true Brother of the Compass and Square
Have a big-belly'd bottle, when harass'd with care!

EPITAPH ON JAMES GRIEVE, LAIRD OF BOGHEAD, TARBOLTON

**This quatrain lampooned the laird of an estate just to
the west of Lochlie, and was probably written in
1783-84.**

Here lies Boghead amang the dead
In hopes to get salvation;
But if such as he in Heav'n may be,
Then welcome—hail! damnation.

THE RUINED FARMER

TUNE: *Go from my window, Love, do*

Probably inspired by the tragedy which overtook the
poet's father in the winter of 1783-84. William Burnes
fell into arrears with the rent of Lochlie and the
landlord, David McLure took the luckless Burnes to
the Sheriff Court. Though Burnes won his appeal to
the Court of Session on 27th January 1784 he died
two weeks later of 'a phthisical consumption'
aggravated by hardship and worry.

The sun he is sunk in the west,
All creatures retired to rest,
While here I sit, all sore beset,
      With sorrow, grief, and woe:
And it's O, fickle Fortune, O!

The prosperous man is asleep,
Nor hears how the whirlwinds sweep;
But Misery and I must watch
      The surly tempests blow:
And it's O, fickle Fortune, O!

There lies the dear Partner of my breast
Her cares for a moment at rest!
Must I see thee, my youthful pride,
      Thus brought so very low?—
And it's O, fickle Fortune, O!

There lie my sweet babes in her arms;
No anxious fear their little hearts alarms;
But for their sake my heart does ache,
      With many a bitter throe:
And it's O, fickle Fortune, O!

I once was by Fortune carest,
I once could relieve the distrest,
Now life's poor support, hardly earn'd,
      My fate will scarce bestow:
And it's O, fickle Fortune, O!

No comfort, no comfort I have!
How welcome to me were the grave!
But then my wife and children dear—
      O, whither would they go!
And it's O, fickle Fortune, O!

O, whither, O, whither shall I turn,
All friendless, forsaken, forlorn?
For, in this world, Rest or Peace
      I never more shall know:
And it's O, fickle Fortune, O!

MARY MORISON

TUNE: *Duncan Davison*

A girl of this name, daughter of the adjutant of the 104th Regiment, died of consumption at the age of 20 in 1791 and her tombstone can still be seen in Mauchline Kirkyard. The story that she was the subject of this poem originated with her sister, who communicated it to the Rev. Dr. Edgar of Mauchline. But Burns described it as 'one of my juvenile works' written in 1784-5 (when this girl was barely fourteen) and it is significant that he makes no mention of the untimely death of the adjutant's daughter when sending this song to George Thomson. Kinsley shrewdly observes that 'Morison is not an uncommon name, and many Morisons are Marys.'

O Mary, at thy window be!
    It is the wish'd the trysted hour.
Those smiles and glances let me see,
    That makes the miser's treasure poor.
How blythely wad I bide the stoure,   *bear the struggle*
    A weary slave frae sun to sun,
Could I the rich reward secure—
    The lovely Mary Morison!

Yestreen, when to the trembling string   *Last night*
    The dance gaed thro the lighted ha',   *went*
To thee my fancy took its wing,
    I sat, but neither heard or saw:
Tho this was fair, and that was braw,   *fine*
    And yon the toast of a' the town,   *the other*
I sigh'd, and said amang them a'—
    'Ye are na Mary Morison!'

O, Mary, canst thou wreck his peace
    Wha for thy sake wad gladly die?
Or canst thou break that heart of his
    Whase only faut is loving thee?   *fault*
If love for love thou wilt na gie,   *give*
    At least be pity to me shown:
A thought ungentle canna be   *cannot*
    The thought o Mary Morison.

EPITAPH ON MY OWN FRIEND AND
MY FATHER'S FRIEND, WM. MUIR
IN TARBOLTON MILL

A true friend of the Burnes family, William Muir
(1745-93) gave lodging to Jean Armour in March 1788
when she was cast out by her own family 'banished
like a martyr — forlorn, destitute, and friendless'.
Burns repaid this kindness by helping Muir's widow,
through Gavin Hamilton. This mock epitaph was
composed in April 1784 (1CPB). With the seven
ensuing epitaphs it was chosen by Burns to complete
the Kilmarnock Edition of 1786.

An honest man here lies at rest,
As e'er God with his image blest:
The friend of man, the friend of truth,
The friend of age, and guide of youth:
Few hearts like his—with virtue warm'd,
Few heads with knowledge so inform'd:
If there's another world, he lives in bliss;
If there is none, he made the best of this.

EPITAPH ON A CELEBRATED
RULING ELDER

Dated April 1784 in 1 CPB where it is annotated
'Epitaph on Wm. Hood, Senr. In Tarbolton.'

Tailor

Here Souter Hood in death does sleep;
To hell if he's gane thither,

possessions
hold together

Satan, gie him thy gear to keep;
He'll haud it weel thegither.

EPITAPH ON A NOISY POLEMIC

The subject of this verse was James Humphrey (1755-
1844) a Mauchline stone-mason employed at Lochlie
and Mossgiel. He had a smattering of book-learning
which induced him to engage in arguments with Burns,
but the shallowness of his knowledge resulted in him
invariably losing the debate. Humphrey was quite
flattered to be the butt of the poet's Muse, and
recalled these occasions with affection to Allan
Cunningham in 1834.

those

Below thir stanes lie Jamie's banes:
O Death, it's my opinion,

garrulous

Thou ne'er took such a bleth'rin bitch
Into thy dark dominion.

EPITAPH ON 'WEE JOHNIE'

Hic Jacet wee Johnie

Allegedly John Wilson (c. 1751-1839), schoolmaster, grocer, pharmacist and session clerk in Tarbolton, the original of 'Dr. Hornbook'.

Whoe'er thou art, O reader, know
That Death has murder'd Johnie,
An here his *body* lies fu low;
For saul he ne'er had onie.

EPITAPH ON MY HONOURED FATHER

One of the groups of epitaphs which Burns selected to complete the Kilmarnock Edition. William Burnes died at Lochlie on 13th February 1784.

O ye whose cheek the tear of pity stains,
    Draw near with pious rev'rence, and attend!
Here lie the loving husband's dear remains,
    The tender father, and the gen'rous friend.
The pitying heart that felt for human woe,
    The dauntless heart that fear'd no human pride,
The friend of man—to vice alone a foe;
    For 'ev'n his failings lean'd to virtue's side,'

EPITAPH FOR ROBERT AIKEN, ESQ.

Robert Aiken, 'Orator Bob' (1739-1807), lawyer in Ayr, a close friend of Burns from 1783, and the recipient of many of the poet's most frank and intimate letters. It was Aiken's spirited defence of Gavin Hamilton before the Presbytery of Ayr in 1785 that inspired 'Holy Willie's Prayer'.

Know thou, O stranger to the fame
Of this much lov'd, much honour'd name!
(For none that knew him need be told)
A warmer heart Death ne'er made cold.

EPITAPH FOR
GAVIN HAMILTON ESQ.

Gavin Hamilton (1751-1805), solicitor in Mauchline
who sub-let Mossgiel to the Burns brothers in 1784,
encouraged Robert to publish his poems and was the
dedicatee of the Kilmarnock Edition. This poetic
dedication aligned Burns with the liberals in the
struggle between the Auld Lichts and the New Lichts.

The poor man weeps—here Gavin sleeps,
    Whom canting wretches blam'd;
But with such as he, where'er he be,
    May I be sav'd or damn'd!

BALLAD ON THE AMERICAN WAR

TUNE: *Killiecrankie*

Probably written in 1784 in the aftermath of the War
of Independence but too politically sensitive for
inclusion in the Kilmarnock Edition. In December
1786 Burns wrote: 'I showed the inclosed political
ballad to my lord Glencairn, to have his opinion
whether I should publish it; as I suspect my political
tenets, such as they are, may be rather heretical in
the opinion of some of my best Friends.'

Frederick, Lord North	When Guilford good our pilot stood,
helm turn	An did our hellim thraw, man;
Boston Tea Party, 1773	Ae night, at tea, began a plea,
	Within America, man:
teapot	Then up they gat the maskin-pat,
dash	And in the sea did jaw, man;
Continental Congress 1774-6	An did nae less, in full Congress,
	Than quite refuse our law, man.
The Great Lakes	
Richard Montgomery	Then thro the lakes Montgom'ery takes,
	I wat he was na slaw, man;
St. Lawrence river	Down Lowrie's Burn he took a turn,
	And Carleton did ca', man:
what matter	But yet, whatreck, he, at Quebec,
	Montgomery-like did fa', man,
	Wi sword in hand, before his band,
	Amang his en'mies a', man.

Ballad On The American War

Poor Tammy Gage within a cage
  Was kept at Boston-ha', man;
Till Willie Howe took o'er the knowe
  For Philadelphia, man;
Wi sword an gun he thought a sin
  Guid Christian bluid to draw, man;
But at New-York, wi knife an fork,
  Sir-Loin he hacked sma', man.

Burgoyne gaed up, like spur an whip,
  Till Fraser brave did fa', man;
Then lost his way, ae misty day,
  In Saratoga shaw, man.
Cornwallis fought as lang's he dought,
  An did the buckskins claw, man;
But Clinton's glaive frae rust to save,
  He hung it to the wa', man.

Then Montague, an Guilford too,
  Began to fear a fa', man;
And Sackville doure, wha stood the stoure,
  The German chief to thraw, man:
For Paddy Burke, like onie Turk,
  Nae mercy had at a', man;
An Charlie Fox threw by the box,
  An lows'd his tinkler jaw, man.

Then Rockingham took up the game,
  Till death did on him ca', man;
When Shelburne meek held up his cheek,
  Conform to gospel law, man:
Saint Stephen's boys, wi jarring noise,
  They did his measures thraw, man;
For North an Fox united stocks,
  An bore him to the wa', man.

Then clubs an hearts were Charlie's cartes,
  He swept the stakes awa, man,
Till the diamond's ace, of Indian race,
  Led him a sair *faux pas*, man:
The Saxon lads, wi loud placads,
  On Chatham's boy did ca', man:
An Scotland drew her pipe an blew,
  'Up, Willie, waur them a', man!'

*Marginal glosses:*

General Gage, governor of Massachusetts

hill, Sir William Howe

A reference to the seizure of the rebels' cattle at Peekshill on Hudson, 1776.

Sir John Burgoyne
Brigadier Simon Fraser

woods
could, Charles Cornwallis
American colonists
Sir Henry Clinton, sword

John Montague, Earl of Sandwich
Lord George Sackville
obstinate, fight
thwart
Edmund Burke

Charles James Fox
let loose

Charles Wentworth, Marquis of Rockingham

Earl of Shelburne

i.e. member of the House of Commons

Fox's East India Bill

cheers
William Pitt the younger

worst

Ballad On The American War

William Wyndham,
Lord Grenville

sly, Henry Dundas
North of
garments
the elder Pitt died in 1778

Behind the throne then Granville's gone,
  A secret word or twa, man;
While slee Dundas arous'd the class
  Be-north the Roman wa', man:
An Chatham's wraith, in heav'nly graith,
  (Inspired bardies saw, man),
Wi kindling eyes, cry'd: 'Willie rise!
  Would I hae fear'd them a', man?'

Golfed
rose, cast clothes

bagpipes
blade

But, word an blow, North, Fox, and Co.
  Gowff'd Willie like a ba', man,
Till Suthron raise, an coost their claise
  Behind him in a raw, man:
An Caledon threw by the drone,
  An did her whittle draw, man;
An swoor fu rude, thro dirt an bluid,
  To mak it guid in law, man.

ADDRESS TO THE UNCO GUID
OR THE RIGIDLY RIGHTEOUS

My Son, these maxims make a rule,
  An lump them ay thegither:
The Rigid Righteous is a fool,
  The Rigid Wise anither;

sifted
chaff

larking

The cleanest corn that e'er was dight
  May hae some pyles o caff in;
So ne'er a fellow-creature slight
  For random fits o daffin.

—SOLOMON.—Eccles. ch. vii. verse 16.

1 CPB (March 1784) contains two observations: 'that every man even the worst, have something good about them' (sic) and 'I have yet found among [Blackguards] some of the noblest Virtues, Magnanimity, Generosity, disinterested friendship and even modesty, in the highest perfection.' In this poem he illustrates the idea of natural sympathy as the root of the moral consciousness.

well-going

hopper
clapper of a mill

O ye, wha are sae guid yoursel,
  Sae pious and sae holy,
Ye've nought to do but mark and tell
  Your neebour's fauts and folly!
Whase life is like a weel-gaun mill,
  Supplied wi store o water;
The heapet happer's ebbing still,
  An still the clap plays clatter!

74

Address To The Unco Guid

Hear me, ye venerable core,   crowd
   As counsel for poor mortals
That frequent pass douce Wisdom's door sober
   For glaikit Folly's portals: silly
I for their thoughtless, careless sakes,
   Would here propone defences— restive
Their donsie tricks, their black mistakes, unlucky in sexual
Their failings and mischances.   adventures

Ye see your state wi theirs compared,
   And shudder at the niffer;   exchange
But cast a moment's fair regard,
   What maks the mighty differ?
Discount what scant occasion gave;
   That purity ye pride in;
And (what's aft mair than a' the lave) rest
   Your better art o hidin.

Think, when your castigated pulse
   Gies now and then a wallop,
What ragings must his veins convulse,
   That still eternal gallop!
Wi wind and tide fair i your tail,
   Right on ye scud your sea-way;
But in the teeth o baith to sail,
   It maks an unco lee-way.   uncommon

See Social Life and Glee sit down,
   All joyous and unthinking,
Till, quite transmugrify'd, they're grown
   Debauchery and Drinking:
O, would they stay to calculate
   Th' eternal consequences,
Or your more dreaded hell to state—
   Damnation of expenses!

Ye high, exalted, virtuous dames,
   Tied up in godly laces,
Before ye gie poor Frailty names,
   Suppose a change o cases:
A dear-lov'd lad, convenience snug,
   A treach'rous inclination—
But, let me whisper i your lug,   ear
   Ye'er aiblins nae temptation.   perhaps

Address To The Unco Guid

Then gently scan your brother man,
　　Still gentler sister woman;
Tho they may gang a kennin wrang,
　　To step aside is human:
One point must still be greatly dark,
　　The moving *Why* they do it;
And just as lamely can ye mark,
　　How far perhaps they rue it.

Who made the heart, 'tis He alone
　　Decidedly can try us:
He knows each chord, its various tone,
　　Each spring, its various bias:
Then at the balance let's be mute,
　　We never can adjust it;
What's done we partly may compute,
　　But know not what's resisted.

THE RONALDS OF THE BENNALS

The Bennals was a 200 acre farm near Lochlie, owned
by William Ronald. His daughters Jean and Anne were
admired by Robert and Gilbert, but these feelings
were not reciprocated. This poem pokes mild fun at
the Ronalds and their wealth. When Ronald went
bankrupt in November 1789 Burns wrote: 'You will
easily guess, that from his insolent vanity in his
sunshine of life, he will feel a little retaliation from
those who thought themselves eclipsed by him . . .'

In Tarbolton, ye ken, there are proper young men,
　　And proper young lasses and a', man:

know
bear the bell

But ken ye the Ronalds that live in the Bennals?
　　They carry the gree frae them a', man.

Their father's a laird, and weel he can spare't,
　　Braid money to tocher them a', man:

Broad, to dower

To proper young men, he'll clink in the hand

Gold

Gowd guineas a hunder or twa, man.

There's ane they ca' Jean, I'll warrant ye've seen
　　As bonie a lass or as braw, man;

well set up

But for sense and guid taste she'll vie wi the best,
　　And a conduct that beautifies a', man.

76

The Ronalds of the Bennals

The charms o the min', the langer they shine
    The mair admiration they draw, man;
While peaches and cherries, and roses and lilies,
    They fade and they wither awa, man.

If ye be for Miss Jean, tak this frae a frien',
    A hint o a rival or twa, man:
The Laird o Blackbyre wad gang through the fire,   would go
    If that wad entice her awa, man.

The Laird o Braehead has been on his speed,
    For mair than a towmond or twa, man: twelve months
The Laird o the Ford will straught on a board,   stretch
    If he canna get her at a', man.

Then Anna comes in, the pride o her kin,
    The boast of our bachelors a', man:
Sae sonsy and sweet, sae fully complete,   pleasant
    She steals our affections awa, man.

If I should detail the pick and the wale   choice
    O lasses that live here awa, man,   around
The faut wad be mine, if they didna shine   fault
    The sweetest and best o them a', man.

I lo'e her mysel, but darena weel tell,
    My poverty keeps me in awe, man;
For making o rhymes, and working at times,
    Does little or naething at a', man.

Yet I wadna choose to let her refuse   would not
    Nor hae't in her power to say na, man: have it
For though I be poor, unnoticed, obscure,
    My stomach's as proud as them a', man.

Though I canna ride in weel-booted pride,
    And flee o'er the hills like a craw, man,
I can haud up my head wi the best o the breed,   hold
    Though fluttering ever so braw, man.   fine

My coat and my vest, they are Scotch o the best;
    O pairs o guid breeks I hae twa, man,   breeches
And stockings and pumps to put on my stumps,
    And ne'er a wrang steek in them a', man.   stitch

The Ronalds of the Bennals

shirts	My sarks they are few, but five o them new—
	Twal' hundred, as white as the snaw, man!
fine linen necktie	A ten-shillings hat, a Holland cravat—
well dressed	There are no monie Poets sae braw, man!
well endowed	I never had frien's weel stockit in means,
	To leave me a hundred or twa, man;
-dowered, prosings	Nae weel-tocher'd aunts, to wait on their drants,
	And wish them in hell for it a', man.
careful	I never was cannie for hoarding o money,
grasping it	Or claughtin't together at a', man;
	I've little to spend and naething to lend,
owe	But devil a shilling I awe, man.

THE TARBOLTON LASSES

Composed in 1784, at the same time as the preceding. Faile is a hamlet in Tarbolton parish.

If ye gae up to yon hill-tap,
  Ye'll there see bonie Peggy:
She kens her father is a laird,
lady   And she forsooth's a leddy.

prepared or dressed There's Sophy tight, a lassie bright,
  Besides a handsome fortune:
Wha canna win her in a night,
  Has little art in courtin.

Gae down by Faile, and taste the ale,
  And tak a look o Mysie:
stubborn, swarthy She's dour and din, a deil within,
perhaps   But aiblins she may please ye.

If she be shy, her sister try,
  Ye'll may be fancy Jenny:
If ye'll dispense wi want o sense
  She kens herself she's bonie.

78

As ye gae up by yon hillside,   that
   Spier in for bonie Bessy: call
She'll gie ye a beck, and bid ye light,   curtsy
   And handsomely address ye.

There's few sae bonie, nane sae guid
   In a' King George' dominion:
If ye should doubt the truth o this,
   It's Bessy's ain opinion!

THE BELLES OF MAUCHLINE

TUNE: *Bonie Dundee*

Written about 1784-5 about Helen Miller and her sister Betty, Jean Markland, Jean Smith (sister of James), Christina Morton and, of course, Jean Armour herself.

In Mauchline there dwells six proper young belles,
   The pride of the place and its neighbourhood a',
Their carriage and dress, a stranger would guess,
   In Lon'on or Paris, they'd gotten it a'.

Miss Miller is fine, Miss Markland's divine,
   Miss Smith she has wit, and Miss Betty is braw,   elegant
There's beauty and fortune to get wi Miss Morton;
   But Armour's the jewel for me o them a'.

O, LEAVE NOVELS

TUNE: *Donald Blue*

Probably composed in 1784-5, before Burns turned his attention to Jean Armour.

O, leave novéls, ye Mauchline belles—
   Ye're safer at your spinning-wheel!
Such witching books are baited hooks
   For rakish rooks like Rob Mossgiel.

O, Leave Novels

Your fine *Tom Jones* and *Grandisons,*
    They make your youthful fancies reel!
They heat your brains, and fire your veins,
    And then you're prey for Rob Mossgiel.

Beware a tongue that's smoothly hung,
    A heart that warmly seems to feel!
That feeling heart but acts a part—
    'Tis rakish art in Rob Mossgiel.

The frank address, the soft caress,
    Are worse than poisoned darts of steel:
The frank address, and politesse,
    Are all finesse in Rob Mossgiel.

THE MAUCHLINE LADY

TUNE: *I had a horse, and I had nae mair*

The lady of this poem is thought to have been Jean Armour herself. 'Stewart Kyle' alludes to the Burns family's move to Lochlie in 1777. The move to Mossgiel took place in February 1784.

When first I came to Stewart Kyle,
    My mind it was na steady:
went, rode   Where'er I gaed, where'er I rade,
    A mistress still I had ay.

But when I cam roun' by Mauchline toun,
    Not dreadin anybody,
My heart was caught, before I thought,
    And by a Mauchline lady.

GREEN GROW THE RASHES O,

Derived from the ancient ballad 'Cou thou me the raschyes grene' first published in 1549, with other versions set down in 1627 and 1740, Burns's version appears in 1 CPB following a prose musing on categorizing young men into the grave and the merry.

CHORUS

> *Green grow the rashes, O;*
> *Green grow the rashes, O;*
> *The sweetest hours that e'er I spend,*
> *Are spent among the lasses, O.*

There's nought but care on ev'ry han',
   In every hour that passes, O:
What signifies the life o man,
   An 'twere na for the lasses, O.

The war'ly race may riches chase,   worldly
   An riches still may fly them, O;
An tho at last they catch them fast,
   Their hearts can ne'er enjoy them, O.

But gie me a cannie hour at e'en,   quiet, evening
   My arms about my dearie, O,
An war'ly cares an war'ly men,
   May a' gae tapsalteerie, O!   topsy-turvy

For you sae douce, ye sneer at this;   sober
   Ye're nought but senseless asses, O:
The wisest man the warl' e'er saw,
   He dearly lov'd the lasses, O.

Auld Nature swears, the lovely dears
   Her noblest work she classes, O:
Her prentice han' she try'd on man,
   An then she made the lasses, O.

MY GIRL SHE'S AIRY

TUNE: *Black Joke*

Composed in 1784, during the poet's brief affair with
Elizabeth Paton of Lairgieside. The affair blossomed
after the death of William Burnes. The result of this
liaison was 'Dear-bought Bess', the poet's first
illegitimate child, born on 22nd May 1785. The Black
Joke of the tune title was a bawdy name for the
female genitalia.

My girl she's airy, she's buxom and gay;
Her breath is as sweet as the blossoms in May;
    A touch of her lips it ravishes quite.
She's always good natur'd, good humour'd and free;
She dances, she glances, she smiles with a glee;
    Her eyes are the lightenings of joy and delight;
Her slender neck, her handsome waist,
Her hair well buckled, her stays well lac'd,
    Her taper white leg with an et, and a, c,   <small>etcetera (i.e. other charms)</small>
For her a, b, e, d, and her c, u, n, t,
And oh, for the joys of a long winter night!!!

EPISTLE TO JOHN RANKINE

ENCLOSING SOME POEMS

The tenant-farmer of Adamhill near Tarbolton,
Rankine (died 1810) was a close friend of Burns in the
latter part of the Lochlie period. He discovered early
on that Elizabeth Paton was pregnant by Burns and
twitted the poet about it. Burns retaliated with these
verses, using the analogy of the poacher to describe
his adulterous activities.

O rough, rude, ready-witted Rankine,
The wale o cocks for fun an drinkin!   <small>pick</small>
There's monie godly folks are thinkin
    Your dreams and tricks
Will send you, Korah-like, a-sinkin   <small>Num. xvi 29-33</small>
    Straught to Auld Nick's.

Ye hae sae monie cracks an cants,   <small>anecdotes</small>
And in your wicked drucken rants,   <small>drunken ravings</small>
Ye mak a devil o the saunts,
    An fill them fou;
And then their failings, flaws, an wants,
    Are a' see thro.

Epistle To John Rankine

Hypocrisy, in mercy spare it!
That holy robe, O, dinna tear it!
Spare't for their sakes, wha aften wear it—
    The lads in black;
But your curst wit, when it comes near it,
    Rives't aff their back.   rips

Think, wicked sinner, wha ye're skaithing: injuring
It's just the Blue-gown badge an claithing
O saunts; tak that, ye lea'e them naething
    To ken them by
Frae onie unregenerate heathen,
    Like you or I.

I've sent you here some rhymin ware,
A' that I bargain'd for, an mair;
Sae, when ye hae an hour to spare,
    I will expect,
Yon sang ye'll sen't, wi cannie care,   send it
    And no neglect.

Tho faith, sma' heart hae I to sing:
My Muse dow scarcely spread her wing!   can
I've play'd mysel a bonie spring,   melody
    An danc'd my fill!
I'd better gaen an sair't the King   have gone, served
    At Bunker's Hill.   one of the first
    battles in the
    American War

'Twas ae night lately, in my fun,
I gaed a rovin wi the gun,   went
An brought a paitrick to the grun'—   partridge
    A bonie hen;
And, as the twilight was begun,
    Thought nane wad ken.   know

The poor, wee thing was little hurt;
I straikit it a wee for sport,   stroked a little
Ne'er thinkin they wad fash me for't;   worry
    But Deil-ma-care!
Somebody tells the Poacher-Court   Kirk Session
    The hale affair.   whole

Epistle To John Rankine

       Some auld, us'd hands had taen a note,
       That sic a hen had got a shot;
       I was suspected for the plot;
             I scorn'd to lie;

lost my fourpence   So gat the whissle o my groat,
             An pay't the fee.

pick   But, by my gun, o guns the wale,
gunpowder   An by my pouther an my hail,
       An by my hen, an by her tail,
             I vow an swear!
       The game shall pay, owre moor an dale,

next   For this, niest year!

incubation   As soon's the clockin-time is by,
chicks   An the wee pouts begun to cry,
I'll   Lord, I'se hae sportin by an by
             For my gowd guinea;

American cattle Tho I should herd the buckskin kye
             For't, in Virginia!

       Trowth, they had muckle for to blame!
       'Twas neither broken wing nor limb,

blows, belly But twa-three chaps about the wame,
             Scarce thro the feathers;

a guinea   An baith a yellow George to claim
tolerate nonsense   An thole their blethers!

       It pits me ay as mad's a hare;
       So I can rhyme nor write nae mair;

tit-for-tat   But pennyworths again is fair,
             When time's expedient:
       Meanwhile, I am, respected Sir,
             Your most obedient.

EPITAPH ON JOHN RANKINE

Composed in 1785 as a sequel to the preceding Epistle.

Ae day, as Death, that gruesome carl, One, fellow
Was driving to the tither warl'   other world
A mix:ie-maxtie motley squad,   jumbled
And monie a guilt-bespotted lad:
Black gowns of each denomination,   preachers
And thieves of every rank and station, lawyers
From him that wears the star and garter,
To him that wintles in a halter: dangles on a noose
Asham'd himself to see the wretches,
He mutters, glowrin at the bitches:—
'By God I'll not be seen behint them,
Nor 'mang the sp'ritual core present them, crowd
Without at least ae honest man,
To grace this damn'd infernal clan!'
By Adamhill a glance he threw,
'Lord God!' quoth he, 'I have it now,
There's just the man I want, i faith!'
And quickly stoppit Rankine's breath.

REPLY TO AN ANNOUNCEMENT BY JOHN RANKINE

Allegedly the poet's answer to Rankine's reactions on learning that Elizabeth Paton was expecting his child.

I am a keeper of the law
In some sma' points, altho not a';
Some people tell me, gin I fa'   if I fall
   Ae way or ither   one, other
The breaking of ae point, tho sma'
   Breaks a' thegither.   together

I hae been in for't ance or twice,
And winna say o'er far for thrice,   will not, too certainly
Yet never met wi that surprise
   That broke my rest.
But now a rumour's like to rise—
   A whaup's i the nest!   curlew

EPITAPH ON THE AUTHOR

This mock epitaph probably belongs to the Mossgiel period.

He who of Rankine sang, lies stiff and deid,
And a green grassy hillock hides his heid:
Alas! alas! a devilish change indeed!

EPISTLE TO DAVIE, A BROTHER POET

JANUARY

David Sillar (1760-1830) was the third of the four sons of Patrick Sillar of Spittalside near Lochlie. Though self-educated he ran his own school. He was a member of the Tarbolton Bachelors' Club. His own inferior verses were published at Kilmarnock in 1789.

While winds frae aff Ben-Lomond blaw,
  And bar the doors wi drivin snaw,
    And hing us owre the ingle,
I set me down to pass the time,
And spin a verse or twa o rhyme,
    In hamely, westlin jingle:
While frosty winds blaw in the drift,
    Ben to the chimla lug,
I grudge a wee the great-folk's gift,
    That live sae bien an snug:
      I tent less, and want less
        Their roomy fire-side;
      But hanker, and canker,
        To see their cursed pride.

It's hardly in a body's pow'r,
To keep, at times, frae being sour,
    To see how things are shar'd;
How best o chiels are whyles in want,
While coofs on countless thousands rant,
    And ken na how to ware't;
But, Davie, lad, ne'er fash your head
    Tho we hae little gear;
We're fit to win our daily bread,
    As lang's we're hale and fier:
      'Mair spier na, nor fear na,'
        Auld age ne'er mind a feg;
      The last o't, the warst o't,
        Is only but to beg.

*Glosses (left margin):*
hang over fire — western — Right to the chimney corner — a little — prosperous — value — chaps, sometimes — fools, roister — spend — trouble — wealth — sound — fig

Epistle to Davie, A Brother Poet

To lie in kilns and barns at e'en,
When banes are craz'd, and bluid is thin,
   Is, doubtless, great distress!
Yet then content could make us blest;
Ev'n then, sometimes, we'd snatch a taste
   Of truest happiness.
The honest heart that's free frae a'
   Intended fraud or guile,
However Fortune kick the ba',
   Has ay some cause to smile;
     And mind still, you'll find still,
     A comfort this nae sma';
   Nae mair then, we'll care then,
     Nae farther we can fa'.

What tho, like commoners of air,
We wander out, we know not where,
   But either house or hal'?   *without (small) Holding*
Yet Nature's charms, the hills and woods,
The sweeping vales, and foaming floods,
   Are free alike to all.
In days when daisies deck the ground,
   And blackbirds whistle clear,
With honest joy our hearts will bound,
   To see the coming year:
     On braes when we please then,   *slopes*
     We'll sit an sowth a tune;   *hum*
     Syne rhyme till't, we'll time till't,   *Then*
     An sing't when we hae done.

It's no in titles nor in rank:
It's no in wealth like Lon'on Bank,
   To purchase peace and rest,
It's no in makin muckle, mair;   *much, more*
It's no in books, it's no in lear,   *learning*
   To make us truly blest:
If happiness hae not her seat
   An centre in the breast,
We may be wise, or rich, or great,
   But never can be blest!
Nae treasures nor pleasures
   Could make us happy lang;
The heart ay's the part ay
   That makes us right or wrang.

Epistle to Davie, A Brother Poet

Think ye, that sic as you and I,
Wha drudge and drive thro wet and dry,
    Wi never ceasing toil;
Think ye, are we less blest than they,
Wha scarcely tent us in their way,
    As hardly worth their while?
Alas! how oft in haughty mood,
    God's creatures they oppress!
Or else, neglecting a' that's guid,
    They riot in excess!
        Baith careless and fearless
           Of either Heaven or Hell;
        Esteeming and deeming
           It a' an idle tale!

Then let us cheerfu acquiesce,
Nor make our scanty pleasures less
    By pining at our state:
And, even should misfortunes come
I here wha sit, hae met wi some,
    An's thankfu for them yet,
They gie the wit of age to youth;
    They let us ken oursel;
They make us see the naked truth—
    The real guid and ill:
        Tho losses and crosses
           Be lessons right severe,
        There's wit there, ye'll get there,
           Ye'll find nae other where.

But tent me, Davie, ace o hearts!
(To say aught less wad wrang the cartes,
    And flatt'ry I detest)
This life has joys for you and I;
And joys that riches ne'er could buy,
    And joys the very best.
There's a' the pleasures o the heart,
    The lover an the frien:
Ye hae your Meg, your dearest part,
    And I my darling Jean!
        It warms me, it charms me
           To mention but her name:
        It heats me, it beets me,
           An sets me a' on flame!

Marginal glosses:
And am
listen to
anything, cards
kindles

Epistle to Davie, A Brother Poet

O all ye Pow'rs who rule above!
O Thou whose very self art love!
　　Thou know'st my words sincere!
The life-blood streaming thro my heart,
Or my more dear immortal part,
　　Is not more fondly dear!
When heart-corroding care and grief
　　Deprive my soul of rest,
Her dear idea brings relief,
　　And solace to my breast.
　　　　Thou Being, All-seeing,
　　　　　O, hear my fervent pray'r!
　　　　Still take her, and make her
　　　　　Thy most peculiar care!

All hail! ye tender feelings dear!
The smile of love, the friendly tear,
　　The sympathetic glow!
Long since, this world's thorny ways
Had number'd out my weary days,
　　Had it not been for you!
Fate still has blest me with a friend
　　In every care and ill;
And oft a more endearing band,
　　A tie more tender still.
　　　　It lightens, it brightens
　　　　　The tenebrific scene,
　　　　To meet with, and greet with
　　　　　My Davie, or my Jean!

O, how that Name inspires my style!
The words come skelpin rank an file,   spanking
　　Amaist before I ken!   Almost, know
The ready measure rins as fine,
As Phoebus an the famous Nine
　　Were glowrin owre my pen.   watching over
My spaviet Pegasus will limp,   spavined
　　Till ance he's fairly het;   hot
And then he'll hilch, an stilt, and jimp,   hobble, limp, jump
　　And rin an unco fit;   uncommon burst
But least then the beast then
　　Should rue this hasty ride,
I'll light now, and dight now   wipe
　　His sweaty, wizen'd hide.

THE TWA HERDS: OR, THE HOLY TULZIE

squabble

unduly

AN UNCO MOURNFU TALE

Blockheads with reason, wicked wits abhor,
But fool with fool is barbarous civil war. — POPE

This satirical lamentation was based on the unseemly quarrel over parish boundaries, between two Auld Licht ministers, Alexander Moodie of Riccarton and John Russel of Kilmarnock. Matters came to a head at the Presbytery of Irvine 'where the reverend divines . . lost all command of temper and abused each other, with a fiery virulence of invective.'

O a' ye pious godly flocks,
Weel fed on pastures orthodox,
Wha now will keep you frae the fox,
      Or worrying tykes?
dogs

tend, stragglers
and old ewes,
stone fences

Or wha will tent the waifs an crocks,
      About the dykes?

shepherds, west
gave

The twa best herds in a' the wast,
That e'er gae gospel horn a blast
These five an twenty simmers past—
sad
      O, dool to tell!—
quarrel
Between
Hae had a bitter, black out-cast
      Atween themsel.

O Moodie, man, an wordy Russell,
How could you raise so vile a bustle?
Ye'll see how New-Light herds will whistle,
      An think it fine!
such a twist
can recall
The Lord's cause gat na sic a twistle
      Sin I hae min'.

O Sirs! whae'er wad hae expeckit
would have so
Your duty ye wad sae negleckit?
Ye wha were no by lairds respeckit
      To wear the plaid,
But by the brutes themselves eleckit,
      To be their guide!

What flock wi Moodie's flock could rank
leg
Sae hale an hearty every shank?
stagnant pool
Nae poison'd, soor Arminian stank
      He let me taste;
Arminius of Leyden
(1609) opposed
Calvinism . The
Scottish liberals
were abused as
'Arminians'
Frae Calvin's fountain-head they drank,—
      O, sic a feast!

The Twa Herds: or, The Holy Tulzie

The thummart, wilcat, brock, an tod   *polecat, wildcat,*
Weel kend his voice thro a' the wood;   *badger and fox*
He smell'd their ilka hole an road,
     Baith out an in;   *every*
An weel he lik'd to shed their bluid,
     An sell their skin.

What herd like Russell tell'd his tale?
His voice was heard thro muir and dale;
He ken'd the Lord's sheep, ilka tail,
     O'er a' the height;
An tell'd gin they were sick or hale,   *if*
     At the first sight.

He fine a mangy sheep could scrub;
Or nobly fling the gospel club;
Or New-Light herds could nicely drub
     And pay their skin;
Or hing them o'er the burning dub,   *hang, puddle*
     Or heave them in.

Sic twa—O! do I live to see't?—
Sic famous twa sud disagree't,   *should have*
An names like villain, hypocrite,
     Ilk ither gi'en   *each other*
While New-Light herds, wi laughin spite,
     Say neither's liein!   *lying*

A' ye wha tent the gospel fauld,   *pay heed to*
Thee Duncan deep, an Peebles shaul',   *shallow*
But chiefly great apostle Auld,   *Robert Duncan*
     We trust in thee,   *(1753-1815)*
That thou wilt work them, hot an cauld,   *William Peebles*
     Till they agree!   *(1753-1826)*

Consider, sirs, how we're beset:
There's scarce a new herd that we get
But comes frae 'mang that cursed set,
     I winna name: *will not*
I hope frae heav'n to see them yet
     In fiery flame!

Dalrymple had been lang our fae,   *William Dalrymple*
M'Gill has wrought us meikle wae,   *(1723-1814); William*
An that curs'd rascal ca'd M'Quhae,   *McGill (1732-1807); much*
     An baith the Shaws,   *woe; William McQuhae*
That aft hae made us black an blae,   *(1737-1823); David (1719*
     Wi vengeful paws.   *-1810) and Andrew (1741-*
                                      1805); blue

The Twa Herds: or, The Holy Tulzie

Patrick Wodrow
(1713-93)

Auld Wodrow lang has hatch'd mischief:
We thought ay death wad bring relief,
But he has gotten to our grief,
    Ane to succeed him,
chap, strike our flesh
greatly

A chield wha'll soundly buff our beef—
    I meikle dread him.

more

And monie mae that I could tell,
Wha fain would openly rebel,
Besides
George Smith (d. 1823)
gambler

Forby turn-coats amang oursel:
    There's Smith for ane—
I doubt he's but a greyneck still,
    An that ye'll fin'!

bogs, hillsides

O! a' ye flocks o'er a' the hills,
By mosses, meadows, moors, an fells,
Come, join your counsel and your skills
frighten
    To cowe the lairds,
An get the brutes the power themsels
    To chuse their herds!

hangman's noose
formidable

Then Orthodoxy yet may prance,
An Learning in a woody dance,
An that fell cur ca'd Common-sense,
    That bites sae sair,
Be banished o'er the sea to France—
    Let him bark there!

Then Shaw's an D'rymple's eloquence,
M'Gill's close, nervous excellence,
M'Quhae's pathetic, manly sense,
    An guid M'Math,
Wha thro the heart can brawly glance,
    May a' pack aff!

HOLY WILLIE'S PRAYER

And send the godly in a pet to pray—POPE

The prototype of this burlesque prayer was William Fisher (1737-1809) of Montgarswood, an elder of Mauchline parish at whose instigation the Kirk Session took action against Gavin Hamilton for failure to observe the Sabbath in the proper manner. Burns described Fisher as 'a rather oldish bachelor, much and justly famed for that polemical chattering which ends in tippling orthodoxy, and for that spiritualised bawdry which refines to liquorish devotion.'

O Thou that in the Heavens does dwell,
Wha, as it pleases best Thysel,
Sends ane to Heaven, an ten to Hell,
    A' for Thy glory,
And no for onie guid or ill
    They've done before Thee!

I bless and praise Thy matchless might,
When thousands Thou hast left in night,
That I am here before Thy sight,
    For gifts an grace
A burning and a shining light
    To a' this place.

What was I, or my generation,
That I should get sic exaltation?   *such*
I, wha deserv'd most just damnation
    For broken laws,
Sax thousand years ere my creation,   *Six*
    Thro Adam's cause!

When from my mither's womb I fell,
Thou might hae plung'd me deep in Hell,
To gnash my gooms, and weep and wail,   *gums*
    In burning lakes,
Whare damned devils roar and yell,
    Chain'd to their stakes.

Yet I am here a chosen sample,
To show Thy grace is great and ample:
I'm here a pillar o Thy temple,
    Strong as a rock,
A guide, a buckler, and example,   *shield*
    To a' Thy flock!

But yet, O Lord! confess I must,
At times I'm fash'd wi fleshy lust;   *irked*
An sometimes, too, in warldly trust,
    Vile self gets in;
But Thou remembers we are dust,
    Defil'd wi sin.

Holy Willie's Prayer

O Lord! yestreen, Thou kens, wi Meg—
Thy pardon I sincerely beg—
O, may't ne'er be a livin plague
    To my dishonour!
An I'll ne'er lift a lawless leg
    Again upon her.

Besides, I farther maun avow,
Wi Leezie's lass, three times I trow—
But, Lord, that Friday I was fou,
    When I cam near her,
Or else, Thou kens, Thy servant true
    Wad never steer her.

Maybe Thou lets this fleshy thorn
Buffet Thy servant e'en and morn,
Lest he owre proud and high should turn,
    That he's sae gifted:
If sae, Thy han' maun e'en be borne,
    Until Thou lift it.

Lord, bless Thy chosen in this place,
For here Thou has a chosen race!
But God confound their stubborn face,
    An blast their name,
Wha bring Thy elders to disgrace
    An open shame.

Lord, mind Gau'n Hamilton's deserts:
He drinks, an swears, an plays at cartes,
Yet has sae monie takin arts,
    Wi great and sma',
Frae God's ain Priest the people's hearts
    He steals awa.

And when we chasten'd him therefore,
Thou kens how he bred sic a splore,
And set the warld in a roar
    O laughin at us;
Curse Thou his basket and his store,
    Kail an potatoes!

Lord, hear my earnest cry and pray'r,
Against that Presbyt'ry o Ayr!
Thy strong right hand, Lord, mak it bare
    Upo' their heads!
Lord, visit them, an dinna spare,
    For their misdeeds!

*Glosses (left margin):*
- last night
- must
- drunk
- would, meddle with
- cards
- many
- row
- do not

O Lord, my God! that glib-tongu'd Aiken,   Robert Aiken
My vera heart and flesh are quakin,
To think how we stood sweatin, shakin,
    An pish'd wi dread,
While he, wi hingin lip, an snakin,   sneering
    Held up his head.

Lord, in Thy day o vengeance try him!
Lord, visit them wha did employ him!
And pass not in Thy mercy by them,
    Nor hear their pray'r,
But for Thy people's sake destroy them,
    An dinna spare.

But, Lord, remember me and mine
Wi mercies temporal and divine,
That I for grace an gear may shine,   wealth
    Excell'd by nane,
And a' the glory shall be Thine—
    Amen, Amen!

EPITAPH ON HOLY WILLIE

Here Holy Willie's sair worn clay   very
    Taks up its last abode;
His saul has ta'en some other way—   soul
    I fear, the left-hand road.

Stop! there he is as sure's a gun!
    Poor, silly body, see him!
Nae wonder he's as black's the grun—   ground
    Observe wha's standing wi him!

Your brunstane Devilship, I see   brimstone
    Has got him there before ye!
But haud your nine-tail cat a wee,   hold back a little
    Till ance you've heard my story.   once

Your pity I will not implore,
    For pity ye have nane.
Justice, alas! has gi'en him o'er,
    And mercy's day is gane.

But hear me, Sir, Deil as ye are,
    Look something to your credit:
A cuif like him wad stain your name,   blockhead
    If it were kent ye did it!

DEATH AND DOCTOR HORNBOOK

A TRUE STORY

The prototype was John Wilson (c.1751-1839), appointed schoolmaster at Tarbolton in 1781. A hornbook consisted of a sheet of paper bearing the alphabet, numbers, Lord's Prayer and rules of spelling, mounted on a wooden board and protected by a thin plate of transparent horn. This primitive teaching aid was in widespread use till about 1800. 'Hornbook' thus became a popular nickname for schoolmasters. Burns was inspired to write this satire in 1785 after hearing Wilson airing his medical knowledge at a meeting of Tarbolton Masonic Lodge.

Some books are lies frae end to end,
And some great lies were never penn'd:
Ev'n ministers, they hae been kend,
    In holy rapture,
A rousing whid at times to vend,
    And nail't wi Scripture.

But this that I am gaun to tell,
Which lately on a night befel,
Is just as true's the Deil's in Hell
    Or Dublin city:
That e'er he nearer comes oursel
    'S a muckle pity!

The clachan yill had made me canty,
I was na fou, but just had plenty:
I stacher'd whyles, but yet took tent ay
    To free the ditches;
An hillocks, stanes, an bushes, kend ay
    Frae ghaists an witches.

The rising moon began to glowr
The distant Cumnock Hills out-owre:
To count her horns, wi a my pow'r,
    I set mysel;
But whether she had three or four,
    I cou'd na tell.

I was come round about the hill,
An todlin down on Willie's mill,
Setting my staff wi a' my skill,
    To keep me sicker;
Tho leeward whyles, against my will,
    I took a bicker.

I there wi *Something* does forgather,
That pat me in an eerie swither;
An awfu scythe, out-owre ae shouther,
    Clear-dangling, hang;
A three-tae'd leister on the ither
    Lay, large an lang.

*Glosses (left margin):*
- lie
- going
- village ale, jolly
- drunk
- staggered sometimes
- took care to avoid
- always
- stare
- above
- steady
- run
- put, ghostly panic
- across one shoulder
- trident

96

BURNS AT THE HOUSE OF FRANCIS GROSE by Robert Scott Lauder
courtesy of the Dick Institute, Kilmarnock

THE ARCHIBALD SKIRVING PORTRAIT OF BURNS

courtesy of the National Galleries of Scotland

Its stature seem'd lang Scotch ells twa,   metres
The queerest shape that e'er I saw,
For fient a wame it had ava;   not a belly at all
   And then its shanks,   legs
They were as thin, as sharp an sma'
   As cheeks o branks.   horse-bridle bits

'Guid-e'en', quo I; 'Friend! hae ye been mawin, Good evening, said
When ither folk are busy sawin?'
It seem'd to mak a kind o stan,   halt
   But naething spak.
At length, says I, 'Friend! whare ye gaun?
   Will ye go back?'

It spak right howe,—'My name is *Death*, hollow
But be na fley'd'—Quoth I, 'Guid faith, frightened
Ye're may be come to stap my breath;
   But tent me, billie: heed, comrade
I red ye weel, tak care o skaith,   counsel, injury
   See, there's a gully!'   large knife

'Gudeman,' quo he, 'put up your whittle, Tenant farmer, blade
I'm no design'd to try its mettle;
But if I did, I wad be kittle   ticklish
   To be mislear'd: mischievous
I wad na mind it, no that spittle
   Out-owre my beard.'

'Weel, weel!' says I, 'a bargain be't;
Come, gie's your hand, an sae we're gree't; agreed
We'll ease our shanks, an tak a seat:
   Come, gie's your news:
This while ye hae been monie a gate, road
   At monie a house.'

'Ay, ay!' quo he, an shook his head,
'It's e'en a lang, lang time indeed
Sin' I began to nick the thread,   cut
   An choke the breath:
Folk maun do something for their bread,
   An sae maun *Death*.'

'Sax thousand years are near-hand fled well-nigh
Sin' I was to the butching bred,   butchery
An monie a scheme in vain's been laid,
   To stap or scar me;   scare
Till ane Hornbook's ta'en up the trade,
   And faith! he'll waur me.'   get the better of

D

Death and Doctor Hornbook

'Ye ken Jock Hornbook i the clachan?
Deil mak his king's-hood in a spleuchan!—
He's grown sae weel acquaint wi *Buchan*
      And ither chaps,
The weans haud out their fingers laughin,
      An pouk my hips.'

scrotum, tobacco-pouch
Dr. William Buchan
(1729-1805) author
of Domestic Medicine;
children, poke

'See, here's a scythe, an there's a dart,
They hae pierc'd monie a gallant heart;
But Doctor Hornbook wi his art
      An cursed skill,
Has made them baith no worth a fart,
      Damn'd haet they'll kill!'

The devil a one

'Twas but yestreen, nae farther gane,
I threw a noble throw at ane;
Wi less, I'm sure, I've hundreds slain;
      But Deil-ma' care!
It just play'd dirl on the bane,
      But did nae mair.'

gone

tinkle

'Hornbook was by wi ready art,
An had sae fortify'd the part,
That when I looked to my dart,
      It was sae blunt,
Fient haet o't wad hae pierc'd the heart
      Of a kail-runt.'

cabbage-stalk

'I drew my scythe in sic a fury,
I near-hand cowpit wi my hurry,
But yet the bauld Apothecary
      Withstood the shock;
I might as weel hae try'd a quarry
      O hard whin-rock.'

tumbled

granite

'Ev'n them he canna get attended,
Altho their face he ne'er had kend it,
Just shite in a kail-blade, an send it,
      As soon's he smells 't,
Baith their disease, and what will mend it,
      At once he tells 't.'

known
cabbage-leaf

'And then a doctor's saws and whittles,
Of a' dimensions, shapes and mettles,
A' kinds o boxes, mugs, and bottles,
      He's sure to hae;
Their Latin names as fast he rattles
      As A B C.'

scalpels

'Calces o fossils, earths, and trees;
True *sal-marinum* o the seas;
The *farina* of beans an pease,
    He has't in plenty;
Aqua-fontis, what you please,
    He can content ye.'

'Forbye some new, uncommon weapons,
Urinus spiritus of capons;
Or mite-horn shavings, filings, scrapings,
    Distill'd *per se;*
Sal-alkali o midge-tail-clippings,
    And monie mae.'   *many more*

'Waes me for Johnie Ged's Hole now,'
Quoth I, 'if that thae news be true!   *these*
His braw calf-ward whare gowans grew,   *pasture, daisies*
    Sae white and bonie,
Nae doubt they'll rive it wi the plew: *split, plough*
    They'll ruin Johnie!'

The creature grain'd an eldritch laugh,   *groaned, unearthly*
And says: 'Ye needna yoke the pleugh,
Kirkyards will soon be till'd eneugh,
    Tak ye nae fear:
They'll a' be trench'd wi monie a sheugh,   *ditch*
    In twa-three year.'

'Whare I kill'd ane, a fair strae death   *straw [bed]*
By loss o blood or want o breath,
This night I'm free to tak my aith,
    That Hornbook's skill
Has clad a score i their last claith,   *cloth*
    By drap an pill.'   *drop*

'An honest wabster to his trade,   *weaver*
Whase wife's twa nieves were scarce weel-bred   *fists*
Gat tippence-worth to mend her head,
    When it was sair;   *aching*
The wife slade cannie to her bed,   *crept quietly*
    But ne'er spak mair.'

'A countra laird had ta'en the batts,   *colic*
Or some curmurring in his guts,   *commotion*
His only son for Hornbook sets,
    An pays him well:
The lad, for twa guid gimmer-pets   *pet ewes*
    Was laird himsel.'

Death and Doctor Hornbook

upset, stomach

'A bonie lass—ye ken her name—
Some ill-brewn drink had hov'd her wame;
She trusts hersel, to hide the shame,
    In Hornbook's care;
Horn set her aff to her lang hame
    To hide it there.

sample

'That's just a swatch o Hornbook's way;
Thus goes he on from day to day,
Thus does he poison, kill, an slay,
    An's weel paid for't;
Yet stop me o my lawfu prey,
    Wi his damn'd dirt.'

'But hark! I'll tell you of a plot,
Tho dinna ye be speakin o't!
I'll nail the self-conceited sot,
    As dead's a herrin;

Next, wager fourpence
reward

Niest time we meet, I'll wad a groat,
    He gets his fairin!'

But just as he began to tell,
The auld kirk-hammer strak the bell

beyond twelve
got us on our feet

Some wee short hour ayont the twal,
    Which rais'd us baith:
I took the way that pleas'd mysel,
    And sae did *Death*.

ON TAM THE CHAPMAN

**Written about Thomas Kennedy of Ayr who died in
Homor, Courtland county, New York in 1846.**

pedlar

As Tam the chapman on a day
Wi Death forgather'd by the way,

sturdy person

Weel pleas'd, he greets a wight so famous,
And Death was nae less pleas'd wi Thomas,
Wha cheerfully lays down his pack,

conversation

And there blaws up a hearty crack:
His social, friendly, honest-heart
Sae tickled Death, they could na part;
Sae, after viewing knives and garters,
Death taks him hame to gie him quarters.

EPISTLE TO J. LAPRAIK

AN OLD SCOTTISH BARD—APRIL 1, 1785

John Lapraik (1727-1807), farmer of Dalfram, Muirkirk, nine miles from Mauchline. The failure of the Ayr Bank (1773) forced him to sell his farm, and in 1785 he was gaoled for debt at Ayr. While in prison he turned to poetry and, encouraged by the success of Burns, he published his own poems at Kilmarnock in 1788. His friendship stimulated Burns to write two of his best verse-epistles.

While briers an woodbines budding green,
An paitricks scraichin loud at e'en,   *partridges*
An morning poussie whiddin seen,   *hare scudding*
      Inspire my Muse,
This freedom, in an unknown frien'
      I pray excuse.

On Fasten-e'en we had a rockin,   *meeting*
To ca' the crack and weave our stockin;   *have a chat*
And there was muckle fun and jokin,
      Ye need na doubt;
At length we had a hearty yokin,   *set-to*
      At 'sang about.'

There was ae sang, amang the rest,
Aboon them a' it pleas'd me best,   *Above*
That some kind husband had addrest
      To some sweet wife:
It thirl'd the heart-strings thro the breast. *thrilled*
      A' to the life.

I've scarce heard ought describ'd sae weel, *Dr. James Beattie (1735-*
What gen'rous, manly bosoms feel;   *1803) professor of Moral*
Thought I, 'Can this be Pope, or Steele,   *Philosophy, Aberdeen*
      Or Beattie's wark?'   *work*
They told me 'twas an odd kind chiel   *chap*
      About Muirkirk.

It pat me fidgin-fain to hear't ,   *tingling with excitement*
An sae about him there I speir't;   *enquired*
Then a' that kent him round declar'd
      He had ingine;   *genius*
That nane excell'd it, few cam near't,
      It was sae fine:

That, set him to a pint of ale,
An either douce or merry tale,   *sober*
Or rhymes an sangs he'd made himsel.
      Or witty catches,
'Tween Inverness and Teviotdale,
      He had few matches.

Epistle To J. Lapraik

swore, oath   Then up I gat, an swoor an aith,
equipment   Tho I should pawn my pleugh an graith,
hawker, pony   Or die a cadger pownie's death,
behind a fence   At some dyke-back,
               A pint an gill I'd gie them baith,
chat   To hear your crack.

But, first an foremost, I should tell,
Amaist as soon as I could spell,
rhyming   I to the crambo-jingle fell;
                Tho rude an rough—
Yet crooning to a body's sel,
                Does weel enough.

I am nae poet, in a sense;
But just a rhymer like by chance.
An hae to learning nae pretence;
                Yet, what the matter?
Whene'er my Muse does on me glance,
                I jingle at her.

Your critic-folk may cock their nose,
And say, 'How can you e'er propose,
You wha ken hardly verse frae prose,
                To mak a sang?'
But, by your leaves, my learned foes,
                Ye're maybe wrang.

What's a' your jargon o your schools,
Your Latin names for horns an stools?
If honest Nature made you fools,
serves   What sairs your grammars?
shovels   Ye'd better taen up spades and shools,
stone-breaking   Or knappin-hammers.

fools   A set o dull, conceited hashes
          Confuse their brains in college-classes,
bullocks   They gang in stirks, and come out asses,
                Plain truth to speak;
then   An syne they think to climb Parnassus
                By dint o Greek!

Gie me ae spark o Nature's fire,
That's a' the learning I desire;
puddle   Then, tho I drudge thro dub an mire
                At pleugh or cart,
My Muse, tho hamely in attire,
                May touch the heart.

Epistle To J. Lapraik

O for a spunk o Allan's glee   spark, Allan Ramsay
Or Fergusson's, the bauld an slee,   sly, Robert Fergusson
Or bright Lapraik's, my friend to be,
      If I can hit it!
That would be lear eneugh for me,   learning
      If I could get it.

Now, sir, if ye hae friends enow,
Tho real friends I b'lieve are few;
Yet, if your catalogue be fow,   full
      I'se no insist:
But, gif ye want ae friend that's true,
      I'm on your list.

I winna blaw about mysel,   brag
As ill I like my faults to tell;
But friends, an folk that wish me well,
      They sometime roose me;   praise
Tho I maun own, as monie still
      As far abuse me.

There's ae wee faut they whyles lay to me,   sometimes
I like the lasses—Gude forgie me!   God
For monie a plack they wheedle frae me   farthing
      At dance or fair;
Maybe some ither thing they gie me,
      They weel can spare.

But Mauchline Race or Mauchline Fair,
I should be proud to meet you there:
We'se gie ae night's discharge to care,
      If we forgather;
And hae a swap o rhymin-ware
      Wi ane anither.

The four-gill chap, we'se gar him clatter,   cup
An kirsen him wi reekin water;   christen, steaming
Syne we'll sit down an take our whitter,   draught
      To cheer our heart;
An faith, we'se be acquainted better
      Before we part.

Awa ye selfish, warly race,   wordly
Wha think that havins, sense, an grace,   manners
Ev'n love an friendship should give place
      To Catch-the-Plack!   Hunt-the-Coin
I dinna like to see your face,
      Nor hear your crack.

Epistle To J. Lapraik

But ye whom social pleasure charms,
Whose hearts the tide of kindness warms,
Who hold your being on the terms,
    'Each aid the others,'
Come to my bowl, come to my arms,
    My friends, my brothers!

But, to conclude my lang epistle,
As my auld pen's worn to the grissle,
make tingle Twa lines frae you would gar me fissle,
    Who am most fervent,
While I can either sing or whistle,
    Your friend and servant.

SECOND EPISTLE TO J. LAPRAIK

APRIL 21, 1785

Lapraik replied to the first epistle in similar vein, sending his son to deliver his verses while Burns was sowing in a field at Mossgiel. This, in turn, provoked the second epistle, dwelling on the bad luck which both poets had experienced and leading up to a declaration on the value of humility and contentment.

new-driven, low While new-ca'd kye rowte at the stake
steam, harrow An pownies reek in pleugh or braik,
This hour on e'enin's edge I take,
    To own I'm debtor
To honest-hearted, auld Lapraik,
    For his kind letter.

very tired Forjesket sair, with weary legs,
Rattlin the corn out-owre the rigs,
distributing Or dealing thro amang the naigs
    Their ten-hours' bite;
My awkward Muse sair pleads and begs,
    I would na write.

feckless, tired girl The tapetless, ramfeezl'd hizzie,
She's saft at best an something lazy:
Quo she, 'Ye ken we've been sae busy
    This month an mair,
That trowth, my head is grown right dizzie,
    An something sair.'

104

Second Epistle To J. Lapraik

Her dowff excuses pat me mad: *dull*
'Conscience,' says I, 'ye thowless jad!   *lazy*
I'll write, an that a hearty blaud,   *screed*
    This vera night;
So dinna ye affront your trade,
    But rhyme it right.

'Shall bauld Lapraik, the king o hearts,
Tho mankind were a pack of cartes,
Roose ye sae weel for your deserts,   *Praise*
    In terms sae friendly;
Yet ye'll neglect to shaw your parts
    An thank him kindly?'

Sae I gat paper in a blink,
An down gaed stumpie in the ink:
Quoth I, 'Before I sleep a wink,   *quill-pen*
    I vow I'll close it:
An if ye winna mak it clink,   *rhyme*
    By Jove, I'll prose it!'

Sae I've begun to scrawl, but whether
In rhyme, or prose, or baith thegither,
Or some hotch-potch that's rightly neither,
    Let time mak proof;
But I shall scribble down some blether   *nonsense*
    Just clean aff-loof.   *off the cuff*

My worthy friend, ne'er grudge an carp,
Tho Fortune use you hard an sharp;
Come, kittle up your moorland harp   *tickle*
    Wi gleesome touch!
Ne'er mind how Fortune waft an warp;   *weft*
    She's but a bitch.

She's gien me monie a jirt an fleg,   *jerk, scare*
Sin' I could striddle owre a rig;   *straddle*
But, by the Lord, tho I should beg
    Wi lyart pow,   *grey head*
I'll laugh an sing, an shake my leg,
    As lang's I dow!   *can*

Now comes the sax-and-twentieth simmer
I've seen the bud upo' the timmer,
Still persecuted by the limmer   *woods*
    Frae year to year;   *jade*
But yet, despite the kittle kimmer,
    I, Rob, am here.   *idle gossip*

Second Epistle To J. Lapraik

Do ye envy the city gent,
Behind a kist to lie an sklent; *counter, cheat*
Or purse-proud, big wi cent. per cent.
    An muckle wame, *belly*
In some bit brugh to represent *borough*
    A bailie's name? *magistrate*

Or is't the paughty feudal thane, *haughty*
Wi ruffl'd sark an glancing cane, *shirt*
Wha thinks himself nae sheep-shank bane,
    But lordly stalks;
While caps an bonnets aff are taen,
    As by he walks?

'O Thou wha gies us each guid gift!
Gie me o wit an sense a lift, *load*
Then turn me, if Thou please adrift,
    Thro Scotland wide;
Wi cits nor lairds I wadna shift, *city people*
    In a' their pride!'

Were this the charter of our state,
'On pain o hell be rich an great,'
Damnation then would be our fate,
    Beyond remead; *remedy*
But, thanks to heaven, that's no the gate *way*
    We learn our creed.

For thus the Royal mandate ran,
When first the human race began:
'The social, friendly, honest man,
    Whate'er he be,
'Tis *he* fulfils great Nature's plan,
    And none but he.'

O mandate glorious and divine!
The followers o the ragged Nine— *the Muses*
Poor, thoughtless devils!—yet may shine
    In glorious light;
While sordid sons o Mammon's line
    Are dark as night!

Tho here they scrape, an squeeze, an growl,
Their worthless nievefu of a soul *fistful*
May in some future carcase howl,
    The forest's fright;
Or in some day-detesting owl
    May shun the light.

Second Epistle To J. Lapraik

Then may Lapraik and Burns arise,
To reach their native, kindred skies,
And sing their pleasures, hopes an joys
    In some mild sphere;
Still closer knit in friendship's ties,
    Each passing year!

EPISTLE TO WILLIAM SIMPSON

SCHOOLMASTER, OCHILTREE—MAY 1785

William Simpson (1758-1815) studied at Glasgow University and was originally intended for the Church, but became a schoolmaster instead. Like Lapraik he was something of a poetaster, whose verse-epistle to Burns provoked this response, describing the psychology of poetic composition.

I gat your letter, winsome Willie;
Wi gratefu heart I thank you brawlie,   handsomely
Tho I maun say't, I wad be silly
    And unco vain,   mighty
Should I believe, my coaxin billie,   fellow
    Your flatterin strain.

But I'se believe ye kindly meant it:
I sud be laith to think ye hinted
Ironic satire, sidelines sklented   squinted sideways
    On my poor Musie;
Tho in sic phraisin terms ye've penn'd it,   wheedling
    I scarce excuse ye.

My senses wad be in a creel,
Should I but dare a hope to speel,
Wi Allan, or wi Gilbertfield,   Allan Ramsay
    The braes of fame;   William Hamilton of
Or Fergusson, the writer-chiel,   Gilbertfield(1665-1751)
    A deathless name.   lawyer, Robert Fergusson

(O Fergusson! thy glorious parts
Ill suited law's dry, musty arts!
My curse upon your whunstane hearts,   whinstone
    Ye E'nbrugh gentry!
The tythe o what ye waste at cartes   tenth
    Wad stow'd his pantry!)   stored

Epistle To William Simpson

Yet when a tale comes i my head,
ache   Or lassies gie my heart a screed—
death   As whiles thy're like to be my dead,
        (O sad disease!)
tickle   I kittle up my rustic reed;
        It gies me ease.

tingle with delight   Auld Coila, now, may fidge fu fain,
    She's gotten bardies o her ain;
spare   Chiels wha their chanters winna hain,
        But tune their lays,
    Till echoes a' resound again
        Her weel-sung praise.

Nae poet thought her worth his while,
    To set her name in measur'd style;
    She lay like some unkend-of-isle
East Indies   Beside New Holland,
    Or whare wild-meeting oceans boil
south of   Besouth Magellan.

Ramsay an famous Fergusson
lift-up   Gied Forth an Tay a lift aboon;
    Yarrow an Tweed, to monie a tune,
        Owre Scotland rings;
    While Irwin, Lugar, Ayr an Doon
        Naebody sings.

Th' Illissus, Tiber, Thames, an Seine,
    Glide sweet in monie a tunefu line:
strain of music   But, Willie, set your fit to mine,
        And cock your crest!
make, brooks   We'll gar our streams an burnies shine
        Up wi the best!

We'll sing auld Coila's plains an fells,
    Her moors red-brown wi heather bells,
slopes, dingles   Her banks an braes, her dens and dells,
        Whare glorious Wallace
bore off the prize   Aft bure the gree, as story tells,
        Frae Suthron billies.

At Wallace' name, what Scottish blood
    But boils up in a spring-tide flood?
    Oft have our fearless fathers strode
        By Wallace' side,
shoes wet with blood   Still pressing onward, red-wat-shod,
        Or glorious dy'd!

Epistle To William Simpson

O, sweet are Coila's haughs an woods,   hollows
Where lintwhites chant amang the buds,   linnets
And jinkin hares, in amorous whids,   darting, gambols
    Their loves enjoy;
While thro the braes the cushat croods   wood-pigeon coos
    With wailfu cry!

Ev'n winter bleak has charms to me,
When winds rave thro the naked tree;
Or frosts on hills of Ochiltree
    Are hoary gray;
Or blinding drifts wild-furious flee,
    Dark'ning the day!

O Nature! a' thy shews an forms
To feeling, pensive hearts hae charms!
Whether the summer kindly warms,
    Wi life an light;
Or winter howls, in gusty storms,
    The lang, dark night!

The Muse, nae poet ever fand her,   found
Till by himsel he learn'd to wander,
Adown some trottin burn's meander,   brook's
    An no think lang:
O sweet to stray, an pensive ponder
    A heart-felt sang!

The warly race may drudge an drive,   wordly
Hog-shouther, jundie, stretch, an strive,   push with the shoulder, jostle
Let me fair Nature's face descrive,
    And I, wi pleasure,
Shall let the busy, grumbling hive
    Bum owre their treasure.   Hum

Fareweel, my rhyme-composing brither!
We've been owre land unkend to ither: unknown
Now let us lay our heads thegither,
    In love fraternal:
May envy wallop in a tether,   dangle at a rope's end
    Black fiend, infernal!

While Highlandmen hate tolls an taxes;
While moorlan herds like guid, fat braxies;   sheep carcases
While Terra Firma, on her axis,
    Diurnal turns;
Count on a friend, in faith an practice,
    In Robert Burns.

Epistle To William Simpson

POSTSCRIPT

pin
almost

My memory's no worth a preen:
I had amaist forgotten clean,
Ye bade me write you what they mean
    By this New-Light,

shepherds

'Bout which our herds sae aft hae been
    Maist like to fight.

striplings

In days when mankind were but callans
At grammar, logic, an sic talents,
They took nae pains their speech to balance,
    Or rules to gie;

Lowland Scots

But spak their thoughts in plain, braid Lallans,
    Like you or me.

those
shirt, shoes
round
went

In thae auld times, they thought the moon,
Just like a sark, or pair o shoon,
Wore by degrees, till her last roon
    Gaed past their viewin;
An shortly after she was done
    They gat a new ane.

fellows

This past for certain, undisputed;
It ne'er cam i their heads to doubt it,
Till chiels gat up an wad confute it,
    An ca'd it wrang;
An muckle din there was about it,
    Baith loud an lang.

maintain
corner

Some herds, weel learn'd upo' the Beuk,
Wad threap auld folk the thing misteuk;
For 'twas the auld moon turn'd a neuk
    An out o sight,

backward looking

An backlins-comin to the leuk,
    She grew mair bright.

flocks

This was deny'd, it was affirm'd;
The herds and hissels were alarm'd;
The rev'rend gray-beards rav'd an storm'd,
    That beardless laddies
Should think they better were inform'd,
    Than their auld daddies.

oaths, blows, cuts
punishment
whack

Frae less to mair, it gaed to sticks;
Frae words an aiths, to clours an nicks;
An monie a fallow gat his licks,
    Wi hearty crunt;
An some, to learn them for their tricks,

burned

    Were hang'd an brunt.

Epistle To William Simpson

This game was play'd in monie lands,
An Auld-Light caddies bure sic hands, *lackeys*
That faith, the youngsters took the sands *fled into the wilderness*
  Wi nimble shanks;
Till lairds forbade, by strict commands,
  Sic bluidy pranks.

But New-Light herds gat sic a cowe, *got such a trouncing*
Folk thought them ruin'd stick-an-stowe; *entirely*
Till now, amaist on ev'ry knowe *knoll*
  Ye'll find ane placed;
An some, their New-Light fair avow,
  Just quite barefac'd.

Nae doubt the Auld-Light flocks are bleatin;
Their zealous herds are vex'd and sweatin;
Mysel, I've even seen them greetin *weeping*
  Wi girnin spite, *snarling*
To hear the moon sae sadly lie'd on
  By word an write.

But shortly they will cowe the louns! *rascals*
Some Auld-Light herds in neebor touns *neighbouring*
Are mind't, in things they ca balloons, *determined*
  To tak a flight;
An stay ae month amang the moons
  An see them right.

Guid observation they will gie them;
An when the auld moon's gaun to lea'e them,
The hindmost shaird, they'll fetch it wi them, *shard*
  Just i their pouch;
An when the New-Light billies see them,
  I think they'll crouch!

Sae, ye observe that a' this clatter
Is naething but a 'moonshine-matter';
But tho dull prose-folk Latin splatter
  In logic tulzie, *quarrel*
I hope we, Bardies, ken some better
  Than mind sic brulzie. *brawl*

A POET'S WELCOME TO HIS
LOVE-BEGOTTEN DAUGHTER

Compared with the sexual boastfulness over this
episode, expressed in 'Epistle to John Rankine', this
poem following the birth of Elizabeth Burns expresses
only warm tenderness. The child was raised at Mossgiel
under the care of the poet's mother. She married John
Bishop and died in January 1817, allegedly in
childbirth.

child, mishap, befall
    Thou's welcome, wean! Mishanter fa' me,
    If thoughts o thee, or yet thy mammie,
    Shall ever daunton me or awe me
          My sweet, wee lady,
    Or if I blush when thou shalt ca' me
          Tyta or daddie!

    What tho they ca' me fornicator,

country gossip
    An tease my name in kintra clatter,
    The mair they talk, I'm kend the better,

tattle
          E'en let them clash!

feeble
    An auld wife's tongue's a feckless matter

give annoyance
          To gie ane fash.

    Welcome my bonie, sweet, wee dochter!
    Tho ye come here a wee unsought for,
    And tho your comin I hae fought for,

church, court
          Baith kirk and queir;
    Yet, by my faith, ye're no unwrought for—
          That I shall swear!

occasion
    Sweet fruit o monie a merry dint,

not all lost
    My funny toil is no a' tint,

askew
    Tho thou cam to the warl' asklent,
          Which fools may scoff at,

farthing
    In my last plack thy part's be in't
          The better half o't.

worse provided
    Tho I should be the waur bestead,

well, finely
    Thou's be as braw and bienly clad,

comfortably
    And thy young years as nicely bred
          Wi education,
    As onie brat o wedlock's bed,
          In a' thy station.

Elizabeth Paton
    Wee image o my bonie Betty,

caress
    As fatherly I kiss and daut thee,
    As dear, and near my heart I set thee
          Wi as guid will,
    As a' the priests had seen me get thee
          That's out o Hell.

Gude grant that thou may ay inherit   God
Thy mither's looks an gracfu merit,
An thy poor, worthless daddie's spirit,
     Without his failins!
'Twill please me mair to see thee heir it,
     Than stocket mailens.   well-stocked farms

And if thou be what I wad hae thee,
An tak the counsel I shall gie thee,
I'll never rue my trouble wi thee—
     The cost nor shame o't—
But be a loving father to thee,
     And brag the name o't.

THE FORNICATOR

TUNE: *Clout the Caldron*

Believed to have been written in celebration of the poet's affair with Elizabeth Paton.

Ye jovial boys who love the joys,
     The blissful joys of Lovers;
Yet dare avow with dauntless brow,
     When th' bony lass discovers;   reveals pregnancy
I pray draw near and lend an ear,
     And welcome in a Frater,   brother (Latin)
For I've lately been on quarantine,
     A proven Fornicator.

Before the Congregation wide
     I pass'd the muster fairly,
My handsome Betsey by my side,
     We gat our ditty rarely;   sermon
But my downcast eye by chance did spy
     What made my lips to water,
Those limbs so clean where I, between,
     Commenc'd a Fornicator.

With rueful face and signs of grace
     I pay'd the buttock-hire,
The night was dark and thro the park
     I could not but convoy her;   accompany
A parting kiss, what could I less,
     My vows began to scatter,
My Betsey fell—lal de dal lal lal,
     I am a Fornicator.

The Fornicator

But for her sake this vow I make,
    And solemnly I swear it,
That while I own a single crown,
    She's welcome for to share it;
And my roguish boy his Mother's joy,
    And the darling of his Pater,
For him I boast my pains and cost,
    Although a Fornicator.

passed on a social disease

Ye wenching blades whose hireling jades
    Have tipt you off blue-boram,
I tell ye plain, I do disdain
    To rank you in the Quorum;
But a bony lass upon the grass

to be a mother (Latin)

    To teach her esse Mater,
And no reward but for regard,
    O that's a Fornicator.

Your warlike Kings and Heros bold,
    Great Captains and Commanders;
Your mighty Cèsars fam'd of old,
    And Conquering Alexanders;
In fields they fought and laurels bought
    And bulwarks strong did batter,
But still they grac'd our noble list
    And ranked Fornicator!!!

THE VISION
DUAN FIRST

Opinion is divided concerning the date of composition.
Dewar considered a time prior to the move to Mossgiel
early in 1784, but Kinsley argued for a date in late
1785, and Burns substituted or added several stanzas
in 1786-7. The division of this poem into Duan was
influenced by Macpherson's 'Ossian' (from Gaelic *dán*,
poetry).

finished
hungry hare

The sun had clos'd the winter day,
The curlers quat their roaring play,
And hunger'd maukin taen her way,
    To kail-yards green,

each

While faithless snaws ilk step betray
    Whare she has been.

The Vision

The thresher's weary flingin-tree,   flail-swingle
The lee-lang day had tired me;   live-long
And when the day had clos'd his e'e,
    Far i the west,
Ben i the spence, right pensivelie,   Back, parlour
    I gaed to rest.   went

There, lanely by the ingle-cheek   -side
I sat an ey'd the spewing reek,   eddying
That fill'd, wi hoast-provoking smeek,   cough, smoke
    The auld clay biggin;   building
An heard the restless rattons squeak   rats
    About the riggin.   roof

All in this mottie, misty clime,   spotty
I backward mus'd on wasted time:
How I had spent my youthfu prime,
    An done naething,
But stringing blethers up in rhyme,   nonsense
    For fools to sing.

Had I to guid advice but harkit,   listened
I might, by this, hae led a market,
Or strutted in a bank and clarkit
    My cash-account:
While here, half-mad, half-fed, half-sarkit,   half-clothed
    Is a' th' amount.

I started, mutt'ring 'Blockhead! coof!'
An heav'd on high my waukit loof,   calloused palm
To swear by a' yon starry roof,
    Or some rash aith,   oath
That I henceforth would be rhyme-proof
    Till my last breath—

When click! the string the snick did draw;   latch
And jee! the door gaed to the wa;
And by my ingle-lowe I saw,   -flame
    Now bleezin bright,
A tight, outlandish hizzie, braw,   hussy
    Come full in sight.

Ye need na doubt, I held my whisht;   peace
The infant aith, half-form'd, was crusht;
I glowr'd, as eerie's I'd been dusht,   stared, touched
    In some wild glen;
When sweet, like modest Worth, she blusht,
    An steppèd ben.   inside

The Vision

Green, slender, leaf-clad holly-boughs
Were twisted, gracefu round her brows;
I took her for some Scottish Muse,
    By that same token;
And come to stop those reckless vows,
    Would soon been broken.

A 'hair-brain'd, sentimental trace'
Was strongly markèd in her face;
A wildly-witty, rustic grace
    Shone full upon her;
Her eye, ev'n turn'd on empty space,
    Beam'd keen with honor.

bright   Down flow'd her robe, a tartan sheen,
barely   Till half a leg was scrimply seen;
And such a leg! my bonie Jean
equal   Could only peer it;
straight, slim   Sae straught, sae taper, tight an clean—
    Nane else came near it.

Her mantle large, of greenish hue,
My gazing wonder chiefly drew;
Deep lights and shades, bold-mingling, threw
    A lustre grand;
And seem'd, to my astonish'd view,
    A well-known land.

Here, rivers in the sea were lost;
There, mountains to the skies were toss't;
Here, tumbling billows mark'd the coast,
    With surging foam;
There, distant shone Art's lofty boast,
    The lordly dome.

Here, Doon pour'd down his far-fetch'd floods;
beats   There, well-fed Irvine stately thuds:
stole   Auld hermit Ayr staw thro his woods,
    On to the shore;
And many a lesser torrent scuds,
    With seeming roar.

Low, in a sandy valley spread,
An ancient borough rear'd her head;
Still, as in Scottish story read,
    She boasts a race
To ev'ry nobler virtue bred,
    And polish'd grace.

The Vision

By stately tow'r, or palace fair,
Or ruins pendent in the air,
Bold stems of heroes, here and there,
    I could discern;
Some seem'd to muse, some seem'd to dare,
    With feature stern.

My heart did glowing transport feel,
To see a race heroic wheel,
And brandish round the deep-dyed steel,
    In sturdy blows;
While, back-recoiling, seem'd to reel
    Their suthron foes.

His Country's Saviour, mark him well!   William Wallace (d. 1305)
Bold Richardton's heroic swell;   Riccarton
The chief, on Sark who glorious fell   John Wallace of Craigie
    In high command;   (d. 1449)
And he whom ruthless fates expel   Sir William Wallace Dunlop,
    His native land.   forced to sell Craigie, 1783.

There, where a sceptr'd Pictish shade
Stalk'd round his ashes lowly laid,
I mark'd a martial race, pourtray'd   the Montgomeries of Coilsfield
    In colours strong:
Bold, soldier-featur'd, undismay'd,
    They strode along.

Thro many a wild, romantic grove,   Barskimming
Near many a hermit-fancied cove
(Fit haunts for friendship or for love,
    In musing mood),
An aged Judge, I saw him rove,   Alexander Boswell (1707-82)
    Dispensing good.

With deep-struck, reverential awe,   Matthew Stewart (1717-35)
The learned Sire and Son I saw: Dugald Stewart (1753-1828)
To Nature's God, and Nature's law,   professors of moral philosophy
    They gave their lore;   Edinburgh University
This, all its source and end to draw,
    That, to adore.

Brydon's brave ward I well could spy,   Willaim Fullarton (1754-1808)
Beneath old Scotia's smiling eye;   ward of Patrick Brydone
Who call'd on Fame, low standing by,
    To hand him on,
Where many a patriot-name on high,
    And hero shone.

The Vision

DUAN SECOND

With musing-deep, astonish'd stare,
I view'd the heavenly-seeming Fair;
A whisp'ring throb did witness bear
    Of kindred sweet,
When with an elder sister's air
    She did me greet.

'All hail! my own inspired Bard!
In me thy native Muse regard!
Nor longer mourn thy fate is hard,
    Thus poorly low!
I come to give thee such reward,
    As we bestow!

'Know, the great Genius of this land
Has many a light aerial band,
Who, all beneath his high command
    Harmoniously,
As arts or arms they understand,
    Their labours ply.

'They Scotia's race among them share:
Some fire the soldier on to dare;
Some rouse the patriot up to bare
    Corruption's heart;
Some teach the bard—a darling care—
    The tuneful art.

' 'Mong swelling floods of reeking gore,
They, ardent, kindling spirits pour;
Or, 'mid the venal Senate's roar,
    They, sightless, stand,
To mend the honest patriot-lore,
    And grace the hand.

'And when the bard, or hoary sage,
Charm or instruct the future age,
They bind the wild poetic rage
    In energy,
Or point the inconclusive page
    Full on the eye.

William Fullarton
George Dempster, M.P.
(1732-1818), Dr. James
Beattie (1735-1803) published
1771

'Hence, Fullarton, the brave and young;
Hence, Dempster's zeal-inspirèd tongue;
Hence, sweet, harmonious Beattie sung
    His *Minstrel* lays;
Or tore, with noble ardour stung,
    The sceptic's bays.

The Vision

'To lower orders are assign'd
The humbler ranks of human-kind,
The rustic bard, the laboring hind,
  The artisan.
All chuse, as various they're inclin'd,
  The various man.

'When yellow waves the heavy grain,
The threat'ning storm some strongly rein
Some teach to meliorate the plain,
  With tillage-skill;
And some instruct the shepherd-train,
  Blythe o'er the hill.

'Some hint the lover's harmless wile;
Some grace the maiden's artless smile;
Some soothe the laborer's weary toil
  For humble gains,
And make his cottage-scenes beguile
  His cares and pains.

'Some, bounded to a district-space,
Explore at large man's infant race,
To mark the embryotic trace
  Of rustic bard;
And careful note each opening grace,
  A guide and guard.

'Of these am I—Coila my name:
And this district as mine I claim,
Where once the Campbells, chiefs of fame,   Loudoun, a Campbell
  Held ruling pow'r: earldom since 1633
I mark'd thy embryo-tuneful flame,
  Thy natal hour.

'With future hope I oft would gaze
Fond, on thy little early ways:
Thy rudely caroll'd, chiming phrase,
  In uncouth rhymes;
Fir'd at the simple, artless lays
  Of other times.

'I saw thee seek the sounding shore,
Delighted with the dashing roar;
Or when the North his fleecy store
  Drove thro the sky,
I saw grim Nature's visage hoar
  Struck thy young eye.

The Vision

'Or when the deep green-mantled earth
Warm cherish'd ev'ry flow'ret's birth,
And joy and music pouring forth
    In ev'ry grove;
I saw thee eye the gen'ral mirth
    With boundless love.

'When ripen'd fields and azure skies
Call'd forth the reapers' rustling noise,
I saw thee leave their ev'ning joys,
    And lonely stalk,
To vent thy bosom's swelling rise,
    In pensive walk.

'When youthful Love, warm-blushing, strong,
Keen-shivering, shot thy nerves along,
Those accents grateful to thy tongue,
    Th' adorèd *Name,*
I taught thee how to pour in song,
    To soothe thy flame.

'I saw thy pulse's maddening play,
Wild-send thee Pleasure's devious way,
Misled by Fancy's meteor-ray,
    By passion driven;
But yet the light that led astray
    Was light from Heaven.

'I taught thy manners-painting strains,
The loves, the ways of simple swains,
Till now, o'er all my wide domains
    Thy fame extends;
And some, the pride of Coila's plains,
    Become thy friends.

James Thomson (1700-48)

William Shenstone (1714-63)
Thomas Gray (1716-71)

'Thou canst not learn, nor can I show,
To paint with Thomson's landscape glow;
Or wake the bosom-melting throe,
    With Shenstone's art;
Or pour, with Gray, the moving flow
    Warm on the heart.

'Yet, all beneath th' unrivall'd rose,
The lowly daisy sweetly blows;
Tho large the forest's monarch throws
    His army-shade,
\ et green the juicy hawthorn grows,
    Adown the glade.

'Then never murmur nor repine;
Strive in thy humble sphere to shine;
And trust me, not Potosi's mine,   in S.W. Bolivia
      Nor king's regard,
Can give a bliss o'ermatching thine,
      A rustic Bard.

'To give my counsels all in one,
Thy tuneful flame still careful fan;
Preserve the dignity of Man,
      With soul erect:
And trust the Universal Plan
      Will all protect.

'And wear thou *this*' —She solemn said,
And bound the holly round my head:
The polish'd leaves and berries red
      Did rustling play;
And, like a passing thought, she fled
      In light away.

EPISTLE TO JOHN GOLDIE, IN KILMARNOCK
AUGUST 1785

John Goldie (1717-1809), son of the miller of Craigmill, Galston — cabinet-maker, inventor, wine-merchant, mathematician, astronomer, theologian, speculator in coalmines and canals, and one of the guarantors for the Kilmarnock Edition — a prime example of the Augustan virtuoso.

O Goudie, terror o the Whigs,
Dread o blackcoats and rev'rend wigs!
Sour Bigotry on his last legs
      Girns an looks back,   snarls
Wishing the ten Egyptian plagues
      May seize you quick.

Poor gapin, glowerin Superstition!   staring
Wae's me, she's in a sad condition!
Fye! bring Black Jock, her state physician,
      To see her water!
Alas! there's ground for great suspicion
      She'll ne'er get better.

Epistle to John Goldie, in Kilmarnock

<table>
<tr><td></td><td>Enthusiasm's past redemption,</td></tr>
<tr><td></td><td>Gane in a gallopin consumption:</td></tr>
<tr><td>intiative</td><td>Not a' her quacks, wi a' their gumption,</td></tr>
<tr><td></td><td style="padding-left:2em">Can ever mend her;</td></tr>
<tr><td></td><td>Her feeble pulse gies strong presumption,</td></tr>
<tr><td></td><td style="padding-left:2em">She'll soon surrender.</td></tr>
</table>

Auld Orthodoxy lang did grapple,

stopper — For every hole to get a stapple;

gags, gullet — But now she fetches at the thrapple,
    An fights for breath:
Haste, gie her name up in the chapel,
    Near unto death!

Rev. Dr. Taylor of Norwich, — 'Tis you an Taylor are the chief

apostle of New Light doctrine — To blame for a' this black mischief;

if — But gin the Lord's ain folk gat leave,

empty —   A toom tar barrel
An twa red peats wad bring relief,
    And end the quarrel.

For me, my skill's but very sma',

at all — An skill in prose I've nane ava;

confidentially — But, quietlenswise, between us twa,
    Weel may ye speed!
And, tho they sud you sair misca',

bother —   Ne'er fash your head!

flog, thoroughly — E'en swinge the dogs, and thresh them sicker!

strike — The mair they squeel ay chap the thicker,

beaker — An still 'mang hands a hearty bicker
    O something stout!

makes, author's — It gars an owthor's pulse beat quicker,
    And helps his wit.

liquor — There's naething like the honest nappy:
Whare'll ye e'er see men sae happy,

pleasant, soft succulent — Or women sonsie, saft and sappy
    'Tween morn and morn,

drop — As them wha like to taste the drappie,
    In glass or horn?

dazed — I've seen me daez't upon a time,

faintest outline — I scarce could wink or see a styme;

half-measure — Just ae half-mutchkin does me prime,
    (Ought less is little,)
Then back I rattle on the rhyme,

sharp, knife —   As gleg's a whittle.

MAN WAS MADE TO MOURN—A DIRGE

TUNE: *Peggy Bawn*

Gilbert, writing to Dr. Currie about his brother: 'He used to remark to me that he could not well conceive a more mortifying picture of human life than a man seeking work. In casting about in his mind how this sentiment might be brought forward the elegy Man wa. made to mourn was composed.'

When chill November's surly blast
    Made fields and forests bare,
One ev'ning, as I wander'd forth
    Along the banks of Ayr,
I spied a man, whose aged step
    Seem'd weary, worn with care,
His face was furrow'd o'er with years,
    And hoary was his hair.

'Young stranger, whither wand'rest thou?'
    Began the rev'rend Sage;
'Does thirst of wealth thy step constrain,
    Or youthful pleasure's rage?
Or haply, prest with cares and woes,
    Too soon thou hast began
To wander forth, with me to mourn
    The miseries of Man.

'The sun that overhangs yon moors,
    Out-spreading far and wide,
Where hundreds labour to support
    A haughty lordling's pride;
I've seen yon weary winter-sun
    Twice forty times return;
And ev'ry time has added proofs,
    That Man was made to mourn.

'O Man! while in thy early years,
    How prodigal of time!
Mis-spending all thy precious hours,
    Thy glorious, youthful prime!
Alternate follies take the sway,
    Licentious passions burn:
Which tenfold force gives Nature's law,
    That Man was made to mourn.

Man Was Made To Mourn—A Dirge

'Look not alone on youthful prime,
　Or manhood's active might;
Man then is useful to his kind,
　Supported is his right:
But see him on the edge of life,
　With cares and sorrows worn,
Then Age and Want—oh! ill-matched pair!—
　Shew Man was made to mourn.

'A few seem favourites of Fate,
　In pleasure's lap carest;
Yet think not all the rich and great
　Are likewise truly blest:
But oh! what crowds in ev'ry land,
　All wretched and forlorn,
Thro weary life this lesson learn,
　That Man was made to mourn.

'Many and sharp the num'rous ills
　Inwoven with our frame!
More pointed still we make ourselves,
　Regret, remorse, and shame!
And Man, whose heav'n-erected face
　The smiles of love adorn,—
Man's inhumanity to man
　Makes countless thousands mourn!

'See yonder poor, o'erlabour'd wight,
　So abject, mean, and vile,
Who begs a brother of the earth
　To give him leave to toil;
And see his lordly fellow-worm
　The poor petition spurn,
Unmindful, tho a weeping wife
　And helpless offspring mourn.

'If I'm design'd yon lordling's slave—
　By Nature's law design'd—
Why was an independent wish
　E'er planted in my mind?
If not, why am I subject to
　His cruelty, or scorn?
Or why has Man the will and pow'r
　To make his fellow mourn?

Man Was Made To Mourn—A Dirge

'Yet let not this too much, my son,
    Disturb thy youthful breast:
This partial view of human-kind
    Is surely not the last!
The poor, oppressèd, honest man
    Had never, sure, been born,
Had there not been some recompense
    To comfort those that mourn!

'O Death! the poor man's dearest friend,
    The kindest and the best!
Welcome the hour my aged limbs
    Are laid with thee at rest!
The great, the wealthy fear thy blow,
    From pomp and pleasure torn;
But, oh! a blest relief for those
    That weary-laden mourn!'

YOUNG PEGGY

TUNE: *The last time I came o'er the Moor*

The subject of this poem was Margaret Kennedy (1766-95), daughter of Robert Kennedy of Daljarrock, factor to the Earl of Cassilis and brother-in-law of Gavin Hamilton. Burns met her at the latter's house and sent her this poem in the autumn of 1785 as 'a small tho' grateful tribute . . . I have, in these verses, attempted some faint sketches of your PORTRAIT in the unimbellished simple manner of descriptive TRUTH. Flattery I leave to your LOVERS.' She was subsequently seduced by Captain Andrew McDoual, by whom she had a daughter in 1794. The gallant Captain denied paternity but in 1798 the Consistorial Court declared in favour of a secret marriage and the child's legitimacy. Tragically, Peggy died before the action was concluded. The Court of Session overturned this judgement but awarded £3,000 to the dead woman, and alimentary provision for the child.

Young Peggy blooms our boniest lass,
    Her blush is like the morning,
The rosy dawn the springing grass
    With early gems adorning.
Her eyes outshine the radiant beams
    That gild the passing shower,
And glitter o'er the crystal streams,
    And cheer each fresh'ning flower.

125

Her lips, more than the cherries bright—
    A richer dye has graced them—
They charm the admiring gazer's sight,
    And sweetly tempt to taste them.
Her smile is as the evening mild,
    When feather'd pairs are courting,
And little lambkins wanton wild,
    In playful bands disporting.

Were Fortune lovely Peggy's foe,
    Such sweetness would relent her;
As blooming Spring unbends the brow
    Of surly, savage Winter.
Detraction's eye no aim can gain,
    Her winning powers to lessen,
And fretful Envy grins in vain
    The poison'd tooth to fasten.

Ye Pow'rs of Honour, Love and Truth
    From ev'ry ill defend her!
Inspire the highly-favour'd youth
    The destinies intend her!
Still fan the sweet connubial flame
    Responsive in each bosom,
And bless the dear parental name
    With many a filial blossom!

THE BRAES O BALLOCHMYLE

Written in 1785 when Sir John Whitefoord (1734-1803) was forced to sell his estate to the Alexander family, in the aftermath of the collapse of the Ayr Bank of Douglas, Heron and Company. 'Maria' was Mary Anne Whitefoord, eldest of Sir John's four daughters. Her sister-in-law, Helen D'Arcy, married Professor Dugald Stewart who owned the Catrine woods mentioned in the song. The music for this song was composed by Allan Masterton, for the *Scots Musical Museum.*

The Catrine woods were yellow seen,
    The flowers decay'd on Catrine lea,
lark Nae lav'rock sang on hillock green,
    But nature sicken'd on the e'e.
Thro faded groves Maria sang,
    Hersel in beauty's bloom the while,
And aye the wild-wood echoes rang:—
    Fareweel the braes o Ballochmyle!

126

The Braes O Ballochmyle

Low in your wintry beds, ye flowers,
  Again ye'll flourish fresh and fair;
Ye birdies, dumb in with'ring bowers,
  Again ye'll charm the vocal air;
But here, alas! for me nae mair
  Shall birdie charm, or floweret smile;
Fareweel the bonie banks of Ayr!
  Fareweel! fareweel! sweet Ballochmyle!

THIRD EPISTLE TO J. LAPRAIK

SEPTEMBER 13, 1785

Composed at harvest-time, hence the reference to 'the staff o bread.'

Guid speed and furder to you, Johnie,
Guid health, hale han's, an weather bonie!   *whole hands*
Now, when ye're nickin down fu cannie   *cutting, skilfully*
      The staff o bread,   *corn*
May ye ne'er want a stoup o bran'y   *cup*
      To clear your head!

May Boreas never thresh your rigs,   *north wind*
Nor kick your rickles aff their legs,   *corn-rigs*
Sendin the stuff o'er muirs an haggs   *bogs*
      Like drivin wrack!   *storm-tossed seaweed*
But may the tapmost grain that wags
      Come to the sack!

I'm bizzie, too, an skelpin at it,   *busy, driving*
But, bitter, daudin showers hae wat it;   *pelting, wet*
Sae my auld stumpie-pen, I gat it,   *quill*
      Wi muckle wark,
An took my jocteleg an whatt it,   *clasp-knife, whittled*
      Like onie clark.

It's now twa month that I'm your debtor,
For your braw, nameless, dateless letter,   *fine*
Abusin me for harsh ill-nature
      On holy men,
While deil a hair yoursel ye're better,
      But mair profane!

127

Third Epistle To J. Lapraik

But let the kirk-folk ring their bells!
Let's sing about our noble sel's:
call We'll cry nae jads frae heathen hills
rouse   To help or roose us,
brewer But browster wives an whisky stills—
                    They are the Muses!

will not yield Your friendship, sir, I winna quat it,
An if ye mak objections at it,
fist Then hand in nieve some day we'll knot it,
                    An witness take,
whisky An, when wi usquabae we've wat it,
                    It winna break.

horse and bridle But if the beast and branks be spar'd
cattle, going, keeper Till kye be gaun without the herd,
grain And a' the vittel in the yard,
thatched   An theckit right,
fire- I mean your ingle-side to guard
                    Ae winter night.

Then Muse-inspirin aqua-vitae
Shall mak us baith sae blythe an witty,
enervated Till ye forget ye're auld an gatty,
jolly   And be as canty
thirty As ye were nine years less than thretty—
                    Sweet ane an twenty!

rigs upset But stooks are cowpet wi the blast,
sun peeps And now the sinn keeks in the wast;
must Then I maun rin amang the rest,
leave my song   An quat my chanter;
Sae I subscribe mysel in haste,
                    Yours, Rab the Ranter.

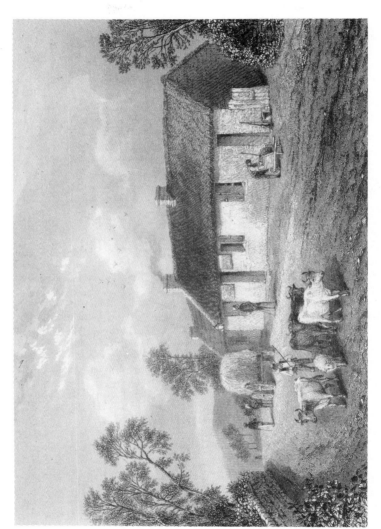

BURNS COTTAGE
The Birthplace of Burns.

LOCHLEA

EPISTLE TO
THE REV. JOHN McMATH

INCLOSING A COPY OF "HOLY WILLIE'S
PRAYER" WHICH HE HAD REQUESTED,
SEPT. 17, 1785

John McMath (1755-1825) was born in Galston,
educated at Glasgow University, and ordained
assistant to Patrick Wodrow, minister of Tarbolton. He
was a New Licht liberal who championed Gavin
Hamilton. He took to drink, resigned in 1791, enlisted
as a private soldier and ended his days on the island of
Mull.

While at the stook the shearers cow'r   *corn-sheaf, stoop*
To shun the bitter blaudin show'r,   *pelting*
Or, in gulravage rinnin, scowr: *horseplay, scour*
      To pass the time,
To you I dedicate the hour
      In idle rhyme.

My Musie, tir'd wi monie a sonnet
On gown an ban', an douse black-bonnet,   *sober*
Is grown right eerie now she's done it,   *fearful*
      Lest they should blame her,
An rouse their holy thunder on it
      And anathem her.

I own 'twas rash, an rather hardy,
That I, a simple, countra Bardie,
Should meddle wi a pack sae sturdy,
      Wha, if they ken me,
Can easy wi a single wordie,
      Louse Hell upon me.

But I gae mad at their grimaces,
Their sighin, cantin, grace-proud faces,   *furious*
Their three-mile prayers, an hauf-mile graces,
      Their raxin conscience,   *elastic*
Whase greed, revenge, an pride disgraces
      Waur nor their nonsense.   *worse than*

There's Gau'n, misca'd waur than a beast,   *Gavin Hamilton*
Wha has mair honor in his breast
Than monie scores as guid's the priest
      Wha sae abus't him:
And may a Bard no crack his jest
      What way they've use't him?

129

E

Epistle To The Rev. John McMath

See him, the poor man's friend in need,
The gentleman in word an deed—
An shall his fame an honor bleed
      By worthless skellums,
An not a Muse erect her head
      To cowe the blellums?

O Pope, had I thy satire's darts
To gie the rascals their deserts,
I'd rip their rotten, hollow hearts,
      An tell aloud
Their jugglin, hocus-pocus arts
      To cheat the crowd!

God knows, I'm no the thing I should be,
Nor am I even the thing I could be,
But twenty times I rather would be
      An atheist clean,
Than under gospel colors hid be
      Just for a screen.

An honest man may like a glass,
An honest man may like a lass;
But mean revenge, an malice fause
      He'll still disdain,
An then cry zeal for gospel laws,
      Like some we ken.

They take Religion in their mouth,
They talk o Mercy, Grace an Truth:
For what? to gie their malice skouth
      On some puir wight;
An hunt him down, o'er right an ruth,
      To ruin streight.

All hail, Religion! Maid divine!
Pardon a Muse sae mean as mine,
Who in her rough imperfect line
      Thus daurs to name thee;
To stigmatise false friends of thine
      Can ne'er defame thee.

Tho blotch't and foul wi monie a stain,
An far unworthy of thy train,
With trembling voice I tune my strain,
      To join with those
Who boldly dare thy cause maintain
      In spite of foes:

---

*Marginal glosses:*

scoundrels
blusterers
Alexander Pope
false
play
pity
straight

Epistle To The Rev. John McMath

In spite o crowds, in spite o mobs,
In spite o undermining jobs,
In spite o dark banditti stabs
    At worth an merit,
By scoundrels, even wi holy robes,
    But hellish spirit!

O Ayr! my dear, my native ground,
Within thy presbyterial bound
A candid lib'ral band is found
    Of public teachers,
As men, as Christians too, renown'd,
    An manly preachers.

Sir, in that circle you are nam'd;
Sir, in that circle you are fam'd;
An some, by whom your doctrine's blam'd
    (Which gies ye honor),
Even, Sir, by them your heart's esteem'd,
    An winning manner.

Pardon this freedom I have ta'en,
An if impertinent I've been,
Impute it not, good Sir, in ane
    Whase heart ne'er wrang'd ye,
But to his utmost would befriend
    Ought that belang'd ye.

TO A MOUSE

ON TURNING HER UP IN HER NEST WITH THE PLOUGH, NOVEMBER 1785

Wee sleekit, cow'rin, tim'rous beastie,   *glossy-coated*
O, what a panic's in thy breastie!
Thou need na start awa sae hasty,
    Wi bickering brattle!   *rushing, scurry*
I wad be laith to rin an chase thee,   *loth*
    Wi murdering pattle!   *plough-scraper*

I'm truly sorry man's dominion
Has broken Nature's social union,
An justifies that ill opinion,
    Which makes thee startle
At me, thy poor, earth-born companion,
    An fellow mortal!

131

To A Mouse

sometimes | I doubt na, whyles, but thou may thieve;
| What then? poor beastie, thou maun live!
odd ear in 24 sheaves | A daimen icker in a thrave
| 'S a sma request;
remainder | I'll get a blessin wi the lave,
| An never miss't!

Thy wee-bit housie, too, in ruin!
feeble | Its silly wa's the win's are strewin!
An naething, now, to big a new ane,
coarse grass | O foggage green!
An bleak December's win's ensuin,
bitter | Baith snell an keen!

Thou saw the fields laid bare an waste,
An weary winter comin fast,
An cozie here, beneath the blast,
     Thou thought to dwell,
ploughshare | Till crash! the cruel coulter past
     Out thro thy cell.

stubble | That wee bit heap o leaves an stibble,
Has cost thee monie a' weary nibble!
Now thou's turn'd out, for a thy trouble,
without, holding | But house or hald,
endure | To thole the winter's sleety dribble,
hoar-frost | An cranreuch cauld!

alone | But Mousie, thou art no thy lane,
In proving foresight may be vain:
The best-laid schemes o mice an men
often go awry | Gang aft agley,
An lea'e us nought but grief an pain,
     For promis'd joy!

Still thou art blest, compar'd wi me!
The present only toucheth thee:
But och! I backward cast my e'e,
     On prospects drear!
An forward, tho I canna see,
     I guess an fear!

THE HOLY FAIR

A robe of seeming truth and trust
Hid crafty observation;
And secret hung, with poison'd crust,
The dirk of defamation:
A mask that like the gorget show'd,
Dye-varying on the pigeon;
And for a mantle large and broad,
He wrapt him in Religion—HYPOCRISY À-LA-MODE

Written in 1785, probably following the annual Communion, held at Mauchline on the second Sunday in August. Burns completely revised the text early in 1786 prior to publication. Several parishes would join forces for the annual sacrament, attracting large numbers of communicants from the surrounding countryside for a 'holy fair' of preachings and prayer-meetings extending over several days prior to the Communion itself (cf. the *Orduighean beaga* of the Free Church in the Highlands and Islands to this day). In Burns's day, however, the holy fair had deteriorated into a curious mixture of solemnity and carnival, symbolic of the double standards of the Church at the time.

Upon a simmer Sunday morn,	
When Nature's face is fair,	
I walkèd forth to view the corn,	
An snuff the caller air.	cool
The rising sun, owre Galston Muirs	
Wi glorious light was glintin;	glancing
The hares were hirplin down the furs,	hopping, furrows
The lav'rocks they were chantin	larks
Fu sweet that day.	
As lightsomely I glowr'd abroad,	gazed
To see a scene sae gay,	
Three hizzies, early at the road,	girls
Cam skelpin up the way.	spanking along
Twa had manteels o dolefu black,	
But ane wi lyart lining;	grey
The third, that gaed a wee a-back,	walked a bit behind
Was in the fashion shining,	
Fu gay that day.	
The twa appear'd like sisters twin,	
In feature, form, an claes;	clothing
Their visage wither'd, lang and thin,	
An sour as onie slaes:	blackthorn (sloes)
The third cam up, hap-step-an-lowp,	hop, step and jump
As light as onie lambie,	
An wi a curchie low did stoop,	curtsey
As soon as e'er she saw me,	
Fu kind that day.	

133

The Holy Fair

Wi bonnet aff, quoth I, 'Sweet lass,
    I think ye seem to ken me;
I'm sure I've seen that bonie face,
    But yet I canna name ye.'
Quo she, an laughin as she spak,
    An taks me by the han's,
bulk   'Ye, for my sake, hae gien the feck
    Of a' the Ten Comman's
rip   A screed some day.'

'My name is Fun—your cronie dear,
    The nearest friend ye hae;
An this is Superstition here,
    An that's Hypocrisy.
going   I'm gaun to Mauchline Holy Fair,
larking   To spend an hour in daffin:
wrinkled   Gin ye'll go there, yon runkl'd pair,
    We will get famous laughin
          At them this day.'

Quoth I, 'Wi a' my heart, I'll do't;
shirt   I'll get my Sunday's sark on,
An meet you on the holy spot;
we'll have   Faith, we'se hae fine remarkin!'
porridge-time Then I gaed hame at crowdie-time,
    An soon I made me ready;
For roads were clad, frae side to side,
    Wi monie a weary body,
          In droves that day.

self-satisfied, kit Here farmers gash, in ridin graith,
jogging   Gaed hoddin by their cotters;
strapping youngsters There swankies young, in braw braid-claith,
    Are springin owre the gutters.
padding, thronging The lasses, skelpin barefit, thrang,
    In silks an scarlets glitter;
thick slice Wi sweet-milk cheese, in monie a whang,
cookies   An farls, bak'd wi butter,
crisp   Fu crump that day.

When by the plate we set our nose,
    Weel heapèd up wi ha'pence,
A greedy glowr black-bonnet throws,   church elder
    An we maun draw our tippence.
Then in we go to see the show:
    On ev'ry side they're gath'rin,
Some carrying dails, some chairs an stools,   planks
    An some are busy bleth'rin   gossiping
          Right loud that day.

Here stands a shed to fend the show'rs,   keep off
    An screen our countra gentry;
There Racer Jess, an twa-three whores,   Janet Gibson, half-witted
    Are blinkin at the entry.   daughter of Poosie Nansie
Here sits a raw o tittlin jads,   whispering jades
    Wi heavin breasts an bare neck;
An there a batch o wabster lads,   weaver
    Blackguardin frae Kilmarnock,   Roistering
          For fun this day.

Here some are thinkin on their sins,
    An some upo their claes;
Ane curses feet that fyl'd his shins,   defiled
    Anither sighs an prays:
On this hand sits a chosen swatch,   sample
    Wi screw'd-up, grace-proud faces;
On that a set o chaps, at watch,
    Thrang winkin on the lasses   busy
          To chairs that day.

O happy is that man, an blest!
    Nae wonder that it pride him!
Whase ain dear lass, that he likes best,
    Comes clinkin down beside him!
Wi arm repos'd on the chair back,
    He sweetly does compose him;
Which, by degrees, slips round her neck,
    An's loof upon her bosom,   and his palm
          Unkend that day.   unknown

135

The Holy Fair

Rev. Alexander Moodie,
(1728-99); climbs
the Devil

Now a' the congregation o'er
    Is silent expectation;
For Moodie speels the holy door,
    Wi tidings o damnation:
Should Hornie, as in ancient days,
    'Mang sons o God present him,

hot home

The vera sight o Moodie's face,
    To 's ain het hame had sent him
        Wi fright that day.

Hear how he clears the points o Faith
    Wi rattlin an thumpin!
Now meekly calm, now wild in wrath,
    He's stampin, an he's jumpin!
His lengthen'd chin, his turn'd-up snout,

unearthly

    His eldritch squeel an gestures,
O how they fire the heart devout,

aphrodisiacs

    Like cantharidian plaisters
        On sic a day!

But hark! the tent has chang'd its voice;
    There's peace an rest nae langer;
For a' the real judges rise,
    They canna sit for anger,

Rev. George Smith (d. 1823)
A New Light moderate
crowds

Smith opens out his cauld harangues,
    On practice and on morals;
An aff the godly pour in thrangs,
    To gie the jars an barrels
        A lift that day.

What signifies his barren shine,
    Of moral powers an reason?
His English style, an gesture fine
    Are a' clean out o season.
Like Socrates or Antonine,
    Or some auld pagan heathen,
The moral man he does define,
    But ne'er a word o faith in
        That's right that day.

The Holy Fair

In guid time comes an antidote
    Against sic poison'd nostrum;
For Peebles, frae the water-fit,
    Ascends the holy rostrum: *William Peebles of Newto*
See, up he's got the word o God,   *on-Ayr*
    An meek an mim has view'd it,   *demure*
While Common-sense has taen the road   *Dr. John MacKenzie of*
    An aff, an up the Cowgate   *Mauchline*
        Fast, fast that day.

Wee Miller niest, the guard relieves,   *Rev. Alexander Miller*
    An Orthodoxy raibles,   *(d. 1804) of Kilmaurs*
Tho in his heart he weel believes,   *recites*
    An thinks it auld wives' fables:
But faith! the birkie wants a manse,   *fellow*
    So, cannilie he hums them;   *humbugs*
Altho his carnal wit an sense
    Like hafflins-wise o'ercomes him   *nearly half*
        At times that day.

                           tavern
Now butt an ben the change-house fills,   *backwards and forwards*
    Wi yill-caup commentators;   *ale-cup*
Here's cryin out for bakes and gills,   *biscuits*
    An there the pint-stowp clatters;
While thick an thrang, an loud an lang,
    Wi logic an wi Scripture,
They raise a din, that in the end
    Is like to breed a rupture
        O wrath that day.

Leeze me on drink! it gies us mair   *Blessings*
    Than either school or college;
It kindles wit, it waukens lear,   *learning*
    It pangs us fou o knowledge: *crams full*
Be't whisky-gill or penny wheep,   *beer sold for a penny*
    Or onie stronger potion,   *a bottle*
It never fails, on drinkin deep,
    To kittle up our notion,   *tickle*
        By night or day.

The Holy Fair

The lads an lasses, blythely bent
  To mind baith saul an body,
Sit round the table, weel content,
  An steer about the toddy:
On this ane's dress, an that ane's leuk,
  They're makin observations;
While some are cozie i the neuk,
  An forming assignations
    To meet some day.

But now the Lord's ain trumpet touts,
  Till a' the hills are rairin,
And echoes back return the shouts;
  Black Russell is na spairin:
His piercin words, like Highlan swords,
  Divide the joints an marrow;
His talk o Hell, whare devils dwell,
  Our vera 'sauls does harrow'
    Wi fright that day!

A vast, unbottom'd, boundless pit,
  Fill'd fou o lowin brunstane,
Whase ragin flame, an scorchin heat,
  Wad melt the hardest whun-stane!
The half-asleep start up wi fear,
  An think they hear it roarin;
When presently it does appear,
  'Twas but some neebor snorin
    Asleep that day.

'Twad be owre lang a tale to tell,
  How monie stories past;
An how they crouded to the yill,
  When they were a' dismist;
How drink gaed round, in cogs an caups,
  Amang the furms an benches;
An cheese an bread, frae women's laps,
  Was dealt about in lunches,
    An dawds that day.

stir

corner

sounds
roaring

Rev. John Russell of
Cromarty (1740-1817)

flaming brimstone

whinstone

neighbour

beakers, cups
forms

full portions
lumps

The Holy Fair

In comes a gawsie, gash guidwife,   *showy, smart*
    An sits down by the fire,
Syne draws her kebbuck an her knife;   *Then, cheese*
    The lasses they are shyer:
The auld guidmen, about the grace,
    Frae side to side they bother;
Till some ane by his bonnet lays,
    An gies them't, like a tether,   *rope*
        Fu lang that day.

Waesucks! for him that gets nae lass,   *Alas*
    Or lasses that hae naething!
Sma need has he to say a grace,
    Or melvie his braw claithing!   *meal-dust*
O wives, be mindfu ance yoursel
    How bonie lads ye wanted;
An dinna, for a kebbuck-heel,   *cheese-rind*
    Let lasses be affronted
        On sic a day!

Now Clinkumbell, wi rattlin tow,   *the bell-ringer, rope*
    Begins to jow an croon;   *swing, toll*
Some swagger hame the best they dow,   *can*
    Some wait the afternoon.
At slaps the billies halt a blink,   *fence-gaps, chaps*
    Till lasses strip their shoon:
Wi faith an hope, an love an drink,
    They're a' in famous tune
        For crack that day.   *chat*

How monie hearts this day converts
    O sinners and o lasses!
Their hearts o stane, gin night, are gane   *by nightfall*
    As saft as onie flesh is: *any*
There's some are fou o love divine;
    There's some are fou o brandy;
An monie jobs that day begin,
    May end in houghmagandie   *fornication*
        Some ither day.

THE TWA DOGS

A TALE

According to Gilbert Burns this poem 'was composed
after the resolution of publishing was nearly taken.
Robert had had a dog, which he called Luath, that was
a great favourite. The dog had been killed by the
wanton cruelty of some person the night before my
father's death. Robert said to me, that he should like
to confer such immortality as he could bestow upon
his old friend . . . Caesar was merely the creature of
the poet's imagination.'

Kyle

'Twas in that place o Scotland's Isle,
That bears the name of auld King Coil,
Upon a bonie day in June,
When wearin thro the afternoon,

busy   Twa dogs, that were na thrang at hame,
encountered   Forgathered ance upon a time.
       The first I'll name, they ca'd him Caesar,
Was keepit for 'his Honor's' pleasure:

ears   His hair, his size, his mouth, his lugs,
Shew'd he was nane o Scotland's dogs;

pupped   But whalpit some place far abroad,
Newfoundland   Whare sailors gang to fish for cod.
       His lockèd, letter'd, braw brass collar
Shew'd him the gentleman an scholar;
But tho he was o high degree,

devil   The fient a pride, nae pride had he;
But wad hae spent an hour caressin,

cur   Ev'n wi a tinkler-gipsy's messin:
smithy   At kirk or market, mill or smiddie,
matted mongrel, ragged   Nae tawted tyke, tho e'er sae duddie,
But he wad stan't, as glad to see him,

pissed   An stroan't on stanes an hillocks wi him.
other   The tither was a ploughman's collie,
fellow   A rhyming, ranting, raving billie,
Wha for his friend an comrade had him,
And in his freaks had Luath ca'd him,

MacPherson's Ossian—   After some dog in Highland sang,
a sly dig at this literary forgery   Was made lang syne—Lord knows how lang.
respectable   He was a gash an faithfu tyke,
ditch, stone wall   As ever lap a sheugh or dyke.
pleasant, white-streaked   His honest, sonsie, baws'nt face
Always, every   Ay gat him friends in ilka place;
shaggy   His breast was white, his tousie back
Weel clad wi coat o glossy black;

jolly   His gawsie tail, wi upward curl,
buttocks   Hung owre his hurdies wi a swirl.

The Twa Dogs

Nae doubt but they were fain o ither,   *happy in each other*
And unco pack an thick thegither;   *confidential*
Wi social nose whyles snuff'd an snowkit;   *now, poke with nose*
Whyles mice an moudieworts they howkit;   *moles, dug up*
Whyles scour'd awa in lang excursion,
An worry'd ither in diversion;
Till tir'd at last wi monie a farce,
They set them down upon their arse,
An there began a lang digression
About the 'lords o the creation.'

CAESAR

I've aften wonder'd, honest Luath,
What sort of life poor dogs like you have;
An when the gentry's life I saw.
What way poor bodies liv'd ava.   *at all*
    Our laird gets in his rackèd rents,   *paid in kind*
His coals, his kain, an a' his stents: *dues*
He rises when he likes himsel;
His flunkies answer at the bell;
He ca's his coach; he ca's his horse;
He draws a bonie silken purse,
As lang's my tail, whare, thro the steeks,   *stitches*
The yellow letter'd Geordie keeks.   *guinea, peeps*
    Frae morn to e'en it's nought but toiling,
At baking, roasting, frying, boiling;
An tho the gentry first are stechin,   *cramming*
Yet ev'n the ha' folk fill their pechan   *servants, stomach*
Wi sauce, ragouts, an sic like trashtrie   *rubbish*
That's little short o downright wastrie.   *wasteful*
Our whipper-in, wee, blastit wonner,   *Hugh Andrew, huntsman*
Poor, worthless elf, it eats a dinner,   *at Coilsfield*
Better than onie tenant-man
His Honor has in a' the lan;
An what poor cot-folk pit their painch in,   *put, paunch*
I own it's past my comprehension.

The Twa Dogs

LUATH

Trowth, Caesar, whyles they're fash't eneugh: *sometimes, bothered*
A cotter howkin in a sheugh, *digging*
Wi dirty stanes biggin a dyke, *building*
Baring a quarry, an sic like; *clearing*
Himsel, a wife, he thus sustains,
A smytrie o wee duddie weans, *litter, brats*
An nought but his han-darg to keep *manual labour*
Them right an tight in thack an rape. *thatch, rope*

An when they meet wi sair disasters,
Like loss o health or want o masters,
Ye maist wad think, a wee touch langer,
An they maun starve o cauld and hunger:
But how it comes, I never kend yet, *knew*
They're maistly wonderfu contented;
An buirdly chiels, an clever hizzies, *stout lads, girls*
Are bred in sic a way as this is.

CAESAR

But then to see how ye're negleckit,
How huff'd, an cuff'd, an disrespeckit!
Lord man, our gentry care as little
For delvers, ditchers, an sic cattle;
They gang as saucy by poor folk, *go*
As I wad by a stinking brock. *badger*

I've notic'd, on our laird's court-day,
(An monie a time my heart's been wae),
Poor tenant bodies, scant o cash,
How they maun thole a factor's snash: *an allusion to the harsh treatment of William Burnes*
He'll stamp an threaten, curse an swear
He'll apprehend them, poind their gear;
While they maun stan, wi aspect humble,
An hear it a', an fear an tremble!

I see how folk live that hae riches;
But surely poor-folk maun be wretches!

142

LUATH

They're no sae wretched's ane wad think:
Tho constantly on poortith's brink,   poverty
They're sae accustom'd wi the sight,
The view o't gies them little fright.
   Then chance and fortune are sae guided,
They're ay in less or mair provided;
An tho fatigu'd wi close employment,
A blink o rest's a sweet enjoyment.
   The dearest comfort o their lives,
Their grushie weans an faithfu wives;   growing
The prattling things are just their pride,
That sweetens a' their fireside.
   An whyles twalpennie worth o nappy
Can mak the bodies unco happy:
They lay aside their private cares,
To mind the Kirk and State affairs;
They'll talk o patronage an priests,
Wi kindling fury i' their breasts,
Or tell what new taxation's comin,
An ferlie at the folk in Lon'on.   wonder
   As bleak-fac'd Hallowmass returns,
They get the jovial, ranting kirns,   harvest-homes
When rural life, of ev'ry station,
Unite in common recreation;
Love blinks, Wit slaps, an social Mirth   glances
Forgets there's Care upo the earth.
   That merry day the year begins,
They bar the door on frosty win's;
The nappy reeks wi mantling ream,   froth
An sheds a heart-inspiring steam;
The luntin pipe, an sneeshin mill,   smoking, snuff-mull
Are handed round wi right guid will;
The cantie auld folks crackin crouse,   jolly, conversing cheerfully
The young anes ranting thro the house—   romping
My heart has been sae fain to see them,   sore
That I for joy hae barkit wi them.

The Twa Dogs

Still it's owre true that ye hae said,
Sic game is now owre aften play'd;
There's monie a creditable stock
O decent, honest, fawsont folk,
Are riven out baith root an branch,
Some rascal's pridefu greed to quench,
Wha thinks to knit himsel the faster
In favor wi some gentle master,
Wha, aiblins thrang a parliamentin,
For Britain's guid his saul indentin—

CAESAR

Haith, lad, ye little ken about it:
For Britain's guid! guid faith! I doubt it.
Say rather, gaun as Premiers lead him:
An saying aye or no's they bid him:
At operas an plays parading,
Mortgaging, gambling, masquerading:
Or maybe, in a frolic daft,
To Hague or Calais taks a waft,
To mak a tour an tak a whirl,
To learn *bon ton,* an see the worl.
There, at Vienna or Versailles,
He rives his father's auld entails;
Or by Madrid he takes the rout,
To thrum guitars an fecht wi nowt;
Or down Italian vista startles,
Whore-hunting amang groves o myrtles;
Then bowses drumlie German-water,
To mak himsel look fair an fatter,
An clear the consequential sorrows,
Love-gifts of Carnival signoras.
For Britain's guid! for her destruction!
Wi dissipation, feud an faction.

*Margin glosses:*
too often
well-doing
perhaps
indenturing
know
going
go on the Grand Tour of Europe
splits
road
fight bulls
courses
muddy spa water

144

The Twa Dogs

LUATH

Hech man! dear sirs! is that the gate	way
They waste sae monie a braw estate!	fine
Are we sae foughten an harass'd	troubled
For gear ta gang that gate at last?	wealth
O would they stay aback frae courts,	
An please themsels wi countra sports,	
It wad for ev'ry ane be better,	
The laird, the tenant, an the cotter!	
For thae frank, rantin, ramblin billies,	those roistering
Fient haet o them's ill-hearted fellows:	not one of
Except for breakin o their timmer,	timber
Or speakin lightly o their limmer,	whore
Or shootin of a hare or moor-cock	
The ne'er-a-bit they're ill to poor folk.	
But will ye tell me, master Caesar,	
Sure great folk's life's a life o pleasure?	
Nae cauld nor hunger e'er can steer them,	
The vera thought o't need na fear them.	

CAESAR

Lord, man, were ye but whyles whare I am,	
The gentles, ye wad ne'er envy 'em!	
It's true, they need na starve or sweat,	
Thro winter's cauld, or simmer's heat;	
They've nae sair wark to craze their banes,	hard
An fill auld age wi grips an granes;	gripes, groans
But human bodies are sic fools,	
For a' their colleges an schools,	
That when nae real ills perplex them,	
They mak enow themsels to vex them;	
An aye the less they hae to start them,	fret
In like proportion, less will hurt them.	
A countra fellow at the pleugh,	
His acre's till'd, he's right eneugh;	
A countra girl at her wheel,	
Her dizzen's dune, she's unco weel;	dozen
But gentlemen, an ladies warst,	worst
Wi ev'n down want o wark are curst.	downright
They loiter, lounging, lank an lazy;	
Tho deil-haet ails them, yet uneasy:	nothing
Their days insipid, dull an tasteless;	
Their nights unquiet, lang an restless.	

The Twa Dogs

An ev'n their sports, their balls an races,
Their galloping through public places,
There's sic parade, sic pomp an art,
The joy can scarcely reach the heart.
  The men cast out in party-matches,
Then sowther a' in deep debauches;
Ae night they're mad wi drink an whoring,
Niest day their life is past enduring.
  The ladies arm-in-arm in clusters,
As great an gracious a' as sisters;
But hear their absent thoughts o ither,
They're a' run deils and jads thegither.
Whyles, owre the wee bit cup and platie,
They sip the scandal-potion pretty;
Or lee-lang nights, wi crabbit leuks
Pore owre the devil's pictur'd beuks;
Stake on a chance a farmer's stackyard,
An cheat like onie unhang'd blackguard.
  There's some exceptions, man an woman;
But this is Gentry's life in common.

By this, the sun was out o sight,
An darker gloamin brought the night;
The bum-clock humm'd wi lazy drone;
The kye stood rowtin i' the loan;
When up they gat an shook their lugs,
Rejoic'd they were na *men* but *dogs;*
An each took aff his several way,
Resolv'd to meet some ither day.

patch up

next

positively

live-long
playing cards

twilight
beetle
cattle, lowing, driving-road
ears

146

THE COTTER'S SATURDAY NIGHT
INSCRIBED TO R. AIKEN, ESQ.

Let not Ambition mock their useful toil,
Their homely joys, and destiny obscure;
Nor Grandeur hear, with a disdainful smile,
The short and simple annals of the poor–GRAY

Composed over the winter of 1785-6, using the Spenserian stanza popular in the eighteenth century, for sentimental poetry extolling the merits of rustic simplicity. It was dedicated to Robert Aiken (1739-1807), addressed in the opening stanza.

My lov'd, my honour'd, much respected friend!
  No mercenary bard his homage pays;
With honest pride, I scorn each selfish end,
  My dearest meed, a friend's esteem and praise:
  To you I sing, in simple Scottish lays,
The lowly train in life's sequester'd scene;
  The native feelings strong, the guileless ways;
What Aiken in a cottage would have been;
Ah! tho his worth unknown, far happier there I ween!

November chill blaws loud wi angry sugh;   *wail*
  The short'ning winter-day is near a close;
The miry beasts retreating frae the pleugh;
  The black'ning trains o craws to their repose:
  The toil-worn Cotter frae his labor goes,—
This night his weekly moil is at an end,
  Collects his spades, his mattocks, and his hoes,
Hoping the morn in ease and rest to spend,
And weary, o'er the moor, his course does hameward bend.

At length his lonely cot appears in view,
  Beneath the shelter of an aged tree;
Th' expectant wee-things, toddlin, stacher through   *stagger*
  To meet their dad, wi flichterin noise and glee.   *fluttering*
  His wee bit ingle, blinkin bonilie,
His clean hearth-stane, his thrifty wifie's smile,
  The lisping infant, prattling at his knee,
Does a' his weary kiaugh and care beguile,   *anxiety*
An makes him quite forget his labor and his toil.

Belyve, the elder bairns come drapping in,   *By and by*
  At service out, amang the farmers roun;
Some ca' the pleugh, some herd, some tentie rin   *drive, heedful run*
  A cannie errand to a neebor town: *neighbouring*
  Their eldest hope, their Jenny, woman grown,
In youthfu bloom, love sparkling in her e'e,
  Comes hame; perhaps, to show a braw new gown,
Or deposits her sair-won penny-fee,   *hard-earned wages*
To help her parents dear, if they in hardship be.

The Cotter's Saturday Night

With joy unfeign'd, brothers and sisters meet,
    And each for other's welfare kindly spiers:
The social hours, swift-wing'd, unnotic'd fleet;
    Each tells the uncos that he sees or hears.
    The parents partial eye their hopeful years;
Anticipation forward points the view;
    The mother, wi her needle and her sheers
Gars auld claes look amaist as weel's the new;
The father mixes a' wi admonition due.

Their master's and their mistress's command,
    The younkers a' are warned to obey;
And mind their labors wi an eydent hand,
And ne'er tho out o sight, to jauk or play;
    'And O! be sure to fear the Lord alway,
And mind your duty, duly, morn and night;
    Lest in temptation's path ye gang astray,
Implore His counsel and assisting might:
They never sought in vain that sought the Lord aright.'

But hark! a rap comes gently to the door;
    Jenny, wha kens the meaning o the same,
Tells how a neebor lad came o'er the moor,
    To do some errands, and convoy her hame.
    The wily mother sees the conscious flame
Sparkle in Jenny's e'e, and flush her cheek;
    With heart-struck anxious care, inquires his name,
While Jenny hafflins is afraid to speak;
Weel-pleas'd the mother hears, it's nae wild, worthless rake.

Wi kindly welcome, Jenny brings him ben;
    A strappin youth, he takes the mother's eye;
Blythe Jenny sees the visit's no ill taen;
    The father cracks of horses, pleughs, and kye.
    The youngster's artless heart o'erflows wi joy,
But blate an laithfu, scarce can weel behave;
    The mother, wi a woman's wiles, can spy
What makes the youth sae bashfu and sae grave;
Weel-pleas'd to think her bairn's respected like the lave.

O happy love! where love like this is found:
    O heart-felt raptures! bliss beyond compare!
I've pacèd much this weary, mortal round,
    And sage experience bids me this declare,—
'If Heaven a draught of heavenly pleasure spare,
One cordial in this melancholy vale,
    'Tis when a youthful, loving, modest pair
In other's arms, breathe out the tender tale,
Beneath the milk-white thorn that scents the ev'ning gale.'

148

The Cotter's Saturday Night

Is there, in human form, that bears a heart,
 A wretch! a villain! lost to love and truth!
That can, with studied, sly, ensnaring art,
 Betray sweet Jenny's unsuspecting youth?
 Curse on his perjur'd arts! dissembling, smooth!
Are honor, virtue, conscience, all exil'd?
 Is there no pity, no relenting ruth,
Points to the parents fondling o'er their child?
Then paints the ruin'd maid, and their distraction wild?

But now the supper crowns their simple board,
 The halesome parritch, chief o Scotia's food;   wholesome porridge
The soupe their only hawkie does afford,   milk, cow
 That, 'yont the hallan snugly chows her cood: beyond partition
 The dame brings forth, in complimental mood,
To grace the lad, her weel-hain'd kebbuck, fell;   -saved, cheese, pungent
 And aft he's prest, and aft he ca's it guid:
The frugal wifie, garrulous, will tell,
How 'twas a towmond auld, sin lint was i' the bell.   twelve month, flax, flower

The chearfu supper done, wi serious face,
 They, round the ingle, form a circle wide;
The sire turns o'er, wi patriarchal grace,
 The big ha'-Bible, ance his father's pride.
 His bonnet rev'rently is laid aside,
His lyart haffets wearing thin and bare;   grey side-locks
 Those strains that once did sweet in Zion glide,
He wales a portion with judicious care;   chooses
And 'Let us worship God!' he says with solemn air.

They chant their artless notes in simple guise,
 They tune their hearts, by far the noblest aim;
Perhaps *Dundee's* wild-warbling measures rise,   three popular
 Or plaintive *Martyrs*, worthy of the name;   Psalm tunes
 Or noble *Elgin* beets the heavenward flame,   fans
The sweetest far of Scotia's holy lays:
 Compar'd with these, Italian trills are tame;
The tickl'd ears no heart-felt raptures raise;
Nae unison hae they, with our Creator's praise.

The priest-like father reads the sacred page,
 How Abram was the friend of God on high;
Or, Moses bade eternal warfare wage
 With Amalek's ungracious progeny;
 Or, how the royal Bard did groaning lie
Beneath the stroke of Heaven's avenging ire;
 Or Job's pathetic plaint, and wailing cry;
Or rapt Isaiah's wild, seraphic fire;
Or other holy Seers that tune the sacred lyre.

149

The Cotter's Saturday Night

Perhaps the Christian volume is the theme:
    How guiltless blood for guilty man was shed;
How He, who bore in Heaven the second name,
    Had not on earth whereon to lay His head;
    How His first followers and servants sped;
The precepts sage they wrote to many a land:
    How he, who lone in Patmos banishèd,
Saw in the sun a mighty angel stand,
And heard great Bab'lon's doom pronounc'd by
    Heaven's command.

Then kneeling down to Heaven's Eternal King,
    The saint, the father, and the husband prays:
Hope 'springs exulting on triumphant wing,'
    That thus they all shall meet in future days,
    There, ever bask in uncreated rays,
No more to sigh or shed the bitter tear,
    Together hymning their Creator's praise,
In such society, yet still more dear;
While circling Time moves round in an eternal sphere.

Compar'd with this, how poor Religion's pride,
    In all the pomp of method, and of art;
When men display to congregations wide
    Devotion's ev'ry grace, except the heart,
    The Power, incens'd, the pageant will desert,
The pompous strain, the sacerdotal stole;
    But haply, in some cottage far apart,
May hear, well-pleas'd, the language of the soul;
And in His Book of Life the inmates poor enroll.

Then homeward all take off their sev'ral way,
    The youngling cottagers retire to rest:
The parent-pair their secret homage pay,
    And proffer up to Heaven the warm request,
    That He who stills the raven's clam'rous nest,
And decks the lily fair in flow'ry pride,
    Would, in the way His wisdom sees the best,
For them and for their little ones provide;
But, chiefly, in their hearts with Grace Divine preside.

From scenes like these, old Scotia's grandeur springs,
    That makes her lov'd at home, rever'd abroad:
Princes and lords are but the breath of kings,
    'An honest man's the noblest work of God';
    And certes, in fair Virtue's heavenly road,
The cottage leaves the palace far behind;
    What is a lordling's pomp? a cumbrous load,
Disguising oft the wretch of human kind,
Studied in arts of Hell, in wickedness refin'd!

The Cotter's Saturday Night

O Scotia! my dear, my native soil!
    For whom my warmest wish to Heaven is sent!
Long may thy hardy sons of rustic toil
    Be blest with health, and peace, and sweet content!
    And O! may Heaven their simple lives prevent
From Luxury's contagion, weak and vile!
    Then, howe'er crowns and coronets be rent,
A virtuous populace may rise the while,
And stand a wall of fire around their much-lov'd Isle.

O Thou! who pour'd the patriotic tide,
    That stream'd thro Wallace's undaunted heart,
Who dar'd to, nobly, stem tyrannic pride,
    Or nobly die, the second glorious part:
    (The patriot's God, peculiarly Thou art,
His friend, inspirer, guardian, and reward!)
    O never, never Scotia's realm desert;
But still the patriot, and the patriot-bard
In bright succession raise, her ornament and guard!

HALLOWEEN

Yes! let the rich deride, the proud disdain,
The simple pleasures of the lowly train:
To me more dear, congenial to my heart,
One native charm, than all the gloss of art—GOLDSMITH

The fourth in the group of ambitious essays in 'manners-painting', this poem deals with ancient customs surrounding Halloween, allegedly obsolete even by Burns's time. This poetic record derives much of its material from the stories and legends told to him by his mother and Betty Davidson. The Feast of All Saints (1st November) coincided with the ancient Celtic pagan festival of Samhuinn, hence the blend of Christian ritual and superstition surviving till modern times.

Upon that night, when fairies light
    On Cassilis Downans dance,   hillocks of Cassilis,
Or owre the lays, in splendid blaze,   Kirkmichael
    On sprightly coursers prance;
Or for Colean the rout is taen,   Culzean Castle, road
    Beneath the moon's pale beams;
There, up the Cove, to stray and rove,   Culzean Bay
    Amang the rocks and streams
        To sport that night:

151

Halloween

Amang the bonie winding banks,
　　Where Doon rins, wimplin, clear:
Where Bruce ance ruled the martial ranks,
　　An shook his Carrick spear;
Some merry, friendly, country-folks
　　Together did convene,
To burn their nits, an pou their stocks,
　　An haud their Halloween
　　　　Fu blythe that night.

The lasses feat an cleanly neat,
　　Mair braw than when they're fine;
Their faces blythe fu sweetly kythe,
　　Hearts leal, an warm, an kin:
The lads sae trig, wi wooer-babs
　　Weel-knotted on their garten;
Some unco blate, an some wi gabs
　　Gar lasses' hearts gang startin
　　　　Whyles fast at night.

Then, first an foremost, thro the kail,
　　Their stocks maun a' be sought ance;
They steek their een, an grape an wale
　　For muckle anes, an straught anes.
Poor hav'rel Will fell aff the drift,
　　An wandered thro the bow-kail,
An pow't, for want o better shift,
　　A runt, was like a sow-tail
　　　　Sae bow't that night.

Then, straught or crooked, yird or nane,
　　They roar an cry a' throu'ther;
The vera wee-things, toddlin, rin,
　　Wi stocks out-owre their shouther:
An gif the custock's sweet or sour,
　　Wi joctelegs they taste them;
Syne coziely, aboon the door,
　　Wi cannie care, they've plac'd them
　　　　To lie that night.

The lasses staw frae 'mang them a',
　　To pou their stalks o corn;
But Rab slips out, an jinks about,
　　Behint the muckle thorn:
He grippet Nelly hard an fast;
　　Loud skirl'd a' the lasses;
But her tap-pickle maist was lost,
　　Whan kiutlin in the fause-house
　　　　Wi him that night.

152

Halloween

The auld guid-wife's weel-hoordet nits   well-hoarded
   Are round an round divided,
An monie làds' an lasses' fates
   Are there that night decided:
Some kindle couthie, side by side,   comfortably
   An burn thegither trimly;
Some start awa wi saucy pride,
   An jump out-owre the chimlie   fireplace
      Fu high that night.

Jean slips in twa, wi tentie e'e;   watchful
   Wha 'twas, she wadna tell;
But this is *Jock*, and this *is* me,
   She says in to hersel: whispers
He bleez'd owre her, an she owre him,
   As they wad never mair part;
Till fuff! he started up the lum,   chimney
   And Jean had e'en a sair heart
      To see't that night.

Poor Willie, wi his bow-kail runt,
   Was burnt wi primsie Mallie;   precise
An Mary, nae doubt, took the drunt,   huff
   To be compar'd to Willie:
Mall's nit lap out, wi pridefu fling,
   An her ain fit, it burnt it;   foot
While Willie lap, an swoor by jing,   leaped
   'Twas just the way he wanted
      To be that night.

Nell had the fause-house in her min',
   She pits hersel an Rob in;
In loving bleeze they sweetly join,
   Till white in ase they're sobbin: ashes
Nell's heart was dancin at the view;
   She whisper'd Rob to leuk for't:
Rob, stownlins, prie'd her bonie mou,   stealthily, mouth
   Fu cozie in the neuk for't,   corner
      Unseen that night.

But Merran sat behint their backs,
   Her thoughts on Andrew Bell;
She lea'es them gashing at their cracks,   chattering
   An slips out by hersel:
She thro the yard the nearest taks,
   An to the kiln she goes then,
An darklins grapit for the bauks,   in the dark, baulks
   ·And in the blue-clue throws then,   ball of blue yarn used for
      Right fear't that night.   divining

Halloween

An ay she win't, an ay she swat— *wound, sweated*
  I wat she made nae jaukin; *bet, trifling*
Till something held within the pat, *pot*
  Guid Lord! but she was quakin!
But whether 'twas the Deil himsel,
  Or whether 'twas a bauk-en, *beam-end*
Or whether it was Andrew Bell,
  She did na wait on talkin
      To spier that night. *ask*

Wee Jenny to her graunie says, *Jenny Broun, the poet's cousin*
  'Will ye go wi me, graunie?
I'll eat the apple at the glass,
  I gat frae uncle Johnie':
She fuff't her pipe wi sic a lunt, *puffed, smoke*
  In wrath she was sae vap'rin,
She notic't na an aizle brunt *burning ember*
  Her braw, new, worset apron *worsted*
      Out thro that night.

'Ye little skelpie-limmer's-face! *hussy*
  I daur you try sic sportin,
As seek the Foul Thief onie place, *Devil*
  For him to spae your fortune: *tell*
Nae doubt but ye may get a sight!
  Great cause ye hae to fear it;
For monie a ane has gotten a fright,
  An liv'd an died deleeret, *delirious*
      On sic a night.

'Ae hairst afore the Sherra-moor, *harvest, Battle of Sheriffmuir, 1715: remember*
  I mind't as weel's yestreen—
I was a gilpey then, I'm sure *young girl*
  I was na past fyfteen:
The simmer had been cauld an wat,
  An stuff was unco green; *grain*
An ay a rantin kirn we gat, *rollicking, harvest-home*
  An just on Halloween
      It fell that night.

'Our stibble-rig was Rab M'Graen, *chief harvester*
  A clever, sturdy fallow
His sin gat Eppie Sim wi wean, *son, child*
  That liv'd in Achmachalla: *a fictitious placename*
He gat hemp-seed, I mind it weel,
  An he made unco light o't;
But monie a day was by himsel, *out of his mind*
  He was sae sairly frighted
      That vera night.'

Halloween

Then up gat fechtin Jamie Fleck,   *fighting*
  An he swoor by his conscience,
That he could saw hemp-seed a peck;   *sow*
  For it ,was a' but nonsense: *all merely*
The auld guidman raught down the pock, *reached, bag*
  An out a handfu gied him;
Syne bad him slip frae 'mang the folk,
  Sometime when nae ane see'd him,
      An try't that night.

He marches thro amang the stacks,
  Tho he was something sturtin;   *staggered*
The graip he for a harrow taks,   *pitchfork*
  An haurls at his curpin: *trails, crupper*
And ev'ry now and then, he says,
  'Hemp-seed I saw thee,
An her that is to be my lass
  Come after me, an draw thee
      As fast this night.'

He whistl'd up *Lord Lennox March*,
  To keep his courage cheery;
Altho his hair began to arch,
  He was sae fley'd an eerie;   *scared, awe-stricken*
Till presently he hears a squeak,
  An then a grane an gruntle;   *groan*
He by his shouther gae a keek,   *glances over his shoulder*
  An tumbled wi a wintle   *somersault*
      Out-owre that night.

He roar'd a horrid murder-shout,
  In dreadfu desperation!
An young an auld come rinnin out,
  An hear the sad narration:
He swoor 'twas hilchin Jean M'Craw. *crippled*
  Or crouchie Merran Humphie— *hump-backed, Marion*
Till stop! she trotted thro them a';
  And wha was it but grumphie   *the pig*
      Asteer that night?   *Astir*

Meg fain wad to the barn gaen,   *would gladly have gone*
  To winn three wechts o naething, *sievefuls*
But for to meet the Deil her lane,   *on her own*
  She pat but little faith in:
She gies the herd a pickle nits,   *shepherd, few*
  An twa red-cheekit apples,
To watch, while for the barn she sets,
  In hopes to see Tam Kipples
      That vera night.

Halloween

careful twist   She turns the key wi cannie thraw,
                                  An owre the threshold ventures;

careful twist	She turns the key wi cannie thraw,
	An owre the threshold ventures;
	But first on Sawnie gies a ca',
	Syne bauldly in she enters:
rat	A ratton rattl'd up the wa',
	An she cry'd Lord preserve her!
	An ran thro midden-hole an a',
	An pray'd wi zeal and fervour,
	Fu fast that night.

urged	They hoy't out Will, wi sair advice;
promised	They hecht him some fine braw ane;
fathomed	It chanc'd the stack he faddom't thrice,
shored up	Was timmer-propt for thrawin;
gnarled	He taks a swirlie, auld moss-oak
beldam	For some black, gruesome carlin;
uttered a curse, aimed a blow	An loot a winze, an drew a stroke,
shreds, flying off his fists	Till skin in blypes cam haurlin
	Aff's nieves that night.

	A wanton widow Leezie was,
lively, kitten	As cantie as a kittlin;
woods	But och! that night, amang the shaws,
	She gat a fearful settlin!
	She thro the whins, an by the cairn,
careering	An owre the hill gaed scrievin;
brook	Whare three lairds' lands met at a burn,
shirt-	To dip her left sark-sleeve in,
	Was bent that night.

Now, waterfall	Whyles owre a linn the burnie plays,
	As thro the glen it wimpl't;
cliff	Whyles round a rocky scaur it strays,
eddy	Whyles in a wiel it dimpl't;
	Whyles glitter'd to the nightly rays,
	Wi bickerin, dancin dazzle;
hid	Whyles cookit underneath the braes,
	Below the spreading hazel
	Unseen that night.

bracken, hillside	Amang the brachens, on the brae,
	Between her an the moon,
heifer, outdoors	The Deil, or else an outler quey,
	Gat up an gae a croon:
sheath	Poor Leezie's heart maist lap the hool;
lark-high	Near lav'rock-height she jumpit,
missed her footing	But mist a fit, an in the pool
ears	Out-owre the lugs she plumpit,
	Wi a plunge that night.

Halloween

In order, on the clean hearth-stane,
   The luggies three are ranged;   wooden dishes
An ev'ry time great care is taen
   To see them duly changed;
Auld uncle John, wha wedlock's joys
   Sin' Mar's-year did desire,   1715, the year of the Jacobite
Because he gat the toom dish thrice,   Rebellion led by the Earl of Mar
   He heav'd them on the fire,   empty
      In wrath that night.

Wi merry sangs, an friendly cracks,
   I wat they did na weary;
And unco tales, an funnie jokes—
   Their sports were cheap an cheery:
Till butter'd sow'ns, wi fragrant lunt, sour pudding, steam
   Set a' their gabs a-steerin;   tongues wagging
Syne, wi a social glass o strunt,   liquor
   They parted aff careerin
      Fu blythe that night.

THE MAUCHLINE WEDDING

**Written in the late autumn of 1785, but not sent to
Mrs Dunlop till 21st August 1788, with a note
explaining that it was written in retaliation for the
poet's rejection by a Miss Miller. Her brother William
married Nansie Bell for the £500 left to her by her
brother, Alexander Bell who had died in Jamaica.**

When Eighty-five was seven month auld,
   And wearing thro the aught,
When rotting rains and Boreas bauld
   Gied farmer-folks a faught;
Ae morning quondam Mason Will,
   Now Merchant Master Miller,
Gaed down to meet wi Nansie Bell
   And her Jamaica siller,
      To wed, that day.

The rising sun o'er Blacksideen
   Was just appearing fairly,
When Nell and Bess got up to dress
   Seven lang half-hours o'er early!
Now presses clink and drawers jink,
   For linnens and for laces;
But modest Muses only *think*
   What ladies' underdress is,
      On sic a day.

157

The Mauchline Wedding

held in place
linen
dare peep

prudent

But we'll suppose the stays are lac'd,
  And bony bosoms steekit;
Tho, thro the lawn—but guess the rest—
  An Angel scarce durst keek it:
Then stockins fine, o silken twine,
  Wi cannie care are drawn up;
And gartened tight, whare mortal wight

. . . .

. . . .

such clothes
narrow, rump

buttocks

But now the gown wi rustling sound,
  Its silken pomp displays;
Sure there's no sin in being vain
  O siccan bony claes!
Sae jimp the waist, the tail sae vast—
  Trouth, they were bony Birdies!
O Mither Eve, ye wad been grave
  To see their ample hurdies
      Sae large that day!!!

fine

countenance
broad
shoulders, wig
powder, unguent

Then Sandy wi 's red jacket bra'
  Comes, whip-jee-whoa! about,
And in he gets the bony twa—
  Lord send them safely out!
And auld John Trot wi sober phiz
  As braid and bra 's a Bailie,
His shouthers and his Sunday's giz
  Wi powther and wi ulzie
      Weel smear'd that day.

THE AULD FARMER'S NEW-YEAR MORNING SALUTATION TO HIS AULD MARE, MAGGIE

ON GIVING HER THE ACCUSTOMED RIPP OF CORN TO HANSEL IN THE NEW—YEAR

be a first gift

Mentioned by Burns in his letter to John Richmond (17th February 1786) and probably composed shortly before.

handful from sheaf, belly
hollow-backed, knobbly

gone, colt
lea

A Guid New-Year I wish thee, Maggie!
Hae, there's a ripp to thy auld baggie:
Tho thou's howe-backit now, an knaggie,
  I've seen the day
Thou could hae gaen like onie staggie,
      Out-owre the lay.

The Auld Farmer's New-Year Morning Salutation To His Auld Mare, Maggie

Tho now thou's dowie, stiff an crazy,	drooping
An thy auld hide as white's a daisie,	
I've seen thee dappl't, sleek an glaizie,	glossy
A bonie gray:	
He should been tight that daur't to raize thee,	ready, excite
Ance in a day.	

Thou ance was i' the foremost rank,	
A filly buirdly, steeve an swank:	elegant, trim, limber
An set weel down a shapely shank,	
As e'er tread yird;	earth
An could hae flown out-owre a stank,	pool
Like onie bird.	

It's now some nine-an-twenty year	
Sin' thou was my guid-father's meere;	father-in-law's mare
He gied me thee, o tocher clear,	dowry
An fifty mark;	
Tho it was sma', 'twas weel-won gear,	
An thou was stark	strong

When first I gaed to woo my Jenny,	went
Ye then was trottin wi your minnie:	mother
Tho ye was trickie, slee, an funnie,	sly
Ye ne'er was donsie;	mischievous
But hamely, tawie, quiet, an cannie,	docile
An unco sonsie.	good-tempered

That day, ye pranc'd wi muckle pride,	
When ye bure hame my bonie bride:	
An sweet an gracefu, she did ride,	
Wi maiden air!	
Kyle-Stewart I could bragged wide,	central Ayrshire
For sic a pair.	

Tho now ye dow but hoyte and hobble,	can, stumble
An wintle like a saumont-coble,	stagger, salmon-boat
That day, ye was a jinker noble,	goer
For heels an win'!	
An ran them till they a' did wauble,	wobble
Far, far, behin'!	

When thou an I were young an skiegh,	skittish
An stable-meals at fairs were driegh,	tedious
How thou wad prance, an snore, an skriegh.	snort, whinny
An tak the road!	
Town's-bodies ran, an stood abiegh,	aback
An ca't thee mad.	

The Auld Farmer's New-Year Morning Salutation To His Auld Mare, Maggie

When thou was corn't, an I was mellow,
We took the road ay like a swallow:
At brooses thou had ne'er a fellow,
    For pith an speed;
But ev'ry tail thou pay't them hollow,
    Where'er thou gaed.

The sma', droop-rumpl't, hunter cattle
Might aiblins waur't thee for a brattle;
But sax Scotch miles thou try't their mettle,
    An gar't them whaizle:
Nae whip nor spur, but just a wattle
    O saugh or hazle.

Thou was a noble fittie-lan',
As e'er in tug or tow was drawn!
Aft thee an I, in aught hours' gaun,
    On guid March-weather,
Hae turn'd sax rood beside our han',
    For days thegither.

Thou never braing't, an fetch't, an fliskit;
But thy auld tail thou wad hae whiskit,
An spread abreed thy well-fill'd brisket,
    Wi pith an pow'r;
Till sprittie knowes wad rair't an riskit
    An slypet owre.

When frosts lay lang, an snaws were deep,
An threaten'd labour back to keep,
I gied thy cog a wee bit heap
    Aboon the timmer:
I ken'd my Maggie wad na sleep,
    For that, or simmer.

In cart or car thou never reestit;
The steyest brae thou wad hae fac't it;
Thou never lap, an sten't, an breastit,
    Then stood to blaw;
But just thy step a wee thing hastit,
    Thou snoov't awa.

My pleugh is now thy bairntime a',
Four gallant brutes as e'er did draw;
Forbye sax mae I've sell't awa,
    That thou hast nurst:
They drew me thretteen pund an twa,
    The vera warst.

---

*Glosses (left margin):*

fed

wedding-races
stamina

short-rumped
perhaps have beaten
sprint
made wheeze
wand
willow

rear left-hand plough-horse

to our own cheek

pulled rashly, stopped
suddenly: capered

rooty knolls would have
roared: cracked, slipped over

dish
edge
knew
ere

steepest slope
leaped, sprang

jogged along

ploughing-team, issue

more

MOSSGIEL

ELLISLAND

The Auld Farmer's New-Year Morning Salutation To
His Auld Mare, Maggie

Monie a sair darg we twa hae wrought,   hard day's work
An wi the weary warl' fought!
An monie an anxious day, I thought
    We wad be beat!
Yet here to crazy age we're brought,
    Wi something yet.

An think na, my auld trusty servan',
That now perhaps thou's less deservin,
An my auld days may end in starvin;
    For my last fow,   bushel
A heapet stimpart, I'll reserve ane   quarter of a peck
    Laid by for you.

We've worn to crazy years thegither;
We'll toyte about wi ane anither;   totter
Wi tentie care I'll flit thy tether   prudent, change
    To some hain'd rig,   reserved space
Whare ye may nobly rax your leather,   stretch your stomach
    Wi sma' fatigue.

ADDRESS TO THE DEIL

O Prince! O chief of many throned pow'rs!
That led th' embattl'd seraphim to war—MILTON

Composed in the winter of 1785-6, in three parts — a mock invocation, a recital of the Devil's occupations and a satirical farewell. The middle part owes much to Burns's recollection of 'an old Maid of my Mother's (Betty Davidson), remarkable for her ignorance, credulity and superstition. She had, I suppose, the largest collection in the county of tales and songs concerning devils, ghosts, fairies, brownies, witches, warlocks, spunkies, kelpies, elf-candles, dead-lights, wraiths, apparitions, cantraips, giants, inchanted towers, dragons, and other trumpery.'

O Thou! whatever title suit thee—
Auld Hornie, Satan, Nick, or Clootie—   cloven-hoofed
Wha in yon cavern grim an sootie,
    Clos'd under hatches,
Spairges about the brunstane cootie,   splashes, brimstone dish
    To scaud poor wretches!   scald

161

F

Address To The Deil

Old Hangman	Hear me, Auld Hangie, for a wee,
	An let poor damned bodies be;
	I'm sure sma' pleasure it can gie,
	Ev'n to a deil,
spank	To skelp an scaud poor dogs like me,
	An hear us squeel.
	Great is thy pow'r an great thy fame;
	Far kend an noted is thy name;
flaming, hollow	An tho yon lowin heugh's thy hame,
	Thou travels far;
backward	An faith! thou's neither lag, nor lame,
bashful, afraid	Nor blate, nor scaur.
Now	Whyles, ranging like a roarin lion,
	For prey, a' holes an corners trying;
	Whyles, on the strong-wing'd tempest flyin
stripping	Tirlin the kirks;
	Whyles, in the human bosom pryin,
	Unseen thou lurks.
	I've heard my rev'rend graunie say,
	In lanely glens ye like to stray;
	Or, where auld ruin'd castles grey
	Nod to the moon,
	Ye fright the nightly wand'rer's way,
unearthly	Wi eldritch croon.
	When twilight did my graunie summon,
sober	To say her pray'rs, douce, honest woman!
beyond, humming	Aft yont the dyke she's heard you bummin,
	Wi eerie drone;
alders	Or, rustlin, thro the boortrees comin,
	Wi heavy groan.
	Ae dreary, windy, winter night,
slanting	The stars shot down wi sklentin light,
	Wi you mysel, I gat a fright:
pond	Ayont the lough;
clump of rushes	Ye, like a rash-buss, stood in sight,
moan	Wi waving sugh.
fist	The cudgel in my nieve did shake,
	Each bristl'd hair stood like a stake;
harsh	When wi an eldritch, stoor 'quaick, quaick,'
	Amang the springs,
	Awa ye squatter'd like a drake,
	On whistling wings.

Address To The Deil

Let warlocks grim, an wither'd hags,
Tell how wi you, on ragweed nags,   ragwort
They skim the muirs an dizzy crags,
      Wi wicked speed;
And in kirkyards renew their leagues,
      Owre howkit dead.   exhumed

Thence, countra wives, wi toil an pain,
May plunge an plunge the kirn in vain;   churn
For O! the yellow treasure's taen
      By witching skill
An dawtit, twal-pint hawkie's gaen   petted, twelve-pint, cow
      As yell's the bill.   dry, bull

Thence, mystic knots mak great abuse
On young guidmen, fond, keen an croose;   husbands, cocksure
When the best wark-lume i' the house,   working tool
      By cantraip wit,   magic
Is instant made no worth a louse,
      Just at the bit.   nick of time

When thowes dissolve the snawy hoord,   thaws, hoard
An float the jinglin icy boord,   surface
Then, water-kelpies haunt the foord,
      By your direction,
An 'nighted trav'llers are allur'd   benighted
      To their destruction.

And aft your moss-traversing spunkies   bog-, demons
Decoy the wight that late an drunk is:
The bleezin, curst, mischievous monkies
      Delude his eyes,
Till in some miry slough he sunk is,
      Ne'er mair to rise.

When Mason's mystic word an grip
In storms an tempests raise you up,
Some cock or cat your rage maun stop,   must
      Or, strange to tell!
The youngest brother ye wad whip
      Aff straught to Hell.   staight

Lang syne in Eden's bonie yard,   garden
When youthfu lovers first were pair'd,
An all the soul of love they shar'd
      The raptur'd hour,
Sweet on the fragrant flow'ry swaird,
      In shady bow'r:

Address To The Deil

scheming	Then you, ye auld, snick-drawing dog!
	Ye came to Paradise incog,
trick	An play'd on man a cursed brogue,
	(Black be your fa'!)
shake	An gied the infant warld a shog,
Almost	'Maist ruin'd a'.
flurry	D'ye mind that day when in a bizz
smoky, scorched wig	Wi reekit duds, an reestit gizz,
smutty face	Ye did present your smoutie phiz
	'Mang better folk,
squinted, Job	An sklented on the man of Uzz
	Your spitefu joke?
	An how ye gat him i' your thrall,
	An brak him out o house an hal',
blotches	While scabs an botches did him gall.
	Wi bitter claw;
scold	An lows'd his ill-tongu'd wicked scaul—
	Was warst ava?
	But a' your doings to rehearse,
fighting	Your wily snares an fechtin fierce,
the Archangel	Sin' that day Michael did you pierce,
	Down to this time,
beat, Lowland, Irish	Wad ding a Lallan tongue, or Erse,
	In prose or rhyme.
	An now, Auld Cloots, I ken ye're thinkin,
roistering	A certain Bardie's rantin, drinkin,
hurrying	Some luckless hour will send him linkin
	To your black Pit;
dodging	But, faith! he'll turn a corner jinkin,
	An cheat you yet.
	But fare-you-weel, Auld Nickie-ben!
	O, wad ye tak a thought an men'!
perhaps, know	Ye aiblins might—I dinna ken—
	Still hae a stake:
sad	I'm wae to think upo' yon den,
	Ev'n for your sake!

SCOTCH DRINK

Gie him strong drink until he wink,
That's sinking in despair;
An liquor guid to fire his bluid,
That's prest wi grief and care:
There let him bowse, and deep carouse,
Wi bumpers flowing o'er,
Till he forgets his loves or debts,
An minds his griefs no more.
—SOLOMON'S PROVERBS, xxxi. 6,7.

Kinsley considered that this poem was probably suggested by Fergusson's 'Caller Water', and it uses the same metre. It was composed in the winter of 1785-6, a copy being sent to Robert Muir of Kilmarnock on 20th March 1786.

Let other poets raise a fracas
Bout vines, and wines, an drucken Bacchus,
An crabbit names an stories wrack us,   torment
    An grate our lug: vex, ear
I sing the juice Scotch bear can mak us,   barley
    In glass or jug.

O thou, my Muse! guid auld Scotch drink!
Whether thro wimplin worms thou jink,   spiral, coils, frisk
Or, richly brown, ream owre the brink,   froth
    In glorious faem,   foam
Inspire me, till I lisp an wink,
    To sing thy name!

Let husky wheat the haughs adorn,   hollows
An aits set up their awnie horn,   oats, bearded
An pease and beans, at e'en or morn,
    Perfume the plain:
Leeze me on thee, John Barleycorn,   Blessings on thee
    Thou king o grain!

On thee aft Scotland chows her cood,   chews, cud
    In souple scones, the wale o food!   choice
Or tumbling in the boiling flood
    Wi kail an beef;
But when thou pours thy strong heart's blood
    There thou shines chief.

Food fills the wame, an keeps us livin;   belly
Tho life's a gift no worth receivin,
When heavy-dragg'd wi pine an grievin;
    But oil'd by thee,
The wheels o life gae down-hill, scrievin,   careering
    Wi rattlin glee.

Scotch Drink

muddled	Thou clears the head o doited Lear,
	Thou cheers the heart o drooping Care;
	Thou strings the nerves o Labour sair,
	At 's weary toil;
	Thou ev'n brightens dark Despair
	Wi gloomy smile.
raiment	Aft, clad in massy siller weed,
	Wi gentles thou erects thy head;
	Yet humbly kind in time o need,
	The poor man's wine:
porridge	His wee drap parritch, or his bread,
	Thou kitchens fine.
	Thou art the life o public haunts;
without, festivals	But thee, what were our fairs and rants?
saints	Ev'n godly meetings o the saunts,
	By thee inspir'd,
	When, gaping, they besiege the tents,
	Are doubly fir'd.
	That merry night we get the corn in,
	O sweetly, then, thou reams the horn in!
steaming	Or reekin on a New-Year mornin
bowl, beaker	In cog or bicker,
	An just a wee drap sp'ritual burn in,
tasty sugar	An gusty sucker!
	When Vulcan gies his bellows breath,
gear	An ploughmen gather wi their graith,
froth	O rare! to see thee fizz an freath
two-eared cup	I' th' lugget caup!
Blacksmith	Then Burnewin comes on like death
stroke	At every chaup.
iron	Nae mercy, then, for airn or steel:
bony, chap	The brawnie, bainie, ploughman chiel,
	Brings hard owrehip, wi sturdy wheel,
	The strong forehammer,
anvil	Till block an studdie ring an reel,
	Wi dinsome clamour.
squalling babies	When skirlin weanies see the light,
babble	Thou maks the gossips clatter bright,
fools	How fumblin cuifs their dearies slight;
woe betide	Wae worth the name!
midwife	Nae howdie gets a social night,
	Or plack frae them.

Scotch Drink

When neebors anger at a plea,   neighbours
An just as wud as wud can be,   wild
How easy can the barley-brie   -brew
     Cement the quarrel!
It's aye the cheapest lawyer's fee,
     To taste the barrel.

Alake! that e'er my Muse has reason,
To wyte her countrymen wi treason!   charge
But monie daily weet their weason   throat
     Wi liquors nice,
An hardly, in a winter season,
     E'er spier her price.   ask

Wae worth that brandy, burnin trash!
Fell source o monie a pain an brash!   illness
Twins monie a poor, doylt, drucken hash   Robs, stupid drunken oaf
     O half his days;
An sends, beside, auld Scotland's cash
     To her warst faes.   foes

Ye Scots, wha wish auld Scotland well!
Ye chief, to you my tale I tell,
Poor, plackless devils like mysel!   penniless
     It sets you ill,   becomes
Wi bitter, dearthfu wines to mell,   meddle
     Or foreign gill.

May gravels round his blather wrench,   bladder
An gouts torment him, inch by inch,
Wha twists his gruntle wi a glunch   face, sneer
     O sour disdain,
Out owre a glass o whisky-punch
     Wi honest men!

O Whisky! soul o plays an pranks!
Accept a Bardie's gratefu thanks!
When wanting thee, what tuneless cranks   creakings
     Are my poor verses!
Thou comes—they rattle i' their ranks,
     At ither's arses!

Thee, Ferintosh! O sadly lost!   A reference to the withdrawal
Scotland lament frae coast to coast!   in 1785 of the exemption
Now colic grips, an barkin hoast   from duty enjoyed by the
     May kill us a';   Ferintosh distillery; as a result
For loyal Forbes' charter'd boast   the price of whisky rose
     Is taen awa!   sharply.

Scotch Drink

<table>
<tr><td>Those
stills</td><td>They curst horse-leeches o th' Excise,
Wha mak the whisky stells their prize!
Haud up thy han', Deil! ance, twice, thrice!</td></tr>
<tr><td>spies</td><td>There, seize the blinkers!
An bake them up in brunstane pies
For poor damn'd drinkers.</td></tr>
</table>

Those
stills

spies

They curst horse-leeches o th' Excise,
Wha mak the whisky stells their prize!
Haud up thy han', Deil! ance, twice, thrice!
    There, seize the blinkers!
An bake them up in brunstane pies
    For poor damn'd drinkers.

Whole breeches
store

Fortune! if thou'll but gie me still
Hale breeks, a scone, an whisky gill,
An rowth o rhyme to rave at will,
    Tak a' the rest,
An deal't about as thy blind skill
    Directs thee best.

BROSE AND BUTTER

According to Prof. J. De L. Ferguson, this was Burns's earliest surviving example of his work as a collector of folk songs. He extensively reworked this old Ayrshire ballad, full of sexual innuendo and double entendres: 'brose and butter' (seminal ejaculation), 'grass', 'stibble' (pubic hair), 'dibble' (penis) 'leather' (vagina), 'Mouse', 'Moudiewart' (penis)

CHORUS

O gie my love brose, lasses;
O gie my love brose and butter;
For nane in Carrick wi him
Can gie a cunt its supper.

loft

Jenny sits up i' the laft,
    Jockie wad fain a been at her;
But there cam a wind out o the west

windows
    Made a' the winnocks to clatter.

lark
partridge

The laverock lo'es the grass,
    The paetrick lo'es the stibble:
And hey, for the gardiner lad,
    To gully awa wi his dibble!

cow

My daddie sent me to the hill
    To pu my minnie some heather;
An drive it in your fill,
    Ye're welcome to the leather.

Brose and Butter

The Mouse is a merry wee beast,
   The Moudiewart wants the een;   *mole*
And O, for a touch o the thing
   I had in my nieve yestreen.   *fist*

We a' were fou yestreen,   *drunk*
   The night shall be its brither;
And hey, for a roaring pin   *erect penis*
     To nail twa wames thegither!   *bellies*

EPISTLE TO JAMES SMITH

Friendship, mysterious cement of the soul!
Sweet'ner of Life, and solder of Society!
I owe thee much—   —BLAIR

James Smith (1765-1823), brother of one of the 'Mauchline Belles', and a draper in Mauchline, who later emigrated to Jamaica. He shared Burns's propensity for amatory pursuits, with similar results, and he was the recipient of some of the poet's letters on the subject of love and marriage couched in the frankest terms. In this verse-epistle Burns develops his rip-roaring denunciation of the censorious, hypocritical bigots of the period. It also contains (ll.37ff.) his intention to publish his poems.

Dear Smith, the slee'st, pawkie thief,   *artful*
That e'er attempted stealth or rief!   *plunder*
Ye surely hae some warlock-breef   *wizard-spell*
     Owre human hearts;
For ne'er a bosom yet was prief   *proof*
     Against your arts.

For me, I swear by sun an moon,
An ev'ry star that blinks aboon,   *above*
Ye've cost me twenty pair o shoon,
     Just gaun to see you;
And ev'ry ither pair that's done,
     Mair taen I'm wi you.   *taken*

That auld, capricious carlin, Nature,   *beldam*
To mak amends for scrimpit stature,   *stunted*
She's turn'd you off, a human-creature
     On her first plan;
And in her freaks, on ev'ry feature
     She's wrote the Man.

Epistle to James Smith

Just now I've taen the fit o rhyme,
seething brain   My barmie noddle's working prime,
stirred   My fancy yerkit up sublime,
                       Wi hasty summon:
                  Hae ye a leisure-moment's time
                       To hear what's comin?

                  Some rhyme a neebor's name to lash;
                  Some rhyme (vain thought!) for needfu cash;
talk   Some rhyme to court the countra clash,
                       An raise a din;
heed   For me, an aim I never fash;
                       I rhyme for fun.

                  The star that rules my luckless lot,
                  Has fated me the russet coat,
                  And damn'd my fortune to the groat;
                       But, in requit,
                  Has blest me with a random-shot
                       O countra wit.

turn   This while my notion's taen a sklent,
                  To try my fate in guid, black prent;
                  But still the mair I'm that way bent,
Softly   Something cries 'Hoolie!
heed   I red you, honest man, tak tent!
                       Ye'll shaw your folly;

                  'There's ither poets, much your betters,
                  Far seen in Greek, deep men o letters,
                  Hae thought they had ensur'd their debtors,
                       A' future ages;
                  Now moths deform, in shapeless tatters,
                       Their unknown pages.'

                  Then farewell hopes o laurel-boughs,
                  To garland my poetic brows!
                  Henceforth I'll rove where busy ploughs
at work   Are whistling thrang;
                  An teach the lanely heights an howes
                       My rustic sang.

careless   I'll wander on, wi tentless heed
                  How never-halting moments speed,
                  Till Fate shall snap the brittle thread;
                       Then, all unknown,
                  I'll lay me with th' inglorious dead,
                       Forgot and gone!

170

Epistle To James Smith

But why o death begin a tale?
Just now we're living sound an hale;
Then top and maintop crowd the sail,
      Heave Care o'er-side!
And large, before Enjoyment's gale,
      Let's tak the tide.

This life, sae far's I understand,
Is a' enchanted fairy-land,
Where Pleasure is the magic-wand,
      That, wielded right,
Maks hours like minutes, hand in hand,
      Dance by fu light.

The magic-wand then let us wield;
For, ance that five-and-forty's speel'd,   *climbed*
See, crazy, weary, joyless Eild,
      Wi wrinkl'd face,
Comes hostin, hirplin owre the field,   *coughing, limping*
      Wi creepin pace.

When ance life's day draws near the gloamin,   *twilight*
Then fareweel vacant, careless roamin;
An fareweel cheerfu tankards foamin,
      An social noise:
An fareweel dear, deluding Woman,
      The joy of joys!

O Life! how pleasant, in thy morning,
Young Fancy's rays the hills adorning!
Cold-pausing Caution's lesson scorning,
      We frisk away,
Like school-boys, at th' expected warning,
      To joy an play.

We wander there, we wander here,
We eye the rose upon the brier,
Unmindful that the thorn is near,
      Among the leaves;
And tho the puny wound appear,
      Short while it grieves.

Some, lucky, find a flow'ry spot,
For which they never toil'd nor swat;   *sweated*
They drink the sweet and eat the fat,
      But care or pain;   *without*
And haply eye the barren hut
      With high disdain.

Epistle To James Smith

With steady aim, some Fortune chase;
Keen Hope does ev'ry sinew brace;
Thro fair, thro foul, they urge the race,
        And seize the prey:
Then cannie, in some cozie place,
        They close the day.

And others, like your humble servan',
Poor wights! nae rules nor roads observin,
To right or left eternal swervin,
        They zig-zag on;
Till, curst with age, obscure an starvin,
        They aften groan.

Alas! what bitter toil an straining—
But truce with peevish, poor complaining!
Is Fortune's fickle *Luna* waning?
        E'en let her gang!
Beneath what light she has remaining,
        Let's sing our sang.

My pen I here fling to the door,
And kneel, ye Pow'rs! and warm implore,
'Tho I should wander *Terra* o'er,
        In all her climes,
Grant me but this, I ask no more,
plenty   Ay rowth o rhymes.

dripping   'Gie dreeping roasts to countra lairds,
        Till icicles hing frae their beards;
clothes   Gie fine braw claes to fine life-guards,
        And maids of honor;
ale, tinkers   And yill an whisky gie to cairds,
sicken   Until they sconner.

George Dempster, M.P.   'A title, Dempster merits it;
        A garter gie to Willie Pitt;
city-dweller   Gie wealth to some be-ledger'd cit,
        In cent, per cent.;
        But give me real, sterling wit,
        And I'm content.

        'While ye are pleas'd to keep me hale
        I'll sit down o'er my scanty meal,
gruel, beefless broth   Be't water brose or muslin-kail,
        Wi cheerfu face,
        As lang's the Muses dinna fail
        To say the grace.'

172

Epistle To James Smith

An anxious e'e I never throws
Behint my lug, or by my nose;   ear
I jouk beneath Misfortune's blows   dodge
    As weel's I may;
Sworn foe to sorrow, care, and prose,
    I rhyme away.

O ye douce folk that live by rule,
Grave, tideless-blooded, calm an cool,   sober
Compar'd wi you—O fool! fool! fool!
    How much unlike!
Your hearts are just a standing pool,
    Your lives, a dyke!   wall

Nae hair-brain'd, sentimental traces
In your unletter'd, nameless faces!
In *arioso* trills and graces
    Ye never stray;
But *gravissimo*, solemn basses
    Ye hum away.

Ye are sae grave, nae doubt ye're wise,
Nae ferly tho ye do despise   marvel
The hairum-scairum, ram-stam boys,   headlong
    The rattling squad:
I see ye upward cast your eyes—
    Ye ken the road!

Whilst I—but I shall haud me there,   hold
Wi you I'll scarce gang onie where—
Then, Jamie, I shall say nae mair,
    But quat my sang,
Content wi you to mak a pair,
    Whare'er I gang.

THE RANTIN DOG, THE DADDIE O'T

TUNE: *Whare'll our gudeman lie*

Burns commented that he wrote this song 'pretty early in life and sent it to a young girl, a very particular acquaintance of mine, who was at that time under a cloud.' But whether Elizabeth Paton or Jean Armour is meant has long been a matter for conjecture. Kinsley draws attention to 'the cheerful impenitence' and the expectation of renewed pleasure, characteristic of Burns.

-linen   O, wha my babie-clouts will buy?
attend to   O, wha will tent me when I cry?
   Wha will kiss me where I lie?—
rollicking   The rantin dog, the daddie o't!

fault   O, wha will own he did the faut?
midwife's ale   O, wha will buy the groanin maut?
name it   O, wha will tell me how to ca't?—
    The rantin dog, the daddie o't!

stool of repentance   When I mount the creepie-chair,
   Wha will sit beside me there?
   Gie me Rob, I'll seek nae mair—
    The rantin dog, the daddie o't!

talk, alone   Wha will crack to me my lane?
desirous   Wha will mak me fidgin fain?
   Wha will kiss me o'er again?—
    The rantin dog, the daddie o't!

THE AUTHOR'S EARNEST CRY AND PRAYER

TO THE SCOTCH REPRESENTATIVES IN THE HOUSE OF COMMONS

Dearest of distillation! last and best—
How art thou lost! —PARODY ON MILTON

Written as a reaction to the passing of the Wash Act of 1784 which aimed at terminating the privileged treatment enjoyed by Scottish distillers under the excise laws. The rigorous application of this Act, together with the growth of illicit distilling, had a serious effect on the legitimate whisky industry. London gin distillers, however, continued to object to whisky imports in England and this led to the Scotch Distillery Act of 1786 which imposed even more swingeing taxes on the whisky trade, but actually provoked the Scots into devising more efficient methods of production which paradoxically resulted in a significant expansion of the industry.

boroughs   Ye Irish lords, ye knights an squires,
sedately   Wha represent our brughs an shires,
   An doucely manage our affairs
    In Parliament,
   To you a simple Bardie's prayers
    Are humbly sent.

The Author's Earnest Cry and Prayer

Alas! my roupet Muse is haerse!   husky, hoarse
Your Honors' hearts wi grief 'twad pierce,
To see her sittin on her arse
   Low i' the dust,
And scriechin out prosaic verse,
   An like to brust!   burst

Tell them wha hae the chief direction,
Scotland an me's in great affliction,
E'er sin' they laid that curst restriction
   On aqua-vitae;   water of life(Latin)
An rouse them up to strong conviction, (cf. *uisge beatha* in Gaelic)
   An move their pity.

Stand forth, an tell yon Premier youth William Pitt the Younger,
The honest, open, naked truth: Prime Minister at the age of 24
Tell him o mine an Scotland's drouth, thirst
   His servants humble:
The muckle deevil blaw you south,
   If ye dissemble!

Does onie great man glunch an gloom? growl
Speak out, an never fash your thumb! care a jot
Let posts an pensions sink or soom swim
   Wi them wha grant 'em:
If honestly they canna come,
   Far better want 'em.

In gath'rin votes you were na slack;
Now stand as tightly by your tack:
Ne'er claw your lug, an fidge your back, scratch, wriggle
   An hum an haw;
But raise your arm, an tell your crack
   Before them a'.

Paint Scotland greetin owre her thrissle; weeping, thistle
Her mutchkin stowp as toom's a whissle; pint-pot, empty
An damn'd excisemen in a bustle,
   Seizin a stell,   still
Triumphant, crushin't like a mussel,
   Or lampit shell!   limpet

Then, on the tither hand, present her—
A blackguard smuggler right behint her,
An cheek-for-chow, a chuffie vintner cheek-by-jowl, fat-faced
   Colleaguing join,
Pickin her pouch as bare as winter pocket
   Of a' kind coin.

The Author's Earnest Cry and Prayer

Is there, that bears the name o Scot,
But feels his heart's bluid rising hot,
To see his poor auld mither's pot
    Thus dung in staves,
An plunder'd o her hindmost groat,
    By gallows knaves?

broken in bits

Alas! I'm but a nameless wight,
Trode i' the mire out o sight!
But could I like Montgomeries fight,
    Or gab like Boswell,
There's some sark-necks I wad draw tight,
    An tie some hose well.

Earls of Eglinton
James Boswell (1740-95)
shirt-

God bless your Honors! can ye see't,
The kind, auld, cantie carlin greet,
An no get warmly to your feet,
    An gar them hear it,
An tell them wi a patriot-heat,
    Ye winna bear it?

jolly matron weep

make

Some o you nicely ken the laws,
To round the period an pause,
An with the rhetoric clause on clause
    To mak harangues:
Then echo thro Saint Stephen's wa's
    Auld Scotland's wrangs.

House of Commons

Dempster, a true blue Scot I'se warran;
Thee, aith-detesting, chaste Kilkerran;
An that glib-gabbet Highland baron,
    The Laird o Graham;
An ane, a chap that's damn'd auldfarran,
    Dundas his name:

George Dempster, M.P.
Sir Adam Ferguson of
Kilkerran; glib-tongued
James Graham, 3rd Duke
of Montrose (1755-1836);
shrewd, Henry Dundas,
Viscount Melville (1742-1811)
Thomas Erskine, M.P. (1750-1823)
Lord Frederick Campbell (1736-1816)
Sir Ilay Campbell (1734-1823)
Sir William Cunninghame of Livingston
Cicero

Erskine, a spunkie Norland billie;
True Campbells, Frederick and Ilay;
An Livistone, the bauld Sir Willie;
    An monie ithers,
Whom auld Demosthenes or Tully
    Might own for brithers.

Hugh Montgomerie, 12th Earl
of Eglinton

Thee sodger Hugh, my watchman stented,
If Bardies e'er are represented;
I ken if that your sword were wanted,
    Ye'd lend your hand;
But when there's ought to say anent it,
    Ye're at a stand.

The Author's Earnest Cry and Prayer

Arouse, my boys! exert your mettle,
To get auld Scotland back her kettle;   *whisky still*
Or faith! I'll wad my new pleugh-pettle,   *plough-scraper*
    Ye'll see't or lang,
She'll teach you, wi a reekin whittle,   *smoking knife*
    Anither sang.

This while she's been in crankous mood,   *fretful*
Her lost Militia fir'd her bluid;   *alluding to the Militia Bill, 1782*
(Deil na they never mair do guid,   *opposed by Dempster*
    Play'd her that pliskie!)   *trick*
An now she's like to rin red-wud   *berserk*
    About her whisky.

An Lord! if ance they pit her till't,   *to it*
Her tartan petticoat she'll kilt,
An durk an pistol at her belt,
    She'll tak the streets,
An rin her whittle to the hilt,   *knife*
    I' the first she meets!

For God-sake, sirs! then speak her fair,
An straik her cannie wi the hair,   *stroke; gently*
An to the Muckle House repair,   *House of Commons*
    Wi instant speed,
An strive, wi a' your wit an lear,   *learning*
    To get remead.   *redress*

Yon ill-tongu'd tinkler, Charles Fox,   *Charles James Fox*
May taunt you wi his jeers and mocks;
But gie him't het, my hearty cocks!   *hot*
    E'en cowe the cadie!   *frighten the lackey*
An send him to his dicing box
    An sportin lady.

Tell yon guid bluid of auld Boconnock's,   *Robert Pitt of Boconnoc,*
I'll be his debt twa mashlum bonnocks,   *grandfather of the Prime Minister*
An drink his health in auld Nanse Tinnock's   *hostess of the Sorn Inn,*
    Nine times a-week,   *Castle St., Mauchline*
If he some scheme, like tea an winnocks,   *a reference to the Commutation Act,*
    Wad kindly seek.   *1784 reducing the import duty on tea
and windows*

Could he some commutation broach,
I'll pledge my aith in guid braid Scotch,   *oath*
He needna fear their foul reproach
    Nor erudition,
Yon mixtie-maxtie, queer hotch-potch,   *mixed-up*
    The 'Coalition.'   *Fox-North administration
of 1783*

The Author's Earnest Cry and Prayer

bitter	Auld Scotland has a raucle tongue;
cudgel	She's just a devil wi a rung;
	An if she promise auld or young
	To tak their part,
	Tho by the neck she would be strung.
	She'll no desert.

the 45 Scottish M.P.s

       And now, ye chosen Five-and-Forty,
       May still your mither's heart support ye;

pettish

       Then, tho a minister grow dorty,
           An kick your place,
       Ye'll snap your fingers, poor an hearty,
           Before his face.

       God bless your Honors, a' your days

sups, broth, scraps   Wi sowps o kail and brats o claes,
jackdaws   In spite o a' the thievish kaes,
Palace of St. James's   That haunt St. Jamie's!
(i.e. the Court)   Your humble Bardie sings an prays,
           While Rab his name is.

POSTSCRIPT

Let half-starved slaves in warmer skies
See future wines, rich-clust'ring, rise;
Their lot auld Scotland ne'er envies,
    But, blythe and frisky,
She eyes her freeborn, martial boys
    Tak aff their whisky.

sun   What tho their Phoebus kinder warms,
While fragrance blooms and Beauty charms,
When wretches range, in famish'd swarms,
    The scented groves;
Or, hounded forth, dishonour arms
    In hungry droves!

shoulder   Their gun's a burden on their shouther;
gunpowder They downa bide the stink o powther;
doubt   Their bauldest thought's a hank'ring swither
    To stan' or rin,
crack, pell-mell Till skelp—a shot—they're aff, a' throw'ther
    To save their skin.

But bring a Scotsman frae his hill,
Clap in his cheek a Highland gill,
Say, such is royal George's will,
    An there's the foe!
He has nae thought but how to kill
    Twa at a blow.

Nae cauld, faint-hearted doubtings tease him;
Death comes, wi fearless eye he sees him;
Wi bluidy han' a welcome gies him;
    An when he fa's,
His latest draught o breathin lea'es him
    In faint huzzas.

Sages their solemn een may steek,   *eyes; close*
An raise a philosophic reek,   *smoke*
An physically causes seek,
    In clime an season;
But tell me whisky's name in Greek:
    I'll tell the reason.

Scotland, my auld, respected mither!
Tho whiles ye moistify your leather,   *sometimes*
Till whare ye sit on craps o heather,   *heather tops*
    Ye tine your dam;   *lose; water*
Freedom an whisky gang thegither
    Tak aff your dram!

SKETCH

First published by Currie from Burns's holograph, but later rejected on doubt being expressed by Gilbert Burns, and subsequent editors wrongly attributed it to Fergusson but Kinsley demonstrated conclusively that Burns was, in fact, its author. Dewar placed it in the poet's Mossgiel period.

Hail, Poesie! thou nymph reserv'd!
In chase o thee, what crowds hae swerv'd
Frae Common Sense, or sunk ennerv'd
    'Mang heaps o clavers;   *idle talk*
And Och! o'er aft thy joes hae starv'd
    'Mid a' thy favors!

Say, Lassie, why thy train amang,
While loud the trumps heroic clang,
And Sock and buskin skelp alang   *symbols of*
    To death or marriage;   *Greek drama*
Scarce ane has tried the Shepherd-sang
    But wi miscarriage?

Sketch

In Homer's craft Jock Milton thrives;
Eschylus' pen Will Shakespeare drives;
Alexander Pope; Wee Pope, the knurlin, 'till him rives
dwarf Horatian fame;
Mrs. Anna In thy sweet sang, Barbauld, survives
Barbauld (1743-1825) E'en Sappho's flame.

But thee, Theocritus, wha matches?
David Herd They're no Herd's ballats, Maro's catches;
(c. 1731-1810) Squire Pope but busks his skinklin patches
glittering O Heathen tatters:
I pass by hunders, nameless wretches,
That ape their betters.

learning In this braw age o wit and lear,
Will nane the Shepherd's whistle mair
Blaw sweetly in his native air
And rural grace;
And wi the far-fam'd Grecian share
A rival place?

lad Yes! there is ane; a Scottish callan!
Allan Ramsay There's ane: come forrit, honest Allan!
partition Thou need na jouk behint the hallan,
fellow A chiel sae clever;
Tantallon Castle The teeth o Time may gnaw Tamtallan,
But thou's for ever.

Thou paints auld Nature to the nines,
In thy sweet Caledonian lines;
golden Nae gowden stream thro myrtles twines
Where Philomel,
While nightly breezes sweep the vines,
Her griefs will tell!

Thy rural loves are Nature's sel;
Nae bombast spates o nonsense swell;
Nae snap conceits, but that sweet spell
O witchin love,
That charm that can the strongest quell,
The sternest move.

flowery; In gowany glens thy burnie strays,
brooklet Where bonie lasses bleach their claes;
woods, slopes Or trots by hazelly shaws and braes
Wi hawthorns gray,
Where blackbirds join the shepherd's lays
At close o day.

TO A LOUSE
ON SEEING ONE ON A LADY'S BONNET
AT CHURCH

Probably written late in 1785; the use of Lunardi to
denote a type of bonnet then the very height of
fashion is an allusion to Vincenzo Lunardi who made
several balloon flights in Scotland that year. Ironically,
the first manned flights in the British Isles were made
in September 1784 by James Tytler, Editor of the
Encyclopaedia Britannica and a collaborator with
Burns in the Scots Musical Museum.

Ha! whare ye gaun' ye crowlin ferlie?   crawling marvel
Your impudence protects you sairly;   marvel
I canna say but ye strunt rarely   strut
   Owre gauze and lace,
Tho faith! I fear ye dine but sparely
   On sic a place.

Ye ugly, creepin, blastit wonner,
Detested, shunn'd by saunt an sinner,
How daur ye set your fit upon her—   foot
   Sae fine a lady!
Gae somewhere else and seek your dinner
   On some poor body.

Swith! in some beggar's hauffet squattle;   Off!, temples squat;
There ye may creep, and sprawl, and sprattle,   scramble
Wi ither kindred, jumping cattle;
   In shoals and nations;
Whare horn nor bane ne'er daur unsettle
   Your thick plantations.

Now haud you there! ye're out o sight,   keep
Below the fatt'rils, snug an tight,   falderols
Na, faith ye yet! ye'll no be right,
   Till ye've got on it—
The vera tapmost, tow'rin height
   O Miss's bonnet.

My sooth! right bauld ye set your nose out,
As plump an grey as onie grozet: gooseberry
O for some rank, mercurial rozet,   resin
   Or fell, red smeddum,   deadly powder
I'd gie you sic a hearty dose o't,
   Wad dress your droddum!   backside

I wad na been surpris'd to spy
You on an auld wife's flainen toy;   flannel cap
Or aiblins some bit duddie boy,   perhaps, small
   On's wyliecoat;   ragged vest
But Miss's fine Lunardi! fye!   balloon bonnet
   How daur ye do't?

181

To A Louse

O Jeany, dinna toss your head,
abroad   An set your beauties a' abread!
Ye little ken what cursed speed
pest   The blastie's makin!
Those   Thae winks an finger-ends, I dread,
Are notice takin!

O wad some Power the giftie gie us
To see oursels as ithers see us!
It wad frae monie a blunder free us,
An foolish notion:
What airs in dress an gait wad lea'e us,
An ev'n devotion!

THE JOLLY BEGGARS—A CANTATA

Burns was with his bosom friend John Richmond in
Poosie Nansie's tavern, Mauchline on the night the
poet saw the 'merry core' of beggars that inspired this
work, often known by its alternative title 'Love and
Liberty.' This event probably took place in September
– October 1785. This cantata, the poet's only
attempt at a larger work capable of being staged, was
clearly influenced by John Gay's Beggar's Opera
(1728). The characters in this work are the vagabonds
who then infested the highways 'who sorn and thieve,
and pilfer and extort alms, from the weak and timid,
to the disgrace of the police, the terror of the
inhabitants, and discredit of humanity.'

RECITATIVO

withered, earth   When lyart leaves bestrow the yird,
bat   Or, wavering like the bauckie-bird,
north wind   Bedim cauld Boreas' blast;
lash   When hailstanes drive wi bitter skyte,
And infant frosts begin to bite,
rime   In hoary cranreuch drest;
crowd   Ae night at e'en a merry core
disorderly vagabonds   O randie, gangrel bodies,
carousal   In Poosie-Nansie's held the splore,
spare rags   To drink their orra duddies:
Wi quaffing and laughing,
roistered   They ranted an they sang,
Wi jumping an thumping,
very, griddle   The vera girdle rang.

The Jolly Beggars — A Cantata

First, niest the fire, in auld red rags,	next
Ane sat, weel brac'd wi mealy bags,	
And knapsack a' in order;	
His doxy lay within his arm;	girlfriend
Wi usquebae an blankets warm	whisky
She blinket on her sodger:	leered
An ay he gies the tozie drab	flushed with drink
The tither skelpin kiss,	smacking
While she held up her greedy gab	mouth
Just like an aumous dish:	alms
Ilk smack still did crack still	
Like onie cadger's whup;	hawker's whip
Then, swaggering an staggering,	
He roar'd this ditty up:—	

AIR

TUNE: *Soldier's Joy*

I am a son of Mars, who have been in many wars,
    And show my cuts and scars wherever I come:
This here was for a wench, and that other in a trench
    When welcoming the French at the sound of the drum.
        Lal de daudle, etc.

My prenticeship I past, where my leader breath'd his last,
    When the bloody die was cast on the heights of Abram:
And I served out my trade when the gallant game was play'd,
    And the Moro low was laid at the sound of the drum.

> Moro Castle, Santiago de Cuba, stormed 1762.

I lastly was with Curtis among the floating batt'ries,
    And there I left for witness an arm and a limb;
Yet let my country need me, with Elliot to head me
    I'd clatter on my stumps at the sound of the drum.

> Admiral Sir Roger Curtis (1746-1816)
> General George Elliot (1717-90)

And now, tho I must beg, with a wooden arm and leg,
    And many a tatter'd rag hanging over my bum,
I'm as happy with my wallet, my bottle and my callet,
    As when I us'd in scarlet to follow a drum.

> girlfriend

What tho, with hoary locks, I must stand the winter shocks,
    Beneath the woods and rocks, oftentimes for a home?
When the tother bag I sell, and the tother bottle tell,
    I could meet a troop of Hell, at the sound of a drum.

The Jolly Beggars — A Cantata

rafters shook   He ended; and the kebars sheuk
Above   Aboon the chorus roar;
rats   While frighted rattons backward leuk.
inmost hole   An seek the benmost bore:
corner   A fairy fiddler frae the neuk,
                     He skirl'd out, *Encore!*
camp whore   But up arose the martial chuck,
                     An laid the loud uproar:—

AIR

TUNE: *Sodger Laddie*

I once was a maid, tho I cannot tell when,
And still my delight is in proper young men:
Some one of a troop of dragoons was my daddie,
No wonder I'm fond of a sodger laddie!
Sing, lal de dal, etc.

The first of my loves was a swaggering blade,
To rattle the thundering drum was his trade;
His leg was so tight, and his cheek was so ruddy,
Transported I was with my sodger laddie.

But the godly old chaplain left him in the lurch
The sword I forsook for the sake of the church;
He risked the soul, and I ventur'd the body,
'Twas then I prov'd false to my sodger laddie.

Full soon I grew sick of my sanctified sot,
The regiment at large for a husband I got;
From the gilded spontoon to the fife I was ready,
I asked no more but a sodger laddie.

northern Ayrshire   But the Peace it reduc'd me to beg in despair,
Till I met my old boy in a Cunningham Fair:
His rags regimental they flutter'd so gaudy,
My heart it rejoic'd at a sodger laddie.

And now I have liv'd—I know not how long!
And still I can join in a cup and a song;
But whilst with both hands I can hold the glass steady,
Here's to thee, my hero, my sodger laddie.

The Jolly Beggars — A Cantata

RECITATIVO

Poor Merry-Andrew in the neuk
    Sat guzzling wi a tinkler-hizzie;   *tinker hussy*
They mind't na wha the chorus teuk,   *cared not*
    Between themselves they were sae busy.
At length, wi drink an courting dizzy,
    He stoiter'd up an made a face;   *struggled*
Then turn'd an laid a smack on Grizzie,
    Syne tun'd his pipes wi grave grimace:—   *Then*

AIR

TUNE: *Auld Sir Symon*

Sir Wisdom's a fool when he's fou: *drunk*
    Sir Knave is a fool in a session: *court*
He's there but a prentice I trow,   *trust*
    But I am a fool by profession.

My grannie she bought me a beuk,   *book*
    An I held awa to the school: *went off*
I fear I my talent misteuk,
    But what will ye hae of a fool?

For drink I would venture my neck;
    A hizzie's the half of my craft:
But what could ye other expect,
    Of ane that's avowedly daft?   *mentally deficient*

I ance was tyed up like a stirk   *once, bullock*
    For civilly swearing and quaffing;
I ance was abus'd i' the kirk,   *rebuked*
    For towsing a lass i' my daffin.   *indecent handling, fun*

Poor Andrew that tumbles for sport
    Let naebody name wi a jeer:
There's even, I'm tauld, i' the Court
    A tumbler ca'd the Premier.

Observ'd ye yon reverend lad
    Mak faces to tickle the mob?
He rails at our mountebank squad—
    It's rivalship just i' the job!

And now my conclusion I'll tell,
    For faith! I'm confoundedly dry:
The chiel that's a fool for himsel,   *fellow*
    Guid Lord! he's far dafter than I.

The Jolly Beggars — A Cantata

RECITATIVO

sturdy beldam
steal money

ducked

Then niest outspak a raucle carlin,
Wha kent fu weel to cleek the sterlin;
For monie a pursie she had hooked,
An had in monie a well been douked:
Her love had been a Highland laddie,
But weary fa' the waefu woodie!
Wi sighs an sobs she thus began
To wail her braw John Highlandman:—

AIR

TUNE: *O, an ye were dead, Guidman*

CHORUS

Sing hey my braw John Highlandman!
Sing ho my braw John Highlandman!
There's not a lad in a' the lan'
Was match for my John Highlandman!

lowland

A Highland lad my love was born,
The lalland laws he held in scorn
But he still was faithfu to his clan,
My gallant, braw John Highlandman.

little kilt
broadsword
ensnare

With his philibeg an tartan plaid,
An guid claymore down by his side,
The ladies' hearts he did trepan,
My gallant, braw John Highlandman.

We rangèd a' from Tweed to Spey,
An liv'd like lords an ladies gay,
For a lalland face he feared none,
My gallant, braw John Highlandman.

They banished him beyond the sea,
But ere the bud was on the tree,
Adown my cheeks the pearls ran,
Embracing my John Highlandman.

But, och! they catch'd him at the last,
And bound him in a dungeon fast:
My curse upon them every one—
They've hang'd my braw John Highlandman!

And now a widow I must mourn
The pleasures that will ne'er return;
No comfort but a hearty can,
When I think on John Highlandman.

The Jolly Beggars — A Cantata

A pigmy scraper on a fiddle,
Wha us'd to trystes an fairs to driddle,   cattle round-ups, dawdle
Her strappin limb an gawsie middle   buxom
      (He reach'd nae higher)
Had hol'd his heartie like a riddle,
      An blawn't on fire.   blown it

Wi hand on hainch and upward e'e,   haunch
He croon'd his gamut, one, two, three
Then in an *arioso* key,
      The wee Apollo
Set off wi *allegretto* glee
      His *giga* solo:—

AIR

TUNE: *Whistle owre the lave o't*   rest of it

CHORUS

I am a fiddler to my trade,
An a' the tunes that e'er I play'd
The sweetest still to wife or maid,
    Was 'Whistle owre the lave o't.'

Let me ryke up to dight that tear,   reach, wipe
An go wi me an be my dear;
An then your every care an fear
    May whistle owre the lave o't.

At kirns an weddins we'se be there,   harvest-homes
An O, sae nicely's we will fare!
We'll bowse about till Daddie Care
    Sing *Whistle owre the lave o't.*

Sae merrily the banes we'll pyke,   bones, pick
An sun oursels about the dyke;   fence
An at our leisure, when ye like,
    We'll—whistle owre the lave o't!

But bless me wi your heav'n o charms,
An while I kittle hair on thairms,   tickle, catguts
Hunger, cauld, an a' sick harms,
    May whistle owre the lave o't.

The Jolly Beggars — A Cantata

tinker

Her charms had struck a sturdy caird,
    As weel as poor gut-scraper;
He taks the fiddler by the beard,
    An draws a roosty rapier;
He swoor by a' was swearing worth,

skewer, plover

    To speet him like a pliver,
Unless he would from that time forth
    Relinquish her for ever.

Wi ghastly e'e, poor Tweedle-Dee

haunches

    Upon his hunkers bended,
An pray'd for grace wi ruefu face,
    An sae the quarrel ended.
But tho his little heart did grieve
    When round the tinkler prest her,
He feign'd to snirtle in his sleeve,
    When thus the caird address'd her:—

AIR

patch

TUNE: *Clout the Cauldron*

My bonie lass, I work in brass,
    A tinkler is my station:
I've travell'd round all Christian ground
    In this my occupation;
I've taen the gold, an been enrolled
    In many a noble squadron;
But vain they search'd when off I march'd
    To go an clout the cauldron.

Despise that shrimp, that wither'd imp,
    With a' his noise an cap'rin;
An take a share wi those that bear
    The budget and the apron!

cup
a Clackmannanshire
whisky distillery
wet, throat

An by that stowp! my faith an houpe!
    And by that dear Kilbaigie!
If e'er ye want, or meet wi scant,
    May I ne'er weet my craigie.

The Jolly Beggars — A Cantata

RECITATIVO

The caird prevail'd: th' unblushing fair
  In his embraces sunk;
Partly wi love oercome sae sair,
  An partly she was drunk.
Sir Violino, with an air
That show'd a man o spunk,   spirit
Wish'd unison between the pair,
  An made the bottle clunk
    To their health that night.

But hurchin Cupid shot a shaft,   urchin
  That play'd a dame a shavie: trick
The fiddler rak'd her fore and aft,
  Behint the chicken cavie.   hen-coop
Her lord, a wight o Homer's craft,
  Tho limpin wi the spavie,   spavin
He hirpl'd up, an lap like daft,   limped, leaped
  An shor'd them *Dainty Davie*   Rev. David Williamson,
    O boot that night.   a celebrated Covenanter; gratis

He was a care-defying blade
  As ever Bacchus listed!
Tho Fortune sair upon him laid,
  His heart, she ever miss'd it.
He had no wish but — to be glad,
  Nor want but — when he thirsted;
He hated nought but — to be sad,
  An thus the Muse suggested
    His sang that night.

AIR

TUNE: *For a' that, an a' that*

CHORUS

For a' that, an a' that,
  An twice as muckle's a' that,
I've lost but ane, I've twa behin',
  I've wife eneugh for a' that

I am a Bard of no regard,
  Wi' gentle folks an a' that,
But Homer-like the glowrin byke,   staring crowd
  Frae town to town I draw that.

The Jolly Beggars — A Cantata

pool	I never drank the Muses' stank,
brook	Castalia's burn, an a' that;
froths	But there it streams, an richly reams—
	My Helicon I ca' that.

Great love I bear to a' the fair,
    Their humble slave an a' that;
But lordly will, I hold it still
thwart   A mortal sin to thraw that.

In raptures sweet this hour we meet,
    Wi mutual love an a' that:
fly, sting But for how lang the flie may stang,
    Let inclination law that!

Their tricks an craft hae put me daft,
    They've taen me in, an a' that;
But clear your decks, an here's the Sex!
jades   I like the jads for a' that.

CHORUS

For a' that. an a' that,
* An twice as muckle's a' that,*
My dearest bluid, to do them guid,
* They're welcome till't for a' that!*

RECITATIVO

walls   So sung the Bard, and Nansie's wa's
    Shook with a thunder of applause,
      Re-echo'd from each mouth!
emptied pockets They toom'd their pocks, they pawn'd their duds,
cover tails They scarcely left to coor their fuds,
burning thirst   To quench their lowin drouth.
throng   Then owre again the jovial thrang
      The Poet did request
untie, choose To lowse his pack, an wale a sang
      A ballad o the best:
      He rising, rejoicing,
Judges v. 12   Between his twa Deborahs,
      Looks round him, an found them
      Impatient for the chorus:—

The Jolly Beggars — A Cantata

TUNE: *Jolly Mortals, fill your Glasses*

CHORUS

A fig for those by law protected!
Liberty's a glorious feast!
Courts for cowards were erected,
Churches built to please the priest!

See the smoking bowl before us,
Mark our jovial, ragged ring!
Round and round take up the chorus,
And in raptures let us sing:

What is title, what is treasure,
What is reputation's care?
If we lead a life of pleasure,
'Tis no matter how or where!

With the ready trick and fable,
Round we wander all the day;
And at night, in barn or stable,
Hug our doxies on the hay.

Does the train-attended carriage
Thro the country lighter rove?
Does the sober bed of marriage
Witness brighter scenes of love?

Life is all a variorum,
We regard not how it goes;
Let them prate about decorum,
Who have character to lose.

Here's to budgets, bags and wallets!
Here's to all the wandering train!
Here's our ragged brats and callets!   wenches
One and all, cry out, Amen!

THE ORDINATION

For sense, they little owe to frugal Heav'n:
To please the mob they hide the little giv'n.

Probably written in early January 1786, it was
mentioned by Burns in his letter of 17th February to
John Richmond. It deals with the ordination of the
Rev. James Mackinlay (1756-1841) at Kilmarnock's
Laigh Kirk. Mackinlay's presentation to the charge
(August 1785) was violently opposed by the
Moderates, and it was not until 6th April 1786 that he
could actually be inducted. This poem was composed
as 'an anticipatory view of the approaching ceremony.'

weavers, shrug, scratch	Kilmarnock wabsters, fidge an claw,
greasy	An pour your creeshie nations;
stretch	An ye who leather rax an draw,
	Of a' denominations;
Haste!	Swith! to the Laigh Kirk, ane an a',
	An there tak up your stations;
later the Angel tavern	Then aff to Begbie's in a raw,
	An pour divine libations
	For joy this day.

	Curst Common-sense, that imp o Hell,
wife of the Rev. Wm. Lindsay	Cam in wi *Maggie Lauder:*
Rev. James Oliphant, High Kirk	But Oliphant aft made her yell,
Rev. John Russel, his successor	An Russel sair misca'd her:
Rev. James Mackinlay	This day Mackinlay taks the flail,
slap	An he's the boy will blaud her!
cleft stick	He'll clap a shangan on her tail,
pelt	An set the bairns to daud her
	Wi dirt this day.

give out a metrical psalm	Mak haste an turn King David owre,
	An lilt wi holy clangor;
	O double verse come gie us four,
a famous psalm tune	An skirl up the *Bangor:*
dust	This day the Kirk kicks up a stoure,
	Nae mair the knaves shall wrang her,
	For Heresy is in her pow'r,
flog	And gloriously she'll whang her,
	Wi pith this day.

	Come, let a proper text be read,
	An touch it aff wi vigour,
laughed	How graceless Ham leugh at his dad,
	Which made Canaan a nigger;
	Or Phineas drove the murdering blade,
	Wi whore-abhorring rigour;
jade	Or Zipporah, the scauldin jade,
	Was like a bluidy tiger,
	I' th' inn that day.

192

KILMARNOCK
From near Riccarton

JOHN WILSON'S PRINTING OFFICE
Kilmarnock

The Ordination

There, try his mettle on the Creed,
 And bind him down wi caution,—
That stipend is a carnal weed   *a luxury like tobacco*
 He taks but for the fashion—
And gie him o'er the flock to feed,
 And punish each transgression;
Especial, rams that cross the breed   *fornicators*
 Gie them sufficient threshin;
     Spare them nae day.

Now auld Kilmarnock, cock thy tail,
 An toss thy horns fu canty;   *joyfully*
Nae mair thou'lt rowte out-owre the dale,   *low*
 Because thy pasture's scanty;
For lapfu's large o gospel kail
 Shall fill thy crib in plenty,
An runts o grace the pick an wale,   *stalks, choice*
 No gi'en by way o dainty,
     But ilka day.   *every*

Nae mair by Babel's streams we'll weep,
 To think upon our Zion;
And hing our fiddles up to sleep,
 Like baby-clouts a-drying!
Come, screw the pegs wi tunefu cheep,
 And o'er the thairms be tryin;   *strings*
Oh, rare! to see our elbucks wheep,   *elbows*
 And a' like lamb-tails flying,
     Fu fast this day!

Lang, Patronage, wi rod o airn,   *a reference to the opposition to*
 Has shor'd the Kirk's undoin;   *the induction of the Rev.*
As lately Fenwick, sair forfairn,   *William Boyd at Fenwick. 1782*
 Has proven to its ruin:
Our patron, honest man! Glencairn,
 He saw mischief was brewin;
An like a godly, elect bairn,
 He waled us out a true ane,   *chose*
     And sound this day.

Now Robertson, harangue nae mair   *Rev. John Robertson (1733-99)*
 But steek your gab for ever;   *shut, mouth*
Or try the wicked town of Ayr,
 For there they'll think you clever;
Or, nae reflection on your lear,   *learning*
 Ye may commence a shaver;   *set up as a barber*
Or to the Netherton repair,   *carpet-making district*
 An turn a carpet weaver,   *of Kilmarnock*
     Aff-hand this day.

The Ordination

Rev. John Mutrie (d. 1785)
Mackinlay's predecessor
The Devil
cat

cauldrons

Mutrie and you were just a match,
  We never had sic twa drones:
Auld Hornie did the Laigh Kirk watch,
  Just like a winkin baudrons,
And ay he catch'd the tither wretch,
  To fry them in his caudrons;
But now his Honor maun detach,
  Wi a his brimstone squadrons,
        Fast, fast this day.

foes
flogging

mighty

James Beattie

See, see auld Orthodoxy's faes
  She's swingein thro the city!
Hark, how the nine-tailed cat she plays!
  I vow it's unco pretty:
There, Learning, with his Greekish face,
  Grunts out some Latin ditty;
And Common-sense is gaun, she says,
  To mak to Jamie Beattie
        Her plaint this day.

subcutaneous tissue

But there's Morality himsel,
  Embracing all opinions;
Hear how he gies the tither yell,
  Between his twa companions!
See, how she peels the skin an fell
  As ane was peelin onions!
Now there, they're packed aff to Hell,
  An banish'd our dominions,
        Henceforth this day.

rope, hoist
crop

O happy day! rejoice, rejoice!
  Come bouse about the porter!
Morality's demure decoys
  Shall here nae mair find quarter:
Mackinlay, Russel, are the boys
  That Heresy can torture;
They'll gie her on a rape a hoyse,
  And cowe her measure shorter
        By th' head some day.

pint-pot

deafen

match

Come, bring the tither mutchkin in,
  And here's — for a conclusion—
To ev'ry New-Light mother's son,
  From this time forth, confusion!
If mair they deave us wi their din
  Or patronage intrusion,
We'll light a spunk, and ev'ry skin,
  We'll rin them aff in fusion,
        Like oil some day.

194

THE INVENTORY

IN ANSWER TO A MANDATE BY THE SURVEYOR OF TAXES

MOSSGIEL, *February 22, 1786*

A poetic reaction to the various taxes introduced by
William Pitt in 1784-86, to restore the country's
fortunes depleted by the recent American War. These
fiscal measures taxed carriages, carriage-horses and
personal servants (at a higher rate for bachelors than
for married men).

Sir, as your mandate did request,
I send you here a faithfu list
O guids an gear, an a' my graith,   chattels
To which I'm clear to gi'e my aith.   oath

 Imprimis, then, for carriage cattle: cart-horses
I hae four brutes o gallant mettle,
As ever drew before a pettle: plough-scraper
My *Lan'-afore's* a guid auld 'has been'   front left-hand horse
An wight an wilfu a' his days been: strong
My *Lan'-ahin's* a weel gaun fillie,   rear left-hand horse
That aft has borne me hame frae Killie,   Kilmarnock
An your auld borough monie a time,   Ayr
In days when riding was nae crime.
But ance, when in my wooing pride
I, like a blockhead, boost to ride,
The wilfu creature sae I pat to, —   must, needs
Lord pardon a' my sins, an that too!
I play'd my fillie sic a shavie,   trick
She's a' bedevil'd wi the spavie.   spavin
My *Fur-ahins's* a wordy beast   rear furrow (right hand) worthy
As e'er in tug or tow was traced.
The fourth's a Highland Donald hastie,
A damn'd red-wud Kilburnie blastie!   stark mad, Kilbirnie pest
Foreby, a cowte, o cowtes the wale,   Besides, colt, pick
As ever ran afore a tail:
If he be spar'd to be a beast,
He'll draw me fifteen pund at least.   fetch £15

Wheel-carriages I ha'e but few,
Three carts, an twa are feckly new   partly
An auld wheelbarrow —mair for token,
Ae leg an baith the trams are broken;   shafts
I made a poker o the spin'le,
An my auld mither brunt the trin'le.   wheel

The Inventory

For men, I've three mischievous boys,
Right devils, fighting — Run-deils for fechtin an for noise:
cattle-drover — A gaudsman ane, a thrasher t'other,
David Hutcheson — Wee Davoc hauds the nowte in fother.
cattle, fodder

I rule them, as I ought, discreetly,
An aften labour them completely;
An ay on Sundays duly, nightly,
catechism, discipline — I on the *Questions* tairge them tightly;
sharp — Till, faith! wee Davoc's grown sae gleg,
Tho scarcely langer than your leg,
rattle — He'll screed you aff 'Effectual Calling,'
As fast as onie in the dwalling.

I've nane in female servan' station,
(Lord keep me ay frae a' temptation!):
I hae nae wife — and that my bliss is—
mistresses — An ye hae laid nae tax on misses;
An then, if kirk folks dinna clutch me,
I ken the deevils darena touch me.

brats — Wi weans I'm mair than weel contented:
Heav'n sent me ane mair than I wanted!
Elizabeth Burns — My sonsie, smirking, dear-bought Bess,
She stares the daddie in her face,
Enough of ought ye like but grace:
But her, my bonie, sweet wee lady,
I've paid enough for her already;
if — An gin ye tax her or her mither,
altogether — By the Lord, ye'se get them a' thegither!

Robert Aiken — But pray, remember, Mr. Aiken,
Nae kind o licence out I'm takin:
Frae this time forth, I do declare
hussy, more — I'se ne'er ride horse nor hizzie mair;
mire and slush, wade — Thro dirt and dub for life I'll paidle,
Ere I sae dear pay for a saddle;
I've sturdy stumps, the Lord be thankit!
ways — And a' my gates on foot I'll shank it.

The Kirk and you may tak you that,
It puts but little in your pat:
pot —
do not, book — Sae dinna put me in your beuk,
Nor for my ten white shillings leuk.

This list wi my ain hand I've wrote it,
The day and date as under notit;
Then know all ye whom it concerns,
I have endorsed — *Subscripsi huic,*   ROBERT BURNS
this (Latin)

196

TO JOHN KENNEDY, DUMFRIES
HOUSE

MOSSGIEL, *March 3, 1786*

John Kennedy (1757-1812), a kinsman of Mrs Gavin
Hamilton, was factor to the Earl of Dumfries at
Dumfries House near Cumnock, when Burns met him
in 1786. These lines accompanied copies of 'To a
Mountain Daisy' and 'The Cotter's Saturday Night'
which Burns sent to him at his request.

Now, Kennedy, if foot or horse
E'er bring you in by Mauchlin Corss   Cross
(Lord, man, there's lasses there wad force   would
   A hermit's fancy;
And down the gate in faith! they're worse,   way
   An mair unchancy):   dangerous

But as I'm sayin, please step to Dow's,   the Whitefoord Arms,
An taste sic gear as Johnie brews,   Mauchline; stuff
Till some bit callan bring me news   stripling
   That ye are there;
An if we dinna hae a bowse,
   I'se ne'er drink mair.   I'll

It's no I like to sit an swallow,   not that
Then like a swine to puke an wallow;
But gie me just a true good fallow,
   Wi right ingine,   wit
And spunkie ance to mak us mellow,   liquor, enough
   An then we'll shine!

Now if ye're ane o warl's folk,   world's
Wha rate the wearer by the cloak,
An sklent on poverty their joke,   look askance
   Wi bitter sneer,
Wi you nae friendship I will troke,   barter
   Nor cheap nor dear.

But if, as I'm informèd weel,
Ye hate as ill's the vera Deil
The flinty heart that canna feel—
   Come, sir, here's tae you!
Hae, there's my haun, I wiss ye weel,
   An Gude be wi you.

ADAM ARMOUR'S PRAYER

Jean Armour's brother (b. 1771) was one of a group of
boys in Mauchline who punished a local whore by
making her 'ride the stang'. According to Dr. A. Edgar
the 'jurr' referred to here was Agnes Wilson, mentioned
in a Kirk Session minute of 6th March 1786 'as being of
lewd and immoral practices... the occasion of a late
disturbance in this place.' 'Geordie' was George Gibson
landlord of Poosie Nansie's, while 'Hav'rel Jean' was his
half-wit daughter, otherwise known as Racer Jess.

God	Gude pity me, because I'm little!
	For though I am an elf o mettle,
weaver's	An can like onie wabster's shuttle
Dodge	Jink there or here,
cabbage-knife	Yet, scarce as lang's a guid kail-whittle,
quite worth	I'm unco queer.
knowest	An now Thou kens our woefu case:
maid	For Geordie's jurr we're in disgrace,
ridden on a rail	Because we stang'd her through the place,
genitalia	An hurt her spleuchan;
dare not	For whilk we daurna show our face
	Within the clachan.
hidden, ravines	An now we're dern'd in dens and hollows,
	And hunted, as was William Wallace,
those	Wi constables — thae blackguard fallows —
	An sodgers baith;
	But Gude preserve us frae the gallows,
	That shamefu death!
	Auld, grim, black-bearded Geordie's sel'—
	O, shake him owre the mouth o Hell!
	There let him hing, an roar, an yell
	Wi hideous din,
	And if he offers to rebel,
	Then heave him in!
glance	When Death comes in wi glimmerin blink,
drunken	An tips auld drucken Nanse the wink,
bottom, smack	May Sautan gie her doup a clink
gate	Within his yett,
	An fill her up wi brimstone drink,
hot	Red-reekin het.
half-witted	Though Jock an hav'rel Jean are merry,
	Some devil seize them in a hurry,
	An waft them in th' infernal wherry
straight	Straught through the lake,
	An gie their hides a noble curry
oak	Wi oil of aik!

Adam Armour's Prayer

As for the jurr — puir worthless body! —
She's got mischief enough already;
Wi stanget hips and buttocks bluidy   ie. from being ridden out of
        She suffer'd sair;   town on a rail
But may she wintle in a woody,   dangle in a noose
        If she whore mair!

THE LASS O BALLOCHMYLE

TUNE: *Ettrick Banks*

The subject of this song was Wilhelmina
Alexander (1753-1843), sister of Claud Alexander of
Ballochmyle. Burns saw her while out walking one
evening and was inspired by her beauty to compose
this song which he sent to her with an effusively
complimentary letter. Miss Alexander ignored the
letter. Ironically she lived out her long life an old
maid, and the poet's letter and this song were the
most treasured possessions of her declining years.

'Twas even: the dewy fields were green,
    On every blade the pearls hang,
The zephyr wanton'd round the bean,
    And bore its fragrant sweets alang,
In ev'ry glen the mavis sang,   thrush
    All Nature list'ning seem'd the while,
Except where greenwood echoes rang,
    Amang the braes o Ballochmyle.   heights

With careless step I onward stray'd,
    My heart rejoic'd in Nature's joy,
When, musing in a lonely glade,
    A maiden fair I chanc'd to spy.
Her look was like the morning's eye,
    Her air like Nature's vernal smile.
Perfection whisper'd, passing by:—
    'Behold the lass o Ballochmyle!'

Fair is the morn in flowery May,
    And sweet is night in autumn mild,
When roving thro the garden gay,
    Or wand'ring in the lonely wild;
But woman, Nature's darling child —
    There all her charms she does compile;
Even there her other works are foil'd
    By the bonie lass o Ballochmyle.

199

O, had she been a country maid,
    And I the happy country swain,
Tho shelter'd in the lowest shed
That ever rose on Scotia's plain!
Thro weary winter's wind and rain
    With joy, with rapture, I would toil,
And nightly to my bosom strain
    The bonie lass o Ballochmyle!

Then Pride might climb the slipp'ry steep,
    Where fame and honours lofty shine;
And thirst of gold might tempt the deep,
    Or downward seek the Indian mine!
Give me the cot below the pine,
    To tend the flocks or till the soil;
And ev'ry day have joys divine
    With the bonie lass o Ballochmyle.

EPISTLE TO JAMES TENNANT
OF GLENCONNER

James Tennant (1755-1835) was the eldest son of John Tennant of Glenconner whose large family prospered in many different fields. A younger brother Charles (1786-1838) — the 'wabster Charlie' of 1.45 — founded the St. Rollox chemical works, Glasgow and amassed the fortune which henceforward placed the Tennant family in the forefront of national affairs. James himself was a miller in Ochiltree.

Auld comrade dear, and brither sinner,
How's a' the folk about Glenconner?

livid, easterly | How do you this blae eastlin wind,
That's like to blaw a body blind?
For me, my faculties are frozen,

torpid | My dearest member nearly dozen'd.
dancing-master, Ochiltree | I've sent you here, by Johnie Simson,
Twa sage philosophers to glimpse on:

Adam Smith (1723-90) | Smith, wi his sympathetic feeling,
Dr. Thomas Reid (1710-96) | An Reid, to common sense appealing.
Philosophers have fought and wrangled,

much | An meikle Greek an Latin mangled,
Till, wi their logic-jargon tir'd
An in the depth of science mir'd,
To common sense they now appeal—

weavers | What wives and wabsters see and feel!

Epistle To James Tennant of Glenconner

But, hark ye, friend! I charge you strictly,
Peruse them, an return them quickly:
For now I'm grown sae cursed douse   serious
I pray and ponder butt the house;   at the back
My shins, my. lane, I there sit roastin,   alone
Perusing Bunyan, Brown an Boston,   John Brown (1722-87)
Till, by and by, if I haud on,   Thomas Boston (1676-1732)
I'll grunt a real gospel groan.
Already I begin to try it,
To cast my e'en up like a pyet   eyes, magpie
When by the gun she tumbles o'er,
Flutt'ring an gasping in her gore:
Sae shortly you shall see me bright,
A burning an a shining light.

My heart-warm love to guid auld Glen,   John Tennant (1725-1810)
The ace an wale of honest men: pick
When bending down wi auld grey hairs
Beneath the load of years and cares,
May He who made him still support him,
An views beyond the grave comfort him!
His worthy fam'ly far and near,
God bless them a' wi grace and gear!   wealth

My auld schoolfellow, preacher Willie,   Rev. Wm. Tennant (d. 1813)
The manly tar, my Mason-billie,   David Tennant (d. 1839)
And Auchenbay, I wish him joy;   John Tennant Jr. (1760-1853)
If he's a parent, lass or boy,
May he be dad, and Meg the mither,   Margaret Colville
Just five-and-forty years thegither!
And no forgetting wabster Charlie,
I'm tauld he offers very fairly.
An, Lord, remember singing Sannock,   Robert Tennant (1774-1841)
Wi hale breeks, saxpence, an a bannock!   whole, breeches
And next, my auld acquaintance, Nancy,   Agnes Tennant (d. 1787)
Since she is fitted to her fancy,
An her kind stars hae airted till her   directed to
A guid chiel wi a pickle siller!   chap, little
My kindest, best respects, I sen' it,
To cousin Kate, an sister Janet:
Tell them, frae me, wi chiels be cautious,
For, faith! they'll aiblins fin' them fashious;   perhaps, troublesome
To grant a heart is fairly civil,
But to grant a maidenhead's the devil!

Epistle To James Tennant of Glenconner

An lastly, Jamie, for yoursel,
May guardian angels tak a spell
An steer you seven miles south o Hell!
But first, before you see Heaven's glory,
May ye get monie a merrie story,
Monie a laugh, and monie a drink,
coin   And ay eneugh o needfu clink!

    Now fare ye weel, an joy be wi you!
For my sake, this I beg it o you:
Assist poor Simson a' ye can;
Ye'll fin' him just an honest man,
leave, song   Sae I conclude, and quat my chanter,
Yours, saint or sinner,
                   ROB THE RANTER

INSCRIBED ON A WORK OF HANNAH MORE'S

PRESENTED TO THE AUTHOR BY A LADY

These lines were included in a letter to Robert Aiken, of 3rd April 1786. The identity of the lady mentioned in the title is not known, but possibilities include Mrs William Campbell of Fairfield, Mrs Cuninghame of Lainshaw and Mrs Maxwell Campbell of Skerrington — all fitting the 'Mrs. C—' mentioned in the letter.

Thou flatt'ring mark of friendship kind,
Still may thy pages call to mind
    The dear, the beauteous donor!
Tho sweetly female ev'ry part,
Yet such a head, and more—the heart
    Does both the sexes honor:
She show'd her taste refin'd and just,
    When she selected thee,
Yet deviating, own I must,
    For sae approving me:
        But, kind still, I'll mind still
          The *giver* in the gift;
regard   I'll bless her, an wiss her
above, rest   A Friend aboon the lift.

TO A MOUNTAIN DAISY

ON TURNING ONE DOWN WITH THE
PLOUGH, IN APRIL, 1786

Originally entitled 'The Gowan', it was written at a
time when Burns was experiencing a great deal of
trouble with the Armour family. He sent it to John
Kennedy on 20th April 1786 with a letter describing
these verses as 'just the native querulous feelings of a
heart which, as the elegantly melting Gray says,
"Melancholy has marked for her own".'

Wee, modest, crimson-tippèd flow'r,
Thou's met me in an evil hour;
For I maun crush amang the stoure   *dust*
    Thy slender stem:
To spare thee now is past my pow'r,
    Thou bonie gem.

Alas! it's no thy neebor sweet,
The bonie lark companion meet,
Bending thee 'mang the dewy weet,   *wet*
    Wi spreckl'd breast!
When upward-springing, blythe, to greet
    The purpling east.

Cauld blew the bitter-biting north
Upon thy early, humble birth;
Yet cheerfully thou glinted forth   *shone*
    Amid the storm,
Scarce rear'd above the parent-earth
    Thy tender form.

The flaunting flow'rs our gardens yield,
High shelt'ring woods and wa's maun shield;   *must*
But thou, beneath the random bield   *shelter*
    O clod or stane,
Adorns the histie stibble-field,   *bare*
    Unseen, alane.

There, in thy scanty mantle clad,
Thy snawie bosom sun-ward spread,
Thou lifts thy unassuming head
    In humble guise;
But now the share uptears thy bed,
    And low thou lies!

Such is the fate of artless maid,
Sweet flow'ret of the rural shade!
By love's simplicity betray'd,
    And guileless trust;
Till she, like thee, all soil'd, is laid
    Low i' the dust.

To A Mountain Daisy

Such is the fate of simple Bard,
On Life's rough ocean luckless starr'd!
Unskilful he to note the card
    Of prudent lore,
Till billows rage, and gales blow hard,
    And whelm him o'er!

Such fate to suffering Worth is giv'n,
Who long with wants and woes has striv'n,
By human pride or cunning driv'n
    To mis'ry's brink;
Till, wrench'd of ev'ry stay but Heav'n,
    He, ruin'd, sink!

Ev'n thou who mourn'st the Daisy's fate,
That fate is thine — no distant date;
Stern Ruin's plough-share drives elate,
    Full on thy bloom,
Till crush'd beneath the furrow's weight,
    Shall be thy doom!

THE LAMENT

OCCASIONED BY THE UNFORTUNATE ISSUE
OF A FRIEND'S AMOUR

TUNE: *Scots Queen*

Alas! how oft does Goodness wound itself,
And sweet Affection prove the spring of Woe! — HOME

The 'friend's amour' of the sub-title was his own ill-
starred affair early in 1786 with Jean Armour. In his
Autobiographical Letter to Dr Moore he wrote: '...a
shocking affair... and had very nearly given [me] one or
two of the principal qualifications for a place among
those who have lost the chart of Rationality.'

O thou pale Orb that silent shines
    While care-untroubled mortals sleep!
Thou seest a wretch who inly pines,
    And wanders here to wail and weep!
With Woe I nightly vigils keep,
    Beneath thy wan, unwarming beam;
And mourn, in lamentation deep,
    How life and love are all a dream!

The Lament

I joyless view thy rays adorn
    The faintly-markèd, distant hill;
I joyless view thy trembling horn,
    Reflected in the gurgling rill:
My fondly-fluttering heart, be still!
    Thou busy pow'r, Remembrance, cease!
Ah! must the agonizing thrill
    For ever bar returning Peace!

No idly-feign'd, poetic pains
    My sad, love-lorn lamentings claim:
No shepherd's pipe — Arcadian strains;
    No fabled tortures quaint and tame.
The plighted faith, the mutual flame,
    The oft-attested Pow'rs above,
The promis'd father's tender name;
    These were the pledges of my love!

Encircled in her clasping arms,
    How have the raptur'd moments flown!
How have I wish'd for Fortune's charms,
    For her dear sake, and her's alone!
And, must I think it! is she gone,
    My secret heart's exulting boast?
And does she heedless hear my groan?
    And is she ever, ever lost?

O! can she bear so base a heart,
    So lost to honour, lost to truth,
As from the fondest lover part,
    The plighted husband of her youth?
Alas! Life's path may be unsmooth!
    Her way may lie thro rough distress!
Then, who her pangs and pains will soothe,
    Her sorrows share, and make them less?

Ye wingèd Hours that o'er us pass'd,
    Enraptur'd more the more enjoy'd,
Your dear remembrance in my breast
    My fondly-treasur'd thoughts employ'd—
That breast, how dreary now, and void,
    For her too scanty once of room!
Ev'n ev'ry ray of Hope destroy'd,
    And not a wish to gild the gloom!

The Lament

The morn, that warns th'approaching day,
   Awakes me up to toil and woe;
I see the hours in long array,
   That I must suffer, lingering slow:
Full many a pang, and many a throe,
   Keen Recollection's direful train,
Must wring my soul, ere Phoebus, low,
   Shall kiss the distant western main.

And when my nightly couch I try,
   Sore-harass'd out with care and grief,
My toil-beat nerves, and tear-worn eye
   Keep watchings with the nightly thief:
Or, if I slumber, Fancy, chief,
   Reigns, haggard-wild, in sore affright:
Ev'n day, all-bitter, brings relief
   From such a horror-breathing night.

O thou bright Queen, who, o'er th' expanse
   Now highest reign'st, with boundless sway!
Oft has thy silent-marking glance
   Observ'd us, fondly-wand'ring, stray!
The time, unheeded, sped away,
   While Love's luxurious pulse beat high,
Beneath thy silver-gleaming ray,
   To mark the mutual-kindling eye.

O! scenes in strong remembrance set!
   Scenes, never, never to return!
Scenes if in stupor I forget,
   Again I feel, again I burn!
From ev'ry joy and pleasure torn,
   Life's weary vale I'll wander thro;
And hopeless, comfortless, I'll mourn
   A faithless woman's broken vow!

DESPONDENCY — AN ODE

Another piece inspired by the melancholy induced by
the dramatic events of March-April 1786, when Jean
and Robert were compeared before the Kirk Session
for fornication, and she was subsequently packed off to
Paisley by her father who tried to nullify their irregular
(though legal in Scots law) marriage by mutilating the
document promising or declaring marraige — the
'unlucky paper' whose destruction 'cut my very veins'.

Opress'd with grief, oppress'd with care,
A burden more than I can bear,
  I set me down and sigh;
O Life! thou art a galling load,
Along a rough, a weary road,
  To wretches such as I!
Dim-backward, as I cast my view,
  What sick'ning scenes appear!
What sorrows yet may pierce me thro,
  Too justly I may fear!
    Still caring, despairing,
      Must be my bitter doom;
    My woes here shall close ne'er
      But with the closing tomb!

Happy! ye sons of busy life,
Who, equal to the bustling strife,
  No other view regard!
Ev'n when the wished end's denied,
Yet while the busy means are plied,
  They bring their own reward:
Whilst I, a hope-abandon'd wight,
  Unfitted with an aim,
Meet ev'ry sad returning night,
  And joyless morn the same.
    You, bustling and justling,
      Forget each grief an pain;
    I, listless yet restless,
      Find ev'ry prospect vain.

Despondency – An Ode

How blest the Solitary's lot,
Who, all-forgetting, all-forgot,
    Within his humble cell—
The cavern, wild with tangling roots—
Sits o'er his newly gather'd fruits,
    Beside his crystal well!
Or haply to his ev'ning thought,
    By unfrequented stream,
The ways of men are distant brought,
    A faint-collected dream;
        While praising, and raising
            His thoughts to Heav'n on high,
        As wand'ring, meand'ring,
            He views the solemn sky.

Than I, no lonely hermit plac'd
Where never human footstep trac'd,
    Less fit to play the part;
The lucky moment to improve,
And just to stop, and just to move,
With self-respecting art:
But ah! those pleasures, loves, and joys,
    Which I too keenly taste,
The Solitary can despise—
    Can want, and yet be blest!
        He needs not, he heeds not,
            Or human love or hate;
        Whilst I here must cry here
            At perfidy ingrate!

O enviable early days,
When dancing thoughtless pleasure's maze
    To care, to guilt unknown!
How ill exchang'd for riper times,
To feel the follies, or the crimes,
    Of others, or my own!
Ye tiny elves that guiltless sport,
    Like linnets in the bush,
Ye little know the ills ye court,
    When manhood is your wish!
        The losses, the crosses,
            That active man enrage;
        The fears all, the tears all,
            Of dim declining Age!

AH, WOE IS ME, MY MOTHER DEAR

Paraphrase of Jeremiah, 15th chap., 10th verse

The closing lines of this poem give the clue to the occasion which inspired it: the Armour affair of early 1786.

Ah, woe is me, my Mother dear!
  A man of strife ye've born me:
For sair contention I maun bear;   must
  They hate, revile, and scorn me.

I ne'er could lend on bill or band,
  That five per cent. might blest me;   might have
And borrowing, on the tither hand,   other
  The deil a ane wad trust me.   would

Yet I, a coin-denyèd wight,   sturdy person
  By Fortune quite discarded,
Ye see how I am, day and night,
  By lad and lass blackguarded!   miscalled

EPITAPH ON A HENPECKED SQUIRE

This epitaph, and the following epigrams, commemorate William Campbell of Netherplace near Mauchline. His domineering wife was Lilias Neilson (d. 1826), daughter of a Glasgow merchant.

As father Adam first was fool'd,
  A case that's still too common,
Here lies a man a woman ruled—
  The Devil ruled the woman.

EPIGRAM ON SAID OCCASION

O Death, had'st thou but spar'd his life,
  Whom we this day lament!
We freely wad exchanged the wife,
  And a' been weel content.
Ev'n as he is, cauld in his graff,   grave
  The swap we yet will do't;
Tak thou the carlin's carcase aff,   old fellow
  Thou'se get the saul o boot.   soul into the bargain

ANOTHER

Artemisa, Queen of Halicarnassus, married her brother
Mausolus. She was so devoted to him that,
following his death c. 353 B.C., she not only erected
the Mausoleum, one of the ancient wonders of the
world, but ingested his ashes in liquor.

One Queen Artemisa, as old stories tell,
When depriv'd of her husband she loved so well,
In respect for the love and affection he'd show'd her,
She reduc'd him to dust and she drank up the powder.
But Queen Netherplace, of a diff'rent complexion.
When call'd on to order the fun'ral direction,
Would have eat her dead lord, on a slender pretence,
Not to show her respect, but—to save the expense!

STANZAS ON NAETHING

EXTEMPORE EPISTLE
TO GAVIN HAMILTON, ESQ.

Though undated, this poem must have been composed
in the spring of 1786, as it deals with matters then
topical: Hamilton's troubles with Daddy Auld and
Mauchline Kirk Session, recently resolved, the poet's
own moral transgressions which were to lead him to
make three penitential appearances in church in July
1786, and his plans to emigrate to Jamaica.

      To you, Sir, this summons I've sent

pony, frothing   (Pray, whip till the pownie is fraething!)
      But if you demand what I want,
        I honestly answer you — naething.

      Ne'er scorn a poor Poet like me
        For idly just living and breathing,
      While people of every degree
        Are busy employed about — naething.

      Poor Centum-per-Centum may fast,
grudge, buttocks   And grumble his hurdies their claithing;
      He'll find, when the balance is cast,
        He's gane to the Devil for — naething.

      The courtier cringes and bows;
        Ambition has likewise its plaything—
      A coronet beams on his brows;
        And what is a coronet? — naething.

complain of   Some quarrel the Presbyter gown,
vestments   Some quarrel Episcopal graithing;
      But every good fellow will own
        The quarrel is a' about — naething.

Stanzas On Naething

The lover may sparkle and glow,
    Approaching his bonie bit gay thing;   little
But marriage will soon let him know
    He's gotten — a buskit-up naething.   tricked-out

The Poet may jingle and rhyme
    In hopes of a laureate wreathing,
And when he has wasted his time,
    He's kindly rewarded with — naething.

The thundering bully may rage,
    And swagger and swear like a heathen;
But collar him fast, I'll engage,
    You'll find that his courage is — naething.

Last night with a feminine Whig —
    A poet she couldna put faith in!
But soon we grew lovingly big,
    I taught her, her terrors were — naething.

Her Whigship was wonderful pleased,
    But charmingly tickled wi ae thing;
Her fingers I lovingly squeezed,
    And kissed her, and promised her — naething.

The priest anathèmas may threat —
    Predicament, sir, that we're baith in;
But when Honor's reveillé is beat,
    The holy artillery's — naething.

And now I must mount on the wave:
    My voyage perhaps there is death in;
But what is a watery grave?
    The drowning a Poet is — naething.

And now, as grim Death's in my thought,
    To you, Sir, I make this bequeathing:
My service as long as ye've ought,
    And my friendship, by God, when ye've — naething.

ON A SCOTCH BARD

GONE TO THE WEST INDIES

Written in the summer of 1786, by which time Burns had fixed to go to Jamaica in October. When that time came, however, his fortunes had improved and the course of his life was changing in a literary direction, and plans to emigrate to the West Indies were dropped. The mood of this poem contrasts with the verses immediately preceding it, evidence of Burns's cyclothymic nature.

sups	A' ye wha live by sowps o drink,
rhyme	A' ye wha live by crambo-clink,
	A' ye wha live and never think
	Come, mourn wi me!
comrade, given the slip	Our billie's gien us a' a jink,
	An owre the sea!

Lament him a' ye rantin core,
Wha dearly like a random-splore;
Nae mair he'll join the merry roar,
In social key;
For now he's taen anither shore,
An owre the sea!

The bonie lasses weel may wiss him,
And in their dear petitions place him:
The widows, wives, an a' may bless him
Wi tearfu e'e,
For weel I wat they'll sairly miss him
That's owre the sea!

O Fortune, they hae room to grumble!
Hadst thou taen aff some drowsy bummle,
Wha can do nought but fyke an fumble,
'Twad been nae plea;
But he was gleg as onie wumble,
That's owre the sea!

Auld, cantie Kyle may weepers wear,
An stain them wi the saut, saut tear:
'Twill make her poor auld heart, I fear,
In flinders flee:
He was her Laureat monie a year,
That's owre the sea!

He saw Misfortune's cauld nor-west
Lang-mustering up a bitter blast;
A jillet brak his heart at last,
Ill may she be!
So, took a berth afore the mast,
An owre the sea.

212

To tremble under Fortune's cummock,   rod
On scarce a bellyfu o drummock,   gruel
Wi his proud, independent stomach,
    Could ill agree;
So, row't his hurdies in a hammock,   rolled, buttocks
    An owre the sea.

He ne'er was gien to great misguiding,
Yet coin his pouches wad na bide in;   pockets
Wi him it ne'er was under hiding;
    He dealt it free;
The Muse was a' that he took pride in,
    That's owre the sea.

Jamaica bodies, use him weel,
An hap him in a cozie biel: shelter, place
Ye'll find him ay a dainty chiel,   fellow
    An fou o glee:
He wad na wrang'd the vera Deil,
    That's owre the sea.

Fareweel, my rhyme-composing billie!   friend
Your native soil was right ill-willie;   unkind
But may ye flourish like a lily,
    Now bonilie!
I'll toast you in my hindmost gillie,   last gill
    Tho owre the sea!

SECOND EPISTLE TO DAVIE

A BROTHER POET

Addressed to David Sillar (1760-1830), see page 86.
This epistle was evidently written some time before
the publication of Burns's poems at the end of July
1786.

Auld Neebor,
I'm three times doubly o'er your debtor
For your auld-farrant, frien'ly letter;   old-fashioned
Tho I maun say't, I doubt ye flatter,   must
    Ye speak sae fair;
For my puir, silly, rhymin clatter   babble
    Some less maun sair.   serve

Second Epistle To Davie

Hale be your heart, hale be your fiddle!
elbow, dance, shake   Lang may your elbuck jink an diddle,
wriggle   To cheer you thro the weary widdle
    O war'ly cares,
grandchildren   Till bairns' bairns kindly cuddle
    Your auld grey hairs!

afraid, foolish   But Davie, lad, I'm red ye're glaikit;
    I'm tauld the Muse ye hae negleckit;
if, whipped   An gif it's sae, ye sud be lickit
fidget   Until ye fyke;
spared   Sic han's as you sud ne'er be faiket,
except   Be hain't wha like.

    For me, I'm on Parnassus' brink,
Tearing, make rhyme   Rivin the words to gar them clink;
Now dazed   Whyles daez't wi love, whyles daez't wi drink,
jades, Freemasons   Wi jads or Masons;
    An whyles, but ay owre late, I think
Fine   Braw sober lessons.

Of a' the thoughtless sons o man,
Commen' to me the Bardie clan;
Except it be some idle plan
    O rhymin clink—
Heaven forbid   The devil-haet that I sud ban!—
    They never think.

Nae thought, nae view, nae scheme o livin,
Nae cares to gie us joy or grievin,
pocket, fist   But just the pouchie put the nieve in,
    An while ought's there,
Helter-skelter, careering   Then, hiltie-skiltie, we gae scrievin,
trouble   An fash nae mair.

Blessings   Leeze me on rhyme! it's ay a treasure,
almost   My chief, amaist my only pleasure;
At hame, a-fiel', at wark or leisure,
hussy   The Muse, poor hizzie!
homespun   Tho rough an raploch be her measure,
    She's seldom lazy.

stick   Haud to the Muse, my dainty Davie:
trick   The warl' may play you monie a shavie,
But for the Muse, she'll never leave ye,
    Tho e'er sae puir;
spavin   Na, even tho limpin wi the spavie
    Frae door to door.

TO GAVIN HAMILTON, ESQ.,
MAUCHLINE

RECOMMENDING A BOY

MOSSGAVILLE, *May 3, 1786*

According to Cromek 'Master Tootie' (1.2) was a rascally
Mauchline cattle-dealer who filed and polished off the
rings on his cows' horns ('auld Crummie's nicks) to
conceal their true age. 'Mossgaville' is the posh
rendering of Mossgiel.

I hold it, Sir, my bounden duty
To warn you how that Master Tootie,
　　Alias Laird M'Gaun,
Was here to hire yon lad away
'Bout whom ye spak the tither day,
　　An wad hae don't aff han';　　　　　　out of hand
But lest he learn the callan tricks—　　　teach, lad
　　As faith! I muckle doubt him —　　　much
Like scrapin out auld Crummie's nicks,
　　An tellin lies about them,
　　　　As lieve then, I'd have then　　　Rather
　　　　　　Your clerkship he should sair,　serve
　　　　If sae be ye may be
　　　　　　Not fitted otherwhere.

Altho I say't, he's gleg enough,　　　　　bright
An 'bout a house that's rude an rough,
　　The boy might learn to swear;
But then wi *you* he'll be sae taught,
An get sic fair example straught,　　　　　straight
　　I hae na onie fear.　　　　　　　　　any
Ye'll catechise him, every quirk,
　　An shore him weel wi 'Hell';　　　　threaten
An gar him follow to the kirk —　　　　　make
　　Ay when ye gang yoursel!　　　　　go
　　　　If ye, then, maun be then　　　must
　　　　　　Frae hame this comin Friday,
　　　　Then please, Sir, to lea'e, Sir,
　　　　　　The orders wi your lady.

To Gavin Hamilton, Esq., Mauchline

John Dow, landlord of the
Whitefoord Arms
miserable, reptile
contractual payment

latch

My word of honour I hae gi'en,
In Paisley John's that night at e'en,
    To meet the 'warld's worm;'
To try to get the twa to gree,
An name the airles an the fee,
    In legal mode an form:
I ken he weel a *snick* can draw,
    When simple bodies let him;
An if a Devil be at a'.
    In faith he's sure to get him.
To phrase you an praise you,
    Ye ken, you Laureat scorns:
The pray'r still you share still,
    Of grateful MINSTREL BURNS.

A DEDICATION

TO GAVIN HAMILTON, ESQ.

**This poem was intended originally to appear at the
end of the Kilmarnock Edition. Its curious position
within that volume is explained by the fact that Burns
added several poems while the book was going through
the press.**

wheedling, flattering
praise

ie. the Duke of Hamilton

Expect na, Sir, in this narration,
A fleechin, fleth'rin Dedication,
To roose you up, an ca' you guid,
An sprung o great an noble bluid,
Because ye're surnam'd like His Grace —
Perhaps related to the race:
Then, when I'm tir'd — and sae are ye,
Wi monie a fulsome, sinfu lie, —
Set up a face how I stop short,
For fear your modesty be hurt.

bellyful
low

cannot

This may do — maun do, Sir, wi them wha
Maun please the great-folk for a wamefou;
For me! sae laigh I need na bow,
For, Lord be thankit, I can plough;
And when I downa yoke a naig,
Then, Lord be thankit, I can beg;
Sae I shall say an that's nae flatt'rin,
It's just sic poet and sic patron.

216

A Dedication

The Poet, some guid angel help him,
Or else, I fear, some ill ane skelp him!   beat
He may do weel for a' he's done yet,
But only he's no just begun yet.

The Patron (sir, ye maun forgie me;
I winna lie, come what will o me),
On ev'ry hand it will allow'd be,
He's just — nae better than he should be.

I readily and freely grant,
He downa see a poor man want;
What's no his ain he winna tak it;   will not
What ance he says, he winna break it;
Ought he can lend he'll no refus't,
Till aft his guidness is abus'd;
And rascals whyles that do him wrang,   sometimes
Ev'n that, he does na mind it lang;
As master, landlord, husband, father,
He does na fail his part in either.

But then, nae thanks to him for a' that;
Nae godly symptom ye can ca' that;
It's naething but a milder feature
Of our poor, sinfu, corrupt nature:
Ye'll get the best o moral works,
'Mang black Gentoos, and pagan Turks,   Hindus
Or hunters wild on Ponataxi,   Cotopaxi, Ecuador
Wha never heard of orthodoxy.
That he's the poor man's friend in need,
The gentleman in work and deed,
It's no thro terror of damnation;
It's just a carnal inclination,
An och! that's nae regeneration.

Morality, thou deadly bane,
Thy tens o thousands thou hast slain!
Vain is his hope, whase stay an trust is
In moral mercy, truth, and justice!

No — stretch a point to catch a plack;   farthing
Abuse a brother to his back;
Steal thro the winnock frae a whore,   window
But point the rake that taks the door;
Be to the poor like onie whunstane,   whinstone
And haud their noses to the grunstane;   grindstone
Ply ev'ry art o legal thieving;
No matter — stick to sound believing.

A Dedication

Learn three-mile pray'rs, an half-mile graces,
Wi weel-spread looves, an lang, wry faces;
Grunt up a solemn, lengthen'd groan,
And damn a' parties but your own;
I'll warrant then, ye're nae deceiver,
A steady, sturdy, staunch believer.

O ye wha leave the springs o Calvin,
For gumlie dubs of your ain delvin!
Ye sons of Heresy and Error,
Ye'll some day squeel in quaking terror,
When Vengeance draws the sword in wrath,
And in the fire throws the sheath;
When Ruin with his sweeping besom,
Just frets till Heav'n commission gies him;
While o'er the harp pale Misery moans,
And strikes the ever-deep'ning tones,
Still louder shrieks, and heavier groans!

Your pardon, sir, for this digression:
I maist forgat my Dedication;
But when divinity comes 'cross me,
My readers still are sure to lose me.

So, Sir, you see 'twas nae daft vapour;
But I maturely thought it proper,
When a' my works I did review,
To dedicate them, Sir, to you:
Because (ye need na tak it ill),
I thought them something like yoursel.

Then patronize them wi your favor,
And your petitioner shall ever —
I had amaist said, ever pray,
But that's a word I need na say;
For prayin, I hae little skill o't;
I'm baith dead-sweer, an wretched ill o't;
But I'se repeat each poor man's pray'r,
That kens or hears about you, Sir —

palms

muddy puddles

almost

mad

very loath, bad at it

knows

A Dedication

'May ne'er Misfortune's gowling bark,
Howl thro the dwelling o the clerk!
May ne'er his gen'rous, honest heart,
For that same gen'rous spirit smart!
May Kennedy's far-honor'd name
Lang beet his hymeneal flame,
Till Hamiltons, at least a dizzen,
Are frae their nuptial labors risen:
Five bonie lasses round their table,
And sev'n braw fellows, stout an able,
To serve their king an country weel,
By word, or pen, or pointed steel!
May Health and Peace, with mutual rays,
Shine on the ev'ning o his days;
Till his wee, curlie John's ier-oe,
When ebbing life nae mair shall flow,
The last, sad, mournful rites bestow!'

    I will not wind a lang conclusion,
With complimentary effusion;
But, whilst your wishes and endeavours
Are blest with Fortune's smiles and favours,
I am, dear sir, with zeal most fervent,
Your much indebted, humble servant.

    But if (which Pow'rs above prevent)
That iron-hearted carl, Want,
Attended, in his grim advances,
By sad mistakes, and black mischances,
While hopes, and joys, and pleasures fly him,
Make you as poor a dog as I am,
Your 'humble servant' then no more;
for who would humbly serve the poor?
But, by a poor man's hopes in Heav'n!
While recollection's pow'r is giv'n.
If, in the vale of humble life,
The victim sad of Fortune's strife,
I thro the tender-gushing tear,
Should recognise my master dear;
I friendless, low, we meet together,
Then, Sir, your hand — my Friend and Brother!

a reference to Hamilton's
position as Clerk of the Court

Helen Kennedy of Daljarrock,
Hamilton's wife
dozen

poetic exaggeration: Hamilton
had two sons & two daughters

great-grandchild

219

A BARD'S EPITAPH

This was the last poem printed in the Kilmarnock
Edition.

Is there a whim-inspirèd fool,
too   Owre fast for thought, owre hot for rule,
modest, cringe   Owre blate to seek, owre proud to snool?
         Let him draw near;
woe   And owre this grassy heap sing dool,
         And drap a tear.

Is there a Bard of rustic song,
Who, noteless, steals the crowds among,
That weekly this area throng?
         O, pass not by!
brother-   But, with a frater-feeling strong,
         Here, heave a sigh.

Is there a man, whose judgment clear
Can others teach the course to steer,
Yet runs, himself, life's mad career,
         Wild as the wave?—
Here pause — and, thro the starting tear,
         Survey this grave.

The poor inhabitant below
Was quick to learn and wise to know,
And keenly felt the friendly glow,
         And softer flame;
But thoughtless follies laid him low,
         And stain'd his name!

Reader, attend! whether thy soul
Soars Fancy's flights beyond the pole,
Or darkling grubs in this earthly hole,
         In low pursuit;
Know, prudent, cautious, self-control
         Is wisdom's root.

EPISTLE TO A YOUNG FRIEND

15 May, 1786

This was addressed to Andrew Hunter Aiken, son of
Robert Aiken, later merchant in Liverpool and
British consul in Riga where he died in 1831.

I lang hae thought, my youthfu friend,
    A something to have sent you,
Tho it should serve nae ither end
    Than just a kind memento:
But how the subject-theme may gang,
    Let time and chance determine:
Perhaps it may turn out a sang;
    Perhaps, turn out a sermon.

Ye'll try the world soon, my lad;
    And, Andrew dear, believe me,
Ye'll find mankind an unco squad,   *strange*
    And muckle they may grieve ye:
For care and trouble set your thought,
    Ev'n when your end's attainèd;
And a' your views may come to nought,
    Where ev'ry nerve is strainèd.

I'll no say, men are villains a':
    The real, harden'd wicked,
Wha hae nae check but human law,
    Are to a few restricked;
But, och! mankind are unco weak,   *mighty*
    An little to be trusted;
If *self* the wavering balance shake,
    It's rarely right adjusted!

Yet they wha fa' in Fortune's strife,
    Their fate we should na censure;
For still, th' important end of life
    They equally may answer:
A man may hae an honest heart,
    Tho poortith hourly stare him;   *poverty*
A man may tak a neebor's part,
    Yet hae nae cash to spare him.

Ay free, aff han', your story tell,
    When wi a bosom cronie;
But still keep something to yoursel
    Ye scarcely tell to onie:
Conceal yoursel as weel's ye can
    Frae critical dissection:
But keek thro ev'ry other man,   *look*
    Wi sharpen'd, sly inspection.

Epistle To A Young Friend

flame

The sacred lowe o weel-plac'd love,
    Luxuriantly indulge it;
But never tempt th' illicit rove,
    Tho naething should divulge it:
I waive the quantum o the sin,
    The hazard of concealing;
But, och! it hardens a' within,
    ·And petrifies the feeling!

To catch Dame Fortune's golden smile,
    Assiduous wait upon her;
And gather gear by ev'ry wile
    That's justify'd by honor:
Not for to hide it in a hedge,
    Nor for a train-attendant;
But for the glorious privilege
    Of being independent.

The fear o Hell's a hangman's whip
    To haud the wretch in order;
But where ye feel your honour grip,
    Let that ay be your border:
Its slightest touches, instant pause —
    Debar a' side-pretences;
And resolutely keep its laws,
    Uncaring consequences.

The great Creator to revere,
    Must sure become the creature;
But still the preaching cant forbear,
    An ev'n the rigid feature:
Yet ne'er with wits profane to range
    Be complaisance extended;
An atheist-laugh's a poor exchange
    For Deity offended!

frolicking

When ranting round in Pleasure's ring,
    Religion may be blinded;
Or if she gie a random sting,
    It may be little minded;
But when on Life we're tempest-driv'n—
    A conscience but a canker —
A correspondence fix'd wi' Heav'n,
    Is sure a noble anchor!

Epistle To A Young Friend

Adieu, dear, amiable youth!
   Your heart can ne'er be wanting!
May prudence, fortitude, and truth,
   Erect your brow undaunting!
In ploughman phrase, 'God send you speed,'
   Still daily to grow wiser;
And may ye better reck the rede,   heed, advice
   Than ever did th' adviser!

LINES WRITTEN ON A BANK-NOTE

Composed in the summer of 1786 when Burns was seriously considering emigration as the solution to his moral and financial problems. Notaphilists may care to learn that this poem was written on a one-guinea note of the Bank of Scotland issued 1st March 1780.

Wae worth thy power, thou cursed leaf!   woe betide
Fell source o a' my woe and grief,   Deadly
For lack o thee I've lost my lass,
For lack o thee I scrimp my glass!
I see the children of affliction
Unaided, through thy curs'd restriction.
I've seen the oppressor's cruel smile
Amid his hapless victims' spoil;
And for thy potence vainly wish'd,
To crush the villain in the dust.
For lack o thee, I leave this much-lov'd shore,
Never, perhaps, to greet old Scotland more.
                        R.B.

KYLE

MY HIGHLAND LASSIE, O

TUNE: *MacLauchlin's Scots-Measure*

In his annotation of his copy of the Scots Musical Museum Burns sentimentalised his relationship with Mary Campbell, to whom he turned for solace after James Armour had broken up his affair with Jean. Joseph Train presented a different picture of her in his notes to Lockhart, based on the recollections of John Richmond: 'Her character was loose in the extreme. She was kept for some time by a brother of Lord Eglinton's, and even while a servant with Gavin Hamilton, and during the period of Burns' attachment it was well known that her meetings with Montgomery were open and frequent.' She died at Greenock in the summer of 1786, whether from a fever or from premature childbirth is a matter of controversy to this day.

CHORUS

Within the glen sae busy, O,
Above, rushy *Aboon the plain sae rashy, O,*
I set me down wi right guid will,
To sing my Highland lassie, O!

highborn ladies Nae gentle dames, tho ne'er sae fair,
Shall ever by my Muse's care:
Their titles a' are empty show;
Gie me my Highland lassie, O!

O, were yon hills and vallies mine,
Yon palace and yon gardens fine,
The world then the love should know
I bear my Highland lassie, O!

But fickle Fortune frowns on me,
must And I maun cross the raging sea;
But while my crimson currents flow,
I'll love my Highland.lassie, O!

Altho thro foreign climes I range,
I know her heart will never change;
For her bosom burns with honour's glow,
My faithful Highland lassie, O!

For her I'll dare the billows' roar,
For her I'll trace a distant shore,
That Indian wealth may lustre throw
Around my Highland lassie, O!

She has my heart, she has my hand,
By secret troth and honor's band!
'Till the mortal stroke shall lay me low,
I'm thine, my Highland lassie, O!

Farewell the glen sae bushy, O!
Farewell the plain sae rashy, O!
To other lands I now must go
To sing my Highland lassie, O!

Manuscript of the Poem
'THE TWA DOGS'

MAUCHLINE

ADDRESS OF BEELZEBUB

HELL, June 1st, Anno Mundi 5790

To the Right Honorable the Earl of Breadalbane, President of the Right Honorable the Highland Society, which met on the 23rd of May last, at the Shakespeare, Covent Garden, to concert ways and means to frustrate the designs of five hundred Highlanders who, as the Society were informed by Mr. M'Kenzie of Applecross, were so audacious as to attempt an escape from their lawful lords and masters whose property they were, by emigrating from the lands of Mr. Macdonald of Glengary to the wilds of Canada, in search of that fantastic thing—LIBERTY.

This Address was provoked by the controversy over whether Highlanders should be encouraged to remain at home or emigrate. Burns took the view that the reaction of Lord Breadalbane and the Highland Society was autocratic. Furthermore, in view of his own decision not to emigrate, he did not credit Highlanders with similar attitudes — that no one left their native soil unless economic necessity dictated. It is ironic that the very gentlemen then trying to prevent emigration should, within a few years, take up the cause with a vengeance and perpetrate the forced exodus know as the Highland Clearances.

Long life, my lord, and health be yours,
Unskaith'd by hunger'd Highland boors!
Lord grant nae duddie, desperate beggar, ragged
Wi dirk, claymore, or rusty trigger,
May twin auld Scotland o a life rob
She likes — as lambkins like a knife!
Faith! you and Applecross were right Thomas MacKenzie of
To keep the Highland hounds in sight! Applecross
I doubt na! they wad bid nae better offer
Than let them ance out owre the water! once
Then up amang thae lakes and seas, these
They'll mak what rules and laws they please:
Some daring Hancock, or a Franklin, John Hancock (1737-93)
May set their Highland bluid a-ranklin; Benjamin Franklin (1706-90)
Some Washington again may head them, George Washington (1732-99)
Or some Montgomery, fearless, lead them; Richard Montgomery (d. 1775)
Till (God knows what may be effected
When by such heads and hearts directed)
Poor dunghill sons of dirt an mire
May to Patrician rights aspire!
Nae sage North now, nor sager Sackville, Lord George Sackville
To watch and premier o'er the pack vile!
An whare will ye get Howes and Clintons,
To bring them to a right repentence?
To cowe the rebel generation,
An save the honor o the nation?

225

H

Address To Beelzebub

They, an be damn'd! what right hae they
To meat or sleep, or light o day?
Far less to riches, pow'r, or freedom,
But what your lordship likes to gie them?

Macdonell of Glengarry — But hear, my lord! Glengary, hear!
Your hand's owre light on them, I fear:
Your factors, grieves, trustees, and bailies,

gaily — I canna say but they do gaylies:
They lay aside a' tender mercies,

strip, sluts, bristles — An tirl the hullions to the birses;
distrained, harried — Yet while they're only poind and herriet,
They'll keep their stubborn Highland spirit.
But smash them! crush them a' to spails,
An rot the dyvors i' the jails!
The young dogs swinge them to the labour:
Let wark an hunger mak them sober!

hussies, at all good-looking — The hizzies, if they're aughtlins fawsont,
the 'red light' district of — Let them in Drury-lane be lesson'd !
London at that time
begging; gates — An if the wives an dirty brats
flogging, rags, vermin — Come thiggin at your doors an yetts,
Flaffin wi duds, an grey wi beas',
Frightin awa your ducks an geese;

bulldog — Get out a horsewhip or a jowler,
The langest thong, the fiercest growler,
An gar the tatter'd gypsies pack
Wi a' their bastards on their back!

Go on, my Lord! I lang to meet you,
An in my 'house at hame' to greet you;

shall not — Wi common lords ye shanna mingle,
innermost corner, fireside — The benmost neuk beside the ingle,
At my right han' assigned your seat,

Polycrates, tyrant of Samos — 'Tween Herod's hip an Polycrate;
6th Century B.C, — Or (if you on your station tarrow),
Diego d'Almagro (1475-1538) — Between Almagro and Pizarro,
Francisco Pizarro (1478-1541) — A seat, I'm sure ye're well deservin't;
the Conquistadores of Peru — An till ye come — your humble servant,

BEELZEBUB

LIBEL SUMMONS

This mock summons to a fictional Court of Equity parodies both the Bachelors' Club, Tarbolton (a serious debating society) and the Kirk Session tribunals on fornication. The text is based on the Hastie MS, with additions from the Egerton MS.

In Truth and Honour's name—Amen
Know all men by these Presents plain:

This fourth o June, at Mauchline given,
The year 'tween eighty five and seven,
We, Fornicators by profession,
As per extractum from each Session,
In way and manner here narrated,
Pro bono Amor congregated;   for the sake of Love
And by our brethren constituted,   (Latin)
A Court of Equity deputed.
With special authoris'd direction
To take beneath our strict protection,
The stays-out-bursting, quondam maiden,
With Growing Life and anguish laden;
Who by the rascal is deny'd,
That led her thoughtless steps aside.
He who disowns the ruin'd Fair-one,
And for her wants and woes does care none;
The wretch that can refuse subsistence
To those whom he has given existence;
He who when at a lass's by-job,   fornication
Defrauds her wi a frig or dry bob;   masturbation
The coof that stands on clishmaclavers   fool; nonsense
When women haflins offer favors:—   partly
All who in any way or manner
Disdain the Fornicator's honor,
We take cognisance thereanent,
The proper Judges competent.

First, Poet Burns he takes the chair,
Allow'd by a', his title's fair;
And pass'd nem. con. without dissension,
He has a duplicate pretension.—
Next, Merchant Smith, our worthy Fiscal,   James Smith
To cow each pertinaceous rascal;   (1765-1823)
In this, as every other state,
His merit is conspicuous great:
Richmond the third, our trusty Clerk,   John Richmond
The minutes regular to mark,   (1765-1846)
And sit dispenser of the law,
In absence of the former twa;

Libel Summons

The fourth our Messenger At Arms,
When failing all the milder terms,
William Hunter, Hunter, a hearty, willing brother,
a Mauchline Weel skill'd in dead and living leather.
shoemaker Without Preamble less or more said,
We, body politic aforesaid,
With legal, due Whereas, and Wherefore,
We are appointed here to care for
The interests of our constituents,
And punish contravening truants,
Keeping a proper regulation
Within the lists of Fornication.

Whereas, our Fiscal, by petition,
Informs us there is strong suspicion,
Alex Dow, John You, Coachman Dow, and Clockie Brown,
Brown a clockmaker Baith residenters in this town;
In other words, you, Jock, and Sandy,
fornication Hae been at wark at Houghmagandie;
And now when facts are come to light,
The matter ye deny outright.

First, You, John Brown, there's witness borne,
And affidavit made and sworn,
That ye hae bred a hurly-burly
genitalia 'Bout Jeany Mitchel's tirlie-whirlie,
And blooster'd at her regulator,
Till a' her wheels gang clitter-clatter.
And farther still, ye cruel Vandal,
A tale might even in hell be scandal!
That ye hae made repeated trials
Wi drugs and draps in doctor's phials,
Mixt, as ye thought, wi fell infusion,
child Your ain begotten wean to poosion.
And yet ye are sae scant o grace,
Ye daur to lift your brazen face,
And offer for to take your aith,
clothing Ye never lifted Jeany's claith.—
But tho ye should yoursel manswear,
slates Laird Wilson's sclates can witness bear,
Ae e'ening of a Mauchline fair,
That Jeany's masts they saw them bare;
For ye had furl'd up her sails,
And was at play—at heads and tails.

228

Libel Summons

Next, Sandy Dow, you're here indicted
To have, as publickly you're wyted,   accused
Been clandestinely upward whirlin
The petticoats o Maggy Borelan,
And giein her canister a rattle,
That months to come it winna settle.
And yet, ye offer your protest,
Ye never herried Maggy's nest;   harried
Tho, it's weel ken'd that at her gyvel   vagina
Ye hae gien mony a kytch and kyvel.   thrust, bang
Then Brown and Dow, before design'd,
For clags and clauses there subjoin'd,   claims
We, Court aforesaid cite and summon,
That on the fifth o July comin,
The hour o cause, in our Court-ha',
At Whitefoord's arms, ye answer Law!

But, as reluctantly we Punish,
An rather, mildly would admonish:
Since Better Punishment prevented,
Than Obstinacy sair repented.

Then, for that ancient Secret's sake,
You have the honor to partake;
An for that noble Badge you wear,
You, Sandie Dow, our Brother dear,
We give you as a Man an Mason,
This private, sober, friendly lesson.

Your Crime, a manly deed we view it,
As Man alone, can only do it;
But, in denial persevering,
Is to a Scoundrel's name adhering.
The best o men, hae been surpris'd;
The best o women been advis'd:
Nay, cleverest Lads hae haen a trick o't,
An, bonniest Lasses taen a lick o't.

Then Brother Dow, if you're asham'd
In such a Quorum to be nam'd,
Your conduct much is to be blam'd.
See, ev'n himsel—there's godly Bryan,   a notorious reprobate
The auld whatreck he has been tryin;   fornication
When such as he put to their han',
What man on character need stan'?
Then Brother dear, lift up your brow,
And, like yoursel, the truth avow;

Libel Summons

Erect a dauntless face upon it,
An say, 'I am the man has done it;
'I Sandie Dow gat Meg wi wean,
'An 's fit to do as much again.'
Ne'er mind their solemn rev'rend faces,
Had they—in proper times an places,
But seen an fun'—I mukle dread it, *much*
They just would done as you an we did.
To tell the truth 's a manly lesson,
An doubly proper in a Mason.

You Monsieur Brown, as it is proven,
Jean Mitchel's wame by you was hoven; *belly, distended*
Without you by a quick repentance
Acknowledge Jean's an your acquaintance,
Depend on't, this shall be your sentence.
Our beadles to the Cross shall take you,
And there shall mither naked make you;
Some canie grip near by your middle,
They shall it bind as tight 's a fiddle;
The raep they round the pump shall tak *rope*
An tye your han's behint your back;
Wi just an ell o string allow'd
To jink an hide you frae the croud: *dodge*
There ye shall stan', a legal seizure,
In during Jeanie Mitchel's pleasure;
So be, her pleasure dinna pass
Seven turnings of a half-hour glass:
Nor shall it in her pleasure be
To louse you out in less than three. *release*

This, our futurum esse Decreet,
We mean it not to keep a secret;
But in our summons here insert it,
And whoso dares, may controvert it.
This, mark'd before the date and place is,
Sigillum est, per, *'The Seal is by . . . '* *(Latin)*
        Burns the Preses.
This Summons and the signet mark,
Extractum est, per, *'Is extracted by' (Latin)*
        Richmond, Clerk.

At Mauchline, idem date of June,
'Tween six and seven, the afternoon,
You twa, in propria personæ,
Within design'd, Sandy and Johny,
This Summons legally have got,
As vide witness underwrote:
Within the house of John Dow, vinter,
Nunc facio hoc, *'I now make this' (Latin)*
        Gullelmus Hunter.

230

EPITAPH ON JOHN DOVE,
INNKEEPER

John Dove or Dow, a native of Paisley, kept the
Whitefoord Arms where the Mauchline Bachelors'
Club met in 1785.

Here lies Johnie Pigeon:
What was his religion
 Whae'er desires to ken   know
To some other warl'
Maun follow the carl,   old chap
 For here Johnie Pigeon had nane!

Strong ale was ablution;
Small beer, persecution;
 A dram was *memento mori;*
But a full flowing bowl
Was the saving his soul,
 And port was celestial glory!

EPITAPH FOR A WAG IN MAUCHLINE

Cunningham and other early editors identified the
subject as James Smith (1765-c-1823), but Kinsley
considers 'Clockie' Brown as more likely - see 'Libel
Summons.'

Lament him, Mauchline husbands a',
 He aften did assist ye;
For had ye staid hale weeks awa',   whole
 Your wives they ne'er had missed ye!

Ye Mauchline bairns, as on ye pass   children
 To school in bands thegither,
O, tread ye lightly on his grass—
 Perhaps he was your father!

WILLIE CHALMERS

William Chalmers, writer and notary-public in Ayr,
drew up the assignation of the poet's property in
favour of his brother Gilbert in 1786 when he was
thinking of emigrating. Chalmers asked Burns to write
a poem for him to give to his sweetheart. The result
was this humorous piece of advice to the young lady.

Wi braw new branks in mickle pride,   fine bridle
 And eke a braw new brechan,   also, collar
My Pegasus I'm got astride,
 And up Parnassus pechin: panting
Whyles owre a bush wi downward crush   sometimes
 The doited beastie stammers;   stupid
Then up he gets, and off he sets
 For sake o Willie Chalmers.

231

Willie Chalmers

well-known

bestowed

I doubt na, lass, that weel kend name
    May cost a pair o blushes:
I am nae stranger to his fame,
    Nor his warm-urged wishes.
Your bonie face, sae mild and sweet,
    His honest heart enamours;
And faith! ye'll no be lost a whit,
    Tho wair'd on Willie Chalmers.

eyes

Auld Truth hersel might swear ye're fair,
    And Honor safely back her:
And Modesty assume your air,
    And ne'er a ane mistak her;
And sic twa love-inspiring een
    Might fire even holy palmers:
Nae wonder then they've fatal been
    To honest Willie Chalmers!

prim-lipped powdered

I doubt na Fortune may you shore
    Some mim-mou'd pouther'd priestie,
Fu lifted up wi Hebrew lore
    And band upon his breastie;
But O! what signifies to you
    His lexicons and grammars?
The feeling heart's the royal blue,
    And that's wi Willie Chalmers.

staring
struggle
scratch, ear, stroke
cough

dunces
spank

Some gapin, glowrin countra laird
    May warsle for your favour:
May claw his lug, and straik his beard,
    And hoast up some palaver.
My bonie maid, befor ye wed
    Sic clumsy-witted hammers,
Seek Heaven for help, and barefit skelp
    Awa wi Willie Chalmers.

not, flatter

Forgive the Bard! my fond regard
    For ane that shares my bosom
Inspires my Muse to gie 'm his dues,
    For deil a hair I roose him.
May powers aboon unite you soon,
    And fructify your amours,
And every year come in mair dear,
    To you and Willie Chalmers!

A DREAM

Thoughts, words, and deeds, the Statute blames with reason;
But surely *Dreams* were ne'er indicted Treason.

On reading in the public papers, the Laureate's Ode,
with the other parade of June 4, 1786, the Author was
no sooner dropt asleep, than he imagined himself
transported to the Birthday Levee; and, in his
dreaming fancy made the following Address:—

**The 'parade' referred to was the national celebration
of the 48th birthday of King George III, and the Ode
was composed by Thomas Warton (1728-90),
Professor of Poetry at Oxford (1757-67) and Poet
Laureate (1785-90). According to Christopher North
'the gods had made him poetical, but not a poet' and
he is remembered today only indirectly, from having
been the cause of this poem. Mrs Dunlop of Dunlop
urged Burns to omit it from his second edition as it
gave offence to 'numbers at London.' But Burns was
unrepentant.**

Guid-mornin to your Majesty!
   May heaven augment your blisses,
On ev'ry new birthday ye see,
   A humble Poet wishes!
My Bardship here, at your Levee,
   On sic a day as this is,
Is sure an uncouth sight to see,
   Amang thae birthday dresses   those
      Sae fine this day.

I see ye're complimented thrang,   effusively
   By monie a lord an lady;
'God save the King' 's a cuckoo sang
   That's unco easy said ay: very
The poets, too, a venal gang,
   Wi rhymes weel-turn'd an ready,
Wad gar you trow ye ne'er do wrang,   make, think
   But ay unerring steady,
      On sic a day.

For me! before a Monarch's face,
   Ev'n there I winna flatter;
For neither pension, post, nor place,
   Am I your humble debtor:
So, nae reflection on your Grace,
   Your Kingship to bespatter;
There's monie waur been o the race,   worse
   And aiblins ane been better   a reference to the
      Than you this day.   Young Pretender

A Dream

'Tis very true, my sovereign King,
　　My skill may weel be doubted;
But facts are chiels that winna ding,
　　An downa be disputed:
Your royal nest, beneath your wing,
　　Is e'en right reft and clouted,
And now the third part o the string,
　　An less, will gang about it
　　　　Than did ae day.

Far be't frae me that I aspire
　　To blame your legislation,
Or say, ye wisdom want, or fire
　　To rule this mighty nation:
But faith! I muckle doubt, my sire,
　　Ye've trusted ministration
To chaps wha in a barn or byre
　　Wad better fill'd their station,
　　　　Than courts yon day.

And now ye've gien auld Britain peace,
　　Her broken shins to plaister;
Your sair taxation does her fleece,
　　Till she has scarce a tester:
For me, thank God, my life's a lease,
　　Nae bargain wearin faster,
Or faith! I fear, that, wi the geese,
　　I shortly boost to pasture
　　　　I' the craft some day.

I'm no mistrusting Willie Pitt,
　　When taxes he enlarges,
(An Will's a true guid fallow's get,
　　A name not envy spairges)
That he intends to pay your debt,
　　An lessen a' your charges;
But, God sake! let nae saving fit
　　Abridge your bonie barges
　　　　An boats this day.

fellows, upset
cannot

torn and patched

go

greatly

cowshed

given

sixpence

behove
croft

spatters

234

A Dream

Adieu, my Liege! may Freedom geck   *toss the head*
  Beneath your high protection;
An may ye rax Corruption's neck,   *stretch*
  And gie her for dissection!
But since I'm here, I'll no neglect,
  In loyal, true affection,
To pay your Queen, wi due respect,
  My fealty an subjection
      This great birthday.

Hail, Majesty most Excellent!
  While nobles strive to please ye,
Will ye accept a compliment,
  A simple Bardie gies ye?
Thae bonie bairntime Heav'n has lent,   *brood*
  Still higher may they heeze ye   *hoist*
In bliss, till Fate some day is sent,
  For ever to release ye
      Frae care that day.

For you, young Potentate o Wales,   *George, Prince of Wales,*
  I tell your Highness fairly,   *later Prince Regent and*
Down Pleasure's stream, wi swelling sails,   *King George IV*
  I'm tauld ye're driving rarely;   *(1762-1830)*
But some day ye may gnaw your nails,   *a reference to 'Prinny's'*
  An curse your folly sairly,   *affair with*
That e'er ye brak Diana's pales,   *Mrs Fitzherbert*
  Or rattl'd dice wi Charlie   *Charles James Fox*
      By night or day.

Yet aft a ragged cowte's been known,   *colt*
  To mak a noble aiver;   *old horse*
So, ye may doucely fill a throne,   *soberly*
  For a' their clish-ma-claver: *gossip*
There, him at Agincourt wha shone,   *Prince Hal (later*
  Few better were or braver;   *Henry V)*
And yet, wi funny, queer Sir John,   *Falstaff*
  He was an unco shaver
      For monie a day.

A Dream

Frederick Augustus,
Duke of York, younger
son of George III and
Bishop of Osnabruck (1764)
the Pope

For you, right rev'rend Osnaburg,
  Nane sets the lawn-sleeve sweeter,
Altho a ribban at your lug
  Wad been a dress completer:
As ye disown yon paughty dog,
  That bears the keys of Peter,
Then swith! an get a wife to hug,
  Or trowth, ye'll stain the mitre
    Some luckless day!

haste!
a reference to the Duke-
Bishop's affair with the former
mistress of Rann the notorious
highwayman.
Prince William, later Duke of
Clarence and King William IV
(1830-7)
his affair with Sarah Martin
at Portsmouth

grappling-iron

Young, royal Tarry-breeks, I learn,
  Ye've lately come athwart her—
A glorious galley, stem an stern,
  Well rigg'd for Venus' barter;
But first hang out that she'll discern
  Your hymeneal charter;
Then heave aboard your grapple-airn,
  An, large upon her quarter,
    Come full that day.

the daughters of George III:
Charlotte, Augusta, Elizabeth,
Mary, Sophia and Amelia

Ye, lastly, bonie blossoms a',
  Ye royal lasses dainty,
Heav'n mak ye guid as weel as braw,
  An gie you lads-a-plenty!
But sneer na British boys awa!

noblemen

For kings are unco scant ay,
An German gentles are but sma',
  They're better just than want ay
    On onie day.

extremely pampered

salted
dish full
tarried
trust
bottom, scraped

God bless you a'! consider now,
  Ye're unco muckle dautet;
But ere the course o life be through,
  It may be bitter sautet:
An I hae seen their coggie fou,
  That yet hae tarrow't at it.
But or the day was done, I trow,
  The laggen they hae clautet
    Fu clean that day.

TO DR. MACKENZIE, MAUCHLINE

MOSSGIEL, An. M. 5790

John Mackenzie (d. 1837) practised medicine in Mauchline, and became a close friend of Burns through the Masonic lodge St. James, Tarbolton. Dr. Mackenzie gave the poet valuable introductions and recommendations prior to his first visit to Edinburgh.

Friday first's the day appointed
By the Right Worshipful Anointed,
  To hold our grand procession;
To get a blaud o Johnie's morals,   screed
An taste a swatch o Manson's barrels   Manson's Inn, where the
  I' the way of our profession.   Tarbolton masonic lodge met

Our Master and the Brotherhood
  Wad a' be glad to see you.
For me, I wad be mair than proud
  To share the mercies wi you.
    If Death, then, wi skaith, then,   harm
      Some mortal heart is hechtin,   menacing
    Inform him, an storm him,
      That Saturday you'll fecht him.   fight

ROBERT BURNS

THE FAREWELL

TO THE BRETHREN OF ST. JAMES'S LODGE, TARBOLTON

TUNE: *Good-night, and joy be wi you a'*

Burns became an apprentice freemason in July 1781, and was 'passed and raised' on 1st October that year. He became Depute-Master on 27th July 1784. It is thought that this song was written for the meeting on 24th June 1786, well before the publication of the Kilmarnock Edition, when Burns was still set on emigrating to Jamaica.

Adieu! a heart-warm, fond adieu;
  Dear Brothers of the *Mystic Tie!*
Ye favoured, ye *enlighten'd* few,
  Companions of my social joy!
Tho I to foreign lands must hie,
  Pursuing Fortune's slidd'ry ba';   slippery
With melting heart and brimful eye,
  I'll mind you still, tho far awa.

The Farewell

Oft have I met your social band,
　　And spent the cheerful, festive night:
Oft, honour'd with supreme command,
　　Presided o'er the *Sons of Light;*
And by that *Hieroglyphic* bright,
　　Which none but *Craftsmen* ever saw!
Strong Mem'ry on my heart shall write
　　Those happy scenes, when far awa.

May Freedom, Harmony, and Love,
　　Unite you in the *Grand Design,*
Beneath th' Omniscient Eye above—
　　The glorious *Architect Divine,*
That you may keep th' *Unerring Line,*
　　Still rising by the *Plummet's Law,*
Till *Order* bright completely shine,
　　Shall be my pray'r when far awa.

And *you,* farewell! whose merits claim
　　Justly that *Highest Badge* to wear:
Heav'n bless your honour'd, noble name,
　　To *Masonry* and *Scotia* dear!
A last request permit me here
　　When yearly ye assemble a',
One *round,* I ask it with a *tear,*
　　To him, *the Bard that's far awa.*

THE FAREWELL

The valiant, in himself, what can he suffer?
Or what does he regard his single woes?
But when, alas! he multiplies himself,
To dearer selves, to the lov'd tender fair,
To those whose bliss, whose beings hang upon him,
To helpless children,—then, Oh then he feels
The point of misery festering in his heart,
And weakly weeps his fortunes like a coward:
Such, such am I!—undone!—THOMSON'S *Edward and Eleanora*

**Written in the summer of 1786, while Burns was still
intent on going abroad.**

Farewell, old Scotia's bleak domains,
Far dearer than the torrid plains,
pineapples　　　Where rich ananas blow!
Farewell, a mother's blessing dear
A brother's sigh, a sister's tear,
　　My Jean's heart-rending throe!
Elizabeth Burns　Farewell, my Bess! Tho thou'rt bereft

238

The Farewell

Of my paternal care,
A faithful brother I have left,   Gilbert Burns
My part in him thou'lt share!
  Adieu too, to you too,
    My Smith, my bosom frien';   James Smith
  When kindly you mind me,
    O, then befriend my Jean!

What bursting anguish tears my heart?
From thee, my Jeany, must I part?
Thou, weeping, answ'rest—'No!'
Alas! misfortune stares my face,
And points to ruin and disgrace—
  I for thy sake must go!
Thee, Hamilton, and Aiken dear,   Gavin Hamilton
  A grateful, warm adieu: Robert Aiken
I with a much-indebted tear
  Shall still remember you!
    All-hail then, the gale then
      Wafts me from thee, dear shore!
    It rustles, and whistles—
      I'll never see thee more!

TAM SAMSON'S ELEGY

An honest man's the noblest work of God — POPE

**Thomas Samson (1722-95) of Kilmarnock, 'a
seedsman of good credit, a zealous sportsman, and a
good fellow.' On one occasion when they had been
out wildfowling, Tam had a foreboding that this would
be his last such outing and expressed a wish to be
buried on the moors. This inspired Burns to write this
epitaph.**

Has auld Kilmarnock seen the Deil?
Or great Mackinlay thrawn his heel?   Rev. James Mackinlay
Or Robertson again grown weel,   Rev. John Robertson
    To preach an read?
'Na, waur than a'!' cries ilka chiel,   worse, every chap
    'Tam Samson's dead!'

Kilmarnock lang may grunt an grane,   groan
An sigh, an sab, an greet her lane,   sob, cry, alone
An cleed her bairns—man, wife, an wean—   clothe, child
    In mourning weed;
To Death she's dearly pay'd the kain: rent in kind
    Tam Samson's dead!

Tam Samson's Elegy

Masons of St. John, Kilwinning
Lodge, Kilmarnock

The Brethren o the mystic level
May hing their head in woefu bevel,
While by their nose the tears will revel,
    Like onie bead;
violent blow
  Death's gien the Lodge an unco devel:
    Tam Samson's dead!

When Winter muffles up his cloak,
And binds the mire like a rock;
When to the loughs the curlers flock,
    Wi gleesome speed,
mark
  Wha will they station at the cock—
    Tam Samson's dead!

crowd
  He was the king of a' the core,
To guard, or draw, or wick a bore,
Or up the rink like Jehu roar
    In time o need;
But now he lags on Death's hog-score:
    Tam Samson's dead!

salmon
  Now safe the stately sawmont sail,
And trouts bedropp'd wi crimson hail,
well-known, supple
  And eels, weel-kend for souple tail,
pike
    And geds for greed,
Since, dark in Death's fish-creel, we wail
    Tam Samson's dead!

partridges
  Rejoice, ye birring paitricks a';
leg-plumed, cockily
  Ye cootie moorcocks, crousely craw;
hares, behind, fine
  Ye maukins, cock your fud fu braw,
    Withouten dread;
foe
  Your mortal fae is now awa:
    Tam Samson's dead!

That woefu morn be ever mourn'd,
Saw him in shootin graith adorn'd,
gear
While pointers round impatient burn'd,
leashes
    Frae couples free'd;
went
  But, och! he gaed and ne'er return'd:
    Tam Samson's dead!

In vain auld age his body batters,
In vain the gout his ancles fetters,
In vain the burns cam down like waters,
    An acre braid!
crying, babbles
  Now ev'ry auld wife, greetin, clatters:
    'Tam Samson's dead!'

Owre monie a weary hag he limpit,   *bog*
An ay the tither shot he thumpit,
Till coward Death behint him jumpit,
     Wi deadly feide;   *enmity*
Now he proclaims wi tout o trumpet: *blast*
     'Tam Samson's dead!'

When at his heart he felt the dagger,
He reel'd his wonted bottle-swagger,
But yet he drew the mortal trigger,
     Wi weel-aim'd heed;
'Lord, five!' he cry'd, an owre did stagger—
     Tam Samson's dead!

Ilk hoary hunter mourn'd a brither;   *Each*
Ilk sportsman-youth bemoan'd a father;
Yon auld gray stane, amang the heather,
     Marks out his head;
Whare Burns has wrote, in rhyming blether,   *nonsense*
     'Tam Samson's dead!'

There, low he lies in lasting rest;
Perhaps upon his mould'ring breast
Some spitefu moorfowl bigs her nest,   *builds*
     To hatch and breed:
Alas! nae mair he'll them molest:
     Tam Samson's dead!

When August winds the heather wave,
And sportsmen wander by yon grave,
Three volleys let his memory crave,
     O pouther an lead,   *gunpowder*
Till Echo answer frae her cave,
     'Tam Samson's dead!'

'Heav'n rest his saul whare'er he be!'
Is th' wish o' monie mae than me: *many more*
He had twa fauts, or maybe three,
     Yet what remead?   *remedy*
Ae social, honest man want we: *One*
     Tam Samson's dead!

THE EPITAPH

Tam Samson's weel-worn clay here lies:
     Ye canting zealots, spare him!
If honest worth in Heaven rise,
     Ye'll mend or ye win near him.

PER CONTRA

Go, Fame, an canter like a filly
Thro a' the streets an neuks o Killie;   *corners, Kilmarnock*
Tell ev'ry social honest billie   *person*
     To cease his grievin;
For, yet unskaith'd by Death's gleg gullie,   *unharmed, sharp knife*
     Tam Samson's leevin!

TO MR. JOHN KENNEDY

These lines brought to a close a letter from Burns written at Kilmarnock in August 1786, following publication of his poems. Even at this date he was still set on emigration.

Farewell, dear friend! may guid luck hit you,
And 'mong her favourites admit you!
threaten, smite   If e'er Detraction shore to smit you,
        May nane believe him!
any   And onie Deil that thinks to get you,
        Good Lord, deceive him!

REPLY TO A TRIMMING EPISTLE RECEIVED FROM A TAILOR

The subject of this reply was Thomas Walker (d. about 1812) of Pool near Ochiltree, a friend of the schoolmaster William Simson. Walker sent a verse-epistle to Burns, in the hope of a similar reply. Burns apparently ignored it, and this provoked Walker to write, after the appearance of the Kilmarnock Edition, criticising the poet's morals. Clearly Simson had a hand in this, a fact not lost on Burns when he responded with these verses.

What ails ye now, ye lousie bitch
thrash   To thresh my back at sic a pitch?
Lord, notching-blade   Losh, man, hae mercy wi your natch!
needle   Your bodkin's bauld:
    I didna suffer half sae much
Rev. William Auld   Frae Daddie Auld.

set   What tho at times, when I grow crouse,
bellies, thrust   I gie their wames a random pouse,
strike   Is that enough for you to souse
        Your servant sae?
nit-picking   Gae mind your seam, ye prick-the-louse,
flea   An jag-the-flae!

writ   King David o poetic brief
Wrocht 'mang the lasses sic mischief
As fill'd his after-life wi grief,
rows   An bluidy rants;
An yet he's rank'd amang the chief
old-time saints   O lang-syne saunts.

canters   And maybe, Tam, for a' my cants,
drunken sprees   My wicked rhymes, an drucken rants,
the Devil   I'll gie auld Cloven Clootie's haunts
        An unco slip yet,
An snugly sit amang the saunts,
        At Davie's hip yet!

Reply to a Trimming Epistle received from a Tailor

But, fegs! the Session says I maun   *faith!, must*
Gae fa' upo' anither plan
Than garrin lasses coup the cran,   *making, upset the cart*
    Clean heels owre body,
An sairly thole their mother's ban   *endure*
    Afore the howdy.   *midwife*

This leads me on to tell for sport
How I did wi the Session sort:
Auld Clinkum at the inner port,   *The Bell-ringer*
    Cried three times, 'Robin!
Come hither lad, and answer for't,
    Ye're blam'd for jobbin!'   *fornication*

Wi pinch I put a Sunday's face on,
An snoov'd awa before the Session   *toddled off*
I made an open, fair confession—
    I scorned to lie—
An syne Mess John, beyond expression,   *Master (of Arts)*
    Fell foul o me.

A fornicator-loun he call'd me,
An said my faut frae bliss expell'd me.
I own'd the tale was true he tell'd me,
    'But, what the matter?'
(Quo' I) 'I fear unless ye geld me,   *castrate*
    I'll ne'er be better!'

'Geld you!' (quo' he) 'an what for no?   *why not*
If that your right hand, leg, or toe
Should ever prove your sp'ritual foe,
    You should remember
To cut it aff—an what for no
    Your dearest member!'

'Na, na,' (quo' I) 'I'm no for that,
Gelding's nae better than 'tis ca't;
I'd rather suffer for my faut,
    A hearty flewit,   *flogging*
As sair owre hips as ye can draw't,
    Tho I should rue it.'

'Or, gin ye like to end the bother,
To please us a'—I've just ae ither: *one another*
When next wi yon lass I forgather,   *have intercourse*
    Whate'er betide it,
I'll frankly gie her 't a' thegither,
    An let her guide it.'

243

Reply to a Trimming Epistle received from a Tailor

But, Sir, this pleas'd them warst of a',
An therefore, Tam, when that I saw,
I said 'Guid night,' an came awa,
    An left the Session:
I saw they were resolvèd a'
    On my oppression.

THE BRIGS OF AYR

INSCRIBED TO JOHN BALLANTINE, ESQ., AYR

Written in the autumn of 1786, when work on the new
bridge was under way. The old bridge dates from c. 1232
and was in a dangerous condition by 1786. The new
bridge, completed in 1788, was constructed by
Alexander Steven, master mason, and John Ballantine,
Dean of Guild and a patron of Burns. Ballantine (1743-
1812) was a merchant and banker, later (1787) Provost
of Ayr.

The simple Bard, rough at the rustic plough,
Learning his tuneful trade from ev'ry bough
(The chanting linnet, or the mellow thrush,
Hailing the setting sun, sweet, in the green thorn bush;
The soaring lark, the perching red-breast shrill,
Or deep-ton'd plovers grey, wild-whistling o'er the hill):
Shall he — nurst in the peasant's lowly shed,
To hardy independence bravely bred,
By early poverty to hardship steel'd,
And train'd to arms in stern Misfortune's field —
Shall he be guilty of their hireling crimes,
The servile, mercenary Swiss of rhymes?
Or labour hard the panegyric close,
With all the venal soul of dedicating prose?
No! though his artless strains he rudely sings,
And throws his hand uncouthly o'er the strings,
He glows with all the spirit of the Bard,
Fame, honest fame, his great, his dear reward.
Still, if some patron's gen'rous care he trace,
Skill'd in the secret to bestow with grace;
When Ballantine befriends his humble name,
And hands the rustic stranger up to fame,
With heartfelt throes his grateful bosom swells:
The godlike bliss, to give, alone excels.

a reference to his
financial support over
the publication of
Burns's poems

'Twas when the stacks get on their winter hap,   wrapping
And thack and rape secure the toil-won crap;   thatch, rope, crop
Potatoe-bings are snuggèd up frae skaith   heaps, harm
O coming Winter's biting, frosty breath;
The bees, rejoicing o'er their summer toils —
Unnumber'd buds' an flowers' delicious spoils,
Sealed up with frugal care in massive waxen piles —   honeycombs
Are doom'd by Man, that tyrant o'er the weak,
The death o devils smoor'd wi brimstone reek: smothered
The thundering guns are heard on ev'ry side,
The wounded coveys, reeling, scatter wide;
The feather'd field-mates, bound by Nature's tie,
Sires, mothers, children, in one carnage lie:
(What warm, poetic heart but inly bleeds,
And execrates man's savage, ruthless deeds!)
Nae mair the flower in field or meadow springs;
Nae mair the grove with airy concert rings,
Except perhaps the robin's whistling glee,
Proud o the height o some bit half-lang tree;   half grown
The hoary morns precede the sunny days,
Mild, calm, serene, widespreads the noontide blaze,
While thick the gossamour waves wanton in the rays.

'Twas in that season, when a simple Bard,
Unknown and poor — simplicity's reward! —
Ae night, within the ancient brugh of Ayr,   one, burgh
By whim inspir'd, or haply prest wi care,
He left his bed, and took his wayward route,
And down by *Simpson's* wheel'd the left about:
(Whether, impell'd by all-directing Fate,
To witness what I after shall narrate;
Or whether, rapt in meditation high,
He wander'd forth, he knew not where nor why):
The drowsy Dungeon-Clock had number'd two,   Tolbooth, Sandgate
And Wallace Tower had sworn the fact was true;
The tide-swoln Firth, with sullen-sounding roar,
Through the still night dash'd hoarse along the shore;
All else was hush'd as Nature's closed e'e;
The silent moon shone high o'er tower and tree;
The chilly frost, beneath the silver beam,
Crept, gently-crusting, o'er the glittering stream.

The Brigs of Ayr

When, lo! on either hand the list'ning Bard,
The clanging sugh of whistling wings is heard;
Two dusky forms dart thro the midnight air,
Swift as the gos drives on the wheeling hare;
Ane on th' Auld Brig his airy shape uprears,
The ither flutters o'er the rising piers:
Our warlock rhymer instantly decried
The Sprites that owre the Brigs of Ayr preside.
(That Bards are second-sighted is nae joke,
And ken the lingo of the sp'ritual folk;
Fays, spunkies, kelpies, a', they can explain them,
An ev'n the vera deils they brawly ken them).
Auld Brig appear'd of ancient Pictish race,
The vera wrinkles Gothic in his face;
He seem'd as he wi Time had wrastl'd lang,
Yet, teughly doure, he bade an unco bang.
New Brig was buskit in a braw new coat,
That he at Lon'on, frae ane Adams got;
In's hand fine taper staves as smooth's a bead,
Wi virls an whirlygigums at the head.
The Goth was stalking round with anxious search,
Spying the time-worn flaws in ev'ry arch;
It chanc'd his new-come neebor took his e'e,
And e'en a vex'd and angry heart had he!
Wi thieveless sneer to see his modish mien,
He, down the water, gies him this guid-een:—

AULD BRIG

'I doubt na, frien, ye'll think ye're nae sheep shank,
Ance ye were streekit owre frae bank to bank!
But gin ye be a brig as auld as me —
Tho faith, that date, I doubt, ye'll never see —
There'll be, if that day come, I'll wad a boddle,
Some fewer whigmeleeries in your noddle.'

NEW BRIG

'Auld Vandal! ye but show your little mense,
Just much about it wi your scanty sense:
Will your poor, narrow foot-path of a street,
Where twa wheel-barrows tremble when they meet,
Your ruin'd, formless bulk o stane an lime,
Compare wi bonie brigs o modern time?
There's men of taste would tak the Ducat stream,
Tho they should cast the vera sark and swim,
E'er they would grate their feelings wi the view
O sic an ugly, Gothic hulk as you.'

The Brigs of Ayr

AULD BRIG

'Conceited gowk! puffed up wi windy pride!   cuckoo
This monie a year I've stood the flood an tide;
And tho wi crazy eild I'm sair forfairn,   eld, worn out
I'll be a brig when ye're a shapeless cairn!
As yet ye little ken about the matter,
But twa-three winters will inform ye better.
When heavy, dark, continued, a'-day rains   day-long
Wi deepening deluges o'erflow the plains;
When from the hills where springs the brawling Coil,   four tributaries of
Or stately Lugar's mossy fountains boil,   the River Ayr
Or where the Greenock winds his moorland course,
Or haunted Garpal draws his feeble source,
Arous'd by blustering winds an spotting thowes,   thaws
In monie a torrent down the snaw-broo rowes;   snow-brew rolls
While crashing ice, borne on the roaring speat,   flood
Sweeps dams, an mills, an brigs, a' to the gate;
And from Glenbuck down to the Ratton-Key,   village in Muirkirk
Auld Ayr is just one lengthen'd tumbling sea —   parish
Then down ye'll hurl (deil nor ye never rise!),   crash
And dash the gumlie jaups up to the pouring skies! muddy splashes
A lesson sadly teaching, to your cost,
That Architecture's noble art is lost!'

NEW BRIG

'Fine architecture, trowth, I needs must say't o't,
The Lord be thankit that we've tint the gate o't!   lost the knack of it
Gaunt, ghastly, ghaist-alluring edifices,
Hanging with threat'ning jut, like precipices;
O'er-arching, mouldy, gloom-inspiring coves,
Supporting roofs fantastic — stony groves;
Windows and doors in nameless sculptures drest,
With order, symmetry, or taste unblest;
Forms like some bedlam statuary's dream,
The craz'd creations of misguided whim;
Forms might be worshipp'd on the bended knee,
And still the second dread Command be free:
Their likeness is not found on earth, in air, or sea!
Mansions that would disgrace the building taste
Of any mason reptile, bird or beast:
Fit only for a doited monkish race,   befuddled
Or frosty maids forsworn the dear embrace,
Or cuifs of later times, wha held the notion,   fools
That sullen gloom was sterling true devotion:
Fancies that our guid brugh denies protection,
And soon may they expire, unblest with resurrection!'

247

The Brigs of Ayr

AULD BRIG

co-evals   'O ye, my dear-remember'd, ancient yealings,
               Were ye but here to share my wounded feelings!

provosts   Ye worthy proveses, an monie a bailie,
               Wha in the paths o righteousness did toil ay;

sober   Ye dainty deacons, an ye douce conveeners,
street-sweepers   To whom our moderns are but causey-cleaners;
               Ye godly councils, wha hae blest this town;
               Ye godly brethren o the sacred gown,

buttocks   Wha meekly gie your hurdies to the smiters;
lawyers (Writers   And (what would now be strange), ye godly Writers;
to the Signet);   A' ye douce folk I've born aboon the broo,
sedate, above,   Were ye but here, what would ye say or do?
water   How would your spirits groan in deep vexation,
               To see melancholy alteration;
               And, agonising, curse the time and place
               When ye begat the base degen'rate race!
               Nae langer rev'rend men, their country's glory,
               In plain braid Scots hold forth a plain, braid story;
               Nae langer thrifty citizens, an douce,
               Meet owre a pint, or in the council-house;

half-witted   But staumrel, corky-headed, graceless gentry,
               The herryment and ruin of the country;
               Men three-parts made by tailors and by barbers,
               Wha waste your weel-hain'd gear on damn'd New Brigs
                    and harbours!'

NEW BRIG

               'Now haud you there! for faith ye've said enough,
make good   And muckle mair then ye can mak to through.
               As for your priesthood, I shall say but little,
Ravens, sort, ticklish   Corbies and clergy are a shot right kittle:
               But, under favour o your langer beard,
               Abuse o magistrates might weel be spar'd;
               To liken them to your auld-warld squad,
               I must needs say, comparisons are odd.
               In Ayr, wag-wits nae mair can hae a handle
               To mouth 'a Citizen' a term o scandal;
               Nae mair the council waddles down the street,
               In all the pomp of ignorant conceit;

haggling   Men wha grew wise priggin owre hops an raisins,
               Or gather'd lib'ral views in bonds and seisins;
               If haply Knowledge, on a random tramp,

threatened   Had shor'd them with a glimmer of his lamp,
               And would to common-sense for once betray'd them,
               Plain, dull stupidity stept kindly in to aid them,'

The Brigs of Ayr

What farther clish-ma-claver might been said,   nonsense
What bloody wars, if Sprites had blood to shed,
No man can tell; but, all before their sight,
A fairy train appear'd in order bright:
Adown the glittering stream they featly danc'd;
Bright to the moon their various dresses glanc'd;
They footed o'er the wat'ry glass so neat,
The infant ice scarce bent beneath their feet;
While arts of minstrelsy among them rung,
And soul-ennobling Bards heroic ditties sung.

O, had McLauchlan, thairm-inspiring sage,   James McLauchlan
Been there to hear this heavenly band engage,   of Inverary
When thro his dear strathspeys they bore with Highland
     rage;
Or when they struck old Scotia's melting airs,
The lover's raptured joys or bleeding cares;
How would his Highland lug been nobler fir'd,
And ev'n his matchless hand with finer touch inspir'd!
No guess could tell what instrument appear'd,
But all the soul of Music's self was heard;
Harmonious concert rung in every part,
While simple melody pour'd moving on the heart.

The Genius of the Stream in front appears,
A venerable chief advanc'd in years;
His hoary head with water-lilies crown'd,
His manly leg with garter-tangle bound.
Next came the loveliest pair in all the ring,
Sweet female Beauty hand in hand with Spring;
Then, crown'd with flow'ry hay, came Rural Joy,
And Summer, with his fervid-beaming eye;
All-cheering Plenty, with her flowing horn,
Led yellow Autumn wreath'd with nodding corn;
Then Winter's time-bleach'd locks did hoary show,
By Hospitality with cloudless brow;
Next followed Courage, with his martial stride,
From where the Feal wild-woody coverts hide;
Benevolence, with mild, benignant air,
A female form, came from the towers of Stair;
Learning and Worth in equal measures trode,
From simple Catrine, their long-lov'd abode;
Last, white-rob'd Peace, crown'd with a hazel wreath,
To rustic Agriculture did bequeath
The broken, iron instruments of death:
At sight of whom our Sprites forgat their kindling wrath.

TO AN OLD SWEETHEART

Addressed to Miss Peggy Thomson of Kirkoswald when emigration was still uppermost in the poet's mind.

Once fondly loved and still remember'd dear,
  Sweet early object of my youthful vows,
Accept this mark of friendship, warm, sincere—
  (Friendship! 'tis all cold duty now allows.)

And when you read the simple artless rhymes,
  One friendly sigh for him—he asks no more—
Who, distant, burns in flaming torrid climes,
  Or haply lies beneath th' Atlantic roar.

THE GLOOMY NIGHT
IS GATH'RING FAST

TUNE: *Roslin Castle*

Burns is said to have written this song after a solitary walk home from Dr. Lawrie's, following what he felt would be his last visit. By now he was all packed and ready to take ship from Greenock and doubtless the thought of leaving Scotland for the uncertainties of the West Indies filled him with foreboding and melancholy.

The gloomy night is gath'ring fast,
Loud roars the wild inconstant blast;
Yon murky cloud is filled with rain,
I see it driving o'er the plain;
The hunter now has left the moor,
The scatt'red coveys meet secure;
While I here wander, prest with care,
Along the lonely banks of Ayr.

The Autumn mourns her rip'ning corn
By early Winter's ravage torn;
Across her placid, azure sky,
She sees the scowling tempest fly;
Chill runs my blood to hear it rave;
I think upon the stormy wave,
Where many a danger I must dare,
Far from the bonie banks of Ayr.

'Tis not the surging billows' roar,
'Tis not that fatal, deadly shore;
Tho death in ev'ry shape appear,
The wretched have no more to fear:
But round my heart the ties are bound;
The heart transpierc'd with many a wound;
These bleed afresh, those ties I tear,
To leave the bonie banks of Ayr.

The Gloomy Night Is Gath'ring Fast

Farewell, old Coila's hills and dales,
Her heathy moors and winding vales;
The scenes where wretched Fancy roves,
Pursuing past unhappy loves!
Farewell my friends! farewell my foes!
My peace with these, my love with those—
The bursting tears my heart declare,
Farewell, my bonie banks of Ayr!

THO CRUEL FATE

TUNE: *The Northern Lass*

The last of the valedictory songs written in the autumn of 1786 before Burns abandoned his plan for emigrating.

Tho cruel fate should bid us part
    Far as the pole and line,
Her dear idea round my heart
    Should tenderly entwine.

Tho mountains rise, and deserts howl,
    And oceans roar between,
Yet dearer than my deathless soul,
    I still would love my Jean.

A FRAGMENT

Sent to John Richmond on 3rd September 1786, with the note announcing 'Armour has just brought me a fine boy and a girl at one throw. God bless the little dears!'

CHORUS

Green grow the rashes O,
Green grow the rashes O,
The lasses they hae wimble bores,
The widows they hae gashes O.

In sober hours I am a priest;
    A hero when I'm tipsey, O;
But I'm a king and ev'ry thing,
    When wi a wanton Gipsey, O.

'Twas late yestreen I met wi ane,
    An wow, but she was gentle, O!
Ae han she pat roun my cravat,
    The tither to my pintle O.

I dought na speak—yet was na fley'd
    My heart play'd duntie, duntie, O;
An ceremony laid aside,
    I fairly fun' her cuntie, O.

              Multa desunt   'More follows'
                                 (Latin)

THE CALF

To the Rev. James Steven, on his text, MALACHI, iv., 2:—
'And ye shall go forth, and grow up as calves of the stall.'

On 8th September 1786 Burns wrote to his close
friend Robert Muir (1758-88), a wine merchant of
Kilmarnock: 'You will have heard that poor Armour
has repaid my amorous mortgages double. A very fine
boy and girl have awakened a thousand feelings that
thrill, some with tender pleasure, and some with fore-
boding anguish, thro' my soul.' The letter was accom-
panied by this poem, 'an extemporaneous production, on
a wager with Mr. Hamilton that I would not produce a
poem on the subject in a given time.' Gavin Hamilton
asked him to compose a poem based on the text of the
sermon that Sunday (3rd September). The Rev. James
Steven (d. 1824) was assistant at Ardrossan and was
probably preaching at Mauchline on exchange.

Right, sir! your text I'll prove it true,
    Tho heretics may laugh;
For instance, there's yoursel just now,
    God knows, an unco *calf.*

And should some patron be so kind
    As bless you wi a kirk,
I doubt na sir, but then we'll find

steer   Ye're still as great a *stirk,*

But, if the lover's raptur'd hour
    Shall ever be your lot,
Forbid it, every heavenly Power,

young bullock   You e'er should be a *stot!*

Tho, when some kind connubial dear

cottage   Your but-an-ben adorns,
The like has been that you may wear
    A noble head of *horns.*

ear   And, in your lug, most reverend James,
rant   To hear you roar and rowte,
Few men o sense will doubt your claims

cattle   To rank among the *nowte.*

And when ye're number'd wi the dead,
    Below a grassy hillock,
With justice they may mark your head—
    'Here lies a famous *bullock!*

NATURE'S LAW

HUMBLY INSCRIBED TO GAVIN HAMILTON, ESQ.

Composed after Jean Armour gave birth to twins on 3rd September 1786.

Great Nature spoke, observant man obey'd — POPE

Let other heroes boast their scars,
    The marks o sturt and strife,   turmoil
And other poets sing of wars,
    The plagues o human life!
Shame fa' the fun: wi sword and gun
    To slap mankind like lumber!
I sing his name and nobler fame
    Wha multiplies our number.

Great Nature spoke, with air benign:—
    'Go on, ye human race;
This lower world I you resign;
    Be fruitful and increase.
The liquid fire of strong desire,
    I've poured it in each bosom;
Here on this hand does Mankind stand,
    And there, is Beauty's blossom!'

The Hero of these artless strains,
    A lowly Bard was he,
Who sung his rhymes in Coila's plains
    With meikle mirth an glee:
Kind Nature's care had given his share
    Large of the flaming current;
And, all devout, he never sought
    To stem the sacred torrent.

He felt the powerful, high behest
    Thrill vital thro and thro;
And sought a correspondent breast
    To give obedience due.
Propitious Powers screen'd the young flow'rs
    From mildews of abortion;
And lo! the Bard—a great reward—
    Has got a double portion!

Auld cantie Coil may count the day,   cheerful
    As annual it returns,
The third of Libra's equal sway,
    That gave another Burns,
With future rhymes, an other times
    To emulate his sire,
To sing auld Coil in nobler style
    With more poetic fire!

Nature's Law

Ye Powers of peace and peaceful song,
    Look down with gracious eyes,
And bless auld Coila large and long,
    With multiplying joys;
Lang may she stand to prop the land,
    The flow'r of ancient nations,
And Burnses spring her fame to sing
    To endless generations!

ON MEETING WITH LORD DAER

Basil William Douglas-Hamilton, Lord Daer (1763-94)
was the second son of the Earl of Selkirk. Lord Daer,
then a student at Edinburgh University, was staying
at the country home of Professor Dugald Stewart at
Catrine when he met Burns on 23rd October, 1786.
This was the poet's first encounter with an aristocrat,
though Lord Daer, admirer of the French Revolution
and staunch advocate of Parliamentary reform, was
hardly typical of his class at that time.

This wot ye all whom it concerns:
I, Rhymer Rab, *alias* Burns,
    October twenty-third,
A ne'er-to-be-forgotten day,
Sae far I sprackl'd up the brae, — *clambered, hillside*
    I dinner'd wi a Lord.

I've been at drucken Writers' feasts, — *drunken, lawyers*
Nay, been bitch-fou 'mang godly Priests— — *drunk*
    Wi rev'rence be it spoken!—
I've even join'd the honor'd jorum,
When mighty Squireships o the Quorum
    Their hydra drouth did sloken. — *thirst, slake*

But wi a Lord—stand out my shin!
A Lord, a Peer, an Earl's son!—
    Up higher yet, my bonnet!
An sic a Lord!—lang Scotch ell twa, — *over six feet*
Our Peerage he looks o'er them a',
    As I look o'er my sonnet.

But O, for Hogarth's magic pow'r, — *William Hogarth (1697-1764) the famous painter and engraver*
To show Sir Bardie's willyart glow'r,
    An how he star'd an stammer'd,
When, goavin's he'd been led wi branks, — *looking dazedly, bridle*
An stumpin on his ploughman shanks,
    He in the parlour hammer'd!

254

On Meeting With Lord Daer

To meet good Stewart little pain is,
Or Scotia's sacred Demosthenes: Dr. Hugh Blair
      Thinks I: 'They are but men!'   (1718-1800)
But 'Burns'!— 'My Lord!'— Good God! I doited   doddered
My knees on ane anither knoited   knocked
      As faltering I gaed ben.   went inside

I sidling shelter'd in a neuk,   corner
An at his Lordship staw a leuk,   stole a glance
      Like some portentous omen:
Except good sense and social glee
An (what supris'd me) modesty
      I marked naught uncommon.

I watch'd the symtoms o the Great—
The gentle pride, the lordly state,
      The arrogant assuming:
The fient a pride, nae pride had he,   not
Nor sauce, nor state, that I could see,
      Mair than an honest ploughman!

Then from his Lordship I shall learn,
Henceforth to meet with unconcern
      One rank as weel's another;
Nae honest, worthy man need care
To meet with noble, youthfu Daer,
      For he but meets a brother.

MASONIC SONG

TUNE: *Shawn-boy;* or *Over the water to Charlie*

Written to celebrate the poet's admission as an honorary member of Lodge St. John Kilwinning, Kilmarnock on 26th October 1786.

Ye sons of old Killie, assembled by Willie   Major William Parker of
    To follow the noble vocation,   Assloss, Right Worshipful
Your thrifty old mother has scarce such another   Master
To sit in that honoured station!
I've little to say, but only to pray,
    (As praying's the *ton* of your fashion);
A prayer from the Muse you well may excuse,
    ('Tis seldom her favourite passion)—

'Ye Powers who preside o'er the wind and the tide,
    Who markèd each element's border,
Who formèd this frame with beneficent aim,
    Whose sovereign statute is order,
Within this dear mansion, may wayward Contention
    Or witherèd Envy ne'er enter!
May secrecy round be the mystical bound,
    And brotherly Love be the centre!'

EPIGRAM ON ROUGH ROADS

Attributed by Scott Douglas to Burns and dated
October 1786. The roads in question are said to have
been those between Kilmarnock and Stewarton.
Kinsley, however, considers it more likely to date
from the Highland tour; the reference to 'this people'
implies residents of a district outside Burns's
native Ayrshire.

I'm now arrived — thanks to the gods!
Thro pathways rough and muddy,
A certain sign that makin roads
Is no this people's study:
Altho I'm not wi Scripture cram'd,
I'm sure the Bible says
That heedless sinners shall be damn'd,
Unless they mend their *ways.*

EPISTLE TO MAJOR LOGAN

Mossgiel, 30th October, 1786

Major William Logan lived in retirement with his sister
Susan at Park, Ayr. At the time this poem was written
he was, in fact, merely a lieutenant on half-pay; his
majority came with service in the West Lowland
Fencibles (1794-99).

fiddle-string	Hail, thairm-inspirin, rattlin Willie!
	Tho Fortune's road be rough an hilly
fellow	To every fiddling, rhyming billie,
	We never heed,
unbroken	But take it like the uncrack'd filly,
	Proud o her speed.
gazing dreamily, sometimes	When, idly goavin, whyles we saunter
	Yirr! Fancy barks, awa we canter,
mishap	Up hill, down brae, till some mishanter,
	Some black bog-hole,
	Arrests us; then the scathe an banter
tolerate	We're forced to thole.
Whole	Hale be your heart! hale be your fiddle!
elbow dance, shake	Lang may your elbuck jink an diddle,
wriggle	To cheer you through the weary widdle
	O this vile warl,
curved stick, saunter	Until you on a cummock driddle,
old man	A grey-hair'd carl.
poverty	Come wealth, come poortith, late or soon,
	Heaven send your heart-strings ay in tune,
fiddle-pegs, above	And screw your temper-pins aboon
	(A fifth or mair),
sorrowful note	The melancholious sairie croon
crabbed	O cankrie Care.

DUNURE CASTLE

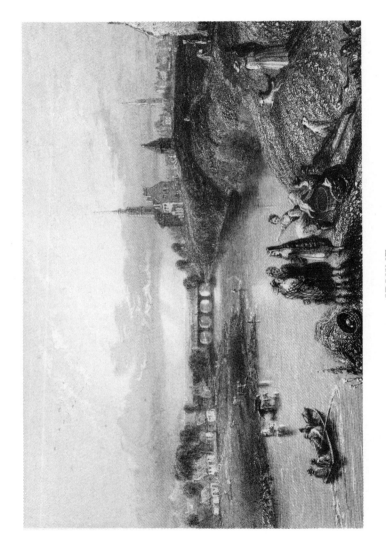

IRVINE

May still your life from day to day
Nae *lente largo* in the play,
But *allegretto forte* gay,
    Harmonious flow,
A sweeping, kindling, bauld strathspey—   bold
    Encore! Bravo!

A' blessings on the cheery gang
Wha dearly like a jig or sang,
An never think o right an wrang
    But square an rule,
But as the clegs o feeling stang,   horseflies, sting
    Are wise or fool.

My hand-wal'd curse keep hard in chase   -picked
The harpy, hoodock, purse-proud race,   grasping
Wha count on poortith as disgrace!
    Their tuneless hearts,
May fireside discords jar a bass
    To a' their parts!

But come, your hand, my careless brither!
I' th' ither warl, if there's anither—
An that there is, I've little swither   doubt
    About the matter —
We, cheek for chow, shall jog thegither—   jowl
    I'se ne'er bid better!

We've faults and failins—granted clearly!
We're frail, backsliding mortals merely;
Eve's bonie squad, priests wyte them sheerly   castigate, wholly
    For our grand fa';
But still, but still, I like them dearly—
    God bless them a'!

Ochon for poor Castalian drinkers,   (i.e. poets)
When they fa' foul o earthly jinkers!   sportsmen
The witching, curs'd, delicious blinkers   oglers
    Hae put me hyte,   furious
An gart me weet my waukrife winkers,   made wet wakeful
    Wi girnin spite.   eyes; snarling

But by yon moon—and that's high swearin!
An every star within my hearin,
An by her een wha was a dear ane   eyes
    I'll ne'er forget,
I hope to gie the jads a clearin,   jades
    In fair play yet!

Epistle To Major Logan

lost
Once
witching
enchanted

My loss I mourn, but not repent it;
I'll seek my pursie whare I tint it;
Ance to the Indies I were wonted,
  Some cantraip hour
By some sweet elf I'll yet be dinted;
  Then *vive l'amour!*

Make my respectful
greeting;
Logan's mother
flatter:
such

Faites mes baissemains respectueusè,
To sentimental sister Susie,
An, honest Lucky: no to roose you,
  Ye may be proud,
That sic a couple Fate allows ye,
  To grace your blood.

Nae mair at present can I measure,
An trowth! my rhymin ware's nae treasure;
But when in Ayr, some half-hour's leisure,
  Be't light, be't dark,
Sir Bard will do himself the pleasure
  To call at Park.

ROBERT BURNS

A WINTER NIGHT

Poor naked wretches, wheresoe'er you are,
That bide the pelting of this pityless storm!
How shall your houseless heads and unfed sides,
Your loop'd and window'd raggedness, defend you
From seasons such as these? – SHAKESPEARE

**Sent to John Ballantine on 20th November 1786 as
his 'first attempt in that irregular kind of measure in
which many of our finest Odes are wrote.'**

the north wind, hard

sun, stare
horizon

When biting Boreas, fell and doure,
Sharp shivers thro the leafless bow'r;
When Phoebus gies a short-liv'd glow'r,
  Far south the lift,
Dim-dark'ning thro the flaky show'r,
  Or whirling drift:

One

brooks

vomited

Ae night the storm the steeples rocked;
Poor Labour sweet in sleep was locked;
While burns, wi snawy wreaths up-choked,
  Wild-eddying swirl;
Or thro the mining outlet bocked,
  Down headlong hurl:

A Winter Night

List'ning the doors an winnocks rattle,   *windows*
I thought me on the ourie cattle,   *shivering*
Or silly sheep, wha bide this brattle   *endure, clatter*
     O winter war,
And thro the drift, deep-lairing, sprattle   *scramble*
     Beneath a scaur.   *rocky outcrop*

Ilk happing bird,- wee, helpless thing!—   *Each hopping*
That in the merry months o spring,
Delighted me to hear thee sing,
     What comes o thee?
Whare wilt thou cow'r thy chittering wing,
     An close thy e'e?

Ev'n you, on murdering errands toil'd,
Lone from your savage homes exil'd,
The blood-stain'd roost, and sheep-cote spoil'd
     My heart forgets,
While pityless the tempest wild
     Sore on you beats!

Now Phoebe, in her midnight reign,   *the moon*
Dark-muffl'd, view'd the dreary plain;
Still crowding thoughts, a pensive train,
     Rose in my soul,
When on my ear this plaintive strain,
     Slow, solemn, stole:—

'Blow, blow, ye winds, with heavier gust!
And freeze, thou bitter-biting frost!
Descend, ye chilly, smothering snows!
Not all your rage, as now united, shows
    More hard unkindness, unrelenting,
    Vengeful malice, unrepenting
Than heaven-illumin'd Man on brother Man bestows!

'See stern Oppression's iron grip,
    Or mad Ambition's gory hand,
Sending, like blood-hounds from the slip,
    Woe, Want, and Murder o'er the land!
Ev'n in the peaceful rural vale,
    Truth, weeping, tells the mournful tale,
How pamper'd Luxury, Flatt'ry by her side,
    The parasite empoisoning her ear,
With all the servile wretches in the rear,
Looks o'er proud Property, extended wide;
    And eyes the simple, rustic hind,
Whose toil upholds the glitt'ring show—
    A creature of another kind,
    Some coarser substance, unrefin'd—
Place'd for her lordly use, thus far, thus vile, below!

'Where, where is Love's fond, tender throe,
With lordly Honor's lofty brow,
   The pow'rs you proudly own?
Is there, beneath Love's noble name,
Can harbour, dark, the selfish aim,
   To bless himself alone?
   Mark Maiden-Innocence a prey
     To love-pretending snares:
   This boasted Honor turns away,
   Shunning soft Pity's rising sway,
Regardless of the tears and unavailing pray'rs!
   Perhaps this hour, in Misery's squalid nest,
   She strains your infant to her joyless breast,
And with a mother's fears shrinks at the rocking blast!'

   'Oh ye! who, sunk in beds of down,
     Feel not a want but what yourselves create,
     Think, for a moment, on this wretched fate,
     Whom friends and fortune quite disown!
Ill-satisfy'd keen nature's clam'rous call,
   Stretch'd on his straw, he lays himself to sleep;
While through the ragged roof and chinky wall,
   Chill, o'er his slumbers, piles the drifty heap!
   Think on the dungeon's grim confine,
   Where Guilt and poor Misfortune pine!
   Guilt, erring man, relenting view!
   But shall thy legal rage pursue
   The wretch, already crushèd low
   By cruel Fortune's undeserved blow?
Affliction's sons are brothers in distress;
A brother to relieve, how exquisite the bliss!'

powdery

   I heard nae mair, for Chanticleer
     Shook off the pouthery snaw,
   And hail'd the morning with a cheer,
     A cottage-rousing craw.

   But deep this truth impress'd my mind:
     Thro all His works abroad,
   The heart benevolent and kind
     The most resembles God.

REPLY TO AN INVITATION

The date and circumstances of composition are unknown. Kinsley places it 'probably in 1785 or 1786.' Bartie is a poetic name, apparently peculiar to Burns, for the Devil.

Sir,
  Yours this moment I unseal,
    And faith! I'm gay and hearty.
  To tell the truth and shame the Deil,
    I am as fou as Bartie.   drunk as the Devil
  But Foorsday, Sir, my promise leal,   Thursday, true
    Expect me o your partie,
  If on a beastie I can speil   climb
    Or hurl in a cartie.   trundle

        Yours,—ROBERT BURNS

    MAUCHLIN, Monday night, 10 o'clock

PRAYER—O THOU DREAD POWER

Written about November 1786, following the poet's visit to the home of the Rev. Dr. George Lawrie (1727-99) in Edinburgh that autumn. Burns was introduced to the blind Dr Blacklock through Lawrie. Subsequently he attended a soiree given by Lawrie, where Burns first hear the spinet, played by the minister's daughter Christina (b. 1766). This was one of several poems given by Burns to the Lawrie family.

O thou dread Power, who reign'st above,
  I know thou wilt me hear,
When for this scene of peace and love
  I make my prayer sincere.

The hoary Sire—the mortal stroke,
  Long, long be pleas'd to spare:
To bless his little filial flock,
  And show what good men are.

She, who her lovely offspring eyes
  With tender hopes and fears—
O, bless her with a mother's joys,
  But spare a mother's tears!

Their hope, their stay, their darling youth,
  In manhood's dawning blush,
Bless him, Thou God of love and truth,
  Up to a parent's wish.

The beauteous, seraph sister-band—
  With earnest tears I pray—
Thou know'st the snares on every hand,
  Guide Thou their steps alway.

When, soon or late, they reach that coast,
  O'er Life's rough ocean driven,
May they rejoice, no wand'rer lost,
  A family in Heaven!

261

THE NIGHT WAS STILL

Another poem presented by Burns to the daughters of
Dr. Lawrie in the late autumn of 1786.

The night was still, and o'er the hill
The moon shone on the castle wa',
The mavis sang, while dew-drops hang
Around her on the castle wa':

Sae merrily they danc'd the ring
evening   Frae eenin till the cock did craw,
And ay the o'erword o the spring
children   Was:--'Irvine's bairns are bonie a'!'

RUSTICITY'S UNGAINLY FORM

Enclosed in a song-book sent to Archibald Lawrie
(1768-1837) on 13th November 1786.

Rusticity's ungainly form
    May cloud the highest mind;
But when the heart is nobly warm,
    The good excuse will find.

Propriety's cold, cautious rules
    Warm Fervour may o'erlook;
But spare poor Sensibility
    Th' ungentle, harsh rebuke.

ADDRESS TO EDINBURGH

An uncomfortable ode, composed in the stiff Augustan
English favoured by poets of the late eighteenth
century, it was written shortly after Burns arrived
in Edinburgh. The opening line of this Address was
seized by a well-known firm of bathroom manu-
facturers who applied the name 'Edina' to one of
their necessary though unpoetic products — according
to Maurice Lindsay!

Edina! Scotia's darling seat!
    All hail thy palaces and tow'rs,
Where once, beneath a Monarch's feet,
    Sat Legislation's sov'reign pow'rs:
From marking wildly-scatt'red flow'rs,
    As on the banks of Ayr I stray'd,
And singing, lone, the ling'ring hours,
    I shelter in thy honor'd shade.

Here Wealth still swells the golden tide,
    As busy Trade his labour plies;
There Architecture's noble pride
    Bids elegance and splendour rise:
Here Justice, from her native skies,
    High wields her balance and her rod;
There Learning, with his eagle eyes,
    Seeks Science in her coy abode.

Address To Edinburgh

Thy sons, Edina, social, kind,
    With open arms the stranger hail;
Their views enlarg'd, their lib'ral mind,
    Above the narrow, rural vale;
Attentive still to Sorrow's wail,
    Or modest Merit's silent claim:
And never may their sources fail!
    And never Envy blot their name!

Thy daughters bright thy walks adorn,
    Gay as the gilded summer sky,
Sweet as the dewy, milk-white thorn,
    Dear as the raptur'd thrill of joy!
Fair Burnet strikes th' adoring eye,
    Heav'n's beauties on my fancy shine:
I see the Sire of Love on high,
    And own His work indeed divine!

Eliza Burnett, Lord
Monboddo's youngest
daughter (1766-90)

There, watching high the least alarms,
    Thy rough, rude fortress gleams afar;
Like some bold vet'ran, grey in arms,
    And mark'd with many a seamy scar:
The pond'rous wall and massy bar,
    Grim-rising o'er the rugged rock,
Have oft withstood assailing war,
    And oft repell'd th' invader's shock.

With awe-struck thought and pitying tears,
    I view that noble, stately dome,
Where Scotia's kings of other years,
    Fam'd heroes! had their royal home:
Alas, how chang'd the times to come!
    Their royal name low in the dust!
Their hapless race wild-wand'ring roam!
    Tho rigid Law cries out, 'Twas just!'

Wild beats my heart to trace your steps,
    Whose ancestors, in days of yore,
Thro hostile ranks and ruin'd gaps
    Old Scotia's bloody lion bore:
Ev'n I, who sing in rustic lore,
    Haply my sires have left their shed,
And fac'd grim Dangers's loudest roar,
    Bold-following where your fathers led!

Address To Edinburgh

Edina! Scotia's darling seat!
All hail thy palaces and tow'rs;
Where once, beneath a Monarch's feet,
Sat Legislation's sov'reign pow'rs,
From marking wildly-scatt'red flow'rs,
As on the banks of Ayr I stray'd,
And singing, lone, the ling'ring hours,
I shelter in thy honor'd shade.

ADDRESS TO A HAGGIS

The closing stanza is said to have been composed ext-
empore during a dinner at the home of John Morrison,
a Mauchline cabinet-maker. The complete poem was
written soon after Burns arrived in Edinburgh,
and appeared in the *Caledonian Mercury* — the first of
Burns's poems to be published in any periodical. Oddly
enough, the earliest recipe for Haggis appeared the
same year, in *Cookery and Pastry* by Susanna
Maciver.

cheerful	Fair fa' your honest, sonsie face,
	Great chieftain o the puddin'-race!
Above	Aboon them a' ye tak your place,
paunch, guts	Painch, tripe, or thairm:
worthy	Weel are ye wordy of a grace
	As lang's my arm.

The groaning trencher there ye fill,
buttocks   Your hurdies like a distant hill,
skewer   Your pin wad help to mend a mill
     In time o need,
While thro your pores the dews distil
     Like amber bead.

wipe   His knife see rustic Labour dight,
skill   An cut you up wi ready slight,
Diggin   Trenching your gushing entrails bright,
     Like onie ditch;
And then, O what a glorious sight,
-steaming   Warm-reekin, rich!

spoon   Then, horn for horn, they stretch an strive:
Deil tak the hindmost, on they drive,
well-swollen bellies, soon   Till a' their weel-swall'd kytes belyve
     Are bent like drums;
burst   The auld Guidman, maist like to rive,
     'Bethankit' hums.

264

Address To A Haggis

Is there that owre his French *ragout,*
Or *olio* that wad staw a sow,   sicken
Or *fricassee* wad mak her spew
    Wi perfect sconner,   disgust
Looks down wi sneering, scornfu view
    On sic a dinner?

Poor devil! see him owre his trash,
As feckless as a wither'd rash,   weak, rush
His spindle shank a guid whip-lash,
    His nieve a nit;   fist, nut
Thro bloody flood or field to dash,
    O how unfit!

But mark the Rustic, haggis-fed,
The trembling earth resounds his tread,
Clap in his walie nieve a blade,   choice
    He'll make it whissle;
An legs an arms, an heads will sned,   trim
    Like taps o thrissle.   tops, thistle

Ye Pow'rs, wha mak mankind your care,
And dish them out their bill o fare,
Auld Scotland wants nae skinking ware   watery
    That jaups in luggies;   splashes, porringers
But, if ye wish her gratefu prayer,
    Gie her a Haggis!

VERSES INTENDED TO BE WRITTEN BELOW A NOBLE EARL'S PICTURE

On 13th January 1787 Burns sent these verses to the Earl of Glencairn with a letter seeking permission to publish them in an Edinburgh newspaper. Lord Glencairn (1749-91) declined, Burns later admitting that he 'does me the honor of giving me his strictures: his hints, with respect to impropriety or indelicacy, I follow implicity.' It was not until 1851 that this poem was actually printed.

Whose is that noble, dauntless brow?
    And whose that eye of fire?
And whose that generous princely mien,
    E'en rooted foes admire?

Stranger! to justly show that brow
    And mark that eye of fire,
Would take His hand, whose vernal tints
    His other works inspire.

Verses Intended To Be Written Below A
Noble Earl's Picture

Bright as a cloudless summer sun,
With stately port he moves;
His guardian Seraph eyes with awe
The noble Ward he loves.

Among the illustrious Scottish sons,
That Chief thou may'st discern:
Mark Scotia's fond-returning eye—
It dwells upon Glencairn.

AND MAUN I STILL ON
MENIE DOAT

TUNE: *Johnny's Grey Breeks*

Early editors assigned this song to 1785-6, but Kinsley
considered, from internal evidence, that it was written,
wholly or in part during his Edinburgh period.

CHORUS

must, dote

And maun I still on Menie doat,
And bear the scorn that's in her e'e?
For it's jet, jet-black, an it's like a hawk,

will not

An it winna let a body be.

Again rejoicing Nature sees
Her robe assume its vernal hues:
Her leafy locks wave in the breeze,
All freshly steep'd in morning dews.

In vain to me the cowslips blaw,
In vain to me the vi'lets spring;

wood

In vain to me in glen or shaw,

linnet

The mavis and the lint-white sing,

The merry ploughboy cheers his team

careful

Wi joy the tentie seedsman stalks;
But life's to me a weary dream,

wakes

A dream of ane that never wauks.

The wanton coot the water skims,
Amang the reeds the ducklings cry,
The stately swan majestic swims,
And ev'ry thing is blest but I.

shuts, fold-gate

The sheep-herd steeks his faulding slap,
And o'er the moorlands whistles shrill;
Wi wild, unequal, wand'ring step,
I meet him on the dewy hill.

266

And Maun I Still On Menie Doat

And when the lark, 'tween light and dark,
   Blythe waukens by the daisy's side,
And mounts and sings on flittering wings,
   A woe-worn ghaist I hameward glide.   ghost

Come winter, with thine angry howl,
   And raging, bend the naked tree;
Thy gloom will soothe my cheerless soul,
   When nature all is sad like me!

TO MISS LOGAN

WITH BEATTIE'S POEMS FOR A NEW-YEAR'S GIFT, JAN. 1, 1787

Dedicated to Susan Logan, sister of Willian Logan of Park and accompanying a copy of The Minstrel by Dr. James Beattie.

Again the silent wheels of time
   Their annual round have driv'n,
And you, tho scarce in maiden prime,
   Are so much nearer Heav'n.

No gifts have I from Indian coasts
   The infant year to hail;
I send you more than India boasts,
   In Edwin's simple tale.

Our sex with guile, and faithless love,
   Is charg'd—perhaps too true;
But may, dear maid, each lover prove
   An Edwin still to you.

RANTIN, ROVIN ROBIN
TUNE: *Dainty Davie*

Possibly written in flippant celebration of his 28th birthday, Burns noted down this autobiographical song in 2CPB about 9th April 1787. Evidently there was some difference of opinion between Burns and George Thomson concerning the chorus, which the poet averred should be sung 'to the low part of the tune; and nothing, since a Highland wench in the Cowgate once bore me three bastards at a birth, has surprised me so much as your opinion on this subject.'

CHORUS

Robin was a rovin boy,
   Rantin, rovin, rantin, rovin,
Robin was a rovin boy,
   Rantin, rovin Robin!

There was a lad was born in Kyle,   at Alloway
But whatna day o whatna style,
I doubt it's hardly worth the while
   To be sae nice wi Robin.

1759	Our monarch's hindmost year but ane
	Was five-and-twenty days begun,
	'Twas then a blast o Janwar win'
	Blew hansel in on Robin.
peered, face	The gossip keekit in his loof,
	Quo scho:—'Wha lives will see the proof,
sturdy, fool	This waly boy will be nae coof:
	I think we'll ca' him Robin.'

'He'll hae misfortunes great an sma
But ay a heart aboon them a'.
He'll be a credit till us a':
    We'll a' be proud o Robin!'

'But sure as three times three mak nine,
every I see by ilka score and line,
This chap will dearly like our kin',
commend   So leeze me on thee, Robin!'

'Guid faith', quo she, 'I doubt you gar
legs apart The bonie lasses lie aspar;
faults, worse But twenty fauts ye may hae waur —
    So blessins on thee. Robin!'

ELEGY ON THE DEATH OF
ROBERT RUISSEAUX

This mock-elegy dates from 1787, the subject being the poet himself. Ruisseaux (French - 'brooks, streams') is a play on Robert's surname.

Now Robin lies in his last lair,
more He'll gabble rhyme, nor sing nae mair;
Cauld poverty wi hungry stare,
frighten   Nae mair shall fear him;
crabbed Nor anxious fear, nor cankert care,
    E'er mair come near him.

bothered To tell the truth, they seldom fash'd him,
Except the moment that they crush'd him;
soon For sune as chance or fate had hush'd 'em,
    Tho e'er sae short,
Then wi a rhyme or sang he lash'd 'em,
    And thought it sport.

country-labour Tho he was bred to kintra-wark,
both stout, strong And counted was baith wight and stark,
Yet that was never Robin's mark
    To mak a man;
scholarly But tell him, he was learn'd and clark,
flattered   Ye roos'd him then!

INSCRIPTION FOR THE HEADSTONE
OF FERGUSSON THE POET

Robert Fergusson (1750-74), a young poet of immense promise, died insane in the Edinburgh mad-house. His Poems were published a year before his tragic death and had a considerable influence on Burns who was appalled to discover that Fergusson's grave was unmarked. On 6th February 1787 he applied to the Canongate Bailies for permission to erect a headstone. The architect, Robert Burn was commissioned to erect the stone for which Burns composed the following quatrain. The additional stanzas were written in 2CPB. Burns did not settle the bill till 1792. Commenting on the delay he wrote of Mr Burn: 'He was two years in erecting it, after I commissioned him for it; and I have been two years paying him, after he sent me his account; so he and I are quits. He had the hardiesse to ask me interest on the sum; but considering that the money was due by one Poet, for putting a tombstone over another, he may, with grateful surprise, thank Heaven that he ever saw a farthing of it.'

No sculptured Marble here, nor pompous lay,
    No storied Urn nor animated Bust:
This simple stone directs pale Scotia's way,
    To pour her sorrows o'er the Poet's dust.

ADDITIONAL STANZAS

She mourns, sweet tuneful youth, thy hapless fate;
    Tho all the powers of song thy fancy fir'd,
Yet Luxury and Wealth lay by in State,
    And, thankless, starv'd what they so much admir'd.

This humble tribute, with a tear, he gives,
    A brother Bard—he can no more bestow:
But dear to fame thy Song immortal lives,
    A nobler monument than Art can show.

APOSTROPHE TO FERGUSSON

Written in a copy of Fergusson's Poems given to the poetess Rebeccah Carmichael on 19th March 1787.

Curse on ungrateful man, that can be pleas'd,
And yet can starve the author of the pleasure!
O thou, my elder brother in misfortune,
By far my elder brother in the Muse,
With tears I pity thy unhappy fate!
Why is the Bard unfitted for the world,
Yet has so keen a relish of its pleasures?

LINES ON FERGUSSON, THE POET

Inscribed in a copy of the World, a periodical to which
Burns subscribed for five years (1785-90). This poem
was first published in the Scots Magazine in November
1803.

Ill-fated genius! Heaven-taught Fergusson!
What heart that feels, and will not yield a tear
To think Life's sun did set e'er well begun
To shed its influence on thy bright career!

O, why should truest Worth and Genius pine
Beneath the iron grasp of Want and Woe,
While titled knaves and idiot-greatness shine
In all the splendour Fortune can bestow?

EPIGRAM ADDRESSED TO
AN ARTIST

Allegedly written by Burns on the back of a small
sketch, during a visit to an artist's studio in
Edinburgh. The unnamed painter was working
on a picture of Jacob's dream.

Dear ——, I'll gie ye some advice,
    You'll tak it no uncivil:
You shouldna paint at angels, man,
    But try to paint the Devil.

ticklish work   To paint an angel's kittle wark,
    Wi Nick there's little danger:
long-known   You'll easy draw a lang-kent face,
    But no sae weel a stranger. — R.B.

ON ELPHINSTONE'S TRANSLATION
OF MARTIAL

James Elphinstone (1721-1809), born in Edinburgh but
resident in Kensington where he ran a boarding school.
In 1782 he published a translation of Martial's Epigrams,
in a letter of 14th January 1788 Burns mentions 'I was
sitting in a merchant's shop... waiting somebody; he
put Elphinstone into my hand, and asked my opinion of
it I begged leave to write it on a blank leaf.'

O thou whom Poesy abhors,
Whom Prose has turnèd out of doors
Heard'st thou yon groan?—Proceed no further:
'Twas laurel'd Martial calling 'Murther!'

TO THE GUIDWIFE OF
WAUCHOPE HOUSE

(MRS. SCOTT)

March, 1787

Elizabeth Scott (1729-89), née Rutherford, was a
niece of the poetess Alison Cockburn and wife of
Walter Scott of Wauchope House near Jedburgh.
She had been lent a copy of the Kilmarnock Edition
in December 1786 and this started a correspondence
between her and the poet who visited Wauchope on
10th May 1787 during his Border tour. Earlier, Mrs.
Scott had sent Burns a long verse-epistle and this was
his reply.

I mind it weel, in early date,   remember
When I was beardless, young, and blate,   bashful
   An first could thresh the barn,
Or haud a yokin at the pleugh,   hold, a day's work
An tho forfoughten sair eneugh,   exhausted
   Yet unco proud to learn;   mighty
When first amang the yellow corn
   A man I reckon'd was,
An wi the lave ilk merry morn   others, each
   Could rank my rig an lass: ridge
     Still shearing, and clearing   reaping
       The tither stookèd raw, row of sheaves
     Wi clavers an havers,   gossip, nonsense
      Wearing the day awa.   away

E'en then, a wish (I mind its pow'r),
A wish that to my latest hour
   Shall strongly heave my breast,
That I for poor auld Scotland's sake
Some usefu plan or book could make,
   Or sing a sang at least.
The rough burr-thistle spreading wide
   Amang the bearded bear,   barley
I turn'd the weeder-clips aside,   -shears
   An spar'd the symbol dear.
     No nation, no station,
      My envy e'er could raise;
     A Scot still, but blot still, without
      I knew nae higher praise.

But still the elements o sang
In formless jumble, right an wrang,
   Wild floated in my brain;
'Till on that hairst I said before,   harvest
My partner in the merry core,   crowd
   She rous'd the forming strain.

To The Guidwife Of Wauchope House

pleasant lass	I see her yet, the sonsie quean
	That lighted up my jingle,
shrewd	Her witching smile, her pauky een
made	That gart my heart-strings tingle!
	I firèd, inspirèd,
glance	At ev'ry kindling keek,
	But, bashing and dashing,
	I fearèd ay to speak.
(Health, each, chap	Hale to the sex! (ilk guid chiel says):
	Wi merry dance on winter days,
	An we to share in common!
	The gust o joy, the balm of woe,
soul	The saul o life, the heav'n below,
	Is rapture-giving Woman.
boors	Ye surly sumphs, who hate the name,
	Be mindfu o your mither;
	She, honest woman, may think shame
	That ye're connected with her!
sad	Ye're wae men, ye're nae men
	That slight the lovely dears;
	The shame ye, disclaim ye,
fellow	Ilk honest birkie swears.
cow-shed	For you, no bred to barn and byre,
	Wha sweetly tune the Scottish lyre,
	Thanks to you for your line!
parti-coloured	The marl'd plaid ye kindly spare,
worn	By me should gratefully be ware;
perfection	'Twad please me to the nine.
proud, covering	I'd be mair vauntie o my hap,
soberly, crupper	Douce hingin owre my curple,
folded	Than onie ermine ever lap,
	Or proud imperial purple.
long health	Farewell then! lang hale then,
lot	An plenty be your fa!
	May losses and crosses
porch	Ne'er at your hallan ca'!

R. BURNS

TO MISS ISABELLA MACLEOD

EDINBURGH, March 16, 1787

Isabella MacLeod of Raasay was the daughter of that laird who entertained Boswell and Johnson during their Hebridean tour. Burns may have been introduced to the MacLeods by Gavin Hamilton. We do not know what the 'tuneful gift' of line 3 was.

The crimson blossom charms the bee,
The summer sun the swallow:
So dear this tuneful gift to me
From lovely Isabella.

Her portrait fair upon my mind
Revolving time shall mellow,
And mem'ry's latest effort find
The lovely Isabella.

No Bard nor lover's rapture this
In fancies vain and shallow!
She is, so come my soul to bliss,
The lovely Isabella.

EPIGRAMS
EXTEMPORE IN THE COURT OF SESSION

Composed in Edinburgh in 1787 during a visit to the Court of Session to hear the case of Campbell v. Montgomerie. Captain James Montgomerie and Mrs Maxwell Campbell became lovers, and Mrs. Campbell bore a child in 1784. Maxwell Campbell sued for damages without divorcing his wife and Montgomerie fled to the West Indies. The Lord Advocate was Ilay Campbell (1734-1823), also referred to in 'The Author's Ernest Cry and Prayer'. Henry Erskine (1746-1817), Dean of the Faculty (1786) was noted for his wit and forensic skill. Both men were friends and patrons of Burns.

LORD ADVOCATE

He clench'd his pamphlets in his fist,
    He quoted and he hinted,
Till in a declamation-mist,
    His argument, he tint it: lost
He gapèd for't, he grapèd for't,   groped
    He fand it was awa, man;   found
But what his common sense came short,
    He eked out wi law, man.

MR. ERSKINE

Collected, Harry stood awee,   a moment
    Then open'd out his arm, man;
His Lordship sat wi ruefu e'e,   eye
    And ey'd the gathering storm, man;
Like wind-driv'n hail it did assail,
    Or torrents owre a linn, man;
The Bench sae wise lift up their eyes,
    Hauf-wauken'd wi the din, man.

273

TO MR. McADAM,
OF CRAIGEN-GILLAN

IN ANSWER TO AN OBLIGING LETTER HE SENT
IN THE COMMENCEMENT OF MY POETIC CAREER

John McAdam (d. 1790) attained celebrity as a leading
agricultural improver. It has been assumed, from the
sub-title, that this verse-epistle was written in 1786;
but McAdam and his family appear only in the addenda
and not the main subscription list in the Edinburgh
Edition. This would date composition to about March
1787, rather than late 1786 as implied in Burns's
annotation in the Glenriddell MS which, long after the
event, may have been due to faulty memory.

drink	Sir, o'er a gill I gat your card,
trust	I trow it made me proud;
	'See wha tak's notice o the Bard!'
danced	I lap, and cry'd fu loud.
	Now deil-ma-care about their jaw,
clumsy	The senseless, gawky million!
	I'll cock my nose aboon them a',
praised	I'm roos'd by Craigen-Gillan!
	'Twas noble, sir;-'twas like yoursel,
	To grant your high protection:
	A great man's smile, ye ken fu well,
	Is ay a blest infection.
Diogenes	Tho, by his banes wha in a tub
Alexander the Great	Match'd Macedonian Sandy!
puddle	On my ain legs thro dirt and dub,
	I independent stand ay;
broth	And when those legs to guid warm kail,
	Wi welcome canna bear me,
stone fence, onion-	A lee dyke-side, a sybow-tail,
	An barley-scone shall cheer me.
	Heaven spare you lang to kiss the breath
	O monie flow'ry simmers,
	An bless your bonnie lasses baith,
lovable, wenches	(I'm tauld they're loosome kimmers!)
Col. Quinton McAdam	An God bless young Dunaskin's laird,
(d. 1805)	The blossom of our gentry,
	An may he wear an auld man's beard,
	A credit to his country!

PROLOGUE

SPOKEN BY MR. WOODS ON HIS BENEFIT NIGHT,
MONDAY, 16th APRIL, 1787

William Woods (1751-1802) began his dramatic career
in Southampton, but moved to Edinburgh in the early
1770s where he became a close friend of Robert
Fergusson, and it was this that drew Burns to him. John
Home's tragedy Douglas (l. 21) roused considerable
patriotic pride at the time of its debut in 1756,
memorable from the cry from the audience 'Whaur's
your Wullie Shakespeare noo?' Harley was the hero
of Henry MacKenzie's The Man of Feeling (1771),
one of the poet's favourite novels.

When by a generous Public's kind acclaim
That dearest need is granted — honest fame;
Where here your favour is the actor's lot,
Nor even the man in private life forgot;
What breast so dead to heavenly Virtue's glow
But heaves impassion'd with the grateful throe?
Poor is the task to please a barb'rous throng:
It needs no Siddons's powers in Southern's song.
But here an ancient nation, fam'd afar
For genius, learning high, as great in war.
Hail, Caledonia! name for ever dear!
Before whose sons I'm honor'd to appear!
Where every science, every nobler art,
That can inform the mind or mend the heart,
Is known (as grateful nations oft have found),
Far as the rude barbarian marks the bound!
Philosophy, no idle pedant dream,
Here holds her search by heaven-taught Reason's beam:
Here History paints with elegance and force
The tide of Empire's fluctuating course;
Here *Douglas* forms wild Shakespeare into plan,
And Harley rouses all the God in man.
When well-form'd taste and sparkling wit unite
With manly lore, or female beauty bright
(Beauty, where faultless symmetry and grace
Can only charm us in the second place),
Witness my heart, how oft with panting fear,
As on this night, I've met these judges here!
But still the hope Experience taught to live:
Equal to judge, you're candid to forgive.
No hundred-headed Riot here we meet,
With Decency and Law beneath his feet;
Nor Insolence assumes fair Freedom's name:
Like CALEDONIANS you applaud or blame!

Sarah Siddons
(1755-1831)

Prologue

O Thou, dread Power, whose empire-giving hand
Has oft been stretch'd to shield the honor'd land!
Strong may she glow with all her ancient fire;
May every son be worthy of his sire;
Firm may she rise, with generous disdain
At Tyranny's, or direr Pleasure's chain;
Still self-dependent in her native shore,
Bold may she brave grim Danger's loudest roar,
Till Fate the curtain drops on worlds to be no more!

ADDRESS TO WM. TYTLER, ESQ., OF WOODHOUSELEE

WITH AN IMPRESSION OF THE AUTHOR'S PORTRAIT

William Tytler (1711-92) was a Writer to the Signet
who collaborated with Johnson in the SMM project
and helped Burns collect material for the later volumes.
The 'impression' accompanying this Address was
allegedly the silhouette by John Miers, though
Kinsley suggests that it may have been the engraving
by John Beugo, from the portrait by Alexander
Nasmyth.

Reverèd defender of beauteous Stuart,
    Of Stuart!—a name once respected,
A name which to love was once mark of a true heart,
    But now 'tis despis'd and neglected!

Tho something like moisture conglobes in my eye,
    Let no one misdeem me disloyal!
A poor friendless wand'rer may well claim a sigh—
    Still more, if that wand'rer were royal.

My Fathers that name have rever'd on a throne;
    My Fathers have fallen right to it:
Those Fathers would spurn their degenerate son,
    That name, should he scoffingly slight it.

Still in prayers for King George I most heartily join
    The Queen, and the rest of the gentry;
Be they wise, be they foolish, is nothing of mine:
    Their title's avow'd by my country.

But why of that epocha make such a fuss
    That gave us the Hanover stem?
If bringing them over was lucky for us,
    I'm sure 'twas as lucky for them.

But loyalty — truce! we're on dangerous ground:
    Who know how the fashions may alter?
The doctrine, to-day, that is loyalty sound,
    To-morrow may bring us a halter!

Bonnie Prince
Charlie

276

Address To Wm. Tytler, Esq., Of Woodhouselee

I send you a trifle, a head of a Bard,
    A trifle scarce worthy your care;
But accept it, good Sir, as a mark of regard,
    Sincere as a saint's dying prayer.

Now Life's chilling evening dim-shades on your eye,
    And ushers the long dreary night;
But you, like the star that athwart gilds the sky,
    Your course to the latest is bright.

EPIGRAM TO MISS AINSLIE
IN CHURCH

Burns met Rachel Ainslie (b. 1768) while on his Border tour with her brother Robert. At Duns parish church early in May 1787 Burns sat next to Miss Ainslie listening to the 'hell-fire and damnation' sermon of Dr. Bowmaker. The lady seemed attentive but agitated, and Burns was moved to inscribe these extempore lines on the fly-leaf of her Bible.

Fair maid, you need not take the hint,
    Nor idle texts pursue;
'Twas guilty sinners that he meant,
    Not angels such as you.

LAMENT FOR THE ABSENCE
OF WILLIAM CREECH, PUBLISHER

William Creech (1745-1815) publisher and bookseller of the High Street, Edinburgh, immortalised by Burns on account of his vanity and meanness. Creech was incredibly slow in settling accounts with the poet for the Edinburgh Edition of 1787 and forced Burns to visit Edinburgh that winter to obtain satisfaction. This Lament, written during the Border tour, reflects their relationship before the quarrel over the delay in payment.

Auld chuckie Reekie's sair distrest,	mother-hen
Down droops her ance weel burnish'd crest,	
Nae joy her bonie buskit nest	trimmed
Can yield ava:	at all
Her darling bird that she lo'es best,	
Willie's awa.	
O, Willie was a witty wight,	
And had o things an unco sleight!	uncommon skill
Auld Reekie ay he keepit tight,	in order
And trig an braw;	trim, handsome
But now they'll busk her like a fright,—	clothe, freak
Willie's awa!	

The stiffest o them a' he bow'd;
The bauldest o them a' he cow'd;
The bauldest o them a' he cow'd;   *daunted*
They durst nae mair than he allow'd—   *dared*
    That was a law:
We've lost a birkie well worth gowd—   *blade, gold*
    Willie's awa!

Now gawkies, tawpies, gowks, and fools,   *boobies, silly girls, dolts*
Frae colleges and boarding schools
May sprout like simmer puddock-stools   *toadstools*
    In glen or shaw: *wood*
He wha could brush them down to mools,   *dust*
    Willie's awa!

The brethren o the Commerce-Chaumer
May mourn their loss wi doolfu clamour: *woeful*
He was a dictionar and grammar
    Among them a'.
I fear they'll now mak monie a stammer:
    Willie's awa!

Nae mair we see his levee door
Philosophers and Poets pour,
And toothy Critics by the score,
    In bloody raw: *row*
The adjutant o a' the core,   *band*
    Willie's awa!

Now worthy Greg'ry's Latin face,
Tytler's and Greenfield's modest grace,
M'Kenzie, Stewart, such a brace
    As Rome ne'er saw,
They a' maun meet some ither place—   *must*
    Willie's awa!

Dr. James Gregory (1753-1821); Alexander Fraser Tytler (1747-1813); Rev. William Greenfield (d.1827); Henry MacKenzie (1745-1831); Dugald Stewart (1753-1828)

Poor Burns ev'n 'Scotch Drink' canna quicken,
He cheeps like some bewilder'd chicken   *chirps*
Scar'd frae its minnie and the cleckin,   *mother, brood*
    By hoodie-craw.   *carrion-crow*
Grief's gien his heart an unco kickin,
    Willie's awa!

Now ev'ry sour-mou'd, girnin blellum,   *ill-tongued, snarling, nag*
And Calvin's folk, are fit to fell him;   *kill*
Ilk self-conceited critic-skellum   *scullion*
    His quill may draw:
He wha could brawlie ward their bellum,   *finely repel, assault*
    Willie's awa!

Lament For The Absence Of William Creech, Publisher

Up wimpling, stately Tweed I've sped,   *meandering*
And Eden scenes on crystal Jed,
And Ettrick banks, now roaring red
    While tempests blaw;
But every joy and pleasure's fled,
    Willie's awa!

May I be Slander's common speech,
A text for Infamy to preach,
And lastly, streekit out to bleach
    In winter snaw,
When I forget thee, Willie Creech,
    Tho far awa!

May never wicked Fortune touzle him,
May never wicked men bamboozle him,
Until a pow as auld's Methusalem
    He canty claw!
Then to the blessed new Jerusalem,
    Fleet-wing awa!

TO SYMON GRAY

Written in May 1787, during Burns's Border tour. Gray met the poet at church in Duns on 6th May. Gray was a retired businessman and amateur versifier who made many charitable bequests and is commemorated in the local literary society. Gray pestered Burns with his poems and these lines were the Bard's answer.

Symon Gray,
You're dull to-day.

Dulness, with redoubted sway,
Has seized the wits of Symon Gray.

Dear Cimon Gray,
    The other day,
When you sent me some rhyme,
I could not then just ascertain
    Its worth, for want of time.

But now today, good Mr. Gray,
    I've read it o'er and o'er,
Tried all my skill, but find I'm still
    Just where I was before.

We auld wives' minions gie our opinions,
    Solicited or no;
Then of its fau'ts my honest thoughts
    I'll give—and here they go.

To Symon Gray

Such damn'd bombast no time that's past
Will show, or time to come,
So, Cimon dear, your song I'll tear,
And with it wipe my bum.

NOTE TO MR. RENTON
OR LAMERTON

Written about 18th May 1787, during the Border tour.
John Renton had invited Burns to visit him at
Mordington House near Berwick, though there is no
record of the visit having taken place.

letter	Your billet, Sir, I grant receipt;
any road	Wi you I'll canter onie gate,
	Tho 'twere a trip to yon blue warl,
fellows, hell	Whare birkies march on burning marl:
	Then, Sir, God willing, I'll attend ye,
	And to His goodness I commend ye.

ROBERT BURNS

BONIE DUNDEE

TUNE: *Adew Dundee*

This is an early example of Burns's collecting frag-
ments of old folk ballads. The opening stanza was
noted down by Burns on the back of a letter dated
1st February 1787, the remaining lines being com-
posed subsequently. The 'haver-meal bannock' was an
ancient Scots euphemism for the foetus (cf. modern
slang 'bun in the oven').

oatmeal	'O, whar gat ye that hauver-meal bannock?'
	'O silly blin' booby, O dinna ye see?
soldier	I gat it frae a young brisk sodger laddie
Perth	Between Saint Johnston and bonie Dundee.
would, that	'O, gin I saw the laddie that gae me't!
dandled	Aft has he doudl'd me upon his knee;
	May Heaven protect my bonie Scots laddie,
	And send him safe hame to his babie and me!
	'My blessin's upon thy sweet, wee lippie!
eyebrow	My blessin's upon thy bonie e'e-brie!
	Thy smiles are sae like my blythe sodger laddie,
	Thou's ay the dearer and dearer to me!
build	'But I'll big a bow'r on yon bonie banks,
winding	Whare Tay rins wimplin by sae clear;
clothe	An I'll cleed thee in the tartan sae fine,
	And mak thee a man like thy daddie dear.'

EPIGRAM AT ROSLIN INN

Composed early in 1787, after breakfast at Roslin to
which Burns and the painter Nasmyth had walked
after a night's carousing in Edinburgh. Nasmyth states
that this epigram, addressed to Mrs Willson the landlady,
was written on the back of the bill.

My blessings on ye, honest wife!
I ne'er was here before;
Ye've wealth o gear for spoon and knife:
Heart could not wish for more.
Heav'n keep you clear o sturt and strife,   trouble
Till far ayont fourscore,   beyond
And by the Lord o death and life,
I'll ne'er gae by your door!

THE BARD AT INVERARAY

Written on 24th June 1787 when Burns was visiting
Dumbarton and the Clyde coast of Argyll. These terse
lines were allegedly inscribed on the window of the
inn at Inveraray, whose landlord was too busy
attending to a large house-party of the Duke of Argyll
to serve Burns and other travellers.

Whoe'er he be that sojourns here,
 I pity much his case,
Unless he come to wait upon
 The lord *their* god, 'His Grace.'

There's naething here but Highland pride,
 And Highland scab and hunger:
If Providence has sent me here,
 'Twas surely in an anger.

ELEGY ON THE DEATH OF
SIR JAMES HUNTER BLAIR

Sir James Hunter Blair (1741-87) was Lord Provost of
Edinburgh in 1784 and created baronet in 1786.
This elegy was written shortly after Blair's death on
1st July 1787.

The lamp of day with ill-presaging glare,
 Dim, cloudy, sank beneath the western wave;
Th' inconstant blast howl'd thro the darkening air,
 And hollow whistled in the rocky cave.

Lone as I wander'd by each cliff and dell,
 Once the lov'd haunts of Scotia's royal train;
Or mus'd where limpid streams, once hallow'd, well,
 Or mould'ring ruins mark the sacred Fane.

Elegy On The Death Of Sir James Hunter Blair

Th' increasing blast roared round the beetling rocks,
    The clouds, swift-wing'd, flew o'er the starry sky,
The groaning trees untimely shed their locks,
    And shooting meteors caught the startled eye.

The paly moon rose in the livid east,
    And 'mong the cliffs disclos'd a stately form
In weeds of woe, that frantic beat her breast,
    And mix'd her wailings with the raving storm.

Wild to my heart the filial pulses glow:
    'Twas Caledonia's trophied shield I view'd,
Her form majestic droop'd in pensive woe,
    The lightning of her eye in tears imbued.

Revers'd that spear redoubtable in war,
    Reclined that banner, erst in fields unfurl'd,
That like a deathful meteor gleam'd afar,
    And brav'd the mighty monarchs of the world.

'My patriot son fills an untimely grave!'
    With accents wild and lifted arms she cried:
'Low lies the hand that oft was stretch'd to save,
    Low lies the heart that swell'd with honor's pride.

'A weeping country joins a widow's tear;
    The helpless poor mix with the orphan's cry;
The drooping Arts surround their patron's bier;
    And graceful Science heaves the heart-felt sigh.

'I saw my sons resume their ancient fire;
    I saw fair Freedom's blossoms richly blow.
But ah! how hope is born but to expire!
    Relentless fate has laid their guardian low.

'My patriot falls, but shall he lie unsung,
    While empty greatness saves a worthless name?
No: every Muse shall join her tuneful tongue,
    And future ages hear his growing fame.

'And I will join a mother's tender cares
    Thro future times to make his virtues last
That distant years may boast of other Blairs!'
    She said, and vanish'd with the sweeping blast.

TO MISS FERRIER

ENCLOSING THE ELEGY ON SIR J. H. BLAIR

Jane Ferrier (1767-1846) was the eldest daughter of
James Ferrier, W.S. and sister of the novelist Susan
Edmondstone Ferrier. She married General Graham
Depute-Governor of Stirling Castle, and published a
volume of engravings of its ancient carvings in 1817.
She was a famous society beauty when Burns met
her in the summer of 1787 and she requested one of
his poems.

Nae heathen name shall I prefix,
   Frae Pindus or Parnassus;
Auld Reekie dings them a' to sticks,   Edinburgh, knocks down
   For rhyme-inspiring lasses.

Jove's tunefu dochters three times three   the Muses
   Made Homer deep their debtor;
But gien the body half an e'e,
   Nine Ferriers wad done better!

Last day my mind was in a bog;
   Down George's Street I stoited;   George St., Edinburgh
A creeping, cauld, prosaic fog   New Town
   My very senses doited.   dulled

Do what I dought to set her free,
   My saul lay in the mire: soul
Ye turned a neuk, I saw your e'e,   corner
   She took the wing like fire!

The mournfu sang I here enclose,   song
   In gratitude I send you,
And pray, in rhyme as weel as prose,
   A' guid things may attend you!

ON THE DEATH OF JOHN McLEOD, ESQ.

BROTHER TO A YOUNG LADY, A PARTICULAR FRIEND OF THE AUTHOR

Son of the laird of Raasay who had died in 1786, young
John McLeod himself died on 20th July 1787. Burns,
who was friendly with John's sister Isabella, sent these
lines from Mossgiel on reading of John's death in a
newspaper. In the Glenriddell MS Burns added the
comment: 'This poetic compliment, what few poetic
compliments are, was from the heart.'

Sad thy tale, thou idle page,
   And rueful thy alarms:
Death tears the brother of her love
   From Isabella's arms.

Sweetly deckt with pearly dew
   The morning rose may blow;
But cold successive noontide blasts
   May lay its beauties low.

On The Death Of John McLeod, Esq.

Fair on Isabella's morn
   The sun propitious smil'd;
But, long ere noon, succeeding clouds
   Succeeding hopes beguil'd.

Fate oft tears the bosom chords
   That Nature finest strung:
So Isabella's heart was form'd,
   And so that heart was wrung.

Dread Omnipotence alone
   Can heal the wound he gave—
Can point the brimful, grief-worn eyes
   To scenes beyond the grave.

Virtue's blossoms there shall blow,
   And fear no withering blast;
There Isabella's spotless worth
   Shall happy be at last.

YON WILD MOSSY MOUNTAINS

TUNE: *Phebe*

Burns noted cryptically 'The song alludes to a part of my private history, which it is of no consequence to the world to know.' From this it has been conjectured that the lassie referred to was a Lanarkshire girl whom the poet encountered on his way to or from Edinburgh in 1787.

Yon wild mossy mountains sae lofty and wide,
That nurse in their bosom the youth o the Clyde,
Where the grouse lead their coveys thro the heather to feed,
And the shepherd tends his flock as he pipes on his reed.

Not Gowrie's rich valley nor Forth's sunny shores
To me hae the charms o yon wild, mossy moors;
For there, by the lanely, sequestered stream,
Resides a sweet lassie, my thought an my dream.

Amang thae wild mountains shall still be my path,
Ilk stream foaming down its ain green, narrow strath;
For there wi my lassie the day-lang I rove,
While o'er us unheeded flie the swift hours o love.

She is not the fairest, altho she is fair;
O nice education but sma' is her share;
Her parentage humble as humble can be;
But I lo'e the dear lassie because she lo'es me.

284

Yon Wild Mossy Mountains

To Beauty what man but maun yield him a prize,
In her armour of glances, and blushes, and sighs?
And when Wit and Refinement hae polish'd her darts,
They dazzle our een, as they flie to our hearts.

But kindness, sweet kindness, in the fond-sparkling e'e
Has lustre outshining the diamond to me,
And the heart beating love as I'm clasp'd in her arms,
O these are my lassie's all-conquering charms!

HIGHLAND HARRY BACK AGAIN

TUNE: *The Highland Watch's Farewell to Ireland*

Written some time after August 1787, Burns noted in
his personal copy of SMM 'the chorus I pickt up from an
old woman in Dunblane; the rest of the song is mine',
but 'Knockhaspie's land' was the name of a field at
Mossgiel.

CHORUS

O, for him back again!
O, for him back again!
I wad gie a' Knockhaspie's land
For Highland Harry back again.

My Harry was a gallant gay,
    Fu stately strade he on the plain,   strode
But now he's banish'd far away:
    I'll never see him back again.

When a' the lave gae to their bed,   rest
    I wander dowie up the glen,   sadly
I set me down and greet my fill,
    And ay I wish him back again.

O, were some villains hangit high,
    And ilka body had their ain,   every
Then I might see the joyfu sight,
    My Highland Harry back again!

IMPROMPTU ON CARRON
IRON WORKS

Written on 26th August 1787 during the Highland tour. The Carron Iron Works, founded in 1759 and world famous for the cannon known as Carronades, was forced into liquidation in 1983.

works   We cam na here to view your warks
          In hopes to be mair wise,
          But only, lest we gang to Hell,
          It may be nae surprise.
          But when we tirl'd at your door

could not permit   Your porter dought na bear us:
gates   Sae may, should we to Hell's yetts come,
comrade   Your billy Satan sair us.

WRITTEN BY SOMEBODY
ON THE WINDOW

OF AN INN AT STIRLING, ON SEEING THE ROYAL
PALACE IN RUIN

Written on or about 27th August 1787 when Burns and William Nicol supped with 'Messrs Doig the Schoolmaster, Bell and Captn. Forrester of the Castle. D a queerish fellow and a pedant, B a joyous, vacant fellow who sings a good song, Forrester a merry swearing kind of man with a dash of the Sodger.'

          Here Stewarts once in glory reign'd,
          And laws for Scotland's weal ordain'd;
          But now unroof'd their palace stands,
          Their sceptre fallen to other hands;
          Fallen indeed, and to the earth,
          Whence grovelling reptiles take their birth.
          The injured Stewart line is gone,

i.e. the House of   A race outlandish fills their throne:
Hanover   An idiot race, to honour lost—
          Who know them best despise them most.

EPITAPH FOR WILLIAM MICHIE

SCHOOLMASTER OF CLEISH PARISH, FIFESHIRE

Ebenezer Michie (1766-1812) was introduced to Burns by William Nicol and they spent a convivial evening together. This mock epitaph was composed when Michie collapsed in a stupor. The Wallace-Chambers edition gives his name as Ebenezer, and reads 'Eben Michie' in the first line, but this version is preferred by other editors.

bones   Here lie Willie Michie's banes:
          O Satan, when ye tak him,
schooling, brats   Gie him the schulin o your weans,
devils   For clever deils he'll mak them!

STRATHALLAN'S LAMENT

James Drummond, 5th Viscount Strathallan (d. 1765), is allegedly the speaker of this lament for his father, William, killed at Culloden in 1746 — a vehicle used by Burns to air his Jacobite sentiments. The tune to which Burns set these words was specially composed for the occasion by Allan Masterton, an Edinburgh schoolmaster, who shared his Jacobite sympathies. Burns passed through Strathallan on 28th August 1787 and wrote this song on his return to Edinburgh.

Thickest night, surround my dwelling!
Howling tempests, o'er me rave!
Turbid torrents wintry-swelling,
Roaring by my lonely cave!
Crystal streamlets gently flowing,
Busy haunts of base mankind,
Western breezes softly blowing,
Suit not my distracted mind.

In the cause of Right engaged,
Wrongs injurious to redress,
Honour's war we strongly waged,
But the heavens deny'd success.
Ruin's wheel has driven o'er us:
Not a hope that dare attend,
The wide world is all before us,
But a world without a friend.

VERSES WRITTEN WITH A PENCIL

OVER THE CHIMNEY-PIECE, IN THE PARLOUR
OF THE INN AT KENMORE, TAYMOUTH

These lines were first published in the Edinburgh Evening Courant of 6th September 1787, allegedly communicated by 'O.B. of Kenmore who, a few days ago, being on a visit to Taymouth, . . . found the following verses (by the celebrated Ayrshire bard) written on the walls of the Hermitage there.' It is more likely that Burns himself contributed the poem to the newspaper. His journal of the Highland tour (29th August 1787) laconically states 'Taymouth — described in rhyme.'

Admiring Nature in her wildest grace,
These northern scenes with weary feet I trace;
O'er many a winding dale and painful step,
Th' abodes of covey'd grouse and timid sheep,
My savage journey, curious, I pursue,
Till fam'd Breadalbane opens to my view.
The meeting cliffs each deep-sunk glen divides:
The woods, wild-scatter'd, clothe their ample sides;
Th' outstretching lake, imbosomed 'mong the hills,
The eye with wonder and amazement fills:
The Tay meand'ring sweet in infant pride,
The palace rising on his verdant side,

Verses Written With A Pencil

The lawns wood-fring'd in Nature's native taste,
The hillocks dropt in Nature's careless haste,
The arches striding o'er the new-born stream,
The village glittering in the noontide beam—

.   .   .   .

Poetic ardors in my bosom swell,
Lone wand'ring by the hermit's mossy cell;
The sweeping theatre of hanging woods,
Th' incessant roar of headlong tumbling floods—

.   .   .   .

Here Poesy might wake her heav'n-taught lyre,
And look through Nature with creative fire;
Here, to the wrongs of Fate half reconcil'd,
Misfortune's lighten'd steps might wander wild;
And Disappointment, in these lonely bounds,
Fine balm to soothe her bitter rankling wounds;
Here heart-struck Grief might heav'nward
      stretch her scan,
And injur'd Worth forget and pardon man.

.   .   .   .

THE BIRKS OF ABERFELDIE

On 30th August 1787 'I composed these stanzas
standing under the falls of Aberfeldy, at, or near,
Moness.' The chorus comes from the traditional
Aberdeenshire ballad 'Birks of Abergeldie'.

CHORUS

Bonie lassie, will ye go,
Will ye go, will ye go?
Bonie lassie, will ye go

birches

To the birks of Aberfeldie?

Now simmer blinks on flow'ry braes,
And o'er the crystal streamlets plays,
Come, let us spend the lightsome days
    In the birks of Aberfeldie!

The little birdies blythely sing,
While o'er their heads the hazels hing,
Or lightly flit on wanton wing
    In the birks of Aberfeldie!

288

AYR
The Twa Brigs

SHANTER FARM AND BAY

The Birks of Aberfeldie

The braes ascend like lofty wa's,   hillsides
The foaming stream, deep-roaring, fa's
O'erhung wi fragrant-spreading shaws,
    The birks of Aberfeldie.

The hoary cliffs are crown'd wi flowers,
White o'er the linns the burnie pours,   cascades, brooks
And, rising, weets wi misty showers   wets
    The birks of Aberfeldie.

Let Fortune's gifts at random flee,
They ne'er shall draw a wish frae me,
Supremely blest wi love and thee
    In the birks of Aberfeldie.

AMANG THE TREES

TUNE: *The King o France he rade a race*

On 31st August, at Dunkeld, Burns met Neil Gow
(1727-1807), the famous fiddler whom he described
as 'a short, stout-built Highland figure, with his greyish
hair shed on his honest social brow — an interesting
face, marking strong common sense, kind open-
heartedness mixed with unmistrusting simplicity.' This
song was intended as a compliment to him.

Amang the trees, where humming bees
    At buds and flowers were hinging, O,   hanging
Auld Caledon drew out her drone,
    And to her pipe was singing, O.
'Twas Pibroch, Sang, Strathspeys and Reels—
    She dirl'd them aff fu clearly, O,   rang
When there cam a yell o foreign squeels,
    That dang her tapsalteerie, O!   knocked upside
                                                  down

Their capon craws an queer 'ha, ha's,'
    They made our lugs grow eerie, O.   ears
The hungry bike did scrape and fyke,   swarm, make a fuss
    Till we were wae and weary, O.   sad
But a royal ghaist, wha ance was cas'd   King James I
    A prisoner, aughteen year awa,   (1394-1437)
He fir'd a Fiddler in the North,   imprisoned in England,
    That dang them tapsalteerie, O!   1406-24

289

K

THE HUMBLE PETITION OF BRUAR WATER

TO THE NOBLE DUKE OF ATHOLE

This poem was sent by Burns to Josiah Walker, tutor of the Marquis of Tullibardine, son of the Duke of Atholl, from Inverness on 5th September 1787. It had been composed two or three days earlier: 'at least part of it, the effusion of the half hour that I spent at Bruar. I don't mean it was extempore, for I have endeavoured, to brush it up as well as Mr Nichol's chat and the jogging of the chaise would allow.' Burns met Walker at the home of Dr. Blacklock in Edinburgh, and renewed the acquaintance at Blair Atholl on his way north during the Highland tour.

My lord, I know, your noble ear
    Woe ne'er assails in vain;
Embolden'd thus, I beg you'll hear
    Your humble slave complain,
How saucy Phoebus' scorching beams,
    In flaming summer-pride,
Dry-withering, waste my foamy streams,
    And drink my crystal tide.

staring

The lightly-jumping, glowrin trouts,
    That thro my waters play,
If, in their random, wanton spouts,
    They near the margin stray;
If, hapless chance! they linger lang,
    I'm scorching up so shallow,
They're left the whitening stanes amang
    In gasping death to wallow.

wept, vexation

Last day I grat wi spite and teen,
    As poet Burns came by,
That, to a Bard, I should be seen
    Wi half my channel dry;
A panegyric rhyme, I ween,

offered

    Ev'n as I was, he shor'd me;
But had I in my glory been,
    He, kneeling, wad ador'd me.

shelving

Here, foaming down the skelvy rocks,
    In twisting strength I rin;
There high my boiling torrent smokes,

fall

    Wild-roaring o'er a linn:
Enjoying large each spring and well,
    As Nature gave them me,
I am, altho I say't mysel,

going

    Worth gaun a mile to see.

The Humble Petition Of Bruar Water

Would, then, my noble master please
　　To grant my highest wishes,
He'll shade my banks wi tow'ring trees
　　And bonie spreading bushes.
Delighted doubly then, my lord,
　　You'll wander on my banks,
And listen monie a grateful bird
　　Return you tuneful thanks.

The sober laverock, warbling wild,　　　　　　　　lark
　　Shall to the skies aspire;
The gowdspink, Music's gayest child,　　　　　　goldfinch
　　Shall sweetly join the choir;
The blackbird strong, the lintwhite clear,　　　linnet
　　The mavis mild and mellow,　　　　　　　　　thrush
The robin, pensive Autumn cheer
　　In all her locks of yellow.

This, too, a covert shall ensure,
　　To shield them from the storm;
And coward maukin sleep secure,　　　　　　　　hare
　　Low in her grassy form:
Here shall the shepherd make his seat
　　To weave his crown of flow'rs;
Or find a shelt'ring, safe retreat,
　　From prone-descending show'rs.

And here, by sweet, endearing stealth,
　　Shall meet the loving pair,
Despising worlds with all their wealth,
　　As empty idle care:
The flow'rs shall vie, in all their charms,
　　The hour of heav'n to grace;
And birks extend their fragrant arms　　　　　　birches
　　To screen the dear embrace.

Here haply, too, at vernal dawn,
　　Some musing Bard may stray,
And eye the smoking, dewy lawn
　　And misty mountain grey;
Or, by the reaper's nightly beam,
　　Mild-chequering thro the trees,
Rave to my darkly dashing stream,
　　Hoarse-swelling on the breeze.

The Humble Petition Of Bruar Water

Let lofty firs and ashes cool,
  My lowly banks o'erspread,
And view, deep-bending in the pool,
  Their shadows' wat'ry-bed:
Let fragrant birks, in woodbines drest,
  My craggy cliffs adorn,
And, for the little songster's nest,
  The close embow'ring thorn!

So may, old Scotia's darling hope,
  Your little angel band
Spring, like their fathers, up to prop
  Their honour'd native land!
So may, thro Albion's farthest ken,
  To social-flowing glasses,
The grace be—'Athole's honest men
And Athole's bonie lasses!'

A HIGHLAND WELCOME

**Written on Sunday 2nd September 1787 when Burns
and Nicol went up the Garry to Dalnacardoch and
Dalwhinnie.**

When Death's dark stream I ferry o'er
  (A time that surely shall come),
In Heaven itself I'll ask no more,
  Than just a Highland welcome.

LINES ON THE FALLS OF FYERS
NEAR LOCH-NESS
WRITTEN WITH A PENCIL ON THE SPOT

**Written on Wednesday 5th September, when Burns
and Nicol came down the east shore of Loch Ness
from Inverness to Foyers.**

AMONG the heathy hills and ragged woods
The roaring Fyers pours his mossy floods;
Till full he dashes on the rocky mounds,
Where, thro a shapeless breach, his steam resounds,
As high in air the bursting torrents flow,
As deep recoiling surges foam below,
Prone down the rock the whitening sheet descends,
And viewless Echo's ear, astonish'd, rends.
Dim-seen through rising mists and ceaseless show'rs,
The hoary cavern, wide-surrounding, lours:
Still thro the gap the struggling river toils,
And still, below, the horrid caldron boils—

. . . .

292

CASTLE GORDON

Written after visiting the seat of Alexander, 4th Duke
of Gordon, and his beautiful and witty Duchess, Jane
Maxwell, near Fochabers on 7th September 1787.
Burns, who had met the Duchess in Edinburgh and
invited to call, left Nicol at the inn. After taking wine
with his hosts Burns rose to leave, and on being pressed
to stay, explained about Nicol. The Duke suggested
sending a servant to fetch Nicol, but Burns insisted on
accompanying the servant. Nicol, furious at being left
behind, was all packed ready to depart. He gave Burns
the option of accompanying him there and then, or
remaining on his own. Burns had little choice but go on
with his angry companion.

Streams that glide in Orient plains,
Never bound by Winter's chains,
　　Glowing here on golden sands,
There immixed with foulest stains
　　From tyranny's empurpled hands;
These, their richly gleaming waves,
I leave to tyrants and their slaves:
Give me the stream that sweetly laves
　　The banks by Castle Gordon.

Spicy forests ever gay,
Shading from the burning ray
　　Hapless wretches sold to toil;
Or, the ruthless native's way,
　　Bent on slaughter, blood, and spoil;
Woods that ever verdant wave,
I leave the tyrant and the slave:
Give me the groves that lofty brave
　　The storms of Castle Gordon.

Wildly here without control
Nature reigns, and rules the whole;
　　In that sober pensive mood,
Dearest to the feeling soul,
　　She plants the forest, pours the flood.
Life's poor day I'll, musing, rave,
And find at night a sheltering cave,
Where waters flow and wild woods wave
　　By bonie Castle Gordon.

THE YOUNG HIGHLAND ROVER

TUNE: *Morag*

Composed about the same time as the preceding. The
Highland rover of this poem was Prince Charles
Edward Stuart.

Loud blaw the frosty breezes,
　　The snaws the mountains cover.
Like winter on me seizes,
　　Since my young Highland rover
　　Far wanders nations over.

The Young Highland Rover

Where'er he go, where'er he stray,
    May Heaven be his warden!
Return him safe to fair Strathspey
    And bonie Castle Gordon!

The trees, now naked groaning,
    Shall soon wi leaves be hinging,
The birdies, dowie moaning,
    Shall a' be blythely singing,
    And every flower be springing:
Sae I'll rejoice the lee-lang day,
    When (by his mighty Warden)
My youth's return'd to fair Strathspey,
    And bonie Castle Gordon.

THENIEL MENZIES' BONIE MARY

AIR: *The Ruffian's Rant* or *Roy's Wife*

The characters of this song appear to be entirely
fictitious and not identifiable although the brig o Dye
and Darlet are places in Kincardineshire. Burns and
Nicol stayed at Stonehaven on 10th September 1787
to meet some of the bard's Burness relatives.

CHORUS
Theniel Menzies' bonie Mary,
    Theniel Menzies' bonie Mary,
Charlie Grigor tint his plaidie,
    Kissin Theniel's bonie.Mary.

In comin by the brig o Dye,
    At Darlet we a blink did tarry;
As day was dawin in the sky,
    We drank a health to bonie Mary.

Her een sae bright, her brow sae white,
    Her haffet locks as brown's a berry,
And ay they dimpl't wi a smile,
    The rosy cheeks o' bonie Mary.

leaped, live-long
exhausted

We lap an danc'd the lee-lang day,
    Till piper-lads were wae and weary;
But Charlie gat the spring to pay,
    For kissin Theniel's bonie Mary.

LADY ONLIE, HONEST LUCKY

TUNE: *The Ruffian's Rant*

The 'Bucky' of this song is the Banffshire fishing village of Buckie, which Burns visited on 7th September 1787. Thorniebank is a farm about a mile south of the village. This is an early example of a traditional song collected by Burns, on his Highland tour, and subsequently reworked by him.

CHORUS
Lady Onlie, honest lucky,
  Brews guid ale at shore o Bucky:
I wish her sale for her guid ale,
  The best on a' the shore o Bucky!

A' the lads o Thorniebank,
  When they gae to the shore o Bucky,
They'll step in an tak a pint,
  Wi Lady Onlie, honest lucky.

Her house sae bien, her curch sae clean—   snug, kerchief
  I wat she is a dainty chuckie,   old dear
And cheery blinks the ingle-gleede   glances, -blaze
  O Lady Onlie, honest lucky.

BLYTHE WAS SHE

TUNE: *Andro and his Cutty Gun*

Burns records that he composed these verses while staying at Ochtertyre with Sir William Murray in October 1787. The 'Phemie' of l.3 was Miss Euphemia Murray of Lentrose (b. 1769), nicknamed the Flower of Strathmore on account of her dazzling beauty. Miss Murray is said not to have appreciated the honour done to her by Burns. Perhaps she objected to the tune to which the poem was set: 'cutty gun' is a phallic metaphor.

CHORUS
Blythe, blythe and merry was she,
  Blythe was she butt and ben,
Blythe by the banks of Earn,
  And blythe in Glenturit glen!

By Oughtertyre grows the aik,   oak
  On Yarrow banks the birken shaw;   birch, wood
But Phemie was a bonier lass
  Than braes o Yarrow ever saw.   slopes

Her looks were like a flow'r in May,
  Her smile was like a simmer morn:
She tripped by the banks o Earn,
  As light's a bird upon a thorn.

Her bonie face it was as meek
  As onie lamb upon a lea.
The evening sun was ne'er sae sweet
  As was the blink o Phemie's e'e.   glance

295

Blythe Was She

The Highland hills I've wander'd wide,
As o'er the Lawlands I hae been,
But Phemie was the blythest lass
That ever trod the dewy green.

ON SCARING SOME WATER-FOUL
IN LOCH TURIT

Burns visited Sir William Murray and his family when
he was touring Clackmannanshire with Dr. Adair in
1787, and this poem refers to one of the sporting
outings he enjoyed during his stay at Ochtertyre.
Euphemia Murray later recalled how Burns recited
these lines after supper one evening.

Why, ye tenants of the lake,
For me your wat'ry haunt forsake?
Tell me, fellow-creatures, why
At my presence thus you fly?
Why disturb your social joys,
Parent, filial, kindred ties?—
Common friend to you and me,
Nature's gifts to all are free:
Peaceful keep your dimpling wave,
Busy feed, or wanton lave;
Or, beneath the sheltering rock,
Bide the surging billow's shock.

Conscious, blushing for our race,
Soon, too soon, your fears I trace.
Man, your proud, usurping foe,
Would be lord of all below:
Plumes himself in freedom's pride,
Tyrant stern to all beside.

The eagle, from the cliffy brow,
Marking you his prey below,
In his breast no pity dwells,
Strong necessity compels:
But Man, to whom alone is giv'n
A ray direct from pitying Heav'n,
Glories in his heart humane—
And creatures for his pleasure slain!

296

In these savage, liquid plains,
Only known to wand'ring swains,
Where the mossy riv'let strays
Far from human haunts and ways,
All on Nature you depend,
And life's poor season peaceful spend.

Or, of Man's superior might
Dare invade your native right,
On the lofty ether borne,
Man with all his powers you scorn;
Swiftly seek, on clanging wings,
Other lakes, and other springs;
And the foe you cannot brave,
Scorn at least to be his slave.

MY PEGGY'S CHARMS

TUNE: *My Peggy's Charms*

**The subject of this song was Margaret Chalmers (1763-
1843), a cousin of Gavin Hamilton, whom Burns may
have known from his Mauchline days. He sent her
these verses in October 1787 and when she raised
objections to publication he pointed out that 'The
poetic compliments I pay cannot be misunderstood.'
She later told Thomas Campbell the poet that Burns
had proposed to her but she gently turned him down
and they remained good, but platonic, friends.**

My Peggy's face, my Peggy's form
The frost of hermit Age might warm.
My Peggy's worth, my Peggy's mind
Might charm the first of human kind.

I love my Peggy's angel air,
Her face so truly heavenly fair,
Her native grace so void of art:
But I adore my Peggy's heart.

The lily's hue, the rose's dye,
The kindling lustre of an eye—
Who but owns their magic sway?
Who but knows they all decay?

The tender thrill, the pitying tear,
The generous purpose, nobly dear,
The gentle look that rage disarms—
These are all immortal charms.

WHERE, BRAVING ANGRY
WINTER'S STORMS

TUNE: *Neil Gow's Lament for Abercairny*

This song was also written for Margaret Chalmers soon
after Burns had visited her at Harvieston in October
1787. '. . . when I think I have met with you, and have
lived more of real life with you in eight days than I
can do with almost anybody I meet with in eight years
— when I think on the improbability of meeting you
in this world again — I could sit down and cry like a
child', he wrote to her a year later, when her marriage
to the banker Lewis Hay was imminent.

Where, braving angry winter's storms,
    The lofty Ochils rise,
Far in their shade my Peggy's charms
    First blest my wondering eyes:
As one who by some savage stream
    A lonely gem surveys,
Astonish'd doubly, marks its beam
    With art's most polish'd blaze.

Blest be the wild, sequester'd glade,
    And blest the day and hour,
Where Peggy's charms I first survey'd,
    When first I felt their pow'r!
The tyrant Death, with grim control
    May seize my fleeting breath,
But tearing Peggy from my soul
    Must be a stronger death.

THE BANKS OF THE DEVON

TUNE: *Bhannerach dhon na chri*

'These verses were composed on a charming girl, a Miss
Charlotte Hamilton, who is now married to Jas.
McKitrick Adair, Esquire, Physician. She is sister of my
worthy friend Gavin Hamilton.' Miss Hamilton (1763-
1806) was living at Harvieston when Burns met her in
1787, the 'clear winding Devon' being the river
bordering the estate. The song was set to a Gaelic
melody which Burns noted down during his visit to
Inverness.

How pleasant the banks of the clear winding Devon,
    With green spreading bushes and flow'rs blooming fair!
But the boniest flow'r on the banks of the Devon
    Was once a sweet bud on the braes of the Ayr.

Mild be the sun on this sweet blushing flower,
    In the gay rosy morn, as it bathes in the dew!
And gentle the fall of the soft vernal shower,
    That steals on the evening each leaf to renew!

O, spare the dear blossom, ye orient breezes,
    With chill, hoary wing as ye usher the dawn!
And far be thou distant, thou reptile that seizes
    The verdure and pride of the garden or lawn!

The Banks Of The Devon

Let Bourbon exult in his gay gilded lilies,
  And England triumphant display her proud rose!
A fairer than either adorns the green vallies,
  Where Devon, sweet Devon, meandering flows.

EPITAPH FOR WILLIAM NICOL, OF
THE HIGH SCHOOL, EDINBURGH

William Nicol (1744-97) was born in Annan and
studied theology and medicine in Edinburgh before
becoming classical master at Edinburgh High School in
1774. He accompanied Burns on his Highland tour and
despite the incident at Blair Atholl remained a close
friend of the poet who named one of his sons in 1791
after him.

Ye maggots, feed on Nicol's brain,
  For few sic feasts you've gotten;
And fix your claws in Nicol's heart,
  For deil a bit o't's rotten.

CA' THE YOWES TO THE KNOWES

In September 1794 Burns wrote to George Thomson:
'. . . it was owing to me that ever it [this song] saw the
light. About seven years ago, I was well acquainted
with a worthy little fellow of a Clergyman, a Mr.
Clunzie, who sung it charmingly . . . when I gave it to
Johnson, I added some stanzas to the song and mended
others.' This vividly illustrates Burns's role as a
preserver and mender of traditional ballads. 'Mr.
Clunzie' was John Clunie (1757-1819), schoolmaster
and precentor at Markinch.

CHORUS
Ca' the yowes to the knowes,   ewes, hillocks
Ca' them where the heather grows,
Ca' them where the burnie rowes,   stream runs
  My bonie dearie!

As I gaed down the water-side,   went
There I met my shepherd lad:
He row'd me sweetly in his plaid,   wrapped
  An he ca'd me his dearie.

'Will ye gang down the water-side,
And see the waves sae sweetly glide
Beneath the hazels spreading wide?
  The moon it shines fu clearly.'

'Ye sall get gowns and ribbons meet,
Cauf-leather shoon upon your feet,
And in my arms thou'lt lie and sleep,
  An ye sall be my dearie.'

Ca' The Yowes To The Knowes

'If ye'll but stand to what ye've said,
I'se gang wi thee, my shepherd lad,
And ye may row me in your plaid,
And I sall be your dearie.'

meander
sky

'While waters wimple to the sea,
While day blinks in the lift sae hie,
Till clay-cauld death sall blin' my e'e,
Ye sall be my dearie.'

ON THE DEATH OF
LORD PRESIDENT DUNDAS

Robert Dundas, Lord Arniston (1713-87) was Lord
Advocate (1754) and Lord President of the Court of
Session (1760-87). On the death of Dundas on 13th
December, Alexander Wood suggested to Burns that he
write an elegy, a task which the poet tackled with less
than his customary enthusiasm, later admitting that
some verses were 'rather commonplace, and others
rather hide-bound.' Burns sent the poem with a
covering letter to Robert Dundas, jnr. 'His Solicitor-
ship never took the smallest notice of the Letter, the
Poem, or the Poet.'

Lone on the bleaky hills, the straying flocks
Shun the fierce storms among the sheltering rocks;
Down foam the rivulets, red with dashing rains;
The gathering floods burst o'er the distant plains;
Beneath the blast the leafless forests groan
The hollow caves return a hollow moan.

Ye hills, ye plains, ye forests, and ye caves,
Ye howling winds, and wintry swelling waves,
Unheard, unseen, by human ear or eye,
Sad to your sympathetic glooms I fly,
Where, to the whistling blast and water's roar
Pale Scotia's recent wound I may deplore!

O heavy loss, thy country ill could bear!
A loss these evil days can ne'er repair!
Justice, the high vicegerent of her God,
Her doubtful balance eyed, and sway'd her rod;
Hearing the tidings of the fatal blow,
She sank, abandon'd to the wildest woe.

Wrongs, injuries, from many a darksome den,
Now gay in hope, explore the paths of men.
See from his cavern grim Oppression rise,
And throw on Poverty his cruel eyes!
Keen on the helpless victim see him fly,
And stifle, dark, the feeble-bursting cry!

300

On The Death Of Lord President Dundas

Mark ruffian Violence, distained with crimes,
Rousing elate in these degenerate times!
View unsuspecting Innocence a prey,
As guileful Fraud points out the erring way;
While subtile Litigation's pliant tongue
The life-blood equal sucks of Right and Wrong!
Hark, injur'd Want recounts th' unlisten'd tale,
And much-wrong'd Mis'ry pours th' unpitied wail!

Ye dark, waste hills, ye brown, unsightly plains.
Congenial scenes, ye soothe my mournful strains.
Ye tempests, rage! ye turbid torrents, roll!
Ye suit the joyless tenor of my soul.
Life's social haunts and pleasures I resign;
Be nameless wilds and lonely wanderings mine,
To mourn the woes my country must endure:
That wound degenerate ages cannot cure.

SYLVANDER TO CLARINDA

Clarinda was Agnes Craig McLehose (1759-1841), estranged wife of a Glasgow lawyer. Burns met her at Edinburgh on 4th December 1787 and a sentimental affair developed between them. Much of this platonic courtship was conducted by letter, using classical noms de plume in the fashion of the time. Frustrated in the physical side of his affair, Burns returned to Ayrshire and renewed his relationship with Jean Armour — a move for which Agnes accused him of 'perfidious treachery.' This was the first of ten poems and songs which Burns wrote in her honour.

When dear Clarinda, matchless fair,
    First struck Sylvander's raptur'd view,
He gaz'd, he listened to despair—
    Alas! 'twas all he dared to do.

Love from Clarinda's heavenly eyes
    Transfix'd his bosom thro and thro,
But still in Friendship's guarded guise—
    For more the demon fear'd to do.

That heart, already more than lost,
    The imp beleaguer'd all *perdu;*   lost (French)
For frowning Honor kept his post—
    To meet that frown he shrunk to do.

His pangs the Bard refus'd to own,
    Tho half he wish'd Clarinda knew;
But Anguish wrung the unweeting groan—
    Who blames what frantic Pain must do?

301

Sylvander To Clarinda

That heart, where motley follies blend,
  Was sternly still to Honor true:
To prove Clarinda's fondest friend
  Was what a lover, sure, might do.

The Muse his ready quill employ'd,
  No nearer bliss he could pursue;
This bliss Clarinda cold deny'd—
  'Send word by Charles how you do!'

The chill behest disarm'd his Muse,
  Till Passion, all impatient grew:
He wrote, and hinted for excuse,
  'Twas, 'cause 'he'd nothing else to do.'

But by those hopes I have above!
  And by those faults I dearly rue!
The deed, the boldest mark of love,
  For thee, that deed I dare to do!

O, could the Fates but name the price
  Would bless me with your charms and you,
With frantic joy I'd pay it thrice,
  If human art and power could do!

Then take, Clarinda, friendship's hand
  (Friendship, at least, I may avow),
And lay no more your chill command,—
  I'll write, whatever I've to do.

                              SYLVANDER

THE BONIE LASS OF ALBANIE
TUNE: *Mary's Dream*

Charlotte Stuart (1753-89) was the daughter of Bonnie
Prince Charlie by his mistress Clementina Walkinshaw
who had followed him to the Continent. The affair
lasted about eight years before the long-suffering
Clementina left the Prince. As his marriage to Princess
Louise of Stolberg was childless, Charles sought to
have his daughter legitimated, under the title of
Duchess of Albany, at Paris on 6th December 1787 —
the occasion for the composition of this song.

mighty sad

My heart is wae, and unco wae,
  To think upon the raging sea,
That roars between her gardens green
  An the bonie lass of Albanie.

This lovely maid's of royal blood,

England, Scotland
and Ireland

  That rulèd Albion's kingdoms three;
But Oh, alas for her bonie face!
  They hae wrang'd the lass of Albanie.

302

The Bonie Lass Of Albanie

In the rolling tide of spreading Clyde
  There sits an isle of high degree,   the isle of Bute
And a town of fame, whose princely name   Rothesay
  Should grace the lass of Albanie.

But there is a youth, a witless youth,   Prince George,
  That fills the place where she should be;   later Prince
We'll send him o'er to his native shore,   Regent and
  And bring our ain sweet Albanie!   King George IV

Alas the day, and woe the day!
  A false usurper wan the gree,   highest honours
Who now commands the towers and lands,
  The royal right of Albanie.

We'll daily pray, we'll nightly pray,
  On bended knees most fervently,
The time may come, with pipe and drum
  We'll welcome hame fair Albanie.

BIRTHDAY ODE
FOR 31st DECEMBER, 1787

Burns attended a dinner in Edinburgh to celebrate the
birthday of 'the King o'er the water.' Those present
did not seriously entertain 'any hope of . . . the
restoration of the house of Stewart; but over their
sparkling wine, they indulged the generous feelings
which the recollection of fallen greatness is calculated
to inspire . . . [Burns] took upon himself the office of
poet-laureate.' (Currie vol. 1 181-2). It is perhaps
worth noting that the sentimental attachment to the
House of Stuart, which was the extent of Burns's
Jacobitism, was shared ironically by none other than
'the witless youth', Prince George himself. Prince
Charles died at Rome a few weeks later, on 31st
January 1788.

Afar the illustrious Exile roams,
  Whom kingdoms on this day should hail,
An inmate in the casual shed,
On transient pity's bounty fed,
  Haunted by busy Memory's bitter tale!
Beasts of the forest have their savage homes,
  But He, who should imperial purple wear,
Owns not the lap of earth where rests his royal head:
  His wretched refuge, dark despair,
While ravening wrongs and woes pursue,
And distant far the faithful few
  Who would his sorrows share!

Birthday Ode For 31st December, 1787

False flatterer, Hope, away,
Nor think to lure us as in days of yore!
We solemnize this sorrowing natal day,
To prove our loyal truth—we can no more—
And, owning Heaven's mysterious sway,
Submissive, low, adore.
Ye honored, mighty Dead,
Who nobly perish'd in the glorious cause,
Your King, your Country, and her laws,

John Graham of
Claverhouse, Viscount
Dundee (1649-89)

From great Dundee, who smiling victory led,
And fell a Martyr in her arms
(What breast of northern ice but warms!)

Arthur Elphinstone,
Lord Balmerino
(1688-1746)

To bold Balmerino's undying name,
Whose soul of fire, lighted at Heaven's high flame,
Deserves the proudest wreath departed heroes claim!
Not unrevenged your fate shall lie,
It only lags, the fatal hour,
Your blood shall with incessant cry,
Awake at last th' unsparing Power;
As from the cliff, with thundering course,
The snowy ruin smokes along
With doubling speed and gathering force,
Till deep it, crushing, whelms the cottage in the vale,
So Vengeance' arm, ensanguin'd, strong,
Shall with resistless might assail,

i.e. the Elector of
Hanover and Duke
of Brunswick-Luneberg

Usurping Brunswick's pride shall lay,
And Stewart's wrongs and yours, with tenfold weight repay.

PERDITION, baleful child of night,
Rise and revenge the injured right
Of Stewart's royal race!
Lead on the unmuzzled hounds of Hell,
Till all the frightened echoes tell
The blood-notes of the chase!
Full on the quarry point their view,
Full on the base, usurping crew,
The tools of faction and the nation's curse!
Hark how the cry grows on the wind;
They leave the lagging gale behind;
Their savage fury, pityless, they pour;
With murdering eyes already they devour!
See Brunswick spent, a wretched prey,
His life one poor despairing day,
Where each avenging hour still ushers in a worse!
Such Havoc howling all abroad,
Their utter ruin bring,
The base apostates to their God,
Or rebels to their King!

THE BONIE MOOR-HEN

TUNE: *Beware of the Ripells*

Composed at the end of 1787. Clarinda, writing on 6th February 1788, urged Burns not to publish this song on the grounds of its indelicacy. Cromek printed it with a row of asterisks at the end, implying that further stanzas had been cut out, but there is no evidence to support this. Clarinda objected to the sexual undertones of the hunting metaphor.

CHORUS

I rede you, beware at the hunting, young men!   counsel
I rede you, beware at the hunting, young men!
Take some on the wing, and some as they spring,
But cannily steal on a bonie moor-hen.   cautiously

The heather was blooming, the meadows were mawn,   mown
Our lads gaed a-hunting ae day at the dawn,   went, one
O'er moors and o'er mosses and monie a glen:
At length they discovered a bonie moor-hen.

Sweet-bruising the dew from the brown heather bells,
Her colours betray'd her on yon mossy fells!
Her plumage outlustered the pride o the spring,
And O as she wanton'd sae gay on the wing.

Auld Phoebus himsel, as he peep'd o'er the hill,
In spite at her plumage he tryèd his skill:
He levell'd his rays where she bask'd on the brae—   hillside
His rays were outshone, and but mark'd where she lay!

They hunted the valley, they hunted the hill,
The best of our lads wi the best o their skill;
But still as the fairest she sat in their sight,
Then whirr! she was over, a mile at a flight.

ON JOHNSON'S OPINION OF HAMPDEN

Burns read Samuel Johnson's Lives of the English Poets some time before August 1790. The lines are a comment on Johnson's statement that Edmund Waller's mother was 'sister to [John] Hampden, the zealot of rebellion.'

For shame!
Let Folly and Knavery
    Freedom oppose:
'Tis suicide, Genius,
    To mix with her foes.

ANNA, THY CHARMS

Anna Stewart of East Craigs was engaged to the poet's
friend Alexander Cunningham but jilted him in favour
of Forrest Dewar, an Edinburgh physician whom she
married on 24th January 1789. At that time Burns
published this poem in the Edinburgh Star. Writing to
Cunningham he said 'I would scorn to put my name to
a Newspaper Poem . . . Had the lady kept her
character, she should have kept her verses; but as she
prostituted the one, I no longer made anything of the
other.'

Anna, thy charms my bosom fire,
    And waste my soul with care;
But ah! how bootless to admire,
    When fated to despair!

Yet in thy presence, lovely Fair,
    To hope may be forgiven:
For sure 'twere impious to despair
    So much in sight of Heaven.

ON BEING APPOINTED TO AN
EXCISE DIVISION

Burns received his commission on 14th July 1788, but
this poem may be rather earlier, dating from his six-
week probationary period. Burns first considered the
Excise as a career late in 1786 when plans to emigrate
were abandoned. In January 1788 he enlisted the help
of Robert Graham of Fintry, a Commissioner of Excise
whom he had met on his Highland tour. He began
training in February 1788.

	Searching auld wives' barrels,
Alas	Ochon, the day!
dirty yeast	That clarty barm should stain my laurels!
	But, what'll ye say?
brats	These movin things ca'd wives an weans
	Wad move the very hearts o stanes!

TO THE WEAVER'S GIN YOU GO

'The chorus of this song is old' wrote Burns in his note
for SMM, 'the rest of it is mine . . . Many beautiful airs
wanted words; in the hurry of other avocations, if I
could string a parcel of rhymes together anything near
tolerable, I was fain to let them pass. He must be an
excellent poet indeed, whose every performance is
excellent.'

CHORUS

should	*To the weaver's gin ye go, fair maids,*
	To the weaver's gin ye go,
warn, go	*I rede you right, gang ne'er at night,*
	To the weaver's gin ye go.
once	My heart was ance as blythe and free
	As simmer days were lang;
western	But a bonie, westlin weaver lad
made	Has gart me change my sang.

306

To The Weaver's Gin You Go

My mither sent me to the town,
   To warp a plaiden wab;
But the weary, weary warpin o't
   Has gart me sigh and sab.   sob

A bonie, westlin weaver lad
   Sat working at his loom;
He took my heart, as wi a net,
   In every knot and thrum.

I sat beside my warpin-wheel,
   And ay I ca'd it roun.   drove
But every shot and every knock,
   My heart it gae a stoun.   ache

The moon was sinking in the west,
   Wi visage pale and wan,
As my bonie, westlin weaver lad
   Convoy'd me thro the glen.

But what was said, or what was done,
   Shame fa' me gin I tell;   befall, if
But Oh! I fear the kintra soon   country
   Will ken as weel's mysel!   know

I'M O'ER YOUNG TO MARRY YET

Another example of an old chorus, with original verses supplied by Burns.

CHORUS

I'm o'er young, I'm o'er young,   far too
*   I'm o'er young to marry yet!*
I'm o'er young, 'twad be a sin
*   To tak me frae my mammie yet.*

I am my mammie's ae bairn,   only child
   Wi unco folk I weary, Sir;   strangers
And lying in a strange bed,
   I'm fley'd it make me eerie, Sir.   afraid, apprehensive

Hallowmass is come and gane,
   The nights are lang in winter, Sir,
And you and I in ae bed,   one
   In trowth, I dare na venture, Sir! truth

Fu loud an shrill the frosty wind
   Blaws thro the leafless timmer, Sir; woods
But if ye come this gate again,   way
   I'll aulder be gin simmer, Sir.   older be by

McPHERSON'S FAREWELL

TUNE: *McPherson's Rant*

James McPherson was the illegitimate son of McPherson of Invershie by a gipsy mother, and was renowned as much for his skill as a fiddler as he was feared as a freebooter. He and his gang terrorised the counties of Aberdeen, Banff and Moray until he was captured by Duff of Braco and tried at Banff. Shortly before his execution in the market place of Banff in November 1700 he played this tune on his fiddle and then smashed the instrument before the assembled crowd.

CHORUS

Sae rantingly, sae wantonly,

went   *Sae dauntingly gaed he,*

He play'd a spring, and danc'd it round

Below the gallow-tree.

Farewell, ye dungeons dark and strong,
     The wretch's destinie!
M'Pherson's time will not be long
     On yonder gallows-tree.

O what is death but parting breath?
     On many a bloody plain
I've dared his face, and in this place
     I scorn him yet again!

Untie these bands from off my hands,
     And bring to me my sword,
And there's no a man in all Scotland
     But I'll brave him at a word.

trouble   I've liv'd a life of sturt and strife;
     I die by treacherie:
It burns my heart I must depart,
     And not avengèd be.

Now farewell light, thou sunshine bright,
     And all beneath the sky!
May coward shame distain his name,
     The wretch that dare not die!

STAY, MY CHARMER

TUNE: *An Gille dubh*

Possibly based on an old ballad collected during the Highland tour.

Stay, my charmer, can you leave me?
Cruel, cruel to deceive me!
Well you know how much you grieve me!
     Cruel charmer, can you go?
     Cruel charmer, can you go?

Stay, My Charmer

By my love so ill-requited,
By the faith you fondly plighted,
By the pangs of lovers slighted,
    Do not, do not leave me so!
    Do not, do not leave me so!

MY HOGGIE

TUNE: *Moss Platt*

Based on a traditional ballad, sung by an old lady in the clachan of Moss Platt in Liddesdale.

What will I do gin my hoggie die?   should, lamb
    My joy, my pride, my hoggie!
My only beast, I had nae mae,   no more
    And vow but I was vogie!   vain
The lee-lang night we watched the fauld,   live-long, fold
    Me and my faithfu doggie;
We heard nocht but the roaring linn,   waterfall
    Amang the braes sae scroggie.   slopes, scrubby

But the houlet cry'd frae the castle wa',   owl
    The blitter frae the boggie,   snipe
The tod reply'd upon the hill: fox
    I trembled for my hoggie.
When day did daw, and cocks did craw,
    The morning it was foggie,
An unco tyke lap o'er the dyke,   strange dog, fence
    And maist has kill'd my hoggie!   almost

JUMPIN JOHN

Stenhouse says that this is 'a fragment of the old humorous ballad, with some verbal corrections,' but the ballad has not been identified.

CHORUS
The lang lad they ca' Jumpin John
Beguil'd the bonie lassie!
The lang lad they ca' Jumpin John
Beguil'd the bonie lassie!

Her daddie forbad, her minnie forbad;   mother
    Forbidden she wadna be: would not
She wadna trow't, the browst she brew'd   believe, liquor
    Wad taste sae bitterlie!

A cow and a cauf, a yowe and a hauf,   ewe, half
    And thretty guid shillins and three: thirty
A vera guid tocher, a cotter-man's dochter,   dowry, daughter
    The lass with the bonie black e'e.

309

UP IN THE MORNING EARLY

'The chorus of this is old,' noted Burns 'the two stanzas
are mine.'

CHORUS

Up in the morning's no for me,
Up in the morning early!
When a' the hills are cover'd wi snaw
I'm sure it's winter fairly!

Cauld blaws the wind frae east to west,
sorely   The drift is driving sairly,
Sae loud and shrill's I hear the blast—
I'm sure it's winter fairly!

The birds sit chittering in the thorn,
    A day they fare but sparely;
evening   And lang's the night frae e'en to morn—
I'm sure it's winter fairly.

THE DUSTY MILLER

An expansion of a traditional fragment.

Hey, the dusty miller,
    And his dusty coat!
He will win a shilling,
Before   Or he win a groat.
Dusty was the coat,
    Dusty was the colour,
Dusty was the kiss
    That I gat frae the miller!

Hey the dusty miller,
    And his dusty sack!
Blessings   Leeze me on the calling
    Fills the dusty peck!
Fills the dusty peck,
    Brings the dusty siller!
I wad gae my coatie
    For the dusty miller!

DUNCAN DAVISON

Based on a snatch of a bawdy ballad which Burns collected on his Border tour. He cleaned up the first four lines and added the rest.

There was a lass, they ca'd her Meg,
    And she held o'er the moors to spin;
There was a lad that follow'd her,
    They ca'd him Duncan Davison.
The moon was dreigh, and Meg was skeigh,   dull, skittish
    Her favour Duncan could na win;
For wi the rock she wad him knock,   distaff
    And ay she shook the temper-pin.   tuning-screw

As o'er the moor they lightly foor,   fared
    A burn was clear, a glen was green;
Upon the banks they eas'd their shanks,
    And ay she set the wheel between:
But Duncan swoor a haly aith,   holy oath
    That Meg should be a bride the morn;   tomorrow
Then Meg took up her spinnin-graith,   -implements
    And flang them a' out o'er the burn.   across the brook

We will big a wee, wee house,   build
    And we will live like king and queen,
Sae blythe and merry's we will be,
    When ye set by the wheel at e'en!   sit beside
A man may drink, and no be drunk;
    A man may fight, and no be slain;
A man may kiss a bonie lass,
    And ay be welcome back again!

WHERE HELEN LIES

This well-known old ballad tells the story of Helen Irvine of Kirkconnel near Springkell. She had two suitors one of whom shot at his rival; but Helen, thrusting herself in front of her lover, Adam Fleming received the fatal wound instead. Fleming killed his assailant on the spot, but fled the country to avoid the legal process and enlisted in the Spanish army. Years later, he returned to Kirkconnel and died by Helen's grave. He was interred alongside her. This tragic event took place in the 16th century. Burns extensively reworked the ballad for both Johnson and Thomson, writing to the latter in 1793 that the original 'is silly, to contemptibility'.

O that I were where Helen lies,
Night and day on me she cries;
O that I were where Helen lies
    In fair Kirkconnel lee.
O Helen fair beyond compare,
A ringlet of thy flowing hair,
I'll wear it still for ever mair
    Until the day I die.

Where Helen Lies

Curs'd be the hand that shot the shot.
And curs'd the gun that gave the crack!
fell   Into my arms bird Helen lap,
    And died for sake o me!
O think na ye but my heart was sair;
My Love fell down and spake nae mair;
much   There did she swoon wi meikle care
    On fair Kirkconnel lee.

I lighted down, my sword did draw,
I cutted him in pieces sma';
I cutted him in pieces sma'
    On fair Kirkconnel lee.
O Helen chaste, thou wert modest,
If I were with thee I were blest
Where thou lies low and takes thy rest
    On fair Kirkconnel lee.

I wish my grave was growing green,
A winding sheet put o'er my e'en,
And I in Helen's arms lying
    In fair Kirkconnel lee!
I wish I were where Helen lies!
Night and day on me she cries:
O that I were where Helen lies
    On fair Kirkconnel lee.

WEARY FA' YOU, DUNCAN GRAY

TUNE: *Duncan Gray*

Based on a traditional song in the Herd MSS.

Woe betide   Weary fa' you, Duncan Gray!
    (Ha, ha, the girdin o't!)
Wae gae by you, Duncan Gray!
    (Ha, ha, the girdin o't!)
rest   When a' the lave gae to their play,
must, live-long   Then I maun sit the lee-lang day,
rock, toe   And jeeg the cradle wi my tae,
    And a' for the girdin o't!

Bonie was the Lammas moon,
    (Ha, ha, the girdin o't!)
staring   Glow'rin a' the hills, aboon,
    (Ha, ha, the girdin o't!)
broke   The girdin brak, the beast cam down,
lost, kerchief, both shoes   I tint my curch and baith my shoon,
awful fool   And, Duncan, ye're an unco loun—
    Wae on the bad girdin o't!

Weary Fa' You, Duncan Gray

But, Duncan, gin ye'll keep your aith,
   (Ha, ha, the girdin o't!),
I'se bless you wi my hindmost breath,
   (Ha, ha, the girdin o't!)
Duncan, gin ye'll keep your aith,
The beast again can bear us baith,   both
And auld Mess John will mend the skaith,   Master, damage
   And clout the bad girdin o't.   patch

THE PLOUGHMAN

**A typical example of Burns's reworking of a traditional
song, known in both polite and bawdy versions.**

CHORUS

*Then up wi't a', my Ploughman lad,
   And hey, my merry Ploughman;
Of a' the trades that I do ken,
   Commend me to the Ploughman.*

The Ploughman he's a bony lad,
   His mind is ever true, jo,   darling
His garters knit below his knee,
   His bonnet it is blue, jo.

My Ploughman he comes hame at e'en,
   He's aften wat and weary: often wet
Cast off the wat, put on the dry,
   And gae to bed, my Dearie.

I will wash my Ploughman's hose,
   And I will dress his o'erlay;   cravat
I will mak my Ploughman's bed,
   And cheer him late and early.

I hac been east, I hae been west,
   I hae been at Saint Johnston,   Perth
The boniest sight that e'er I saw
   Was th' Ploughman laddie dancin.

Snaw-white stockins on his legs,
   And siller buckles glancin;
A gude blue bonnet on his head,
   And O but he was handsome!

Commend me to the Barn yard,
   And the Corn-mou, man;
I never gat my Coggie fou   corn measure (slang:
   Till I met wi the Ploughman.   womb)

HEY TUTI TATEY

Composed from some traditional fragments, set to an old air.

CHORUS

Hey tuti tatey, How tuti taiti,
Hey tuti taiti, wha's fou now.   drunk

Landlady count the lawin,   reckoning
The day is near the dawin,   dawning
Ye're a' blind drunk, boys,
     And I'm jolly fou.

Cog an ye were ay fou,   cup, full
Cog an ye were ay fou;
I wad sit and sing to you,
     If ye were ay fou.

Weel may we a' be,
Ill may we never see!
God bless the king
     And the Companie!

RAVING WINDS AROUND
HER BLOWING

TUNE: *M'Grigor of Roro's Lament*

'I composed these verses', says Burns, 'on Miss Isabella McLeod of Raza, alluding to her feelings on the death of her sister, and the still more melancholy death of her sister's husband, the late Earl of Loudon, who shot himself out of sheer heart-break at some mortifications he suffered, owing to the deranged state of his finances.' The sister was Miss Flora McLeod of Raasay.

Raving winds around her blowing,
Yellow leaves the woodlands strowing,
By a river hoarsely roaring,
Isabella stray'd deploring—

'Farewell hours that late did measure
Sunshine days of joy and pleasure!
Hail, thou gloomy night of sorrow—
Cheerless night that knows no morrow!

'O'er the Past too fondly wandering,
On the hopeless Future pondering,
Chilly Grief my life-blood freezes,
Fell Despair my fancy seizes.

'Life, thou soul of every blessing,
Load to Misery most distressing,
Gladly how would I resign thee,
And to dark Oblivion join thee!'

MUSING ON THE ROARING OCEAN

TUNE: *Druimionn dubh*

Composed 'out of compliment to a Mrs McLachlan, whose husband is an officer in the East Indies,' and first published in the second volume of Johnson's Museum.

Musing on the roaring ocean,
    Which divides my love and me,
Wearying heav'n in warm devotion
    For his weal where'er he be.

Hope and Fear's alternate billow
    Yielding late to Nature's law,
Whispering spirits round my pillow,
    Talk of him that's far awa .

Ye whom sorrow never wounded,
    Ye who never shed a tear,
Care-untroubled, joy-surrounded,
    Gaudy day to you is dear!

Gentle night, do thou befriend me!
    Downy sleep, the curtain draw!
Spirits kind, again attend me,
    Talk of him that's far awa!

TO DAUNTON ME

Derived from an old Jacobite ballad, dating from the Rebellion of 1715, the singer being forced to part from her Highland lad and marry an old man — a variation on the age-old theme of the elderly lover and his young bride.

REFRAIN

To daunton me, to daunton me,
An auld man shall never daunton me!

The blude-red rose at Yule may blaw,
The simmer lilies bloom in snaw,
The frost may freeze the deepest sea,
But an auld man shall never daunton me.

To daunton me, and me sae young,
Wi his fause heart and flatt'ring tongue
That is the thing you ne'er shall see,
For an auld man shall never daunton me.

For a' his meal and a' his maut,   malt
For a' his fresh beef and his saut,   salt
For a' his gold and white monie,
An auld man shall never daunton me.

315

wealth, cattle, sheep	His gear may buy him kye and yowes,
knolls	His gear may buy him glens and knowes;
	But me he shall not buy nor fee,
	For an auld man shall never daunton me.
limps, can	He hirples twa-fauld as he dow,
mouth, bald pate	Wi his teethless gab and his auld beld pow,
eye	And the rain rains down frae his red blear'd e'e—
	That auld man shall never daunton me!

INTERPOLATION

Your friendship much can make me blest,
  Oh, why that bliss destroy!
Why urge the only, one request
  You know I will deny!

Your thought, if love must harbour there,
  Conceal it in that thought;
Nor cause me from my bosom tear
  The very friend I sought.

O'ER THE WATER TO CHARLIE

Based on a traditional Jacobite song.

CHORUS
We'll o'er the water, we'll o'er the sea,
  We'll o'er the water to Charlie;

good fortune *Come weal, come woe, we'll gather and go.*
  And live or die wi Charlie.

Come boat me o'er, come row me o'er,
  Come boat me o'er to Charlie;

halfpenny I'll gie John Ross anither bawbee
  To boat me o'er to Charlie.

I lo'e weel my Charlie's name,
  Tho some there be abhor him:

the Devil But O, to see auld Nick gaun hame,
foes   And Charlie's faes before him!

I swear and vow by moon and stars,
  And sun that shines so early!
If I had twenty thousand lives,

often   I'd die as aft for Charlie.—

UP AND WARN A' WILLIE

A satirical ballad on the Battle of Sherriffmuir
(November 1715) between the Hanoverians under
Argyll and the Jacobites under the Earl of Mar. Burns
extensively revised it for SMM. Burns got the song
from Tom Neil of Edinburgh. The title was the cryptic
slogan used by the clansmen as a call to arms. Both
sides claimed victory. The Jacobites routed the
Hanoverian left wing commanded by General
Whetham, while Argyll drove the Jacobite left-wing
back 2 miles. Argyll was nearly encircled by the
Highlanders, but both sides tired and withdrew
without forcing the decision.

Up and warn a' Willie,
  Warn, warn a';
To hear my cantie Highland sang,   joyful, song
  Relate the thing I saw, Willie.

When we gaed to the braes o Mar,   went
  And to the wapon-shaw, Willie,   review of arms
Wi true design to serve the king
  And banish whigs awa, Willie.
Up and warn a', Willie,
  Warn, warn a';
For Lords and lairds came there bedeen   early
  And wow but they were braw, Willie.   handsome

But when the standard was set up
  Right fierce the wind did blaw, Willie;
The royal nit upon the tap   nut, top
  Down to the ground did fa', Willie.
Up and warn a', Willie,
  Warn, warn a';
Then second-sighted Sandie said
  We'd do nae gude at a', Willie.

But when the army join'd at Perth,
  The bravest ere ye saw, Willie,
We didna doubt the rogues to rout,
  Restore our king and a', Willie.
Up and warn a' Willie,
  Warn, warn a';
The pipers play'd frae right to left
  O whirry whigs awa, Willie.

But when we march'd to Sherramuir   Sheriffmuir
  And there the rebels saw, Willie;
Brave Argyle attack'd our right,
  Our flank and front and a', Willie.
Up and warn a', Willie,
  Warn, warn a',
Traitor Huntly soon gave way   Earl of Huntly
  Seaforth, St. Clair and a' Willie.   Earl of Seaforth

Up An Warn A' Willie

MacDonnell of Glengarry

But brave Glengary on our right,
    The rebel's left did claw, Willie,
He there the greatest slaughter made
    That ever Donald saw, Willie.
Up and warn a', Willie,
    Warn, warn a',

General Whetham, breeches run

And Whittam shat his breeks for fear
    And fast did rin awa, Willie.

For he ca'd us a Highland mob
    And soon he'd slay us a', Willie;

bridge

But we chas'd him back to Stirling brig
    Dragoons and foot and a', Willie.
Up and warn a' Willie,
    Warn, warn a',
At length we rallied on a hill
    And briskly up did draw, Willie.

A ROSE—BUD BY MY EARLY WALK

TUNE: *A Rose-bud*

Composed on Miss Jean Cruikshank, daughter of William Cruikshank (d. 1795), Latin master at the High School of Edinburgh. Jean was only twelve years old at the time of composition, but even at that tender age she was an accomplished musician, able to sing Burns's songs to her own accompaniment.

A rose-bud, by my early walk

footpath

Adown a corn-inclosèd bawk,
Sae gently bent its thorny stalk,
    All on a·dewy morning.
Ere twice the shades o dawn are fled,
In a' its crimson glory spread,
And drooping rich the dewy head,
    It scents the early morning.

Within the bush her covert nest
A little linnet fondly prest,
The dew sat chilly on her breast,
    Sae early in the morning.
She soon shall see her tender brood,
The pride, the pleasure o the wood,
Amang the fresh green leaves bedew'd,
    Awake the early morning.

So thou, dear bird, young Jeany fair,
On trembling string or vocal air,
Shall sweetly pay the tender care

guards

    That tents thy early morning!
So thou, sweet rose-bud, young and gay,
Shall beauteous blaze upon the day,
And bless the parent's evening ray
    That watch'd thy early morning!

318

REVISION FOR CLARINDA

This was Burn's revision of a poem by Mrs Agnes
McLehose entitled 'To a Blackbird singing on a Tree',
composed at Morningside in 1784 and which she sent
to him on 19th January 1788. He sent his revision to
her accompanied by a letter two days later. It later
appeared in SMM 1788 entitled 'To a Blackbird, by a
Lady'.

Go on, sweet bird, and soothe my care,
Thy tuneful notes will hush Despair;
Thy plaintive warblings void of art
Thrill sweetly thro my aching heart.
Now chuse thy mate, and fondly love,
And all the charming transport prove;
While I a lovelorn exile live,
Nor transport or receive or give.

For thee is laughing Nature gay;
For thee she pours the vernal day;
For me in vain is Nature drest,
While joy's a stranger to my breast!
These sweet emotions all enjoy;
Let love and song thy hours employ!
Go on, sweet bird, and soothe my care;
Thy tuneful note will hush Despair.

AND I'LL KISS THEE YET
BONIE PEGGY ALISON

TUNE: *The Braes o Balquhidder*

Controversy continues to range over the subject of
this song. Alison Begbie seems the likelier contender,
though arguments in favour of Mary Campbell are
occasionally put forward.

CHORUS
And I'll kiss thee yet, yet,
And I'll kiss thee o'er again,
And I'll kiss thee yet, yet,
My bonie Peggy Alison.

Ilk care and fear, when thou art near	each
I ever mair defy them, O!	more
Young kings upon their hansel throne	good-luck
Are no sae blest as I am, O!	

When in my arms, wi a' thy charms,	
I clasp my countless treasure, O!	
I seek nae mair o Heav'n to share	no more
Than sic a moment's pleasure, O!	such

And by thy een sae bonie blue	eyes
I swear I'm thine for ever, O!	
And on thy lips I seal my vow,	
And break it shall I never, O!	

319

RATTLIN, ROARIN WILLIE

William Dunbar (d.1807) was a Writer to the Signet and 'colonel' of the Crochallan Fencibles, the Edinburgh drinking club with which Burns was associated and for which many of the bawdy ballads in the Merry Muses were produced. This song, based on the traditional Border ballad 'Rattling, Rovin Willie,' conveys something of Dunbar's rumbustious good humour. The Crochallan Fencibles, named jokingly after the militia regiments raised at the time of the American War, met in the tavern kept by Dawnie Douglas, a habitual singer of Crodh Chailein (Colin's Cattle).

roistering

O, rattlin, roarin Willie,
  O, he held to the fair,
An for to sell his fiddle
  An buy some other ware;
But parting wi his fiddle,

sale

  The saut tear blin't his e'e—
And rattlin, roarin Willie,
  Ye're welcome hame to me.

O Willie, come sell your fiddle,
  O, sell your fiddle sae fine!
O Willie, come sell your fiddle,
  And buy a pint o wine!
If I should sell my fiddle,
  The warld would think I was mad;

rollicking

For monie a rantin day
  My fiddle an I hae had.

As I cam by Crochallan,

cautionsly peeped inside

  I cannilie keekit ben;
Rattlin, roaring Willie,

table-end

  Was sittin at yon boord-en';
Sitting at yon boord-en',
  And amang guid companie;
Rattlin, roarin Willie,
  Ye're welcome hame to me.

CLARINDA, MISTRESS OF MY SOUL

In a letter to Agnes McLehose, Burns wrote: 'My song was a real affair. It was un petit egaremen du coeur . . . but circumstances are too romantic to be credited.' The melody to which this is sung was specially composed by J.G.C. Schetky of Darmstadt, who came to Edinburgh in 1772.

Clarinda, mistress of my soul,
  The measur'd time is run!
The wretch beneath the dreary pole
  So marks his latest sun.

OLD BRIG O DOON

NEW BRIG O DOON
with Burns Monument

Clarinda, Mistress Of My Soul

To what dark cave of frozen night
    Shall poor Sylander hie,
Depriv'd of thee, his life and light,
    The sun of all his joy?

We part—but, by these precious drops
    That fill thy lovely eyes,
No other light shall guide my steps
    Till thy bright beams arise!

She, the fair sun of all her sex,
    Has blest my glorius day;
And shall a glimmering planet fix
    My worship to its ray?

THE WINTER IT IS PAST

Based on a ballad about the notorious Irish
highwayman Johnson, hanged in 1750 for armed
robbery at the Curragh, Kildare. Burns omitted two
stanzas referring to this incident and subjected the rest
to considerable variation.

The winter it is past, and the simmer comes at last,
    And the small birds sing on ev'ry tree:
The hearts of these are glad, but mine is very sad,
    For my true love is parted from me.

The rose upon the brier, by the waters running clear
    May have charms for the linnet or the bee:
Their little loves are blest, and their little hearts at rest,
    But my lover is parted from me.

VERSES TO CLARINDA

SENT WITH A PAIR OF WINE-GLASSES

Composed shortly before leaving Edinburgh in March
1788, these verses accompanied a present of wine-
glasses on 17th March.

Fair Empress of the Poet's soul
    And Queen of Poetesses,
Clarinda, take this little boon,
    This humble pair of glasses:

And fill them up with generous juice,
    As generous as your mind;
And pledge them to the generous toast,
    'The whole of human kind!'

'To those who love us!' second fill:
    But not to those whom *we* love,
Lest we love those who love not us!
    A third— 'To thee and me, love!'

321

THE CHEVALIER'S LAMENT

AIR: *Captain O'Kean*

This lament Burns puts into the mouth of Prince
Charles Edward Stuart after the battle of Culloden. A
draft of the opening lines was sent to Robert Cleghorn
on 31st March 1788, as 'Captain O'Kean' was a
favourite tune of his. Cleghorn thought that the verses
'fit the tune to a hair.'

The small birds rejoice in the green leaves returning,
The murmuring streamlet winds clear thro the vale,
The primroses blow in the dews of the morning,
And wild scatter'd cowslips bedeck the green dale:
But what can give pleasure, or what can seem fair,
When the lingering moments are number'd by care?
No flow'rs gaily springing, nor birds sweetly singing,
Can soothe the sad bosom of joyless despair!

The deed that I dar'd, could it merit their malice,
A king and a father to place on his throne?
His right are these hills, and his right are those valleys,
Where the wild beasts find shelter, tho I can find none!
But 'tis not my suff'rings this wretched, forlorn—
My brave gallant friends, 'Tis your ruin I mourn!
Your faith prov'd so loyal in hot bloody trial,
Alas! can I make it no better return?

EPITAPH ON ROBERT MUIR

Robert Muir (1758-88), a Kilmarnock wine merchant
whom Burns first met in 1786, became a close friend.
He was one of the first to be apprised of the birth of
Jean Armour's first pair of twins. He subscribed for 72
copies of the Kilmarnock Edition and 40 of the first
Edinburgh Edition. He died of tuberculosis on 22nd
April 1788.

What man could esteem, or what woman could love,
    Was he who lies under this sod:
If such Thou refusest admission above,
    Then whom wilt Thou favour, Good God?

EPISTLE TO HUGH PARKER

Hugh Parker, brother of Major William Parker, was a
Kilmarnock banker to whom Burns wrote this verse-
epistle complaining of the smoke in the hut near the
tower of Isle, where he lived while the farmhouse at
Ellisland was being erected. Jenny Geddes was Burns's
horse, named after the woman who, on 23rd August
1637, threw her foot-stool at the Bishop of Edinburgh
in St. Giles Cathedral while trying to introduce The
Book of Common Prayer.

In this strange land, this uncouth clime,
A land unknown to prose or rhyme;
hackles | Where words ne'er cros't the Muses's heckles,
Nor limpit in poetic shackles:

Epistle To Hugh Parker

A land that Prose did never view it,
Except when drunk he stacher't thro it: staggered
Here, ambush'd by the chimla cheek   chimney
Hid in an atmosphere of reek,
I hear a wheel thrum i' the neuk,   spin, corner
I hear it—for in vain I leuk: look
The red peat gleams, a fiery kernel
Enhuskèd by a fog infernal.
Here, for my wonted rhyming raptures,
I sit and count my sins by chapters;
For life and spunk like ither Christians,   spirit
I'm dwindled down to mere existence:
Wi nae converse but Gallowa' bodies,
Wi nae kend face but Jenny Geddes.   known
Jenny, my Pegasean pride,
Dowie she saunters down Nithside,   gloomily
And ay a westlin leuk she throws,   westering
While tears hap o'er her auld brown nose!   cover
Was it for this, wi cannie care,   cautious
Thou bure the Bard through many a shire?   bore
At howes or hillocks never stumbled,   hollows
And late or early never grumbled?
O, had I power like inclination,
I'd heeze thee up a constellation!   elevate
To canter with the Sagitarre,
Or loup the Ecliptic like a bar,   leap
Or turn the Pole like any arrow;
Or, when auld Phoebus bids good-morrow,
Down the Zodiac urge the race,
And cast dirt on his godship's face:
For I could lay my bread and kail   wager, broth
He'd ne'er cast saut upo' thy tail!—   salt
Wi a' this care and a' this grief,
And sma', sma' prospect of relief,
And nought but peat reek i' my head,
How can I write what ye can read?—
Tarbolton, twenty-fourth o June,
Ye'll find me in a better tune;
But till we meet and weet our whistle,   wet
Tak this excuse for nae epistle.

                        ROBERT BURNS

VERSES IN FRIARS'
CARSE HERMITAGE

Burns took up residence at Ellisland on 13th June 1788 and may have been introduced to Robert Riddell of Glenriddell (1755-94) by his landlord, Patrick Miller of Dalswinton at that time. Within two weeks he was composing these verses in the summer-house on Riddell's estate, to which he had been given a key. This poem was but the first of several inspired by the friendship between Burns and Captain Riddell.

Thou whom chance may hither lead,
Be thou clad in russet weed,
Be thou deckt in silken stole,
Grave these maxims on thy soul.
Life is but a day at most,
Sprung from night in darkness lost;
Hope not sunshine every hour,
Fear not clouds will always lour.

Happiness is but a name,
Make content and ease thy aim.
Ambition is a meteor-gleam;
Fame a restless idle dream;
Pleasures, insects on the wing
Peace, th' tend'rest flow'r of spring,
Those that sip the dew alone—
Make the butterflies thy own;
Those that would the bloom devour—
Crush the locusts, save the flower.

For the future be prepar'd:
Guard wherever thou can'st guard;
But, thy utmost duly done,
Welcome what thou can'st not shun.
Follies past, give thou to air,
Make their consequence thy care.
Keep the name of Man in mind,
And dishonour not thy kind.
Reverence with lowly heart
Him, whose wondrous work thou art;
Keep His Goodness still in view—
Thy trust, and thy example, too.

Stranger, go! Heaven by thy guide!
Quod the Beadsman on Nidside.

WRITTEN IN FRIARS' CARSE HERMITAGE, ON NITHSIDE

Later Version

This version was composed some months later, and
was sent to Mrs Dunlop on 7th December 1788. Both
versions were subsequently put into the Glenriddell MS.

Thou whom chance may hither lead,
Be thou clad in russet weed,
Be thou deckt in silken stole,
Grave these counsels on thy soul.

Life is but a day at most,
Sprung from night,—in darkness lost:
Hope not sunshine ev'ry hour,
Fear not clouds will always lour.

As Youth and Love, with sprightly dance
Beneath thy morning star advance,
Pleasure with her siren air
May delude the thoughtless pair:
Let Prudence bless Enjoyment's cup,
Then raptur'd sip, and sip it up.

As thy day grows warm and high,
Life's meridian flaming nigh,
Dost thou spurn the humble vale?
Life's proud summits would'st thou scale?
Check thy climbing step, elate,
Evils lurk in felon wait:
Dangers, eagle-pinioned, bold,
Soar around each cliffy hold;
While cheerful Peace, with linnet song,
Chants the lowly dells among.

As the shades of ev'ning close,
Beck'ning thee to long repose;
As life itself becomes disease,
Seek the chimney-nook of ease:
There ruminate with sober thought,
On all thou'st seen, and heard, and wrought;
And teach the sportive younkers round,
Saws of experience, sage and sound:
Say, man's true, genuine estimate,
The grand criterion of his fate,
Is not, Art thou high or low?
Did thy fortune ebb or flow?
Did many talents gild thy span?
Or frugal Nature grudge thee one?
Tell them, and press it on their mind,
As thou thyself must shortly find,

Written In Friars' Carse Hermitage, On Nithside

The smile or frown of awful Heav'n,
To Virtue or to Vice is giv'n;
Say, to be just, and kind, and wise—
There solid self-enjoyment lies;
That foolish, selfish, faithless ways
Lead to be wretched, vile, and base.

Thus resign'd and quiet, creep
To the bed of lasting sleep:
Sleep, whence thou shalt ne'er awake,
Night, where dawn shall never break;
Till future life, future no more,
To light and joy the good restore,
To light and joy unknown before.
Stranger, go! Heav'n be thy guide!
Quod the Beadsman of Nithside.

THE FÊTE CHAMPETRE

TUNE: *Killiecrankie*

William Cunninghame (b.1757) gave a supper and ball
to celebrate his majority and inheritance of his
grandfather's estates of Annbank and Enterkin. Most
of the respectable families of Ayrshire were invited
and the event attracted widespread attention. The
dissolution of Parliament was imminent and it was
suspected that Cunninghame was using the 'fête' to
canvas votes. In the event, however, he stood down.
The other would-be candidates were Sir John
Whitefoord ('Glencaird') and James Boswell, Johnson's
biographer.

House of Commons

O, wha will to Saint Stephen's House,
    To do our errands there, man?
O, wha will to Saint Stephen's House
O, th' merry lads of Ayr, man?
Or will ye send a man o law?
    Or will ye send a sodger?

James Boswell

Great Bear (i.e.
Samuel Johnson)

Or him wha led o'er Scotland a'
    The meikle Ursa-Major?

Come, will ye court a noble lord,
    Or buy a score o lairds, man?
For Worth and Honour pawn their word.
    Their vote shall be Glencaird's, man.
Ane gies them coin, ane gies them wine,

talk

    Anither gies them clatter;
Annbank, wha guess'd the ladies' taste,
    He gies a Fête Champetre.

326

The Fête Champetre

When Love and Beauty heard the news
    The gay green-woods amang, man,
Where, gathering flowers, and busking bowers,   dressing
    They heard the blackbird's sang, man:
A vow, they seal'd it with a kiss,
    Sir Politics to fetter:
As their alone, the patent bliss,
    To hold a Fête Champetre.

Then mounted Mirth on gleesome wing,
    O'er hill and dale she flew, man;
Ilk wimpling burn, ilk crystal sprint,   each winding
    Ilk glen and shaw she knew, man   wood
She summon'd every social sprite,
    That sports by wood or water,
On th' bonie banks of Ayr to meet,
    And keep this Fête Champetre.

Cauld Boreas, wi his boisterous crew
    Were bound to stakes like kye, man;   cattle
And Cynthia's car, o silver fu,
    Clamb up the starry sky, man: climbed
Reflected beams dwell in the streams,
    Or down the current shatter;
The western breeze steals through the trees
    To view this Fête Champetre.

How many a robe sae gaily floats,
    What sparkling jewels glance, man,
To harmony's enchanting notes,
    As moves the mazy dance, man!
The echoing wood, the winding flood,
    Like Paradise did glitter,
When angels met at Adam's yett   gate
    To hold their Fête Champetre.

When Politics came there, to mix
    And make his ether-stane, man,   adder-
He circled round the magic ground,
    But entrance found he nane, man:
He blush'd for shame, he quat his name,   left
    Forswore it, every letter,
Wi humble prayer to join and share
    This festive Fête Champetre.

TO ALEX. CUNNINGHAM
ELLISLAND, NITHSDALE, JULY 27, 1788

Cunningham (d.1812) was a law student whom Burns
met in Edinburgh. 'Anna' was Anne Stewart (see
'Anna, Thy Charms')

My godlike friend—nay, do not stare:
    You think the phrase is odd-like?
But 'God is Love,' the saints declare,
    Then surely thou art god-like!

And is thy ardour still the same?
    And kindled still in Anna?
Others may boast a partial flame,
    But thou art a volcano!

Even Wedlock asks not love beyond
    Death's tie-dissolving portal;
But thou, omnipotently fond,
    May'st promise love immortal!

Thy wounds such healing powers defy,
    Such symptoms dire attend them,
That last great antihectic try—
    Marriage perhaps may mend them.

Sweet Anna has an air—a grace,
    Divine, magnetic, touching!
She takes, she charms—but who can trace
    The process of bewitching?

MALLY'S MEEK, MALLY'S SWEET

TUNE: *Deil flee o'er the water*

This song formed part of the Law MS, sent to James
Johnson from Mauchline in August 1788.

CHORUS

Mally's meek, Mally's sweet,
    Mally's modest and discreet,
Mally's rare, Mally's fair
    Mally's ev'ry way complete.

As I was walking up the street,
    A barefit maid I chanc'd to meet;
But O, the road was very hard
    For that fair maiden's tender feet!

It were mair meet that those fine feet
    Were weel laced up in silken shoon!
An 'twere more fit that she should sit
    Within yon chariot gilt aboon!

Her yellow hair, beyond compare,
    Comes tumbling down her swan-like neck,
And her twa eyes, like stars in skies,
    Would keep a sinking ship frae wreck!

OF A' THE AIRTS
THE WIND CAN BLAW

TUNE: *Miss Admiral Gordon's Strathspey*

Burns's notes in SMM say 'This air is by Marshall; the
song I composed out of compliment to Mrs. Burns.
N.B. It was during the honeymoon.' William Marshall,
who wrote the music, was butler to the Duke of
Gordon.

Of a' the airts the wind can blaw
   I dearly like the west,
For there the bonie lassie lives,
   The lassie I lo'e best.
There wild woods grow, and rivers row
   And monie a hill between,
But day and night my fancy's flight
   Is ever wi my Jean.

I see her in the dewy flowers—
   I see her sweet and fair.
I hear her in the tunefu birds—
   I hear her charm the air.
There's not a bonie flower that springs
   By fountain, shaw, or green,
There's not a bonie bird that sings,
   But minds me o my Jean.

O, WERE I ON PARNASSUS HILL

Included in the Law MS of August 1788, it too was
'made out of compliment to Mrs Burns' (Jean Armour).
Corsincon is a hill in the parish of New Cumnock
which Burns could see from Ellisland.

O, were I on Parnassus hill,
Or had o Helicon my fill,
That I might catch poetic skill
    To sing how dear I love thee!
But Nith maun by my Muse's well,
My Muse maun be thy bonie sel,
On Corsincon I'll glowr and spell,
    And write how dear I love thee.

Then come, sweet Muse, inspire my lay!
For a' the lee-lang simmer's day   live-long
I couldna sing, I couldna say,
    How much, how dear I love thee.
I see thee dancing o'er the green,
    Thy waist sae jimp, thy limbs sae clean,   tiny
Thy tempting lips, thy roguish een—
    By Heav'n and Earth I love thee!

O, Were I On Parnassus Hill

By night, by day, a-field, at hame,
The thoughts o thee my breast inflame,
And ay I muse and sing thy name—
I only live to love thee.
Tho I were doom'd to wander on,
Beyond the sea, beyond the sun,
Till my last weary sand was run,
Till then—and then— I'd love thee!

THE BANKS OF NITH

Described in the Law MS as 'Mr Burns's words', this
song was composed on 20th August 1788. In a letter
to Mrs. Dunlop the following day Burns wrote: 'The
following is the first Compliment I have paid the Nith
and was the work of an hour as I jogged up his banks
yesterday morning . . .'

The Thames flows proudly to the sea,
where royal cities stately stand;
But sweeter flows the Nith to me,
the Red Comyn   Where Cummins ance had high command.
When shall I see that honor'd land,
That winding stream I love so dear?
Must wayward Fortune's adverse hand
For ever—ever keep me here?

How lovely, Nith, thy fruitful vales,
Where bounding hawthorns gayly bloom,
And sweetly spread thy sloping dales,
Where lambkins wanton thro the broom!
Tho wandering now must be my doom,
Far from thy bonie banks and braes,
May there my latest hours consume,
Amang my friends of early days!

EPISTLE TO ROBERT GRAHAM, ESQ., OF FINTRY

REQUESTING A FAVOUR

Rough drafts of this verse-epistle were sent to Mrs.
Dunlop on 2nd August and 5th September 1788;
the finished poem was sent to Robert Graham on 10th
September. Although Mrs. Dunlop gave it a good
appraisal, it must be admitted that the flattery of a
patron he scarcely knew and owed little as yet, with an
equally insecure posture of independence, is absurd.

When Nature her great masterpiece design'd,
And fram'd her last, best work, the human mind,
Her eye intent on all the wondrous plan,
She form'd of various parts the various Man.

Epistle To Robert Graham, Esq., Of Fintry

The useful many first, she calls them forth—
Plain plodding Industry and sober Worth:
Thence peasants, farmers, native sons of earth,
And merchandise' whole genus take their birth:
Each prudent cit a warm existence finds,   *city-dweller*
And all mechanics' many-apron'd kinds.
Some other rarer sorts are wanted yet—
The lead and buoy are needful to the net:
The *caput mortuum* of gross desires   *dregs in a chemistry*
Makes a material for mere knights and squires;   *experiment*
The martial phosphorus is taught to flow;
She kneads the lumpish philosophic dough,
Then marks th' unyielding mass with grave designs—
Law, physic, politics, and deep divines;
Last, she sublimes th' Aurora of the poles,
The flashing elements of female souls.

The order'd system fair before her stood;
Nature, well pleas'd, pronounc'd it very good;
Yet ere she gave creating labour o'er,
Half-jest, she tried one curious labour more.
Some spumy, fiery, *ignis fatuus* matter,   *wandering fire due to*
Such as the slightest breath of air might scatter;   *spontaneous combustion*
With arch-alacrity and conscious glee   *of gas from decaying*
(Nature may have her whim as well as we: *vegetation*
Her Hogarth-art, perhaps she meant to show it),
She forms the thing and christens it — a Poet:
Creature, tho oft the prey of care and sorrow,
When blest to-day, unmindful of to-morrow;
A being form'd t' amuse his graver friends,
Admir'd and prais'd — and there the wages ends;
A mortal quite unfit for Fortune's strife,
Yet oft the sport of all the ills of life;
Prone to enjoy each pleasure riches give,
Yet haply wanting wherewithal to live;
Longing to wipe each tear, to heal each groan,
Yet frequent all unheeded in his own.
But honest Nature is not quite a Turk:
She laugh'd at first, then felt for her poor work:
Viewing the propless climber of mankind,
She cast about a standard tree to find;
In pity for his helpless woodbine state,
She clasp'd his tendrils round the truly great:
A title, and the only one I claim,
To lay strong hold for help on bounteous Graham.

Epistle To Robert Graham, Esq., Of Fintry

Pity the hapless Muses' tuneful train!
Weak, timid landsmen on life's stormy main,
There hearts no selfish, stern, absorbent stuff,
That never gives — tho humbly takes — enough:
The little Fate allows, they share as soon,
Unlike sage, proverb'd Wisdom's hard-wrung boon.
The world were blest did bliss on them depend —
Ah, that 'the friendly e'er should want a friend!'
Let Prudence number o'er each sturdy son,
Who life and wisdom at one race begun,
Who fell by reason and you give by rule,
(Instinct's a brute, and Sentiment a fool!)
Who make poor 'will do' wait upon 'I should' —
We own they're prudent, but who owns they're good?
Ye wise ones, hence! ye hurt the social eye,
God's image rudely etch'd on base alloy!
But come ye who the godlike pleasure know,
Heaven's attribute distinguish'd — to bestow!
Whose arms of love would grasp the human race:
Come thou who giv'st with all a courtier's grace—
Friend of my life, true patron of my rhymes,
Prop of my dearest hopes for future times!
Why shrinks my soul, half blushing, half afraid,
Backward, abash'd to ask thy friendly aid?
I know my need, I know thy giving hand,
I tax thy friendship at thy kind command.
the Muses   But there are such who court the tuneful Nine—
(Heavens! should the branded character be mine!)
Whose verse in manhood's pride sublimely flows,
Yet vilest reptiles in their begging prose.

Mark, how their lofty independent spirit
Soars on the spurning wing of injur'd merit!
Seek you the proofs in private life to find?
Pity the best of words should be but wind!
So, to heaven's gates the lark's shrill song ascends,
But grovelling on the earth the carol ends.
In all the clam'rous cry of starving want,
They dun Benevolence with shameless front;
Oblige them, patronise their tinsel lays —
They persecute you all your future days!
Ere my poor soul such deep damnation stain,
My horny fist assume the plough again!

332

Epistle To Robert Graham, Esq., Of Fintry

The pie-bald jacket let me patch once more!
On eighteenpence a week I've liv'd before.
Tho, thanks to Heaven, I dare even that last shift,
I trust, meantime, my boon is in thy gift:
That, plac'd by thee upon the wish'd-for height,
With man and nature fairer in her sight,
My Muse may imp her wing for some sublimer flight.

an exaggeration: 18d represented half a week's wages of an Ayrshire farm labourer

THE DAY RETURNS

TUNE: *Seventh of November*

Composed, wrote Burns 'out of compliment to one of the happiest and worthiest married couples in the world, Robert Riddel, Esq. of Glenriddel, and his lady. At their fire-side I have enjoyed more pleasant evenings than at all the houses of fashionable people in this country put together; and to their kindness and hospitality I am indebted for many of the happiest hours of my life.'

The day returns, my bosom burns,
    The blissful day we twa did meet:
Tho winter wild in tempest toil'd,
    Ne'er summer-sun was half sae sweet.
That a' the pride that loads the tide,
    And crosses o'er the sultry line,
Than kingly robes, than crowns and globes,
    Heav'n gave me more — it made thee mine!

While day and night can bring delight,
    Or Nature aught of pleasure give,
While joys above my mind can move,
    For thee, and thee alone, I live!
When that grim foe of Life below
    Comes in between to make us part,
The iron hand that breaks our band,
    It breaks my bliss, it breaks my heart!

THE BLUE-EYED LASSIE

The subject of this song was Jean Jaffray (1773-1850) daughter of the Rev. Andrew Jaffray of Ruthwell and later Lochmaben. She was about fifteen years old when this was written.

I gaed a waefu gate yestreen,
    A gate I fear I'll dearly rue:
I gat my death frae twa sweet een,
    Twa lovely een o bonie blue!
'Twas not her golden ringlets bright,
    Her lips like roses wat wi dew,
Her heaving bosom, lily-white:
    It was her een sae bonie blue.

went, doleful, way

eyes

333

The Blue-Eyed Lassie

She talk'd, she smil'd, my heart she wyl'd;
  She charm'd my soul I wist na how;
And ay the stound, the deadly wound,
  Cam frae her een sae bonie blue.
But 'spare to speak, and spare to speed;'

perhaps
  She'll aiblins listen to my vow:
Should she refuse, I'll lay my dead
  To her twa een sae bonie blue.

A MOTHER'S LAMENT

Sent to Mrs Dunlop on 27th September 1788 with a
letter: 'I was on horseback this morning, for between
my wife and my farm is just 46 miles, by three o'clock.
As I jogged on in the dark, I was taken with a Poetic-
fit, as follows.' It was composed for Mrs. Fergusson of
Craigdarroch, whose son died on 5th November 1787,
but Burns transcribed it in 1791 for the Afton Lodge
collection, wherein it was annotated as commemor-
ating Alexander Gordon Stewart of Afton, who died at
Strasbourg military academy on 5th December 1787,
aged sixteen.

Fate gave the word — the arrow sped,
  And pierc'd my darling's heart,
And with him all the joys are fled
  Life can to me impart.

By cruel hands the sapling drops,
  In dust dishonor'd laid:
So fell the pride of all my hopes,
  My age's future shade.

The mother linnet in the brake
  Bewails her ravish'd young;
So I, for my lost darling's sake,
  Lament the live-day long.

Death, oft I've fear'd thy fatal blow!
  Now fond I bare my breast;
O, do thou kindly lay me low
  With him I love, at rest!

THE LAZY MIST

Burns sent a copy of this to Dr. Blacklock on 15th
November 1788.

The lazy mist hangs from the brow of the hill,
Concealing the course of the dark winding rill.
How languid the scenes, late so sprightly, appear!
As Autumn to Winter resigns the pale year!

The Lazy Mist

The forests are leafless, the meadows are brown,
And all the gay foppery of summer is flown.
Apart let me wander, apart let me muse,
How quick Time is flying, how keen Fate pursues!

How long I have liv'd, but how much liv'd in vain!
How little of life's scanty span may remain!
What aspects old Time in his progress has worn!
What ties cruel Fate in my bosom has torn!

How foolish, or worse, till our summit is gain'd!
And downward, how weaken'd, how darken'd, how pain'd!
Life is not worth having with all it can give:
For something beyond it poor man, sure, must live.

WHISTLE O'ER THE LAVE O'T

The air was traditional, but Burns set it to entirely new words, and it is regarded as one of Burns's finest restorations of an old lyrical motif.

First when Maggie was my care,
Heav'n, I thought, was in her air;
Now we're married, speir nae mair,   ask no more
But — whistle o'er the lave o't!   rest

Meg was meek, and Meg was mild,
Sweet and harmless as a child:
Wiser men than me's beguil'd—
Whistle o'er the lave o't!

How we live, my Meg and me,
How we love, and how we gree,
I care na by now few may see—
Whistle o'er the lave o't!

Wha I wish were maggot's meat,
Dish'd up in her winding-sheet,
I could write (but Meg may see't)
Whistle o'er the lave o't!

TAM GLEN

TUNE: *The Merry Beggars*

Sent to Johnson for SMM on 15th November 1788. The 'Valentine's dealing' (line 21) refers to the old custom of drawing lots for sweethearts on St. Valentine's day.

My heart is a-breaking, dear tittie,   sister
    Some counsel unto me come len',
To anger them a' is a pity,
    But what will I do wi Tam Glen?

Tam Glen

fine
poverty, shift

must not

I'm thinking, wi sic a braw fellow
  In poortith I might make a fen';
What care I in riches to wallow,
  If I mauna marry Tam Glen?

There's Lowrie the laird o Dumeller:
  'Guid day to you' — brute! he comes ben,
He brags and he blaws o his siller,
  But when will he dance like Tam Glen?

mother, deafen

My minnie does constantly deave me,
  And bids me beware o young men.
They flatter, she says, to deceive me—
  But wha can think sae o Tam Glen?

if
£55 sterling

My daddie says, gin I'll forsake him,
  He'd gie me guid hunder marks ten.
But if it's ordain'd I maun take him,
  O, wha will I get but Tam Glen?

mouth, start

Yestreen at the Valentines' dealing,
  My heart to my mou gied a sten,
For thrice I drew ane without failing,
  And thrice it was written 'Tam Glen!'

drenched, shirt-sleeve
stalking
breeches

The last Hallowe'en I was waukin
  My droukit sark-sleeve, as ye ken—
His likeness came up the house staukin,
  And the very grey breeks o Tam Glen!

Come, counsel, dear tittie, don't tarry!
  I'll gie ye my bonie black hen,
Gif ye will advise me to marry
  The lad I lo'e dearly, Tam Glen.

TO THE BEAUTIFUL
MISS ELIZA J———N

ON HER PRINCIPLES OF LIBERTY AND EQUALITY

The identity of the dedicatee is not known, though Kinsley considered Elizabeth Johnston, a friend of Dr. Blacklock, a possiblity.

How, 'Liberty!' Girl, can it be by thee nam'd?
'Equality,' too! Hussey, are not asham'd?
Free and Equal indeed, while mankind thou enchainest,
And over their hearts a proud Despot so reignest.

SKETCH FOR AN ELEGY

Regarded by most editors as 'the fragment' of an Elegy
which Burns originally composed for Matthew
Henderson in 1788, and revised and completed in 1790
(see next poem). Craigdarroch was Alexander
Fergusson (see 'The Whistle'). 'Black James' may have
been Boswell, but more probably Dr. Gregory or
Sibbald the Edinburgh book-seller.

Craigdarroch, fam'd for speaking art
And every virtue of the heart,
Stops short, nor can a word impart
    To end his sentence,
When mem'ry strikes him like a dart
    With auld acquaintance.

Black James — whase wit was never laith,
But, like a sword had tint the sheath,
Ay ready for the work o death—
    He turns aside,
And strains wi suffocating breath
    His grief to hide.

Even Philosophic Smellie tries   William Smellie
To cloak the stream that floods his eyes: (1740-95)
So Moses wi a hazel-rice   Burns's printer
    Came o'er the stane;
But, tho it cost him speaking twice,
    It gush'd amain.

Go to your marble graffs, ye great,   graves
In a' the tinkler-trash of state!
But by thy honest turf I'll wait,
    Thou man of worth,
And weep the ae best fallow's fate
    E'er lay in earth!

ELEGY ON
CAPTAIN MATTHEW HENDERSON
A GENTLEMAN WHO HELD THE PATENT
FOR HIS HONOURS IMMEDIATELY
FROM ALMIGHTY GOD!
Should the poor be flattered—SHAKESPEARE

Captain Henderson (1737-88) was the son of David
Henderson of Tannoch (Ayrshire) and Tannoch-
side (Lanarkshire) and was connected by marriage
with James Boswell. Henderson dissipated his family
wealth and estates in high living in Edinburgh and
died in reduced circumstances in November 1788. He
and Burns were fellow-lodgers for a time in a house in
St. James Square, Edinburgh.

O Death! thou tyrant fell and bloody!
The meikle Devil wi a woodie   great, noose
Haurl thee hame to his black smiddie,   Trail, smithy
    O'er hurcheon hides,   hedgehog
And like stock-fish come o'er his studdie   beaten, anvil
    Wi thy auld sides!

337

Elegy On Captain Matthew Henderson

gone
one
	He's gane, he's gane! he's frae us torn,
	The ae best fellow e'er was born!
	Thee, Matthew, Nature's sel' shall mourn,
	    By wood and wild,
	Where, haply, Pity strays forlorn,
	    Frae man exil'd.

neighbours, stars
mould
eagles
 	
children
	Ye hills, near neebors o the starns,
	That proudly cock your cresting cairns!
	Ye cliffs, the haunts of sailing yearns,
	    Where Echo slumbers!
	Come join ye, Nature's sturdiest bairns,
	    My wailing numbers!

every, wood-pigeon
woods, hollows
brooks, meandering
pattering
strong, bursts
cascade
	Mourn, ilka grove the cushat kens!
	Ye hazly shaws and briery dens!
	Ye burnies, wimplin down your glens,
	    Wi toddlin din,
	Or foaming, strang, wi hasty stens,
	    Frae lin to lin!

	Mourn, little harebells o'er the lea;
	Ye stately foxgloves, fair to see;
	Ye woodbines, hanging bonilie,
	    In scented bowers;
	Ye roses on your thorny tree,
	    The first o flowers!

hares, scudding	At dawn, when every grassy blade
	Droops with a diamond at his head;
	At ev'n, when beans their fragrance shed,
	    I' th' rustling gale,
	Ye maukins, whidden thro the glade,
	    Come join my wail!

crop
cloud
 	
partridge
	Mourn, ye wee songsters o the wood;
	Ye grouse that crap the heather bud;
	Ye curlews, calling thro a clud;
	    Ye whistling plover;
	And mourn, ye whirring paitrick brood;
	    He's gane for ever!

Roar	Mourn, sooty coots, and speckled teals;
	Ye fisher herons, watching eels;
	Ye duck and drake, wi airy wheels
	    Circling the lake;
	Ye bitterns, till the quagmire reels,
	    Rair for his sake!

Elegy On Captain Matthew Henderson

Mourn, clam'ring craiks, at close o day,   *corncrakes*
'Mang fields o flow'ring clover gay!
And when you wing your annual way
    Frae our cauld shore,
Tell thae far warlds wha lies in clay,   *those*
    Wham we deplore.

Ye houlets, frae your ivy bower   *owls*
In some auld tree, or eldritch tower,   *haunted*
What time the moon, wi silent glowr   *glare*
    Sets up her horn,
Wail thro the dreary midnight hour,
    Till waukrife morn!   *sleepless*

O rivers, forests, hills, and plains!
Oft have ye heard my canty strains: *joyful*
But now, what else for me remains
    But tales of woe?
And frae my een the drapping rains
    Maun ever flow.   *Must*

Mourn, Spring, thou darling of the year!
Ilk cowslip cup shall kep a tear: *catch*
Thou, Simmer, while each corny spear
    Shoots up its head,
Thy gay, green, flowery tresses shear,
    For him that's dead!

Thou, Autumn, wi thy yellow hair,
In grief thy sallow mantle tear!
Thou, Winter, hurling thro the air
    The roaring blast,
Wide o'er the naked world declare
    The worth we've lost!

Mourn him, thou Sun, great source of light!
Mourn, Empress of the silent night!
And you, ye twinkling starnies bright,   *starlets*
    My Matthew mourn!
For through your orbs he's ta'en his flight,
    Ne'er to return.

O Henderson! the man! the brother!
And art thou gone, and gone for ever?
And hast thou crost that unknown river,
    Life's dreary bound?
Like thee, where shall I find another,
    The world around?

Elegy On Captain Matthew Henderson

Go to your sculptur'd tombs, ye Great,
In a' the tinsel trash o state!
But by thy honest turf I'll wait,
    Thou man of worth!
And weep the ae best fellow's fate
    E'er lay in earth!

THE EPITAPH

Stop, passenger! my story's brief,
    And truth I shall relate, man:
I tell nae common tale o grief,
    For Matthew was a great man.

If thou uncommom merit hast,
    Yet spurn'd at Fortune's door, man;
A look of pity hither cast,
    For Matthew was a poor man.

If thou a noble sodger art,
    That passest by this grave, man;
There moulders here a gallant heart,
    For Matthew was a brave man.

If thou on men, their works and ways,
    Canst throw uncommon light, man;
Here lies wha weel had won thy praise,
    For Matthew was a bright man.

If thou, at Friendship's sacred ca'.
    Wad life itself resign, man;
Thy sympathetic tear maun fa',
    For Matthew was a kind man.

If thou art staunch, without a stain,
    Like the unchanging blue, man;
This was a kinsman o thy ain,
    For Matthew was a true man.

If thou hast wit, and fun, and fire,
    And ne'er guid wine did fear, man;
This was thy billie, dam, and sire,
    For Matthew was a queer man.

If onie whiggish, whingin sot,
    To blame poor Matthew dare, man;
May dool and sorrow be his lot!
    For Matthew was a rare man.

comrade
whining
sadness

AULD LANG SYNE

'Light be the turf on the breast of the heaven-inspired Poet who composed this glorious Fragment' wrote Burns to Mrs. Dunlop on 7th December 1788. In a note to George Thomson (1793) he describes it as 'the old song of the olden times, and which has never been in print, nor even in manuscript, until I took it down from an old man's singing.' To what extent Burns reworked this traditional ballad has been the subject of speculation for many years. The tune itself has been known in print since 1700.

CHORUS

For auld lang syne, my dear,   old long ago
For auld lang syne,
We'll tak a cup o kindness yet,
For auld lang syne!

Should auld acquaintance be forgot,
And never brought to mind?
Should auld acquaintance be forgot,
And auld lang syne?

And surely ye'll be your pint-stowp,   pay for
And surely I'll be mine,
And we'll tak a cup o kindness yet,
For auld lang syne!

We twa hae run about the braes,   hillsides
And pou'd the gowans fine,   pulled, daisies
But we've wander'd monie a weary fit,
Sin auld lang syne.

We twa hae paidl'd in the burn   waded, stream
Frae morning sun till dine,   noon, dinner-time
But seas between us braid hae roar'd   broad
Sin auld lang syne.

And there's a hand my trusty fiere,
And gie's a hand o thine,
And we'll tak a right guid-willie waught,   goodwill drink
For auld lang syne.

EPITAPH FOR JOHN HUNTER, WRITER IN AYR

John Hunter, W.S. of Doonholm was famed for his stature. Burns enclosed this epitaph in a letter to Mrs. Dunlop on 7th December 1788.

Here lies a Scots mile of a chiel,   fellow
If he's in heaven, Lord, fill him weel!

THE SILVER TASSIE

TUNE: *The Secret Kiss*

'Two other old Stanzas which please me mightily' was Burns's description of this old Jacobite ballad, and it was originally published in SMM as an anonymous traditional song. By September 1793, however, he was claiming it as his own, adding 'the first half stanza of the song is old, the rest is mine.'

goblet

Queeensferry

must

Go fetch to me a pint o wine,
    And fill it in a silver tassie;
That I may drink, before I go,
    A service to my bonie lassie:
The boat rocks at the Pier o Leith,
    Fu loud the wind blaws frae the Ferry,
The ship rides by the Berwick-law,
    And I maun leave my bony Mary.

The trumpets sound, the banners fly,
    The glittering spears are ranked ready,
The shouts o war are heard afar,
    The battle closes deep and bloody.
It's not the roar o sea or shore,
    Wad make me langer wish to tarry;
Nor shouts o war that's heard afar—
    It's leaving thee, my bony Mary!

ODE, SACRED TO THE MEMORY OF MRS. OSWALD OF AUCHENCRUIVE

The daughter of a wealthy plantation owner in Jamaica, Mary Ramsay married Richard Oswald who made his money by speculation during the Seven Years' War (1756-63). In 1764 he bought the estate of Auchencruive, but after her husband's death Mrs. Oswald preferred to live in London. Following her own death in 1788, her funeral cortege passed through Dumfriesshire on its way to St. Quivox. Burns was lodging at Bailie Whigham's Inn, Sanquhar but was forced to give up his room to the funeral party and ride on a further twelve miles on a wild January night to the next inn, at New Cumnock. As soon as he had thawed out he sat down and composed this savage satire in the white heat of anger.

Dweller in yon dungeon dark,
Hangman of creation, mark!
Who in widow-weeds appears,
Laden with unhonoured years.
Noosing with care a bursting purse,
Baited with many a deadly curse?

342

Ode, Sacred To The Memory Of Mrs. Oswald Of Auchencruive

STROPHE

View the wither'd beldam's face:
Can thy keen inspection trace
Aught of Humanity's sweet, melting grace?
Note that eye, 'tis rheum o'erflows—
Pity's flood there never rose.
See these hands, ne'er stretch'd to save,
Hands that took, but never gave.
Keeper of Mammon's iron chest,
Lo, there she goes, unpitied and unblest,
She goes, but not to realms of everlasting rest!

ANTISTROPHE

Plunderer of Armies! lift thine eyes
(A while forbear, ye torturing fiends),
Seest thou whose step, unwilling, hither bends?
No fallen angel, hurl'd from upper skies!
'Tis thy trusty, quondam Mate,
Doom'd to share thy fiery fate:
She, tardy, hell-ward plies.

a reference to Richard Oswald's war-profiteering

EPODE

And are they of no more avail,
Ten thousand glittering pounds a-year?
In other worlds can Mammon fail,
Omnipotent as he is here?
O, bitter mockery of the pompous bier!
While down the wretched vital part is driven,
The cave-lodged beggar, with a conscience clear,
Expires in rags, unknown, and goes to Heaven.

VERSICLES ON SIGN-POSTS

These random jottings were written in 2CPB at the end of December 1788. The second versicle was later incorporated in his ode to Robert Graham of Fintry in 1791, but the others were apparently never utilised.

He looked just as your sign-post Lions do,
With aspect fierce, and quite as harmless too.

So heavy, passive to the tempest's shocks,
Dull on the sign-post stands the stupid ox.

His face with smile eternal drest
Just like the landlord to his guest,
High as they hang with creaking din,
To index out the Country Inn.

A head, pure, sinless quite of brain and soul,
The very image of a barber's poll:
coiffeured   Just shows a human face, and wears a wig,
And looks, when well friseur'd, amazing big.

PEGASUS AT WANLOCKHEAD

When Burns, mounted on his new horse Pegasus, called
at the smithy in Wanlockhead one frosty day in the
winter of 1788-9 the smith was too busy to frost the
horse's shoes. Burns composed these lines extempore
and addressed them to John Taylor, a man of standing
in the community who immediately spoke to the
smith and rectified the matter.

With Pegasus upon a day
    Apollo, weary flying,
(Through frosty hills the journey lay),
    On foot the way was plying.

Poor slipshod, giddy Pegasus
    Was but a sorry walker;
To Vulcan then Apollo goes
    To get a frosty caulker.

Obliging Vulcan fell to work,
    Threw by his coat and bonnet,
And did Sol's business in a crack—
    Sol paid him with a sonnet.

Ye Vulcan's sons of Wanlockhead,
    Pity my sad disaster!
My Pegasus is poorly shod—
    I'll pay you like my master.

TO JOHN TAYLOR, Ramage's, 3 o'clock

A SONNET UPON SONNETS

This appears to have been Burns's first attempt at writing
a sonnet, a fourteen-line poem popularised by Shake-
speare, and appropriately takes this verse form itself as
the subject.

Fourteen, a sonneteer thy praises sings;
What magic myst'ries in that number lie!
Your hen hath fourteen eggs beneath her wings
That fourteen chickens to the roost may fly.
Fourteen full pounds the jockey's stone must be;
His age fourteen — a horse's prime is past.
Fourteen long hours too oft the Bard must fast;
Fourteen bright bumpers — bliss he ne'er must see!
Before fourteen — e'en thirteen's strength is vain.
Fourteen good years — a woman gives us life;
Fourteen good men — we lose that life again.
What lucubrations can be more upon it?
Fourteen good measur'd verses make a sonnet.

344

THE CARES O LOVE

HE

The cares o Love are sweeter far
Than onie other pleasure;   any
And if sae dear its sorrows are,
Enjoyment, what a treasure!

SHE

I fear to try, I dare na try
A passion sae ensnaring;
For light's her heart and blythe's her sang
That for nae man is caring.

LOUIS, WHAT RECK I BY THEE

Probably written in December 1788, when Jean Armour joined Burns in Dumfriesshire. Louis and Geordie were Louis XVI of France and George III respectively. There is an unconscious element of irony about these lines penned only months before the dramatic outbreak of the French Revolution.

Louis, what reck I by thee,
Or Geordie on his ocean?
Dyvor beggar louns to me!   bankrupt, chaps
I reign in Jeanie's bosom.

Let her crown my love her law,
And in her breast enthrone me,
Kings and nations — swith awa!   haste away
Reif randies, I disown ye!   Thieving rascals

NEW YEAR'S DAY

TO MRS. DUNLOP

Written on 1st January 1789 and sent to Mrs. Dunlop who commented on this poem on 22nd January.

This day Time winds th' exhausted chain,
To run the twelvemonth's length again:
I see the old, bald-pated fellow,
With ardent eyes, complexion sallow,
Adjust the unimpair'd machine
To wheel the equal, dull routine.

The absent lover, minor heir,
In vain assail him with their prayer:
Deaf as my friend, he sees them press,   a reference to Mrs. Dunlop's
Nor makes the hour one moment less.   deafness
Will you (the Major's with the hounds;   Andrew Dunlop (d. 1804)
The happy tenants share his rounds;

New Year's Day

Mrs. Dunlop's 5th daughter
the youngest daughter, reading
Gray's Elegy

Coila's fair Rachel's care to-day,
And blooming Keith's engaged with Gray)
From housewife cares a minute borrow
(That grandchild's cap will do to-morrow),
And join with me a-moralising;
This day's propitious to be wise in!

 First, what did yesternight deliver?
'Another year has gone for ever.'
And what is this day's strong suggestion?
'The passing moment's all we rest on!'
Rest on for what? what do we here?
Or why regard the passing year?
Will Time, amus'd with proverb'd lore,
Add to our date one minute more?
A few days may — a few years must —
Repose us in the silent dust:
Then, is it wise to damp our bliss?
Yes — all such reasonings are amiss!
The voice of Nature loudly cries,
And many a message from the skies,
That something in us never dies
That on this frail uncertain state
Hang matters of eternal weight;
That future in worlds unknown
Must take its hue from this alone,
Whether as heavenly glory bright
Or dark as Misery's woeful night.

 Since, then, my honor'd first of friends,
On this poor being all depends,
Let us th' important Now employ,
And live as those who never die.
Tho' you, with days and honours crown'd,
Witness that filial circle round
(A sight life's sorrows to repulse,
A sight pale Envy to convulse),
Others now claim your chief regard:
Yourself, you wait your bright reward.

ELEGY ON THE YEAR 1788

January 1, 1789

Written on 1st January 1789 and sent to the Edinburgh Courant, it provides an interesting reflection on the previous twelve months. The Regency crisis, which arose in November 1788 as a result of the King's insanity centred on the desire of Fox to give Prince George full powers, whereas Pitt argued for a regency with severely limited powers. See also 'Ode on the Departed Regency Bill.'

For lords or kings I dinna mourn;   do not
E'en let them die — for that they're born;
But O, prodigious to reflect,
A Towmont, sirs, is gane to wreck!   Twelvemonth
O Eighty-eight, in thy sma' space
What dire events hae taken place!
Of what enjoyments thou hast reft us!
In what a pickle thou has left us!

    The Spanish empire's tint a head,   Charles III of Spain died
An my auld teethless Bawtie's dead;   13th December 1788
The tulyie's teugh 'tween Pitt and Fox,   tough struggle
An our guidwife's wee birdie cocks;
The tane is game, a bluidie devil,   one
But to the hen-birds unco civil;   a reference to Fox's
The tither's dour — has nae sic breedin,   womanising; stubborn
But better stuff ne'er claw'd a midden.

    Ye ministers, come mount the poupit,   pulpit
An cry till ye be hoarse an roupet,   husky
For Eighty-eight, he wished you weel,
An gaed ye a' baith gear an meal: gave, both, wealth
E'en monie a plack, and monie a peck,   coin
Ye ken yoursels, for little feck!   know, return
    Ye bonie lasses, dight your e'en,   wipe
For some o you hae tint a frien':
In Eighty-eight, ye ken, was taen,
What ye'll ne'er hae to gie again.   virginity

    Observe the vera nowte an sheep,   cattle
How dowff an dowilie they creep!   dull, languid
Nay, even the yirth itsel does cry,   earth
For Embro wells are grutten dry!   Edinburgh, wept

    O Eighty-nine, thou's but a bairn,
An no owre auld, I hope, to learn!
Thou beardless boy, I pray tak care,   Prince George
Thou now has got thy Daddie's chair:
Nae handcuff'd, mizzl'd, half-shackl'd Regent,
But, like himsel, a full free agent,
Be sure ye follow out the plan
Nae waur than he did, honest man!   worse
As muckle better as ye can.   much

ROBIN SHURE IN HAIRST

TUNE: *Rob shear'd in hairst*

The subject is not Burns himself, as the name Robin
might suggest, but his friend Robert Ainslie (1766-
1838), born at Berrywell, near Duns. The last line
refers to the quills and pen-knife, traditional tools
of the law which was Ainslie's profession.

CHORUS

reaped, harvest	*Robin shure in hairst,*
	I shure wi him:
not a sickle	*Fient a heuk had I,*
stuck	*Yet I stack by him.*
went	I gaed up to Dunse,
weave, web, tweed	To warp a wab o plaiden,
gate	At his daddie's yett,
	Wha met me but Robin!
bold	Was na Robin bauld,
	Tho I was a cotter?
	Play'd me sick a trick,
Elder's daughter	An me the Eller's dochter!
	Robin promis'd me
food	A' my winter vittle:
Devil have it (i.e. nothing)	Fient haet he had but three
goose-quills, knife	Guse-feathers and a whittle!

COME REDE ME, DAME

TUNE: *The Quaker's Wife*

The opening lines are traditional, but the rest is Burns's
own work and dates from January 1789.

	Come rede me, dame, come tell me dame,
	'My damè come tell me truly,
tool, hammered home	'What length of graith, when weel ca'd hame,
	'Will sair a woman duly?'
wench, clutched, vulva	The carlin clew her wanton tail,
	Her wanton tail sae ready—
	I learn'd a sang in Annandale,
	Nine inch will please a lady—
country	But for a koontrie cunt like mine,
	In sooth, we're nae sae gentle;
thumb-breadth	We'll tak tway thumb-bread to the nine,
	And that's a sonsy pintle:
Blessings	O Leeze me on my Charlie lad,
	I'll ne'er forget my Charlie!
testicles and penis	Tway roarin handfu's and a daud,
press forcibly	He nidge't it in fu rarely.

348

Come Rede Me, Dame

But weary fa' the laithron doup,   lazy buttocks
  And may it ne'er be thrivin!
It's no the length that maks me loup,   leap
  But it's the double drivin.
Come nidge me, Tam, come nudge me, Tam,
  Come nidge me o'er the nyvel!   navel
Come lowse and lug your battering ram, loose and pull
  And thrash him at my gyvel!   vagina

CALEDONIA

TUNE: *Caledonian Hunt's Delight of Mr. Gow*

Sent to Johnson for SMM on 23rd January 1789. The 'Cameleon-Savage' (l. 25) has been taken to mean the Picts in war-paint, but it is more likely that Burns meant 'Camelon', near Falkirk, legendary capital of Pictland.

There was on a time, but old Time was then young,
  That brave Caledonia, the chief of her line,
From some of your northern deities sprung
  (Who knows not that brave Caledonia's divine?)
From Tweed to the Orcades was her domain,   Orkney
  To hunt, or to pasture, or do what she would.
Her heav'nly relations there fixed her reign,
  And pledg'd her their godheads to warrant it good.

A lambkin in peace but a lion in war,
  The pride of her kindred the heroine grew.
Her grandsire, old Odin, triumphantly swore:— an illusion to the old
  'Whoe'er shall provoke thee, th' encounter shall rue!' belief that the Picts
With tillage or pasture at times she would sport, came from Scandinavia
  To feed her fair flocks by her green rustling corn;
But chiefly the woods were her fav'rite resort,
  Her darling amusement the hounds and the horn.

Long quiet she reign'd, till thitherward steers
  A flight of bold eagles from Adria's strand.   Roman legions
Repeated, successive, for many long years,
  They darken'd the air, and they plunder'd the land.
Their pounces were murder, and horror their cry;
  They'd conquer'd and ravag'd a world beside.
She took to her hills, and her arrows let fly—
  The daring invaders, they fled or they died!

The Cameleon-Savage disturb'd her repose,   painted Picts
  With tumult, disquiet, rebellion, and strife.
Provok'd beyond bearing, at last she arose,
  And robb'd him at once of his hopes and his life.
The Anglian lion, the terror of France,
  Oft, prowling, ensanguin'd the Tweed's silver flood, Pictish victory over
But, taught by the bright Caledonian lance,   Ecgfrith at
  He learned to fear in his own native wood.   Nechtansmere, 685 AD

Caledonia

The fell Harpy-Raven took wing from the north,

Danes   The fell Harpy-Raven took wing from the north,
The scourge of the seas, and the dread of the shore;
Norwegians   The wild Scandinavian Boar issued forth
To wanton in carnage and wallow in gore;
O'er countries and kingdoms their fury prevail'd,
No arts could appease them, no arms could repel;
Scots victories in 1263   But brave Caledonia in vain they assail'd,
and 990.   As Largs well can witness, and Loncartie tell.

Thus bold, independent, unconquer'd, and free,
Her bright course of glory for ever shall run,
For brave Caledonia immortal must be,
I'll prove it from Euclid as clear as the sun:—
Rectangle-triangle, the figure we'll chuse:
The upright is Chance, and old Time is the base,
But brave Caledonia's the hypothenuse;
Then, *ergo*, she'll match them, and match them always!

AT WHIGHAM'S INN, SANQUHAR

Edward Whigham (1750-1823) was landlord of the Queensberry Arms at Sanquhar and these lines were inscribed on a window-pane. Burns often called there while travelling between Mauchline and Ellisland.

Envy, if thy jaundiced eye
Through this window chance to spy,
To thy sorrow thou shalt find,
All that's generous, all that's kind
Friendship, virtue, every grace,
Dwelling in this happy place.

TO WILLIAM STEWART

Written in Brownhill Inn, probably early in 1789. William Stewart was the son of the publican at Closeburn, and became factor of Closeburn Castle, not far from Ellisland. His brother-in-law, Mr. Bacon, was landlord of Brownhill Inn.

Brownhill Monday even:
Dear Sir,

fireside corner   In honest Bacon's ingle-neuk,
must   Here maun I sit and think;
folk   Sick o the warld and warld's fock,
And sick, damn'd sick o drink!

I see, I see there is nae help,
But still down I maun sink;
low   Till some day, *laigh enough,* I yelp,
'Wae worth that cursed drink!'

To William Stewart

Yestreen, alas! I was sae fu,   drunk
   I could but yisk and wink;   belch
And now, this day, sair, sair I rue,
   The weary, weary drink,

Satan, I fear thy sooty claws,
   I hate thy brunstane stink,   brimstone
And ay I curse the luckless cause,
   The wicked soup o drink.

In vain I would forget my woes
   In idle rhyming clink,
For past redemption damm'd in Prose
   I can do nought but drink.

For you, my trusty, well-try'd friend,
   May Heaven still on you blink;
And may your life flow to the end,
   Sweet as a dry man's drink!

ROBT. BURNS

IN THE KIRK OF LAMINGTON

An example of poetic graffiti which, on this occasion roused the anger of the beadle who discovered that the window had been thus defaced, after Burns had sat nearby, possibly in late February 1789. The minister was the Rev. Thomas Mitchell (d. 1811).

As cauld a wind as ever blew,
A cauld kirk, and in't but few,
As cauld a minister's ever spak—
Ye'se a' be het or I come back!   You'll all be hot

SWEET AFTON

Composed before 5th February 1789 when Burns sent these lines to Mrs. Dunlop with the comment: 'There is a small river, Afton, that falls into Nith, near New Cumnock; which has some charming wild, romantic scenery on its banks...'

Flow gently, sweet Afton, among thy green braes!   slopes
Flow gently, I'll sing thee a song in thy praise!
My Mary's asleep by thy murmuring stream—
Flow gently, sweet Afton, disturb not her dream!

Thou stock dove whose echo resounds thro the glen,
Ye wild whistling blackbirds in yon thorny den,
Thou green-crested lapwing, thy screaming forbear—
I charge you, disturb not my slumbering Fair.

Sweet Afton

How lofty, sweet Afton, thy neighbouring hills,
Far mark'd with the courses of clear, winding rills!
There daily I wander, as noon rises high,
My flocks and my Mary's sweet cot in my eye.

How pleasant thy banks and green vallies below,
Where wild in the woodlands the primroses blow
There oft, as mild Ev'ning weeps over the lea,
birch The sweet-scented birk shades my Mary and me.

Thy crystal stream, Afton, how lovely it glides,
cottage And winds by the cot where my Mary resides!
wash How wanton thy waters her snowy feet lave,
As, gathering sweet flowerets, she stems thy clear wave!

Flow gently, sweet Afton, among thy green braes!
Flow gently, sweet river, the theme of my lays!
My Mary's asleep by thy murmuring stream—
Flow gently, sweet Afton, disturb not her dream!

ODE ON THE DEPARTED
REGENCY BILL

King George III's first bout of insanity occurred between November 1788 and February 1789 and gave rise to a dangerous political crisis in which the supporters of William Pitt and Charles James Fox were polarized for and against restriction of the powers of regency to be given to Prince George and conducted a campaign of passionate ferocity. The King's recovery resolved the crisis and the Regency Bill was abandoned. Burns wrote these lines in March 1789.

Daughter of Chaos' doting years,
Nurse of ten thousand hopes and fears!
Whether thy airy, unsubstantial shade
(The rights of sepulture now duly paid)
Spread abroad its hideous form
On the roaring civil storm,
Deafening din and warring rage
Factions wild with factions wage;
Or under-ground, deep-sunk, profound,
Among the demons of the earth,
With groans that make the mountains shake,
Thou mourn thy ill-starr'd, blighted birth,
Or in the uncreated Void,
Where seeds of future being fight,
With lighten'd step thou wander wide
To greet thy mother—Ancient Night,
And as each jarring, monster-mass is past,
Fond recollect what once thou wast:
In manner due, beneath this sacred oak,
Hear, Spirit, hear! thy presence I invoke!

AYR
Market Cross

KIRK ALLOWAY

Ode On The Departed Regency Bill

By a Monarch's heaven-struck fate;
By a disunited State;
By a generous Prince's wrongs;
By a Senate's war of tongues;
By a Premier's sullen pride
Louring on the changing tide;
By dread Thurlow's powers to awe—   Edward, Lord Thurlow (1731-
Rhetoric, blasphemy and law;   1806)
By the turbulent ocean,
A Nation's commotion;
By the harlot-carresses
Of Borough addresses;
By days few and evil;
(Thy portion, poor devil!)
By Power, Wealth, and Show,
  (The Gods by men adored),
By nameless Poverty,
  (Their Hell abhorred),
By all they hope, by all they fear,
Hear! and Appear!
Stare not on me, thou ghostly Power,
Nor, grim with chain'd defiance, lour!
No Babel-structure would I build
  Where, Order exil'd from his native sway,
Confusion might the REGENT-sceptre wield,
  While all would rule and none obey:
Go, to the world of Man relate
  The story of thy sad, eventful fate;
And call presumptuous Hope to hear
And bid him check his blind career;
And tell the sore-prest sons of Care,
    Never, never to despair!
Paint Charles's speed on wings of fire,   Fox
The object of his fond desire,
Beyond his boldest hopes, at hand.
Paint all the triumph of the Portland Band;   followers of the Duke of
(Hark! how they lift the joy-exulting voice,   Portland
And how their num'rous creditors rejoice!)
  But just as hopes to warm enjoyment rise,
  Cry 'Convalescence!' and the vision flies.

Then next pourtray a dark'ning twilight gloom
  Eclipsing sad a gay, rejoicing morn,
While proud Ambition to th' untimely tomb
  By gnashing, grim, despairing fiends is borne!
Paint Ruin, in the shape of high Dundas   Henry Dundas, Viscount
  Gaping with giddy terror o'er the brow: Melville (1742-1811)
In vain he struggles, the Fates behind him press,
  And clam'rous Hell yawns for her prey below!

Ode On The Departed Regency Bill

How fallen That, whose pride late scaled the skies!
And This, like Lucifer, no more to rise!
Again pronounce the powerful word:
See Day, triumphant from the Night, restored!

Then know this truth, ye Sons of Men!
(Thus ends thy moral tale):
Your darkest terrors may be vain,
Your brightest hopes may fail!

THE WOUNDED HARE

On 21st April 1789 Burns wrote to Mrs. Dunlop: 'Two
mornings ago as I was at a very early hour, sowing in the
fields, I heard a shot, and presently a poor little hare
limped by me, apparently very much hurt. You will
easily guess, this set my humanity in tears and my
indignation in arms. The following was the result.'

Inhuman man! curse on thy barb'rous art,
And blasted by thy murder-aiming eye;
May never pity soothe thee with a sigh,
Nor never pleasure glad thy cruel heart!

Go live, poor wanderer of the wood and field,
The bitter little of life that remains!
No more the thickening brakes and verdant plains
To thee shall home, or food, or pastime yield.

Seek, mangled wretch, some place of wonted rest,
No more of rest, but now of dying bed!
The sheltering rushes whistling o'er thy head,
The cold earth with thy bloody bosom prest.

Oft as by winding Nith I, musing, wait
The sober eve, or hail the cheerful dawn,
I'll miss thee sporting o'er the dewy lawn,
And curse the ruffian's aim, and mourn thy hapless fate.

A NEW PSALM FOR THE CHAPEL OF
KILMARNOCK

ON THE THANKSGIVING-DAY FOR
HIS MAJESTY'S RECOVERY

Thursday 23rd April (St. George's Day) was declared a
day of public thanksgiving for the King's recent
recovery from insanity. Burns looked on 'the whole
business as a solemn farce or pageant mummery.' This
'psalm', signed Duncan McLeerie, was sent to the
Edinburgh Star.

O, sing a new song to the Lord!
Make, all and every one,
A joyful noise, ev'n for the King
His restoration!

354

A New Psalm For The Chapel Of Kilmarnock

The sons of Belial in the land
  Did set their heads together.
'Come, let us sweep them off,' said they,
  'Like an o'erflowing river!'

They set their heads together, I say,
  They set their heads together:
On right, on left and every hand,
  We saw none to deliver.

Thou madest strong two chosen ones,
  To quell the Wicked's pride:
That Young Man, great in Issachar,   William Pitt
  The burden-bearing tribe.   Genesis xlix. 14-15

And him, among the Princes, chief   Lord Thurlow
  In our Jerusalem,
The Judge that's mighty in Thy law,
  The man that fears Thy name.

Yet they, even they, with all their strength,
  Began to faint and fail;
Even as two howling, rav'ning wolves
  To dogs do turn their tail.

Th' ungodly o'er the just prevail'd;
  For so Thou hadst appointed,
That Thou might'st greater glory give
  Unto Thine own anointed!

And now Thou hast restored our State,
  Pity our Kirk also;
For she by tribulations
  Is now brought very low!

Consume that high-place, Patronage,
  From off Thy holy hill;
And in Thy fury burn the book
  Even of that man M'Gill!   Rev. Dr. William McGill
                               (1732-1807)

Now hear our prayer, accept our song,
  And fight Thy chosen's battle!
We seek but little, Lord, from Thee;
  Thou kens we get as little!

ON JOHN McMURDO, ESQ.

Said to have been inscribed on a window-pane in John
McMurdo's house at Drumlanrig.

Blest be McMurdo to his latest day!
No envious cloud o'ercast his evening ray!
No wrinkle furrow'd by the hand of care,
Nor ever sorrow, add one silver hair!
O may no son the father's honor stain,
Nor ever daughter give the mother pain!

TO JOHN McMURDO, ESQ.,
OF DRUMLANRIG

SENT WITH SOME OF THE AUTHOR'S POEMS

John McMurdo (1743-1803) was chamberlain to the
Duke of Queensberry at Drumlanrig Castle. Burns
lent him his collection of bawdry, later known as the
Merry Muses.

O, could I give thee India's wealth,
    As I this trifle send!
Because thy Joy in both would be
    To share them with a friend!

But golden sands did never grace
    The Heliconian stream;
Then take what gold could never buy—
    An honest Bard's esteem.

INSCRIBED TO THE RIGHT HON.
C. J. FOX

Charles James Fox (1749-1806) was the enfant terrible
of late-18th century politics, best remembered as the
champion of the American colonists and the French
revolutionaries and the ardent advocate of the liberty
of the people against Tory autocracy.

How Wisdom and Folly meet, mix, and unite,
How Virtue and Vice blend their black and their white,
How Genius, th' illustrious father of fiction,
Confounds rule and law, reconciles contradiction,
I sing: If these mortals, the critics, should bustle,
I care not, not I: let the critics go whistle!

But now for a Patron, whose name and whose glory,
At once may illustrate and honor my story:—

356

Inscribed To The Right Hon. C. J. Fox

Thou first of our orators, first of our wits,
Yet whose parts and acquirements seem mere lucky hits;
With knowledge so vast, and with judgment so strong,
No man, with the half of 'em e'er could go wrong;
With passions so potent, and fancies so bright,
No man with the half of 'em e'er could go right;
A sorry, poor, misbegot son of the Muses,
For using thy name, offers fifty excuses.

Good Lord, what is Man! For as simple he looks,
Do but try to develop his hooks and his crooks!
With his depths and his shallows, his good and his evil,
All in all, he's a problem must puzzle the Devil.

On his one ruling passion Sir Pope hugely labors,   *Alexander*
That, like th' old Hebrew walking-switch eats up its neighbours,   *Pope*
Human Nature his show-box—your friend, would you know him?   *peep-show*
Pull the string, Ruling Passion – the picture will show him.
What pity, in rearing so beauteous a system,
One trifling particular, *Truth,* should have miss'd him!
For, spite of his fine theoretic positions,
Mankind is a science defies definitions.

Some sort all our qualities each to its tribe,
And think Human Nature they truly describe;
Have you found this, or t'other? There's more in the wind,
As by one drunken fellow his comrades you'll find.
But such is the flaw, of the depth of the plan
In the make of that wonderful creature called Man,
No two virtues, whatever relation they claim,
Nor even two different shades of the same,
Though like as was ever twin brother to brother,
Possessing the one shall imply you've the other.

But truce with abstraction, and truce with a Muse
Whose rhymes you'll perhaps, Sir, ne'er deign to peruse!
Will you leave your justings, your jars, and your quarrels,
Contending with Billy for proud-nodding laurels?   *William Pitt*
My much-honor'd Patron, believe your poor Poet,
Your courage, much more than your prudence, you show it.
In vain with Squire Billy for laurels you struggle:
He'll have them by fair trade — if not, he will smuggle:
Nor cabinets even of kings would conceal 'em,
He'd up the back-stairs, and by God he would steal 'em!
Then feats like Squire Billy's you ne'er can achieve 'em;
It is not, out-do him — the task is, out-thieve him!

TO PETER STUART

Peter Stuart (d. 1805) founded the London Star in
1788, the first regular evening paper in the Metropolis.
Soon after he fell out with his partners and formed
the Morning Star. Burns's connection with him dates
from this period.

Dear Peter, Dear Peter,
We poor sons of metre
know   Are often negleckit, ye ken;
For instance, your sheet, man,
(Tho glad I'm to see't, man),
not one   I get it no ae day in ten.

R. B.

ON THE DUCHESS OF GORDON'S
REEL DANCING

Though written in Burns's style, this poem was
probably not by him. It was published under his
name in the London Star on 31st March 1789,
but Burns wrote to the paper on 13th April
disclaiming the 'silly verses on the Duchess of
Gordon.' The Duchess was one of his patrons and
he was at considerable pains not to risk giving her
offence.

petticoat   She kiltit up her kirtle weel
ankles   To show her bonie cutes sae sma',
And walloped about the reel,
dancer   The lightest louper o them a'!

salivating, senile, bullocks While some, like slav'ring, doited stots
Lurching, mud   Stoit'ring out thro the midden dub,
Caught   Fankit their heels amang their coats
made   And gart the floor their backsides rub;

Gordon, the great, the gay, the gallant,
hare, fence   Skip't like a maukin owre a dyke:
stripling   Deil take me, since I was a callant,
If, eyes   Gif e'er my een beheld the like!

DELIA

Submitted by Burns to the London Star, 18th May
1789: 'your insertion of the inclosed trifle will be
succeeded by future communications.'

Fair the face of orient day,
Fair the tints of op'ning rose;
But fairer still my Delia dawns,
More lovely far her beauty blows.

Delia

Sweet the Lark's wild-warbled lay,
Sweet the tinkling rill to hear;
But, Delia, more delightful still,
Steal thine accents on mine ear.

The flower-enamour'd busy Bee
The rosy banquet loves to sip;
Sweet the streamlet's limpid lapse
To the sun-brown'd Arab's lip;

But, Delia, on thy balmy lips
Let me, no vagrant insect, rove!
O let me steal one liquid kiss!
For Oh! my soul is parch'd with love!

THE KIRK'S ALARM

TUNE: *Come rouse, Brother Sportsmen*

The Rev. William McGill (1732-1807), one of the New
Licht ministers in Ayr and a friend of Burns and his
father, incurred the wrath of the Auld Lichts on the
publication of his treatise The Death of Jesus Christ
(1786). The General Assembly ordered an enquiry at
Ayr in July 1789. McGill hastily recanted and the case
was dropped after he made a grovelling apology to the
Presbytery. The wretched affair provoked this satire,
written in the autumn of 1789.

Orthodox! orthodox! wha believe in John Knox—
    Let me sound an alarm to your conscience:
A heretic blast has been blown i' the Wast,
    That what is not sense must be nonsense—
Orthodox! That what is not sense must be nonsense.

Doctor Mac! Doctor Mac, you should stretch on a rack,   Dr. McGill
    To strike wicked Writers wi terror:
To join Faith and Sense, upon onie pretence,
    Was heretic, damnable error—
Doctor Mac! 'Twas heretic, damnable error.

Town of Ayr! Town of Ayr! it was rash, I declare,
    To meddle wi mischief a-brewing:
Provost John is still deaf to the Church's relief,   John Ballantine
    And Orator Bob is its ruin—   Robert Aiken
Town of Ayr! And Orator Bob is its ruin.

D'rymple mild! D'rymple mild! tho your heart's like a child!   William
    An your life like the new-driven snaw,   Dalrymple
Yet that winna save ye, auld Satan, just have ye,
    For preaching that three's ane an twa —
Dr'ymple mild! For preaching that three's ane an twa.

359

The Kirk's Alarm

Calvin's sons! Calvin's sons! seize your sp'ritual guns,
    Ammunition you never can need;
Your hearts are the stuff will be powther enough,
    And your skulls are storehouses o lead
Calvin's sons! Your skulls are storehouses o lead.

powder

Rumble John! Rumble John! mount the steps with a groan,
    Cry, 'The Book is wi heresy cramm'd;'
Then lug out your ladle, deal brimstone like adle,
    And roar ev'ry note of the damn'd—
Rumble John! And roar ev'ry note of the damn'd.

Rev. John Russel

pull, cow's urine

Simper James! Simper James, leave the fair Killie dames—
    There's a holier chase in your view:
I'll lay on your head, that the pack you'll soon lead,
    For puppies like you there's but a few—
Simper James! For puppies like you there's but few.

*Rev. James
MacKinlay*

Singet Sawnie! Singet Sawnie, are ye herdin the penny,
    Unconscious what evils await?
Wi a jump, yell, and howl, alarm ev'ry soul,
    For the Foul Fiend is just at your gate,
Singet Sawnie! The Foul Fiend is just at your gate.

*Rev. Alexander
Moodie*

Shrivelled

Daddie Auld! Daddie Auld, there's a tod in the fauld,
    A tod meikle waur than the clerk;
Tho ye do little skaith, ye'll be in at the death,
    And gif ye canna bite, ye may bark,
Daddie Auld! For gif ye canna bite, ye may bark.

*Rev. William Auld
fox, much worse
damage
if*

Jamie Goose! Jamie Goose! ye hae made but toom roose,
    In hunting the wicked Lieutenant;
But the Doctor's your mark, for the Lord's haly ark,
    He has cooper'd an ca'd a wrang pin in't,
Jamie Goose! He has cooper'd an ca'd a wrang pin in't.

*Rev. James Young
empty, flattery*

knocked

Davie Rant! Davie Rant, wi a face like a saunt,
    And a heart that wad poison a hog,
Raise an impudent roar, like a breaker lee-shore,
    Or the kirk will be tint in a bog.
Davie Rant! Or the kirk will be tint in a bog.

Rev. David Grant

lost

Poet Willie! Poet Willie, gie the Doctor a volley,
    Wi your 'Liberty's Chain' and your wit;
O'er Pegasus' side ye ne'er laid a stride,
    Ye but smelt, man, the place where he shit,
Poet Willie! Ye but smelt, man, the place where he shit.

William Peebles

Andro Gowk! Andro Gowk! ye may slander the Book,
    An the Book no the waur, let me tell ye;
Ye are rich, an look big, but lay by hat an' wig,
    An ye'll hae a calf's head o sma' value,
Andro Gowk! Ye'll hae a calf's head o sma' value.

*Andrew Mitchell,
cuckoo*

The Kirk's Alarm

Barr Steenie! Barr Steenie! what mean ye? what mean ye?　Rev. Stephen Young
　If ye meddle nae mair wi the matter,
Ye may hae some pretence, to havins and sense,
　Wi people wha ken ye nae better,
Barr Steenie! Wi people wha ken ye nae better.

Irvine-side! Irvine-side, wi your turkey-cock pride　Rev. George Smith
　Of manhood but sma' is your share:
Ye've the figure, 'tis true, ev'n your faes maun allow,　foes
　An your friends daurna say ye hae mair,　dare not
Irvine-side! Your friends daurna say ye hae mair.

Muirland Jock! Muirland Jock, whom the Lord gave a stock　John Sheppard
　Wad act up a tinkler in brass;
If ill-manners were wit, there's no mortal so fit
　To prove the poor Doctor an ass,
Muirland Jock! To prove the poor Doctor an ass.

Holy Will! Holy Will, there was wit i' your skull,　William Fisher
　When ye pilfer'd the alms o the poor;
The timmer is scant when ye're taen for a saunt,　material, taken
　Wha should swing in a rape for an hour,　rope
Holy Will! Ye should swing in a rape for an hour.

Poet Burns! Poet Burns, wi your priest-skelpin turns,　bashing
　Why desert ye your auld native shire?
Your Muse is a gipsy, yet were she e'en tipsy,
　She could ca' us nae waur than we are—　worse
Poet Burns! ye could ca' us nae waur than we are.

PRESENTATION STANZAS TO CORRESPONDENTS

Afton's Laird! Afton's Laird, when your pen can be spared,　John Logan
　A copy of this I bequeath,
On the same sicker score as I mention'd before,
　To that trusty auld worthy, Clackleith—　James Johnson
Afton's Laird! To that trusty auld worthy, Clackleith.

Factor John! Factor John, whom the Lord made alone,　John McMurdo or
　And ne'er made anither thy peer,　John Kennedy
Thy poor servant, the Bard, in respectful regard,
　He presents thee this token sincere.
Factor John! He presents thee this token sincere.

SONNET TO ROBERT GRAHAM, ESQ.,
OF FINTRY

ON RECEIVING A FAVOUR, AUG. 10, 1789

The poet's repeated importuning of the Commissioner of the Board of Excise eventually paid off. Mr. Graham's 'warmest exertions' obtained for Burns an appointment to the Dumfries division of the Excise. The favour referred to in the sub-title was Burns's commission, dated 14th July 1789.

I call no Goddess to inspire my strains:
A fabled Muse may suit a Bard that feigns.
Friend of my life! my ardent spirit burns,
And all the tribute of my heart returns,
For boons accorded, goodness ever new,
The gift still dearer, as the giver you.
Thou orb of day! thou other paler light!
And all ye many sparkling stars of night!
If aught that giver from my mind efface,
If I that giver's bounty e'er disgrace,
Then roll to me along your wand'ring spheres
Only to number out a villain's years!
I lay my hand upon my swelling breast,
And grateful would, but cannot, speak the rest.

THE KEEKIN GLASS

Said to have been written on the back of a letter at Dalswinton, about 1789, on hearing that a drunken judge on the Dumfries bench had pointed to one of Patrick Miller's beautiful daughters and — his vision 'much affected' — asked 'Wha's yon howlet-faced thing in the corner?'

owl-face   How daur ye ca' me 'Howlet-face'
            Ye blear-e'ed, withered spectre?
mirror   Ye only spied the keekin glass,
            An there ye saw your picture.

INSCRIPTION ON A GOBLET

Said by Cunningham to have been written on a goblet belonging to John Syme, on the second book of Kings, iv. 40.

There's Death in the cup, so beware!
    Nay, more—there is danger in touching;
But who can avoid the fell snare?
    The man and his wine's so bewitching!

ON ANDREW TURNER

'A vain coxcomb of an English commercial traveller'who
tried to patronise Burns over a bottle of wine in the
King's Arms, Dumfries. Burns was asked by his friends,
whose party had been interrupted by Turner, to give an
example of his impromptu versifying. On hearing the
Englishman's age and name he produced the following.

In Se'enteen Hunder'n Forty-Nine,
The Deil gat stuff to make a swine,
   An coost it in a corner;   cast
But wilily he chang'd his plan,
An shap'd it something like a man,
   An ca'd it Andrew Turner.

KIRK AND STATE EXCISEMEN

Probably composed in 1789, following his appointment
to the Excise, and putting the principle of taxation into
proper perspective.

Ye men of wit and wealth, why all this sneering
'Gainst poor Excisemen? Give the cause a hearing.
What are your Landlord's rent-rolls? Taxing ledgers!
What Premiers? What ev'n Monarchs? Mighty Gaugers!
Nay, what are Priests (those seeming godly wise-men)?
What are they, pray, but Spiritual Excisemen!

A GRACE BEFORE DINNER

O Thou who kindly dost provide
   For ev'ry creature's want!
We bless the God of Nature wide,
   For all Thy goodness lent.

And if it please Thee, heavenly Guide,
   May never worse be sent;
But, whether granted or denied,
   Lord, bless us with content.

A GRACE AFTER DINNER

O Thou, in whom we live and move,
   Who made the sea and shore,
Thy goodness constantly we prove,
   And, grateful, would adore.

And, if it please Thee, Power above!
   Still grant us with such store
The friend we trust, the fair we love,
   And we desire no more.

363

WILLIE BREW'D A PECK O MAUT

In the autumn of 1789 Burns and Allan Masterton (d.
1799), writing master in Edinburgh High School,
visited William Nicol, then on holiday at Moffat. 'We
had such a joyous evening'. wrote Burns,' that Mr.
Masterton and I each in our own way should celebrate
the business.' The result was this Bacchanal – words by
Burns and music by Masterton. The Willie, Rob and
Allan of the first verse are Nicol, Burns and Masterton
respectively.

CHORUS

We are na fou, we're nae that fou,
    But just a drappie in our e'e!
The cock may crae, the day may daw,
    And ay we'll taste the barley bree!

O, Willie brew'd a peck o maut,
    And Rob and Allan cam to see.
Three blyther hearts, that lee-lang night,
    Ye wad na found in Christendie.

Here are we met, three merry boys,
    Three merry boys I trow are we;
And monie a night we've merry been,
    And monie mae we hope to be!

It is the moon, I ken her horn,
    That's blinkin in the lift sae hie:
She shines sae bright to wyle us hame,
    But, by my sooth, she'll wait a wee!

Wha first shall rise to gang awa,
    A cuckold, coward loun is he!
Wha first beside his chair shall fa',
    He is the King amang us three!

drunk
droplet
dawn
brew

live-long

know
glinting, sky

bit

fool

THE FIVE CARLINS

TUNE: *Chevy Chase*

In the Parliamentary election of September 1789 the
candidates for the Dumfriesshire burghs (Dumfries,
Lochmaben, Annan, Kirkcudbright and Sanquhar)
were Sir James Johnstone of Westerhall, and Captain
Patrick Miller of Dalswinton (son of the poet's
landlord), representing the Tory and Whig interests
respectively. Though Whig by nature, Burns disliked
young Miller and heartily detested the Duke of
Queensberry his patron and gradually swung to the
Tory side during the election campaign.

matrons

There was five carlins in the South:
    They fell upon a scheme,
To send a lad to London town,
    To bring them tidings hame.

The Five Carlins

Nor only bring them tidings hame,
    But do their errands there:
And aiblins gowd and honor baith   *perhaps, gold, both*
    Might be that laddie's share.

There was Maggie by the banks o Nith,   *Dumfries*
    A dame wi pride eneugh;
And Marjorie o the Monie Lochs,   *Lochmaben*
    A carlin auld and teugh.   *tough*

And Blinkin Bess of Annandale,   *Annan*
    That dwelt near Solway-side;
And Brandy Jean, that took her gill,   *Kirkcudbright*
    In Galloway sae wide.

And Black Joan, frae Crichton Peel,   *Sanquhar*
    O gipsy kith an kin:
Five wighter carlins were na found   *more powerful*
    The South countrie within.

To send a lad to London town,
    They met upon a day;
And monie a knight, and monie a laird,
    This errand fain wad gae.

O, monie a knight, and monie a laird,
    This errand fain wad gae;
But nae ane could their fancy please,
    O, ne'er a ane but tway!

The first ane was a belted Knight,   *Sir James Johnstone*
    Bred of a Border band;
And he wad gae to London Town,
    Might nae man him withstand.

And he wad do their errands weel,
    And meikle he wad say;   *much, would*
And ilka ane at London court   *everyone*
    Wad bid to him guid-day.

The neist cam in a Soger youth,   *Captain Miller*
    Wha spak wi modest grace;
And he wad gae to London Town,
    If sae their pleasure was.

He wad na hecht them courtly gifts,   *promise*
    Nor meikle speech pretend;
But he wad hecht an honest heart,
    Wad ne'er desert his friend.

Now, wham to chuse, and wham refuse,
    At strife thae carlins fell;
For some had gentlefolk to please,
    And some wad please themsel.

prim-mouthed

Then out spak mim-mou'd Meg o Nith,
    And she spak up wi pride,
And she wad send the Soger lad,
    Whatever might betide.

King George III

For the auld Guidman o London court
    She didna care a pin;
But she wad send the Soger lad,
    To greet his eldest son.

oath

Then up sprang Bess o Annandale,
    And swore a deadly aith,
Says: 'I will send the belted Knight,
    Spite of you carlins baith!

'For far-off fowls hae feathers fair,
    And fools o change are fain:
But I hae tried this Border Knight,
    And I'll try him yet again.'

gossips

Then Brandy Jean spak owre her drink,
    'Ye weel ken, kimmers a',
The auld Guidman o London court,
    His back's been at the wa';

cup
hostile

And monie a friend that kiss'd his caup
    Is now a fremit wight;
But it's ne'er be sae wi Brandy Jean,—
    I'll send the Border Knight.

stern

Says Black Joan frae Crichton Peel,
    A carlin stoor and grim:—
'The auld Guidman, and the young Guidman,
    For me may sink or swim!

'For fools will prate o right or wrang,
    While knaves laugh in their slieve;
But whae blaws best the horn shall win—
    I'll spier nae courtier's leave!'

ask

Then slow raise Marjorie o the Lochs,
    And wrinkled was her brow,
Her ancient weed was russet gray,
    Her auld Scots heart was true:—

'There's some great folk set light by me,
    I set as light by them;
But I will send to London town
    Wham I lo'e best at hame.'

turmoil

Sae how this sturt and strife may end,
    There's naebody can tell;
God grant the King and ilka man
    May look weel to himsel!

ELECTION BALLAD FOR WESTERHA'

TUNE: *Up on waur them a' Willie*

Composed in late 1789 about Sir James Johnstone (1726-94) but really attacking the Duke of Queensberry. Despite (or because of) this poetic 'support', Johnstone, who had represented the Dumfriesshire burghs since 1784, lost to Captain Miller, son of Burns's landlord, Patrick Miller of Dalswinton. Johnstone sat in Parliament for Weymouth (1791-94).

CHORUS

Up and waur them a', Jamie,
Up and waur them a'!
The Johnstones hae the guidin o't:
Ye turncoat Whigs, awa!

The Laddies by the banks o Nith
    Wad trust his Grace wi a', Jamie;
But he'll sair them, as he sair'd the King—   serve
    Turn tail and rin awa, Jamie.

The day he stude his country's friend,   stood
    Or gied her faes a claw, Jamie,   foes, scratch
Or frae puir man a blessin wan—   won
    That day the Duke ne'er saw, Jamie.

But wha is he, his country's boast?
    Like him there is na twa, Jamie!
There's no a callant tents the kye,   youth, tends, cattle
    But kens o Westerha', Jamie.   knows

To end the wark, here's Whistlebirk—   Alex Birtwhistle
    Lang may his whistle blae, Jamie!   Provost of Kirkcudbright
And Maxwell true, o sterling blue;   Robert Maxwell,
    And we'll be Johnstones a', Jamie.   Provost of Lochmaben

TO MISS CRUIKSHANK

A VERY YOUNG LADY

WRITTEN ON THE BLANK LEAF OF A BOOK,
PRESENTED TO HER BY THE AUTHOR

Addressed to Jean Cruikshank, daughter of William Cruikshank of the High School, Edinburgh. The melody was composed by David Sillar.

Beauteous Rosebud, young and gay,
Blooming on thy early May,
Never may'st thou, lovely flower,
Chilly shrink in sleety shower!
Never Boreas' hoary path,
Never Eurus' pois'nous breath,

To Miss Cruikshank

Never baleful stellar lights,
Taint thee with untimely blights!
Never, never reptile thief
Riot on thy virgin leaf!
Nor even Sol too fiercely view
Thy bosom blushing still with dew!

May'st thou long, sweet crimson gem,
Richly deck thy native stem;
Till some ev'ning, sober, calm,
Dropping dews and breathing balm,
While all around the woodland rings,
And ev'ry bird thy requiem sings,
Thou, amid the dirgeful sound,
Shed thy dying honours round,
And resign to parent Earth
The loveliest form she e'er gave birth.

THE WHISTLE – A BALLAD

The contest here described took place at Friars' Carse
on 16th October 1789. The prize was a little ebony
whistle brought to Scotland by a Dane in the service
of Prince George of Denmark who married Princess
(later Queen) Anne in 1683. He lost it in a drinking
contest to Sir Robert Lawrie, first baronet of
Maxwelton, one of whose daughters married Walter
Riddell of Glenriddell. The whistle thus passed into the
Riddell family. Sir Robert Lawrie, 3rd baronet,
attempted to emulate his grandfather in this drinking
contest with Robert Riddell and Alexander Fergusson
of Craigdarroch. The latter consumed upwards of 5
bottles of claret before blowing the victory blast.
John McMurdo was the judge and Burns a witness and
recorder of the event. The 'good Scottish King' (l.3)
was James VI, whose daughter Anne also married a
Prince George of Denmark, but that took place almost
a century earlier.

I sing of a Whistle, a Whistle of worth,
I sing of a Whistle, the pride of the North,
Was brought to the court of our good Scottish King,
And long with this Whistle all Scotland shall ring.

Odin (Scandinavia)

Old Loda, still rueing the arm of Fingal,
The God of the Bottle sends down from his hall:
'This Whistle's your challenge, to Scotland get o'er,
And drink them to Hell, Sir! or ne'er see me more!'

Old poets have sung, and old chronicles tell,
What champions ventur'd, what champions fell:

the Danish contestant

The son of the great Loda was conqueror still,
And blew on the Whistle their requiem shrill.

368

The Whistle — A Ballad

Till Robert, the lord of the Cairn and the Scaur, Sir Robert Lawrie
Unmatch'd at the bottle, unconquer'd in war,
He drank his poor god-ship as deep as the sea;
No tide of the Baltic e'er drunker than he.

Thus Robert, victorious, the trophy has gain'd;
Which now in his house has for ages remain'd;
Till three noble chieftains, and all of his blood,
The jovial contest again have renew'd.

Three joyous good fellows, with hearts clear of flaw;
Craigdarroch, so famous for wit, worth, and law;
And trusty Glenriddel, so skill'd in old coins;
And gallant Sir Robert, deep-read in old wines.

Craigdarroch began, with a tongue smooth as oil,
Desiring Glenriddel to yield up the spoil;
Or else he would muster the heads of the clan,
And once more, in claret, try which was the man.

'By the gods of the ancients!' Glenriddel replies,
'Before I surrender so glorious a prize,
I'll conjure the ghost of the great Rorie More, Ruairidh Mór MacLeod of
And bumper his horn with him twenty times o'er.' MacLeod whose drinking
horn at Dunvegan holds 2
litres.

Sir Robert, a soldier, no speech would pretend,
But he ne'er turn'd his back on his foe, or his friend;
Said, 'Toss down the Whistle, the prize of the field,'
And, knee-deep in claret, he'd die ere he'd yield.

To the board of Glenriddel our heroes repair,
So noted for drowning of sorrow and care;
But for wine and for welcome, not more known to fame,
Than the sense, wit, and taste, of a sweet lovely dame. Elizabeth Kennedy,
who married Riddell,
1784

A Bard was selected to witness the fray,
And tell future ages the feats of the day;
A Bard who detested all sadness and spleen,
And wish'd that Parnassus a vineyard had been.

The dinner being over, the claret they ply,
And ev'ry new cork is a new spring of joy;
In the bands of old friendship and kindred so set,
And the bands grew the tighter the more they were wet.

Gay Pleasure ran riot as bumpers ran o'er;
Bright Phoebus ne'er witness'd so joyous a core,
And vow'd that to leave them he was quite forlorn,
Till Cynthia hinted he'd seen them next morn.

Six bottles a-piece had well wore out the night,
When gallant Sir Robert, to finish the fight,
Turn'd o'er in one bumper a bottle of red,
And swore 'twas the way that their ancestor did.

The Whistle — A Ballad

Then worthy Glenriddel, so cautious and sage,
No longer the warfare ungodly would wage:
A high Ruling Elder to wallow in wine!
He left the foul business to folks less divine.

The gallant Sir Robert fought hard to the end;
But who can with Fate and quart bumpers contend?
Though Fate said, a hero should perish in light;
So uprose bright Phoebus—and down fell the knight.

Next uprose our Bard, like a prophet in drink:—
'Craigdarroch, thou'lt soar when creation shall sink!
But if thou would flourish immortal in rhyme,
Come — one bottle more — and have at the sublime!

'Thy line, that have struggled for freedom with Bruce,
Shall heroes and patriots ever produce:
So thine be the laurel, and mine be the bay;
The field thou hast won, by yon bright God of Day!'

ANSWER TO AN INVITATION

Allegedly lines written extempore on a page torn from Burns's Excise-book, and preserved at Craigdarroch, according to Cromek, but long suspect as Burns had not yet begun his Excise career. The invitation was to the contest over the whistle, subject of the previous poem.

The King's most humble servant, I
    Can scarcely spare a minute;
But I'll be wi you by an bye,
    Or else the deil's be in it.

EPISTLE TO DR. BLACKLOCK

ELLISLAND, 21st October, 1789

Thomas Blacklock (1721-91), blinded by smallpox as a baby, was the son of an Annan bricklayer. Largely self-educated, he studied divinity in Edinburgh and was ordained minister of Kirkcudbright in 1762. He retired to Edinburgh in 1765 and devoted the rest of his life to running a boarding school. The friend of Samuel Johnson, David Hume and Benjamin Franklin, Dr. Blacklock was a man of broad culture and one of Edinburgh's arbiters of taste. A minor poet, his chief contribution to Scottish literature was to encourage Burns and deflect him from emigration. Robert Heron (1764-1807), assistant to Hugh Blair, was the drunken hack whose memoir of Burns was a subtle exercise in in character assassination.

proud
cheerful
knew, little excursion
set you up

Wow, but your letter made me vauntie!
And are ye hale, and weel, and cantie?
I kend it still, your wee bit jauntie
        Wad bring ye to:
Lord send you ay as weel's I want ye,
        And then ye'll do!

370

Epistle To Dr. Blacklock

The Ill-Thief blaw the Heron south,   Devil
And never drink be near his drouth!   thirst
He tauld mysel by word o mouth,   told
      He'd tak my letter:
I lippen'd to the chiel in trowth,   trusted, chap
      And bade nae better.

But aiblins, honest Master Heron   perhaps
Had, at the time, some dainty fair one
To ware his theologic care on,
      And holy study,
And, tired o sauls to waste his lear on,   souls, learning
      E'en tried the body.

But what d'ye think, my trusty fier?   friend
I'm turn'd a gauger — Peace be here!
Parnassian queires, I fear, I fear,   choirs
      Ye'll now disdain me,
And then my fifty pounds a year
      Will little gain me!

Ye glaikit, gleesome, dainty damies,   giddy
Wha, by Castalia's wimplin streamies,   meandering
Lowp, sing, and lave your pretty limbies,   leap
      Ye ken, ye ken,
That strang necessity supreme is
      'Mang sons o men.

I hae a wife and twa wee laddies;
They maun hae brose and brats o duddies: must have, scraps of clothing
Ye ken yoursels my heart right proud is—
      I need na vaunt—
But I'll sned besoms, thraw saugh woodies,   prune, brooms
      Before they want.   weave, willow twigs

Lord help me thro this warld o care!
I'm weary-sick o't late and air!   early
Not but I hae a richer share
      Than monie ithers;
But why should ae man better fare,
      And a' men brithers?

Come, firm Resolve, take thou the van,
Thou stalk o carl-hemp in man!   male-hemp
And let us mind, faint heart ne'er wan   remember
      A lady fair:
Wha does the utmost that he can,
      Will whyles do mair.   sometimes

Epistle To Dr. Blacklock

But to conclude my silly rhyme
(I'm scant o verse and scant o time):
To make a happy fireside clime
       To weans and wife,
That's the true pathos and sublime
      Of human life.

My compliments to sister Beckie,
And eke the same to honest Lucky:
I wat she is a daintie chuckie,
      As e'er tread clay:
And gratefully, my guid auld cockie,
      I'm yours for ay.

ROBERT BURNS

children (gloss for "weans")

hen (gloss for "chuckie")

THOU LINGERING STAR

Tune: *Mary weep no more for me*

**This melancholy poem was composed around the third
anniversary of the death of Mary Campbell. Burns sent
it on 8th November 1789 to Mrs Dunlop as 'a Song I
made the other day, of which your opinion, as I am
too much interested in the subject of it, to be a Critic.'**

Thou ling'ring star, with less'ning ray,
    That lov'st to greet the early morn,
Again thou usher'st in the day
    My Mary from my soul was torn.
O Mary dear departed shade!
    Where is thy place of blissful rest?
See'st thou thy lover lowly laid?
    Hear'st thou the groans that rend his breast?

That sacred hour can I forget?
    Can I forget the hallow'd grove,
Where, by the winding Ayr, we met,
    To live one day of parting love?
Eternity cannot efface
    Those records dear of transports past,
Thy image at our last embrace—
    Ah! little thought we 'twas our last!

Ayr, gurgling, kiss'd his pebbled shore,
    O'erhung with wild-woods, thickening green;
The fragrant birch and hawthorn hoar,
    'Twin'd amorous round the raptur'd scene;
The flowers sprang wanton to be prest,
    The birds sang love on every spray,
Till too, too soon, the glowing west,
    Proclaim'd the speed of winged day.

Thou Lingering Star

Still o'er these scenes my mem'ry wakes,
    And fondly broods with miser-care;
Time but th' impression stronger makes,
    As streams their channels deeper wear.
O Mary! dear departed shade!
    Where is thy place of blissful rest?
See'st thou thy lover lowly laid?
    Hear'st thou the groans that rend his breast?

ON THE LATE CAPTAIN GROSE'S PEREGRINATIONS THRO SCOTLAND

COLLECTING THE ANTIQUITIES OF THAT KINGDOM

Captain Francis Grose (1731-91), son of a Swiss jeweller in London, was successively an Army officer, Richmond Herald in the College of Arms and paymaster of the Surrey Militia - a position that almost bankrupted him. He is best remembered for his Antiquities of England and Wales (1773-87) and the two-volume sequel on Scotland. Burns met him while he was gathering Scottish material in Annandale and Nithsdale, at Friars' Carse in July 1789.

Hear, Land o Cakes, and brither Scots   i.e. oatcakes
Frae Maidenkirk to Johnie Groat's,   Wigtownshire to Caithness
If there's a hole in a' your coats,
        I rede you tent it: advise, look after
A chield's amang you takin notes,   chap
        And faith he'll prent it:

If in your bounds ye chance to light
Upon a fine, fodgel wight,   dumpy
O stature short but genius bright,
        That's he, mark weel:
And wow! he has an unco sleight   uncommon skill
        O cauk and keel.   chalk, pencil

By some auld, houlet-haunted biggin,   owl , building
Or kirk deserted by its riggin,   roof
It's ten to ane ye'll find him snug in
        Some eldritch part,   haunted
Wi deils, they say, Lord safe's! colleaguin   save us
        At some black art.

Ilk ghaist that haunts auld ha' or chamer,   each, chamber
Ye gipsy-gang that deal in glamour,   magic
And you, deep-read in hell's black grammar,
        Warlocks and witches:
Ye'll quake at his conjuring hammer,
        Ye midnight bitches!

On The Late Captain Grose's Peregrinations Thro Scotland

It's tauld he was a sodger bred,
And ane wad rather fa'n than fled;
But now he's quat the spurtle-blade,
    And dog-skin wallet,
And taen the—Antiquarian trade,
    I think they call it.

He has a fouth o auld nick-nackets:
Rusty airn caps and jinglin jackets
Wad haud the Lothians three in tackets,
    A towmont guid;
And parritch-pats and auld saut-backets,
    Before the Flood.

Of Eve's first fire he has a cinder;
Auld Tubalcain's fire-shool and fender;
That which distinguishèd the gender
    O Balaam's ass;
A broomstick o the witch of Endor,
    Weel shod wi brass.

Forbye, he'll shape you aff fu gleg
The cut of Adam's philibeg;
The knife that nicket Abel's craig
    He'll prove you fully,
It was a faulding jocteleg,
    Or lang-kail gullie.

But wad ye see him in his glee—
For meikle glee and fun has he—
Then set him down, and twa or three
    Guid fellows wi him;
And port, O port! shine thou a wee,
    And then ye'll see him!

Now, by the Pow'rs o verse and prose!
Thou art a dainty chield, O Grose!—
Whae'er o thee shall ill suppose,
    They sair misca' thee;
I'd take the rascal by the nose,
    Wad say, 'Shame fa' thee.'

---

**Marginal glosses:**

would have
given up, sword

fund, nick-nacks
iron
shoenails
twelvemonth
porridge-pots, salt-boxes

Genesis iv. 22

Numbers xxii. 21
I Samuel xxviii. 7

Besides, smartly
kilt
slit, throat

clasp-knife

much

little

miscall

befall

LINES WRITTEN UNDER THE PICTURE
OF THE CELEBRATED MISS BURNS

Margaret Burns (d. 1792), the poet's 'poor namesake', was a celebrated Edinburgh prostitute, originally from Durham. She and a Sally Anderson kept a brothel in Rose Street which caused great annoyance to their neighbours. The ladies were prosecuted and 'banished forth of the city and liberties for ever.' Miss Burns appealed to the Court of Session which overturned the sentence on 22nd December 1789, but she died at Rosslyn soon afterwards.

Cease ye prudes, your envious railing!
Lovely Burns has charms—confess!
True it is, she had one failing;
Had ae woman ever less?

I'LL TELL YOU A TALE OF A WIFE

TUNE: *Auld Sir Symon*

Sent to Provost Maxwell of Lochmaben on 20th December 1789, a satire on puritanical hypocrisy

I'll tell you a tale of a Wife,
    And she was a Whig and a Saunt;   saint
She liv'd a most sanctify'd life,
    But whyles she was fash'd wi her —   troubled
      Fal lal &c.

Poor woman! she gaed to the Priest,
    And till him she made her complaint;
'There 's naething that troubles my breast
    'Sae sair as the sins O my —.

'Sin that I was herdin at hame,   tending cattle
    Till now I'm three score and ayont,   beyond
'I own it wi sin and wi shame
    'I've led a sad life wi my —.

He bade her to clear up her brow,
    And no be discourag'd upon 't;
For holy gude women enow
    Were mony times waur't wi their —.

It's naught but Beelzebub's art,
    But that 's the mair sign of a saunt,
He kens that ye 're pure at the heart,
    Sae levels his darts at your —.

What signifies Morals and Works,
    Our works are no wordy a runt!   worthy
It 's Faith that is sound, orthodox,
    That covers the fauts o your —.   faults

I'll Tell You A Tale Of A Wife

Were ye o the Reprobate race
Created to sin and be brunt,
O then it would alter the case
If ye should gae wrang wi your —.

elected

But you that is Called and Free
Elekit and chosen a saunt,
Will 't break the Eternal Decree
Whatever ye do wi your —?

And now with a sanctify'd kiss
Let's kneel and renew covenant:
It 's this—and it 's this—and it 's this—
That settles the pride o your —.

Devotion blew up to a flame;
No words can do justice upon 't;
The honest auld woman gaed hame
Rejoicing and clawin her —.

Then high to her memory charge;
And may he who takes it affront,
Still ride in Love's channel at large,
And never make port in a —!!!

These lines quoted casually in a letter to Ainslie, 29th July 1787, are apparently an alternative to the last stanza.

Then ho, for a merry good fellow,
And hey, for a glass of good strunt;
May never We Sons of Apollo
E'er want a good friend and a —.

PROLOGUE SPOKEN AT THE THEATRE OF DUMFRIES

ON NEW YEAR'S DAY EVENING, 1790

George S. Sutherland, manager of the Dumfries theatre company, was the recipient of these lines on 31st December 1789, with a note: 'Jogging home yester night, it occured to me that as your next night is the first night of the New Year, a few lines allusive to the Season, by way of Prologue, Interlude or what you please, might take very well...' Burns sent a copy to his brother on 11th January 1790 reporting that Sutherland had 'spouted to his Audience with great applause.'

No song nor dance I bring from yon great city
That queens it o'er our taste—the more's the pity!
Tho, by-the-bye, abroad why will you roam?
Good sense and taste are natives here at home.
But not for panegyric I appear:
I come to wish you all a good New Year!

Prologue Spoken At The Theatre Of Dumfries

Old Father Time deputes me here before ye,
Not for to preach, but tell his simple story.
The sage grave Ancient cough'd, and bade me say:
'You're one year older this important day,'
If wiser too— he hinted some suggestion,
But 'twould be rude, you know, to ask the question;
And with a would-be-roguish leer and wink,
He bade me on you press this one word—think!

Ye sprightly youths, quite flush with hope and spirit,
Who think to storm the world by dint of merit,
To you the dotard has a deal to say,
In his sly, dry, sententious, proverb way!
He bids you mind, amid your thoughtless rattle,
That the first blow is ever half the battle;
That, tho some by the skirt may try to snatch him,
Yet by the forelock is the hold to catch him;
That, whether doing, suffering, or forbearing,
You may do miracles by persevering.

Last, tho not least in love, ye youthful fair,
Angelic forms, high Heaven's peculiar care!
To you old Bald-pate smoothes his wrinkled brow,
And humbly begs you'll mind the important—now!
To crown your happiness he asks your leave.
And offers, bliss to give and to receive.

For our sincere, tho haply weak endeavours,
With grateful pride we own your many favours;
And howsoe'er our tongues may ill reveal it,
Believe our glowing bosoms truly feel it.

NITHSDALE'S WELCOME HAME

William Maxwell, 5th Earl of Nithsdale was sentenced
to death after the 1715 Rebellion, but escaped from
the Tower of London and died in Rome in 1744. His
titles and estates were forfeited, but they were restored
to his son, and his grand-daughter Winifred Constable-
Maxwell began rebuilding Terregles mansion in 1789.
Burns met her that year and identified with her as
'Common Sufferers in a Cause where even to be
unfortunate is glorious, the Cause of Heroic Loyalty.'
Lady Winifred, touched by this poem, gave Burns a
snuff-box in 1791.

The noble Maxwells and their powers
    Are coming o'er the border;
And they'll gae big Terreagles' towers,   build
    And set them a' in order;
And they declare Terreagles fair,
    For their abode they choose it:
There's no a heart in a' the land
    But's lighter at the news o't!

377

Nithsdale's Welcome Hame

Tho stars in skies may disappear,
And angry tempests gather,
The happy hour may soon be near
That brings us pleasant weather;
The weary night o care and grief
May hae a joyfu morrow;
So dawning day has brought relief—
Fareweel our night o sorrow!

GREEN SLEEVES

A reworking of the famous ballad of Tudor times. The
air itself was still widely popular in Burns's day.

ribbons   Green sleeves and tartan ties
Mark my truelove where she lies;
before   I'll be at her or she rise,
My fiddle and I thegither.—

Be it by the chrystal burn,
Be it by the milk-white thorn,
I shall rouse her in the morn,
My fiddle and I thegither.—

TO ALEXANDER FINDLATER

Alexander Findlater (1754-1839) was a native of
Burntisland, the son of an exciseman and himself
Excise Supervisor at Dumfries (1787-97) 'a gentleman
of great information and the first worth.' Although it
is undated, this verse-epistle may date around
February 1790.

Ellisland Saturday morning

Dear Sir,

           our Lucky humbly begs
taste, fresh   Ye'll prie her caller, new-laid eggs:
Lord grant the Cock may keep his legs,
        Aboon the Chuckies;
tickle, gad-flies   And wi his kittle, forket clegs,
backsides   Claw weel their dockies!

Had Fate that curst me in her ledger,
Exciseman   A Poet poor, and poorer Gager,
Soldier   Created me that feather'd Sodger,
        A generous Cock,
How I wad craw and strut and roger
cackling   My kecklin Flock!

378

To Alexander Findlater

Buskit wi mony a bien, braw feather,   clad, snug
I wad defied the warst o weather:
When corn or bear I could na gather   barley
  To gie my burdies;
I'd treated them wi caller heather,
  And weel-knooz'd hurdies   well-rounded buttocks

Nae cursed Clerical Excise
On honest Nature's laws and ties;
Free as the vernal breeze that flies
  At early day,
We'd tasted Nature's richest joys,
  But stint or stay.

But as this subject's something kittle,   ticklish
Our wisest way 's to say but little;
And while my Muse is at her mettle,
  I am, most fervent,
Or may I die upon a whittle!   knife
  Your Friend and Servant—
  Robt. Burns.

TO A GENTLEMAN

WHO HAD SENT A NEWSPAPER, AND
OFFERED TO CONTINUE IT FREE OF EXPENSE

Kinsley casts doubt on the assumption, by previous
editors, that the gentleman in question was Peter
Stuart, editor of the Edinburgh Star and Evening
Advertiser, although there seems no reason to doubt
this. Stuart wrote to Burns in May 1789 seeking a
regular contribution and offering him 'a small salary
quite as large as his Excise emoluments.' Burns
declined to become too firmly committed to any one
paper, but he agreed to send occasional poems. In
return Stuart put him on the free list. This poem,
written early in 1790, takes this gesture as its pretext
even though Stuart's decision was taken six or seven
months earlier. Burns uses it as a vehicle for reviewing
recent events.

Kind Sir, I've read your paper through,
And faith, to me, 'twas really new!
How guessed ye, Sir, what maist I wanted?
This monie a day I've grain'd and gaunted, groaned, gaped
To ken what French mischief was brewin; know
Or what the drumlie Dutch were doin;   muddy
That vile doup-skelper, Emperor Joseph, bottom-smacker
If Venus yet had got his nose off;   succumbed to V.D.
Or how the collieshangie works   war of attrition
Atween the Russians and the Turks;
Or if the Swede, before he halt,   Gustavus III (1746-92)
Would play anither Charles the Twalt, Charles XII (1697-1718)

To A Gentleman

If Denmark, any body spak o't;
Or Poland, wha had now the tack o't;
How cut-throat Prussian blades were hingin,
How libbet Italy was singin;
If Spaniard, Portuguese, or Swiss,
Were saying or takin aught amiss;
Or how our merry lads at hame
In Britains's court kept up the game:
How royal George—the Lord leuk o'er him!—
Was managing St. Stephen's quorum;
If sleekit Chatham Will was livin,
Or glaikit Charlie got his nieve in;
How Daddie Burke the plea was cookin;
If Warren Hastings' neck was yeukin,
How cesses, stents, and fees were rax'd,
Or if bare arses yet were tax'd;
The news o princes, dukes, and earls,
Pimps, sharpers, bawds, and opera-girls;
If that daft buckie, Geordie Wales,
Was threshin still at hizzies' tails;
Or if he was grown oughtlins douser,
And no a perfect kintra cooser:
A' this and mair I never heard of,
And, but for you, I might despair'd of.
So, gratefu, back your news I send you,
And pray a' guid things may attend you!

ELLISLAND, *Monday Morning, 1790*

Glosses:
- lease of it
- hanging
- Italian castrati
- House of Commons
- William Pitt
- Charles James Fox
- Edmund Burke
- the long drawn-out impeachment of Hastings (1788-95)
- the Prince of Wales
- any more sedate
- country stallion

ELEGY ON WILLIE NICOL'S MARE

Sent to William Nicol on 9th February 1790 with a covering letter: 'That d-mned mare of yours is dead. I would freely have given her price to have saved her; she has vexed me beyond description... I refused fifty-five shillings for her... I fed her up and had her in first order for Dumfries fair; when four or five days before, she was seized with an unaccountable disorder in the sinews...'

Peg Nicholson was a good bay mare
    As ever trod on airn;
But now she's floating down the Nith,
    And past the mouth o Cairn.

Peg Nicholson was a good bay mare,
    An rode thro thick and thin;
But now she's floating down the Nith,
    And wanting even the skin.

Glosses:
- iron
- Cairn Water 4 miles south of Ellisland

380

Elegy On Willie Nicol's Mare

Peg Nicholson was a good bay mare,
   And ance she bore a priest;
But now she's floating down the Nith,
   For Solway fish a feast.

Peg Nicholson was a good bay mare,
   An the priest he rode her sair;
And much oppress'd, and bruis'd she was,
   As priest-rid cattle are.

I LOVE MY LOVE IN SECRET

**A revision of a fragment of verse and chorus, with new
lines added by Burns.**

CHORUS

*My Sandy O, my Sandy O,
My bonie, bonie Sandy O!
Tho the love that I owe
To thee I dare na show,
Yet I love my love in secret, my Sandy, O!*

My Sandy gied to me a ring   gave
Was a' beset wi diamonds fine;
But I gied him a far better thing,
I gied my heart in pledge o his ring.

My Sandy brak a piece o gowd,   gold
While down his cheeks the saut tears row'd, salt, rolled
He took a hauf, and gied it to me,   half
And I'll keep it till the hour I die.

SWEET TIBBIE DUNBAR

TUNE: *Johny McGill*

Another ancient fragment reworked by Burns.

O, wilt thou go wi me, sweet Tibbie Dunbar?
O, wilt thou go wi me, sweet Tibbie Dunbar?
Wilt thou ride on a horse, or be drawn in a car,
Or walk by my side, O sweet Tibbie Dunbar?

I care na thy daddie, his lands and his money;
I care na thy kin, sae high and sae lordly;
But sae that thou'lt hae me for better or waur, worse
And come in thy coatie, sweet Tibbie Dunbar.

THE TAYLOR FELL THRO THE BED

An old song to which Burns added the second and
fourth stanzas to transform it and give it new life and
meaning.

The Taylor fell thro the bed, thimble an a',
The Taylor fell thro the bed, thimble an a';
The blankets were thin and the sheets they were sma',
The Taylor fell thro the bed, thimble an a'.

The sleepy bit lassie she dreaded nae ill,
The sleepy bit lassie she dreaded nae ill;
The weather was cauld and the lassie lay still,
She thought that a Taylor could do her nae ill.

fourpence

Gie me the groat again, cany young man,
Gie me the groat again, cany young man;
The day it is short and the night it is lang,
The dearest siller that ever I wan.

alone

There's somebody weary wi lying her lane,
There's somebody weary wi lying her lane,

sad

There's some that are dowie, I trow wad be fain
To see the bit Taylor come skippin again.

AY WAUKIN, O

Listed as 'Mr Burns's old words' in Law MS no. 20, and
based on a fragment in Herd's MSS.

CHORUS

awake

Ay waukin, O,
  Waukin still and weary:
Sleep I can get nane
  For thinking on my dearie.

Simmer's a pleasant time:
  Flowers of every colour,

crag

The water rins owre the heugh,
  And I long for my true lover.

When I sleep I dream,

apprehensive

  When I wauk I'm eerie,
Sleep I can get nane,
  For thinkin on my dearie.

Lanely night comes on,

rest

  A' the lave are sleepin,
I think on my bonie lad,

blur, crying

  And I bleer my een wi greetin.

382

BEWARE O BONIE ANN

The subject was Ann Masterton, daughter of Burns's
friend and composer, Allan Masterton.

Ye gallants bright, I rede you right,   counsel
    Beware o bonie Ann!
Her comely face sae fu o grace,
    Your heart she will trepan: ensnare
Her een sae bright, like stars by night,   eyes
    Her skin is like the swan.
Sae jimply lac'd, her genty waist,   tightly, neat
    That sweetly ye might span.

Youth, Grace, and Love attendant move,
    And Pleasure leads the van:
In a' their charms, and conquering arms,
    They wait on bonie Ann.
The captive bands may chain the hands
But Love enslaves the man:
Ye gallants braw, I rede you a',
    Beware o bonie Ann!

MY WIFE'S A WANTON, WEE THING

The first half is traditional, but Burns added the last
eight lines.

My wife's a wanton, wee thing,
My wife's a wanton, wee thing,
My wife's a wanton, wee thing,
    She winna be guided by me.   will not

She play'd the loon or she was married,   fool
She play'd the loon or she was married,
She play'd the loon or she was married,
    She'll do it again or she die.

She sell'd her coat and she drank it,
She sell'd her coat and she drank it,
She row'd hersell in a blanket,   rolled
    She winna be guided for me.

She mind't na when I forbade her,
She mind't na when I forbade her,
I took a rung and I claw'd her,
    And a braw gude bairn was she.   child

LASSIE LIE NEAR ME

Probably based on a traditional ballad, although no
earlier version has been traced.

CHORUS

Near me, near me,
Lassie lie near me;
Lang hast thou lien thy lane,
Lassie lie near me.

Lang hae we parted been,
  Lassie my dearie;
Now we are met again,
  Lassie lie near me.

A' that I hae endur'd,
  Lassie, my dearie,
Here in thy arms is cur'd,
  Lassie lie near me.

THE GARD'NER WI HIS PAIDLE

TUNE: *The Gardener's March*

In his annotated copy of SMM Burns wrote 'the title
of the song only is old, the rest is mine.'

When rosy May comes in wi flowers,
To deck her gay, green-spreading bowers,
Then busy, busy are his hours,
spade   The gard'ner wi his paidle.

The crystal waters gently fa',
The merry birds are lovers a',
The scented breezes round him blaw—
           The gard'ner wi his paidle.

When purple morning starts the hare
To steal upon her early fare,
must   Then thro the dew he maun repair—
           The gard'ner wi his paidle.

When Day, expiring in the west,
The curtain draws o Nature's rest,
He flies to her arms he lo'es best,
           The gard'ner wi his paidle.

SANQUHAR
with Crichton Peel

TARBOLTON
procession of St. James Lodge

ON A BANK OF FLOWERS

TUNE: *The Bashful Lover*

This song is based on a poem of the same name by
Theobald in The Tea-Table Miscellany. The situation
is a familiar one in Restoration and eighteenth century
pastoral.

On a bank of flowers in a summer day,
    For summer lightly drest,
The youthful, blooming Nelly lay,
    With love and sleep opprest;
When Willie, wand'ring thro the wood,
    Who for her favour oft had sued—
      He gaz'd, he wish'd,
      He fear'd, he blush'd,
And trembled where he stood.

Her closèd eyes, like weapons sheath'd,
    Were seal'd in soft repose;
Her lips, still as she fragrant breath'd,
    It richer dyed the rose.
The springing lilies, sweetly prest,
Wild-wanton kiss'd her rival breast:
      He gaz'd, he wish'd,
      He fear'd, he blush'd,
His bosom ill at rest.

Her robes, light-waving in the breeze,
    Her tender limbs embrace;
Her lovely form, her native ease,
    All harmony and grace.
Tumultuous tides his pulses roll,
A faltering, ardent kiss he stole;
      He gaz'd, he wish'd,
      He fear'd, he blush'd,
And sigh'd his very soul.

As flies the partridge from the brake
    On fear-inspirèd wings,
So Nelly starting, half-awake,
    Away affrighted springs.
But Willie, follow'd — as he should,
He overtook her in the wood;
      He vow'd, he pray'd,
      He found the maid
Forgiving all, and good.

MY LOVE, SHE'S BUT A LASSIE YET

TUNE: *Miss Farquharson's Reel*

Burns took the title from a snatch of old song and added the rest from his own composition.

My love, she's but a lassie yet,
My love, she's but a lassie yet!
We'll let her stand a year or twa,
She'll no be half sae saucy yet!
I rue the day I sought her, O!
I rue the day I sought her, O!
Wha gets her need na say he's woo'd,
But he may say he has bought her. O.

drop

Go

Come draw a drap o the best o't yet,
Come draw a drap o the best o't yet!
Gae seek for pleasure whare ye will,
But here I never miss'd it yet,
We're a' dry wi drinkin o't,
We're a' dry wi drinkin o't!
The minister kiss't the fiddler's wife—
He could na preach for thinkin o't!

CAULD FROSTY MORNING

That Burns had a hand in this, there can be no doubt but it is well below his usual standard. Kinsley considers that Burns attempted here to produce a Scottish version of the well-known song by Colley Cibber 'Twas past twelve o'clock on a fine summer morning.'

'Twas past ane o'clock in a cauld frosty morning,
    When cankert November blaws over the plain,
I heard the kirk-bell repeat the loud warning,
    As, restless, I sought for sweet slumber in vain:
Then up I arose, the silver moon shining bright;
    Mountains and valleys appearing all hoary white;
Forth I would go, amid the pale, silent night,
    And visit the Fair One, the cause of my pain.—

Sae gently I staw to my lovely Maid's chamber,
    And rapp'd at her window, low down on my knee;
Begging that she would awauk from sweet slumber,
    Awauk from sweet slumber and pity me:
For, that a stranger to a' pleasure, peace and rest,
    Love into madness had fired my tortur'd breast;
And that I should be of a' men the maist unblest,
    Unless she would pity my sad miserie!

Cauld Frosty Morning

My True-love arose and whispered to me,
    (The moon looked in, and envy'd my Love's charms;)
'An innocent Maiden, ah, would you undo me!'
    I made no reply, but leapt into her arms:
Bright Phebus peep'd over the hills and found me there;
    As he has done, now, seven lang years and mair:
A faithfuller, constanter, kinder, more loving Pair,
    His sweet-chearing beam nor enlightens nor warms.

JAMIE, COME TRY ME

'Mr. Burns's old words' in Law MS, no. 34. It is thought that this song is modelled on the air of this name, published in Oswald's 'Curious Scots Tunes' (1742), although no original words have been traced.

CHORUS

Jamie, come try me,
    Jamie, come try me!
If thou would win my love,
    Jamie, come try me!

If thou should ask my love,
    Could I deny thee?
If thou would win my love,
    Jamie, come try me!

If thou should kiss me, love,
    Wha could espy thee?
If thou wad be my love,
    Jamie, come try me!

THE CAPTAIN'S LADY

The old broadside The Liggar Lady, or some variant of it was probably the basis of this song.

CHORUS

O, mount and go, mount and make ye ready!
O, mount and go, and be the Captain's Lady!

When the drums do beat,
    And the cannons rattle,
Thou shalt sit in state,
    And see thy love in battle.

When the vanquish'd foe
    Sues for peace and quiet,
To the shades we'll go,
    And in love enjoy it:

JOHNIE COPE

One of several extant versions of an old Jacobite ballad,
Burns reworked it for SMM. It deals with the Battle of
Prestonpans (1745) when the army of Bonnie Prince
Charlie defeated the Hanoverian troops of General Sir
John Cope.

CHORUS

Hey Johnie Cope are ye wauking yet,
Or are ye sleeping I would wit:
O haste ye get up for the drums do beat,
O fye Cope rise in the morning.

Sir John Cope trode the north right far,
near   Yet ne'er a rebel he cam naur,
Until he landed at Dunbar
Right early in a morning.

He wrote a challenge for Dunbar,
if you dare   Come fight me Charlie an ye daur;
If it be not by the chance of war
I'll give you a merry morning.

When Charlie look'd the letter upon
He drew his sword and scabbard from—
'So Heaven restore to me my own,
'I'll meet you, Cope, in the morning.'

Cope swore with many a bloody word
That he would fight them gun and sword,
But he fled frae his nest like an ill scar'd bird,
And Johnie he took wing in the morning.

It was upon an afternoon,
Sir Johnie march'd to Preston town;
He says, my lads come lean you down,
And we'll fight the boys in the morining.

But when he saw the Highland lads
Wi tartan trews and white cokauds,
cudgels, goads   Wi swords and guns and rungs and gauds,
O Johnie he took wing in the morning.

On the morrow when he did rise,
He look'd between him and the skies;
He saw them wi their naked thighs,
Which fear'd him in the morning.

O then he flew into Dunbar,
Crying for a man of war;
He thought to have pass'd for a rustic tar,
And gotten awa in the morning.

Sir Johnie into Berwick rade,
Just as the devil had been his guide;
Gien him the warld he would na stay'd
To foughten the boys in the morning.

388

Johnie Cope

Says the Berwickers unto Sir John,
O what's become of all your men,
In faith, says he, I dinna ken,
I left them a' this morning.

Says Lord Mark Car, ye are na blate,   bashful
To bring us the news o your ain defeat;
I think you deserve the back o the gate,
Get out o my sight this morning.

O DEAR MINNY

This variant of 'O dear mother, what shall I do' in
Herd's MSS was reworked by Burns.

CHORUS

O dear minny, what shall I do?
O dear minny, what shall I do?
O dear minny, what shall I do?
Daft thing, doylt thing, do as I do.

If I be black, I canna be lo'ed;
If I be fair, I canna be gude;
If I be lordly, the lads will look by me:
O dear minny, what shall I do.

CARL, AN THE KING COME

It is uncertain how much of this song was original and
how much was traditional. Several versions of it were
published in the eighteenth century. 'Carl' is Bonnie
Prince Charlie.

CHORUS

Carl, an the King come,   if
Carl, an the King come,
Thou shalt dance and I will sing,
Carl, an the King come!

An somebodie were come again,
Then somebodie maun cross the main,   must
And every man shall hae his ain,
Carl, an the King come!

I trow we swapped for the worse: believe
We gae the boot and better horse,
An that we'll tell them at the Cross,
Carl, an King come!

Coggie, an the King come,
Coggie, an the King come,
I'll be fou, an thou'se be toom,   drunk, empty
Coggie, an the King come!

389

THERE'S A YOUTH IN THIS CITY

'The first half-stanza of the song is old; the rest is mine.
This air is claimed by Niel Gow who calls it his lament
for his brother' wrote Burns in his Notes for SMM.

There's a youth in this city, it were a great pity
    That he from our lasses should wander awa;
For he's bonie and braw, weel-favor'd witha',
    An his hair has a natural buckle an a'.

His coat is the hue o his bonnet sae blue,
    His fecket is white as the new-driven snaw,
His hose they are blae, and his shoon like the slae,
    And his clear siller buckles, they dazzle us a'.

For beauty and fortune the laddie's been courtin:
    Weel-featur'd, weel-tocher'd, weel-mounted, an braw,
But chiefly the siller that gars him gang till her—
    The penny's the jewel that beautifies a'!

There's Meg wi the mailen, that fain wad a haen him,
    And Susie, wha's daddie was laird o the Ha',
There's lang-tocher'd Nancy maist fetters his fancy,
    But the laddie's dear sel', he loes dearest of a'.

Marginal glosses:
handsome
curl

waistcoat
blue, sloe
silver

well-endowed
money, makes

farm, gladly
would have
almost
self

MY HEART'S IN THE HIGHLANDS

TUNE: *Failte na miosg*

The refrain is traditional, the rest Burns's own
composition.

CHORUS

My heart's in the Highlands, my heart is not here
My heart's in the Highlands, a-chasing the deer,
A-chasing the wild deer, and following the roe—
My heart's in the Highlands, wherever I go!

Farewell to the Highlands, farewell to the North,
The birthplace of valour, the country of worth!
Wherever I wander, wherever I rove,
The hills of the Highlands for ever I love.

Farewell to the mountains, high-cover'd with snow,
Farewell to the straths and green valleys below,
Farewell to the forests and wild-hanging woods,
Farewell to the torrents and loud-pouring floods!

JOHN ANDERSON, MY JO

This is a sanitised version of an old bawdy ballad. One
of the traditional variants was included in the Merry
Muses.

John Anderson my jo, John,	darling
When we were first acquent,	acquainted
Your locks were like the raven,	
Your bonie brow was brent;	smooth
But now your brow is beld, John,	bald
Your locks are like the snaw,	
But blessings on your frosty pow,	pate
John Anderson, my jo!	
John Anderson my jo, John,	
We clamb the hill thegither,	climbed, together
And monie a cantie day, John,	happy
We've had wi ane anither;	
Now we maun totter down, John,	must
And hand in hand we'll go,	
And sleep thegither at the foot,	
John Anderson my jo!	

AWA, WHIGS, AWA

Modelled on a fragment in the Herd MSS, this Jacobite
song lampoons the Whigs, exponents of the Revolution
of 1688 and ancestors of the Liberals.

CHORUS

Awa, Whigs, awa!
Awa, Whigs, awa!
Ye're but a pack o traitor louns,
Ye'll do nae guid at a'.

Our thrissles flourish'd fresh and fair,	thistles
And bonie bloom'd our roses;	
But Whigs cam like a frost in June,	
An wither'd a our posies.	
Our ancient crown's fa'n in the dust—	
Deil blin' them wi the stoure o't,	dust
An write their names in the black beuk	book
Wha gae the Whigs the power o't!	
Our sad decay in church and state	
Surpasses my descriving.	
The Whigs cam o'er us for a curse,	
An we hae done wi thriving.	
Grim Vengeance lang has taen a nap,	taken
But we may see him waukin—	waking
Gude help the day when Royal heads	God
Are hunted like a maukin!	hare

391

I'LL MAK YOU BE FAIN TO FOLLOW ME

Burns reworked the first twelve lines of an old ballad and completed them with four of his own.

soldier   As late by a sodger I chanced to pass,
I heard him a courtin a bony young lass;

darling   My hinny, my life, my dearest, quo he,
I'll mak you be fain to follow me.
Gin I should follow you, a poor sodger lad,

wenches   Ilk ane o my cummers wad think I was mad;
For battles I never shall lang to see,
I'll never be fain to follow thee.

To follow me, I think ye may be glad,
A part o my supper, a part o my bed,
A part o my bed, wherever it be,
I'll mak you be fain to follow me.
Come try my knapsack on your back,
Alang the king's high-gate we'll pack;

Perth   Between Saint Johnston and bony Dundee,
I'll mak you be fain to follow me.

KISSIN MY KATIE

TUNE: *The Bob o Dumblane*

Although clearly based on an old song, no traditional version appears to have been preserved.

heckling-comb   O, merry hae I been teethin a heckle
moulding a horn spoon   An merry hae I been shapin a spoon!
patching   O, merry hae I been cloutin a kettle,
An kissin my Katie when a' was done!

knock   O, a the lang day I ca' at my hammer,
An a' the lang day I whistle and sing!

mistress   O, a' the lang night I cuddle my kimmer,
An a' the lang night as happy's a king!

sadness, earnings   Bitter in dool, I lickit my winnins
O marrying Bess, to gie her a slave:

shroud   Blest be the hour she cool'd in her linens,
And blythe be the bird that sings on her grave!
Come to my arms, my Katie, my Katie,
An come to my arms, and kiss me again!

Drunken   Drucken or sober, here's to thee, Katie,
An blest be the day I did it again!

392

THE WHITE COCKADE

Burns transformed an old song into a specifically
Jacobite ballad. The white cockade was the badge
of the Jacobite Army.

CHORUS

O he's a ranting, roving lad,
He is a brisk an a bonny lad,
Betide what may, I will be wed,
And follow the boy wi the White Cockade.

My love was born in Aberdeen,
The boniest lad that e'er was seen,
But now he makes our hearts fu sad,
He takes the field wi his White Cockade.

I'll sell my rock, my reel, my tow,   distaff, flax fibre
My gude gray mare and hawkit cow;   spotted
To buy mysel a tartan plaid,
To follow the boy wi the White Cockade.

EPPIE ADAIR

TUNE: *My Appie*

Based on a traditional chorus, as the title of the tune
implies.

CHORUS

An O my Eppie, my jewel, my Eppie!
Wha wadna be happy wi Eppie Adair?

By love and by beauty,
By law and by duty,
I swear to be true to
My Eppie Adair!

A' pleasure exile me,
Dishonor defile me,
If e'er I beguile thee,
My Eppie Adair!

THE BATTLE OF SHERRAMUIR

TUNE: *The Cameron Rant*

The battle of Sheriffmuir took place on 13th November
1715 between the Jacobites, under the Earl of Mar, and
the Hanoverian troops led by the Duke of Argyll.
Though the battle was indecisive it brought the
rebellion to an end. This song was based on Barclay's
'Dialogue between Will Lick-Ladle and Tom Clean-
Cogue, twa shephards wha were feeding their Flocks
on the Ochil Hills on the day the Battle of Sheriff-Muir
was fought.'

'O, cam ye here the fight to shun,
   Or herd the sheep wi me, man?
Or were ye at the Sherra-moor,
   Or did the battle see, man?'

sore, tough	'I saw the battle, sair and teugh,
bloody, ditch	And reekin-red ran monie a sheugh;
gave sigh	My heart, for fear, gae sough for sough,
clouds	To hear the thuds, and see the cluds
clothing	O clans frae woods, in tartan duds,
grasped	Wha glaum'd at kingdoms three, man.

      La, la, la, la, *etc.*

the Hanoverian badge	'The red-coat lads wi black cockauds,
not slow	To meet them were na slaw, man;
	They rush'd and push'd, and bluid outgush'd,
trunk	And monie a bouk did fa', man!
	The great Argyle led on his files,
wot, shone	I wat they glanc'd for twenty miles;
mowed, skittles	They hough'd the clans like nine-pin kyles,
	They hack'd and hash'd, while braid-swords clashed,
	And thro they dash'd, and hew'd and smash'd,
ill-fated	Till fey men died awa, man.

      La, la, la, la, *etc.*

kilts	'But had ye seen the philibegs,
flaring, trousers	And skyrin tartan trews, man;
	When in the teeth they daur'd our Whigs,
	And Covenant trueblues, man!
	In lines extended lang and large,
bayonets, shield	When baig'nets o'erpower'd the targe,
	And thousands hasten'd to the charge,
	Wi Highland wrath and frae the sheath
	Drew blades o death, till, out o breath.
pigeons	They fled like frightened dows, man!'

      La, la, la, la, *etc.*

	'O, how Deil, Tam, can that be true?
went	The chase gaed frae the north, man!
	I saw mysel, they did pursue
	The horseman back to Forth, man:
	And at Dunblane, in my ain sight,

The Battle Of Sherramuir

They took the brig wi a' their might,
And straught to Stirling wing'd their flight;
But, cursed lot! the gates were shut,
And monie a huntit poor red-coat,
    For fear amaist did swarf, man!'   swoon
      La, la, la, la, *etc.*

My sister Kate came up the gate   road
    Wi crowdie unto me, man: gruel
She swoor she saw some rebels run
    To Perth and to Dundee, man!
Their left-hand general had nae skill;
The Angus lads had nae good will
That day their neebors' bluid to spill;
For fear, by foes, that they should lose
Their cogs o brose; they scar'd at blows,
    And hameward fast did flee, man.
      La, la, la, la, *etc.*

'They've lost some gallant gentlemen,
    Amang the Highland clans, man!
I fear my Lord Panmure is slain,
    Or in his en'mies' hands, man.
Now wad ye sing this double flight,
Some fell for wrang, and some for right,
But monie bade the world guid-night;
Say, pell and mell, wi muskets' knell
How Tories fell, and Whigs to Hell
    Flew off in frightened bands, man!
      La, la, la, la, *etc.*

SANDY AND JOCKIE

TUNE: *Jenny's Lamentation*

The opening couplet is traditional, the latter being Burns's contribution.

Twa bonie lads were Sandy and Jockie;
Jockie was lo'ed but Sandy unlucky;
Jockie was laird baith of hills and of valleys,
But Sandy was nought but the king o gude fellows.

YOUNG JOCKIE WAS THE BLYTHEST LAD

Probably all of this song but the title and the opening
lines are Burns's own composition. Another version,
entitled 'Willie was a wanton Wag' by William Hamilton
was published in The Tea-Table Miscellany.

Young Jockie was the blythest lad,
round about   In a' our town or here awa:
goad   Fu blythe he whistled at the gaud
Fu lightly danc'd he in the ha'.

praised, eyes   He roos'd my een sae bonie blue,
trimly   He roos'd my waist sae genty sma';
mouth   An ay my heart cam to my mou,
When ne'er a body heard or saw.

My Jockie toils upon the plain,
Thro wind and weet, thro frost and snaw;
look, longingly   And o'er the lea I leuk fu fain,
oxen, drive   When Jockie's owsen hameware ca'.

An ay the night comes round again,
When in his arms he taks me a';
own   An ay he vows he'll be my ain,
As lang's he has a breath to draw.

wakeful mother   # WAUKRIFE MINNIE

'I pickt up this old song and tune from a country girl
in Nithsdale. I never met with it elsewhere in Scotland,'
wrote Burns.

going   'Whare are you gaun, my bonie lass?
honey   Whare are you gaun, my hinnie?'
She answer'd me right saucilie—
'An errand for my minnie!'

'O whare live ye, my bonie lass?
O, whare live ye, my hinnic?'
brookside;   'By yon burnside, gin ye maun ken,
if must know   In a wee house wi my minnie!'

went, evening   But I foor up the glen at e'en,
To see my bonie lassie;
And lang before the grey morn cam,
half   She was na hauf sae saucy.

woe befall   O, weary fa' the waukrife cock,
polecat   And the foumart lay his crawin!
He wauken'd the auld wife frae her sleep,
shortly before dawn   A wee blink or the dawin.

396

A Waukrife Minnie

An angry wife I wat she raise,   wot
 And o'er the bed she brought her,
And wi a meikle hazel-rung   big, -rod
 She made her a weel-pay'd dochter. well-thrashed daughter

'O, fare, thee—weel, my bonie lass,
 O, fare, thee—weel, my hinnie!
Thou art a gay and a bonie lass,
 But thou has a waukrife minnie!'

THO WOMEN'S MINDS

TUNE: *For a' that, an a' that*

This is a variation of the song in 'The Jolly Beggars'
(ll. 208-35).

CHORUS

For a' that, an a' that,
 And twice as meikle's a' that, much as
The bonie lass that I loe best   love
 She'll be my ain for a' that!

Tho women's minds like winter winds
 May shift and turn, an a' that,
The noblest breast adores them maist— most
 A consequence, I draw that.

Great love I bear to a' the fair,
 Their humble slave, an a' that;
But lordly will, I hold it still
 A mortal sin to thraw that.   contradict

In rapture sweet this hour we meet,
 Wi mutual love an a' that,
But for how lang the flie may stang, fly, sting
 Let inclination law that!

Their tricks an craft hae put me daft, mad
 They've taen me in an a' that,
But clear your decks, and here's— 'The Sex!'
 I like the jads for a' that!   jades

397

KILLIECRANKIE

TUNE: *An ye had been whare I hae been*

This is the reworking of an old Jacobite song about
the battle fought on 27th July 1689 between the
Highlanders led by James Graham of Claverhouse,
Viscount Dundee and the Anglo-Dutch troops
commanded by General Hugh Mackay of Scourie.
The speaker is one of Mackay's men saved only by
the deaths, in pursuit, of Haliburton of Pitcur and
Claverhouse himself.

CHORUS

An ye had been whare I hae been,
Ye wad na been sae cantie, O!
An ye had seen what I hae seen,
On the braes o Killiecrankie O!

fine
spruce

'Whare hae ye been sae braw, lad?
  Whare hae ye been sae brankie, O?
Whare hae ye been sae braw, lad?
  Cam ye by Killiecrankie, O?

'I faught at land, I faught at sea,
  At hame I faught my auntie, O;
But I met the Devil an Dundee,
  On the braes o Killiecrankie, O.

ditch
knock
Else, hawk

'The bauld Pitcur fell in a furr,
  An Clavers gat a clankie, O,
Or I had fed an Athole gled,
  On the braes o Killiecrankie, O!'

THE CAMPBELLS ARE COMIN

The melody and first line of the chorus came from a
Jacobite song of the 1715 Rebellion, but the verses by
Burns allude to the imprisonment of Mary, Queen of
Scots in Lochleven Castle in 1567. 'Great Argyle' was
the 5th Earl of Argyll who came to her rescue.

CHORUS

The Campbells are comin, Oho! Oho!
The Campbells are comin, Oho! Oho!
The Campbells are comin to bonie Lochleven,
The Campbells are comin Oho! Oho!

Upon the Lomonds I lay, I lay,
Upon the Lomonds I lay, I lay,
I looked down to bonie Lochleven,
  And saw three bonie perches play

Great Argyle he goes before,
He maks his cannons and guns roar,
Wi sound o trumpet, pipe and drum
  The Campbells are comin Oho, Oho!

The Campbells Are Comin

The Campbells they are a' in arms
Their loyal faith and truth to show,
Wi banners rattling in the wind
The Campbells are comin Oho, Oho!

SCOTS PROLOGUE FOR MRS. SUTHERLAND

ON HER BENEFIT NIGHT AT THE THEATRE, DUMFRIES

In a letter to Mrs Dunlop in March 1790 Burns refers
to George Sutherland 'Manager of a company of
Comedians at present in Dumfries. The following is a
Prologue I made for his wife, Mrs Sutherland's benefit
night. You are to understand that he is getting a new
Theatre built here, by subscription.' Burns was closely
involved with the theatre at this time, and was clearly
(ll. 5-6) contemplating play-writing though nothing
ever came of it.

What needs this din about the town o Lon'on,
How this new play an that new sang is comin?   song
Why is outlandish stuff sae meikle courted?   much
Does nonsense mend, like brandy—when imported?
Is there nae poet, burning keen for fame,
Will bauldly try to gie us plays at hame?
For Comedy abroad he need na toil:
A knave and fool are plants of every soil.
Nor need he hunt as far as Rome or Greece
To gather matter for a serious piece:
There's themes enow in Caledonian story
Would show the tragic Muse in a' her glory.

    Is there no daring Bard will rise and tell
How glorious Wallace stood, how hapless fell?
Where are the Muses fled that could produce
A drama worthy o the name o Bruce?
How here, even here, he first unsheath'd the sword
'Gainst mighty England and her guilty lord,
And after monie a bloody, deathless doing,
Wrench'd his dear country from the jaws of Ruin!
O, for a Shakespeare, or an Otway scene
To paint the lovely, hapless Scottish Queen!

Vain all th' omnipotence of female charms
'Gainst headlong, ruthless, mad Rebellion's arms!
She fell, but fell with spirit truly Roman,
To glut the vengeance of a rival woman:
A woman (tho the phrase may seem uncivil),
As able—and as cruel—as the Devil!

399

Scots Prologue For Mrs. Sutherland

One Douglas lives in Home's immortal page,
But Douglasses were heroes every age:
And tho your fathers, prodigal of life,
A Douglas followed to the martial strife,
Perhaps, if bowls row right, the Right succeeds,
Ye yet may follow where a Douglas leads!

As ye hae generous done, if a' the land
Would take the Muses' servants by the hand;
Not only hear, but patronise, befriend them,
And where ye justly can commend, commend them;
And aiblins, when they winna stand the test,
Wink hard, and say: 'The folks hae done their best!'
Would a' the land do this, then I'll be caition,
Ye'll soon hae Poets o the Scottish nation
Will gar Fame blaw until her trumpet crack,
And warsle Time, an lay him on his back!

For us and for our stage, should onie spier:—
'Whase aught thae chiels maks a' this bustle here?
My best leg foremost, I'll set up my brow:—
'We have the honour to belong to you!'
We're your ain bairns, e'en guide us as ye like,
But like good mithers, shore before ye strike;
And gratefu still, I trust ye'll ever find us,
For gen'rous patronage, and meikle kindness
We've got frae a' professions, setts an ranks:
God help us! we're but poor—ye'se get but thanks!

make
beat

ask
Whose, those chaps

own children
warn

LAMENT OF MARY QUEEN OF SCOTS

ON THE APPROACH OF SPRING

Sent on 6th June 1790 to Mrs Dunlop who shared the poet's sympathies for the great tragic heroine of Scottish history.

Now Nature hangs her mantle green
    On every blooming tree,
And spreads her sheets o daisies white
    Out o'er the grassy lea;
Now Phœbus cheers the crystal streams,
    And glads the azure skies:
But nought can glad the weary wight
    That fast in durance lies.

larks

hawk

Now laverocks wake the merry morn,
    Aloft on dewy wing;
The merle, in his noontide bow'r,
    Makes woodland echoes ring;

400

Lament Of Mary Queen Of Scots

The mavis wild wi monie a note,
   Sings drowsy day to rest:
In love and freedom they rejoice,
   Wi care nor thrall opprest.

Now blooms the lily by the bank,
   The primrose down the brae,
The hawthorn's budding in the glen,
   And milk-white is the slae:
The meanest hind in fair Scotland
   May rove their sweets amang;
But I, the Queen of a' Scotland,
   Maun lie in prison strang.   *must*

I was the Queen o bonie France,
   Where happy I hae been;
Fu lightly rase I in the morn,   *rose*
   As blythe lay down at e'en:
And I'm the sov'reign of Scotland,
   And monie a traitor there;
Yet here I lie in foreign bands,
   And never-ending care.

But as for thee, thou false woman,   *Elizabeth of England*
   My sister and my fae,   *foe*
Grim vengeance yet shall whet a sword
   That thro thy soul shall gae!   *go*
The weeping blood in woman's breast
   Was never known to thee;
Nor th' balm that drops on wounds of woe
   Frae woman's pitying e'e.

My son! my son! may kinder stars   *King James VI and I*
   Upon thy fortune shine;
And may those pleasures gild thy reign,
   That ne'er wad blink on mine!   *would*
God keep thee frae thy mother's faes,
   Or turn their hearts to thee;
And where thou meet'st thy mother's friend,
   Remember him for me!

O! soon, to me, may summer suns
   Nae mair light up the morn!
Nae mair to me the autumn winds
   Wave o'er the yellow corn!
And, in the narrow house of death,
   Let winter round me rave;
And the next flow'rs that deck the spring,
   Bloom on my peaceful grave.

ON SENSIBILITY

Included in a letter to Mrs Dunlop written on 9th July
1790, offering the poet's condolences on the death of
her son-in-law, James Henri, were some stanzas of this
poem on which he was then working. The
complete poem followed with a letter of 30th
July. Nevertheless, he sent a copy to Clarinda a
year later, telling her that it was 'just composed.'

Sensibility how charming,
  Thou, my friend, canst truly tell!
But Distress with horrors arming
  Thou alas! hast known too well!

Fairest flower, behold the lily
  Blooming in the sunny ray:
Let the blast sweep o'er the valley,
  See it prostrate in the clay.

Hear the woodlark charm the forest,
  Telling o'er his little joys;
But alas! a prey the surest
  To each pirate of the skies!

Dearly bought the hidden treasure
  Finer feelings can bestow:
Chords that vibrate sweetest pleasure
  Thrill the deepest notes of woe.

ELECTION BALLAD

AT CLOSE OF THE CONTEST FOR
REPRESENTING THE DUMFRIES BURGHS 1790

Addressed to R. Graham Esq., of Fintry

The general election was held on 12th July 1790 and
this ballad was composed soon afterwards.

Fintry, my stay in worldly strife,
Friend o my Muse, friend of my life,
      Are ye as idle's I am?
country fling   Come, then! Wi uncouth kintra fleg!
O'er Pegasus I'll fling my leg,
      And ye shall see me try him!

go run   But where shall I gae rin or ride,
splash   That I may splatter nane beside?
would not   I wad na be uncivil:
In manhood's various paths and ways
doddering creature   There's ay some doytin body strays,
      And I ride like a devil.

402

Election Ballad

Thus I break aff wi a' my birr,   *force*
An down yon dark, deep alley spur,
     Where Theologies dander: *saunter*
Alas! curst wi eternal fogs,
And damn'd in everlasting bogs,
     As sure's the Creed I'll blunder!

I'll stain a band, or jaup a gown,   *splash*
Or rin my reckless, guilty crown
     Against the haly door!   *holy*
Sair do I rue my luckless fate,   *sore*
When, as the Muse an Deil wad hae't,
     I rade that road before!   *rode*

Suppose I take a spurt, and mix
Amang the wilds o Politics—
     Electors and elected—
Where dogs at Court (sad sons o bitches!)   *Elections had to be held at*
Septennially a madness touches,   *least every seven years*
     Till all the land's infected?

All hail, Drumlanrig's haughty Grace,   *William Douglas, 4th Duke*
Discarded remnant of a race   *of Queensberry (1724-1810)*
     Once godlike—great in story!
Thy fathers' virtues all contrasted,
The very name of Douglas blasted,
     Thine that inverted glory!

Hate, envy, oft the Douglas bore;
But thou hast superadded more,
     And sunk them in contempt!
Follies and crimes have stain'd the name;
But, Queensberry, thine the virgin claim,
     From aught that's good exempt!

I'll sing the zeal Drumlanrig bears,
Who left the all-important cares
     Of fiddlers, whores, and hunters,
And, bent on buying Borough Towns,
Came shaking hands wi wabster-loons,   *weaver rascals*
     And kissing barefit bunters.   *harlots*

Combustion thro our boroughs rode,
Whistling his roaring pack abroad
     Of mad unmuzzled lions,
As Queensberry buff and blue unfurl'd,   *the Whig colours*
And Westerha' and Hopeton hurl'd,   *Sir James Johnstone of*
     To every Whig defiance.   *Westerhall, Earl of Hopetoun,*
                                          his patron

Election Ballad

But cautious Queensberry left the war
(Th' unmanner'd dust might soil his star;
    Besides, he hated bleeding).
But left behind him heroes bright,
Heroes in Cæsarean fight
    Or Ciceronian pleading.

the famous cannon of
Edinburgh Castle

O, for a throat like huge Mons-Meg,
To muster o'er each ardent Whig
    Beneath Drumlanrig's banner!
Heroes and heroines commix,
All in the field of politics,
    To win immortal honor!

John McMurdo

M'Murdo and his lovely spouse
(Th' enamour'd laurels kiss her brows!)
    Led on the Loves and Graces:
She won each gaping burgess' heart,

in secret (Latin)

While he, *sub rosa,* played his part
    Among their wives and lasses.

Alexander Fergusson

Craigdarroch led a light-arm'd core:
Tropes, metaphors, and figures pour,

the Icelandic volcano
Robert Riddell

    Like Hecla streaming thunder.
Glenriddel, skill'd in rusty coins,
Blew up each Tory's dark designs,
    And bared the treason under.

David Staig (1740-1824)
provost of Dumfries

In either wing two champions fought:
Redoubted Staig, who set at nought
    The wildest savage Tory;

allegedly Sheriff of Dumfriesshire
double-quart bottle

And Welsh, who ne'er yet flinch'd his ground,
High-wav'd his magnum-bonum round
    With Cyclopeian fury.

Captain Miller

Miller brought up th' artillery ranks,
The many-pounders of the Banks,
    Resistless desolation!

Sir Robert Lawrie

While Maxwelton, that baron bold,
'Mid Lawson's port entrench'd his hold,
    And threaten'd worse damnation.

To these what Tory hosts oppos'd,
With these what Tory warriors clos'd,
    Surpasses my descriving:
Squadrons, extended long and large,
With furious speed rush to the charge,
    Like furious devils driving.

Election Ballad

What verse can sing, what prose narrate
The butcher deeds of bloody Fate
      Amid this mighty tulyie?   struggle
Grim Horror girn'd, pale Terror roar'd,   snarled
As Murther at his thrapple shor'd,   windpipe, menaced
      And Hell mix'd in the brulyie.   brawl

As Highland craigs by thunder cleft,   crags
When lightnings fire the stormy lift,   sky
      Hurl down with crashing rattle,
As flames among a hundred floods—
      Such is the rage of Battle!

The stubborn Tories dare to die:
As soon the rooted oaks would fly
      Before th' approaching fellers!
The Whigs come on like Ocean's roar,
When all his wintry billows pour
      Against the Buchan Bullers.   a landmark near Peterhead

Lo, from the shades of Death's deep night,
Departed Whigs enjoy the fight,
      And think on former daring!
The muffled murtherer of Charles   Oliver Cromwell
The Magna Charter flag unfurls,   Magna Carta
      All deadly gules its bearing.

Nor wanting ghosts of Tory fame: John Scrimgeour, Viscount
Bold Scrimgeour follows gallant Graham, Dudhope (d.1668)
      Auld Covenanters shiver—   Graham of Claverhouse (d.1689)
Forgive! forgive! much-wrong'd Montrose! Marquis of Montrose (1612-50)
Now Death and Hell engulph thy foes,
      Thou liv'st on high for ever!

Still o'er the field the combat burns;
The Tories, Whigs, give way by turns;
      But Fate the word has spoken;
For woman's wit and strength o man,
Alas! can do but what they can;
      The Tory ranks are broken.

O, that my een were flowing burns!   eyes, brooks
My voice, a lioness that mourns
      Her darling cubs' undoing!
That I might greet, that I might cry,   weep
While Tories fall, while Tories fly,
      And furious Whigs pursuing!

Election Ballad

Sir James Johnstone

What Whig but melts for good Sir James,
Dear to his country, by the names,

Sir James's son William
married the daughter of
William Pulteney, one of
the country's richest men

    Friend, Patron, Benefactor?
Not Pulteney's wealth can Pulteney save;
And Hopeton falls!—the generous, brave-
    And Stewart bold as Hector.

William Pitt
Edward, Baron Thurlow
Henry Dundas, Viscount
Melville
Edmund Burke

Thou, Pitt, shalt rue this overthrow,
And Thurlow growl this curse of woe,
    And Melville melt in wailing!
Now Fox and Sheridan rejoice,
And Burke shall Sing:—'O Prince, arise!
    Thy power is all prevailing!'

For your poor friend, the Bard, afar
He sees and hears the distant war,
    A cool spectator purely:
So, when the storm the forest rends,
The robin in the hedge descends.
    And, patient chirps securely.

Now, for my friends' and brethren's sakes,

Scotland

And for my dear-lov'd Land o Cakes,
    I pray with holy fire:—
Lord, send a rough-shod troop o Hell

would

O'er a' wad Scotland buy or sell,
    To grind them in the mire!

ON THE BIRTH OF A POSTHUMOUS CHILD

BORN IN PECULIAR CIRCUMSTANCES OF FAMILY DISTRESS

James Henri, husband of Susan Dunlop, died on 22nd
June 1790 and his son was born posthumously on 15th
November. On hearing this news 'out skipt I among
the broomy banks of Nith to muse over my joy by
retail . . . I extempore almost poured out to him . . .
the following' as he wrote to Mrs Dunlop senior.

much

    Sweet flow'ret pledge o meikle love,
        And ward o monie a prayer,
    What heart o stane wad thou na move,
        Sae helpless, sweet, and fair!

limps

    November hirples o'er the lea,
        Chill, on thy lovely form:
    And gane, alas! the shelt'ring tree,
        Should shield thee frae the storm.

On The Birth Of A Posthumous Child

May He who gives the rain to pour,
    And wings the blast to blaw,
Protect thee frae the driving show'r,
    The bitter frost and snaw!

May He, the friend of Woe and Want,
    Who heals life's various stounds,
Protect and guard the mother plant,
    And heal her cruel wounds!

But late she flourish'd, rooted fast,
    Fair on the summer morn,
Now feebly bends she in the blast,
    Unshelter'd and forlorn.

Blest be thy bloom, thou lovely gem,
    Unscath'd by ruffian hand!
And from thee many a parent stem
    Arise to deck our land!

YESTREEN I HAD A PINT O WINE

TUNE: *Banks of Banna*

This song was probably written in 1790 when Burns was having an affair with Anne Park, niece of Mrs Hyslop who kept the Globe Inn in Dumfries. Anne gave birth to a daughter at Leith on 31st March 1791. Nine days later Jean Armour presented Burns with a son, christened after William Nicol. With remarkable forbearance Jean raised the little girl Elizabeth as one of her own family, Anne having died in or as the result of childbirth.

Yestreen I had a pint o wine,   Last night
    A place where body saw na;
Yestreen lay on this breast o mine
    The gowden locks of Anna.   golden

The hungry Jew in wilderness
    Rejoicing o'er his manna
Was naething to my hiney bliss   honey
    Upon the lips of Anna.

Ye Monarchs take the East and West
    Frae Indus to Savannah:
Gie me within my straining grasp
    The melting form of Anna!

There I'll despise Imperial charms,
    An Empress or Sultana,
While dying raptures in her arms,   orgasmic
    I give and take wi Anna!

407

Yestreen I Had A Pint O' Wine

Awa , thou flaunting God of Day!
Awa , thou pale Diana!

Each, go

Ilk Star, gae hide thy twinkling ray,
When I'm to meet my Anna!

Come, in thy raven plumage, Night
(Sun, Moon, and Stars, withdrawn a',)
And bring an Angel-pen to write
My transports with my Anna!

POSTSCRIPT

The Kirk an State may join, an tell

such, must not

To do sic things I maunna:
The Kirk an State may gae to Hell,
And I'll gae to my Anna.

eye

She is the sunshine o my e'e,

without, cannot

To live but her I canna:
Had I on earth but wishes three,
The first should be my Anna.

BURNS GRACE AT KIRKCUDBRIGHT

**Traditionally ascribed to Burns, from the collection of
James Grierson of Dalgoner, and alternatively known
as the Selkirk Grace, from the Earl of Selkirk in whose
presence Burns is said to have delivered it extempore.**

Some have meat and cannot eat.
Some cannot eat that want it:
But we have meat and we can eat,
Sae let the Lord be thankit.

GRACE AFTER MEAT

**This grace, and the variant which follows, was
composed in the Globe Inn, Dumfries 'for these many
years . . . my Howff' (to Thomson, 1796). William
'Jock' Hyslop and his wife Meg were the hosts, and
Anna Park, mother of Elizabeth Burns was their neice.**

Lord, we thank, and Thee alone,
For temporal gifts we little merit!
At present we will ask no more—
Let William Hislop bring the spirit.

GRACE BEFORE AND AFTER MEAT

An apocryphal tale goes that Burns once forgot to
order dinner for Nicol, Masterton and himself. Meg
Hyslop produced a sheep's head which she and Jock
intended for themselves. Nicol 'fined' Burns for his
neglect by ordering him to compose a grace. When
they had eaten he was commanded to compose thanks.
These stanzas were allegedly the result.

O Lord, when hunger pinches sore,
Do Thou stand us in stead,
And send us, from Thy bounteous store,
A tup or wether head!

O Lord, since we have feasted thus,
Which we so little merit,
Let Meg now take away the flesh,
And Jock bring in the spirit!

GODLY GIRZIE

TUNE: *Wat ye wha I met yestreen*

Burns annotated this as 'A new Song — from an old
story' and sent it to William Stewart. The 'Cragie hills'
(l.8) lie in Craigie parish between Kilmarnock and
Tarbolton.

The night it was a haly night,	holy
The day had been a haly day;	
Kilmarnock gleam'd wi candle light,	
As Girzie hameward took her way.	
A man o sin, ill may he thrive!	
And never haly-meeting see!	
Wi godly Girzie met belyve,	bye and by
Amang the Cragie hills sae hie.	high
The chiel was wight, the chiel was stark,	fellow, strong
He wad na wait to chap nor ca',	knock
And she was faint wi haly wark,	work
She had na pith to say him na.	strength
But ay she glower'd up to the moon,	stared
And ay she sigh'd most piouslie;	
'I trust my heart's in heaven aboon,	
'Whare'er your sinfu pintle be.'	

409

TAM O SHANTER

A TALE

Of Brownyis and of Bogillis full is this Buke.—GAWIN DOUGLAS

Composed for Francis Grose to accompany an engraving of Alloway Kirk, and published in the second volume of Antiquities of Scotland in April 1791. It was written in fulfilment of a promise to Grose in 1789 but not carried out before the winter of 1790. In November that year Burns sent the first fragment to Mrs. Dunlop. Grose received the complete poem at the beginning of December. Like 'Halloween' it draws heavily on the lore of witchcraft which Burns imbibed from Betty Davidson. The story is loosely based on Douglas Graham of Shanter (1739-1811), whose wife Helen was a superstitious shrew. He was prone to drunkenness on market-day and on one such occasion the wags of Ayr clipped his horse's tail — a fact he explained away by this story of witches which mollified his credulous wife.

pedlars	When chapman billies leave the street,
thirsty neighbours	And drouthy neebors, neebors meet;
	As market-days are wearing late,
road	An folk begin to tak the gate;
ale	While we sit bousing at the nappy,
drunk, mighty	An getting fou and unco happy,
	We think na on the lang Scots miles,
bogs, pools, openings	The mosses, waters, slaps, and styles,
	That lie between us and our hame,
	Whare sits our sulky, sullen dame,
	Gathering her brows like gathering storm,
	Nursing her wrath to keep it warm.
found	This truth fand honest Tam o Shanter,
one	As he frae Ayr ae night did canter:
	(Auld Ayr, whom ne'er a town surpasses,
	For honest men and bonie lasses).
	O Tam, had'st thou but been sae wise,
to have taken	As taen thy ain wife Kate's advice!
good-for-nothing	She tauld thee weel thou was a skellum,
chattering, babbler	A blethering, blustering, drunken blellum;
	That frae November till October,
every meal-grinding	Ae market-day thou was nae sober;
Hugh Broun of Ardlochan	That ilka melder wi the miller,
money	Thou sat as lang as thou had siller;
nag	That ev'ry naig was ca'd a shoe on,
John Niven of Carrick	The smith and thee gat roarin fou on;
	That at the Lord's house, even on Sunday,
Jean Kennedy, who kept a pub in Kirkoswald	Thou drank wi Kirkton Jean till Monday.
	She prophesied that, late or soon,
	Thou would be found, deep drown'd in Doon,
wizards, dark	Or catch'd wi warlocks in the mirk,
in decay since 1690, when Alloway parish was joined to Ayr	By Alloway's auld, haunted kirk.

Tam O Shanter

Ah, gentle dames, it gars me greet,   makes, weep
To think how monie counsels sweet,
How monie lengthen'd, sage advices
The husband frae the wife despises!

But to our tale:—Ae market-night,
Tam had got planted unco right,
Fast by an ingle, bleezing finely,
Wi reaming swats, that drank divinely;   foaming, ale
And at his elbow, Souter Johnie,   John Davidson (1786-1806)
His ancient, trusty, drouthy cronie: a cobbler
Tam lo'ed him like a very brither;
They had been fou for weeks thegither.
The night drave on wi sangs and clatter;
And ay the ale was growing better:
The landlady and Tam grew gracious,
Wi secret favours, sweet and precious:
The Souter tauld his queerest stories;   told
The landlord's laugh was ready chorus:
The storm without might rair and rustle,   roar
Tam did na mind the storm a whistle.

Care, mad to see a man sae happy,
E'en drown'd himsel amang the nappy.
As bees flee hame wi lades o treasure,   loads
The minutes wing'd their way wi pleasure:
Kings may be blest but Tam was glorious,
O'er a' the ills o life victorious!

But pleasures are like poppies spread:
You seize the flow'r, its bloom is shed;
Or like the snow falls in the river,
A moment white — then melts for ever;
Or like the borealis race,   Aurora or Northern Lights
That flit ere you can point their place;
Or like the rainbow's lovely form
Evanishing amid the storm.
Nae man can tether time or tide,
The hour approaches Tam maun ride: must
That hour, o night's black arch the key-stane,
That dreary hour Tam mounts his beast in:
And sic a night he taks the road in,   such
As ne'er poor sinner was abroad in.

The wind blew as 'twad blawn its last;   would have blown
The rattling showers rose on the blast;
The speedy gleams the darkness swallow'd;
Loud, deep, and lang the thunder bellow'd;
That night, a child might understand,
The Deil had business on his hand.

411

Tam O Shanter

Weel mounted on his gray mare Meg,
A better never lifted leg,
Tam skelpit on thro dub and mire,
Despising wind, and rain, and fire;
Whiles holding fast his guid blue bonnet,
Whiles crooning o'er an auld Scots sonnet,
Whiles glow'ring round wi prudent cares,
Lest bogles catch him unawares:
Kirk-Alloway was drawing nigh,
Whare ghaists and houlets nightly cry.

By this time he was cross the ford,
Whare in the snaw the chapman smoor'd;
And past the birks and meikle stane,
Whare drunken Charlie brak's neck-bane;
And thro the whins, and by the cairn,
Whare hunters fand the murder'd bairn;
And near the thorn, aboon the well,
Whare Mungo's mither hang'd hersel.
Before him Doon pours all his floods;
The doubling storm roars thro the woods;
The lightnings flash from pole to pole,
Near and more near the thunders roll:
When, glimmering thro the groaning trees,
Kirk-Alloway seem'd in a bleeze,
Thro ilka bore the beams were glancing,
And loud resounded mirth and dancing.

Inspiring bold John Barleycorn,
What dangers thou canst make us scorn!
Wi tippenny, we fear nae evil;
Wi usquabae, we'll face the Devil!
The swats sae ream'd in Tammie's noddle,
Fair play, he car'd na deils a boddle.
But Maggie stood, right sair astonish'd,
Till, by the heel and hand admonish'd,
She ventur'd forward on the light;
And, vow! Tam saw an unco sight!

Warlocks and witches in a dance:
Nae cotillion, brent new frae France,
But hornpipes, jigs, strathspeys, and reels,
Put life and mettle in their heels.
A winnock-bunker in the east,
There sat Auld Nick, in shape o beast;
A touzie tyke, black, grim and large,
To gie them music was his charge:
He screw'd the pipes and gart them skirl,
Till roof and rafters a' did dirl.

## Glosses (left margin)

spanked, puddle
Now
staring
bogies
ghosts, owls
Slaphouse Burn
smothered
birches, big
Cambusdoon
St. Mungo's Well
every chink
twopenny beer
whisky
brain
farthing
wondrous
brand
window seat
shaggy dog
made, squeal
ring

Tam O Shanter

Coffins stood round, like open presses,   cupboards
That shaw'd the dead in their last dresses;
And, by some devilish cantraip sleight,   magic device
Each in its cauld hand held a light:
By which heroic Tam was able
To note upon the haly table,
A murderer's banes, in gibbet-airns;   -irons
Twa span-lang, wee, unchristen'd bairns; babies
A thief new-cutted frae a rape—   rope
Wi his last gasp his gab did gape;   mouth
Five tomahawks, wi bluid red-rusted.
Five scymitars, wi murder crusted;
A garter which a babe had strangled;
A knife a father's throat had mangled--
The grey-hairs yet stack to the heft;
Whom his ain son o life bereft--
Wi mair of horrible and awefu,
Which even to name wad be unlawfu.

As Tammie glowr'd, amaz'd and curious, stared
The mirth and fun grew fast and furious;
The piper loud and louder blew,
The dancers quick and quicker flew,
They reel'd, they set, they cross'd, they cleekit, took hold
Till ilka carlin swat and reekit,   beldam, sweated, steamed
And coost her duddies to the wark,   stripped off clothes
And linket at it in her sark!   tripped, chemise

Now Tam, O Tam! had thae been queans, these, girls
A' plump and strapping in their teens!
Their sarks, instead o creeshie flannen, greasy flannel
Been snaw-white seventeen hunder linen!— fine (1700 thread gauge)
Thir breeks o mine, my only pair,   These breeches
That ance were plush, o guid blue hair, once
I wad hae gien them off my hurdies,   buttocks
For ae blink o the bonie burdies!   one, glimpse, maidens
But wither'd beldams, auld and droll,
Rigwoodie hags wad spean a foal,   Withered, abort
Louping and flinging on a crummock, Leaping, cudgel
I wonder did na turn thy stomach!

But Tam kend what was what fu brawlie: knew, well
There was ae winsome wench and wawlie, comely, choice
That night enlisted in the core,   crew
Lang after kend on Carrick shore
(For monie a beast to dead she shot, death
An perish'd monie a bonie boat,
And shook baith meikle corn and bear, barley
And kept the country-side in fear).

Tam O Shanter

short shift, coarse cloth   Her cutty sark, o Paisley harn,
That while a lassie she had worn,
In longtitude tho sorely scanty,
proud   It was her best, and she was vauntie . . .
Ah! little kend thy reverend grannie,
bought   That sark she coft for her wee Nannie,
3s4d sterling   Wi twa pund Scots ('twas a' her riches),
Wad ever grac'd a dance of witches!

must curb   But here my Muse her wing maun cour,
Sic flights are far beyond her power:
To sing how Nannie lap and flang
(A souple jade she was and strang),
And how Tam stood like ane bewitch'd,
And thought his very een enrich'd;
fidgeted, fondly   Even Satan glowr'd, and fidg'd fu fain,
jerked   And hotch'd and blew wi might and main:
then   Till first ae caper, syne anither,
lost   Tam tint his reason a' thegither,
And roars out, 'Weel done, Cutty-sark!'
And in an instant all was dark:
And scarcely had he Maggie rallied,
When out the hellish legion sallied.

fret   As bees bizz out wi angry fyke,
hive   When plundering herds assail their byke;
hare's   As open pussie's mortal foes,
When, pop! she starts before their nose;
As eager runs the market-crowd,
When 'Catch the thief!' resounds aloud:
So Maggie runs, the witches follow,
unearthly   Wi monie an eldritch skriech and hollow.

Ah, Tam! Ah, Tam! thou'll get thy fairin!
In hell they'll roast thee like a herrin!
In vain thy Kate awaits thy comin!
Kate soon will be a woefu woman!
Now, do thy speedy utmost, Meg,
bridge   And win the key-stane of the brig;
There, at them thou thy tail may toss,
A running stream they dare na cross!
But ere the key-stane she could make,
not   The fient a tail she had to shake;
For Nannie, far before the rest,
Hard upon noble Maggie prest,
aim   And flew at Tam wi furious ettle;
But little wist she Maggie's mettle!
whole   Ae spring brought off her master hale,
But left behind her ain grey tail:
clawed   The carlin claught her by the rump,
And left poor Maggie scarce a stump.

Tam O Shanter

Now, wha this tale o truth shall read,
Ilk man, and mother's son, take heed:
Whene'er to drink you are inclin'd,
Or cutty sarks rin in your mind,
Think! ye may buy the joys o'er dear:
Remember Tam o Shanter's mare.

ON CAPTAIN GROSE

WRITTEN ON AN ENVELOPE, ENCLOSING
A LETTER TO HIM

Addressed 'extempore and anonymous' to Adam de
Cardonnel Lawson, a numismatist and antiquary who
assisted Grose. The basis of these lines is an oyster-
dredging song from the Firth of Forth with a dog-
Latin chorus.

Ken ye ought o Captain Grose? *Igo and ago,*
If he's among his friends or foes? *Iram, coram, dago.*

Is he south or is he north? *Igo and ago,*
Or drownèd in the river Forth? *Iram, coram, dago*

Is he slain by Hielan bodies? *Igo and ago,*
And eaten like a wether haggis? *Iram, coram, dago.*   sheep

Is he to Abra'm's bosom gane? *Igo and ago,*
Or haudin Sarah by the wame? *Iram, coram, dago.*   holding,
                                                      belly
Where'er he be, the Lord be near him! *Igo and ago,*
As for the Deil, he daur na steer him, *Iram, coram, dago.*   dare not

But please transmit th' enclosèd letter, *Igo and ago,*
Which will oblige your humble debtor, *Iram, coram, dago.*

So may ye hae auld stanes in store, *Igo and ago,*
The very stanes that Adam bore, *Iram, coram, dago.*

So may ye get in glad possession, *Igo and ago,*
The coins o Satan's coronation! *Iram, coram, dago.*

EPIGRAM ON
FRANCIS GROSE THE ANTIQUARY

Captain Grose was in Ireland in 1790-1 gathering material
for a projected work on the antiquities of that country,
when he died at Dublin in May 1791.

The Devil got notice that Grose was a-dying,
So whip! at the summons, old Satan came flying;
But when he approach'd where poor Francis lay moaning,
And saw each bed-post with its burthen a-groaning,
Astonish'd, confounded, cries Satan — 'By God,
I'll want him ere take such a damnable load!'

415

ELEGY ON THE LATE
MISS BURNET OF MONBODDO

Elizabeth Burnett, referred to in the 'Address to Edinburgh' died of TB on 17th June 1790. Burns laboured for several months to produce a satisfactory elegy which he sent to Alexander Cunningham on 23rd January 1791. A more polished copy was sent to Mrs. Dunlop on 7th February.

Life ne'er exulted in so rich a prize
As Burnet, lovely from her native skies;
Nor envious Death so triumph'd in a blow,
As that which laid th' accomplish'd Burnet low.

Thy form and mind, sweet maid, can I forget?
In richest ore the brightest jewel set!
In thee, high Heaven above was truest shown,
For by His noblest work the Godhead best is known.

In vain ye flaunt in summer's pride, ye groves!
  Thou crystal streamlet with thy flowery shore,
Ye woodland choir that chaunt your idle loves,
  Ye cease to charm: Eliza is no more.

Ye healthy wastes immix'd with reedy fens,
  Ye mossy streams with sedge and rushes stor'd,
Ye rugged cliffs o'erhanging dreary glens,
  To you I fly: ye with my soul accord.

Princes whose cumb'rous pride was all their worth,
  Shall venal lays their pompous exit hail,
And thou, sweet Excellence! forsake our earth,
  And not a Muse with honest grief bewail?

We saw thee shine in youth and beauty's pride,
  And Virtue's light, that beams beyond the spheres;
But, like the sun eclips'd at morning tide,
  Thou left us darkling in a world of tears.

The parent's heart that nestled fond in thee,
  That heart how sunk, a prey to grief and care!
So deckt the woodbine sweet yon aged tree,
  So, rudely ravish'd, left it bleak and bare.

FRIARS' CARSE

MRS BURNS
and Grandchild Sarah Burns Hutchinson

EPISTLE TO JOHN MAXWELL, ESQ., OF TERRAUGHTIE

ON HIS SEVENTY-FIRST BIRTHDAY

John Maxwell (1720-1814) was a joiner of Dumfries who prospered, enabling him to buy back Terraughty, the family estate west of Dumfries which had been sold because of financial problems. Later he acquired Portrack, north of Dumfries and, by his second marriage, Munches near Dalbeattie. By the 1790s he was one of the leading gentlemen of Dumfriesshire and the Stewartry. His 71st birthday occurred on 7th February 1791.

Health to the Maxwell's vet'ran Chief!
Health ay unsour'd by care or grief!
Inspir'd, I turn'd Fate's sibyl leaf
    This natal morn;
I see thy life is stuff o prief,   proof
    Scarce quite half-worn.

This day thou metes threescore eleven,
And I can tell that bounteous Heaven
(The second-sight, ye ken, is given   know
    To ilka Poet)   every
On thee a tack o seven times seven   lease
    Will yet bestow it.

If envious buckies view wi sorrow   youngsters
Thy lengthen'd days on thy blest morrow,
May Desolation's lang-teeth'd harrow,
    Nine miles an hour,
Rake them, like Sodom and Gomorrah,
    In brunstane stoure!   brimstone dust

But for thy friends, and they are monie,
Baith honest men and lasses bonie,
May couthie Fortune, kind and cannie   loving, careful
    In social glee,
Wi mornings blythe, and e'enings funny,
    Bless them and thee!

Fareweel, auld birkie! Lord be near ye,   fellow
And then the Deil, he daurna steer ye!   dare not
Your friends ay love, your foes ay fear ye!
    For me, shame fa' me,
If neist my heart I dinna wear ye,   next, do not
    While Burns they ca' me!

417

TO THE MEMORY OF THE
UNFORTUNATE MISS BURNS 1791

Margaret Burns, the celebrated Edinburgh prostitute,
died at Roslin within three years of her banishment
from the city. Burns deplored this harshly puritanical
treatment of his namesake. This 'epitaph on a certain
frail sister' was composed a year before her death.

Like to a fading flower in May,
    Which Gardner cannot save,
So Beauty must, sometime, decay
    And drop into the grave.

Fair Burns, for long the talk and toast
    Of many a gaudy Beau,
That Beauty has forever lost
    That made each bosom glow.

Think, fellow sisters, on her fate!
    Think, think how short her days!
Oh! think, and, e'er it be too late,
    Turn from your evil ways.

Beneath this cold, green sod lies dead
    That once bewitching dame
That fired Edina's lustful sons,
    And quench'd their glowing flame.

THERE'LL NEVER BE PEACE TILL
JAMIE COMES HAME

A development of an old Jacobite song; 'Jamie' is, of
course, King James VIII and III, the Old Pretender.

By yon castle wa' at the close of the day,
I heard a man sing, tho his head it was grey,
And as he was singing, the tears doon came,—
'There'll never be peace till Jamie comes hame!'

'The Church is in ruins, the State is in jars,
Delusion, oppressions, and murderous wars,
We dare na weel say't, but we ken wha's to blame—
There'll never be peace till Jamie comes hame!

'My seven braw sons for Jamie drew sword,
But now I greet round the green beds in the yerd; *weep, kirkyard*
It brak the sweet heart o my faithfu auld dame—
There'll never be peace till Jamie comes hame!

'Now life is a burden that bows me down,
Sin I tint my bairns, and he tint his crown; *lost, children*
But till my last moments my words are the same—
There'll never be peace till Jamie comes hame!'

OUT OVER THE FORTH

Perhaps based on a fragment in the Herd MSS and mentioned in a letter to Alexander Cunningham on 11th March 1791.

Out over the Forth, I look to the north –
    But what is the north, and its Highlands to me?
The south nor the east gie ease to my breast,
    The far foreign land, or the wide rolling sea!

But I look to the west, when I gae to rest,
    That happy my dreams and my slumbers may be;
For far in the west lives he I loe best,
    The man that is dear to my babie and me.

YE FLOWERY BANKS

In his letter of 11th March 1791 to Cunningham, Burns wrote: 'I have this evening sketched out a Song. . . intended to sing to a Strathspey reel.'

Ye flowery banks o bonie Doon,
    How can ye blume sae fair?   bloom
How can ye chant, ye little birds,
    And I sae fu o care?

Thou'll break my heart, thou bonie bird,
    That sings upon the bough:
Thou minds me o the happy days
    When my fause Luve was true!   false

Thou'll break my heart, thou bonie bird,
    That sings beside thy mate:
For sae I sat, and sae I sang,
    And wist na o my fate!

Aft hae I rov'd by bonie Doon,   Often
    To see the woodbine twine,
And ilka bird sang o its luve,
    And sae did I o mine.

Wi lightsome heart I pu'd a rose
    Frae aff its thorny tree,
And my fause luver staw my rose,   stole
    But left the thorn wi me.

THE BANKS O DOON

An extensive revision of the previous song, which Burns sent to Johnson for publication in SMM.

Ye banks and braes o bonie Doon,   slopes
    How can ye bloom sae fresh and fair?
How can ye chant, ye little birds,
    And I sae weary fu o care!

419

The Banks O Doon

Thou'll break my heart, thou warbling bird,
That wantons thro the flowering thorn!
Thou minds me o departed joys,
Departed never to return.

Aft hae I rov'd by bonie Doon
To see the rose and woodbine twine,
And ilka bird sang o its luve,
And fondly sae did I o mine.
Wi lightsome heart I pu'd a rose.
Fu sweet upon its thorny tree!
And my fause luver staw my rose—
But ah! he left the thorn wi me.

every (margin note, left of "And ilka bird sang o its luve")

EPIGRAM ON MR. JAMES GRACIE

**James Gracie (1756-1814), manager of the Dumfries
Commercial Bank and Dean of Guild, was captain in
the Dumfries Volunteers. A week before he died, Burns
wrote to Gracie thanking him for the offer of an
outing in his carriage.**

Gracie, thou art a man of worth,
O, be thou Dean for ever!
May he be damn'd to Hell henceforth,
Who fauts thy weight or measure!

THE SONG OF DEATH

TUNE: *Oran an Aoig*

**Writing to Mrs. Dunlop in May 1791, Burns mentions this
song 'which to a lady the descendant of Wallace. . . and
herself the mother of several soldiers, needs neither
preface nor apology.'**

Farewell, thou fair day, thou green earth and ye skies,
Now gay with the broad setting sun!
Farewell, loves and friendships, ye dear tender ties—
Our race of existence is run!
Thou grim King of Terrors! thou Life's gloomy foe!
Go, frighten the coward and slave!
Go, teach them to tremble, fell tyrant, but know,
No terrors hast thou to the brave!

Thou strik'st the dull peasant—he sinks in the dark,
Nor saves e'en the wreck of a name!
Thou strik'st the young hero—a glorious mark,
He falls in the blaze of his fame!
In the field of proud honour, our swords in our hands,
Our king and our country to save,
While victory shines on Life's last ebbing sands,
O, who would not die with the brave?

ADDRESS TO THE SHADE
OF THOMSON

ON CROWNING HIS BUST AT EDNAM,
ROXBURGHSHIRE, WITH A WREATH OF BAYS

James Thomson (1700-48) the poet and precursor of
Romanticism, was born at Ednam. In 1791 David
Erskine, 11th Earl of Buchan proposed to commemorate
Thomson, by erecting a bust of him on Ednam Hill and
decorating it with a laurel wreath. Lord Buchan wrote to
Burns inviting him to attend the crowning ceremony on
22nd September and soliciting an ode for the occasion.
As the harvest season was in full swing by that time
Burns tactfully declined the prospect of an arduous
75-mile journey overland. In the event, the ceremony was
a fiasco, the bust having got broken in a midnight frolic
during Race Week, and Lord Buchan had to substitute a
copy of Thomson's poem 'The Seasons.'

While virgin Spring by Eden's flood
　　Unfolds her tender mantle green,
Or pranks the sod in frolic mood,
　　Or tunes Eolian strains between.

While Summer, with a matron grace,
　　Retreats to Dryburgh's cooling shade,
Yet oft, delighted, stops to trace
　　The progress of the spikey blade:

While Autumn, benefactor kind,
　　By Tweed erects his aged head,
And sees, with self-approving mind,
　　Each creature on his bounty fed.

While maniac Winter rages o'er
　　The hills whence classic Yarrow flows,
Rousing the turbid torrent's roar,
　　Or sweeping, wild, a waste of snows.

So long, sweet Poet of the year!
　　Shall bloom that wreath thou well has won;
While Scotia, with exulting tear,
　　Proclaims that Thomson is her son.

ON SOME COMMEMORATIONS
OF THOMSON

Composed in the autumn of 1791 in the aftermath of
the farcical ceremony at Ednam.

Dost thou not rise, indignant Shade,
　　And smile wi spurning scorn,
When they wha wad hae starved thy life
　　Thy senseless turf adorn?

421

On Some Commemorations Of Thomson

such   They wha about thee mak sic fuss
                      Now thou art but a name,
             Wad seen thee damn'd ere they had spar'd
One farthing, belly   Ae plack to fill thy wame.

climbed, slope   Helpless, alane, thou clamb the brae
much   Wi meikle honest toil,
grasped   And claucht th' unfading garland there,
                      Thy sair-won, rightful spoil.

And wear it there! and call aloud
     This axiom undoubted:—
Would thou hae Nobles' patronage?
     First learn to live without it!

'To whom hae much, more shall be given,'
     Is every great man's faith;
But he, the helpless, needful wretch,
     Shall lose the mite he hath.

LOVELY DAVIES

Deborah Duff Davies was the daughter of Dr. Daniel
Davies of Tenby, Pembrokeshire and a relation of the
Riddell family. Burns met her at Friars' Carse and
corresponded with her thereafter. The petite Miss
Davies was also the inspiration of 'Bonie Wee
Thing'. She died of consumption at an early age.

O, how shall I, unskilfu, try
     The Poet's occupation?
The tunefu Powers, in happy hours
     That whisper inspiration,
must, more   Even they maun dare an effort mair
     Than aught they ever gave us,
Ere they rehearse in equal verse
     The charms o lovely Davies.

Each eye, it cheers, when she appears,
     Like Phoebus in the morning,
When past the shower, and every flower
     The garden is adorning!
As the wretch looks o'er Siberia's shore,
     When winter-bound the wave is,
Sae droops our heart, when we maun part
     Frae charming, lovely Davies.

Lovely Davies

Her smile's a gift frae 'boon the lift,   above, horizon
That makes us mair than princes.
A sceptred hand, a king's command,
Is in her darting glances.
The man in arms 'gainst female charms,
Even he her willing slave is:
He hugs his chain, and owns the reign
Of conquering lovely Davies.

My Muse to dream of such a theme
Her feeble powers surrenders;
The eagle's gaze alone surveys
The sun's meridian splendours.
I wad in vain essay the strain—
The deed too daring brave is!
I'll drap the lyre, and, mute, admire
The charms o lovely Davies.

LAMENT FOR JAMES, EARL OF GLENCAIRN

James Cunningham, 14th Earl of Glencairn (1749-91) was the second son of the 13th Earl, but his brother having predeceased him he succeeded to the title on the death of his father in 1775. From 1780 to 1784 he was one of the Scottish representative peers in the House of Lords. He was greatly impressed by the Kilmarnock Edition and gave Burns a warm welcome when he arrived in Edinburgh, armed with an introduction from Dalrymple of Orangefield. The Earl introduced Burns into Edinburgh society and gave him the patronage necessary for success. It was due to his influence that the members of the Caledonian Hunt subscribed 'universally, one and all' to the first Edinburgh Edition. The Earl went to Portugal in the autumn of 1790 for his health's sake, but returned to England where he died at Falmouth soon after landing, on 30th January 1791. Burns named his third surviving son (b. 1794) in memory of his early patron.

The wind blew hollow frae the hills;
By fits the sun's departing beam
Look'd on the fading yellow woods,
That wav'd o'er Lugar's winding stream.
Beneath a craigy steep, a Bard,   craggy precipice
Laden with years and meikle pain,   much
In loud lament bewail'd his lord,
Whom Death had all untimely ta'en.

423

Lament For James, Earl Of Glencairn

oak

He lean'd him to an ancient aik,
  Whose trunk was mould'ring down with years;
His locks were bleached white with time,
  His hoary cheek was wet wi tears;
And as he touch'd his trembling harp.
And as he tun'd his doleful sang,
The winds, lamenting thro their caves,
  To echo bore the notes alang:—

choir

'Ye scatter'd birds that faintly sing,
  The reliques o the vernal quire!
Ye woods that shed on a' the winds
  The honours o the aged year!
A few short months, and, glad and gay,

eye

  Again ye'll charm the ear and e'e;
But nocht in all revolving time
  Can gladness bring again to me.

'I am a bending agèd tree,
  That long has stood the wind and rain;
But now has some a cruel blast,
  And my last hold of earth is gane;
Nae leaf o mine shall greet the spring,
  Nae simmer sun exalt my bloom;

must

But I maun lie before the storm,
  And ithers plant them in my room.

'I've seen sae monie changefu years,
  On earth I am a stranger grown:
I wander in the ways of men,
  Alike unknowing and unkown:
Unheard, unpitied, unreliev'd,

alone, load

  I bear alane my lade o care;
For silent, low, on beds of dust,
  Lie a' that would my sorrows share.

'And last (the sum of a' my griefs!)
  My noble master lies in clay;
The flow'r amang our barons bold,
  His country's pride, his country's stay:
In weary being now I pine,
  For a' the life of life is dead,
And hope has left my agèd ken,
  On forward wing for ever fled.

'Awake thy last sad voice, my harp!
  The voice of woe and wild despair!
Awake, resound thy latest lay,
  Then sleep in silence evermair!

424

Lament For James, Earl Of Glencairn

And thou, my last, best, only friend,
    That fillest an untimely tomb,
Accept this tribute from the Bard
    Thou brought from Fortune's mirkest gloom.   darkest

'In Poverty's low barren vale,
    Thick mists obscure involv'd me round;
Though oft I turn'd the wistful eye,
    Nae ray of fame was to be found;
Thou found'st me, like the morning sun
    That melts the fogs in limpid air:
The friendless Bard and rustic song
    Became alike thy fostering care.

'O, why was Worth so short a date,
    While villains ripen grey with time!
Must thou, the noble, gen'rous, great,
    Fall in bold manhood's hardy prime?
Why did I live to see that day,
    A day to me so full of woe?
O, had I met the mortal shaft
    Which laid my benefactor low!

'The bridegroom may forget the bride
    Was made his wedded wife yestreen;   last night
The monarch may forget the crown
    That on his head an hour has been;
The mother may forget the child
    That smiles sae sweetly on her knee;
But I'll remember thee, Glencairn,
    And a' that thou has done for me!'

LINES TO SIR JOHN WHITEFORD, BART.

SENT WITH THE FOREGOING POEM

Sir John Whiteford (1734-1803), a friend of Glencairn
and a patron of Burns (see 'The Vision') wrote to the
poet on 16th October acknowledging these lines
with the view that 'temporal misfortunes shall
receive an eternal recompense. Let us cherish this
hope for our departed friend, and moderate our
grief. . . knowing that he cannot come to us, but we
may go to him.'

Thou, who thy honour as thy God rever'st,
Who, save thy mind's reproach, nought earthly fear'st,
To thee this votive off'ring I impart,
The tearful tribute of a broken heart.
The Friend thou valued'st, I, the Patron lov'd;
His worth, his honour, all the world approved:
We'll mourn till we too go as he has gone,
And tread the shadowy path to that dark world unknown.

425

ON GLENRIDDELL'S FOX BREAKING
HIS CHAIN

A FRAGMENT, 1791

Captain Robert Riddell of Glenriddell kept a pet fox
in a dog-kennel — something which Burns with his
libertarian principles abhorred. When the fox escaped
Burns seized the opportunity to compose these lines
on his favourite theme of Liberty. Though undated,
this poem was probably written at Ellisland.

Thou, Liberty, thou art my theme:
Not such as idle poets dream,
Who trick thee up a heathen goddess
That a fantastic cap and rod has!
Such stale conceits are poor and silly:
I paint thee out a Highland filly,
A sturdy, stubborn, handsome dapple,
As sleek's a mouse, as round's an apple,
That, when thou pleasest can do wonders,
But when thy luckless rider blunders,
Or if thy fancy should demur there,
Wilt break thy neck ere thou go further.

These things premis'd, I sing a Fox—
Was caught among his native rocks,
And to a dirty kennel chained—
How he his liberty regained.

Glenriddell! a Whig without a stain,
A Whig in principle and grain,
Could'st thou enslave a free-born creature,
A native denizen of Nature?
How could'st thou, with a heart so good
(A better ne'er was sluiced with blood),
Nail a poor devil to a tree,
That ne'er did harm to thine or thee?

The staunchest Whig Glenriddell was,
Quite frantic in his country's cause;

poetic name for a fox

And oft was Reynard's prison passing,
And with his brother-Whigs canvassing
The rights of men, the powers of women,
With all the dignity of Freemen.

Sir Reynard daily heard debates
Of princes', kings', and nations' fates,
With many rueful, bloody stories
Of tyrants, Jacobites, and Tories:
From liberty how angels fell,
That now are galley-slaves in Hell;

Genesis x. 8-10

How Nimrod first the trade began
Of binding Slavery's chains on man;

Queen of Assyria who killed
her husband

How fell Semiramis — God damn her!—
Did first, with sacrilegious hammer

426

On Glenriddell's Fox Breaking His Chain

(All ills till then were trivial matters),
For Man dethron'd forge hen-peck fetters:
How Xerxes, that abandoned Tory,
Thought cutting throats was reaping glory,
Until the stubborn Whigs of Sparta
Taught him great Nature's Magna Charta;
How mighty Rome her fiat hurl'd
Resistless o'er a bowing world,
And, kinder than they did desire,
Polish'd mankind with sword and fire:
With much too tedious to relate
Of ancient and of modern date,
But ending still, how Billy Pitt
(Unlucky boy!) with wicked wit
Has gagg'd old Britain, drain'd her coffer,
As butchers bind and bleed a heifer.

William Pitt who devised
new fiscal measures
including income tax
at 3d in the £

Thus wily Reynard, by degrees,
In kennel listening at his ease,
Suck'd in a mighty stock of knowledge,
As much as some folks at a college;
Knew Britain's rights and constitution,
Her aggrandisement, diminution;
How Fortune wrought us good from evil:
Let no man, then, despise the Devil,
As who should say: 'I ne'er can need him,'
Since we to scoundrels owe our Freedom.

LINES TO CAPTAIN RIDDELL

ON RETURNING A NEWSPAPER

Though undated, these lines belong to 1791 and are a
charming relic of the friendship between Burns and
Riddell, who also founded the communal library
known as the Monkland Friendly Society. Riddell
gave a great many of his old books and Burns bought
most of the others from his friend Peter Hill, book-
seller in Edinburgh. At Riddell's instigation Burns
contributed an article about the society to Sir John
Sinclair's Statistical Account.

Your News and Review Sir,
I've read through and through, Sir,
With little admiring or blaming:
The Papers are barren
Of home-news or foreign—
No murders or rapes worth the naming.

427

Lines To Captain Riddell

Our friends, the Reviewers,
Those chippers and hewers,
Are judges of mortar and stone, Sir;
But of meet or unmeet,
In a fabric complete,
I'll boldly pronounce they are none, Sir.

My goose-quill too rude is
To tell all your goodness
Bestow'd on your servant, the Poet;
Would to God I had one
Like a beam of the sun,
And then all the world, Sir, should know it!

ELLISLAND, Monday morning

REPLY TO A NOTE FROM
CAPTAIN RIDDELL

[Dear Bard
          To ride this day is vain
For it will be a steeping rain
     So come and sit with me
Wee'l twa or three leaves fill up with scraps
And whiles fill up the time with Crack
     And spend the day with glee.

R. R.]

Dear Sir, at onie time or tide
I'd rather sit wi you than ride,
     Tho 'twere wi royal Geordie:
And trowth! your kindness, soon and late

makes, backward   Aft gars me to myself look blate—
     The Lord in Heaven reward ye!

ELLISLAND   R. BURNS

428

GRIM GRIZZEL

Burns wrote this parody about 1791. The origin of this burlesque is mentioned in a note: 'Passing lately through Dunblane, while I stopped to refresh my horse, the following ludicrous epitaph, which I pickt up from an old tombstone among the ruins of the ancient Abbey, struck me particularly, being myself a native of Dumfriesshire.' The tombstone apostrophized: 'Here lyes with Dethe auld Grizzel Grimme, Lincluden's ugly witche. O Dethe, an what a taste hast thou Cann lye with siche a bitche!'

Grim Grizzel was a mighty Dame
    Weel kend on Cluden-side:
Grim Grizzel was a mighty Dame
    O meikle fame and pride.

When gentles met in gentle bowers
    And nobles in the ha',
Grim Grizzel was a mighty Dame,
    The loudest o them a'.

Where lawless Riot rag'd the night
    And Beauty durst na gang,
Grim Grizzel was a mighty Dame
    Wham nae man e'er wad wrang.

Nor had Grim Grizzel skill alane
    What bower and ha' require;
But she had skill, and meikle skill,   *much*
    In barn and eke in byre.   *also, cow-shed*

Ae day Grim Grizzel walked forth,
    As she was wont to do,
Alang the banks o Cluden fair
    Her cattle for to view.

The cattle shat o'er hill and dale
    As cattle will incline,
And sair it grieved Grim Grizzel's heart   *sore*
    Sae muckle muck to tine.   *lose*

And she has ca'd on John o Clods,
    Of her herdsmen the chief,
And she has ca'd on John o Clods,
    And tell'd him a' her grief:—

'Now wae betide thee, John o Clods!
    I gie thee meal and fee,
And yet sae meikle muck ye tine
    Might a' be gear to me!   *wealth*

'Ye claut my byre, ye sweep my byre,
    The like was never seen;
The very chamber I lie in
    Was never half sae clean.

Grim Grizzel

cattle, pasture

heed
before
every

go

then

eyes

folded
One
dare, so bold

Mud-

routed

'Ye ca' my kye adown the loan
    And there they a' discharge:
My Tammy's hat, wig, head and a'
    Was never half sae large!

'But mind my words now, John o Clods,
    And tent me what I say:
My kye shall shit ere they gae out,
    That shall they ilka day.

'And mind my words now, John o Clods,
    And tent now wha ye serve;
Or back ye'se to the Colonel gang,
    Either to steal or starve.'

Then John o Clods he lookèd up
    And syne he lookèd down;
He lookèd east, he lookèd west,
    He lookèd roun and roun.

His bonnet and his rowantree club
    Frae either hand di fa';
Wi lifted een and open mouth
    He naething said at a'.

At length he found his trembling tongue,
    Within his mouth was fauld:-
'Ae silly word frae me, madam,
    Gin I daur be sae bauld.

'Your kye will at nae bidding shite,
    Let me do what I can;
Your kye will at nae bidding shite
    Of onie earthly man.

'Tho ye are great Lady Glaur-hole,
    For a' your power and art
Tho ye are great Lady Glaur-hole,
    They winna let a fart.'

'Now wae betide thee, John o Clods!
    An ill death may ye die!
My kye shall at my bidding shite,
    And that ye soon shall see.'

Then she's ta'en Hawkie by the tail,
    And wrung wi might and main,
Till Hawkie rowted through the woods
    Wi agonising pain.

'Shite, shite, ye bitch,' Grim Grizzel roar'd,
    Till hill and valley rang;
'And shite, ye bitch,' the echoes roar'd
    Lincluden wa's amang.

TO ROBERT GRAHAM, ESQ.,
OF FINTRY

Robert Graham, 12th laird of Fintry in Angus (1749-1815) was a distant kinsman of James Graham of Claverhouse. Burns first met him at Blair Atholl on 31st August 1787 during his Highland tour. In that year Graham was appointed a Commissioner of the Scottish Board of Excise and through his 'warmest exertions' he secured for Burns an Excise appointment in 1788.

Late crippl'd of an arm, and now a leg;
About to beg a pass for leave to beg;
Dull, listless, teas'd, dejected, and deprest
(Nature is adverse to a cripple's rest);
Will generous Graham list to his Poet's wail
(It soothes poor Misery, hearkening to her tale),
And hear him curse the light he first survey'd,
And doubly curse the luckless rhyming trade?

Thou, Nature! partial Nature! I arraign;
Of thy caprice maternal I complain:
The lion and the bull thy care have found,
One shakes the forests, and one spurns the ground;
Thou giv'st the ass his hide, the snail his shell;
Th' envenom'd wasp, victorious, guards his cell;
Thy minions kings defend, control, devour,
In all th' omnipotence of rule and power.
Foxes and statesmen subtile wiles ensure;
The cit and polecat stink, and are secure;   city-dweller
Toads with their poison, doctors with their drug,
The priest and hedgehog in their robes, are snug;
Ev'n silly woman has her warlike arts,
Her tongue and eyes — her dreaded spear and darts.

But O thou bitter step-mother and hard,
To thy poor, fenceless, naked child — the Bard!
A thing unteachable in world's skill,
And half an idiot too, more helpless still:
No heels to bear him from the op'ning dun,
No claws to dig, his hated sight to shun;
No horns, but those by luckless Hymen worn,   god of marriage
And those, alas! not, Amalthea's horn;   daughter of Melissus of Crete
No nerves olfact'ry, Mammon's trusty cur,
Clad in rich Dulness' comfortable fur;
In naked feeling, and in aching pride,
He bears th' unbroken blast from ev'ry side:
Vampyre booksellers drain him to the heart,   an insulting reference
And scorpion critics cureless venom dart.   to Creech

Critics — appall'd, I venture on the name;
Those cut-throat bandits in the paths of fame;   Alexander Monroe (1697-1767),
Bloody dissectors, worse than ten Monroes: son (1733-1817) and grandson
He hacks to teach, they mangle to expose.   (1773-1859) professors of
anatomy, Edinburgh.

431

To Robert Graham, Esq., Of Fintry

His heart by causeless wanton malice wrung,
By blockheads' daring into madness stung;
His well-won bays, than life itself more dear,
By miscreants torn, who ne'er one sprig must wear;
Foil'd, bleeding, tortur'd in th' unequal strife,
The hapless Poet flounders on thro life:
Till, fled each hope that once his bosom fir'd,
And fled each Muse that glorious once inspir'd,
Low sunk in squalid, unprotected age,
Dead even resentment for his injur'd page,
He heeds or feels no more the ruthless critic's rage!
So, by some hedge, the gen'rous steed deceas'd,
For half-starv'd snarling curs a dainty feast,
By toil and famine wore to skin and bone,
Lies, senseless of each tugging bitch's son.

O Dulness! portion of the truly blest!
Calm shelter'd haven of eternal rest!
Thy sons ne'er madden in the fierce extremes
Of Fortune's polar frost, or torrid beams.
If mantling high she fills the golden cup,
With sober, selfish ease they sip it up:
Conscious the bounteous meed they well deserve,
They only wonder 'some folks' do not starve
The grave, sage hern thus easy picks his frog,
And thinks the mallard a sad, worthless dog.
When Disappointment snaps the clue of hope,
And thro disastrous night they darkling grope,
With deaf endurance sluggishly they bear,
And just conclude 'that fools are fortune's care.'
So, heavy, passive to the tempest's shocks,
Strong on the sign-post stands the stupid ox.

Not so the idle Muses' mad-cap train;
Not such the workings of their moon-struck brain:
In equanimity they never dwell;
By turns in scoring heav'n, or vaulted hell.

I dread thee, Fate, relentless and severe,
With all a poet's, husband's father's fear!
Already one strong hold of hope is lost:
Glencairn, the truly noble, lies in dust
(Fled, like the sun eclips'd as noon appears,
And left us darkling in a world of tears).
O! hear my ardent, grateful, selfish pray'r!
Fintry, my other stay, long bless and spare!
Thro a long life his hopes and wishes crown,
And bright in cloudless skies his sun go down!
May bliss domestic smooth his private path;
Give energy to life; and soothe his latest breath,
With many a filial tear circling the bed of death!

WILLIAM SMELLIE — A SKETCH

William Smellie (1740-95) was Burns's printer and a founder of the Crochallan Fencibles. The son of a Duddingston stone-mason, he was an antiquary, natural historian, and prolific writer, best remembered as first Editor of the Encyclopaedia Britannica. 'Many letters from Burns to Smellie. . . being totally unfit for publication. . . have been burnt,' wrote Kerr.

Crochallan came:
The old cock'd hat, the brown surtout the same,   overcoat
His grisly beard just bristling in its might
('Twas four long nights and days to shaving-night):
His uncomb'd, hoary locks, wild-staring, thatch'd
A head for thought profound and clear unmatch'd;
Yet, tho his caustic wit was biting rude,
His heart was warm, benevolent, and good.

THOU GLOOMY DECEMBER

This and the following song were written for Clarinda on the eve of her departure for Jamaica. Burns had been in Edinburgh early in December and sent these songs to her on 27th of that month 'Nancy' is, of course, Agnes McLehose herself.

Ance mair I hail thee, thou gloomy December!
   Ance mair I hail thee wi sorrow and care!
Sad was the parting thou makes me remember:
   Parting wi Nancy, O, ne'er to meet mair!

Fond lovers' parting is sweet, painful pleasure,
   Hope beaming mild on the soft parting hour;
But the dire feeling, O farewell for ever!
   Anguish unmingled and agony pure!

Wild as the winter now tearing the forest,
   Till the last leaf o the summer is flown—
Such is the tempest has shaken my bosom,
   Till my last hope and last comfort is gone!

Still as I hail thee, thou gloomy December,
   Still shall I hail thee wi sorrow and care;
For sad was the parting thou makes me remember;
   Parting wi Nancy, O, ne'er to meet mair!

SAE FAR AWA

TUNE: *Dalkeith Maiden Bridge*

Traditionally associated song with the parting of Burns and Nancy McLehose when she was leaving for Jamaica in 1791.

O, sad and heavy should I part
   But for her sake sae far awa,
Unknowing what my way may thwart—
   My native land sae far awa.

Sae Far Awa

Thou that of a' things Maker art,
 That formed this Fair sae far awa,
Gie body strength, then I'll ne'er start
 At this my way sae far awa!

How true is love to pure desert!
 So mine in her sae far awa,
And nocht shall heal my bosom's smart,
 While, O, she is sae far awa!

Nane other love, nane other dart
 I feel, but hers sae far awa;
But fairer never touch'd a heart
 Than hers, the Fair sae far awa.

AE FOND KISS

TUNE: *Rory Dall's Port*

As Maurice Lindsay has said, 'a song so genuine in its
resigned passion that it relegates the other nine songs
he had written for her, full of "sensibility" and
drawing-room manners. to the realms of the insig-
nificant.' In January 1792 Nancy sailed from Greenock
aboard the Roselle – ironically the ship that should
have carried Burns himself to Jamaica five years earlier.

Ae fond kiss, and then we sever!
Ae farewell, and then forever!
Deep in heart-wrung tears I'll pledge thee,
Warring sighs and groans I'll wage thee.
Who shall say that Fortune grieves him,
While the star of hope she leaves him?
Me. nae cheerfu twinkle lights me,
Dark despair around benights me.

I'll ne'er blame my partial fancy:
Naething could resist my Nancy!
But to see her was to love her
Love but her, and love for ever.
Had we never lov'd sae kindly,
Had we never lov'd sae blindly,
Never met – or never parted –
We had ne'er been broken-hearted.

every

Fare-thee-weel, thou first and fairest!
Fare-thee-weel, thou best and dearest!
Thine be ilka joy and treasure,
Peace, Enjoyment, Love and Pleasure!
Ae fond kiss, and then we sever!
Ae farewell, alas, for ever!
Deep in heart-wrung tears I'll pledge thee,
Warring sighs and groans I'll wage thee.

THERE WAS TWA WIVES

TUNE: *Take Your Old Cloak About You*

Burns's revision of a popular ballad, which he sent
to Robert Cleghorn about January 1792, describing it
as 'a new Edition of an old Cloaciniad song, a species of
composition which I have heard you admire.'

There was twa wives, and twa witty wives,
    As e'er play'd houghmagandie,   fornication
And they coost oot, upon a time,   cast
    Out o'er a drink o brandy;
Up Maggy rose, and forth she goes,
    And she leaves auld Mary flytin,   scolding
And she farted by the byre-en'
    For she was gaun a shiten.

She farted by the byre-en',
    She farted by the stable;
And thick and nimble were her steps   rapid
    As fast as she was able:
Till at yon dyke-back the hurly brak,   diarrhoea
    But raxin for some dockins,   reaching, dock-leaves
The beans and pease cam down her thighs,
    And she cackit a' her stockins.   fouled

SAW YE BONIE LESLEY

TUNE: *The Collier's 'Bony Dochter'*

Lesley Baillie (d. 1843) was the daughter of Robert
Baillie of Mayfield, Ayrshire. In a letter of 22nd
August 1792 Burns wrote to Mrs Dunlop that Mr.
Baillie and his two daughters, on their way to
England, had visited him a few days earlier — 'on
which I took my horse. . . and convoyed them
fourteen or fifteen miles and dined and spent the day
with them. 'Twas about nine, I think, when I left
them; and riding home I composed the following
ballad.' It was modelled on the old ballad 'My bonie
Lizie Bailie.'

O, saw ye bonie Lesley,
    As she gaed o'er the Border?
She's gane, like Alexander,
    To spread her conquests farther!

To see her is to love her,
    And love but her for ever;
For Nature made her what she is,
    And never made anither!

Thou art a queen, fair Lesley—
    Thy subjects, we before thee!
Thou art divine, fair Lesley—
    The hearts o men adore thee.

Saw Ye Bonie Lesley

not harm

The Deil he could na skaith thee,
  Or aught that wad belang thee;
He'd look into thy bonie face,
  And say:— 'I canna wrang thee!'

The Powers aboon will tent thee,
  Misfortune sha'na steer thee:
Thou'rt like themsel sae lovely,
  That ill they'll ne'er let near thee.

Return again, fair Lesley,
  Return to Caledonie!
That we may brag we hae a lass
  There's nane again sae bonie.

CRAIGIEBURN WOOD

This was Burns's first contribution to SMM vol.iv. The
subject was Jean Lorimer (1775-1831), daughter of
William Lorimer of Kemmishall on the Nith two miles
south of Ellisland. She was courted by a fellow-
exciseman, John Gillespie, for whom Burns composed
several poems. Unmoved by these effusions Jean
eloped to Gretna Green with a young spendthrift
named Whelpdale who, after three weeks of marriage,
abandoned his bride to escape his creditors. She
returned to her father's home. She later became Burns's
Chloris, for whom he wrote at least two dozen songs
including some of his very best. Craigieburn was Jean's
birthplace, near Moffat. James Hogg, the Ettrick
Shepherd, alleged that Burns himself had an ongoing
affair and stayed with her every time his business took
him to Moffat.

CHORUS

Beyond thee, dearie, beyond thee, dearie,
  And O, to be lying beyond thee!
O, sweetly, soundly, weel may he sleep
  That's laid in the bed beyond thee!

Sweet closes the ev'ning on Craigieburn Wood
  And blythely awaukens the morrow;
But the pride o the spring on the Craigieburn Wood
  Can yield me naught but sorrow.

I see the spreading leaves and flowers,
  I hear the wild birds singing;
But pleasure they hae nane for me,
  While care my heart is wringing.

Craigieburn Wood

I can na tell, I maun na tell,   *must*
   I daur na for your anger;   *dare not*
But secret love will brak my heart,
   If I conceal it langer.

I see thee gracefu, straight, and tall,
   I see thee sweet and bonie;
But O, what will my torment be,
   If thou refuse thy Johnie!

To see thee in another's arms
   In love to lie and languish,
'Twad be my dead, that will be seen—
   My heart wad burst wi anguish!

But, Jeanie, say thou wilt be mine,
   Say thou lo'es nane before me,
And a' my days o life to come
   I'll gratefully adore thee.

FRAE THE FRIENDS AND LAND
I LOVE

Burns alleged that this was a traditional ballad to which he merely added the last four lines, though no original has ever been traced. Dewar considered this a subterfuge whereby Burns might distance himself from authorship of such an avowedly Jacobite song, but the only overtly Jacobite lines are the last— those very lines which he claimed as his own.

Frae the friends and land I love   *From*
   Driv'n by Fortune's felly spite,   *deadly*
Frae my best belov'd I rove,
   Never mair to taste delight!
Never mair maun hope to find
   Ease frae toil, relief frae care.
When remembrance wracks the mind,
   Pleasures but unveil despair.

Brightest climes shall mirk appear,
   Desert ilka blooming shore,   *each*
Till the Fates, nae mair severe,
   Friendship, love, and peace restore;
Till Revenge, wi laurell'd head,
   Bring our banish'd hame again,
And ilk loyal, bonie lad
   Cross the seas, and win his ain!   *own*

HUGHIE GRAHAM

TUNE: *Druimionn dubh*

Many versions exist of this old ballad; this one, according to Burns, 'was from oral tradition in Ayrshire, where, when I was a boy, it was a popular song.' Burns extensively revised it, compressed the opening, and added eight lines of his own. Though set in Stirling a local touch was added by the inclusion of the Whitefoords, a prominent Ayrshire family in Burns's day.

Our lords are to the mountains gane,
 A hunting o the fallow deer;

arrested And they hae gripet Hughie Graham
 For stealing o the bishop's mare.

And they hae tied him hand and foot,
 And led him up thro Stirling town;
The lads and lasses met him there,

fool Cried, Hughie Graham thou art a loun.

release O lowse my right hand free, he says,
 And put my braid sword in the same;
He's no in Stirling town this day,

Dare Daur tell the tale to Hughie Graham.

Up then bespake the brave Whitefoord,
 As he sat by the bishop's knee;

young bullocks Five hundred white stots I'll gie you,
 If ye'll let Hughie Graham gae free.

O haud your tongue, the bishop says,
 And wi your pleading let me be;
For tho ten Grahams were in his coat,
 Hughie Graham this day shall die.

Up then bespake the fair Whitefoord,
 As she sat by the bishop's knee;
Five hundred white pence I'll gie you,
 If ye'll gie Hughie Graham to me.

O haud your tongue now lady fair,
 And wi your pleading let me be;
Altho ten Grahams were in his coat,
 Its for my honor he maun die.

hillock They've taen him to the gallows knowe,
 He looked to the gallows tree,
Yet never color left his cheek,
 Nor ever did he blin' his e'e.

At length he looked round about,
 To see whatever he could spy;
And there he saw his auld father,
 And he was weeping bitterly.

438

Hughie Graham

O haud your tongue, my father dear,   hold
   And wi your weeping let it be;
Thy weeping's sairer on my heart,   sorer
   Than a' that they can do to me.

And ye may gie my brother John
   My sword that's bent in the middle clear,
And let him come at twelve o'clock
   And see me pay the bishop's mare.

And ye may gie my brother James
   My sword that's bent in the middle brown;
And bid him come at four o'clock,
   And see his brother Hugh cut down.

Remember me to Maggy my wife,
   The niest time ye gang o'er the moor;   next, go
Tell her, she staw the bishop's mare,   stole
   Tell her, she was the bishop's whore.

And ye may tell my kith and kin,
   I never did disgrace their blood;
And when they meet the bishop's cloak,
   To mak it shorter by the hood.

JOHN COME KISS ME NOW

**This widely popular song has been traced back to late
medieval times and numerous versions have been
recorded before Burns revised it and added a stanza,
for SMM.**

CHORUS

O John, come kiss me now, now, now;
   O John, my luve, come kiss me now;
O John, come kiss me by and by,
   For weel ye ken the way to woo.   know

O some will court and compliment,
   And ither some will kiss and daut;   caresss
But I will mak o my gudeman,
   My ain gudeman, it is nae faute.

O some will court and compliment,
   And ither some will prie their mou,   prise, mouth
And some will hause in ithers arms,   embrace
   And that's the way I like to do.

COCK UP YOUR BEAVER

This is a revision of an old fragment in the Herd MSS
(II. 205).

When first my brave Johnie lad came to this town,
He had a blue bonnet that wanted the crown,
But now he has gotten a hat and a feather—
beaver-hat   Hey, brave Johnie lad, cock up your beaver!

spruce   Cock up your beaver, and cock it fu sprush!
We'll over the border and gie them a brush:
There's somebody there we'll teach better behaviour—
Hey, brave Johnie lad, cock up your beaver!

MY TOCHER'S THE JEWEL

The last four lines, annotated 'Stanza of an old song,
tune bonie Dundee' were included in a collection of
poetic scraps sent by Burns to Tytler of Woodhouselee,
probably in August 1787 as 'a sample of the old pieces
that are still to be found among our Peasantry in the
West.'

O, meikle thinks my luve o my beauty,
     And meikle thinks my luve o my kin;
finely   But little thinks my luve I ken brawlie
dowry   My tocher's the jewel has charms for him.
It's a' for the apple he'll nourish the tree,
honey   It's a' for the hiney he'll cherish the bee!
much, money   My laddie's sae meikle in luve wi the siller,
     He canna hae luve to spare for me!

bargain penny   Your proffer o luve's an airle-penny,
     My tocher's the bargain ye wad buy;
if   But an ye be crafty, I am cunnin,
     Sae ye wi anither your fortune may try.
timber   Ye're like to the timmer o yon rotten wood,
     Ye're like to the bark o yon rotten tree:
Ye'll slip frae me like a knotless thread,
     An ye'll crack ye're credit wi mair nor me!

GUIDWIFE, COUNT THE LAWIN

According to Burns, the chorus of this song was part
of an old ballad, but the verses were his own work.

CHORUS

Then, guidwife, count the lawin,   mistress, reckoning
The lawin, the lawin!
Then, guidwife, count the lawin,
   And bring a coggie mair!   another jug

Gane is the day, and mirk's the night,   dark's
But we'll ne'er stray for faut o light,   lack
For ale and brandy's stars and moon,
And blude-red wine's the risin sun.

There's wealth and ease for gentlemen,
And semple folk maun fecht and fen';   simple, must fight
But here we're a' in ae accord,   one
For ilka man that's drunk's a lord.   each

My coggie is a haly pool   holy
That heals the wounds o care and dool, woe
And Pleasure is a wanton trout:
An ye drink it a', ye'll find him out!

WHAT CAN A YOUNG LASSIE DO WI
AN AULD MAN

Listed in the Gray MS as 'Mr B——'s words,' and signed
in SMM as his work.

What can a young lassie, what shall a young lassie,
   What can a young lassie do wi an auld man?
Bad luck on the penny that tempted my minnie   mother
   To sell her puir Jenny for siller an lan'!   money

He's always compleenin frae mornin to eenin;
   He hoasts and he hirples the weary day lang; coughs, limps
He's doylt and he's dozin, his blude it is frozen— senile
   O, dreary's the night wi a crazy auld man!

He hums and he hankers, he frets and he cankers, crabs
   I never can please him do a' that I can.
He's peevish an jealous o a' the young fellows—
   O, dool on the day I met wi an auld man!   woe

My auld auntie Katie upon me taks pity,
   I'll do my endeavour to follow her plan;
I'll cross him an wrack him, until I heartbreak him,
   And then his auld brass will buy me a new pan.

THE BONIE LAD THAT'S FAR AWA

Burns modelled this song on the seventeenth century
ballad 'The Unconstant Shepherd or the Forsaken
Lass's Lamentation.'

go, fine

O how can I be blythe and glad,
  Or how can I gang brisk and braw,
When the bonie lad that I lo'e best
  Is o'er the hills and far awa?

It's no the frosty winter wind,
  It's no the driving drift and snaw;
But ay the tear comes in my e'e,
  To think on him that's far awa.

put, from

My father pat me frae his door,
  My friends they hae disown'd me a'!:
But I hae ane will tak my part—
  The bonie lad that's far awa.

bandeaux, gave

A pair o glooves he bought to me,
  And silken snoods he gae me twa,
And I will wear them for his sake,
  The bonie lad that's far awa.

clothe, birch wood

O, weary Winter soon will pass,
  And Spring will cleed the birken shaw,
And my sweet babie will be born,
  And he'll be hame that's far awa!

I DO CONFESS THOU ART SAE FAIR

In his annotated copy of SMM Burns wrote: 'This song
is altered from a poem by Sir Robert Ayton, private
Secretary to Mary and Anne, queens of Scotland... I
think I have improved the simplicity of the
sentiments, by giving them a Scots dress.'

head over heels

I do confess thou art sae fair,
  I wad been o'er the lugs in luve,
Had I na found the slightest prayer
  That lips could speak thy heart could muve.

I do confess thee sweet, but find
  Thou art so thriftless o thy sweets,
Thy favours are the silly wind

every

  That kisses ilka thing it meets.

See yonder rosebud rich in dew,
  Amang its native briers sae coy,

loses

How sune it tines its scent and hue,
  When pu'd and worn a common toy!

Sic fate ere lang shall thee betide,
  Tho thou may gaily bloom awhile,
And sune thou shalt be thrown aside,
  Like onie common weed, an vile.

442

GALLOWAY TAM

Burns's hand in this traditional ballad is uncertain, despite the note in the Law MS (annotations for SMM) 'Mr Burns's old words.'

O Galloway Tam came here to woo,
    I'd rather we'd gin him the brawnit cow;   *given, brindled*
For our lass Bess may curse and ban
    The wanton wit o Galloway Tam.

O Galloway Tam came here to shear,   *clip fleeces*
    I'd rather we'd gin him the gude gray mare;
He kist the gudewife and strack the gudeman,   *wife, struck,*
    And that's the tricks o Galloway Tam.   *husband*

AS I CAM DOWN BY YON CASTLE WA'

Communicated by Burns to Johnson as 'a very popular Ayrshire song'. Kinsley admits this to the canon although there is no evidence that Burns corrected the words in any way, and it retains the rough vigour of the original.

As I cam down by yon castle wa',
    And in by yon garden green,
O there I spied a bony bony lass,
    But the flower-borders were us between.

A bony bony lassie she was,
    As ever mine eyes did see:
O five hundred pounds would I give,
    For to have such a pretty bride as thee.

To have such a pretty bride as me,
    Young man ye are sairly mista'en;
Tho ye were king o fair Scotland,
    I wad disdain to be your queen.

Talk not so very high, bony lass,
    O talk not so very, very high:
The man at the fair that wad sell,
    He maun learn at the man that wad buy.

I trust to climb a far higher tree,
    And herry a far richer nest:
Tak this advice o me, bony lass,
    Humility wad set thee best.

LORD RONALD MY SON

Sent by Burns to Johnson, this is a fragment of the
widespread old ballad 'Lord Randal'. Much longer
versions were in print before Burns's time and it seems
that he reduced these two stanzas to make a song.

O where hae ye been, Lord Ronald, my son?
O where hae ye been, Lord Ronald, my son?
I hae been wi my sweetheart, mother, make my bed soon;
For I'm weary wi the hunting, and fain wad lie down.

What got ye frae your sweetheart, Lord Ronald, my son?
What got ye frae your sweetheart, Lord Ronald, my son?
I hae got deadly poison, mother, make my bed soon;
For life is a burden that soon I'll lay down.—

I HAE BEEN AT CROOKIEDEN

There were several traditional ballads by the name of
'Highland Laddie.' Burns believed this to be the oldest
of them and revised it extensively. Nevertheless, the
reference to 'Willie' (l. 3) — the Duke of Cumberland
and victor of Culloden — puts this version no earlier
than 1746.

I hae been at Crookieden
   My bonie laddie, Highland laddie!
Viewing Willie and his men—
   My bonie laddie, Highland laddie!
There our foes that burnt and slew—
   My bonie laddie, Highland laddie!
There at last they gat their due—
   My bonie laddie, Highland laddie!

corner

Satan sits in his black neuk—
   My bonie laddie, Highland laddie!
Breaking sticks to roast the Duke—
   My bonie laddie, Highland laddie!

gave

The bloody monster gae a yell—
   My bonie laddie, Highland laddie!

went

And loud the laugh gaed round a' Hell.
   My bonie laddie, Highland laddie!

IT IS NA, JEAN, THY BONIE FACE

TUNE: *The Maid's Complaint*

Burns took some old English verses and 'gave them
their Scots dress.' This poem was written for Jean
Armour.

It is na, Jean, thy bonie face
   Nor shape that I admire,
Altho thy beauty and thy grace
awaken
   Might weel awauk desire.

444

It Is Na, Jean, Thy Bonie Face

Something in ilka part o thee   each
    To praise, to love, I find;
But, dear as is thy form to me,
    Still dearer is thy mind.

Nae mair ungen'rous wish I hae,
    Nor stronger in my breast,
Than, if I canna mak thee sae,
    At least to see thee blest.

Content am I, if Heaven shall give
    But happiness to thee,
And, as wi thee I wish to live,
    For thee I'd bear to dee.   die

MY EPPIE MACNAB

'The old song with this title has more wit than decency' says Burns in his SMM notes. The bawdy version first appeared in print about 1806 in the Giblet Pye.

O, saw ye my dearie, my Eppie Macnab?
O, saw ye my dearie, my Eppie Macnab?
    'She's down in the yard, she's kissin the laird,
She winna come hame to her ain Jock Rab!'   will not, own

O, come thy ways to me, my Eppie Macnab!
O, come thy ways to me, my Eppie Macnab!
    Whate'er thou hast done, be it late, be it soon,
Thou's welcome again to thy ain Jock Rab.

What says she, my dearie, my Eppie Macnab?
What says she, my dearie, my Eppie Macnab?
    'She lets thee to wit that she has thee forgot,
And forever disowns thee, her ain Jock Rab.'

O, had I ne'er seen thee, my Eppie Macnab!
O, had I ne'er seen thee, my Eppie Macnab!
    As light as the air, and as fause as thou's fair,   false
Thou's broken the heart o thy ain Jock Rab!

'INDEED WILL I,' QUO FINDLAY

TUNE: *Lass, an I come near thee*

Although the immediate model for this nocturnal dialogue was a broadside 'Wha's that at my chamber door?' the theme behind it can be traced back through medieval ballads to the Song of Solomon itself.

'Wha is that at my bower-door?'
'O, wha is it but Findlay!'
go your way   'Then gae your gate, ye'se nae be here.'   you shall not
must, said   'Indeed maun I!' quo Findlay.

'What mak ye, sae like a thief?'
'O come and see!' quo Findlay.
'Before the morn ye'll work mischief?'
'Indeed will I,' quo Findlay.

If   'Gif I rise and let you in' —
'Let me in!' quo Findlay—
awake   'Ye'll keep me waukin wi your din?'
'Indeed will I!' quo Findlay.

'In my bower if you should stay'—
'Let me stay!' quo Findlay—
stay   'I fear ye'll bide till break o day?'
'Indeed will I!' quo Findlay.

'Here this night if ye remain'—
'I'll remain!' quo Findlay—
'I dread ye'll learn the gate again?'
'Indeed will I!' quo Findlay.

'What may pass within this bower'—
('Let it pass!' quo Findlay)
'Ye maun conceal till your last hour'—
'Indeed will I!' quo Findlay.

BONIE WEE THING

Dedicated to that petite beauty Deborah Duff Davies, to whom he sent this song with one of his more turgid epistles on 6th April 1793. In another letter to her, about two month later, he wrote: 'I am a good deal luckier than most poets. When I sing of Miss Davies or Miss Lesley Baillie, I have only to feign the passion — the charms are real.'

CHORUS

Bonie wee thing, cannie wee thing,
Lovely wee thing, wert thou mine,
I wad wear thee in my bosom
lose   *Lest my jewel it should tine.*

Bonie Wee Thing

Wishfully I look and languish
    In that bonie face o thine,
And my heart it stounds wi anguish,
    Lest my wee thing be na mine.

Wit and Grace and Love and Beauty
    In ae constellation shine!
To adore thee is my duty,
    Goddess o this soul o mine!

GEORDIE — AN OLD BALLAD

**Numerous versions of this song have survived. Burns
appears to have collected it during his Highland tour
and probably revised it before sending it to Johnson.
Geordie has been identified as George Gordon, 4th
Earl of Huntly, imprisoned in Edinburgh Castle (1554)
for failing to catch a Highland reiver, but Kinsley
thought the 6th Earl more likely. He rebelled against
James VI (1589), was imprisoned as a traitor, but
amnestied during the Kings's wedding celebrations.
The identity of Sir Charles Hay has never been
traced.**

There was a battle in the north,
    And nobles there was many,
And they hae kill'd Sir Charlie Hay,
    And they laid the wyte on Geordie   blame

O he has written a lang letter,
    He sent it to his lady;
Ye maun cum up to Enbrugh town   must
    To see what words o Geordie.

When first she look'd the letter on,
    She was baith red and rosy;
But she had na read a word but twa,
    Till she wallow't like a lily,   paled

Gar get to me my gude grey steed,   Make ready
    My menzie a' gae wi me;   retinue
For I shall neither eat nor drink,
    Till Enbrugh town shall see me.

And she has mountit her gude grey steed,
    Her menzie a' gaed wi her;
And she did neither eat nor drink
    Till Enbrugh town did see her.

And first appear'd the fatal block,
    And syne the aix to head him;   axe, behead
And Geordie cumin down the stair,
    And bands o airn upon him.   iron

447

Geordie — An Old Ballad

But tho he was chain'd in fetters strang,
 O airn and steel sae heavy,
There was na ane in a' the court,
fine Sae braw a man as Geordie.

O she's down on her bended knee,
wot I wat she's pale and weary,
O pardon, pardon, noble king,
 And gie me back my Dearie!

I hae born seven sons to my Geordie dear,
 The seventh ne'er saw his daddie:
O pardon, pardon, noble king,
 Pity a waefu lady!

headsman Gar bid the headin-man mak haste!
 Our king reply'd fu lordly:
O noble king, tak a' that's mine,
 But gie me back my Geordie.

The Gordons cam and the Gordons ran,
strong And they were stark and steady;
And ay the word amang them a'
 Was, Gordons keep you ready.

An aged lord at the king's right hand
 Says, noble king, but hear me:
Gar her tell down five thousand pound
 And gie her back her Dearie.

Some gae her marks, some gae her crowns,
 Some gae her dollars many;
And sh's tell'd down five thousand pound,
 And she's gotten again her Dearie.

glanced She blinkit blythe in her Geordie's face,
 Says, dear I've bought thee, Geordie:
should have, trunks But there sud been bluidy bouks on the green,
Ere, lost Or I had tint my laddie.

He claspit her by the middle sma',
 And he kist her lips sae rosy:
The fairest flower o woman-kind
 Is my sweet, bonie Lady!

DUMFRIES
Market Place

ANNAN

THE PLOUGHMAN'S LIFE

TUNE: *Rinn m'eudail mo mhealladh*

Several versions of this old ballad exist. Burns rejected the third and fourth stanzas in the Herd MSS, in which the girl's mood changes dramatically, and he changed the remaining lines extensively to suit the rhythm of the old Gaelic air.

As I was a-wand'ring ae morning in spring,   one
I heard a young ploughman sae sweetly to sing;
And as he was singin, thir words he did say,—
There's nae life like the ploughman's in the month o sweet May.

The lav'rock in the morning she'll rise frae her nest,   lark
And mount i' the air wi the dew on her breast,
And wi the merry ploughman she'll whistle and sing,
And at night she'll return to her nest back again.

THE WEARY PUND O TOW

Burns took a rather artless ballad, published in The Charmer (1782) and transformed it into a neat and witty domestic comedy. Tow is the flax fibre for spinning by breaking, beating and heckling (dressing).

CHORUS

The weary pund, the weary pund,   dressed flax fibre
   The weary pund o tow!
I think my wife will end her life
   Before she spin her tow.

I bought my wife a stane o lint
   As guid as e'er did grow,
And a' that she has made o that
   Is ae puir pund o tow.   one

There sat a bottle in a bole   hole
   Beyont the ingle low;
And ay she took the tither souk   suck
   To drouk the stourie tow.   drench, dusty

Quoth I: — 'For shame, ye dirty dame,
   Gae spin your tap o tow!'
She took the rock, and wi a knock   distaff
   She brake it o'er my pow.   pate

At last her feet — I sang to see't!—
   Gaed foremost o'er the knowe,   Went, knoll
And or I wad anither jad,   ere, wed, jade
   I'll wallop in a tow.

449

Q

I HAE A WIFE O MY AIN

Traditionally this ballad has been assigned to 1788, soon
after Burns finally settled down to married life, but
Kinsley doubts this, and places it in 1792 along with
other adaptations and revisions of old ballads.

I hae a wife o my ain,
    I'll partake wi naebody;
I'll take cuckold frae nane,
    I'll gie cuckold to naebody.

I hae a penny to spend,
    There—thanks to naebody.
I hae naething to lend,
    I'll borrow frae naebody.

I am naebody's lord,
    I'll be slave to naebody.
I'll hae a guid braid sword,
blows   I'll tak dunts frae naebody.

I'll be merry and free,
    I'll be sad for naebody.
Naebody cares for me,
    I care for naebody.

WHEN SHE CAM BEN, SHE BOBBED

A revision of an old ballad in Herd MSS (II. 206-7).
Traditionally the laird of this song was a close friend of
King Charles II. Cockpen, Midlothian belonged in
Burns's day to the factor of Lord Cockburn and later
to the Earl of Dalhousie.

O, when she cam ben, she bobbed fu law,
O, when she cam ben, she bobbed fu law,
And when she cam ben, she kiss'd Cockpen,
then   And syne she deny'd she did it at a'!

And was na Cockpen right saucy witha'?
And was na Cockpen right saucy witha'?
daughter In leaving the dochter o a lord
And kissin a collier lassie an a'!

O, never look down, my lassie, at a'!
O, never look down, my lassie, at a'!
Thy lips are as sweet, and thy figure complete,
As the finest dame in castle or ha'.

Tho thou hast nae silk, and holland sae sma',
Tho thou hast nae silk, and holland sae sma',
shirt   Thy coat and thy sark are thy ain handywark,
handsome And lady Jean was never sae braw.

O, FOR ANE-AND-TWENTY, TAM

In a letter to George Thomson on 19th October 1794
Burns claimed this song as his own.

CHORUS

An O, for ane-and-twenty, Tam!
And hey, sweet ane-and-twenty, Tam!
I'll learn my kin a rattlin sang,
An I saw ane-and-twenty, Tam.   If

They snool me sair, and haud me down,   snub, sorely, hold
  And gar me look like bluntie, Tam;   make, fool
But three short years will soon wheel roun—
  And then comes ane-and-twenty, Tam!

A gleib o lan, a claut o gear   parcel, handful of money
  Was left me by my auntie, Tam.
At kith or kin I needna spier,   enquire
  An I saw ane-and-twenty, Tam.

They'll hae me wed a wealthy coof,   fool
  Tho I mysel hae plenty, Tam;
But hear'st thou, laddie—there's my loof: palm
  I'm thine at ane-and-twenty, Tam.

O, KENMURE'S ON AND AWA, WILLIE

Believed to be based on a Galloway ballad, although no
authentic version earlier than 1810 is known in
published form, Burns re-wrote it for SMM in 1792.
William Gordon, 6th Viscount Kenmure raised the
Jacobite standard at Lochmaben in 1715 and
commanded the rebels in southern Scotland. He was
beheaded at the Tower and his title attainted. Burns
stayed with his grandson the 7th Viscount at Kenmure
Castle on 27th July 1793 when he and John Syme made
their tour through Galloway.

O, Kenmure's on and awa, Willie,
  O, Kenmure's on and awa!
An Kenmure's lord's the bravest lord
  That ever Galloway saw!
Success to Kenmure's band, Willie,
  Success to Kenmure's band!
There's no a heart that fears a Whig
  That rides by Kenmure's hand.

Here's Kenmure's health in wine, Willie,
  Here's Kenmure's health in wine!
There's ne'er a coward o Kenmure's blude,
  Nor yet o Gordon's line.
O, Kenmure's lads are men, Willie,
  O, Kenmure's lads are men!
Their hearts and swords are metal true,
  And that their faes shall ken.   foes

O, Kenmure's On And Awa, Willie

The'll live or die wi fame, Willie,
They'll live or die wi fame!
But soon wi sounding Victorie
May Kenmure's lord come hame!
Here's him that's far awa, Willie,
Here's him that's far awa!
And here's the flower that I lo'e best,

the Jacobite rose   The rose that's like the snaw!

BESSY AND HER SPINNIN-WHEEL

TUNE: *Sweet's the lass that loves me*

**Henderson links this, one of Burns's most charming
pastorals, to 'The loving Lass and Spinning-wheel' in
The Tea-Table Miscellany but Kinsley dismisses this
relationship.**

Blessings
distaff
clothes, snugly
covers, well
sit
low

O, leeze me on my spinnin-wheel!
And leeze me on my rock and reel,
Frae tap to tae that cleeds me bien,
And haps me fiel and warm at e'en!
I'll set me down, and sing and spin,
While laigh descends the summer sun,
Blest wi content, and milk and meal—
O, leeze me on my spinnin-wheel

either, brooks
thatched cottage
birch

cool
glances, shelter

On ilka hand the burnies trot,
And meet below my theekit cot.
The scented birk and hawthorn white
Across the pool their arms unite,
Alike to screen the birdie's nest
And little fishes' caller rest.
The sun blinks kindly in the biel,
Where blythe I tùrṇ my spinnin-wheel.

oaks, pigeons
woeful
linnets, slopes

corncrake, clover
partridge, meadow
darting, shieling

On lofty aiks the cushats wail,
And Echo cons the doolfu tale.
The lintwhites in the hazel braes,
Delighted, rival ither's lays.
The craik amang the claver hay,
The paitrick whirrin o'er the ley,
The swallow jinkin round my shiel,
Amuse me at my spinnin-wheel.

Aboon

Wi sma' to sell and less to buy,
Aboon distress, below envy,
O, wha wad leave this humble state
For a' the pride of a' the great?
Amid their flaring, idle toys,
Amid their cumbrous, dinsome joys,
Can they the peace and pleasure feel
Of Bessy at her spinnin-wheel?

452

MY COLLIER LADDIE

Though Stenhouse claimed that this song was largely Burns's it is likely to have been traditional with revisions and additions. Coalmining was already a major Ayrshire industry in Burns's day, particularly in the vicinity of Kilmarnock. It was thought that the girl herself was a mineworker but Kinsley has pointed out that 5d (l. 17) was a farm labourer's daily wage, whereas miners (including girls) got 4d per 30cwt of coal raised from the coal-face - a good daily average.

'O, whare live ye, my bonie lass,
    And tell me how they ca' ye?'
'My name,' she says, 'is Mistress Jean,
    And I follow the collier laddie.'

'O, see you not yon hills and dales
    The sun shines on sae brawlie?   *finely*
They a' are mine, and they shall be thine,
    Gin ye'll leave your collier laddie!

'An ye shall gang in gay attire,
    Weel buskit up sae gaudy,   *dressed*
And ane to wait on every hand,
    Gin ye'll leave your collier laddie!

'Tho ye had a' the sun shines on,
    And the earth conceals sae lowly,
I wad turn my back on you and it a',
    And embrace my collier laddie.

'I can win my five pennies in a day,
    An spend it at night fu brawlie,
And make my bed in the collier's neuk,   *corner*
    And lie down wi my collier laddie.

'Loove for loove is the bargain for me,
    Tho the wee cot-house should haud me,   *keep*
And the warld before me to win my bread—
    And fair fa' my collier laddie!'

THE SHEPHERD'S WIFE

Burns's emendation of an old ballad in the Herd MSS, with minor changes and refinements.

The Shepherd's wife cries o'er the knowe,   *knoll*
    Will ye come hame, will ye come hame;
The Shepherd's wife cries o'er the knowe,
    Will ye come hame again een, jo?   *darling*

What will I get to my supper,
    Gin I come hame, gin I come hame?   *If*
What will I get to my supper,
    Gin I come hame again een, jo?

453

The Shepherd's Wife

porridge

Ye'se get a panfu o plumpin parridge,
  And butter in them, and butter in them,
Ye'se get a panfu o plumpin parridge,
  Gin ye'll come hame again een, jo.

can
will not, cannot

Ha, ha how! that's naething that dow,
  I winna come hame, I canna come hame;
Ha, ha how! that's naething that dow,
  I winna come hame gin een, jo.

The Shepherd's wife &c.
What will I get &c.

steaming

A reekit fat hen, weel fryth'd i' the pan,
  Gin ye'll come hame, gin ye'll come hame,
A reekin fat hen weel fryth'd i' the pan,
  Gin ye'll come hame again een jo.

Ha, ha, how! &c.
The Shepherd's wife &c.
What will I get &c.

A weel made bed and a pair o clean sheets,
  Gin ye'll come hame, gin ye'll come hame,
A weel made bed and a pair o clean sheets,
  Gin ye'll come hame again een jo.—

Ha, ha, how! &c.
The Shepherd's wife &c.
What will I get &c.

A luving wife in lily-white linens,
  Gin ye'll come hame, gin ye'll come hame,
A luving wife in lily-white linens,
  Gin ye'll come hame again een, jo.

Ha, ha, how! that's something that dow,
  I will come hame, I will come hame;
Ha, ha, how! that's something that dow,
  I will come hame again een, jo.

JOHNIE BLUNT

Johnson's note in the index to SMM suggests that the hero of this ballad 'lived somewhere in Crawford Muirs,' but the name is proverbial for any dull-witted person. Burns reworked a traditional version of this familiar song.

There liv'd a man in yonder glen,
  And John Blunt was his name, O;

malt

He maks gude maut, and he brews gude ale,
  And he bears a wondrous fame, O.

454

Johnie Blunt

The wind blew in the hallan ae night,
  Fu snell out o'er the moor, O;   bitter
'Rise up, rise up, auld Luckie,' he says,
  'Rise up and bar the door, O.'

They made a paction tween them twa,
  They made it firm and sure, O,
Wha'er sud speak the foremost word.   should
  Should rise and bar the door, O.

Three travellers that had tint their gate,   lost way
  As thro the hills they foor, O,   travelled
They airted by the line o light   were guided
  Fu straught to Johnie Blunt's door, O. straight

They haurl'd auld Luckie out o her bed, hauled
  And laid her on the floor, O;
But never a word auld Luckie wad say,
  For barrin o the door, O.

'Ye've eaten my bread, ye hae druken my ale, drunk
  'And ye'll mak my auld wife a whore, O—'
Aha, Johnie Blunt! he hae spoke the first word.
  Get up and bar the door, O.

THE COUNTRY LASS

Acknowledged by Burns to Thomson in a letter of 19th
October 1794. This song, says Cunningham 'has the
air and tone of the ancient lyrics of Caledonia. It
hovers between the dramatic and the sentimental, and
partakes of the character of both.'

In simmer, when the hay was mawn   mown
  And corn wav'd green in ilka field,   every
While claver blooms white o'er the ley clover meadow
  And roses blaw in ilka bield   shelter
Blythe Bessie in the milking shiel   shieling
  Says;— 'I'll be wed, come o't what will!'
Out spake a dame in wrinkled eild:— eld
  'O guid advisement comes nae ill.

'It's ye hae wooers monie ane,   many a one
  And lassie, ye're but young, ye ken! know
Then wait a wee, and cannie wale   bit, prudently choose
  A routhie butt, a routhie ben.   well-stocked kitchen,
There's Johnie o the Buskie-Glen,   parlour
  Fu is his barn, fu is his byre.   cow-shed
Tak this frae me, my bonie hen:
  It's plenty beets the luver's fire!'   fans

The Country Lass

'For Johnie o the Buskie-Glen
I dinna care a single flie:

crops, kine
He lo'es sae weel his craps and kye,
He has nae love to spare for me.
But blythe's the blink o Robie's e'e,
And weel I wat he lo'es me dear:

one glimpse
Ae blink o him I wad na gie
For Buskie-Glen and a' his gear.'

fight
'O thoughtless lassie, life's a faught!
quietest way, sore
The canniest gate, the strife is sair.
full-handed, fighting
But ay fu-han't is fechtin best:
A hungry care's an unco care.
But some will spend and some will spare,

must
An wilfu folk maun hae their will.
Syne as ye brew, my maiden fair,

ale
Keep mind that ye maun drink the yill!'

'O, gear will buy me rigs o land,
And gear will buy me sheep and kye!

lawful
But the tender heart o leesome loove
gold, silver
The gowd and siller canna buy!
We may be poor, Robie and I;
Light is the burden luve lays on;
Content and loove brings peace and joy:
What mair hae Queens upon a throne?'

FAIR ELIZA

Writing to Johnson in July 1788 Burns asked: 'Have
you never a fair goddess that leads you a wild-goose-
chase of amorous devotion? Let me know a few of her
qualities . . . and chuse your air, and I shall task my
Muse to celebrate her.' In the original version (Hastie
MSS) the girl's name was Rabina (!), mercifully
changed to Eliza before publication in SMM.

Turn again, thou fair Eliza!
One glance
Ae kind blink before we part!
Rew on thy despairing lover—
Canst thou break his faithfu heart?
Turn again, thou fair Eliza!
If to love thy heart denies,
For pity hide the cruel sentence
Under friendships's kind disguise!

456

Fair Eliza

Thee, dear maid, hae I offended?
The offence is loving thee.
Canst thou wreck his peace for ever,
Wha for thine wad gladly die?
While the life beats in my bosom,
Thou shalt mix in ilka throe,   every
Turn again, thou lovely maiden,
Ae sweet smile on me bestow!

Not the bee upon the blossom
In the pride o sinny noon,
Not the little sporting fairy,
All beneath the simmer moon,
Not the Poet, in the moment
Fancy lightens in his e'e,
Kens the pleasure, feels the rapture,   Knows
That thy presence gies to me.

YE JACOBITES BY NAME

An old Jacobite song, Burns's hand in it seems uncertain.

Ye Jacobites by name, give an ear, give an ear!
Ye Jacobites by name, give an ear,
Ye Jacobites by name,
Your fautes I will proclaim,   faults
Your doctrines I maun blame — you shall hear!   maun

What is Right, and what is Wrang, by the law, by the law?
What is Right, and what is Wrang, by the law?
What is Right, and what is Wrang?
A short sword and a lang,
A weak arm and a strang, for to draw!

What makes heroic strife, famed afar, famed afar?
What makes heroic strife famed afar?
What makes heroic strife?
To whet th' assassin's knife,
Or hunt a Parent's life, wi bluidy war!

Then let your schemes alone, in the State, in the State!
Then let your schemes alone, in the State!
Then let your schemes alone,
Adore the rising sun,
And leave a man undone, to his fate!

THE POSIE

In a letter of 19th October 1794 to Thomson, Burns wrote: 'My composition, the air was taken down from Mrs. Burns's voice. It is well known in the West Country, but the old words are trash.'

O, luve will venture in where it daur na weel be seen!
O, luve will venture in, where wisdom ance hath been!
But I will doun yon river rove amang the wood sae green,
pluck, own   And a' to pu a posie to my ain dear May!

The primrose I will pu, the firstling o the year,
And I will pu the pink, the emblem o my dear,
For she's the pink o womankind, and blooms without a peer—
And a' to be a posie to my ain dear May!

I'll pu the budding rose, when Phoebus peeps in view,
balmy,   For it's like a baumy kiss o her sweet, bonie mou.
mouth   The hyacinth's for constancy wi its unchanging blue—
And a' to be a posie to my ain dear May!

The lily it is pure, and the lily it is fair,
And in her lovely bosom I'll place the lily there.
The daisy's for simplicity and unaffected air—
And a' to be a posie to my ain dear May!

The hawthorn I will pu, wi its locks o siller gray,
Where, like an aged man, it stands at break o day;
will not   But the songster's nest within the bush I winna tak away—
And a' to be a posie to my ain dear May!

The woodbine I will pu, when the e'ening star is near,
And the diamond draps o dew shall be her een sae clear!
The violet's for modesty, which weel she fa's to wear—
And a' to be a posie to my ain dear May!

I'll tie the posie round wi the silken band o luve,
And I'll place it in her breast, and I'll swear by a' above,
That to my latest draught o life the band shall ne'er remove
And this will be a posie to my ain dear May!

WILLIE WASTLE

This song has elements of the traditional children's game 'I'm the King of the Castle' and the seventeenth century verses 'I William of the Wastle', said to have been inspired by the Parliamentary siege of Hume Castle, Roxburghshire in 1651. 'Wastle' is probably the cake-shaped roundel of heraldry. Linkumdoddie was a cottage on the modern A702 road 5 miles north of Broughton, where the Logan Water joins the Tweed. It was inhabited in Burns's day by a weaver named Gideon Thomson.

Willie Wastle dwalt on Tweed,
  The spot they ca'd it Linkumdoddie.
Willie was a wabster guid   weaver
  Could stown a clue wi onie body.   have stolen
He had a wife was dour and din,   stubborn, saturnine
  O, Tinkler Maidgie was her mither!
Sic a wife as Willie had,
  I wad na gie a button for her.

She has an e'e (she has but ane),   eye
  The cat has twa the very colour,
Five rusty teeth, forbye a stump,   as well as
  A clapper-tongue wad deave a miller;   deafen
A whiskin beard about her mou,   mouth
  Her nose and chin they threaten ither: each other
Sic a wife as Willie had,
  I wad na gie a button for her.

She's bow-hough'd, she's hem-shin'd,   bandy-legged, shins like haims
  Ae limpin leg a hand-breed shorter;   hand's-breadth
She's twisted right, she's twisted left,
  To balance fair in ilka quarter;   each
She has a hump upon her breast,
  The twin o that upon her shouther: shoulder
Sic a wife as Willie had,
  I wad na gie a button for her.

Auld baudrans by the ingle sits,   Old cat
  An wi her loof her face a-washin;   paw
But Willie's wife is nae sae trig,   trim
  She dights her grunzie wi a hushion;   wipes, snout, footless stocking
Her walie nieves like midden-creels,   ample fists
  Her face wad fyle the Logan Water: foul
Sic a wife as Willie had,
  I wad na gie a button for her.

LADY MARY ANN

Several editors have based this song on the true story of
John Urquhart of Craigston (d. 1634) who, as a boy, was
married off on Elizabeth Innes, the plain daughter of his
guardian who had designs on his estates. Kinsley, however,
casts doubt on this, in view of the names mentioned in
the text, though they have not been identified with any
real persons.

O, Lady Mary Ann looks o'er the Castle wa',
She saw three bonie boys playing at the ba',
The youngest he was the flower amang them a'
    My bonie laddie's young, but he's growin yet!

'O father, O father, an ye think it fit,
We'll send him a year to the college yet;
We'll sew a green ribbon round about his hat,
    And that will let them ken he's to marry yet!'

know

Lady Mary Ann was a flower in the dew,
Sweet was its smell and bonie was its hue,
And the longer it blossom'd the sweeter it grew,
    For the lily in the bud will be bonier yet.

Young Charlie Cochran was the sprout of an aik,
Bonie and bloomin and straucht was its make;

straight

The sun took delight to shine for its sake,
    And it will be the brag o the forest yet.

The simmer is gane when the leaves they were green,
And the days are awa that we hae seen;
But far better days I trust will come again,
    For my bonie laddie's young, but he's growin yet.

SUCH A PARCEL OF ROGUES
IN A NATION

Feelings ran high (and continue to do so) over the Act
of Union, 1707 which suppressed Scotland's
Parliament and her existence as an independent
political entity. The 'parcel of rogues' were the 31
Scottish commissioners who sold out to England, and
were well rewarded with land and money for their
treachery. The Sark and the Tweed are the rivers
marking the western and eastern borders with
England.

Fareweel to a' our Scottish fame,
    Fareweel our ancient glory!
Fareweel ev'n to the Scottish name,
    Sae famed in martial story!

runs

Now Sark rins over Solway sands,
    An Tweed rins to the ocean,
To mark where England's province stands—
    Such a parcel of rogues in a nation!

460

Such A Parcel Of Rogues In A Nation

What force or guile could not subdue
Thro many warlike ages
Is wrought now by a coward few
For hireling traitor's wages.
The English steel we could disdain,
Secure in valour's station;
But English gold has been our bane—
Such a parcel of rogues in a nation!

O, would , or I had seen the day
That Treason thus could sell us,
My auld grey head had lien in clay,
Wi Bruce and loyal Wallace!
But pith and power, till my last hour,
I'll mak this declaration:—
'We're bought and sold for English gold'—
Such a parcel of rogues in a nation!

KELLYBURN BRAES

An allegedly traditional ballad similar to this appears in Cromek's Remains of Nithsdale and Galloway Song (1810), in which case 'Kellyburn' may refer to Kello Water which rises in the Cumnock Hills and runs into the Nith near Sanquhar. The theme of the nagging wife whom even the Devil could not control is ancient and widespread in folklore.

There lived a carl in Kellyburn Braes   *old man*
(Hey, and the rue grows bonie wi thyme!)
And he had a wife was the plague o his days
(And the thyme it is wither'd, and rue is in prime!).

Ae day as the carl gaed up the lang glen   *one*
(Hey, and the rue grows bonie wi thyme!),
He met wi the Devil, says:— 'How do you fen?'
(And the thyme it is wither'd, and rue is in prime!).

'I've got a bad wife, sir, that's a' my complaint
(Hey, and the rue grows bonie wi thyme),
For, saving your presence, to her ye're a saint'
(And the thyme it is wither'd, and rue is in prime!).

'It's neither your stot nor your staig I shall crave   *bullock, colt*
(Hey, and the rue grows bonie wi thyme!),
'But gie me your wife, man, for her I must have'
(And the thyme it is wither'd, and rue is in prime!).

Kellyburn Braes

'O welcome most kindly!' the blythe carl said
    Hey, and the rue grows bonie wi thyme),
worse   'But if ye can match her ye're waur than ye're ca'd,'
    (And the thyme it is wither'd, and rue is in prime!).

The Devil has got the auld wife on his back
    (Hey, and the rue grows bonie wi thyme!),
And like a poor pedlar he's carried his pack
    (And the thyme it is wither'd, and rue is in prime!).

porch   He's carried her hame to his ain hallan-door
    (Hey, and the rue grows bonie wi thyme!),
go   Syne bade her gae in for a bitch and a whore
    (And the thyme it is wither'd, and rue is in prime!).

Then straight he makes fifty, the pick o his band
    (Hey, and the rue grows bonie wi thyme!),
Turn out on her guard in the clap o a hand
    (And the thyme it is wither'd, and rue is in prime!).

beldam   The carlin gaed thro them like onie wud bear,
    (Hey, and the rue grows bonie wi thyme!),
Whae'er she gat hands on cam ne'er her nae mair
    (And the thyme it is wither'd, and rue is in prime!).

smoking   A reekit wee devil looks over the wa'
    (Hey, and the rue grows bonie wi thyme!):—
'O help, maister, help, or she'll ruin us a'!'
    (And the thyme it is wither'd, and rue is in prime!).

The Devil he swore by the edge o his knife
    (Hey, and the rue grows bonie wi thyme!),
He pitied the man that was tied to a wife
    (And the thyme it is wither'd, and rue is in prime!).

The Devil he swore by the kirk and the bell
    (Hey, and the rue grows bonie wi thyme!),
He was not in wedlock, thank Heav'n, but in Hell,
    (And the thyme it is wither'd and rue is in prime!).

Then Satan has travell'd again wi his pack
    (Hey, and the rue grows bonie wi thyme!),
And to her auld husband he's carried her back
    (And the thyme it is wither'd, and rue is in prime!).

most   'I hae been a Devil the feck o my life
    (Hey, and the rue grows bonie wi thyme!),
But ne'er was in Hell till I met wi a wife'
    (And the thyme it is wither'd, and rue is in prime!).

LOVE FOR LOVE

A stanza composed by Burns to accompany an old
ballad in The Tea-Table Miscellany (i.187-8).

Let loove sparkle in her e'e,
Let her lo'e nae man but me:
That's the tocher guid I prize,   dowry
There the luver's treasure lies.

THE SLAVE'S LAMENT

There is absolutely no truth in the canard that this
song was based on an original African melody. Kinsley
has traced its origins to a seventeenth century
broadside in the Roxburghe Ballads.

It was in sweet Senegal that my foes did me enthral
    For the lands of Virginia, —ginia, O!
Torn from that lovely shore, and must never see it more,
    And alas! I am weary, weary, O!

All on that charming coast is no bitter snow and frost
    Like the lands of Virginia, —ginia, O!
There streams for ever flow, and flowers for ever blow,
    And alas! I am weary, weary, O!

The burden I must bear, while the cruel scourge I fear,
    In the lands of Virginia, —ginia, O!
And I think on friends most dear with the bitter, bitter tear,
    And alas! I am weary, weary, O!

MY BONIE BELL

Signed in SMM as Burns's work.

The smiling Spring comes in rejoicing,
    And surly Winter grimly flies.
Now crystal clear are the falling waters,
    And bonie blue are the sunny skies.
Fresh o'er the mountains breaks forth the morning,
    The ev'ning gilds the ocean's swell:
All creatures joy in the sun's returning,
    And I rejoice in my bonie Bell.

The flowery Spring leads sunny Summer,
    The yellow Autumn presses near;
Then in his turn comes gloomy Winter,
    Till smiling Spring again appear.
Thus seasons dancing, life advancing,
    Old Time and Nature their changes tell;
But never ranging, still unchanging,
    I adore my bonie Bell.

THE GALLANT WEAVER

Another reworking of a traditional ballad. The river Cart runs through Paisley, centre of Scotland's textile industry in the eighteenth century.

runs   Where Cart rins rowin to the sea
By monie a flower and spreading tree,
There lives a lad, the lad for me—
    He is a gallant weaver!
O, I had wooers aught or nine,
They gied me rings and ribbons fine,
And I was fear'd my heart wad tine,
    And I gied it to the weaver.

marriage settlement   My daddie sign'd my tocher-band
To gie the lad that has the land,
But to my heart I'll add my hand,
    And give it to the weaver.
While birds rejoice in leafy bowers,
While bees delight in opening flowers,
While corn grows green in summer showers,
    I love my gallant weaver.

HEY, CA' THRO

Possibly collected by Burns while journeying in Fife at the close of the Highland tour in 1787. Dysart, Buckhaven, Largo and Leven were, in Burns's day, fishing villages on the south coast of Fife, on the Firth of Forth. The chorus was allegedly sung as the fishing-boats were hauled up on the beach.

CHORUS

Hey, ca' thro, ca' thro,
much   *For we hae mickle ado!*
Hey, ca' thro, ca' thro,
                  For we hae mickle ado!

old men   Up wi the carls o Dysart
    And the lads o Buckhaven,
wenches   And the kimmers o Largo,
    And the lasses o Leven!

We hae tales to tell,
    An we hae sangs to sing;
We hae pennies to spend,
    An we hae pints to bring.

We'll live a' our days,
    And them that comes behin',
Let them do the like,
wealth   And spend the gear they win!

O, CAN YE LABOUR LEA

A bawdy version collected in Nithsdale appears in the
Merry Muses. Burns cleaned up the original and
grafted on 'an auld sang o my Mither's' to produce this
ballad.

CHORUS

O, can ye labour lea, young man,
  O, can ye labour lea?
Gae back the gate ye came again   Go, way
  Ye'se never scorn me!

I fee'd a man at Michaelmas
  Wi airle-pennies three;   coins exchanged on
But a' the faut I had to him   making a bargain
  He couldna labour lea.

O, clappin's guid in Febarwar,   caressing
  An kissin's sweet in May;
But what signifies a young man's love,
  An't dinna last for ay?   ever

O, kissin is the key o love
  And clappin is the lock;
An makin of's the best thing,
  That e'er a young thing got!

THE DEUK'S DANG O'ER MY DADDIE

The theme of the wife's nagging arising out of frus-
tration at her husband's impotence is an old one in
folk tales. Burns probably took some lines from an
old ballad, but this song is substantially his own.
'Paidlin' here has a double meaning, both
pottering about and sexual foreplay.

The bairns gat out wi an unco shout:—   mighty
  'The deuk's dang o'er my daddie, O!'   duck, beaten
'The fien-ma-care', quo the feirrie auld wife,   devil-may-care, lusty
  'He was but a paidlin body, O!   wading
He paidles out, and he paidles in,
  An he paidles late and early, O!
This seven lang years I hae lien by his side,
  An he is but a fusionless carlie, O!'   useless old fellow

'O, haud your tongue, my feirrie auld wife,   hold
  O, haud your tongue, now Nansie, O!
I've seen the day, and sae hae ye,
  Ye wad na been sae donsie, O.   testy
I've seen the day ye butter'd my brose,   enjoyed coitus
  And cuddl'd me late and early, O;
But downa-do's come o'er me now.   'can't-do' has
  And och, I find it sairly, O!'

465

AS I WENT OUT AE MAY MORNING

A pastourelle dialogue collected by Burns for Johnson
in 1792, with minor improvements.

one | As I went out ae May morning,
     | A May morning it chanc'd to be;
beautiful | There I was aware of a weelfar'd Maid
dancing | Cam linkin o'er the lea to me.

O but she was a weelfar'd maid,
The boniest lass that's under the sun;
asked if | I spier'd gin she could fancy me,
But her answer was, I am too young.

To be your bride I am too young,
fool | To be your loun wad shame my kin,
So therefore pray young man begone,
For you never, never shall my favor win.

birches | But amang yon birks and hawthorns green,
bloom, hang | Where roses blaw and woodbines hing,
O there I learn'd my bonie lass
That she was not a single hour too young.

The lassie blush'd, the lassie sigh'd,
And the tear stood twinklin in her e'e;
O kind Sir, since ye hae done me this wrang,
It's pray when will ye marry me.

It's of that day tak ye nae heed,
For that's ae day ye ne'er shall see;
For ought that pass'd between us twa,
Ye had your share as weel as me.

She wrang her hands, she tore her hair,
She cried out most bitterlie,
O what will I say to my mammie,
When I gae hame wi my big bellie!

malt, must | O as ye maut, so maun ye brew,
barrel | And as ye brew, so maun ye tun;
But come to my arms, my ae bonie lass,
For ye never shall rue what ye now hae done!

SHE'S FAIR AND FAUSE

TUNE: *The Lads of Leith*

Traditionally regarded as written about Anne Stewart,
the inconstant mistress of Alexander Cunningham (see
'Anna, thy Charms'), but Kinsley dismisses this,
suggesting that Burns may have Scotticized an English
lyric.

She's fair and fause that causes my smart; false
 I lo'ed her meikle and lang;
She's broken her vow, she's broken my heart;
 And I may e'en gae hang.

A coof cam in wi routh o gear, fool, plenty, money
And I hae tint my dearest dear; lost
But Woman is but warld's gear,
 Sae let the bonie lass gang! go

Whae'er ye be that Woman love,
 To this be never blind:
Nae ferlie 'tis, tho fickle she prove, marvel
 A woman has't by kind. nature

O Woman lovely, Woman fair,
An angel form's faun to thy share, fallen
'Twad been o'er meikle to gien thee mair! have given
 I mean an angel mind.

THE DEIL'S AWA WI TH' EXCISEMAN

TUNE: *The Hemp-dresser*

Lockhart claims that Burns composed these verses
extempore while waiting for his colleague John Lewars
to bring up reinforcements before seizing the brig
Rosamond at Sarkfoot on the Solway on 28th
February 1792. Burns more probably composed it
after the event, and sang it at an Excise dinner in
Dumfries the following month.

CHORUS

The Deil's awa, the Deil's awa,
 The Deil's awa wi th' Exciseman!
He's danc'd awa, he's danc'd awa,
 He's danc'd awa wi th' Exciseman!

The Deil cam fiddlin thro the town,
 And danc'd awa wi th' Exciseman,
And ilka wife cries:— 'Auld Mahoun, every
 I wish you luck o the prize man!'

'We'll mak our maut, and we'll brew our drink, malt
 We'll laugh, sing, and rejoice, man,
And monie braw thanks to the meikle black Deil, fine, great
 That danc'd awa wi th' Exciseman.

The Deil's Awa Wi Th' Exciseman

There's threesome reels, there's foursome reels,
There's hornpipes and strathspeys, man,
But the ae best dance e'er cam to the land
Was *The Deil's awa wi th' Exciseman.*

THE HUE AND CRY OF JOHN LEWARS

A poor man ruined and undone by Robbery and Murder. Being an aweful WARNING to the young men of this age, how they look well to themselves in this dangerous, terrible WORLD.

Despite the above annotation, this poem was probably written on the love affair of John Lewars, the poet's Excise colleague.

A thief, and a murderer! stop her who can!
Look well to your lives and your goods!
Good people, ye know not the hazard you run,
'Tis the far-famed and much-noted Woods.

While I looked at her eye, for the devil is in it,
In a trice she whipt off my poor heart:
Her brow, cheek and lip — in another sad minute,
My peace felt her murderous dart.

Her features, I'll tell you them over — but hold!
She deals with your wizards and books;
And to peep in her face, if but once you're so bold,
There's witchery kills in her looks.

But softly — I have it — her haunts are well known,
At midnight so slily I'll watch her;
And sleeping, undrest, in the dark, all alone
Good lord! the dear Thief how I'll catch her!

WILL YE GO TO THE INDIES,
MY MARY

TUNE: *Ewe-Bughts, Marion*

Burns took the old ballad 'Will ye go to the Ewe-Bughts, Marion?' and set his own words to it, sending these verses to Thomson on 27th October 1792 as a 'farewell of a dear girl.... when I was thinking of going to the West Indies.... all my earlier love-songs were the breathings of ardent Passion.... Their uncouth simplicity was, as they say of wines, their RACE.' Thomson marked the manuscript 'This is a very poor song which I do not mean to include in my collection'; but he published it thirty years later, in Select Melodies.

Will ye go to the Indies, my Mary,
And leave auld Scotia's shore?
Will ye go to the Indies, my Mary,
Across th' Atlantic's roar?

468

Will Ye Go To The Indies, My Mary

O, sweet grows the lime and the orange,
  And the apple on the pine;
But a' the charms o the Indies
  Can never equal thine.

I hae sworn by the Heavens to my Mary,
  I hae sworn by the Heavens to be true,
And sae may the Heavens forget me,
  When I forget my vow!

O, plight me your faith, my Mary,
  And plight me your lily-white hand!
O, plight me your faith, my Mary,
  Before I leave Scotia's strand!

We hae plighted our troth, my Mary,
  In mutual affection to join;
And curst be the cause that shall part us!
  The hour and the moment o time!

MY WIFE'S A WINSOME WEE THING

AIR: *My Wife's a Wanton Wee Thing*

A later version of the song 'My Wife's a Wanton Wee Thing', sung to the same tune, Burns sent these verses to Thomson on 8th November 1792. Thomson was dissatisfied with them and not only tinkered with the lines but added a stanza of his own. Burns acquiesced as part of a bargain that Thomson would not meddle with 'Bonie Lesley.' Later editors, however, have ignored Thomson and printed this song in Burns's original form.

CHORUS

She is a winsome wee thing,
She is a handsome wee thing,
She is a lo'esome wee thing,
    This sweet wee wife o mine!

I never saw a fairer,
I never lo'ed a dearer,
And neist my heart I'll wear her,   next
  For fear my jewel tine.

The warld's wrack we share o't;   wreckage
The warstle and the care o't,   struggle
Wi her I'll blythely bear it,
And think my lot divine.

469

HIGHLAND MARY

TUNE: *Katherine Ogie*

In his letter of 14th November 1792 to Thomson, Burns
wrote 'I agree with you that the song, K. Ogie, is very
poor stuff, and unworthy, altogether unworthy, of so
beautiful an air.' He tried to mend the original but
gave it up and substituted verses of his own. 'The
Subject of the song is one of the most interesting
passages of my youthful days' — see 'My Highland
Lassie O,' for details about Mary Campbell.

slopes   Ye banks and braes and streams around
                The castle o Montgomery,
            Green be your woods, and fair your flowers,
muddly   Your waters never drumlie!
            There Summer first unfald her robes,
                And there the longest tarry!
            For there I took the last fareweel
                O my sweet Highland Mary!

birch   How sweetly bloom'd the gay, green birk,
                How rich the hawthorn's blossom,
            As underneath their fragrant shade
                I clasp'd her to my bosom!
            The golden hours on angel wings
                Flew o'er me and my dearie:
            For dear to me as light and life
                Was my sweet Highland Mary.

       Wi monie a vow and lock'd embrace
                Our parting was fu tender;
            And, pledging aft to meet again,
                We tore oursels asunder.
       But O! fell Death's untimely frost,
                That nipt my flower sae early!
       Now green's the sod, and cauld's the clay,
                That wraps my Highland Mary!

       O, pale, pale now, those rosy lips
                I aft hae kiss'd sae fondly;
       And clos'd for ay, the sparkling glance
                That dwalt on me sae kindly;
       And mouldering now in silent dust
                That heart that lo'ed me dearly!
       But still within my bosom's core
                Shall live my Highland Mary.

AT THE GLOBE TAVERN, DUMFRIES

TUNE: *Killiecrankie*

The first stanza was inscribed on a window-pane at
the Globe Inn, probably as a comment on the French
Revolutionary War, 1792-3. Socrates drank hemlock
in execution of his sentence of death; Leonidas, hero of
Thermopylae, preferred to die for Sparta than rule over
it; and Cato, strengthened by Plato's treatise on
immortality, committed suicide rather than flee or
surrender to Caesar.

I murder hate by field or flood,
    Tho Glory's name may screen us;
In wars at hame I'll spend my blood—
    Life-giving wars of Venus.
The deities that I adore
    Are Social Peace and Plenty:
I'm better pleas'd to make one more,
    Than be the death of twenty.

I would not die like Socrates,
    For all the fuss of Plato;
Nor would I with Leonidas,
    Nor yet would I with Cato:
The zealots of the Church and State
    Shall ne'er my mortal foes be;
But let me have bold Zimri's fate,
    Within the arms of Cozbi.

THE RIGHTS OF WOMAN

AN OCCASIONAL ADDRESS
SPOKEN BY MISS FONTENELLE ON HER
BENEFIT NIGHT, NOVEMBER 26, 1792

Louisa Fontenelle (1773-99) was a London actress who
came to the Theatre Royal, Edinburgh in 1789 and
joined George Sutherland's touring company, which
played in Dumfries in the winters of 1792 and 1793.
She married John Brown Williamson, manager of the
Dumfries Theatre in 1796 and emigrated with him to
the United States. She died of yellow fever at Charles-
ton, S.C. on 30th October 1799. These lines, mirrored
on fellow exciseman Tom Paine's Rights of Man
(1791-2), place Burns in the forefront of the
feminist movement.

While Europe's eye is fix'd on mighty things,
The fate of empires and the fall of kings;
While quacks of State must each produce his plan,
And even children lisp the Rights of Man;
Amid this mighty fuss just let me mention,
The Rights of Woman merit some attention.

The Rights of Woman

First, in the sexes' intermix'd connexion,
One sacred Right of Woman is Protection:
The tender flower that lifts its head elate,
Helpless must fall before the blasts of fate,
Sunk on the earth, defac'd its lovely form,
Unless your shelter ward th' impending storm.

Our second Right — but needless here is caution—
To keep that right inviolate's the fashion:
Each man of sense has it so full before him,
He'd die before he'd wrong it —'tis Decorum!

There was, indeed, in far less polish'd days,
A time, when rough rude Man had naughty ways:
Would swagger, swear, get drunk, kick up a riot,
Nay, even thus invade a lady's quiet!
Now, thank our stars! these Gothic times are fled;
Now, well-bred men — and you are all well-bred—
Most justly think (and we are much the gainers)
Such conduct neither spirit, wit, nor manners.
For Right the third, our last, our best, our dearest:
That right to fluttering female hearts the nearest,
Which even the Rights of Kings, in low prostration,
Most humbly own— 'tis dear, dear Admiration!
In that blest sphere alone we live and move;
There taste that life of life— Immortal Love.
Smiles, glances, sighs, tears, fits, flirtations, airs—
'Gainst such an host what flinty savage dares?
When awful Beauty joins with all her charms,
Who is so rash as rise in rebel arms?
But truce with kings, and truce with constitutions,
With bloody armaments and revolutions;
Let Majesty your first attention summon,
Ah! ça ira! THE MAJESTY OF WOMAN!

French
Revolutionary
slogan

472

HERE'S A HEALTH TO THEM
THAT'S AWA

Based on an old Jacobite song, Burns published this song in the Edinburgh Gazeteer in 1792, up-dating its political flavour to the period at the outbreak of the French Revolutionary Wars. The personalities mentioned in this poem were outspoken radicals who, like Burns, sympathized with the Revolution — at least in its early stages.

Here's a health to them that's awa,
Here's a health to them that's awa!
And wha winna wish guid luck to our cause,
May never guid luck be their fa'!
It's guid to be merry and wise,
It's guid to be honest and true,
It's guid to support Caledonia's cause,
And bide by the buff and the blue.   the Whig colours

Here's a health to them that's awa,
Here's a health to them that's awa!
Here's a health to Charlie, the chief o the clan,   Charles James Fox
Altho that his band be sma'!
May Liberty meet wi success,
May Prudence protect her frae evil!
May tyrants and Tyranny tine i' the mist
And wander their way to the Devil!

Here's a health to them that's awa,
Here's a health to them that's awa;
Here's a health to Tammie, the Norlan' laddie,   Thomas Erskine
That lives at the lug o the Law!   (1750-1823) defence
Here's freedom to them that wad read,   lawyer of Tom Paine
Here's freedom to them that would write!
There's nane ever fear'd that the truth should be heard,
But they whom the truth would indite!

Here's a health to them that's awa,
An here's to them that's awa!
Here's to Maitland and Wycombe! let wha does na like 'em   James Maitland,
Be built in a hole in the wa'!   8th Earl of
Here's timmer that's red at the heart,   Lauderdale
Here's fruit that is sound at the core,   (1759-1839)
And may he that wad turn the buff and blue coat   John Petty,
Be turn'd to the back o the door!   Earl of Wycombe
     (1765-1809)

Here's a health to them that's awa,
Here's a health to them that's awa,
Here's Chieftain M'Leod, a chieftain worth gowd,   Col. Norman McLeod
Tho bred amang mountains o snaw!   of McLeod (1754-1801)
Here's friends on baith sides o the Firth,
And friends on baith sides o the Tweed,
And wha wad betray old Albion's right,
May they never eat of her bread!

THE LEA-RIG

TUNE: *My ain kind dearie, O.*

Burns re-fashioned the traditional ballad of this name, and sent the result to Thomson on 26th October 1792. Thomson complained of its brevity, and Burns sent this expanded version on 1st December.

	When o'er the hill the eastern star
folding, darling	Tells bughtin time is near, my jo,
oxen	And owsen frae the furrow'd field
dull	Return sae dowf and weary, O,
birches	Down by the burn, where scented birks
	Wi dew are hangin clear, my jo,
	I'll meet thee on the lea-rig,
own	My ain kind dearie,O!
darkest	At midnight hour in mirkest glen,
frightened	I'd rove, and ne'er be eerie, O,
went	If thro that glen I gaed to thee,

My ain kind dearie, O!
Altho, the night were ne'er sae wild,
  And I were ne'er sae weary, O,
I'll meet thee on the lea-rig,
  My ain kind dearie, O!

The hunter lo'es the morning sun,
  To rouse the mountain deer, my jo;
At noon the fisher takes the glen
  Adown the burn to steer, my jo:
Gie me the hour o gloamin grey—
  It maks my heart sae cheery, O,
To meet thee on the lea-rig,
  My ain kind dearie, O!

AULD ROB MORRIS

Modelled on a traditional dialogue song, between a mother and daughter, originally published in The Tea-Table Miscellany, Burns adapted the situation to illustrate the theme of love versus wealth.

dwells	There's Auld Rob Morris that wons in yon glen,
pick	He's the king o guid fellows and wale o auld men:
gold, oxen, cattle	He has gowd in his coffers, he has owsen and kine,
one, darling	And ae bonie lassie, his dautie and mine.

She's fresh as the morning, the fairest in May,
She's sweet as the ev'ning amang the new hay,
As blythe and as artlesss as the lambs on the lea.
And dear to my heart as the light to my e'e.

But O, she's an heiress, auld Robin's a laird,
And my daddie has nocht but a cot-house and yard! cottage
A wooer like me maunna hope to come speed: must not
The wounds I must hide that will soon be my dead.

The day comes to me, but delight brings me nane;
The night comes to me, but my rest it is gane;
I wander my lane like a night-troubled ghaist, alone, ghost
And I sigh as my heart it wad burst in my breast.

O, had she but been of a lower degree,
I then might hae hop'd she wad smil'd upon me!
O, how past descriving had then been my bliss,
As now my distraction no words can express!

DUNCAN GRAY

Like the earlier version 'Weary Fa' You' this song was based on an old ballad in the Herd collection, and was sent to Thomson on 4th December 1792.

Duncan Gray cam here to woo
        (Ha, ha, the wooing o't!)
On blythe Yule-night when we were fou drunk
        (Ha, ha, the wooing o't!).
Maggie coost her head fu high, tossed
Look'd asklent and unco skeigh, disdainfully, very skittish
Gart poor Duncan stand abeigh, Made, off
        Ha, ha, the wooing o't!

Duncan fleech'd, and Duncan pray'd: wheedled
        (Ha, ha, the wooing o't!)
Meg was deaf as Ailsa Craig,
        (Ha, ha, the wooing o't!),
Duncan sigh'd baith out and in, both
Grat his e'en baith blear't an blin', Wept, blurred
Spak o lowpin o'er a linn— leaping, waterfall
        Ha, ha, the wooing o't!

Time and Chance are but a tide
        (Ha, ha, the wooing o't!):
Slighted love is sair to bide
        (Ha, ha, the wooing o't!).
'Shall I like a fool,' quoth he,
'For a haughty hizzie die? hussy
She may gae to—France for me!'
        Ha, ha, the wooing o't!

Duncan Gray

How it comes, let doctors tell,
(Ha, ha, the wooing o't!):
healthy   Meg grew sick, as he grew hale,
(Ha, ha, the wooing o't!).
Something in her bosom wrings,
For relief a sigh she brings,
eyes   And O! her een they spak sic things!—
Ha, ha, the wooing o't!

Duncan was a lad o grace
(Ha, ha, the wooing o't!),
Maggie's was a piteous case,
(Ha, ha, the wooing o't!):
Duncan could na be her death,
smothered   Swelling pity smoor'd his wrath;
proud, jolly   Now they're crouse and canty baith—
Ha, ha, the wooing o't!

WHY SHOULD NA POOR FOLK MOWE

TUNE: *The Campbells are comin*

Sent to Robert Cleghorn on 12th December 1792 as 'a
song, just finished this moment.' A copy was sent to
Thomson in July 1794. This song celebrates the levelling
power of copulation, reducing the high and the mighty to
the same basic human level. The Duke of Brunswick
(1735-1806), brother-in-law of King George III, led the
Austrians and Prussians against France in 1792, but was
defeated by 'the cannonade of Valmy'. The second last
stanza refers to the second Partition of Poland which
took place in 1792. Catherine II was notorious for her
immorality and frequently satirised in Britain in terms
far coarser than Burns used here. She made her lover
Stanislaus Poniatowski puppet ruler of the rump of
Poland, before absorbing it in 1793.

CHORUS

copulate   *And why shouldna poor folk mowe, mowe, mowe,*
And why shouldna poor folk mowe:
money   *The great folk hae siller, and houses and lands,*
Poor bodies hae naething but mowe.

hot—   When Princes and Prelates and het-headed zealots
rage   All Europe hae set in a lowe,
The poor man lies down, nor envies a crown,
And comforts himsel with a mowe.

When Brunswick's great Prince cam a cruising to France
Republican billies to cowe,
Bauld Brunswick's great Prince wad hae shawn better sense,
At hame with his Princess to mowe.

476

Why Should Na Poor Folk Mowe

Out over the Rhine proud Prussia wad shine,
  To *spend* his best blood he did vow;
But Frederic had better ne'er forded the water,   Frederick
  But *spent* as he docht in a mowe.   should have

By sea and by shore! the Emperor swore,
  In Paris he'd kick up a row;
But Paris sae ready just leugh at the laddie   laughed
  And bade him gae tak him a mowe.

Auld Kate laid her claws on poor Stanislaus,   Empress Catherine
  And Poland has bent like a bow: of Russia (1729-96)
May the deil in her ass ram a huge prick o brass!
  And damn her in hell with a mowe!

But truce with commotions and new-fangled notions,
  A bumper I trust you'll allow:
Here's George our gude king and Charlotte his queen,   toast
  And lang may they tak a gude mowe!

WHILE PROSE-WORK AND RHYMES

TUNE: *The Campbells are comin*

Although this glorification of copulation was not published till the Barke-Goodsir Smith edition of The Merry Muses in 1959, it has all the hallmarks of Burns about it. Its opening stanza refers to the charge made against Burns in 1792-3 of sympathising with the French Revolution. It was clearly intended as a companion to the foregoing song.

While Prose-work and rhymes
  Are hunted for crimes,
And things are — the devil knows how;
  Aware o my rhymes,
  In these kittle times,   ticklish
The subject I chuse is a mowe.   copulation

Some cry, Constitution!
  Some cry, Revolution!
And Politicks kick up a rowe;
  But Prince and Republic,
  Agree on the Subject,
No treason is in a good mowe.

Th' Episcopal lawn,
  And Presbyter band,
Hae lang been to ither a cowe;
  But still the proud Prelate,
  And Presbyter zealot
Agree in an orthodox mowe.

477

Poor Justice, 'tis hinted—
Ill natur'dly squinted,
The Process — but mum — we'll allow
Poor Justice has ever
For Cunt had a favour,
While Justice could tak a gude mowe.

Now fill to the brim—
To her, and to him,
Wha willingly do what they dow;
And ne'er a poor wench
Want a friend at a pinch,
Whose   Whase failing is only a mowe.

THE TREE OF LIBERTY

Controversy continues to rage over this revolutionary song, and Kinsley urged caution in attribution. On the other hand, it was first published by Chambers from a holograph, apparently now lost, and accords with Burns's Jacobin sympathies in 1792-3.

HEARD ye o the tree o France,
don't know   I watna what 's the name o't;
Around it a' the patriots dance,
knows   Weel Europe kens the fame o't.
once   It stands where ance the Bastile stood,
A prison built by kings, man;
When Superstition's hellish brood
Kept France in leading strings, man.

Upo' this tree there grows sic fruit,
Its virtues a' can tell, man;
above   It raises man aboon the brute,
It maks him ken himsel, man.
If   Gif ance the peasant taste a bit,
He 's greater than a lord, man,
An wi the beggar shares a mite
O a' he can afford, man.

This fruit is worth a' Afric's wealth,
To comfort us 'twas sent, man:
give   To gie the sweetest blush o health,
An mak us a' content, man.
eyes   It clears the een, it cheers the heart,
Maks high and low gude friends, man;
And he wha acts the traitor's part
It to perdition sends, man.

The Tree Of Liberty

My blessings aye attend the chiel
  Wha pitied Gallia's slaves, man,   France
And staw a branch, spite o the deil,   stole
  Frae yont the western waves, man.   America
Fair Virtue water'd it wi care,
  And now she sees wi pride, man,
How weel it buds and blossoms there,
  Its branches spreading wide, man.

But vicious folks aye hate to see
  The works o Virtue thrive, man;
The courtly vermin 's banned the tree,   cursed
  And grat to see it thrive, man;   wept
King Loui' thought to cut it down.
  When it was unco sma', man;   quite small
For this the watchman cracked his crown,
  Cut aff his head an a', man.

A wicked crew syne, on a time,   then
  Did tak a solemn aith, man,   oath
It ne'er should flourish to its prime,
  I wat they pledged their faith, man.   wot
Awa they gaed wi mock parade,   went
  Like beagles hunting game, man,
But soon grew weary o the trade
  And wished they'd been at hame, man.

For Freedom, standing by the tree,
  Her sons did loudly ca', man:
She sang a sang o liberty,
  Which pleased them ane and a', man.
By her inspired, the new-born race
  Soon drew the avenging steel, man;
The hirelings ran — her foes gied chase,
  And banged the despot weel, man.

Let Britain boast her hardy oak,
  Her poplar and her pine, man,
Auld Britain ance could crack her joke,   once
  And o'er her neighbours shine, man.
But seek the forest round and round,
  And soon 'twill be agreed, man,
That sic a tree can not be found,
  'Twixt London and the Tweed, man.

Without this tree, alake this life
  Is but a vale o woe, man;
A scene o sorrow mixed wi strife,
  Nae real joys we know, man.

The Tree Of Liberty

We labour soon, we labour late,
　　To feed the titled knave, man;
And a' the comfort we're to get
beyond　　Is that ayont the grave, man.

such, believe Wi plenty o sic trees, I trow,
　　The warld would live in peace, man;
The sword would help to mak a plough,
　　The din o war wad cease, man.
Like brethren in a common cause,
　　We'd on each other smile, man;
And equal rights and equal laws
　　Wad gladden every isle, man.

woe betide, fool Wae worth the loon wha wadna eat
wholesome　　Sic halesome dainty cheer, man;
shoes I'd gie my shoon frae aff my feet,
　　To taste sic fruit, I swear, man.
Syne let us pray, auld England may
　　Sure plant this far-famed tree, man;
And blythe we'll sing, and hail the day
　　That gave us liberty, man.

WANDERING WILLIE

A remodelling of an old song in the Herd collection, published in SMM (1787). The earliest version by Burns was written in an undated letter to John McMurdo (c.1792), and a revised version was sent to Thomson on 27th March 1793.

Here awa, there awa, wandering Willie,
　　Here awa, there awa, haud awa hame!
one Come to my bosom, my ae only dearie,
　　And tell me thou bring'st me my Willie the same.
Loud tho the Winter blew cauld at our parting,
　　'Twas na the blast brought the tear to my e'e,
Welcome now Simmer, and welcome my Willie,
　　The Simmer to Nature, my Willie to me!

Rest, ye wild storms in the cave of your slumber—
　　How your wild howling a lover alarms!
Wauken, ye breezes, row gently, ye billows,
　　And waft my dear laddie ance mair to my arms.
But O, if he's faithless, and minds na his Nannie,
　　Flow still between us, thou wide-roaring main!
May I never see it, may I never trow it,
　　But, dying, believe that my Willie's my ain!

THE BROW WELL
near Dumfries

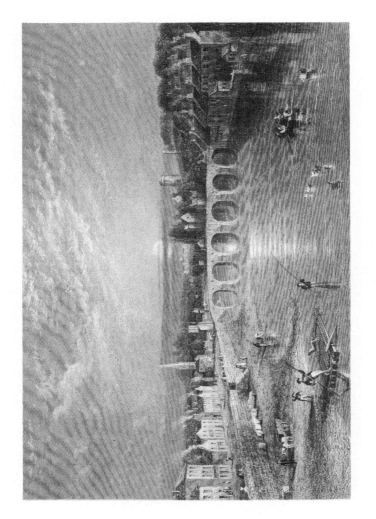

DUMFRIES

BRAW LADS O GALLA WATER

Based on 'Braw, braw lads of Galla Water' in Herd MSS
(ii. 202) and in SMM, 1788, this version was sent to
Thomson in January 1793.

Braw, braw lads on Yarrow braes,
    They rove amang the blooming heather;
But Yarrow braes nor Ettrick shaws   slopes, woods
    Can match the lads o Galla Water.

But there is ane, a secret ane,   one
    Aboon them a' I loe him better;   Above
And I'll be his, and he'll be mine,
    The bonie lad o Galla Water.

Altho his daddie was nae laird,
    And tho I hae nae meikle tocher,   not much dowry
Yet, rich in kindest, truest love,
    We'll tent our flocks by Galla Water.   tend

It ne'er was wealth, it ne'er was wealth,
    That coft contentment, peace, and pleasure: bought
The bands and bliss o mutual love,
    O, that's the chiefest warld's treasure!

POORTITH CAULD

TUNE: *Cauld Kail in Aberdeen*

Sent to Thomson early in January 1793 along with the
foregoing. It is likely that this song was written for
Jean Lorimer (see 'Craigieburn Wood').

CHORUS

O, why should Fate sic pleasure have,   such
    Life's dearest bands untwining?
Or why sae sweet a flower as love
    Depend on Fortune's shining?

O poortith cauld and restless Love,   poverty
    Ye wrack my peace between ye!
Yet poortith a' I could forgive,
    An 'twere na for my Jeanie.

The warld's wealth when I think on,
    Its pride and a' the lave o't—   rest
My curse on silly coward man,
    That he should be the slave o't!

R

Poortith Cauld

Her e'en sae bonie blue betray
    How she repays my passion;
by-word always   But prudence is her o'erword ay:
    She talks o rank and fashion.

O, wha can prudence think upon,
    And sic a lassie by him?
O, wha can prudence think upon,
    And sae in love as I am?

How blest the wild-wood Indian's fate!
    He woos his artless dearie—
demons   The silly bogles, Wealth and State,
frightened   Can never make him eerie.

LORD GREGORY

Burns wrote these verses as a much more preferable alternative to the traditional ballad 'The Lass of Lochryan' and the poem of the same name by John Wolcot under the nom de plume of Peter Pindar.

dark   O, mirk, mirk is this midnight hour,
    And loud the tempest's roar!
doleful   A waefu wanderer seeks thy tower—
    Lord Gregory, ope thy door.
An exile frae her father's ha',
    And a' for sake o thee,
At least some pity on me shaw,
    If love it may na be.

Lord Gregory mind'st thou not the grove
    By bonie Irwine side,
Where first I own'd that virgin love
    I lang, lang had denied?
How aften didst thou pledge and vow,
    Thou wad for ay be mine!
And my fond heart, itsel sae true,
    It ne'er mistrusted thine.

Hard is thy heart, Lord Gregory,
    And flinty is thy breast:
Thou bolt of Heaven that flashest by,
    O, wilt thou bring me rest!
Ye mustering thunders from above,
    Your willing victim see,
But spare and pardon my fause love,
    His wrangs to Heaven and me!

ON HEARING A THRUSH SING IN
HIS MORNING WALK

Composed in January 1793 and sent to Alexander
Cunningham on 20th February. This was one of
Burns's first essays in the sonnet 14-line form.

Sing on, sweet thrush, upon the leafless bough,
Sing on, sweet bird, I listen to thy strain:
See aged Winter, 'mid his surly reign,
At thy blythe carol, clears his furrowed brow.
So in lone Poverty's dominion drear
Sits meek Content with light, unanxious heart,
Welcomes the rapid moments, bids them part,
Nor asks if they bring ought to hope or fear.
I thank thee, Author of this opening day,
Thou whose bright sun now gilds yon orient skies!
Riches denied, Thy boon was purer joys:
What wealth could never give nor take away!
Yet come, thou child of Poverty and Care,
The mite high Heav'n bestow'd, that mite with thee I'll share.

EPITAPH FOR
MR. GABRIEL RICHARDSON

Reproduced by Alexander Cunningham from the lines
engraved by Burns on a crystal goblet owned by
Gabriel   Richardson   (1759-1820).   Richardson
complained to Burns that he had to pay more tax on
his brewery than brewers outside the burgh of
Dumfries. Burns took up the case with Provost Staig in
January 1793. That tax was consequently adjusted
and   Burns   celebrated   with   this   mock-epitaph.
Richardson became Provost himself in 1801.

Here Brewer Gabriel's fire's extinct,
And empty all his barrels:
He's blest—if as he brew'd, he drink—
In upright, honest morals.

ON COMMISSARY GOLDIE'S BRAINS

Colonel Thomas Goldie of Goldielea — 'Colonel Tam'
of Burns's second Heron election ballad — was
president of the Loyal Natives, the right-wing political
club in Dumfries and commissary of the sheriff-court,
an official dealing with adultery, divorce and the
confirmation of testaments.

Lord, to account who does Thee call,
Or e'er dispute Thy pleasure?
Else why within so thick a wall,
Enclose so poor a treasure?

ON GENERAL DUMOURIER'S
DESERTION

FROM THE FRENCH REPUBLICAN ARMY

Charles François Dumouriez (1739-1823) was a career officer in the French Army who joined the revolutionaries and won the battle of Valmy which repelled the Austro-German invasion of 1792. Having won the battle of Jemappes and conquered Belgium, he was defeated by the Austrians at Neerwinden on 18th March 1793. Denounced as a traitor and recalled to Paris he chose instead to go over to the Royalist side, and eventually settled in England. Burns misspelled his surname.

You're welcome to Despots, Dumourier!

Dumouriez's   You're welcome to Despots, Dumourier!
second-in-command

emissary of the   How does Dampiere do?
Convention   Ay, and Beurnonville too?

Why did they not come along with you, Dumourier?

I will fight France with you, Dumourier,
I will fight France with you, Dumourier,
I will fight France with you,
I will take my chance with you,
By my soul, I'll dance with you, Dumourier!

Then let us fight about, Dumourier!
Then let us fight about, Dumourier!
Then let us fight about
Till Freedom's spark be out,
Then we'll be damn'd, no doubt, Dumourier.

ON THE COMMEMORATION OF
RODNEY'S VICTORY

Admiral George Brydges Rodney (1718-92) confronted the French navy off Dominica in the West Indies on 12th April 1792 and destroyed several warships. This decisive victory restored British control of the Atlantic and was enthusiastically celebrated at the time. These lines were probably composed extempore at a celebration in the King's Arms, Dumfries but not published in the Advertiser till the following year.

Instead of a song, boys, I'll give you a toast:
Here's to the mem'ry of those on the Twelfth that we lost!—
That we lost, did I say? — no, by Heav'n, that we found!
For their fame it shall live while the world goes round.
The next in succession I'll give you: The King!
And who would betray him, on high may he swing!
And here's the grand fabric, the Free Constitution,
As built on the base of our great Revolution!
And, longer with Politics not to be cramm'd,
Be Anarchy curs'd, and be Tyranny damn'd!
And who would to Liberty e'er prove disloyal,
May his son be a hangman— and himself his first trial!

THANKSGIVING FOR A NATIONAL VICTORY

This quotation appears in all major editions except Kinsley (1968) — usually linked to the preceding poem. Though the national victory is unspecified it is thought to refer to one of the naval victories in the early stages of the French Revolutionary War. Kinsley rejected it on account of its similarity to lines beginning 'Ye bloody Whigs' which were nailed to the door of a Manchester church on the day of thanksgiving after Culloden in 1746.

Ye hypocrites! are these your pranks?
To murder men, and give God thanks?
Desist, for shame! Proceed no further:
God won't accept your thanks for Murther!

OPEN THE DOOR TO ME OH

TUNE: *Open the door softly*

Sent to Thomson in April 1793 and published in SC as 'altered by Robert Burns.'

OH, open the door, some pity to shew,
  If love it may na be, Oh;
Tho thou hast been false, I'll ever prove true,
  Oh, open the door to me, Oh.

Cauld is the blast upon my pale cheek,
  But caulder thy love for me, Oh:
The frost that freezes the life at my heart,
  Is nought to my pains frae thee, Oh.

The wan moon sets behind the white wave,
  And time is setting with me, Oh:
False friends, false love, farewell! for mair
  I'll ne'er trouble them, nor thee, Oh.

She has open'd the door, she has open'd it wide,
  She sees his pale corse on the plain, Oh:
My true love! she cried, and sank down by his side,
  Never to rise again, Oh.

485

YOUNG JESSIE

TUNE: *Open the door softly*

Sent to Thomson in April 1793 and published in his
Select Collection of Original Scottish Airs, along with
the preceding song. The subject was Jessie Staig
(1775-1801), daughter of Provost David Staig of
Dumfries.

True hearted was he, the sad swain o the Yarrow,
　　And fair are the maids on the banks of the Ayr;
But by the sweet side o the Nith's winding river
　　Are lovers as faithful, and maidens as fair:
To equal young Jessie seek Scotia all over—
　　To equal young Jessie you seek it in vain!
Grace, beauty, and elegance fetter her lover,
　　And maidenly modesty fixes the chain.

Fresh is the rose in the gay, dewy morning,
　　And sweet is the lily at evening close;
But in the fair presence o lovely young Jessie,
　　Unseen is the lily, unheeded the rose.
Love sits in her smile, a wizard ensnaring;
　　Enthron'd in her een he delivers his law;
And still to her charms she alone is a stranger;
　　Her modest demeanour's the jewel of a'.

FAREWELL, THOU STREAM

TUNE: *Nansie's to the greenwood gane*

Burns wrote these words for the air that accompanied
Allan Ramsay's song 'The last time I came o'er the
moor.' He then sent a copy to Maria Riddell, with her
name in the second line (April 1793), but in December
he sent a revised version to Mrs. Dunlop with 'Eliza'
substituted, after the bitter quarrel with the Riddell
family.

Farewell, thou stream that winding flows
　　Around Eliza's dwelling!
O Mem'ry, spare the cruel throes
　　Within my bosom swelling:
Condemn'd to drag a hopeless chain
　　And yet in secret languish,
To feel a fire in every vein,
　　Nor dare disclose my anguish!

Love's veriest wretch, unseen, unknown,
　　I fain my griefs would cover:
The bursting sigh, th' unweeting groan
　　Betray the hapless lover.

Farewell, Thou Stream

I know thou doom'st me to despair,
  Nor wilt, nor canst relieve me;
But, O Eliza, hear one prayer—
  For pity's sake forgive me!
The music of thy voice I heard,
  Nor wist while it enslav'd me!
I saw thine eye, yet nothing fear'd,
  Till fears no more had sav'd me!
Th' unwary sailor thus, aghast
  The wheeling torrent viewing,
'Mid circling horrors sinks at last
  In overwhelming ruin.

THE SOLDIER'S RETURN

TUNE: The Mill, Mill, O

An ancient piece of bawdry had been refined by
Ramsay as 'Beneath a green Shade' (1733) and this
was Burns's exercise in the same process of refine-
ment.

When wild War's deadly blast was blawn,
  And gentle Peace returning,
Wi monie a sweet babe fatherless
  And monie a widow mourning
I left the lines and tented field,
  Where lang I'd been a lodger,
My humble knapsack a' may wealth,
  A poor but honest sodger.   soldier

A leal, light heart was in my breast,   true
  My hand unstain'd wi plunder,
And for fair Scotia, hame again,
  I cheery on did wander:
I thought upon the banks o Coil,
  I thought upon my Nancy,
And ay I mind't the witching smile
  That caught my youthful fancy.

At length I reach'd the bonie glen,
  Where early life I sported.
I pass'd the mill and trysting thorn,
  Where Nancy aft I courted.
Wha spied I but my ain dear maid,
  Down by her mother's dwelling,
And turn'd me round to hide the flood
  That in my e'en was swelling!

487

The Soldier's Return

Wi alter'd voice, quoth I: — 'Sweet lass,
    Sweet as yon hawthorn's blossom,
O, happy, happy may he be,
    That's dearest to thy bosom!
My purse is light, I've far to gang,
    And fain would be thy lodger;
I've served my king and country lang—
    Take pity on a sodger.'

Sae wistfully she gaz'd on me,
    And lovelier was than ever.
Quo she — 'A sodger ance I lo'ed,
    Forget him shall I never:
Our humble cot, and hamely fare,
    Ye freely shall partake it;
That gallant badge — the dear cockade —
    Ye're welcome for the sake o't!'

She gaz'd, she redden'd like a rose,
    Syne, pale like onie lily, *Then*
She sank within my arms, and cried:—
    'Art thou my ain dear Willie?'
'By Him who made yon sun and sky,
    By whom true love's regarded,
I am the man! And thus may still
    True lovers be rewarded!

'The wars are o'er, and I'm come hame,
    And find thee still true-hearted.
Tho poor in gear, we're rich in love, *wealth*
    And mair, we'se ne'er be parted.'
Quo she:— 'My grandsire left me gowd, *gold*
    A mailen plenish'd fairly! *farm, well-stocked*
And come, my faithfu sodger lad,
    Thou'rt welcome to it dearly!'

For gold the merchant ploughs the main,
    The farmer ploughs the manor;
But glory is the sodger's prize,
    The sodger's wealth is honour!
The brave poor sodger ne'er despise,
    Nor count him as a stranger:
Remember he's his country's stay
    In day and hour of danger.

MEG O THE MILL

TUNE: *O bonie lass, will ye lie in a barrack?*

This was indubitably Burns's own composition, which
he sent to Thomson in April 1793: '. . .my song "O
ken ye what Meg o' the mill has gotten" pleases myself
so much, that I cannot without disgust try my hand at
another song to the air; so I shall not attempt it.'
Thomson commented 'he does not generally praise his
own songs so much.'

O ken ye what Meg o the mill has gotten?
An ken ye what Meg o the mill has gotten?
She's gotten a coof wi a claute o siller,   dolt, hoard,
And broken the heart o the barley miller!   money

The miller was strappin, the miller was ruddy,
A heart like a lord, and a hue like a lady.
The laird was a widdifu, bleerit knurl!—   gallows-worthy,
She's left the guid fellow, and taen the churl!   dwarf

The miller, he hecht her a heart leal and loving;   offered, loyal
The laird did address her wi matter mair moving:
A fine pacing-horse wi a clear, chained bridle,
A whip by her side, and a bonie side-saddle!

O, wae on the siller—it is sae prevailing!   woe
And wae on the love that is fixed on a mailen!   farm
A tocher's nae word in a true lover's parl,   dowry, speech
But gie me my love, and a fig for the warl!

MEG O THE MILL

TUNE: *O ken ye what, Meg, etc*

'Written for this work by Robert Burns' (SMM). Never-
theless it seems probable that it was merely a revision of
a traditional ballad, before Burns composed the pre-
ceding version.

O, ken ye what Meg o the Mill has gotten?   know
An ken ye what Meg o the Mill has gotten?
A braw new naig wi the tail o a rottan,   nag, rat
And that's what Meg o the Mill has gotten!

O, ken ye what Meg o the Mill lo'es dearly?
An ken ye what Meg o the Mill lo'es dearly?
A dram o guid strunt in a morning early,
And that's what Meg o the Mill lo'es dearly!

O, ken ye how Meg o the Mill was married?
An ken ye how Meg o the Mill was married;
The priest he was oxter'd, the clark he was carried,   held up by
And that's how Meg o the Mill was married!   the armpits

O, ken ye how Meg o the Mill was bedded?
An ken ye how Meg o the Mill was bedded?
The groom gat sae fu he fell awald beside it,   drunk,
And that's how Meg o the Mill was bedded!   backwards

BLYTHE HAE I BEEN ON YON HILL

TUNE: *Merrily dance the Quaker*

The subject of this song is Lesley Baillie, in whose honour Burns had previously written 'Saw ye Bonie Lesley,' and he sent her a copy in May 1793. By September of that year he was describing it as 'one of the finest songs I ever made in my life; and, besides, is composed on a young lady, positively the most beautiful, lovely woman in the world.'

Blythe hae I been on yon hill
    As the lambs before me,
every   Careless ilka thought, and free.
    As the breeze flew o'er me.
Now nae langer sport and play,
    Mirth or sang can please me:
Lesley is sae fair and coy,
    Care and anguish seize me.

Heavy, heavy is the task,
    Hopeless love declaring!
Trembling, I dow nocht but glow'r,
    Sighing, dumb despairing!
will not, throes   If she winna ease the thraws
    In my bosom swelling,
    Underneath the grass-green sod,
must   Soon maun be my dwelling.

LOGAN BRAES

TUNE: *Logan Water*

'Composed in three-quarters of an hour's lucubrations in my elbow-chair' — Burns to Thomson (25th June 1793). The Logan Water rises in the hills on the Ayrshire-Lanarkshire border and flows eastwards to join the river Nethan in Lesmahagow parish.

O Logan, sweetly didst thou glide
    That day I was my Willie's bride,
since then   And years sin syne hae o'er us run
    Like Logan to the simmer sun.
But now thy flowery banks appear
muddy   Like drumlie winter, dark and drear,
must, foes   While my dear lad maun face his faes
hillsides   Far, far frae me and Logan braes.

Again the merry month of May
Has made our hills and vallies gay;
The birds rejoice in leafy bowers,
The bees hum round the breathing flowers;
Blythe Morning lifts his rosy eye,
And Evening's tears are tears o joy:
My soul delightless a' surveys,
While Willie's far frae Logan braes.

Logan Braes

Within yon milk-white hawthorn bush,
Amang her nestlings sits the thrush:
Her faithfu mate will share her toil,
Or wi his song her cares beguile.
But I wi my sweet nurslings here,
Nae mate to help, nae mate to cheer,
Pass widow'd' nights and joyless days,
While Willie's far frae Logan braes.

O, wae be to you, Men o State,   woe
That brethren rouse in deadly hate!
As ye make monie a fond heart mourn,
Sae may it on your heads return!
Ye mind na 'mid your cruel joys
The widow's tears, the orphan's cries
But soon may peace bring happy days,
And Willie hame to Logan braes!

EPIGRAM ON MISS DAVIES

Composed about Deborah Davies, previously the
subject of 'Bonie Wee Thing,' and again commenting
flatteringly on her smallness of stature.

Ask why God made the gem so small,
And why so huge the granite?
Because God meant mankind should set
That higher value on it.

EPIGRAM ON A COUNTRY LAIRD

NOT QUITE SO WISE AS SOLOMON

The subject of this and the following was David
Maxwell of Cardoness (d.1825) 'a stupid, money-
loving dunderpate of a Galloway laird,' as Burns
commented to Mrs Dunlop when sending her these
lines in June 1793.

Bless Jesus Christ, O Cardoness,
With grateful lifted eyes,
Who taught that not the soul alone
But body too shall rise!

For had He said 'The soul alone
From death I will deliver,'
Alas, alas! O Cardoness,
Then hadst thou lain for ever.

491

ON BEING SHOWN A BEAUTIFUL
COUNTRY SEAT

BELONGING TO THE SAME LAIRD

This epigram on Maxwell of Cardoness was composed
during Burns's tour of Galloway with John Syme in
July-August 1793.

We grant they're thine, those beauties all,
    So lovely in our eye:
Keep them, thou eunuch, Cardoness,
    For others to enjoy.

LINES INSCRIBED IN A LADY'S
POCKET ALMANAC

Written, in fact, in John Syme's copy of the Della
Cruscan British Album which Burns had borrowed in
June 1793.

Grant me, indulgent Heaven, that I may live,
To see the miscreants feel the pains they give!
Deal Freedom's sacred treasures free as air,
Till Slave and Despot be but things that were!

O, WERE MY LOVE

TUNE: *Hughie Graham*

The second stanza comes from a fragment in the Herd
MSS. Writing to Thomson in June 1793 Burns said. 'It
is too short... I have often tried to eke a stanza to it,
but in vain. After balancing myself for a musing five
minutes, on the hind-legs of my elbow-chair, I
produced [the first lines], far inferior to the foregoing,
I frankly confess.'

O, were my love yon lilac fair
    Wi purple blossoms to the spring,
And I a bird to shelter there,
    When wearied on my little wing.
How I wad mourn when it was torn
    By Autumn wild and Winter rude!
But I wad sing on wanton wing,
    When youthfu May its bloom renew'd.

O, gin my love were yon red rose,
    That grows upon the castle wa',
And I mysel a drap o dew
    Into her bonie breast to fa',
O, there, beyond expression blest,
    I'd feast on beauty a' the night,
Seal'd on her silk-saft faulds to rest,
    Till fley'd awa by Phoebus' light!

492

BONIE JEAN

In a letter of April 1793 to Thomson, Burns mentioned some Scots airs which he had picked up from country lasses. 'They please me vastly; but your learned lugs would perhaps be displeased with the very feature for which I like them — I call them Simple; you would pronounce them Silly.' He enclosed a 'beautiful little air' and some lines set to it. The subject was Jean McMurdo, daughter of the chamberlain of Drumlanrig.

There was a lass, and she was fair!
　　At kirk and market to be seen
When a' our fairest maids were met,
　　The fairest maid was bonie Jean.

And ay she wrought her country wark,
　　And ay she sang sae merrilie:
The blythest bird upon the bush
　　Had ne'er a lighter heart than she!

But hawks will rob the tender joys,
　　That bless the little lintwhite's nest,   linnet
And frost will blight the fairest flowers,
　　And love will break the soundest rest.

Young Robie was the brawest lad,   finest
　　The flower and pride of a' the glen,
And he had owsen, sheep, and kye,   oxen, cattle
　　And wanton naigies nine or ten.   horses .

He gaed wi Jeanie to the tryste,   cattle-fair
　　He danc'd wi Jeanie on the down,
And, lang ere witless Jeanie wist,   realised
　　Her heart was tint, her peace was stown!   lost, stolen

As in the bosom of the stream,
　　The moonbeam dwells at dewy e'en.
So, trembling pure, was tender love
　　Within the breast of bonie Jean.

And now she works her country's wark,
　　And ay she sighs wi care and pain,
Yet wist na what her ail might be,   ailment
　　Or what wad make her weel again.   would

But did na Jeanie's heart loup light,   leap
　　And didna joy blink in her e'e;   glance
As Robie tauld a tale of love
　　Ae e'enin on the lily lea?

While monie a bird sang sweet o love,
　　And monie a flower blooms o'er the dale,
His cheek to hers he aft did lay,
　　And whisper'd thus his tender tale.

'O Jeanie fair, I lo'e thee dear.
 O canst thou think to fancy me?
cottage   Or wilt thou leave thy mammie's cot,
 And learn to tent the farms wi me?

cow-shed   'At barn or byre thou shalt na drudge,
 Or naething else to trouble thee,
 But stray amang the heather-bells,
 And tent the waving corn wi me.'

Now what could artless Jeanie do?
 She had nae will to say him na!
 At length she blush'd a sweet consent,
 And love was ay between them twa.

EPIGRAMS AGAINST THE
EARL OF GALLOWAY

John Stewart, 7th Earl of Galloway (1736-1806), was
a Scottish representative peer from 1774 to 1790,
Burns heartily detested him, both personally and for
his High Tory political viewpoint. The Earl was savagely
lampooned in Burns's third Election Ballad, 'John
Bushby's Lamentation,' as well as in these epigrams.
This impression is oddly at variance with all other
published references to the Earl who was noted for his
great piety and generosity to his servants. The Earl was
later quoted as saying 'it would not become him, when
his good old master the King despised and disregarded
the paltry attacks of a Peter Pindar, to feel himself hurt
by those of a licentious, rhyming ploughman.'

What dost thou in that mansion fair?
Move away   Flit, Galloway, and find
 Some narrow, dirty, dungeon cave,
 The picture of thy mind.

No Stewart art thou, Galloway:
 The Stewarts all were brave.
 Besides, the Stewarts were but fools,
 Not one of them a knave.

Bright ran thy line, O Galloway,
 Thro many a far-famed sire!
 So ran the far-famed Roman way,
 And ended in a mire.

Spare me thy vengeance, Galloway!
 In quiet let me live:
 I ask no kindness at thy hand,
 For thou has none to give.

EPITAPH ON A LAPDOG

While Burns was staying with Gordon of Kenmure late in July 1793, Mrs Gordon's lap-dog Echo died. She asked Burns to write an epitaph for him, and though he disliked the subject he tried to please the lady.

In wood and wild, ye warbling throng,
    Your heavy loss deplore:
Now half extinct your powers of song—
    Sweet Echo is no more.

Ye jarring, screeching things around,
    Scream your discordant joys:
Now half your din of tuneless sound
    With Echo silent lies.

EPIGRAM ON THE LAIRD OF LAGGAN

Syme records Burns's bouts of ill-humour during their Galloway tour. While these displays of bad temper are inexplicable they resulted in some savage epigrams. John Morine of Laggan bought Ellisland when Burns moved to Dumfries. Morine disagreed with Burns over the value of some manure and insisted on the fences being repaired. On removals day Burns sent Adam Armour back to Ellisland to smash every pane of glass there on which he had inscribed verses in diamond-point, paying his brother-in-law six shillings for carrying out his orders.

When Morine, deceas'd, to the Devil went down,
'Twas nothing would serve him but Satan's own crown.
'Thy fool's head,' quoth Satan, 'that crown shall wear never:
I grant thou'rt as wicked, but not quite so clever.'

PHILLIS THE FAIR

Phillis of the title was the younger daughter of John McMurdo of Drumlanrig and, like the following, this song was set to Robin Adair, 'a crinkum-crankum' Gaelic tune which Burns got from a 'musical Highlander in Breadalbane's Fencibles,' quartered at Dumfries in 1793.

While larks, with little wing, fann'd the pure air,
Viewing the breathing Spring, forth I did fare.
    Gay, the sun's golden eye
    Peep'd o'er the mountains high;
'Such thy bloom,' did I cry, 'Phillis the fair.'

In each bird's careless song, glad, I did share;
While yon wild flowers among, chance led me there.
    Sweet to the opening day,
    Rosebuds bent the dewy spray;
'Such they bloom,' did I say — 'Phillis the fair!'

Down in the shady walk, doves cooing were;
I mark'd the cruel hawk caught in a snare.
    So kind may Fortune be!
    Such make his destiny,
He who would injure thee, Phillis the fair!

HAD I A CAVE

TUNE: *Robin Adair*

Burns wrote to Thomson in August 1793: 'I succeeded so ill in my last attempt [supra] that I have ventured, in this morning's walk, one essay more . . .'

Had I a cave on some wild distant shore,
Where the winds howl to the wave's dashing roar,
There would I weep my woes,
There seek my lost repose,
Till grief my eyes should close,
Ne'er to wake more!

Falsest of womankind, can'st thou declare
All my fond, plighted vows fleeting as air?
To thy new lover hie,
Laugh o'er thy perjury,
Then in thy bosom try
What peace is there!

WHISTLE AN I'LL COME TO YOU, MY LAD

Derived from an old fragment in the Herd collection, this song was sent to Thomson in August 1793. He showed these verses to Pietro Urbani (1749-1816), the Milanese composer who was in Galloway at the time of Burns's tour in that district, who begged a copy which the poet declined to supply. 'I understand he looks with rather an evil eye on your work. . .'

CHORUS
O, whistle an I'll come to ye, my lad!
O, whistle an I'll come to ye, may lad!
Tho father an mother an a' should gae mad,
O, whistle an I'll come to ye, my lad!

take care	But warily tent when ye come to court me,
-gate, ajar	And come nae unless the back-yett be a-jee;
Then, -stile	Syne up the back-style, and let naebody see,
	And come as ye were na comin to me,
	And come as ye were na comin to me!
	At kirk, or at market, whene'er ye meet me,
Go	Gang by me as tho that ye car'd na a flie;
	But steal me a blink o your bonie black e'e,
	Yet look as ye were na lookin to me,
	Yet look as ye were na lookin to me!
	Ay vow and protest that ye care na for me,
sometimes, a little	And whyles ye may lightly my beauty a-wee;
	But court na anither tho jokin ye be,
lure	For fear that she wyle your fancy frae me,
	For fear that she wyle your fancy frae me!

496

ADOWN WINDING NITH

TUNE: *The Muckin o Geordies's Byre*

The subject of this song is, again, Phillis McMurdo. A
pretty footpath along the east bank of the Nith north
of Dumfries is known as Burns Walk to this day.

CHORUS
Awa wi your belles and your beauties—
They never wi her can compare!
Whaever has met wi my Phillis,
Has met wi the Queen o the Fair.

Adown winding Nith I did wander,
To mark the sweet flowers as they spring.
Adown winding Nith I did wander,
Of Phillis to muse and to sing.

The Daisy amus'd my fond fancy,
So artless, so simple, so wild:
'Thou emblem,' said I, 'o my Phillis'—
For she is Simplicity's child.

The rosebud's the blush o my charmer,
Her sweet balmy lip when 'tis prest.
How fair and how pure is the lily!
But fairer and purer her breast.

Yon knot of gay flowers in the arbour,
They ne'er wi my Phillis can vie:
Her breath is the breath of the woodbine,
Its dew-drop o diamond her eye.

Her voice is the song o the morning,
That wakes thro the green-spreading grove,
When Phoebus peeps over the mountains
On music, and pleasure, and love.

But Beauty, how frail and how fleeting!
The bloom of a fine summer's day!
While Worth in the mind o my Phillis
Will flourish without a decay.

BY ALLAN STREAM

TUNE: *Allan Water*

'I walked out yesterday evening with a volume of
the Museum in my hand, when turning up "Allan
Water" . . .It appeared to me rather unworthy of so
fine an air; and recollecting that it is on your list, I
sat, and raved, under the shade of an old thorn, till
I wrote one to suit the measure. I may be wrong;
but I think it not in my worst style.' — letter to
Thomson, 19th August 1793. Allan Water winds
through Strathallan, Perthshire; Ben Ledi (2873 ft)
towers over the Trossachs to the west.

By Allan stream I chanc'd to rove,
 While Phoebus sank beyond Benledi;
The winds were whispering thro the grove,
 The yellow corn was waving ready;
I listen'd to a lover's sang,
many   An thought on youthfu pleasures monie,
And ay the wild-wood echoes rang:—
 'O, my love Annie's very bonie!'

'O, happy be the woodbine bower,
demon, frightful Nae nightly bogle make it eerie!
Nor ever sorrow stain the hour,
 The place and time I met my dearie!
Her head upon my throbbing breast,
 She, sinking, said:— 'I'm thine for ever!'
While monie a kiss the seal imprest—
 The sacred vow we ne'er should sever.'

-slope The haunt o Spring's the primrose-brae.
 The Summer joys the flocks to follow.
How cheery thro her short'ning day
 Is Autumn in her weeds o yellow!
But can they melt the glowing heart,
 Or chain the soul in speechless pleasure,
Or thro each nerve the rapture dart,
 Like meeting her, our bosom's treasure?

COME, LET ME TAKE THEE

TUNE: *Alley Croker*

'That tune, Cauld Kail in Aberdeen is such a favourite
of yours,' wrote Burns to Thomson on 28th August
1793, 'that I once more roved out yesterevening for a
gloamin-shot at the Muses; when the Muse that presides
o'er the shores of Nith . . . whispered me the following.'
Jean Lorimer is thought to have been the subject.

Come, let me take thee to my breast,
 And pledge we ne'er shall sunder,
And I shall spurn as vilest dust
 The world's wealth and grandeur!
And do I hear my Jeanie own
 That equal transports move her?
I ask for dearest life alone,
 That I may live to love her.

Come, Let Me Take Thee

Thus in my arms, wi a' her charms,
I clasp my countless treasure,
I'll seek nae mair o Heav'n to share
Than sic a moment's pleasure!
And by the e'en sae bonie blue
I swear I'm thine for ever,
And on thy lips I seal my vow,
And break it shall I never!

DAINTY DAVIE

Thomson and Burns disagreed violently on the musical setting of this song. '... nothing, since a Highland wench in the Cowgate once bore me three bastards at a birth, has surprised me so much as your opinion on this subject.' Thomson's dogmatism hardened against Burns's self-assurance and he was unmoved by the poet's colourful (and wholly fictitious) comparison.

CHORUS

Meet me on the Warlock Knowe,   wizard knoll
Dainty Davie, Dainty Davie!
There I'll spend the day wi you,
My ain dear Dainty Davie.   own

Now rosy May comes in wi flowers
To deck her gay, green-spreading bowers;
And now comes in the happy hours
To wander wi my Davie.

The crystal waters round us fa'
The merry birds are lovers a',
The scented breezes round us blaw
A wandering wi my Davie.

When purple morning starts the hare
To steal upon her early fare,
Then thro the dews I will repair
To meet my faithfu Davie.

When day, expiring in the west,
The curtain draws o Nature's rest,
I flee to his arms I loe the best:
And that's my ain dear Davie!

SCOTS WHA HAE

TUNE: *Hey Tutti Taitie*

Burns visited the field of Bannockburn, near Stirling on 26th August 1787. 'I said a fervent prayer for Old Caledonia over the hole in a blue whinstone, where Robert de Bruce fixed his royal standard . . .' Burns introduced the tune, popularly believed to have been Bruce's march at the battle. 'Urbani begged me to make soft verses for it ; but I had no idea of giving myself any trouble on the subject, till the accidental recollection of that glorious struggle for Freedom . . . roused my rhyming Mania.' The theme of Liberty was uppermost in Burns's mind, as the French Republic was then just a year old.

Sir William Wallace (d.1305)
King Robert I (1306-28)

look menacingly
Edward II (1307-27)

Scots, wha hae wi Wallace bled,
Scots, wham Bruce has aften led,
Welcome to your gory bed
    Or to victorie!
Now's the day, and now's the hour:
See the front o battle lour,
See approach proud Edward's power—
    Chains and slaverie!

Wha will be a traitor knave?
Wha can fill a coward's grave?
Wha sae base as be a slave?—
    Let him turn, and flee!
Wha for Scotland's King and Law
Freedom's sword will strongly draw,
Freeman stand, or Freeman fa',
    Let him follow me!

By Oppression's woes and pains,
By your sons in servile chains,
We will drain your dearest veins,
    But they shall be free!
Lay the proud usurpers low!
Tyrants fall in every foe!
Liberty's in every blow!—
    Let us do, or die!

ON MARIA RIDDELL

Maria Banks Woodley Riddell (1772-1808) was the youngest daughter of William Woodley, Governor of the Leeward Islands. She married Walter Riddell in 1790 and settled at Goldielea (renamed Woodley Park) near Dumfries in 1792. Burns probably met her at Friars' Carse, home of her brother-in-law and gave her an introduction to Smellie who published her Voyages to the Madeira and Leeward and Caribee Islands. By April 1793 Maria had become 'thou first of Friends, and most accomplished of Women.' These lines are believed to date from August 1793.

'Praise Woman still,' his lordship roars,
'Deserv'd or not, no matter!'
But thee whom all my soul adores,
There Flattery cannot flatter!
Maria, all my thought and dream,
Inspires my vocal shell:
The more I praise my lovely theme,
The more the truth I tell.

AS DOWN THE BURN

TUNE: *Down the Burn Davie*

This was the 'single elegant stanza' which Thomson commissioned from Burns in August 1793 as a substitute for the concluding 'objectionable verses' of the traditional ballad, 'so that this most exquisite song may no longer be excluded from good company.'

As down the burn they took their way,   brook
And thro the flowery dale;
His cheek to hers he aft did lay,
And love was ay the tale,
With:—'Mary, when shall we return,
Sic pleasure to renew?'
Quoth Mary:—'Love, I like the burn,
And ay shall follow you.'

PASSION'S CRY

*I cannot but remember such things were,
And were most dear to me—*

Burns began composing this poem in 1788 during his affair with Clarinda. He revised it in 1789 and completed it in 1793. It represents one of Burns's essays in Augustan composition, not really his métier.

In vain would Prudence, with decorous sneer,
Point out a cens'ring world, and bid me fear:
Above that world on wings of love I rise:
I know its worst and can that worst despise.
'Wronged, injured, shunned, unpitied, unredrest;
'The mocked quotation of the scorner's jest'
Let Prudence' direst bodements on me fall,
Clarinda, rich reward! o'erpays them all.

501

As low-borne mists before the sun remove,
So shines, so reigns unrivalled mighty Love.
In vain the laws their feeble force oppose;
Chained at his feet, they groan Love's vanquished foes;
In vain Religion meets my shrinking eye;
I dare not combat, but I turn and fly:
Conscience in vain upbraids th' unhallowed fire;
Love grasps his scorpions, stifled they expire:
Reason drops headlong from his sacred throne,
Thy dear idea reigns, and reigns alone;
Each thought intoxicated homage yields,
And riots wanton in forbidden fields.

By all on High, adoring mortals know!
By all the conscious villain fears below!
By, what, Alas! much more my soul alarms,
My doubtful hopes once more to fill thy arms!
E'en shouldst thou, false, forswear each guilty tie,
Thine, and thine only, I must live and die!!!

THE PRIMROSE

TUNE: *Todlin Hame*

The English original was written by Robert Herrick in the mid-17th century. Burns's revision of the first six lines is, however, minimal.

Dost ask me, why I send thee here,
This firstling of the infant year?
Dost ask me, what this primrose shews,
Bepearled thus with morning dews?—

    I must whisper to thy ears,
    The sweets of love are wash'd with tears.

This lovely native of the dale
Thou seest, how languid, pensive, pale:
Thou seest this bending stalk so weak,
That each way yielding doth not break?

    I must tell thee, these reveal,
    The doubts and fears that lovers feel.

THOU HAS LEFT ME EVER, JAMIE

TUNE: *Fee him, father, fee him*

Sent to Thomson in September 1793 with the note
'I composed them [two stanzas] at the time in which
Patie Allan's mither died — that was, "About the back
o' midnight" — and by the leaside of a bowl of
punch . . . '.

Thou has left me ever, Jamie,
  Thou has left me ever!
Thou has left me ever, Jamie,
  Thou hast left me ever!
Aften hast thou vow'd that Death
  Only should us sever;
Now thou'st left thy lass for ay—
  I maun see thee never, Jamie,   must
  I'll see thee never!

Thou hast me forsaken, Jamie,
  Thou hast me forsaken!
Thou hast me forsaken, Jamie,
  Thou hast me forsaken!
Thou canst love another jo,
  While my heart is breaking;
Soon my weary een I'll close,
  Never mair to waken, Jamie,
  Never mair to waken!

BEHOLD THE HOUR, THE BOAT, ARRIVE

TUNE: *Oran gaoil*

The first version of this song was sent to Clarinda on
27th December 1791 when her departure for the West
Indies was imminent. It is a Scotticized version of an
English song 'Behold the fatal hour arrive' (1774).

Behold the hour, the boat, arrive!
  My dearest Nancy, O, fareweel!
Severed frae thee, can I survive,   from
  Frae thee whom I hae lov'd sae weel?

Endless and deep shall be my grief,
  Nae ray of comfort shall I see,
But his most precious, dear belief,
  That thou wilt still remember me.

Along the solitary shore,
  Where flitting sea-fowl round me cry,
Across the rolling, dashing roar,
  I'll westward turn my wistful eye.

'Happy thou Indian grove,' I'll say,
  'Where now my Nancy's path shall be!
While thro your sweets she holds her way,
  O, tell me, does she muse on me?'

503

BEHOLD THE HOUR, THE BOAT
ARRIVE
(Second Version)

The second version, from which 'dearest Nancy' and
the Scotticisms were removed, was sent to Thomson
in September 1793.

Behold the hour, the boat arrive!
  Thou goest, the darling of my heart!
Sever'd from thee, can I survive?
  But fate has will'd and we must part.
I'll often greet the surging swell,
  Yon distant Isle will often hail:—
'E'en here I took the last farewell;
  There, latest mark'd her vanish'd sail.'

Along the solitary shore,
  While flitting sea-fowl round me cry,
Across the rolling, dashing roar,
  I'll westward turn my wistful eye:—
'Happy, thou Indian grove,' I'll say,
  'Where now my Nancy's path may be!
While thro thy sweets she loves to stray,
  O, tell me, does she muse on me?'

WHERE ARE THE JOYS?
TUNE: *Saw ye my father*

Probably the song sent to Janet Miller of Dalswinton,
eldest daughter of Burns's former landlord, on 9th
September 1793. In an accompanying letter Burns
wrote: 'I have taken the liberty to make you the
Heroine . . . I have formed a little love-story for
you . . .' Miss Miller married the 28th Earl of Mar in
1795.

Where are the joys I hae met in the morning,
  That danc'd to the lark's early sang?
Where is the peace that awaited my wand'ring
  At e'ening the wild-woods amang?

Nae mair a-winding the course o yon river
  And marking sweet flowerets sae fair,
Nae mair I trace the light footsteps o Pleasure,
  But Sorrow and sad-sighing Care.

Is it that Summer's forsaken our vallies,
  And grim, surly Winter is near?
No, no, the bees humming round the gay roses
  Proclaim it the pride o the year.

Fain wad I hide what I fear to discover,
  Yet lang, lang, too well hae I known:
A' that has caused the wreck in my bosom,
  Is Jenny, fair Jenny alone!

Where Are The Joys?

Time cannot aid me, my griefs are immortal,
Not Hope dare a comfort bestow,
Come then, enamor'd and fond of my anguish,
Enjoyment I'll seek in my woe!

EPITAPH ON A NOTED COXCOMB

CAPTAIN WM. RODDICK, OF CORBIETON

Sent to Maria Riddell in October 1793 and later
inscribed with other epigrams in the Glenriddell MS,
parodying lines from Henry Mackenzie's The Man
of Feeling (1771).

Light lay the earth on Billy's breast,
His chicken heart's so tender;
But build a castle on his head—
His scull will prop it under.

THINE AM I, MY FAITHFUL FAIR

TUNE: *The Quaker's Wife*

Originally sent to Maria Riddell in 1793, 'Nancy' refers,
of course, to Clarinda. In September 1794 he
instructed Thomson to delete 'Nancy' and substitute
'Chloris', as his interest had switched to Jean Lorimer
by that time.

Thine am I, my faithful Fair,
Thine my lovely Nancy!
Ev'ry pulse along my veins,
Ev'ry roving fancy!

To thy bosom lay my heart,
There to throb and languish.
Tho despair had wrung its core,
That would heal its anguish.

Take away those rosy lips
Rich with balmy treasure!
Turn away thine eyes of love,
Lest I die with pleasure!
What is life when wanting love?
Night without a morning!
Love the cloudless summer's sun,
Nature gay adorning.

BONIE MARY

TUNE: *Minnie's ay glowerin o'er me*

Sent to Cleghorn, with the following ballad, on 25th October 1793: 'Mair for taiken of my violent propensity to Baudy...' Kinsley comments that bawdry on the theme of pubic hair is common in Scottish folk literature.

CHORUS

Come cowe me, minnie, come cowe me;
Come cowe me, minnie, come cowe me;
The hair o my arse is grown into my cunt,
And they canna win to, to mowe me.

When Mary cam over the Border,
When Mary cam over the Border;
hedgehog   As eith 'twas approachin the Cunt of a hurchin,
Her arse was in sic a disorder.

But wanton Wattie cam west on't,
But wanton Wattie cam west on't,
much   He did it sae tickle, he left nae as meikle
build   'S a spider wad bigget a nest on't.

And was nae Wattie a Clinker,
He mow'd frae the queen to the tinkler,
Alexander the Great   Then sat down, in grief, like the Macedon chief
more   For want o mae warlds to conquer.

And O, what a jewel was Mary!
And O, what a jewel was Mary!
Her face it was fine, and her bosom divine,
thatched   And her cunt it was theekit wi glory.

ACT SEDERUNT OF THE SESSION— A SCOTS BALLAD

TUNE: *O'er the muir amang the heather*

'The Law is good for something, since we can make a Baudy-song out of it', wrote Burns to Cleghorn. Thus Burns neatly combined his delight in Bawdry with his penchant for fine legal phraseology. An Act Sederunt is an ordinance for regulating the forms of procedure before the Court of Session, used here loosely as synonymous with the judgment of a law-court.

In Edinburgh town they've made a law,
In Edinburgh at the Court o Session,
defaulters   That standing pricks are fauteors a',
And guilty of a high transgression.

CHORUS

Act sederunt o the Session,
Decreet o the Court o Session,
That standing pricks are fauteors a',
And guilty of a high transgresssion.

506

And they've provided dungeons deep,
  Ilk lass has ane in her possession;   Each
Untill the wretches wail and weep,
  They there shall lie for their transgression.

CHORUS
Act Sederunt o the Session,
Decreet o the Court o Session,
The rogues in pouring tears shall weep,
By act Sederunt o the Session.

TO CAPTAIN GORDON, ON BEING ASKED WHY I WAS NOT TO BE OF THE PARTY WITH HIM AND HIS BROTHER KENMURE AT SYME'S

Adam Gordon of the 81st Regiment, was third son of John Gordon of Kenmure. His elder brother John was M.P. for Kirkcudbright in 1784-6. The title of Viscount Kenmure, attainted since 1716, was restored to him in 1824. Burns met 'noble Kenmure' in 1793, during his Galloway tour with Syme. Tiresias (l.16) was blinded by Juno for saying that women got greater sexual enjoyment than men did.

Dost ask, dear Captain, why from Syme
  I have no invitation,
When well he knows he has with him
  My first friends in the nation?

Is it because I love to toast,
  And round the bottle hurl?
No! there conjecture wild is lost,
  For *Syme* by God's no churl!

Is 't lest with bawdy jests I bore,
  As oft the matter of fact is?
No! *Syme* the theory can't abhor
  Who loves so well the practice.

Is it a fear I should avow
  Some heresy seditious?
No! *Syme* (but this entre nous)
  Is quite an old Tiresias.

In vain Conjecture thus would flit
  Thro mental clime and season:
In short, dear Captain, Syme 's a Wit
  Who asks of Wits a reason?

Yet must I still the sort deplore
  That to my griefs adds one more,
In balking me the social hour
  With you and noble Kenmure.

ON MRS. RIDDELL'S BIRTHDAY

NOVEMBER 4, 1793

Written when the friendship with Maria Riddell was
at its height. A month later, however, it was violently
disrupted as a result of the poet's disorderly conduct
during a drunken party, at Friars' Carse — the 'Rape
of the Sabines' incident. See also the 'Monody.'

Old Winter, with his frosty beard,
Thus once to Jove his prayer preferred:—
'What have I done of all the year,
To bear this hated doom severe?
My cheerless suns no pleasure know;
Night's horrid car drags dreary slow;
My dismal months no joys are crowning,
But spleeny, English hanging, drowning.

'Now Jove, for once be mighty civil:
To counterbalance all this evil
Give me, and I've no more to say,
Give me Maria's natal day!
That brilliant gift shall so enrich me,
Spring, Summer, Autumn, cannot match me.'
' 'Tis done!' says Jove; so ends my story,
And Winter once rejoiced in glory.

ADDRESS

SPOKEN BY MISS FONTENELLE ON-HER
BENEFIT NIGHT, DECEMBER 4, 1793,
AT THE THEATRE, DUMFRIES

Burns sent these lines to Louisa Fontenelle on 1st
December: 'May it be a prologue to an overflowing
House! If all the Town put together, have half the
ardour for your success and welfare, of my individual
wishes, my prayer will most certainly be granted.'

Still anxious to secure your partial favor,
And not less anxious, sure, this night than ever,
A Prologue, Epilogue, or some such matter,
'Twould vamp my bill, said I, if nothing better:
So sought a Poet roosted near the skies;
Told him I came to feast my curious eyes;
Said, nothing like his works was ever printed;
And last, my prologue-business slily hinted.
'Ma'am, let me tell you,' quoth my man of rhymes,
'I know your bent—these are no laughing times:
Can you—but, Miss, I own I have my fears—
Dissolve in pause, and sentimental tears?
With laden sighs, and solemn-rounded sentence,
Rouse from his sluggish slumbers, fell Repentance?
Paint Vengeance as he takes his horrid stand,
Waving on high the desolating brand,
Calling the storms to bear him o'er a guilty land?'

508

Address

I could no more! Askance the creature eyeing:—
'D'ye think,' said I, 'this face was made for crying?
I'll laugh, that's poz—nay more, the world shall know it; possible
And so, your servant! gloomy Master Poet!'
   Firm as my creed, Sirs, 'tis my fix'd belief
That Misery's another word for Grief.
I also think (so may I be a bride!)
That so much laughter, so much life enjoy'd.

Thou man of crazy care and ceaseless sigh,
Still under bleak Misfortune's blasting eye;
Doom'd to that sorest task of man alive—
To make three guineas do the work of five;
Laugh in Misfortune's face—the beldam witch—
Say, you'll be merry tho you can't be rich!

Thou other man of care, the wretch in love!
Who long with jiltish arts and airs hast strove;
Who, as the boughs all temptingly project,
Measur'st in desperate thought—a rope—thy neck—
Or, where the beetling cliff o'erhangs the deep,
Peerest to meditate the healing leap:
Would'st thou be cur'd, thou silly, moping elf?
Laugh at her follies—laugh e'en at thyself;
Learn to despise those frowns now so terrific,
And love a kinder: that's your grand specific.

To sum up all: be merry, I advise;
And as we're merry, may we still be wise!

ON SEEING MISS FONTENELLE IN A FAVOURITE CHARACTER

Possibly sent to Miss Fontenelle along with the 'Address' in December 1793.

Sweet näiveté of feature,
   Simple, wild, enchanting elf,
Not to thee, but thanks to Nature
   Thou art acting but thyself.

Wert thou awkward, stiff, affected,
   Spurning Nature, torturing art,
Loves and Graces all rejected
   Then indeed thou'd'st act a part.

HUSBAND, HUSBAND, CEASE YOUR STRIFE

TUNE: *My Jo Janet*

This was an Anglicization of the traditional ballad 'My
Jo Janet' sent to Thomson in December 1793. Though
this is one of Burns's better English songs it lacks the
naturalism of the original.

'Husband, husband, cease your strife,
    Nor longer idly rave, sir!
Tho I am your wedded wife,
    Yet I am not your slave, sir.'
'One of two must still obey,
    Nancy, Nancy!
Is it Man or Woman, say,
    My spouse Nancy?'

'If 'tis still the lordly word,
    Service and obedience,
I'll desert my sov'reign lord,
    And so, good-bye, allegiance!'
'Sad will I be, so bereft,
    Nancy, Nancy!
Yet I'll try to make a shift,
    My spouse Nancy!'

'My poor heart, then break it must,
    My last hour I am near it:
When you lay me in the dust,
    Think, how you will bear it?'
'I will hope and trust in Heaven,
    Nancy, Nancy!
Strength to bear it will be given,
    My spouse Nancy.'

'Well, sir, from the silent dead,
    Still I'll try to daunt you:
Ever round your midnight bed
    Horrid sprites shall haunt you!'
'I'll wed another like my dear
    Nancy, Nancy!
Then all Hell will fly for fear,
    My spouse Nancy!'

TO MISS GRAHAM OF FINTRY

Anne Graham (d. 1852) was the eldest daughter of
Robert Graham of Fintry, the poet's patron in the
Excise. These lines accompanied a copy of A Select
Collection of Scottish Airs which Burns sent to her
on 31st January 1794.

Here, where the Scottish Muse immortal lives,
   In sacred strains and tuneful numbers join'd,
Accept the gift! Though humble he who gives,
   Rich is the tribute of the grateful mind.

So may no ruffian feeling in thy breast,
   Discordant, jar thy bosom-chords among!
But Peace attune thy gentle soul to rest,
   Or love ecstatic wake his seraph song!

Or Pity's notes in luxury of tears,
   As modest Want the tale of woe reveals;
While conscious Virtue all the strains endears,
   And heaven-born Piety her sanction seals!

MONODY

ON A LADY FAMED FOR HER CAPRICE

Maria Riddell rebuked Burns for his outrageous
behaviour at Friars' Carse in December 1793 and the
rift between them was confirmed by her letter to him
on 12th January 1794, as a result of which Burns
composed this tasteless libel. In a letter to Clarinda in
June 1794 he described the subject of this poem as
'a woman of fashion in this country, with whom, at
one period, I was well acquainted. By some scandalous
conduct to me ... she steered so far to the north of my
good opinion, that I have made her the theme of several
ill natured things.' The 'scandalous conduct' was her
temerity in rebuking Burns!

How cold is that bosom which Folly once fired!
   How pale is that cheek where the rouge lately glisten'd!
How silent that tongue which the echoes oft tired!
   How dull is that ear which to flatt'ry so listen'd!

If sorrow and anguish their exit await,
   From friendship and dearest affection remov'd,
How doubly severer, Maria, thy fate!
   Thou diedst unwept, as thou livedst unlov'd.

Loves, Graces, and Virtues, I call not on you:
   So shy, grave, and distant, ye shed not a tear.
But come, all ye offspring of Folly so true,
   And flowers let us cull for Maria's cold bier!

We'll search through the garden for each silly flower,
   We'll roam thro' the forest for each idle weed,
But chiefly the nettle, so typical, shower,
   For none e'er approach'd her but rued the rash deed.

511

Monody

We'll sculpture the marble, we'll measure the lay:
    Here Vanity strums on her idiot lyre!
There keen Indignation shall dart on his prey,
    Which spurning Contempt shall redeem from his ire!

THE EPITAPH

Here lies, now a prey to insulting neglect,
    What once was a butterfly, gay in life's beam:
Want only of wisdom denied her respect,
    Want only of goodness denied her esteem.

WILT THOU BE MY DEARIE?

TUNE: *The Sutor's Dochter*

First published in the Morning Chronicle on 10th May
1794, though written earlier. Patrick Miller Jr. of
Dalswinton had offered Burns a position with this
newspaper in April 1794. He declined, but contributed
occasional verses to it.

Wilt thou be my dearie?
When Sorrow wrings thy gentle heart,
O, wilt thou let me cheer thee?
By the treasure of my soul—
    That's the love I bear thee—
I swear and vow that only thou
    Shall ever be my dearie!
Only thou, I swear and vow,
    Shall ever be my dearie!

Lassie, say thou lo'es me,
Or, if thou wilt na be my ain,
    Say na thou'lt refuse me!
If it winna, canna be,
    Thou for thine may choose me,
Let me, lassie, quickly die,
    Trusting that thou lo'es me!
Lassie, let me quickly die,
    Trusting that thou lo'es me!

KIRK ALLOWAY

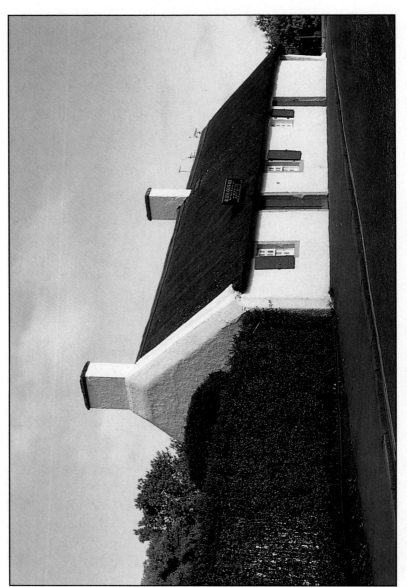

BURNS COTTAGE, ALLOWAY

SONNET ON THE DEATH OF
ROBERT RIDDELL

OF GLENRIDDELL AND FRIARS' CARSE

Although estranged from the Riddell family after the 'Sabine Women' incident, Burns was moved by the sudden death of Robert Riddell, on 20th April 1794, to write this sonnet — 'a small heart-felt tribute to the memory of the man I loved.'

No more, ye warblers of the wood, no more,
  Nor pour your descant grating on my soul!
  Thou young-eyed Spring, gay in thy verdant stole,
More welcome were to me grim Winter's wildest roar!

How can ye charm, ye flowers, with all your dyes?
  Ye blow upon the sod that wraps my friend.
  How can I to the tuneful strain attend?
That strain flows round the untimely tomb where Riddell lies.

Yes, pour, ye warblers, pour the notes of woe,
  And sooth the Virtues weeping o'er his bier!
  The man of worth—and 'hath not left his peer'!—
Is in his 'narrow house,' for ever darkly low.

Thee, Spring, again with joy shall others greet;
Me, memory of my loss will only meet.

INSCRIPTION AT FRIARS' CARSE
HERMITAGE

TO THE MEMORY OF ROBERT RIDDELL

Alleged to have been inscribed on the window of the Hermitage on Burns's first visit there after the death of Robert Riddell.

To Riddell, much lamented man,
  This ivied cot was dear:
Wand'rer, dost value matchless worth?
  This ivied cot revere.

HERE IS THE GLEN

Sent to Thomson about May 1794 with a letter describing how Burns 'got an air, pretty enough composed by Lady Elizabeth Heron of Heron . . . Cree is a beautiful romantic stream; and as her Ladyship is a particular friend of mine, I have written the following song to it.' Lady Elizabeth (1745-1811) was a daughter of the Earl of Dundonald and married Patrick Heron. The Cree forms the western boundary of Kirkcudbrightshire.

Here is the glen, and here the bower
  All underneath the birchen shade,
The village-bell has toll'd the hour—
  O, what can stay my lovely maid?

513

S

'Tis not Maria's whispering call—
  'Tis but the balmy-breathing gale,
Mixed with some warbler's dying fall
  The dewy star of eve to hail!

It is Maria's voice I hear—
  So calls the woodlark in the grove
His little faithful mate to cheer:
  At once 'tis music and 'tis love!

And art thou come? And art thou true?
  O, welcome, dear, to love and me,
And let us all our vows renew
  Along the flowery banks of Cree!

PINNED TO MRS. WALTER RIDDELL'S CARRIAGE

Offered to Patrick Miller as a contribution to the Morning Chronicle. Burns subsequently inserted these scurrilous lines in the Glenriddell MS after Elizabeth Riddell had returned the collection at Burns's request.

If you rattle along like your mistress's tongue,
  Your speed will out-rival the dart;
But, a fly for your load, you'll break down on the road,
  If your stuff be as rotten's her heart.

ON HEARING IT ASSERTED FALSEHOOD

IS EXPRESSED IN THE REV. DR. BABINGTON'S VERY LOOKS

William Babington (1746-1818), a native of Ireland, became priest of the Episcopal Congregation of Dumfries in 1772 and a D.D. of Trinity College, Dublin in 1781. Burns had a twinkle in his eye when he composed this epigram as Dr. Babington was a much-loved member of the community: Chairman of Dumfries and Galloway Infirmary for 28 years. Syme, Bushby, McMurdo and De Peyster were close friends and members of his congregation.

That there is a falsehood in his looks
  I must and will deny:
They tell their Master is a knave,
  And sure they do not lie.

YE TRUE LOYAL NATIVES

A conservative political club formed on 18th January
1793 for 'Supporting the Laws and Constitution of the
Country.' Some verses attacking Burns and his friends
John Syme, Dr James Maxwell and James Mundell were
composed by a club member and circulated in Dumfries.
This was Burns's riposte.

Ye true 'Loyal Natives' attend to my song:
In uproar and riot rejoice the night long!
From Envy and Hatred your core is exempt,
But where is your shield from the darts of Contempt?

ODE FOR GENERAL WASHINGTON'S
BIRTHDAY

George Washington was born in Virginia on 22nd
February 1732, but the first draft of this ode was
composed about 25th June 1794 and sent to Mrs
Dunlop from Castle Douglas during Burns's visit to
Galloway. Washington, recently entered on his second
term as president of the United States, was merely
the pretext for this ode whose subject was Liberty—
'. . . how dear the theme is to me.'

No Spartan tube, no Attic shell,
　No lyre Æolian I awake.
'Tis Liberty's bold note I swell:
　Thy harp, Columbia, let me take!　　　　　　i.e. America
See gathering thousands, while I sing,
A broken chain, exulting, bring
　And dash it in a tyrant's face,
And dare him to his very beard,
And tell him he no more is fear'd,
　No more the despot of Columbia's race!
A tyrant's proudest insults brav'd,
They shout a People freed! They hail an Empire sav'd!

Where is man's godlike form?
　Where is that brow erect and bold,
　That eye that can unmov'd behold
The wildest rage, the loudest storm
That e'er created Fury dared to raise?
Avaunt! thou caitiff, servile, base,
That tremblest at a despot's nod,
Yet, crouching under the iron rod,
Canst laud the arm that struck th' insulting blow!
Art thou of man's Imperial line?
Dost boast that countenance divine?
　Each skulking feature answers: No!
But come, ye sons of Liberty,
Columbia's offspring, brave as free,
In danger's hour still flaming in the van,
Ye know, and dare maintain the Royalty of Man!

515

Ode For General Washington's Birthday

Alfred, on thy starry throne
    Surrounded by the tuneful choir,
    The Bards that erst have stuck the patriot lyre,
    And rous'd the freeborn Briton's soul of fire,
No more thy England own!
Dare injured nations from the great design
    To make detested tyrants bleed?
    Thy England execrates the glorious deed!
    Beneath her hostile banners waving,
    Every pang of honour braving,
England in thunder calls: 'the Tyrant's cause is mine!'

That hour accurst how did the fiends rejoice,
    And Hell thro all her confines raise the exulting voice!
    That hour which saw the generous English name
Link't with such damned deeds of everlasting shame!

Thee, Caledonia, thy wild heaths among,
Fam'd for the martial deed, the heaven-taught song,
    To thee I turn with swimming eyes!
Where is that soul of Freedom fled?
    Immingled with the mighty dead
    Beneath the hallow'd turf where Wallace lies!
Hear it not, Wallace, in thy bed of death!
    Ye babbling winds, in silences weep!
    Disturb not ye the hero's sleep,
Nor give the coward secret breath!
Is this the ancient Caledonian form,
Firm as the rock, resistless as her storm?
Show me that eye which shot immortal hate,
    Blasting the Despot's proudest bearing!
Show me that arm which, nerv'd with thundering fate,
    Crush'd Usurpation's boldest daring!
Dark-quench'd as yonder sinking star,
No more that glance lightens afar,
That palsied arm no more whirls on the waste of war.

EPITAPH FOR MR. WALTER RIDDELL

Walter Riddell (1764-1802), younger brother of
Robert Riddell, inherited estates in Antigua from his
first wife Ann Doig (d. 1788) and married Maria
Woodley in 1790. Burns always had a poor opinion of
Maria's husband, who incurred some of his spleen when
Maria sided with the Riddells over the 'Sabine Rape'
incident.

So vile was poor Wat, such a miscreant slave,
That the worms ev'n damn'd him when laid in his grave
'In his scull there's a famine' a starved reptile cries,
'And his heart it is poison!' another replies.

516

MY LUVE IS LIKE A RED, RED ROSE

This is an amalgam of several old ballads and illustrates
Burns's genius for reworking folk material and producing
a poetic gem of the first rank. It was first published by
Pietro Urbani in April 1794.

O, my luve is like a red, red rose,
That's newly sprung in June.
O, my luve is like the melodie,
That's sweetly play'd in tune.

As fair art thou, my bonie lass,
So deep in luve am I,
And I will luve thee still, my dear,
Till a' the seas gang dry.

Till a' the seas gang dry, my dear,
And the rocks melt wi the sun!
And I will luve thee still, my dear,
While the sands o life shall run.

And fare thee weel, my only luve!
And fare thee weel, a while!
And I will come again, my luve,
Tho it were ten thousand mile!

ON THE SEAS AND FAR AWAY

TUNE: *O'er the hills and far away*

The quality of this song is uneven and Thomson was
very critical of it. Burns later withdrew it with the
comment 'Making a poem is like begetting a son; you
cannot know whether you have a wise man or a fool,
untill you produce him to the world and try him.'

CHORUS

On the seas and far away,
On stormy seas and far away—
Nightly dreams and thoughts by day,
Are ay with him that's far away.

How can my poor heart be glad
When absent from my sailor lad?
How can I the thought forego—
He's on the seas to meet the foe?
Let me wander, let me rove,
Still my heart is with my love.
Nightly dreams, and thoughts by day,
Are with him that's far away.

On The Seas And Far Away

When in summer noon I faint,
As weary flocks around me pant,
Haply in this scorching sun
My sailor's thund'ring at his gun.
Bullets, spare my only joy!
Bullets, spare my darling boy!
Fate, do with me what you may,
Spare but him that's far away!
   On the seas and far away,
   On stormy seas and far away—
   Fate, do with me what you may,
   Spare but him that's far away!

At the starless, midnight hour
When Winter rules with boundless power,
As the storms the forests tear,
And thunders rend the howling air,
Listening to the doubling roar
Surging on the rocky shore,
All I can — I weep and pray
For his weal that's far away.
   On the seas and far away,
   On stormy seas and far away,
   All I can — I weep and pray
   For his weal that's far away.

Peace, thy olive wand extend
And bid wild War his ravage end;
Man with brother-man to meet,
And as a brother kindly greet!
Then may Heav'n with prosperous gales
Fill my sailor's welcome sails,
To my arms their charge convey,
My dear lad that's far away!
   On the seas and far away!
   On stormy seas and far away,
   To my arms their charge convey,
   My dear lad that's far away!

TO DR. MAXWELL

ON MISS JESSIE STAIG'S RECOVERY

Jessie Staig, daughter of the provost of Dumfries, was gravely ill and her own doctor gave her only hours to live. Dr. Maxwell was then called in 'and his prescriptions in a few hours altered her situation, and have now cured her.' (Burns to Mrs. Dunlop, September, 1794). Unhappily, the 'Angel' died in 1801 in her 26th year. William Maxwell (1760-1834), son of James Maxwell of Kirkconnell, was educated by the Jesuits at Dinant and studied medicine in Paris, serving in the National Guard at the execution of Louis XVI. He returned to Scotland and settled in Dumfries in 1794. His 'Jacobinism' endeared him to Burns and they became close friends. He attended the poet during his final illness.

Maxwell, if merit here you crave,
 That merit I deny:
You save fair Jessie from the grave!—
 An Angel could not die!

CA' THE YOWES TO THE KNOWES

(Second Version)

The first version had been sent to SMM but Burns was not satisfied with it. Writing to Thomson in September 1794 Burns said 'In a solitary stroll which I took today, I tried my hand on a few pastoral lines. . . Here it is, with all its crudities and imperfections on its head.' The 'Clouden' is a tributary of the Nith and the 'silent towers' are the ruins of Lincluden Abbey.

CHORUS

Ca' the yowes to the knowes,   ewes, knolls
Ca' them where the heather grows,
Ca' them where the burnie rowes,   streamlet
 My bonie dearie.

Hark, the mavis e'ening sang   thrush
Sounding Clouden's woods amang
Then a-faulding let us gang,
 My bonie dearie.

We'll gae down by Clouden side,   go
Thro the hazels, spreading wide
O'er the waves that sweetly glide
 To the moon sae clearly.

Yonder Clouden's silent towers
Where, at moonshine's midnight hours,
O'er the dewy bending flowers
 Fairies dance sae cheery.

Ghaist nor bogle shalt thou fear—   Ghost, demon
Thou'rt to Love and Heav'n sae dear
Nocht of ill may come thee near,
 My bonie dearie.

519

SAE FLAXEN WERE HER RINGLETS

TUNE: *Oonagh's Waterfall*

The 'blackguard Irish song' which 'Our friend Cunning-
ham sings delightfully' was a urolagniac piece of
bawdry in the Merry Muses. 'The air is charming, and
I have often regretted the want of decent verses to it,'
wrote Burns to Thomson in September 1794, sub-
mitting these lines dedicated to Chloris.

Sae flaxen were her ringlets,
  Her eyebrows of a darker hue,
Bewitching o'er-arching
  Twa laughing een o bonie blue.
Her smiling, sae wyling,
  Wad make a wretch forget his woe!
What pleasure, what treasure,
  Unto those rosy lips to grow!
Such was my Chloris' bonie face,
  When first that bonie face I saw,
And ay my Chloris' dearest charm—
  She says she lo'es me best of a'!

Like harmony her motion,
  Her pretty ankle is a spy
Betraying fair proportion
  Wad make a saint forget the sky!
Sae warming, sae charming,
  Her faultless form and gracefu air,
Ilk feature—auld Nature
do no more   Declar'd that she could dae nae mair!
Hers are the willing chains o love
  By conquering beauty's sovereign law,
And ay my Chloris' dearest charm—
  She says she lo'es me best of a'.

Let others love the city,
  And gaudy show at sunny noon!
Gie me the lonely valley,
  The dewy eve, and rising moon,
Fair beaming, and streaming
  Her silver light the boughs amang,
While falling, recalling,
  The amorous thrush concludes his sang!
Then, dearest Chloris, wilt thou rove
  By wimpling burn and leafy shaw,
And hear my vows o truth and love,
  And say thou lo'es me best of a'?

ON A SWEARING COXCOMB

Here cursing, swearing Burton lies,
A buck, a beau, or 'Dem my eyes!'
Who in his life did little good,
And his last words were, 'Dem my blood!'

ON A SUICIDE

Alexander Cunningham says that the subject of these
lines was 'a melancholy person of the name of Glen-
dinning', buried near Dumfries. Dr. Copland Hutchison
claimed to have seen Burns write this epitaph and push
the paper into the earth over the grave.

Here lies in earth a root of Hell,
  Set by the Deil's ain dibble;   planting-stick
This worthless body damned himsel,
  To save the Lord the trouble.

ON AN INNKEEPER NICKNAMED
'THE MARQUIS'

According to Cunningham, 'This personage was landlord
of a respectable public-house in Dumfries. . . and the
little court or alley where his change-house stood is
still called "The Marquis's Close".'

Here lies a mock Marquis, whose titles were shamm'd,
If ever he rise, it will be to be damn'd.

ON JOHN BUSHBY, ESQ., TINWALD
DOWNS

Legend has it that Burns and Bushby were good friends
but fell out when Burns was scalded by a very hot
pudding which Bushby jokingly claimed was cold.
Thereafter Burns satirised him and his friends in 'John
Bushby's Lamentation' and this mock-epitaph.

Here lies John Bushby — honest man,
Cheat him, Devil — if you can!

ON CAPTAIN LASCELLES

Edward Lascelles (1740-1820) was M.P. for
Northallerton (1761-74) but on losing his seat entered
the Army and eventually rose to the rank of colonel.
He regained his seat in 1790 and became 1st Earl of
Harewood in 1812.

When Lascelles thought fit from this world to depart
Some friends warmly thought of embalming his heart.
A bystander whispers — 'Pray don't make so much o't—
The subject is poison, no reptile will touch it.'

ON WM. GRAHAM, ESQ., OF MOSSKNOWE

William Graham (1756-1832) married Grace Gordon, grand-daughter of the Earl of Aboyne and was laird of Mossknowe, between Annan and Ecclefechan.

'Stop, thief!' Dame Nature call'd to Death,
As Willie drew his latest breath:
'How shall I make a fool again?
My choicest model thou hast ta'en.'

EPIGRAM AT BROWNHILL INN

William Stewart's sister Catherine was the wife of Mr. Bacon, the landlord of the inn at Brownhill about five miles north of Ellisland, hence this punning epigram which was preserved by an English commercial traveller named Ladyman who dined with Burns at this inn.

At Brownhill we always get dainty good cheer
And plenty of bacon each day in the year;
We've a' thing that's nice, and mostly in season,
But why always bacon — come, tell me the reason?

YOU'RE WELCOME, WILLIE STEWART

William Stewart (1749-1812) was the son of the publican at Closeburn, Dumfriesshire and father of 'lovely Polly Stewart'. Burns often visited him on Excise duties and engraved these lines on a crystal tumbler. 'The landlady [Stewart's mother] being very wroth at what she considered the disfigurement of her glass, a gentleman present appeased her by paying down a shilling, and carried off the relic.' This engraved glass was eventually acquired by Sir Walter Scott and is now on display at Abbotsford.

CHORUS
You're welcome, Willie Stewart!
You're welcome, Willie Stewart!
There's ne'er a flower that blooms in May,
That's half sae welcome's thou art!

Come, bumpers high! express your joy!
The bowl we maun renew it—
The tappet hen, gae bring her ben,
To welcome Willie Stewart!

May foes be strong, and friends be slack!
Ilk action, may he rue it!
May woman on him turn her back,
That wrangs thee, Willie Stewart!

must
6-pint pewter vessel

Each

522

LOVELY POLLY STEWART

TUNE: *Ye're welcome, Charlie Stewart*

Polly Stewart (1775-1847) was daughter of William Stewart, factor of Closeburn Estate, Dumfriesshire. She had an erratic life, first marrying her cousin, by whom she had three sons. When he absconded she contracted a 'quasimatrimonial alliance' with a farmer George Welsh (great uncle of Jane Welsh Carlyle). She left him in 1806, went off with a Swiss soldier called Fleitz and wandered all over Europe, before dying in Florence.

CHORUS

O lovely Polly Stewart,
 O charming Polly Stewart,
There's ne'er a flower that blooms in May,
 That's half so fair as thou art!

The flower it blaws, it fades, it fa's,
 And art can ne'er renew it;
But Worth and Truth, eternal youth
 Will gie to Polly Stewart!

May he whase arms shall fauld thy charms
 Possess a leal and true heart!
To him be given to ken the heaven
 He grasps in Polly Stewart!

O, SAW YOU MY DEAR, MY PHILLY

TUNE: *When she cam ben she bobbet*

Composed as a variant of 'My Eppie McNab', and submitted to Thomson in the autumn of 1794.

O, saw ye my Dear, my Philly?
O, saw ye my Dear, my Philly?
She's down i' the grove, she's wi a new love,
She winna come hame to her Willy.

What says she my Dear, my Philly?
What says she my Dear, my Philly?
She lets thee to wit she has thee forgot,
And for ever disowns thee, her Willy.

O, had I ne'er seen thee, my Philly!
O, had I ne'er seen thee, my Philly!
As light as the air, and fause as thou's fair,
Thou's broken the heart o thy Willy.

false

523

HOW LANG AND DREARY IS THE NIGHT

TUNE: *Cauld Kail*

'I met with some such words in a Collection of songs
somewhere, which I altered and enlarged, and to please
you and to suit your favourite air . . . I have taken a
stride or two across my room, and have arranged it
anew . . .' (to Thomson, 19th October 1794)

CHORUS

For O, her lanely nights are lang,
And O, her dreams are eerie,
And O, her widow'd heart is sair,
That's absent frae her dearie!

How lang and dreary is the night,
   When I am frae my dearie!
I restless lie frae e'en to morn,
   Tho I were ne'er sae weary:

When I think on the lightsome days
   I spent wi thee, my dearie,
And now what seas between us roar,
   How can I be but eerie?

How slow ye move, ye heavy hours,
   The joyless day how dreary!
It was na sae ye glinted by,
   When I was with my dearie!

Marginal glosses: from, evening — fearful — glanced

HOW LONG AND DREARY IS THE NIGHT

Second Version

How long and dreary is the night,
   When I am frae my dearie!
I sleepless lie frae e'en to morn,
   Tho I were ne'er sae weary:
I sleepless lie frae e'en to morn,
   Tho I were ne'er sae weary!

When I think on the happy days
   I spent wi you, my dearie:
And now what lands between us lie,
   How can I be but eerie?
And now what lands between us lie,
   How can I be but eerie?

How slow ye move, ye heavy hours,
   As ye were wae and weary!
It was na sae — ye glinted by,
   When I was wi my dearie!
It was na sae — ye glinted by,
   When I was wi my dearie!

524

LET NOT WOMEN E'ER COMPLAIN

TUNE: *Duncan Gray*

Sent to Thomson on 19th October 1794 in response
to the demand for 'English songs' to old Scottish airs.
'These English songs gravel me to death. I have not
that command of the language that I have of my
native tongue,' wrote Burns, self-deprecatingly.

Let not women e'er complain
    Of inconstancy in love!
Let not women e'er complain
    Fickle man is apt to rove!
Look abroad thro Nature's range,
Nature's mighty law is change:
Ladies, would it not seem strange
    Man should then a monster prove?

Mark the winds, and mark the skies,
    Ocean's ebb and ocean's flow.
Sun and moon but set to rise,
    Round and round the seasons go.
Why then ask of silly man
To oppose great Nature's plan?
We'll be constant, while we can—
    You can be no more, you know!

THE WINTER OF LIFE

Sent to Thomson on 19th October as verses to 'a
Musical curiosity — an East Indian air, which you
would swear was a Scottish one.'

But lately seen in gladsome green,
    The woods rejoiced the day;
Thro gentle showers, the laughing flowers
    In double pride were gay;
But now our joys are fled
    On winter blasts awa,
Yet maiden May in rich array,
    Again shall bring them a'.

But my white pow — nae kindly thowe   pate
    Shall melt the snaws of Age!
My trunk of eild, but buss and bield,   eld, bush, shelter
    Sinks in Time's wintry rage.
O, Age has weary days
    And nights o sleepless pain!
Thou golden time o youthfu prime,
    Why comes thou not again?

SLEEP'ST THOU

TUNE: *Deil tak the wars*

'I have been out in the country, taking dinner with a
friend where I met with [Chloris]... As usual, I got
into song; and returning home, I composed the
following...' (Burns to Thomson, 19th October 1794).

wakest   Sleep'st thou, or wauk'st thou, fairest creature?
          Rosy Morn now lifts his eye,
each   Numbering ilka bud, which Nature
          Waters wi the tears o joy.
          Now to the streaming fountain
          Or up the heathy mountain
     The hart, hind, and roe, freely, wildly-wanton stray;
          In twining hazel bowers,
          His lay the linnet pours,
lark   The laverock to the sky
          Ascends, wi sangs o joy.
     While the sun and thou arise to bless the day!

     Phoebus, gliding the brow of morning,
          Banishes ilk darksome shade,
     Nature, gladdening and adorning:
          Such to me my lovely maid!
          When frae my Chloris parted,
          Sad, cheerless, broken-hearted,
     The night's gloomy shades, cloudy, dark, o'ercast my sky;
          But when she charms my sight
          In pride of Beauty's light,
          When thro my very heart
          Her beaming glories dart,
     'Tis then — 'tis then I wake to life and joy!

ON SEEING MRS. KEMBLE IN YARICO

George Colman's drama Yarico, first performed in 1787,
centred on the love affair of an English merchant, Inkle,
and a beautiful savage, here played by Mrs. Stephen
Kemble (1763-1841) at Dumfries in October 1794. The
allusion in the last line is to Moses striking the rock of
Horeb to give water to the Israelites.

Kemble, thou cur'st my unbelief
     Of Moses and his rod:
At Yarico's sweet notes of grief
     The rock with tears had flow'd.

TO THE HONORABLE MR. R. MAULE
OF PANMURE, ON HIS HIGH PHAETON

This epigram was sent to Mrs. Dunlop on 29th October 1794 and was provoked by the activities of the Caledonian Hunt in Dumfries, in particular the spectacle of William Ramsay Maule (1771-1852), Earl of Panmure, 'driving away in his fine and elegant Phaeton on the Race Ground at Tinwald Downs October '94.' Despite this epigram Lord Panmure settled an annuity of £60 on Jean Armour in 1817.

Thou fool, in the Phaeton towering,
    Art proud when that Phaeton's praised?
This the pride of a Thief's exhibition
    When higher his pillory's rais'd.

THE CHARMING MONTH OF MAY
TUNE: *Daintie Davie*

A reworking, in English, of an old Scottish ballad in The Tea-Table Miscellany, sent to Thomson in November 1794.

CHORUS

Lovely was she by the dawn,
    Youthful Chloe, charming Chloe,
Tripping o'er the pearly lawn,
    The youthful, charming Chloe!

It was the charming month of May,
When all the flow'rs were fresh and gay,
One morning, by the break of day,
    The youthful, charming Chloe,
From peaceful slumber she arose,
Girt on her mantle and her hose,
And o'er the flow'ry mead she goes—
    The youthful, charming Chloe!

The feather'd people you might see
Perch'd all around on every tree!
In notes of sweetest melody
    They hail the charming Chloe,
Till, painting gay the eastern skies,
The glorious sun began to rise,
Outrival'd by the radiant eyes
    Of youthful, charming Chloe.

LASSIE WI THE LINT-WHITE LOCKS

TUNE: *Rothiemurchie's Rant*

Sent to Thomson in November 1794, who commented
that he would 'scarcely conceive a woman to be a
beauty, on reading that she had lint-white locks!' Despite
the mention of Cynthia (1.17) this song was written for
Jean Lorimer.

CHORUS
Lassie wi the lint-white locks,
Bonie lassie, artless lassie,

tend
Wilt thou wi me tent the flocks—
Wilt thou be my dearie, O?

clothes, meadow
Now Nature cleeds the flowery lea,
And a' is young and sweet like thee,
O, wilt thou share its joys wi me,
And say thou'lt be my dearie, O?

meandering brook
The primrose bank, the wimpling burn,
The cuckoo on the milk-white thorn,
The wanton lambs at early morn
Shall welcome thee, my dearie, O.

each
And when the welcome simmer shower
Has cheer'd ilk drooping little flower,
We'll to the breathing woodbine-bower
At sultry noon, my dearie, O.

the moon
When Cynthia lights wi silver ray
The weary shearer's hameward way,
Thro yellow waving fields we'll stray,
And talk o love, my dearie, O.

And when the howling wintry blast
Disturbs my lassie's midnight rest,
Enclasped to my faithfu breast,
I'll comfort thee, my dearie, O.

AH, CHLORIS

TUNE: *Major Graham*

Burns took the opening line of Sedley's song 'Ah,
Chloris, cou'd I now but sit' and provided new
words for Jean Lorimer.

Ah, Chloris, since it may not be
That thou of love wilt hear,
If from the lover thou maun flee,
Yet let the friend be dear!

Altho I love my Chloris mair
Than ever tongue could tell,
My passion I will ne'er declare—
I'll say I wish thee well.

Ah, Chloris

Tho a' my daily care thou art,
And a' my nightly dream,
I'll hide the struggle in my heart,
And say it is esteem.

PHILLY AND WILLY

TUNE: *The Sow's tail to Geordie*

These verses were meant 'to be in the alternate way of
a lover and his Mistress chanting together.' He had
intended to use Thomson's name, but dropped the idea
as 'Geordie' was already associated with the bawdy
ballad whose tune he borrowed. Thomson thought his
wife's name Katherine was unpoetical anyway — so Willy
and Philly were substituted.

CHORUS

HE AND SHE
For a' the joys that gowd can gie,
I dinna care a single flie!
The lad/lass I love's the lad/lass for me,
And that's my ain dear Willy/Philly

HE
O Philly, happy be that day,
When roving thro the gather'd hay,
My youthfu heart was stown away,
And by thy charms, my Philly!

SHE
O Willy, ay I bless the grove
When first I own'd my maiden love
Whilst thou did pledge the Powers above,
To be my ain dear Willy.

HE
As songsters of the early year
Are ilka day mair sweet to hear,   every
So ilka day to me mair dear
And charming is my Philly.

SHE
As on the brier the budding rose
Still richer breathes and fairer blows,
So in my tender bosom grows
The love I bear my Willy.

HE
The milder sun and bluer sky,
That crown my harvest cares wi joy,
Were ne'er sae welcome to my eye
As is a sight o Philly.

529

Philly and Willy

	SHE	The little swallow's wanton wing,
		Tho wafting o'er the flowery spring,
such		Did ne'er to me sic tidings bring
		As meeting o my Willy.

HE   The bee that thro the sunny hour
Sips nectar in the op'ning flower,
Compar'd wi my delight is poor
    Upon the lips o Philly

SHE   The woodbine in the dewy weet,
When ev'ning shades in silence meet
Is nocht sae fragrant or sae sweet
    As is a kiss o Willy.

HE   Let Fortune's wheel at random rin,
lose   And fools may tyne, and knaves may win,
My thoughts are a' bound up on ane,
    And that's my ain dear Philly.

gold SHE What's a' the joys that gowd can gie?
I dinna care a single flie!
The lad I love's the lad for me,
    And that's my ain dear Willy.

CANST THOU LEAVE ME THUS, MY KATIE?

TUNE: *Roy's Wife*

This song, composed during the night of 19th-20th
November 1794 and sent to Thomson the following
morning may have been intended as a compliment to
Thomson's wife, though in one version 'Betty' was
substituted, leading some editors improbably to link
the song with Elizabeth Riddell.

CHORUS

Canst thou leave me thus, my Katie!
   Canst thou leave me thus, my Katie!
Well thou know'st my aching heart,
   And canst thou leave me thus, for pity?

Is this thy plighted, fond regard:
   Thus cruelly to part, my Katie?
Is this thy faithful swain's reward:
   An aching broken heart, my Katie?

Farewell! And ne'er such sorrows tear
   That fickle heart of thine, my Katie!
Thou may'st find those will love thee dear,
   But not a love like mine, my Katie.

BEHOLD, MY LOVE, HOW GREEN THE GROVES

TUNE: *My lodging is on the cold ground*

Sent to Thomson in November 1794 and allegedly written for Chloris.

Behold, my love, how green the groves,
   The primrose banks how fair;
The balmy gales awake the flowers,
   and wave thy flowing hair.

The lav'rock shuns the palace gay,   lark
   And o'er the cottage sings:
For Nature smiles as sweet, I ween,
   To Shepherds as to Kings.

Let minstrels sweep the skilfu strings,
   In lordly lighted ha':
The Shepherd stops his simple reed,
   Blythe in the birken shaw.   birch wood

The Princely revel may survey
   Our rustic dance wi scorn;
But are their hearts as light as ours,
   Beneath the milk-white thorn?

The shepherd, in the flowery glen;
   In shepherd's phrase, will woo:
The courtier tells a finer tale,
   But is his heart as true?

These wild-wood flowers I've pu'd, to deck
   That spotless breast o thine:
The courtier's gems may witness love,
   But, 'tis na love like mine.

CONTENTED WI LITTLE AND CANTIE WI MAIR

TUNE: *Lumps o Puddins*

Composed on 18th November 1794, this song was regarded by Burns as a self-portrait and when he sat to Alexander Reid the following summer for his portrait miniature, he had some idea of linking it to this song 'in order that the portrait of my face and the picture of my mind may go down the stream of Time together.'

Contented wi little, and cantie wi mair,   joyful
Whene'er I forgather wi Sorrow and Care,
I gie them a skelp, as they're creepin alang,   smack
Wi a cog o guid swats and an auld Scottish sang.   cup, ale

Contented Wi Little And Cantie Wi Mair

clasp
soldier, fight

dare

I whyles claw the elbow o troublesome Thought;
But Man is a soger, and Life is a faught.
My mirth and guid humour are coin in my pouch,
And my Freedom's my lairdship nae monarch daur touch.

twelvemonth
shoulders

A towmond o trouble, should that be my fa',
A night o guid fellowship sowthers it a':
When at the blythe end o our journey at last,
Wha the Deil ever thinks o the road he has past?

stumble, stagger
go

Blind Chance, let her snapper and stoyte on her way;
Be't to me, be't frae me, e'en let the jade gae!
Come Ease, or come Travail, come Pleasure or Pain,
My warst word is:— 'Welcome, and welcome again!'

MY NANIE'S AWA

TUNE: *There'll never be peace till Jamie comes hame*

Sent to Thomson on 9th December 1794.

hillsides
every, wood

Now in her green mantle blythe Nature arrays,
And listens the lambkins that bleat o'er the braes,
While birds warble welcome in ilka green shaw,
But to me it's delightless — my Nanie's awa.

The snawdrap and primrose our woodlands adorn,
And violets bathe in the weet o the morn,
They pain my sad bosom, sae sweetly they blaw;
They mind me o Nanie — and Nanie's awa!

lark

Thou lav'rock that springs frae the dews of the lawn
The shepherd to warm o the grey-breaking dawn,
And thou mellow mavis, that hails the night-fa',
Give over for pity — my Nanie's awa.

Come Autumn, sae pensive in yellow and grey,
And soothe me wi tidings o Nature's decay!
The dark, dreary Winter, and wild-driving snaw
Alane can delight me — now Nanie's awa.

DUMFRIES EPIGRAMS

This group of epigrams, dating from 1794-5, survives only in the transcript of John Syme of Ryedale.

The subject of this is not known but could be William Copland of Collieston, mentioned in the Second Election Ballad.

C———d faithful likeness, friend Painter,
  would'st seize?
Keep out Worth, Wit and Wisdom: Put in what
  you please.

The only lady who fits this description was Elizabeth, second daughter of the Rev. William Inglis, minister of the Loreburn Street congregation, whose sermons Burns enjoyed above all others.

Extempore on Miss E.I——, a Lady of a figure indicating amazonian strength.

Should he escape the slaughter of thine Eyes,
Within thy strong Embrace he struggling dies.

The Loyal Natives were formed in January 1793 from among the more reactionary citizens of Dumfries. Their scurrilous verses lampooning Burns and other radicals provoked this response.

To a Club in Dumfries who styled themselves the Dumfries Loyal Natives and exhibited violent party work and intemperate Loyalty. . . 10th June 1794.

Pray, who are these *Natives* the Rabble so ven'rate?
They're our true ancient *Natives*, and they breed
    undegen'rate
The ignorant savage that weather's the storm,
When the *man* and the Brute differed but in the form.

The identity of 'Billy' has mercifully passed into oblivion! Possibly the subject was Captain William Roddick whom Burns satirised in 'Epitaph on a Noted Coxcomb' or William Graham of Mossknowe.

On an old acquaintance who seemed to pass the Bard without notice.

[i]   Dost hang thy head, Billy, asham'd that thou
             knowest me?
         'Tis paying in kind a just debt that thou owest me.

[ii]   Dost blush, my dear Billy, asham'd of thyself,
             A Fool and a Cuckold together?
         The fault is not thine, insignificant elf,
             Thou was not consulted in either.

Commissary Goldie was President of the Loyal Natives and thus raised a special animosity in the poet.

Immediate extempore on being told by W L of the Customs Dublin that Com. Goldie did not seem disposed to push the bottle.

Friend Commissar, since we're met and are happy,
Pray why should we part without having more nappy!   ale
Bring in t'other bottle, for faith I am dry—
Thy drink thou can't part with and neither can I.

Dumfries Epigrams

The subject of this quatrain was Edmund Burke
(1729-97) the celebrated Irish orator and politician.
Warren Hastings' trial for maladministration in India
ended with his acquittal in April 1795.

*On Mr. Burke by an opponent and a friend to Mr.
Hastings*

Oft I have wonder'd that on Irish ground
No poisonous Reptile ever has been found:
Revealed the secret stands of great Nature's work:
She preserved her poison to create a Burke!

James Swan, elected a bailie of Dumfries in 1794, was
re-elected in 1795 but ceased to be a magistrate in
October 1796 and was voted off the Council a year
later, so Burns's prophecy came true.

*At the election of Magistrates for Dumfries, 1794,
John M'Murdo, Esqr., was chosen Provost and a Mr.
Swan one of the Baillies; and at the Entertainment
usually given on the occasion Burns, seeing the
Provost's Supporters on the Bench, took his pencil
and wrote the following.*

Baillie Swan, Baillie Swan,
Let you do what you can,
God ha' mercy on honest Dumfries:
But e'er the year's done,
Good Lord! Provost John
Will find that his *Swans* are but *Geese.*

ON CHLORIS

REQUESTING ME TO GIVE HER A SPRIG OF
BLOSSOMED THORN

At one time these lines were attributed to Charles
Dibdin, but the truth is that Dibdin borrowed Burns's
lines and added a stanza of his own. 'Chloris' was, of
course, Jean Lorimer.

From the white-blossom'd sloe my dear Chloris requested
A sprig, her fair breast to adorn:
No, by Heaven! I exclaim'd, 'let me perish for ever
Ere I plant in that bosom a thorn!'

ODE TO SPRING

TUNE: *The tither morn*

This mock pastoral was sent to Thomson in January
1795 — allegedly composed some years earlier 'when I
was younger, and by no means the saint I am now', as
a wager with a friend that he could compose an Ode to
Spring on an original plan.

When maukin bucks, at early fucks,   buck-hares
 In dewy glens are seen, Sir;
And birds, on boughs, take off their mows, complete, copulation
 Amang the leaves sae green, Sir;
Latona's sun looks liquorish on
Dame Nature's grand impetus,
Till his pego rise, then westward flies
To roger Madam Thetis.

Yon wandering rill that marks the hill,
 And glances o'er the brae, Sir,   hillside
Slides by a bower where many a flower
 Sheds fragrance on the day, Sir;
There Damon lay, with Sylvia gay,
 To love they thought no crime, Sir;
The wild-birds sang, the echoes rang,
 While Damon's arse beat time, Sir.

First wi the thrush, his thrust and push
 Had compass large and long, Sir;
The blackbird next, his tuneful text,
 Was bolder, clear and strong, Sir:
The linnet's lay came then in play,
 And the lark that soar'd aboon, Sir; above
Till Damon, fierce, mistim'd his arse,
 And fuck'd quite out o tune, Sir.

A MAN'S A MAN FOR A' THAT

TUNE: *For a' that*

Sent to Thomson in January 1795. The intense
contempt of rank has made this a revolutionary song
with a central place in the psalmody of radicalism.

Is there for honest poverty
 That hings his head, an a' that?   hangs
The coward slave, we pass him by—
 We dare be poor for a' that!
For a' that, an a' that,
 Our toils obscure, an a' that,
The rank is but the guinea's stamp,
 The man's the gowd for a' that.   gold

535

A Man's A Man For A' That

coarse woollen cloth

What though on hamely fare we dine,
  Wear hoddin grey, an a' that?
Gie fools their skills, and knaves their wine—
  A man's a man for a' that.
For a' that, an a' that,
  Their tinsel show, an a' that,
The honest man, tho e'er sae poor,
  Is king o men for a' that.

fellow

fool

Ye see yon birkie ca'd 'a lord,'
  Wha struts, an stares, an a' that?
Tho hundreds worship at his word,
  He's but a cuif for a' that.
For a' that, an a' that,
  His ribband, star, an a' that,
The man o independent mind,
  He looks an laughs at a' that.

above
must not

A prince can mak a belted knight,
  A marquis, duke, an a' that!
But an honest man's aboon his might—
  Guid faith, he mauna fa' that!
For a' that, an a' that,
  Their dignities, an a' that,
The pith o sense an pride o worth,
  Are higher rank than a' that.

have priority

Then let us pray that come it may
  (As come it will for a' that),
That Sense and Worth o'er a' the earth,
  Shall bear the gree an a' that.
For a' that, an a' that,
  It's comin yet for a' that,
That man to man, the world, o'er
  Shall brithers be for a' that.

CRAIGIEBURN WOOD

(Second Version)

This version was composed in the winter of 1794-5 and sent to Thomson on 15th January 1795.

Sweet fa's the eve on Craigieburn,
  And blythe awakes the morrow
But a' the pride o Spring's return
  Can yield me nocht but sorrow.

I see the flowers and spreading trees,
  I hear the wild birds singing;
But what a weary wight can please,
  And Care his bosom is wringing?

Craigieburn Wood

Fain, fain would I my griefs impart,
　　Yet dare na for your anger;
But secret love will break my heart,
　　If I conceal it langer.
If thou refuse to pity me,
　　If thou shalt love another,
When yon green leaves fade frae the tree,
　　Around my grave they'll wither.

DOES HAUGHTY GAUL INVASION THREAT?

TUNE: *Push about the Jorum*

At the end of January 1795 the Volunteer movement
to raise forces for home defence got under way. Burns
played a prominent part in the formation of the
Dumfries Volunteers. It is probable that Burns wrote
this song in March and it was published in various
newspapers in May. The occasion of the song was the
rumoured invasion of Britain by Napoleon's forces.
Corsincon and Criffel are hills, on the Ayrshire
border and the Stewarty side of the Nith estuary
respectively.

Does haughty Gaul invasion threat?
　　Then let the loons beware, Sir!　　　　　　fools
There's wooden walls upon our seas
　　And volunteers on shore, Sir!
The Nith shall run to Corsincon,
　　And Criffel sink in Solway,
Ere we permit a foreign foe
　　On British ground to rally!

O, let us not, like snarling tykes,　　　　　　dogs
　　In wrangling be divided,
Till, slap! come in an unco loon,　　　　　　uncommon
　　And wi a rung decide it!　　　　　　　　cudgel
Be Britain still to Britain true,
　　Amang ourselves united!
For never but by British hands
　　Maun British wrangs be righted!　　　　　Must

The kettle o the Kirk and State,
　　Perhaps a clout may fail in't;　　　　　　patch
But Deil a foreign tinkler loon
　　Shall ever ca' a nail in't!
Our fathers' blude the kettle bought,
　　And wha wad dare to spoil it,
By Heav'ns! the sacrilegious dog
　　Shall fuel be to boil it!

> The wretch that would a tyrant own,
>   And the wretch, his true-sworn brother,
> Who would set the mob above the throne,
>   May they be damn'd together!
> Who will not sing *God Save the King*
>   Shall hang as high's the steeple;
> But while we sing *God Save the King,*
>   We'll ne'er forget the people!

O, LET ME IN THIS AE NIGHT

Thomson rejected the first draft of this song in August 1793. Burns began again in September 1794 and completed it early in February 1795.

CHORUS

one

> *O, let me in this ae night,*
> *This ae, ae, ae night!*
> *O, let me in this ae night,*
> *And rise, and let me in!*

> O lassie, are ye sleepin yet,

awake

> Or are you waukin, I wad wit?

foot

> For Love has bound me hand an fit,

darling

>   And I would fain be in, jo.

> Thou hear'st the winter wind an weet:

shines

> Nae star blinks thro the driving sleet!
> Tak pity on my weary feet,
>   And shield me frae the rain, jo.

> The bitter blast that round me blaws,
> Unheeded howls, unheeded fa's:
> The cauldness o thy heart's the cause
>   Of a' my care and pine, jo.

HER ANSWER

CHORUS

> *I tell you now this ae night,*
> *This ae, ae, ae night,*
> *And ance for a' this ae night,*
> *I winna let ye in, jo.*

> O, tell na me o wind an rain,
> Upbraid na me wi cauld disdain,

go way

> Gae back the gate ye cam again,
>   I winna let ye in, jo!

bitterest, darkest

> The snellest blast at mirkest hours,
> That round the pathless wand'rer pours
> Is nocht to what poor she endures,
>   That's trusted faithless man, jo.

538

O, Let Me In This Ae Night

The sweetest flower that deck'd the mead,
Now trodden like the vilest weed—
Let simple maid the lesson read!
    The weird may be her ain, jo.

The bird that charm'd his summer day,
And now the cruel fowler's prey,
Let that to witless woman say:—
    'The gratefu heart of man,' jo.

FROM ESOPUS TO MARIA

Esopus (an actor in Imperial Rome) conceals the
identity of James Williamson (d. 1802) manager of a
theatrical company which played occasionally behind
the George Inn, Dumfries. When the company was
playing at Whitehaven, the 'bad Earl of Lonsdale'
imprisoned the entire troupe as vagrants. Burns used
this incident to hit back at Maria Riddell and Lord
Lonsdale. Williamson had, like Burns, been admitted
to the Riddell social circle.

From those drear solitudes and frowsy cells,
Where Infamy with sad Repentance dwells;
Where turnkeys make the jealous portal fast,
And deal from iron hands the spare repast;
Where truant 'prentices, yet young in sin,
Blush at the curious stranger peeping in;
Where strumpets, relics of the drunken roar,
Resolve to drink, nay half—to whore—no more;
Where tiny thieves, not destin'd yet to swing,
Beat hemp for others, riper for the string:
From these dire scenes my wretched lines I date,
To tell Maria her Esopus' fate.

'Alas! I feel I am no actor here!'
'Tis real hangmen real scourges bear!
Prepare, Maria, for a horrid tale
Will turn thy very rouge to deadly pale;
Will make thy hair, tho erst from gipsy poll'd,
By barber woven and by barber sold
Though twisted smooth with Harry's nicest care,
Like hoary bristles to erect and stare!

The hero of the mimic scene, no more
I start in Hamlet, in Othello roar;
Or, haughty Chieftain, 'mid the din of arms,
In Highland bonnet woo Malvina's charms:

539

From Esopus To Maria

nickname of the French
revolutionaries, but here
signifying kilted
Highlanders

While sans-culottes stoop up the mountain high,
And steal me from Maria's prying eye.
Blest Highland bonnet! once my proudest dress,
Now, prouder still, Maria's temples press!
I see her wave thy towering plumes afar,
And call each coxcomb to the wordy war!

I see her face the first of Ireland's sons,
And even out-Irish his Hibernian bronze!

Captain Gillespie
Col. McDougal of Logan,
'a noted Lothario'

The crafty Colonel leaves the tartan'd lines
For other wars, where he a hero shines;

Maitland Bushby (b. 1767)
Sheriff of Wigtownshire

The hopeful youth, in Scottish senate bred,
Who owns a Bushby's heart without the head,
Comes 'mid a string of coxcombs to display
That *Veni, vidi, vici,* is his way;

prison ships

The shrinking Bard adown the alley skulks,
And dreads a meeting worse than Woolwich hulks,
Though there, his heresies in Church and State

Thomas Muir (1765-98)
Thomas Palmer
tried for sedition (1793)
and transported to Australia

Might well award him Muir and Palmer's fate:
Still she, undaunted, reels and rattles on,
And dares the public like a noontide sun.
What scandal called Maria's jaunty stagger
The ricket reeling of a crooked swagger?

Whose spleen (e'en worse than Burns's venom, when
He dips in gall unmix'd his eager pen.
And pours his vengeance in the burning line),
Who christen'd thus Maria's lyre-divine,
The idiot strum of Vanity bemus'd,
And even th' abuse of Poesy abus'd?

a slighting reference to
Maria's own poems

Who called her verse a Parish Workhouse, made
For motley foundling Fancies, stolen or strayed?

A Workhouse! Ah, that sound awakes my woes,
And pillows on the thorn my rack'd repose!
In durance vile here must I wake and weep,
And all my frowsy couch in sorrow steep:
That straw where many a rogue has lain of yore,
And vermin'd gipsies litter'd heretofore.

James Lowther, Earl of
Lonsdale (1736-1802)

Why Lonsdale, thus thy wrath on vagrants pour?
Must earth no rascal save thyself endure?
Must thou alone in guilt immortal swell,
And make a vast monopoly of Hell?
Thou know'st the Virtues cannot hate thee worse:
The Vices also, must they club their curse?
Or must no tiny sin to others fall,
Because thy guilt's supreme enough for all?

540

From Esopus To Maria

Maria, send me too thy griefs and cares,
In all of thee sure thy Esopus shares:
As thou at all mankind the flag unfurls,
Who on my fair one Satire's vengeance hurls!
Who calls thee, pert, affected, vain coquette,
A wit in folly, and a fool in wit!
Who says that fool alone is not thy due,
And quotes thy treacheries to prove it true!

Our force united on thy foes we'll turn,
And dare the war with all of woman born:
For who can write and speak as thou and I?
My periods that decyphering defy,
And thy still matchless tongue that conquers all reply!

EPIGRAM ON MISS JEAN SCOTT

According to local tradition Jeanie Scott was the daughter of the postmaster of Ecclefechan, whom Burns met while detained by a snowstorm in February 1795. He is said to have inscribed these lines on a window-pane.

O had each Scot of ancient times
  Been, Jeanie Scott, as thou art,
The bravest heart on English ground
  Had yielded like a coward.

O, WAT YE WHA'S IN YON TOWN?

TUNE: *I'll gang nae mair to yon town*

Burns was trapped at Ecclefechan by a snowstorm on 7th February 1795, while on Excise duties and whiled away the time working on this song. 'Jean' in this context could be Jean Armour, Jean Lorimer or Jean Scott — see the foregoing, — though later he claimed that the subject of this song was Lucy Johnston, wife of Richard Oswald of Auchencruive.

CHORUS

O, wat ye wha's in yon town   wot
  Ye see the e'enin sun upon?
The dearest maid's in yon town,
  That e'enin sun is shining on!

Now haply down yon gay green shaw   that, wood
  She wanders by yon spreading tree.
How blest ye birds that round her blaw!
  Ye catch the glances o her e'e.

How blest ye birds that round her sing,
  And welcome in the blooming year!
And doubly welcome be the Spring,
  The season to my Jeanie dear!

541

O, Wat Ye Wha's In Yon Town?

slopes

The sun blinks blythe in yon town,
   Among the broomy braes sae green;
But my delight in yon town,
   And dearest pleasure is, my Jean.

Without my Love, not a' the charms
   O Paradise could yield my joy;
But gie me Jeanie in my arms,
   And welcome Lapland's dreary sky!

My cave wad be a lover's bower,
   Tho raging winter rent the air,
And she a lovely little flower,
   That I wad tent and shelter there.

O, sweet is she in yon town
   The sinking sun's gane down upon!
A fairer than's in yon town
   His setting beam ne'er shone upon.

If angry Fate be sworn my foe,
   And suff'ring I am doom'd to bear,
I'd careless quit aught else below,
   But spare, O spare me Jeanie dear!

For, while life's dearest blood is warm,
   Ae thought frae her shall ne'er depart,
And she, as fairest is her form,
   She has the truest, kindest heart.

ON CHLORIS BEING ILL

TUNE: *Ay wauken, O*

Burns and Maria Riddell were reconciled in the spring of 1795 and he sent this song to her in March, and to Thomson a month later, although the subject was Jean Lorimer.

CHORUS
Long, long the night,
   Heavy comes the morrow,
While my soul's delight
   Is on her bed of sorrow.

Can I cease to care,
   Can I cease to languish,
While my darling fair
   Is on the couch of anguish!

Ev'ry hope is fled,
Ev'ry fear is terror;
Slumber ev'n I dread,
Ev'ry dream is horror.

Hear me, Powers Divine:
O, in pity, hear me!
Take aught else of mine,
But my Chloris spare me!

EPITAPH FOR MR. W. CRUIKSHANK

William Cruikshank (d. 1795), a native of Duns,
graduated M.A. Edinburgh University and became
Rector of the High School in the Canongate and, in
1772, Latin master at Edinburgh High School. Burns
first met him in 1786-7, through William Nicol, and
stayed with the Cruikshank family at the end of his
Highland tour. It was for Cruikshank's daughter Jean
that Burns wrote 'The Rosebud'.

Now honest William's gaen to Heaven   gone
I wat na gin't can mend him;   if it
The fauts he had in Latin lay,   faults
For nane in English kent them.   knew

BALLADS ON MR. HERON'S ELECTION, 1795

TUNE: *For a' that*

Patrick Heron (1736-1803) was a partner in Douglas,
Heron & Co, the Ayr bank which failed so disastrously
in 1773. Twenty years later Heron bounced back as
Whig candidate in the Election of 1795. Burns met
him at Kerroughtree, Heron's estate near Creetown, in
June 1794 and helped his Election campaign by
writing four satirical political ballads.

BALLAD FIRST

Wham will we send to London town,
To Parliament and a' that?
Or wha in a' the country round
The best deserves to fa' that?
For a' that, and a' that,
Thro Galloway and a' that,
Where is the Laird or belted Knight
That best deserves to fa' that?

Wha sees Kerroughtree's open yett—
And wha is't never saw that?—
Wha ever wi Kerroughtree met,
And has a doubt of a' that?
For a' that, and a' that,
Here's Heron yet for a' that!
The independent patriot,
The honest man, and a' that!

Tho wit and worth, in either sex,
Saint Mary's Isle can shaw that,
Wi Lords and Dukes let Selkirk mix,
And weel does Selkirk fa' that.
For a' that, and a' that,
Here's Heron yet for a' that!
The independent commoner
Shall be the man for a' that.

But why should we to Nobles jeuk,
And it against the law, that,
And even a Lord may be a gowk,
Wi ribban, star, and a' that?
For a' that, and a' that,
Here's Heron yet for a that!
A Lord may be a lousy loon,
Wi ribban, star, and a' that.

A beardless boy comes o'er the hills
Wi's uncle's purse and a' that;
But we'll hae ane frae 'mang oursels,
A man we ken, and a' that.
For a' that, and a' that,
Here's Heron yet for a' that!
We are na to be bought and sold,
Like nowte, and naigs, and a' that.

Then let us drink:—'The Stewartry,
Kerroughtree's laird, and a' that,
Our representative to be':
For weel he's worthy a' that!
For a' that, and a' that!
Here's Heron yet for a' that!
A House of Commons such as he,
They wad be blest that saw that.

Dunbar Douglas, 4th Earl
of Selkirk (1722-99)

bow

cuckoo

fool

Thomas Gordon of Balmaghie (d. 1806)
James Murray of Broughton (1727-99)

know

cattle, horses

Kirkcudbrightshire

THE BACHELORS' CLUB, TARBOLTON

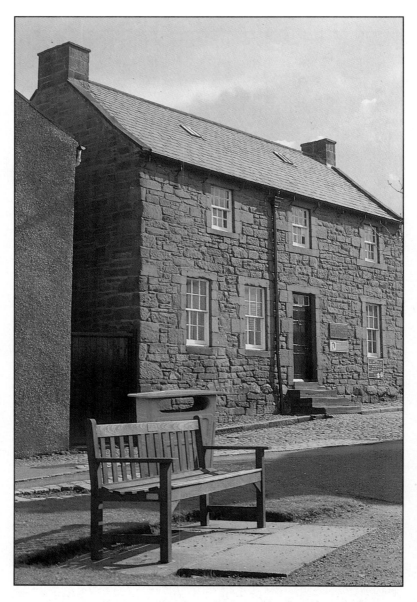

BURNS HOUSE IN THE MILL VENNEL, DUMFRIES
(now Burns Street)

BALLAD SECOND

THE ELECTION

TUNE: *Fy, Let Us A' to The Bridal*

Fy, let us a' to Kirkcudbright,
  For there will be bickerin there;
For Murray's light horse are to muster — Murray of Broughton
An O, how the heroes will swear! — uncle of the Tory candidate
And there will be Murray commander,
  An Gordon the battle to win: — Gordon of Balmaghie
Like brothers, they'll stan' by each other,
  Sae knit in alliance and kin.

An there'll be black-nebbit Johnie, — John Bushby (d. 1802)
  The tongue o the trump to them a': — sheriff-clerk of Dumfries
Gin he get na Hell for his haddin, — If, inheritance
  The Deil gets nae justice ava! — at all
And there'll be Kempleton's birkie, — William Bushby, brother of John
  A boy no sae black at the bane;
But as to his fine nabob fortune— — veiled reference to his wealth
We'll e'en let the subject alane! — acquired in India in questionable
— circumstances

An there'll be Wigton's new sheriff—
  Dame Justice fu brawly has sped:
She's gotten the heart of a Bushby,
  But Lord! what's become o the head?
An there'll be Cardoness, Esquire, — David Maxwell of Cardoness
  Sae mighty in Cardoness' eyes:
A wight that will weather damnation,
  For the Devil the prey would despise.

An there'll be Douglasses doughty, — Sir William Douglas and his
  New christening towns far and near: — brother James; Carlinwark
Abjuring their democrat doings — (now Castle Douglas); Newton
An kissing the arse of a peer! — Stewart (briefly Newton Douglas)
An there'll be Kenmure sae generous, — John Gordon, Viscount Kenmure
  Wha's honor is proof to the storm: — (1750-1840)
To save them from stark reprobation
  He lent them his name to the firm!

But we dinna mention Redcastle, — Walter Lawrie of Redcastle
  The body—e'en let him escape!
He'd venture the gallows for siller, — money
  An 'twere na the cost o the rape! — rope
An whare is our King's Lord Lieutenant, — George Stewart, Lord Garlies
  Sae famed for his gratefu return?
The billie is getting his Questions — fellow
  To say at St. Stephens the morn! — House of Commons

Ballad Second

An there'll be lads of the gospel:
  Muirhead, wha's as guid as he's true;
An there'll be Buittle's Apostle,
  Wha's mair o the black than the blue;
An there'll be folk frae St. Mary's,
  A house o great merit and note:
The Deil ane but honors them highly,
  The Deil ane will gie them his vote!

An there'll be wealthy young Richard,
  Dame Fortune should hang by the neck:
But for prodigal thriftless bestowing,
  His merit had won him respect.
An there'll be rich brither nabobs;
  Tho nabobs, yet men o the first!
An there'll be Collieston's whiskers,
  An Quinton—o lads no the warst!

An there'll be Stamp-Office Johnie:
  Tak tent how ye purchase a dram!
An there'll be gay Cassencarry,
  An there'll be Colonel Tam;
An there'll be trusty Kerroughtree,
  Wha's honour was ever his law:
If the virtues were pack't in a parcel,
  His worth might be sample for a'!

An can we forget the auld Major,
  Wha'll ne'er be forgot in the Greys?
Our flatt'ry we'll keep for some other:
  Him only it's justice to praise!
An there'll be maiden Kilkerran,
  An also Barskimming's guid Knight.
An there'll be roaring Birtwhistle—
  Yet luckily roars in the right!

An there frae the Niddlesdale border
  Will mingle the Maxwells in droves:
Teuch Johnie, Staunch Geordie, and Wattie
  That girns for the fishes an loaves!
An there'll be Logan's McDoual—
  Sculdudd'ry an he will be there!
An also the wild Scot o Galloway,
  Sogering, gunpowther Blair!

Then hey the chaste interest of Broughton.
  An hey for the blessings 'twill bring!
It may send Balmaghie to the Commons—
  In Sodom 'twould mak him a King!
An hey for the sanctified Murray
  Our land wha wi chapels has stor'd;
He founder'd his horse among harlots,
  But gie'd the auld naig to the Lord!

Rev. James Muirhead (1742-1805)
Rev. George Maxwell (1762-1807)

the family of the Earl of Selkirk

Oswald of Auchencruive
(1771-1841)

D & J Anderson of St. Germains

William Copland of Collieston
Quinton McAdam of Craigengillan

John Syme of Ryedale
(1755-1831)
Col. Mackenzie of Cassencarry
Thomas Goldie of Goldielea
Patrick Heron

Major Basil Heron, Patrick's brother

Sir Adam Fergusson of Kilkerran
Sir William Miller of Barskimming
Alexander Birtwhistle, provost
of Kirkcudbright

Maxwells of Terraughty,
Carruchan and the Grove

Andrew McDoual of Logan

Major Blair of Dunskey

546

BALLAD THIRD

JOHN BUSHBY'S LAMENTATION

TUNE: *Babes in the Wood*

John Bushby, was a Dumfries lawyer and sheriff-clerk, formerly a partner of Douglas, Heron & Co. and manager of the Dumfries branch of this ill-fated bank. His brother William, 'the gamesome billie' is alleged to have absconded with some of the bank's funds and used it to build a fortune in India. Bushby was not bothered by these lampoons, though he observed 'that he could not conceive why the poor devil [Burns] had thought proper to run a muck against all those who could best do him a service, and none of whom, as far as he knew, held him at ill will.' The 'lamentation' was for Gordon of Balmaghie who lost the Election.

'Twas in the Seventeen Hunder year
  O grace, and Ninety-Five,
That year I was the wae'est man   saddest
  Of onie man alive.   any

In March the three-an-twentieth morn,
  The sun raise clear an bright;
But O, I was a waefu man,   woeful
  Ere to-fa' o the night!

Yerl Galloway lang did rule this land   Earl
  Wi equal right and fame,
Fast knit in chaste and holy bands,   Lady Euphemia Stewart, the
  With Broughton's noble name.   Earl's daughter, married Alexander
                            Murray of Broughton

Yerl Galloway's man o men was I,
  And chief o Broughton's host:
So twa blind beggars, on a string,
  The faithfu tyke will trust!   dog

But now Yerl Galloway's sceptre's broke,
  And Broughton's wi the slain,
And I my ancient craft may try,   legal profession
  Sin' honesty is gane.

'Twas by the banks o bonie Dee,
  Beside Kirkcudbright's towers,
The Stewart and the Murray there
  Did muster a' their powers.

Then Murray on the auld grey yaud,   mare
  Wi winged spurs did ride:
That auld grey yaud a' Nidsdale rade,
  He staw upon Nidside.   stole

An there had na been the Yerl himsel,
  O, there had been nae play!
But Garlies was to London gane,   the Earl's eldest son
  And say the kye might stray.   cattle

Gordon of Balmaghie

And there was Balmaghie, I ween—
  In front rank he wad shine;
But Balmaghie had better been
  Drinkin Madeira wine.

Viscount Kenmure

And frae Glenkens cam to our aid
  A chief o doughty deed!
In case that worth should wanted be,
  O Kenmure we had need.

Rev. James Muirhead
Rev. George Maxwell

And by our banners march'd Muirhead,
  And Buittle was na slack,
Whase haly priesthood nane could stain,
  For wha could dye the black?

And there was grave squire Cardoness,
  Look'd on till a' was done:
Sae in the tower o Cardoness
  A howlet sits at noon.

comrade

And there I led the Bushby clan:
  My gamesome billie, Will,
And my son Maitland, wise as brave,
  My footsteps follow'd still.

a side-swipe at the
failed bank of 1773

The Douglas and the Heron's name,
  We set nought to their score;
The Douglas and the Heron's name
  Had felt our weight before.

But Douglasses o weight had we,
  The pair o lusty lairds,
For building cot-houses sae fam'd,

cabbage patches

  And christenin kail-yards.

Walter Sloan Lawrie

And then Redcastle drew his sword
  That ne'er was stain'd wi gore,
Save on a wand'rer lame and blind,
  To drive him frae his door.

William Copland

And last cam creepin Collieston,
  Was mair in fear than wrath;
Ae knave was constant in his mind—
  To keep that knave frae scaith.

HERON ELECTION: BALLAD FOURTH

THE TROGGER

Pedlar

Written in May-June 1796 when Patrick Heron was up for re-election, following the dissolution of Parliament. On this occasion his Tory opponent was Montgomery Stewart, (d.1833), younger son of the Earl of Galloway.

CHORUS

TUNE: *Buy Broom Besoms*

Buy braw troggin frae the banks o Dee!   fine wares
Wha wants troggin let him come to me!

Wha will buy my troggin, fine election ware,
Broken trade o Broughton, a' in high repair?   James Murray of Broughton

There's a noble Earl's fame and high renown,   Galloway
For an auld sang—it's thought the guids were stown.   stolen

Here's the worth o Broughton in a needle's e'e;
Here's a reputation tint by Balmaghie.   Gordon of Balmaghie, lost

Here's its stuff and lining, Cardoness's head—   Maxwell of Cardoness
Fine for a soger, a' the wale o lead.   pick

Here's a little wadset, Buittle's scrap o truth,   mortgage
Pawn'd in a gin-shop, quenching holy drouth.   thirst

Here's an honest conscience might a prince adorn,   John Bushby's estate,
Frae the downs o Tinwald, so was never worn!   Tinwald Downs

Here's armorial bearings frae the manse o Urr: a reference to Rev.
The crest, a sour crab-apple rotten at the core.   Dr. James Muirhead

Here is Satan's picture, like a bizzard gled   buzzard hawk
Pouncing poor Redcastle, sprawlin like a taed.   Walter Sloan Lawrie, toad

Here's the font where Douglas stane and mortar names,
Lately used at Caily christening Murray's crimes.   Cally House, Gatehouse of Fleet

Here's the worth and wisdom Collieston can boast: William Copland of Collieston
By a thievish midge they had been nearly lost.

Here is Murray's fragments o the Ten Commands,
Gifted by Black Jock to get them aff his hands.   John Bushby

Saw ye e'er sic troggin?—if to buy ye're slack,
Hornie's turnin chapman: he'll buy a' the pack!   the Devil

TO THE WOODLARK

TUNE: *Loch Erroch Side*

Supposedly written by Burns at the request of Mrs John McMurdo of Drumlanrig and sent to Thomson in April 1795.

O, stay, sweet warbling wood-lark, stay,
Nor quit for me the trembling spray!
A hapless lover counts thy lay,
    Thy soothing, fond complaining.
Again, again that tender part,
That I may catch thy melting art!

would   For surely that wad touch her heart,
    Wha kills me wi disdaining.

Say, was thy little mate unkind,
And heard thee as the careless wind?

naught   O, nocht but love and sorrow join'd
such   Sic notes o woe could wauken!
Thou tells o never-ending care,
O speechless grief and dark despair—

no more   For pity's sake, sweet bird, nae mair,
    Or my poor heart is broken!

THEIR GROVES O SWEET MYRTLE

TUNE: *Humours of Glen*

A tribute to Jean Armour, sent to Thomson in April 1795.

Their groves o sweet myrtle let foreign lands reckon,
    Where bright-beaming summers exalt the perfume!

bracken   Far dearer to me yon lone glen o green breckan,
brook   Wi the burn stealing under the lang, yellow broom;
Far dearer to me are yon humble broom bowers,
    Where the blue-bell and gowan lurk lowly, unseen;
For there, lightly tripping among the wild flowers,
    A-list'ning the linnet, aft wanders my Jean.

Tho rich is the breeze in their gay, sunny vallies,
    And cauld Caledonia's blast on the wave,
Their sweet-scented woodlands that skirt the proud palace,
    What are they?—The haunt of the tyrant and slave!
The slave's spicy forests and gold-bubbling fountains
    The brave Caledonian views wi disdain:
He wanders as free as the winds of his mountains,
    Save Love's willing fetters—the chains o his Jean.

'TWAS NA HER BONIE BLUE E'E

TUNE: *Laddie, lie near me*

These verses, addressed to Chloris, were requested by
Thomson who wanted some decent lines to the
traditional tune.

'Twas na her bonie blue e'e was my ruin:
Fair tho she be, that was ne'er my undoin.
'Twas the dear smile when naebody did mind us,
'Twas the bewitching, sweet, stoun glances o kindness! stolen

Sair do I fear that to hope is denied me, Sore
Sair do I fear that despair maun abide me; must
But tho fell Fortune should fate us to sever,
Queen shall she be in my bosom for ever.

Chloris, I'm thine wi a passion sincerest,
And thou hast plighted me love o the dearest,
And thou'rt the angel that never can alter—
Sooner the sun in his motion would falter!

HOW CRUEL ARE THE PARENTS

TUNE: *John Anderson, my jo*

Burns rewrote this song, which had appeared in several
eighteenth century miscellanies.

How cruel are the parents
 Who riches only prize,
And to the wealthy booby
 Poor Woman sacrifice!
Meanwhile the hapless daughter
 Has but a choice of strife:
To shun a tyrant father's hate
 Become a wretched wife!

The ravening hawk pursuing,
 The trembling dove thus flies:
To shun impelling ruin
 Awhile her pinions tries,
Till, of escape despairing,
 No shelter or retreat,
She trusts the ruthless falconer,
 And drops beneath his feet.

551

MARK YONDER POMP

TUNE: *Deil tak the wars*

Sent to Thomson in May 1795; yet another song to Chloris.

Mark yonder pomp of costly fashion
Round the wealthy, titled bride!
But, when compar'd with real passion,
Poor is all that princely pride.
What are the showy treasures?
What are the noisy pleasures?
The gay, gaudy glare of vanity and art!
The polish'd jewel's blaze
May draw the wond'ring gaze,
And courtly grandeur bright
The fancy may delight,
But never, never can come near the heart!

But did you see my dearest Chloris
In simplicity's array,
Lovely as yonder sweet opening flower is,
Shrinking from the gaze of day?

O, then, the heart alarming
And all resistless charming,
In love's delightful fetters she chains the willing soul!
Ambition would disown
The world's imperial crown!
Ev'n Avarice would deny
His worshipp'd deity,
And feel thro every being love's raptures roll!

O, LAY THY LOOF IN MINE, LASS

TUNE: *The Shoemaker's March*

Traditionally believed to be a tribute to Jessie Lewars who nursed Burns during his last illness, although Johnson actually had it some time before May 1795.

CHORUS

palm

> O, lay thy loof in mine, lass,
> In mine, lass, in mine, lass,
> And swear on thy white hand, lass,
> That thou wilt be my ain!

A slave to Love's unbounded sway,

much grief
He aft has wrought me meikle wae;
But now he is my deadly fae,

own
Unless thou be my ain.

many
There's monie a lass has broke my rest,
glimpse
That for a blink I hae lo'ed best;
But thou art queen within my breast,
For ever to remain.

552

ADDRESS TO THE TOOTHACHE

First published in the Belfast News Letter of 11th
September 1797. It has been argued that this Address
was written in 1786-7 but Kinsley has argued plausibly
for May-June 1795, when Burns was enduring 'the
delightful sensations of an omnipotent Tooth-ache,
while fifty troops of infernal spirits are riding past
from ear to ear along my jaw-bones.'

My curse upon your venom'd stang,   sting
That shoots my tortur'd gums alang,
An thro my lug gies monie a twang   ear, twinge
     Wi gnawing vengeance,
Tearing my nerves wi bitter pang,
     Like racking engines!

A'down my beard the slavers trickle,   saliva
I throw the wee stools o'er the mickle,
While round the fire the giglets keckle,   cackle
     To see me loup,   dance
An raving mad, I wish a heckle   heckling-comb
     Were i' their doup!   backside

When fevers burn, or ague freezes,
Rheumatics gnaw, or colic squeezes,
Our neebors sympathise to ease us,   neighbours
     Wi pitying moan;
But thee!—thou hell o a' diseases—
     They mock our groan!

Of a' the numerous human dools—   woes
Ill-hairsts, daft bargains, cutty-stools, harvests, mad
Or worthy frien's laid i' the mools,   crumbling earth
     Sad sight to see!
The tricks o knaves, or fash o fools— annoyance
     Thou bear'st the gree!   takest the prize

Whare'er that place be priests ca' Hell,
Whare a' the tones o misery yell,
An ranked plagues their numbers tell,
     In dreadfu raw,   row
Thou, Toothache, surely bear'st the bell,
     Amang them a'!

O thou grim, mischief-making chiel,   fellow
That gars the notes o discord squeel, makes
Till human kind aft dance a reel
     In gore, a shoe-thick,
Gie a' the faes o Scotland's weal   Give, foes
     A towmond's toothache! twelve month's

FORLORN MY LOVE, NO COMFORT NEAR

AIR: *Let me in this ae night*

The first draft was sent to Thomson in June 1795 —
'I have written it within this hour; so much for the
speed of my Pegasus; but what say you to his bottom?'
A revised version was sent on 3rd August.

CHORUS

O wert thou, love, but near me,
But near, near, near me,
How kindly thou would cheer me,
And mingle sighs with mine, love!

Forlorn my love, no comfort near,
Far, far from thee I wander here;
Far, far from thee, the fate severe,
    At which I most repine, love.

Around me scowls a wintry sky,
Blasting each bud of hope and joy,
And shelter, shade, nor home have I
    Save in these arms of thine, love.

Cold, alter'd friendship's cruel part,
To poison fortune's ruthless dart!
Let me not break thy faithful heart,
    And say that fate is mine, love!

But, dreary tho the moments fleet,
O, let me think we yet shall meet!
That only ray of solace sweet
    Can on thy Chloris shine, love!

NOW SPRING HAS CLAD THE GROVE IN GREEN

TUNE: *Auld lang syne*

Some detached stanzas were sent to Maria Riddell in
the summer of 1795 which 'I intend to interweave in
some disastrous tale of a Shepherd despairing beside a
clear stream.' The song was completed by 3rd August.

Now spring has clad the grove in green,
    And strew'd the lea wi flowers;
The furrow'd, waving corn is seen
    Rejoice in fostering showers;
every   While ilka thing in nature join
    Their sorrows to forego,
O, why thus all alone are mine
    The weary steps o woe!

554

Now Spring Has Clad The Grove In Green

The trout within yon wimpling burn   meandering brook
   Glides swift, a silver dart,
And, safe beneath the shady thorn,
   Defies the angler's art:
My life was ance that careless stream
   That wanton trout was I,
But Love wi unrelenting beam
   Has scorch'd my fountains dry.

The little floweret's peaceful lot,
   In yonder cliff that grows,
Which, save the linnet's flight, I wot,
   Nae ruder visit knows,
Was mine, till Love has o'er me past,
   And blighted a' my bloom;
And now beneath the withering blast
   My youth and joy consume.

The waken'd lav'rock warbling springs,   lark
   And climbs the early sky,
Winnowing blythe his dewy wings
   In Morning's rosy eye:
As little reck't I Sorrow's power,
   Until the flowery snare
O witching Love, in luckless hour,
   Made me the thrall o care!

O, had my fate been Greenland snows
   Or Afric's burning zone,
Wi Man and Nature leagu'd my foes,
   So Peggy ne'er I'd known!

The wretch, whose doom is 'hope nae mair,'
   What tongue his woes can tell,
Within whose bosom, save Despair,
   Nae kinder spirits dwell!

THE BRAW WOOER

TUNE: *The Lothian Lassie*

Sent to Thomson on 3rd July 1795, it is one of Burns's
best genre songs, expressing 'the inter-play of character,
motife and mask . . . . with ruthless economy.'

Last May a braw wooer cam down the lang glen,   fine
   And sair wi his love he did deave me.   sore, deafen
I said there was naething I hated like men:
   The deuce gae wi'm to believe me, believe me—   go
   The deuce gae wi'm to believe me!

555

The Braw Wooer

eyes
He spak o the darts in my bonie black e'en,
    And vow'd for my love he was diein.
I said, he might die when he liket for Jean:
    The Lord forgie me for liein, for liein—
    The Lord forgie me for liein!

well-stocked farm A weel-stocket mailen, himself for the laird,
    And marriage aff-hand were his proffers:
let, know
worse I never loot on that I kenn'd it, or car'd,
    But thought I might hae waur offers, waur offers—
    But thought I might hae waur offers.

But what wad ye think? In a fortnight or less
    (The Deil tak his taste to get near her!)
a pass through the He up the Gate-Slack to my black cousin, Bess!
Lowther Hills
jade   Guess ye how, the jad! I could bear her, could bear her—
    Guess ye how, the jad! I could bear her.

next But a' the niest week, as I petted wi care,
in upper Nithsdale   I gaed to the tryste o Dalgarnock,
And wha but my fine fickle lover was there?
stared, wizard   I glowr'd as I'd seen a warlock, a warlock—
    I glowr'd as I'd seen a warlock.

glance But owre my left shouther I gae him a blink,
    Lest neebours might say I was saucy.
My wooer he caper'd as he'd been in drink,
    And vow'd I was his dear lassie, dear lassie—
    And vow'd I was his dear lassie!

enquired, loving I spier'd for my cousin fu couthy and sweet:
If   Gin she had recover'd her hearin?
shoes, shapeless And how her new shoon fit her auld, schachl'd feet?
    But heavens! how he fell a swearin, a swearin—
    But heavens! how he fell a swearin!

He begged, for gudesake, I wad be his wife,
    Or else I wad kill him wi sorrow;
So e'en to preserve the poor body in life,
must   I think I maun wed him to-morrow, to-morrow—
    I think I maun wed him to-morrow!

WHY, WHY TELL THY LOVER

TUNE: *Caledonian Hunt's delight*

Sent to Thomson on 3rd July 1795.

Why, why tell thy lover
    Bliss he never must enjoy?
Why, why undeceive him,
    And give all his hopes the lie?
O, why, while Fancy, raptur'd, slumbers,
    'Chloris, Chloris,' all the theme,
Why, why wouldst thou, cruel,
    Wake thy lover from his dream?

INSCRIPTION FOR AN ALTAR OF INDEPENDENCE

AT KERROUGHTREE, THE SEAT OF MR HERON

Lines addressed to Patrick Heron, about July 1795.

Thou of an independent mind,
With soul resolv'd, with soul resign'd,
Prepar'd Power's proudest frown to brave,
Who wilt not be, nor have a slave,
Virtue alone who dost revere,
Thy own reproach alone dost fear:
Approach this shrine, and worship here.

INSCRIPTION

WRITTEN ON THE BLANK LEAF OF A COPY OF THE LAST EDITION OF MY POEMS, PRESENTED TO THE LADY WHOM, IN SO MANY FICTITIOUS REVERIES OF PASSION, BUT WITH THE MOST ARDENT SENTIMENTS OF REAL FRIENDSHIP, I HAVE SO OFTEN SUNG UNDER THE NAME OF 'CHLORIS'

Sent to Alexander Cunningham on 3rd August, 1795

'Tis Friendship's pledge, my young, fair Friend,
    Nor thou the gift refuse;
Nor with unwilling ear attend
    The moralising Muse.

Since thou in all thy youth and charms
    Must bid the world adieu
(A world 'gainst peace in constant arms),
    To join the friendly few;

Since, thy gay morn of life o'ercast,
    Chill came the tempest's lour
(And ne'er Misfortune's eastern blast
    Did nip a fairer flower);

Since life's gay scenes must charm no more
    Still much is left behind,
Still nobler wealth hast thou in store—
    The comforts of the mind!

Thine is the self-approving glow
    Of conscious honor's part;
And (dearest gift of Heaven below)
    Thine Friendship's truest heart!

The joys refin'd of sense and taste,
    With every Muse to rove:
And doubly were the Poet blest,
    These joys could he improve.   R.B.

557

O, THIS IS NO MY AIN LASSIE

TUNE: *This is no my ain house*

'This is a great favourite of mine,' Burns told Thomson
in September 1793, 'and if you will send me your set
of it, I shall task my Muse to her highest effort.'
Nevertheless two years elapsed before he produced
these verses.

O, this is no my ain lassie,
   Fair tho the lassie be:
Weel ken I my ain lassie—
   Kind love is in her e'e.

I see a form, I see a face,
Ye weel may wi the fairest place:
It wants to me the witching grace,
   The kind of love that's in her e'e.

She's bonie, blooming, straight, and tall,
And lang has had my heart in thrall;
And ay it charms my very saul,
   The kind love that's in her e'e.

sly
glance
bright

A thief sae pawkie is my Jean,
To steal a blink by a' unseen!
But gleg as light are lover's een,
   When kind love is in the e'e.

It may escape the courtly sparks,
It may escape the learned clerks;
But well the watching lover marks
   The kind love that's in her e'e.

O, BONIE WAS YON ROSY BRIER

TUNE: *I wish my love was in a mire*

Copies of this song were sent to Alexander Cunningham
and Maria Riddell early in August 1795.

O, bonie was yon rosy brier
   That blooms sae far frae haunt o man,
And bonie she—and ah, how dear!—
   It shaded frae the e'enin sun!

Yon rosebuds in the morning dew,
   How pure among the leaves sae green!
But purer was the lover's vow

last night

   They witness'd in their shade yestreen.

All in its rude and prickly bower,
   That crimson rose how sweet and fair!
But love is far a sweeter flower
   Amid life's thorny path o care.

The pathless wild and wimpling burn,
Wi Chloris in my arms, be mine,
And I the warld nor wish nor scorn—
Its joy and griefs alike resign!

O, THAT'S THE LASSIE O
MY HEART

TUNE: *Morag*

**Burns's poetic activities suffered a series of severe
setbacks: recurring toothache and a prolonged bout
of rheumatic fever over the last three months of 1795.
In addition his three year-old daughter, Elizabeth
Riddell Burns, died in September. This song was
probably written about August 1795 but a copy not
sent to Robert Cleghorn till January 1796 — 'since I
saw you, I have been much the child of disaster.'**

CHORUS
*O, that's the lassie o my heart,
My lassie ever dearer!
O, that's the queen o womankind,
And ne'er a ane to peer her!*   one

O, wat ye wha that lo'es me,   wot
And has my heart a keeping?
O, sweet is she that lo'es me
As dews o summer weeping,
In tears the rosebuds steeping!

If thou shalt meet a lassie
In grace and beauty charming,
That e'en thy chosen lassie,
Erewhile thy breast sae warming,
Had ne'er sic powers alarming:—   such

If thou hadst heard her talking
(And thy attention's plighted),
That ilka body talking   every
But her by thee is slighted,
And thou art all-delighted:—

If thou hast met this fair one,
When frae her thou has parted,
If every other fair one
But her thou hast deserted,
And thou art broken-hearted.

559

TO JOHN SYME OF RYEDALE

WITH A PRESENT OF A DOZEN OF PORTER

John Syme (1755-1831), Army officer and later Writer
to the Signet, suffered from the collapse of the Ayr
bank, but obtained the sinecure of Collector of Stamps
for Dumfries and Galloway. His office was on the
ground floor of the house in Bank Street where Burns
lived in 1791-3.

O had the malt thy strength of mind,
 Or hops the flavour of thy wit,
'Twere drink for the first of human kind—
 A gift that ev'n for Syme were fit.

JERUSALEM TAVERN, DUMFRIES

APOLOGY FOR DECLINING AN
INVITATION TO DINE

*On refusing to dine with him, after having been
promised the first of company, and the first of
Cookery, 17th December, 1795.*

No more of your guests, be they titled or not,
 And cookery the first in the nation:
Who is proof to thy personal converse and wit,
 Is proof to all other temptation.

ON MR PITT'S HAIR - POWDER TAX

The tax on hair-powder was one of the imposts levied
in 1795 to meet the cost of the French Revolutionary
War. 'Guinea' here is a play on words, that being the
amount of the tax levied in each instance.

Pray Billy Pitt explain thy rigs,
 This new poll-tax of thine!
'I mean to mark the Guinea pigs
 'From other common swine.'

THE SOLEMN LEAGUE AND
COVENANT

Burns inscribed these lines in the volume of the
Statistical Account (1794) describing the martyred
Covenanters of Balmaghie, the two David Hallidays,
who were shot in 1685.

The Solemn League and Covenant
 Now brings a smile, now brings a tear.
But sacred Freedom, too, was theirs:
 If thou'rt a slave, indulge thy sneer.

560

THE BOB O DUMBLANE

Sent by Burns to Johnson late in 1795 for the fifth
volume of SMM but omitted on grounds of indelicacy.
The original song was by Ramsay and Burns claimed to
have heard it from the hostess of the principal inn in
Dunblane in 1787.

Lassie, lend me your braw hemp-heckle,	flax comb
And I'll lend you my thripplin kame:	separating comb
My heckle is broken, it canna be gotten,	
And we'll gae dance the Bob o Dumblane.	go

Twa gaed to the wood, to the wood, to the wood,	went
Twa gaed to the wood, three cam hame:	
An't be na weel bobbit, weel bobbit, weel bobbit,	
An't be na weel bobbit, we'll bob it again.	

TO COLLECTOR MITCHELL

John Mitchell (1731-1806), studied for the Ministry
but entered the Excise instead and was appointed
Collector at Dumfries in 1788. Burns met him in May
1789 when he called on him with Graham of Fintry's
introduction. Thereafter Mitchell took an active
interest in the poet's career.

Friend of the Poet tried and leal,	true
Wha wanting thee might beg or steal;	
Alake, alake, the meikle Deil	great
Wi a' his witches	
Are at it, skelpin jig and reel	spanking
In my poor pouches!	pockets

I modestly fu fain wad hint it,	would
That One-pound-one, I sairly want it;	a guinea
If wi the hizzie down ye sent it,	maid
It would be kind;	
And while my heart wi life-blood dunted,	throbbed
I'd bear't in mind!	

So may the Auld Year gang out moanin	
To see the New come laden, groanin,	
Wi doubly plenty o'er the loanin	down the lane
To thee and thine:	
Domestic peace and comfort crownin	
To hale design!	whole

POSTSCRIPT

Ye've heard this while how I've been licket,	a reference to his
And by fell Death was nearly nicket:	grave illness of
Grim loon! He got me by the fecket,	December, 1795, waistcoat
And sair me sheuk;	sore
But by guid luck I lap a wicket,	leaped, fence
And turn'd a neuk.	corner

To Collector Mitchell

health, welfare
more careful

once and all

But by that health, I've got a share o't,
And by that life, I'm promis'd mair o't,
My hale and weel, I'll take a care o't,
    A tentier way;
Then farewell folly, hide and hair o't.
    For ance and ay!

THE DEAN OF THE FACULTY

A NEW BALLAD

TUNE: *The Dragon of Wantley*

Composed some time after 12th January 1796, when
Robert Dundas was elected Dean of the Faculty of
Advocates. His defeated rival was Burns's friend Henry
Erskine. 'Old Harlaw' was the battle fought in 1411
between the Lord of the Isles and the Earl of Mar (an
ancestor of Erskine). Mary Queen of Scots was
defeated at Langside in 1568.

Dire was the hate at Old Harlaw,
    That Scot to Scot did carry;
And dire the discord Langside saw
    For beauteous, hapless Mary.
But Scot to Scot ne'er met so hot,
    Or were more in fury seen, Sir,
That 'twixt Hal and Bob for the famous job,
    Who should be the Faculty's Dean, sir.

This Hal for genius, wit, and lore
    Among the first was number'd;
But pious Bob, 'mid learning's store
    Commandment the tenth remember'd:
Yet simple Bob the victory got,
    And won his heart's desire:
Which shows that Heaven can boil the pot,
    Tho the Deil piss in the fire.

Squire Hal, besides, had in this case
    Pretensions rather brassy;
For talents, to deserve a place,
    Are qualifications saucy.
So their worships of the Faculty,
    Quite sick of Merit's rudeness,
Chose one who should owe it all, d'ye see,
    To their gratis grace and goodness.

562

The Dean Of The Faculty

As once on Pisgah purg'd was the sight   Deuteronomy iii. 27
   Of a son of Circumcision,
So, may be, on this Pisgah height,
   Bob's purblind mental vision.
Nay, Bobby's mouth may be open'd yet,
   Till for eloquence you hail him,
And swear that he has the Angel met   Numbers xxii. 22
   That met the Ass of Balaam.

In your heretic sins may you live and die,
   Ye heretic Eight-and-Thirty!   Dundas's opponents
But accept, ye sublime majority,
   My congratulations hearty!
With your honors, as with a certain King,
   In your servants this is striking,
The more incapacity they bring
   The more they're to your liking.

A LASS WI A TOCHER

TUNE: *Ballinamona Ora*

Thomson planned to publish a volume of Irish airs. Writing in February 1796 Burns promised 'I shall cheerfully undertake the task of finding verses for them . . . . the other day I strung up a kind of rhapsody to another Hibernian melody which I admire much.'

CHORUS
Then hey for a lass wi a tocher,
Then hey for a lass wi a tocher,
Then hey for a lass wi a tocher,
   The nice yellow guineas for me!

Awa wi your witchcraft o Beauty's alarms,
The slender bit beauty you grasp in your arms!
O, gie me the lass that has acres o charms!   give
O, gie me the lass wi the weel-stockit farms!

Your Beauty's a flower in the morning that blows,
And withers the faster the faster it grows;
But the rapturous charm o the bonie green knowes,   hillocks
Ilk spring they're new deckit wi bonie white yowes!   Each, ewes

And e'en when this Beauty your bosom has blest,
The brightest o Beauty may cloy when possess'd;
But the sweet, yellow darlings wi Geordie impress'd,   guineas
The langer ye hae them, the mair they're carest!

563

EPISTLE TO COLONEL DE PEYSTER

Colonel Arentz Schuyler de Peyster was born in New
York in 1736 and served in the British Army from
1755 till April 1794. He married Rebecca Blair, John
McMurdo's sister-in-law, and settled at Mavis Grove
near Dumfries, where he became Major-Commandant
of the Volunteers. This verse-epistle was written in
answer to an enquiry about the poet's health. De
Peyster published his own poems Miscellanies of an
Officer in 1813. He died in 1822.

My honor'd Colonel, deep I feel
Your interest in the Poet's weal:
Ah! now sma' heart hae I to speel
 The steep Parnassus,
Surrounded thus by bolus pill
 And potion glasses.

O, what a canty warld were it,
Would pain and care and sickness spare it,
And Fortune favor worth and merit
 As they deserve,
And ay rowth—roast-beef and claret!—
 Syne, wha wad starve?

Dame Life, tho fiction out may trick her,
And in paste gems and frippery deck her,
Oh! flickering, feeble, and unsicker
 I've found her still:
Ay, wandering, like the willow-wicker,
 'Tween good and ill!

Then that curst carmagnole Auld Satan,
Watches, like baudrons by a ratton,
Our sinfu saul to get a claut on
 Wi felon ire;
Syne, whip! his tail ye'll ne'er cast saut on—
 He's aff like fire.

Ah Nick! Ah Nick! it is na fair,
First showing us the tempting ware,
Bright wines and bonie lasses rare,
 To put us daft;
Syne weave, unseen, thy spider snare
 O Hell's damn'd waft!

Poor Man, the flie, aft bizzes by,
And aft, as chance he comes thee nigh,
Thy damn'd auld elbows yeuks wi joy
 And hellish pleasure.
Already in thy fancy's eye
 Thy sicker treasure!

---

**Glosses (left margin):**

welfare
climb

jolly

plenty
Then, would

unsure

nickname for a French
revolutionary, hence a rascal
in general; cats, rat; grasp

salt

send us mad

web

itches

sure

564

Epistle To Colonel De Peyster

Soon, heels o'er gowdie, in he gangs,   topsy-turvy, goes
And, like a sheep-head on a tangs,   singeing-tongs
Thy girning laugh enjoys his pangs   snarling
    And murdering wrestle,
As, dangling in the wind, he hangs
    A gibbet's tassle.

But lest you think I am uncivil
To plague you with this draunting drivel,
Adjuring a' intentions evil,
    I quat my pen: leave
The Lord preserve us frae the Devil!
    Amen! Amen!

HERE'S A HEALTH TO ANE I LOE DEAR

Sent to Thomson in April 1796. A copy went to Alexander Cunningham on 12th July 'as the last I made or probably will make for some time.' He died just nine days later. The subject of this song was Jessie Lewars (1778-1855), younger daughter of John Lewars, Supervisor of Excise at Dumfries.

CHORUS
Here's a health to ane I loe dear!   one, love
   Here's health to ane I loe dear!
Thou art sweet as the smile when fond lovers meet,
   And soft as their parting tear, Jessie—
   And soft as their parting tear!

Altho thou maun never be mine,   must
   Altho even hope is denied,
'Tis sweeter for thee despairing
   Than ought in the world beside, Jessie—
   Than ought in the world beside!

I mourn thro the gay, gaudy day,
   As hopeles I muse on thy charms;
But welcome the dream o sweet slumber!
   For then I am lockt in thine arms, Jessie—
   For then I am lockt in thine arms!

VERSICLES TO JESSIE LEWARS

Jessie Lewars, last of the poet's heroines, lived with her brother John Lewars, Jr. who, like his father, was an Excise colleague of Burns. Their house was in Mill Vennel (now Burns Street) opposite the poet's residence. Jessie helped to nurse Burns during his last illness.

THE TOAST

Fill me with the rosy wine;
Call a toast, a toast divine:
Give the Poet's darling flame,
Lovely Jessie be her name:
Then thou mayest freely boast
Thou hast given a peerless toast.

THE MENAGERIE

Talk not to me of savages
    From Afric's burning sun!
No savage e'er can rend my heart
    As, Jessie, thou hast done.

But Jessie's lovely hand in mine,
    A mutual faith to plight—
Not even to view the heavenly choir
    Would be so blest a sight.

JESSIE'S ILLNESS

Say, sages, what's the charm on earth
    Can turn Death's dart aside?
It is not purity and worth,
    Else Jessie had not died!

ON HER RECOVERY

But rarely seen since Nature's birth
    The natives of the sky!
Yet still one seraph's left on earth,
    For Jessie did not die.

INSCRIPTION
TO MISS JESSIE LEWARS

Burns asked Johnson for a set of volumes of the Scots
Musical Museum which he presented to Jessie, placing
this inscription on the back of the title-page of the
first volume. Jessie took charge of the poet's four sons
for some time after Burns died.

Thine be the volumes, Jessie fair,
And with them take the Poet's prayer:
That Fate may in her fairest page,
With ev'ry kindliest, best presage
Of future bliss enrol thy name;
With native worth, and spotless fame,
With wakeful caution, still aware
Of ill—but chief, Man's felon snare!
All blameless joys on earth we find,
And all the treasures of the mind—
These be thy guardian and reward!
So prays thy faithful friend, the Bard.

DUMFRIES, *June 26*, 1796   ROBERT BURNS

O, WERT THOU IN THE CAULD
BLAST

TUNE: *Lenox love to Blantyre*

Written for Jessie Lewars, by way of thanking her for
nursing the poet during his final illness, and surely
some of the most poignant lines ever penned.

O, wert thou in the cauld blast
    On yonder lea, on yonder lea,
My plaidie to the angry airt,   quarter
    I'd shelter thee, I'd shelter thee.
Or did Misfortune's bitter storms
    Around thee blaw, around thee blaw,
Thy bield should be my bosom,   shelter
    To share it a', to share it a'.

Or were I in the wildest waste,
    Sae black and bare, sae black and bare,
The desert were a Paradise,
    If thou wert there, if thou wert there.
Or were I monarch o the globe,
    Wi thee to reign, wi thee to reign,
The brightest jewel in my crown
    Wad be my queen, wad be my queen.   Would

567

FAIREST MAID ON DEVON BANKS
TUNE: *Rothiemurchie*

This song accompanied a letter to Thomson on 12th July 1796, written from the Brow: 'After all my boasted independence, curst necessity compels me to implore you for five pounds — A cruel scoundrel of a Haberdasher to whom I owe an account, taking it into his head that I am dying, has commenced a process, and will infallibly put me into jail — Do, for God's sake, send me that sum, and that by return of post . . . upon returning health, I hereby promise and engage to furnish you with five pounds' worth of the neatest song-genius you have seen . . .' To his credit, Thomson responded promptly. The 'Crystal Devon' is the Clackmannanshire river.

CHORUS
Fairest maid on Devon banks,
　　Crystal Devon, winding Devon,
Wilt thou lay that frown aside,
　　And smile as thou wert wont to do?

Full well thou know'st I love thee dear—
Couldst thou to malice lend an ear!
O, did not Love exclaim:—'Forbear,
　　Nor use a faithful lover so!'

Then come, thou fairest of the fair,
Those wonted smiles, O, let me share,
And by thy beauteous self I swear
　　No love but thine my heart shall know!

REMORSEFUL APOLOGY

Early editors assumed that these lines were addressed to Maria Riddell after the quarrel of 1793-4 but Kinsley has tentatively identified the recipient as Simon McKenzie, who attended the inaugural meeting of the Dumfries Volunteers on 31st January 1796.

The friend whom, wild from Wisdom's way,
　　The fumes of wine infuriate send
(Not moony madness more astray),
　　Who but deplores that hapless friend?

Mine was th' insensate frenzied part—
　　Ah! why should I such scenes outlive?
Scenes so abhorrent to my heart!
　　'Tis thine to pity and forgive.

LINES WRITTEN ON WINDOWS OF
THE GLOBE TAVERN, DUMFRIES

These three short pieces were probably written extempore at the Globe, the Poet's 'favourite howff.'

The greybeard, old wisdom, may boast of his treasures,
　　Give me with gay folly to live;
I grant him his calm-blooded, time-settled pleasures,
　　But folly has raptures to give.

Lines Written on Windows of the Globe Tavern

My bottle is a holy pool,
That heals the wounds o care an dool;   woe
And pleasure is a wanton trout,
An ye drink it, ye'll find him out.

In politics if thou would'st mix,
   And mean thy fortunes be;
Bear this in mind, be deaf and blind,
   Let great folks hear and see.

THE TOADEATER

Burns produced several variants of this epigram, of
which the most notable are given here. James McClure
claimed that Burns delivered these lines during a
dinner-party at Terraughty. Syme annotated his copy:
'Extempore on a young fellow W.I. who had made
about £10,000 by a lucky speculation and who
vaunted of keeping the highest company, &c. N.B. he
was of low extraction.'

Of Lordly acquaintance you boast,
   And the Dukes that you dined with yestreen;
Yet an insect's an insect at most,
   Tho it crawl on the curl of a Queen!

ALTERNATIVE VERSION

No more of your titled acquaintances boast,
   Nor of the gay groups you have seen;
A crab louse is but a crab louse at last,
   Tho stack to the _____ of a Queen.   stuck

THE LOVELY LASS O INVERNESS

This and the following fifty songs were published
posthumously in the SMM of 1796 and 1803 and are
believed to date from the last three years of the poet's
life. This ballad was based on a Jacobite original;
'Drumossie' alludes to the battle of Culloden, near
Inverness, in 1746.

The lovely lass of Inverness,
   Nae joy nor pleasure can she see;
For e'en to morn she cries 'Alas!'
   And ay the saut tear blin's her e'e:—   salt, eye

'Drumossie moor, Drumossie day—
   A waefu day it was to me!   sad
For there I lost my father dear,
   My father dear and brethren three.

'Their winding-sheet the bluidy clay,
   Their graves are growin green to see,
And by them lies the dearest lad
   That ever blest a woman's e'e.

'Now wae to thee, thou cruel lord,   Duke of Cumberland
   A bluidy man I trow thou be,
For monie a heart thou hast made sair
   That ne'er did wrang to thine or thee!'

569

AS I STOOD BY YON ROOFLESS TOWER

TUNE: *Cumnock Psalms*

Burns sent to Thomson in September 1794 a copy of
'a droll Scots song, more famous for its humor than
delicacy, called The grey goose and the gled.' Later he
composed these lines to the same tune. The 'roofless
tower' was Lincluden Abbey, north of Dumfries on
the banks of the Nith.

CHORUS

A lassie all alone, was making her moan
Lamenting our lads beyond the sea:—
'In the bluidy wars they fa', and our honor's
gane an a',
And broken-hearted we maun die.'

As I stood by yon roofless tower,
    Where the wa'flow'r scents the dewy air,

owl — Where the houlet mourns in her ivy bower,
    And tells the midnight moon her care:

The winds were laid, the air was still,
    The stars they shot along the sky,

fox — The tod was howling on the hill,
    And the distant-echoing glens reply.

brook — The burn, adown its hazelly path,
    Was rushing by the ruin'd wa',
Hasting to join the sweeping Nith,

Whose — Whase roaring seemed to rise and fa'.

The cauld blae North was streaming forth
    Her lights, wi hissing, eerie din:

Athwart, horizon — Athort the lift they start and shift,
lost — Like Fortune's favors, tint as win.

fold — Now, looking over firth and fauld,
the moon — Her horn the pale-faced Cynthia rear'd,
When lo! in form of minstrel auld

ghost — A stern and stalwart ghaist appear'd.

such — And frae his harp sic strains did flow,
    Might rous'd the slumbering Dead to hear,
But O, it was a tale of woe
    As ever met a Briton's ear!

He sang wi joy his former day,
    He, weeping, wail'd his latter times:
But what he said—it was nae play!
    I winna ventur't in my rhymes.

THE LASS O ECCLEFECHAN

TUNE: *Jack o Latin*

Says Cunningham: '. . . during the Poet's first visit to
Annandale, an old song, called "The Lass of
Ecclefechan," was sung to him, with which he was so
amused that he wrote it down, and, at a leisure
moment, rendered the language more delicate, and the
sentiments less warm' for SMM. A less delicate version
was preserved in the Merry Muses.

'Gat ye me, O, gat ye me,	
Gat ye me wi naething?	
Rock an reel, an spinning wheel,	Distaff
A mickle quarter basin:	big
Bye attour, my gutcher has	Moreover, goodsir
A heich house and a laich ane,	high, low
A' forbye my bonie sel,	All besides
The toss o Ecclefechan!'	toast
'O, haud your tongue now, Lucky Lang,	hold
O, haud your tongue and jauner!	jabber
I held the gate till you I met,	kept to the straight path
Syne I began to wander:	Then
I tint my whistle and my sang,	lost
I tint my peace and pleasure;	
But your green graff, now Lucky Lang,	grave
Wad airt me to my treasure.'	Would direct

THE WREN'S NEST

Burns took down this song from his own wife's lips
and, after revision, sent this fragment to Johnson for
SMM.

The Robin cam to the wren's nest	
And keekit in and keekit in,	peeped
O weel's me on your auld pow,	pate
Wad ye be in, wad ye be in.	Would
Ye'se ne'er get leave to lie without,	
And I within, and I within,	
As lang's I hae an auld clout	cloth
To row you in, to row you in.	roll

O AN YE WERE DEAD GUDEMAN

A revision of a traditional ballad in Herd MS, rejecting
part of the original and developing the theme of the
cuckold's horns.

CHORUS

O an ye were dead gudeman,	if
A green turf on your head, gudeman,	
I wad bestow my widowhood	would
Upon a rantin Highlandman.	rollicking

O An Ye Were Dead Gudeman

There's sax eggs in the pan, gudeman,
There's sax eggs in the pan, gudeman;
There's ane to you, and twa to me,
And three to our John Highlandman.

A sheep-head's in the pot, gudeman,
A sheep-head's in the pot, gudeman;
broth   The flesh to him the broo to me,
An the horns become your brow, gudeman.

CHORUS TO THE LAST VERSE

cudgel   *Sing round about the fire wi a rung she ran,*
An round about the fire wi a rung she ran:
stall   *Your horns shall tie you to the straw,*
And I shall bang your hide, gudeman.

TAM LIN

Several versions of this ancient ballad are known from the 16th century, but these lines communicated by Burns to SMM are the most complete version extant. An unpolished, original version was also taken down by Robert Riddell, possibly from the same source. Carterhaugh is a plain near Selkirk, where the Ettrick and Yarrow meet.

O I forbid you, maidens a'
gold   That wear gowd on your hair,
go   To come, or gae by Carterhaugh,
For young Tom-lin is there.

There's nane that gaes by Carterhaugh
But they leave him a wad;
Either their rings, or green mantles,
Or else their maidenhead.

petticoat   Janet has kilted her green kirtle,
above   A little aboon her knee;
braided   And she has broded her yellow hair
brow   A little aboon her bree;
And she's awa to Carterhaugh
As fast as she can hie.

When she cam to Carterhaugh
Tom-lin was at the well,
found   And there she fand his steed standing
But away was himsel.

plucked   She had na pu'd a double rose,
two   A rose but only tway,
Till up then started young Tom-lin,
Says, Lady, thou's pu nae mae.

Tam Lin

Why pu's thou the rose, Janet,
  And why breaks thou the wand?
Or why comes thou to Carterhaugh
  Withoutten my command?

Carterhaugh it is my ain,   own
  Ma daddie gave it me;
I'll come and gang by Carterhaugh
  And ask nae leave at thee.

Janet has kilted her green kirtle
  A little aboon her knee,
And she has snooded her yellow hair,   banded
  A little aboon her bree,
And she is to her father's ha,
  As fast as she can hie.

Four and twenty ladies fair
  Were playing at the ba,
And out then cam the fair Janet,
  Ance the flower amang them a'.

Four and twenty ladies fair
  Were playing at the chess,
And out then cam the fair Janet,
  As green as onie glass.

Out then spak an auld grey knight,
  Lay o'er the castle-wa,
And says, Alas, fair Janet for thee
  But we'll be blamed a'.

Haud your tongue ye auld-fac'd knight,
  Some ill death may ye die,
Father my bairn on whom I will,   child
  I'll father nane on thee.

Out then spak her father dear,
  And he spak meek and mild,
And ever alas, sweet Janet, he says,
  I think thou gaes wi child.

If that I gae wi child, father,
  Mysel maun bear the blame;   must
There's ne'er a laird about your ha,
  Shall get the bairn's name.

If my Love were an earthly knight,
  As he's an elfin grey;
I wad na gie my ain true-love
  For nae lord that ye hae.

Tam Lin

The steed that my true-love rides on,
  Is lighter than the wind;
silver Wi siller he is shod before,
gold   Wi burning gowd behind.

Janet has kilted her green kirtle
  A little aboon her knee;
And she has snooded her yellow hair
  A little aboon her brie;
And she's awa to Carterhaugh
  As fast as she can hie.

When she cam to Carterhaugh,
  Tom-lin was at the well;
And there she fand his steed standing,
  But away was himsel.

She had na pu'd a double rose,
  A rose but only tway,
Till up then started young Tom-lin,
  Says, Lady thou pu's nae mae.

Why pu's thou the rose Janet,
  Amang the groves sae green,
And a' to kill the bonie babe
  That we gat us between.

O tell me, Tom-lin she says,
  For's sake that died on tree,
If e'er ye was in holy chapel,
  Or Christendom did see.

Roxbrugh he was my grandfather,
  Took me with him to bide,
once And ance it fell upon a day
woe   That wae did me betide.

Ance it fell upon a day,
  A cauld day and a snell,
bitter When we were frae the hunting come
  That frae my horse I fell.

The queen o Fairies she caught me,
  In yon green hill to dwell,
that And pleasant is the fairy-land;
  But, an eerie tale to tell!
strange

Ay at the end of seven years
  We pay a tiend to hell;
tithe I am sae fair and fu of flesh
  I'm fear'd it be mysel.

574

Tam Lin

But the night is Halloween, lady,
    The morn is Hallowday;
Then win me, win me, an ye will,
    For weel I wat ye may.

Just at the mirk and midnight hour   dark
    The fairy folk will ride;
And they that wad their truelove win,   would
    At Milescross they maun bide.

But how shall I thee ken, Tom-lin,
    O how my truelove know,
Amang sae mony unco knights   mighty
    The like I never saw.

O first let pass the black, Lady,
    And syne let pass the brown;   then
But quickly run to the milk-white steed,
    Pu ye his rider down:

For I'll ride on the milk-white steed,
    And ay nearest the town;
Because I was an earthly knight
    They gie me that renown.

My right hand will be glov'd, lady,
    My left hand will be bare;
Cockt up shall my bonnet be,
    And kaim'd down shall my hair;   combed
And thae's the tokens I gie thee,   those are
    Nae doubt I will be there.

They'll turn me in your arms, lady,
    Into an ask and adder,   viper
But hald me fast and fear me not,
    I am your bairn's father.

They'll turn me to a bear sae grim,
    And then a lion bold;
But hold me fast and fear me not,
    As ye shall love your child.

Again they'll turn me in your arms
    To a red het gaud of airn;   hot goad iron
But hold me fast and fear me not,
    I'll do you nae harm.

And last they'll turn me, in your arms,
    Into the burning lead;
Then throw me into well-water,
    O throw me in wi speed!

Tam Lin

And then I'll be your ain truelove,
    I'll turn a naked knight:
Then cover me wi your green mantle,
    And cover me out o sight.

Gloomy, gloomy was the night,
    And eerie was the way,
As fair Jenny in her green mantle
    To Milescross she did gae.

About the middle o the night
    She heard the bridles ring;
This lady was as glad at that
    As any earthly thing.

First she let the black pass by,
    And syne she let the brown;
But quickly she ran to the milk-white steed,
    And pu'd the rider down.

Sae weel she minded what he did say
    And young Tom-lin did win;
Syne cover'd him wi her green mantle
    As blythe's a bird in spring.

Out then spak the queen o Fairies,
    Out of a bush o broom;
Them that has gotten young Tom-lin,
    Has gotten a stately groom.

Out then spak the queen o Fairies,
    And an angry queen was she;
Shame betide her ill-fard face,
    And an ill death may she die,
For she's ta'en awa the boniest knight
    In a' my companie.

known   But had I kend, Tom-lin, she says,
    What now this night I see,
eyes   I wad hae taen out thy twa grey een,
wood   And put in twa een o 'ree.

FUNERAL OF ROBERT BURNS Dumfries 1796

BURNS MONUMENT AND MUSEUM
Kay Park, Kilmarnock

HAD I THE WYTE?

TUNE: *Come kiss with me*

Based on a traditional fragment in the Herd collection
and a bawdy version in the Merry Muses, which Burns
had a hand in, even if he did not wholly compose it as
well.

Had I the wyte? had I the wyte?   Was I to blame?
Had I the wyte? she bade me!
She watch'd me by the hie-gate side, high road
 And up the loan she shaw'd me; lane, showed
And when I wadna venture in,   would not
 A coward loon she ca'd me!   fool
Had Kirk and State been in the gate, way
 I'd lighted when she bade me.

Sae craftilie she took me ben   inside
 And bade me mak nae clatter:— no noise
'For our ramgunshoch, glum guidman surly
 Is o'er ayont the water.'   away beyond
Whae'er shall say I wanted grace
 When I did kiss and dawte her, fondle
Let him be planted in my place,
 Syne say I was the fauter!   Then, trangressor

Could I for shame, could I for shame,
 Could I for shame refus'd her?
And wadna manhood been to blame would not have been
 Had I unkindly used her?
He claw'd her wi the ripplin'-kame, wool-comb
 And blae and bluidy bruis'd her— blue
When sic a husband was frae hame.
 What wife but wad excus'd her!

I dighted ay her e'en sae blue,   wiped, eyes
 An bann'd the cruel randy,   cursed, scoundrel
And, weel I wat, her willin mou   wot, mouth
 Was sweet as sugarcandie.
At gloamin-shot, it was, I wot,   sunset
 I lighted—on the Monday;
But I cam thro the Tyseday's dew, Tuesday's
 To wanton Willie's brandy.

U

COMIN THRO THE RYE

TUNE: *Miller's Wedding*

This was a revision and expansion of an old song in the
collection of Thomas Mansfield formed in 1770-80.
Various bawdy versions were current in the eighteenth
century, and there was even an English pantomime
song 'If a body meet a body' entered at Stationers'
Hall on 6th June 1796.

CHORUS

O, Jenny's a' sweet, poor body,
Jenny's seldom dry:
She draigl't a' her petticoatie,
Comin thro the rye!

Comin thro the rye, poor body,
Comin thro the rye,
She draigl't a' her petticoatie,
Comin thro the rye!

If   Gin a body meet a body
Comin thro the rye,
Gin a body kiss a body,
Need a body cry?

Gin a body meet a body
Comin thro the glen,
Gin a body kiss a body,
know   Need the warld ken?

THE ROWIN 'T IN HER APRON

A ballad collected by Burns in the vicinity of
Dumfries, dealing with the story of the aftermath of
the 1715 Rebellion. 'Young Terreagles' (l.25) was
John, Lord Maxwell who died in 1776.

Our young lady's a huntin gane,
Sheets nor blankets has she ta'en,
before   But she's born her auld son or she cam hame,
rolled   And she's row'd him in her apron.

Her apron was o the hollan fine,
Laid about wi laces nine;
lose   She thought it a pity her babie should tyne,
And she's row'd him in her apron.

Her apron was o the hollan sma,
Laid about wi laces a',
She thought it a pity her babe to let fa,
And she row'd him in her apron.

Her father says within the ha,
Amang the knights and nobles a,
I think I hear a babie ca,
In the chamber amang our young ladies.

578

The Rowin 't In Her Apron

O father dear it is a bairn,
I hope it will do you nae harm,
For the daddie I lo'ed, and he'll lo'e me again,
    For the rowin 't in my apron.

O he is a gentleman, or is he a clown,
That has brought thy fair body down,
I would not for a' this town
    The rowin 't in thy apron.

Young Terreagles he's nae clown,
He is the toss of Edinborrow town,   toast
And he'll buy me a braw new gown   fine
    For the rowin 't in thy apron.

Its I hae castles, I hae towers,
I hae barns, I hae bowers,
A' that is mine it shall be thine,
    For the rowin 't in thy apron.

CHARLIE, HE'S MY DARLING

The original was a street-ballad of about 1775, which
Burns reduced in length and greatly refined. The
'Young Chevalier' was Prince Charles Edward Stuart,
the Young Pretender.

CHORUS
    An Charlie he's my darling,
    My darling, my darling,
    Charlie he's my darling—
    The Young Chevalier!

'Twas on a Monday morning
    Right early in the year,
That Charlie came to our town—
    The Young Chevalier!

As he was walking up the street
    The city for to view,
O, there he spied a bonie lass
    The window looking thro!

Sae light's he jimpèd up the stair,   jumped
    And tirl'd at the pin;   rattled on the latch
And wha sae ready as hersel
    To let the laddie in!

579

He set his Jenny on his knee,
  All in his Highland dress;
finely, knew   For brawlie weel he kend the way
  To please a bonie lass.

It's up yon heathery mountain
scrubby   And down the scroggy glen,
dare not go   We daurna gang a-milking
  For Charlie and his men!

THE COOPER O CUDDY

TUNE: *Bab at the bowster*

Ascribed to Burns on the basis of the Hastie MS and in his characteristic comic style. The terminology of the barrelmaker's trade is used here very humorously with sexual overtones, though less explicit than 'Cuddy the Cooper' in the Merry Muses.

CHORUS
We'll hide the cooper behint the door,
Behint the door, behint the door,
We'll hide the cooper behint the door,
basket   *And cover him under a mawn, O.*

here about   The Cooper o Cuddy came here awa,
knocked hoops   He ca'd the girrs out o'er us a',
  An our guidwife has gotten a ca',
  That's anger'd the silly guidman, O.

He sought them out, he sought them in,
  Wi 'Deil hae her!' an' 'Deil hae him!'
senile, blind   But the body he was sae doited and blin,
knew not, going   He wist na where he was gaun, O.

They cooper'd at e'en, they cooper'd at morn,
  Till our guidman has gotten the scorn:
each, cuckold's horn   On ilka brow she's planted a horn,
shall   And swears that there they shall stan', O!

LEEZIE LINDSAY

This fragment, collected by Burns, was sent to
Johnson for SMM. The complete ballad was not
published till 1806 and has since become a popular
song.

Will ye go to the Highlands, Leezie Lindsay,
Will ye go to the Highlands wi me;
Will ye go to the Highlands, Leezie Lindsay,
My pride and my darling to be.

FOR THE SAKE O SOMEBODY

Based on Allan Ramsay's lovers' dialogue in The Tea-
Table Miscellany and composed by Burns for SMM.
'Somebody' was a synonym for Bonnie Prince Charlie.

My heart is sair—I dare na tell—   sore
My heart is sair for Somebody:
I could wake a winter night
For the sake o Somebody.
    O-hon! for Somebody!
    O-hey! for Somebody!
I could range the world around
For the sake o Somebody.

Ye Powers that smile on virtuous love,
O, sweetly smile on Somebody!
Frae ilka danger keep him free,   each
And send me safe my Somebody!
    O-hon! for Somebody!
    O-hey! for Somebody!
I wad do—what wad I not? —
For the sake o Somebody!

THE CARDIN O'T, THE SPINNIN O'T

TUNE: *Queensberry's Scots Measure*

Allegedly based on a traditional ballad no longer extant.

The cardin o't, the spinnin o't,
The warpin o't, the winnin o't!
When ilka ell cost me a groat,   each yard, fourpence
The tailor staw the lynin o't.   stole

I coft a stane o haslock woo,   bought the soft wool from
    To mak a wab to Johnie o't,   the lamb's neck, web
For Johnie is my only jo—   darling
    I lo'e him best of onie yet!

For tho his locks be lyart gray,   withered
    And tho his brow be beld aboon,   bald above
Yet I hae seen him on a day
    The pride of a' the parishen.   whole parish

581

SUTORS O SELKIRK

This old ballad was allegedly composed for a group of
Selkirk tailors who enlisted in the army of James IV,
decimated at Flodden in 1513. The blame for this
disaster was popularly, though unjustly, laid on the
Earl of Home. The Forest and the Merse allude to
Ettrick Forest and Berwickshire respectively.

Cobblers

Its up wi the Sutors o Selkirk,
 And down wi the Earl o Hume;

fine

And here is to a' the braw laddies
 That wear the single sol'd shoon:
Its up wi the Sutors o Selkirk,

true

 For they are baith trusty and leal;
And up wi the lads o the Forest,
 And down wi the Merse to the deil.

TIBBIE FOWLER

Herd's MSS contain two unrelated fragments of this
song. Burns collected it in its entirety and corrected it,
with some stanzas of his own.

CHORUS

pulling
cannot
money

Wooin at her, pu'in at her,
 Courtin at her, canna get her:
Filthy elf, it's for her pelf,
 That a' the lads are wooin at her.

Tibbie Fowler o the glen,
 There's o'er mony wooin at her,
Tibbie Fowler o the glen,
 There's o'er mony wooin at her.

Ten cam east and ten cam west,
 Ten cam rowin o'er the water;

fence

Twa came down the lang dyke side,
 There's twa and thirty wooin at her.

out front, inside

There's seven but, and seven ben,
 Seven in her pantry wi her,
Twenty head about the door,
 There's ane and forty wooin at her.

pendants, ears

She's got pendles in her lugs,
 Cockle-shells wad set her better;

silver

High-heel'd shoon and siller tags,
 And a' the lads are wooin at her.

Be a lassie e'er sae black,
 An she hae the name o siller,

If, money
Tinto Hill, Lanarkshire

Set her upo' Tintock-tap,
 The wind will blaw a man till her.

582

Tibbie Fowler

Be a lassie e'er sae fair,
  An she want the pennie siller;
A flie may fell her in the air,
  Before a man be even till her.

kill

THERE'S THREE TRUE GUDE FELLOWS

TUNE: *Three guid fellows ayont the glen*

The three of this title were Alexander Cunningham, Robert Cleghorn and William Dunbar, whom Burns regarded as 'Dear [to me] as the ruddy drops that warm my heart . . . I have a good mind to make verse on you all.'

There's three true gude fellows,
There's three true gude fellows,
There's three true gude fellows
  Down ayont the glen.

beyond

Its now the day is dawin,
But or night do fa' in,
Whase cock's best at crawin,
  Willie thou sall ken.

dawning
before nightfall
Whose
shall know

THE LASS THAT MADE THE BED TO ME

Derived from a version of the Restoration ballad 'The Cumberland Lass.'

When Januar wind was blawin cauld,
  As to the North I took my way,
The mirksome night did me enfauld,
  I knew na where to lodge till day.
But by guid luck a maid I met
  Just in the middle o my care,
And kindly she did me invite
  To walk into a chamber fair.

dark, enfold

I bow'd fu low unto this maid,
  And thank'd her for her courtesie;
I bow'd fu low unto this maid,
  An bade her make a bed to me.
She made the bed baith large and wide,
  Wi twa white hands she spread it down,
She put the cup to her rosy lips,
  And drank:—'Young man, now sleep ye soun.'

both

583

The Lass That Made The Bed To Me

She snatch'd the candle in her hand,
  And frae my chamber went wi speed,
But I call'd her quickly back again
  To lay some mair below my head:
A cod she laid below my head,
  And served me with due respeck,
And, to salute her wi a kiss,
  I put my arms about her neck.

'Haud aff your hands, young man!' she said,
  'And dinna sae uncivil be;
Gif ye hae onie luve for me,
  O, wrang na my virginitie!'
Her hair was like the links o gowd,
  Her teeth were like the ivorie,
Her cheeks like lilies dipt in wine,
  The lass that made the bed to me!

Her bosom was the driven snaw,
  Twa drifted heaps sae fair to see;
Her limbs the polish'd marble stane,
  The lass that made the bed to me!
I kiss'd her o'er and o'er again,
  And ay she wist na what to say.
I laid her 'tween me and the wa'—
  That lassie thocht na lang till day.

Upon the morrow, when we raise,
  I thank'd her for her courtesie;
But ay she blush'd and ay she sigh'd,
  And said:—'Alas, ye've ruined me!'
I clasp'd her waist, and kiss'd her syne,
  While the tear stood twinkling in her e'e,
I said:—'My lassie, dinna cry,
  For ye ay shall mak the bed to me.'

She took her mither's holland sheets,
  An made them a' in sarks to me,
Blythe and merry may she be,
  The lass that made the bed to me!
The bonie lass made the bed to me,
  The braw lass made the bed to me!
I'll ne'er forget till the day I die,
  The lass that made the bed to me.

Glosses:
more
pillow

do not
If

gold

thought it not long

arose

then
eye

shirts

584

THE REEL O STUMPIE

A traditional piece of bawdry which Burns refashioned
to fit the well-known air of the title.

Wap and rowe, wap and row, wrap, roll
 Wap and row the feetie o't, feet
I thought I was a maiden fair,
 Till I heard the greetie o't. crying

My daddie was a Fiddler fine,
 My minnie she made mantie O; mother, gown
And I mysel a thumpin quine, strapping wench
 And danc'd the reel o Stumpie O.

I'LL AY CA' IN BY YON TOWN

TUNE: *I'll gang nae mair to yon town*

Ascribed to Burns on the basis of the Hastie MS.

CHORUS
I'll ay ca' in by yon town
 And by yon garden green again!
I'll ay ca' in by yon town,
 And see my bonie Jean again.

There's nane shall ken, there's nane can guess know
 What brings me back the gate again, way
But she, my fairest faithfu lass,
 And stow'nlins we sall meet again. stealthily

She'll wander by the aiken tree, oaken
 When trystin time draws near again; meeting
And where her lovely form I see,
 O haith! she's doubly dear again.

THE RANTIN LADDIE

The earliest published version of an old ballad known
generally as 'Lord Aboyne', possibly collected by
Burns on his tour of the northeast in 1787.

Aften hae I play'd at the cards and the dice,
 For the love of a bonie rantin laddie; rollicking
But now I maun sit in my father's kitchen neuk, must, corner
 Below a bastart babie.

For my father he will not me own,
 And my mother she neglects me,
And a' my friends hae lightlyed me, slandered
 And their servants they do slight me.

But had I a servant at my command,
 As aft-times I've had many,
That wad rin wi a letter to bonie Glenswood,
 Wi a letter to my rantin laddie.

585

The Rantin Laddie

Oh, is he either a laird, or a lord,
    Or is he but a cadie,
That ye do him ca' sae aften by name,
    Your bonie, bonie rantin laddie.

lackey

Indeed he is baith a laird and a lord,
    And he never was a cadie;
But he is the Earl o bonie Aboyne,
    And he is my rantin laddie.

O ye'se get a servant at your command,
    As aft-times ye've had many,
That sall rin wi a letter to bonie Glensswood,
    A letter to your rantin laddie.

shall run

When lord Aboyne did the letter get,
    O but he blinket bonie;
But or he had read three lines of it,
    I think his heart was sorry.

O wha is he daur be sae bauld,
    Sae cruelly to use my lassie?

dare, bold

   *   *   *   *   *   *   *   *
     *   *   *   *   *   *   *

For her father he will not her know,
    And her mother she does slight her,
And a' her friends hae lightlied her,
    And their servants they neglect her.

Go raise to me my five hundred men,
    Make haste and make them ready;
With a milkwhite steed under every ane,
    For to bring hame my lady.

As they cam in thro Buchan shire,
    They were a company bonie,
With a gude claymore in every hand,
    And O, but they shin'd bonie.

O MAY, THY MORN

TUNE: *The Rashes*

A blend of love and conviviality in Burns's finest lyric style.

O May, thy morn was ne'er sae sweet
    As the mirk night o December!
For sparkling was the rosy wine,
    And private was the chamber,
And dear was she I dare na name,
    But I will ay remember:

dark

And here's to them that, like oursel,
  Can push about the jorum!
And here's to them that wish us weel—
  May a' that's guid watch o'er 'em!
And here's to them, we dare na tell,
  The dearest o the quorum!

AS I CAM O'ER THE CAIRNEY MOUNT

Burns took an original but bawdy ballad and expurgated it to produce this beautiful song.

CHORUS
O my bonie Highland lad,
  My winsome, weelfar'd Highland laddie;   handsome
Wha wad mind the wind and rain,
  Sae weel row'd in his tartan plaidie.   well wrapped

As I cam o'er the Cairney mount,
  And down amang the blooming heather,
Kindly stood the milkin-shiel   -shed
  To shelter frae the stormy weather.

Now Phebus blinkit on the bent,   bent-grass
  And o'er the knowes the lambs were bleating: knolls
But he wan my heart's consent,   won
  To be his ain at the neist meeting.   next

HIGHLAND LADDIE

One of a number of songs bearing this title, this version dates from 1745. Burns added opening lines of his own.

    She
The bonniest lad that e'er I saw,
  Bonie laddie, highland laddie,
Wore a plaid and was fu braw,   handsome
  Bonie Highland laddie.

On his head a bonnet blue,
  Bonie &c.
His royal heart was firm and true,
  Bonie &c.

Highland Laddie

He
Trumpets sound and cannons roar,
Bonie lassie, Lawland lassie,
And a' the hills wi echoes roar,
Bonie Lawland lassie.

Glory, Honor now invite
Bonie &c.
For freedom and my King to fight
Bonie &c.

She
The sun a backward course shall take,
Bonie laddie &c.
Ere ought thy manly courage shake;
Bonie laddie &c.

Go, for yourself procure renown,
Bonie &c.
And for your lawful King his crown,
Bonie Highland laddie.

THE HIGHLAND BALOU

A versification by Burns of an old Gaelic nursery song
'Cagaran Gaolach.'

lullaby   Hee balou, my sweet wee Donald,
Picture o the great Clanronald!
Finely knows   Brawlie kens our wanton Chief
Wha gat my young Highland thief.

Blessings, throat   Leeze me on thy bonie craigie!
horse   An thou live, thou'll steal a naigie,
Travel the country thro and thro,
And bring hame a Carlisle cow!

Thro the Lawlands, o'er the Border,
further   Weel, my babie, may thou furder,
Harry, fools, low Herry the louns o the laigh Countrie,
Then   Syne to the Highlands hame to me!

BANNOCKS O BEAR MEAL

Ascribed to Burns, on the basis of the Hastie MS, but
probably as taken down by him without revision.

CHORUS
Bannocks o bear meal,   barley
Bannock o barley,
Here's to the Highlandman's
Bannocks o barley!

Wha in a brulyie will   brawl
First cry 'A parley?'
Never the lads wi the
Bannocks o barley!

Wha, in his wae days,   sad
Were loyal to Charlie?   Prince Charles
Wha but the lads wi the   Edward Stuart
Bannocks o barley!

WAE IS MY HEART

Another old ballad, more or less as taken down, with
some slight revision.

Wae is my heart, and the tear's in my e'e;   Sad, eye
Lang, lang Joy's been a stranger to me:
Forsaken and friendless my burden I bear,
And the sweet voice o pity ne'er sounds in my ear.

Love thou has pleasures—and deep hae I lov'd!
Love thou has sorrows and sair hae I prov'd!
But this bruised heart that now bleeds in my breast,
I can feel by its throbbings, will soon be at rest.

O, if I were where happy I hae been,
Down by yon stream and yon bonie castle green!
For there he is wand'ring and musing on me,
Wha wad soon dry the tear frae his Phillis' e'e!

HERE'S HIS HEALTH IN WATER

TUNE: *The Job of Journey-work*

A song of illicit love with Jacobite overtones, it refers to the toast to the 'King o'er the water' (i.e. the English Channel) — hence the custom of raising glasses over a bowl of water, or drinking the toast in water.

Altho my back be at the wa',
transgressor   And tho he be the fautor,
Altho my back be at the wa',
     Yet, here's his health in water!

sadly go   O, wae gae by his wanton sides,
finely   Sae brawly's he could flatter!
sore   Till for his sake I'm slighted sair,
suffer, country gossip   And dree the kintra clatter!
But, tho my back be at the wa',
     Yet, here's his health in water!

both   He follow'd me baith out and in,
corners, Kilmarnock   Thro a' the nooks o Killie;
He follow'd me baith out an in,
erect penis   Wi a stiff stanin pillie.
But when he gat atween my legs,
splash   We made an unco splatter;
oath, believe, softened   An haith, I trow, I soupled it,
boldly, work vigorously   Tho bauldly he did blatter;
But now my back is at the wa',
     Yet here's his health in water.

GUDE WALLACE

This popular ballad was derived from an episode in Blind Harry's 'Schir Willyame Wallace.' Burns reworked it and added seven stanzas of his own, particularly the Lochmaben episode which he probably collected locally.

own   O for my ain king, quo gude Wallace,
     The rightfu king o fair Scotland;
Between me and my Sovereign Blude
sown   I think I see some ill seed sawn.

that, leaped   Wallace out over yon river he lap,
     And he has lighted low down on yon plain,
And he was aware of a gay ladie,
     As she was at the well washing.

tidings   What tydins, what tydins, fair lady, he says,
     What tydins hast thou to tell unto me;
What tydins, what tydins, fair lady, he says,
     What tydins hae ye in the South Countrie.

Gude Wallace

Low down in yon wee Ostler house,
   There is fyfteen Englishmen,
And they are seeking for gude Wallace,
   It's him to take and him to hang.

There's nocht in my purse, quo gude Wallace.
   There's nocht, not even a bare pennie;
But I will down to yon wee Ostler house
   Thir fyfteen Englishmen to see.

And when he cam to yon wee Ostler house,
   He bad benedicite be there;   *good fortune*

. . . .
. . . .

Where was ye born, auld crookit Carl,   *old man*
   Where was ye born, in what countrie;
I am a true Scot born and bred,
   And an auld, crookit carl just sic as ye see.   *such*

I wad gie fyfteen shilling to onie crookit carl,
   To onie crookit carl just sic as ye,
If ye will get me gude Wallace,
   For he is the man I wad very fain see.

He hit the proud Captain alang the chafft-blade,   *jawbone*
   That never a bit o meat he ate mair;
And he sticket the rest at the table where they sat,   *stabbed*
   And he left them a' lyin sprawlin there.

Get up, get up, gudewife, he says,
   And get to me some dinner in haste;
For it will soon be three lang days
   Sin I a bit o meat did taste.

The dinner was na weel readie,
   Nor was it on the table set,
Till other fyfteen Englishmen
   Were a' lighted about the yett.   *gate*

Come out, come out now, gude Wallace,
   This is the day that thou maun die;   *must*
I lippen nae sae little to God, he says,   *depend*
   Altho I be but ill wordie.   *unworthy*

The gudewife had an auld gudeman,   *husband*
   By gude Wallace he stiffly stood,
Till ten o the fyfteen Englishmen
   Before the door lay in their blude.

The other five to the greenwood ran,
   And he hang'd these five upon a grain: *bough*
And on the morn wi his merry men a'
   He sat at dine in Lochmaben town.

THE AULD MAN'S MARE'S DEAD

This song by Peter Birnie, an itinerant fiddler in Fife
c.1710, was revised by Burns for SMM in 1795. The
poor old horse seems to have been a veritable catalogue
of veterinary ailments.

CHORUS

The auld man's mare's dead,
The poor man's mare's dead,
The auld man's mare's dead,

above   *A mile aboon Dundee,*

-eared, pinch-lipped   She was cut-luggit, painch-lippit,
-bellied, stanchion-footed   Steel-waimit, staincher-fittit,
lantern-jawed, long-necked   Chanler-chaftit, lang-neckit,
       Yet the brute did die.

haunch-bone, knots, corners   Her lunzie-banes were knaggs and neuks,
cramps, wryneck   She had the cleeks, the cauld, the crooks,
urethritis, itch   The jawpish and the wanton yeuks,
eye disease of animals   And the howks aboon her e'e.

rode   My Master rade me to the town,
hitching-rail   He ty'd me to a staincher round,
chopin (Scots measure)   He took a chappin till himsel,
not drop gave   But fient a drap gae me.

THE TAYLOR

Burns reworked an old ballad 'The Taylor of
Hogerglen's Wedding' and added a final chorus of his
own.

The Taylor he cam here to sew,
well knew   And weel he kend the way to woo,
pried, mouth   For ay he pree'd the lassie's mou
As he gaed but and ben O.

CHORUS

For weel he kend the way O
The way O, the way O,
For weel he kend the way O
The lassie's heart to win O.

rose, shook, clothes   The Taylor rase and sheuk his duds,
fleas, clouds   The flaes they flew awa in cluds,
blows   And them that stay'd gat fearfu thuds,
The Taylor prov'd a man O.

CHORUS

twilight   *For now it was the gloamin,*
The gloamin, the gloamin,
For now it was the gloamin
gone   *When a' the rest are gaun O.*

592

THERE GROWS A BONIE BRIER-BUSH

No original of this ballad has been traced, but it has all
the hallmarks of Burns's revision of a folk-song he had
collected.

There grows a bonie brier-bush in our kail-yard,   *vegetable-*
There grows a bonie brier-bush in our kail-yard;   *patch*
And below the bonie brier-bush there's a lassie and a lad,
And they're busy, busy courtin in our kail-yard.

We'll court nae mair below the buss in our kail-yard,   *bush*
We'll court nae mair below the buss in our kail-yard;
We'll awa to Athole's green, and there we'll no be seen,
Whare the trees and the branches will be our safe-guard.

Will ye go to the dancin in Carlyle's ha',
Will ye go to the dancin in Carlyle's ha';
Whare Sandy and Nancy I'm sure will ding them a'?   *beat*
I winna gang to the dance in Carlyle-ha'.   *will not go*

What will I do for a lad, when Sandy gangs awa?
What will I do for a lad, when Sandy gangs awa?
I will awa to Edinburgh and win a pennie fee,
And see an onie bonie lad will fancy me.   *if any bonny*

He's comin frae the North that's to fancy me,
He's comin frae the North that's to fancy me;
A feather in his bonnet and a ribbon at his knee,
He's a bonie, bonie laddie and yon be he.

HERE'S TO THY HEALTH
TUNE: *Laggan Burn*

The manuscript of this song (now at Alloway) bears
Burns's annotation '. . . as far as I can recollect, the
compilation of an illiterate Millwright, about thirty or
forty years ago, somewhere in Ayrshire.'

Here's to thy health, my bonie lass!
    Guid night and joy be wi thee!
I'll come nae mair to thy bower-door   *no more*
    To tell thee that I lo'e thee.
O, dinna think, my pretty pink,
    But I can live without thee:
I vow and swear I dinna care   *do not*
    How lang ye look about ye!

Thou'rt ay sae free informing me
    Thou hast nae mind to marry,   *desire*
I'll be as free informing thee
    Nae time hae I to tarry:
I ken thy freens try ilka means   *friends, every*
    Frae wedlock to delay thee
(Depending on some higher chance),
    But fortune may betray thee.

I ken they scorn my low estate,
　　But that does never grieve me,
For I'm as free as any he—
a little money　　Sma' siller will relieve me!
I'll count my health my greatest wealth
　　Sae lang as I'll enjoy it.
I'll fear nae scant, I'll bode nae want
　　As lang's I get employment.

But far off fowls hae feathers fair,
　　And, ay until ye try them,
Tho they seem fair, still have a care—
　　They may prove as bad as I am!
twelve　　But at twel at night, when the moon shines bright,
My dear, I'll come and see thee,
For the man that loves his mistress weel,
　　Nae travel makes him weary.

IT WAS A' FOR OUR RIGHTFU KING

**Burns rewrote the chap-book ballad 'Mally Stewart'
(c. 1746) which deals with an episode in the Williamite
War of 1689-90 in Ireland. The 'rightfu king' was
King James VII and II.**

It was a' for our rightfu King
　　We left fair Scotland's strand;
It was a' for our rightfu King
　　We e'er saw Irish land, my dear—
　　We e'er saw Irish land.

Now a' is done that men can do,
　　And a' is done in vain,
My Love and Native Land fareweel,
must　　For I maun cross the main, my dear—
　　For I maun cross the main.

He turn'd him right and round about
　　Upon the Irish shore,
gave　　And gae his bridle reins a shake,
　　With adieu for evermore, my dear—
　　And adieu for evermore!

The soger frae the war returns,
　　The sailor frae the main,
But I hae parted frae my love,
　　Never to meet again, my dear—
　　Never to meet again.

It Was A' For Our Rightfu King

When day is gane, and night is come,
And a' folk bound to sleep,
I think on him that's far awa
    The lee-lang night, and weep, my dear—
    The lee-lang night and weep.

THE HIGHLAND WIDOW'S LAMENT

Attributed to Burns (on the basis of the Hastie MS).
Not surprisingly, he seldom admitted authorship of
Jacobite songs at a time when expression of such
sentiments could still be dangerous.

O, I am come to the low countrie—
    Ochon, ochon, ochrie!—   alas, alack
Without a penny in my purse
    To buy a meal to me.

It was na sae in the Highland hills—
    Ochon, ochon, ochrie!—
Nae woman in the country wide
    Sae happy was as me.

For then I had a score o kye—   cattle
    Ochon, ochon, ochrie!—
Feeding on yon hill sae high
    And giving milk to me.

And there I had three score o yowes—   ewes
    Ochon, ochon, ochrie!—
Skipping on yon bonie knowes   knolls
    And casting woo to me.   wool

I was the happiest of a' the clan—
    Sair, sair may I repine!—
For Donald was the brawest man,
    And Donald he was mine.

Till Charlie Stewart cam at last   Prince Charles Edward Stuart
    Sae far to set us free:
My Donald's arm was wanted then
    For Scotland and for me.

Their waefu fate what need I tell?   sad
    Right to the wrang did yield;
My Donald and his country fell
    Upon Culloden field.

Ochon! O Donald, O!
    Ochon, ochon, ochrie!
Nae woman in the warld wide,
    Sae wretched now as me!

O, STEER HER UP AN HAUD HER GAUN

Apparently a reconstruction of a traditional fragment
in The Tea-Table Miscellany.

guide, hold, going   O, steer her up, an haud her gaun—
dear   Her mither's at the mill, jo,
if, will not   An gin she winna tak a man
    E'en let her tak her will, jo.
offer   First shore her wi a gentle kiss,
order, drink   And ca' anither gill, jo,
    An gin she tak the thing amiss,
scold   E'en let her flyte her fill, jo.

bashful   O, steer her up, an be na blate,
    An gin she tak it ill, jo,
    Then leave the lassie till her fate,
    And time nae langer spill, jo!
    Ne'er break your heart for ae rebute,
    But think upon it still, jo,
    That gin the lassie winna do't,
    Ye'll find anither will, jo.

WEE WILLIE GRAY

A nursery jingle (other versions are 'Wee Totum Fogg'
and the English 'Tommy Tacket'), revised by Burns
according to James Johnson.

    Wee Willie Gray an his leather wallet,
    Peel a willow-wand to be him boots and jacket!
trousers   The rose upon the brier will be him trouse an doublet—
    The rose upon the brier will be him trouse an doublet!

    Wee Willie Gray an his leather wallet,
shirt, neck-tie   Twice a lily-flower will be him sark and gravat!
    Feathers of a flie wad feather up his bonnet—
    Feathers of a flie wad feather up his bonnet!

GUDEEN TO YOUR KIMMER

Burns appears to have taken the fragments of two
traditional ballads and welded them together, with
extensive revision to produce this song for SMM. Part
of this was preserved in the Herd MSS, which Burns
probably examined during his stay in Edinburgh.

CHORUS
We're a' noddin, nid nid noddin,
    We're a' noddin at our house at hame,
We're a' noddin, nid nid noddin,
    W'ere a' noddin at our house at hame.

Good evening, wench   Gudeen to you kimmer
    And how do ye do?
    Hiccup, quo kimmer,
drunk   The better that I'm fou,

596

Gudeen To You Kimmer

Kate sits i' the neuk,   corner
    Suppin hen-broo ;   -brew
Deil tak Kate
    An she be na noddin too!

How's a' wi you, kimmer,
    And how do ye fare?
A pint o the best o't,
    And twa pints mair.   more

How's a' wi you, kimmer,
    And how do ye thrive;
How mony bairns hae ye?   children
    Quo kimmer, I hae five.

Are they a' Johny's?
    Eh! atweel no:
Twa o them were gotten   conceived
    When Johny was awa.

Cats like milk
    And dogs like broo;
Lads like lasses weel,
    And lasses lads too.

O, AY MY WIFE SHE DANG ME

Based on a traditional piece of bawdry, revised for SMM.

CHORUS

O, ay my wife she dang me,   struck
    An aft my wife she bang'd me!
If ye gie a woman a' her will,
    Guid faith! she'll soon o'er-gang ye. dominate

On peace an rest my mind was bent,
    And, fool I was! I married;
But never honest man's intent
    Sae cursedly miscarried.

Some sairie comfort at the last,   sorry
    When a' thir days are done, man: their
My 'pains o hell' on earth is past,
    I'm sure o bliss aboon, man.   above

SCROGGAM

David Murison suggests that the title comes from 'scrag 'em', one of the cries of the London street-mob, and may have been derived from a traditional English lynching ballad. Ruffum ('rough 'em') has the same source but Kinsley thought it may have also had sexual connotations.

dwelt

There was a wife wonn'd in Cockpen,
    Scroggam!
She brew'd guid ale for gentlemen:

a Catholic priest
or monk

    Sing Auld Cowl, lay you down by me—
      Scroggam, my dearie, ruffum!

daughter

The guidwife's dochter fell in a fever,
    Scroggam!
The priest o the parish fell in anither:
    Sing Auld Cowl, lay you down by me—
      Scroggam, my dearie, ruffum!

They laid the twa i' the bed thegither,
    Scroggam!

the one, the other

That the heat o the tane might cool the tither;
    Sing Auld Cowl, lay you down by me—
      Scroggam, my dearie, ruffum!

O, GUID ALE COMES

Stenhouse claimed this as wholly Burns's work, but Johnson's annotation 'Corrected by R. Burns' is probably more accurate.

CHORUS

O, guide ale comes, and guid ale goes,

makes
shoes
above

Guid ale gars me sell my hose,
Sell my hose, and pawn my shoon—
Guid ale keeps my heart aboon!

oxen

I had sax owsen in a pleugh,
And they drew a' weel eneugh:
I sell'd them a' just ane by ane—
Guid ale keeps the heart aboon!

keeps
copulate, wench
stool of repentance

Guid ale hauds me bare and busy,
Gars me moop wi the servant hizzie,
Stand i' the stool when I hae dune—
Guid ale keeps the heart aboon!

598

MY LORD A-HUNTING HE IS GANE

TUNE: *My lady's gown, there's gairs upon't*

Burns wrote to Johnson in May 1795 saying he hoped
to procure the air, for which he subsequently wrote
these words, published in SMM, 1803. The tune was
composed by the Ayrshire musician James Gregg. The
Kennedy family, Earls of Cassilis, were the chief family
in Carrick.

CHORUS

My lady's gown, there's gairs upon't,　　　　　　stripes
And gowden flowers sae rare upon't;
But Jenny's jimps and jirkinet,　　　　　　skirts, bodice
My lord thinks meikle mair upon't!　　　　　　much more

My lord a-hunting he is gane,
But hounds or hawks wi him are nane;
By Colin's cottage lies his game,
If Colin's Jenny be at hame.

My lady's white, my lady's red,
And kith and kin o Cassillis' blude;
But her ten-pund lands o tocher guid　　　　　　dowry
Were a' the charms his lordship lo'ed.

Out o'er yon muir, out o'er yon moss,　　　　　　bog
Whare gor-cocks thro the heather pass,　　　　　　red grouse
There wons auld Colin's bonie lass,
A lily in a wilderness.

Sae sweetly move her genty limbs,
Like music notes o lovers' hymns!
The diamond-dew in her een sae blue,
Where laughing love sae wanton swims!

My lady's dink, my lady's drest,　　　　　　trim
The flower and fancy o the west;
But the lassie that a man lo'es best,
O, that's the lass to mak him blest!

SWEETEST MAY

TUNE: *Kinloch of Kinloch*

This is a revision of 'There's my Thumb I'll ne'er
beguile thee', published by Ramsay in Tea-Table
Miscellany.

Sweetest May let love inspire thee;
Take a heart which he designs thee;
As thy constant slave regard it;
For its faith and truth reward it.

Proof o shot to Birth or Money,
Not the wealthy, but the bonie;
Not high-born, but noble-minded,
In Love's silken band can bind it.

599

JOCKIE'S TA'EN THE PARTING KISS

TUNE: *Bonie lass tak a man*

A Scottish version of an English song published as a
'Scotch' ballad in 1776.

Jockie's ta'en the parting kiss,
O'er the mountain he is gane,
And with him is a' my bliss—
Nought but griefs with me remain.
Spare my luve, ye winds that blaw,
Plashy sleets and beating rain!
Spare my luve, thou feathery snaw,
Drifting o'er the frozen plain!

When the shades of evening creep
O'er the day's fair, gladsome e'e,
Sound and safely may he sleep,
Sweetly blythe his waukening be!
He will think on her he loves,
Fondly he'll repeat her name;
For where'er he distant roves,
Jockie's heart is still at hame.

BONIE PEG-A-RAMSAY

Peg-a-Ramsay or Peggy Ramsay is a well-known figure
in Anglo-Saxon bawdry from medieval times onward.
Burns here conceals the lady's legendary sexual prowess
until the punch-line — the milling metaphor was a
familiar euphemism in his day for sexual activity.

Cauld is the e'enin blast
the north wind   O Boreas o'er the pool
dawn   An dawin, it is dreary,
birches, Christmas   When birks are bare at Yule.

O, cauld blaws the e'enin blast,
When bitter bites the frost,
dark   And in the mirk and dreary drift
The hills and glens are lost!

Ne'er sae murky blew the night
That drifted o'er the hill,
But bonie Peg-a-Ramsay
Gat grist to her mill.

OVER SEA, OVER SHORE

'A cento of old catchwords' (Henley and Henderson).

There was a bonie lass, and a bonie, bonie lass,
And she lo'ed her bonie laddie dear,
Till War's loud alarms tore her laddie frae her arms
Wi monie a sigh, and a tear.

Over Sea, Over Shore

Over sea, over shore, where the cannons loudly roar,
He still was a stranger to fear,
And nocht could him quail, or his bosom assail,
But the bonie lass he loed sae dear.

THERE'S NEWS, LASSES, NEWS

TUNE: *Captain Mackenzie's Reel*

A blend of nursery rhyme chorus, old fragments from
the Herd collection and original lines.

CHORUS

The wean wants a cradle,	baby
And the cradle wants a cod,	pillow
I'll no gang to my bed,	go
Until I get a nod.	

There's news, lasses, news,
Guid news I've to tell!
There's a boatfu o lads
Come to our town to sell!

'Father,' quo she, 'Mither,' quo she,
'Do what you can:
I'll no gang to my bed
Until I get a man!'

I hae as guid a craft rig	croft-ridge
As made o yird and stane;	earth, stone
And waly fa' the ley-crap	woe befall, meadow crop
For I maun till'd again.	must plough it

O, THAT I HAD NE'ER BEEN MARRIED

The first eight lines are 'an old Scots ballad' which
Burns quoted to Mrs Dunlop, and added the final
stanza to complete an eloquently simple expression of
fear and want. The air dates from the seventeenth
century.

CHORUS

Ance crowdie, twice crowdie,	gruel
Three times crowdie in a day!	
Gin ye crowdie onie mair,	If, any more
Ye'll crowdie a' my meal away.	

O, that I had ne'er been married,	
I wad never had nae care!	
Now I've gotten wife an bairns,	children
An they cry 'Crowdie' ever mair	

Waefu Want and Hunger fley me,	Woeful, thrash
Glowrin by the hallan en';	Staring, porch-end
Sair I fech them at the door,	Sore, fight
But ay I'm eerie they come ben.	afraid, inside

THE GERMAN LAIRDIE

Burns's abridged version of a lengthy political ballad, current in the period following the accession of George Louis, Elector of Hanover as King of Great Britain in 1714. The Whigs were the ascendant party at the time. The Revolution referred to in 1.9 was the overthrow of the old Stuart dynasty in 1688.

CHORUS

Sing heedle liltie, teedle liltie,
Andum tandum tandie;
Sing fal de dal, de dal lal lal,
Sing howdle liltie dandie.

What merriment has taen the whigs,
I think they be gaen mad, Sir,
Wi playing up their whiggish jigs,
Their dancin may be sad, Sir.

The Revolution principles
Has put their heads in bees, Sir;
They're a' fa'n out amang themsels,
Deil tak the first that grees, Sir.

a spin

wins

EPITAPH FOR HUGH LOGAN OF LOGAN

Hugh Logan (1739-1802), laird of Logan near Cumnock, enjoyed quite a reputation as a man who delighted in wine, women and song — a man very much after Burns's own heart.

Here lyes Squire Hugh — Ye harlot crew,
Come mak your water on him,
I'm sure that he well pleas'd would be
To think ye pish'd upon him.

MUIRLAND MEG

TUNE: *Saw Ye My Eppie McNab*

Muirland Meg, alias Meg Hog or Monkery Meg, kept a brothel at Dumfries Whitesands and died c. 1811.

Amang our young lassies there's Muirland Meg,
She'll beg or she work, and she'll play or she beg,
At thretten her maidenhead flew to the gate,
And the door o her cage stands open yet.

thirteen

Her kittle black een they wad thirl you thro,
Her rose-bud lips cry, miss me now;
The curls and links o her bonie black hair,
Wad put you in mind that the lassie has mair.

skittish eyes, thrill

locks

An armfu o love is her bosom sae plump,
A span o delight is her middle sae jimp;
A taper, white leg, and a thumpin thie,
And a fiddle near by, an ye play a wee!

neat
thigh
a little

602

Muirland Meg

Love's her delight, and kissin's her treasure,
She'll·stick at nae price, and ye gie her gude measure.   if
As lang's a sheep-fit, and as girt's a goose-egg,   sheep-foot, broad
And that's the measure o Muirland Meg.

THE PATRIARCH

TUNE: *The auld cripple Dow*

A curious safety-valve for the extreme puritanism of
Scottish Calvinism has been the abundance of comic —
not to say coarse — verse with biblical themes. This
composition by Burns belongs to an old and well-
established genre.

As honest Jacob on a night,
  Wi his beloved beauty,
Was duly laid on wedlock's bed,
  And noddin at his duty:
    Tal de dal, &c.

'How lang' she says, 'ye fumblin wretch,
  Will ye be fuckin at it?
My eldest wean might die of age,
  Before that ye could get it.

'Ye pegh, and grane, and groazle there,   pant, groan, breathe heavily
  And mak an unco splutter,   mighty
And I maun ly and thole you here,   must, endure
  And fient a hair the better.'   not

Then he, in wrath, put up his graith,   tool
  'The deevil's in the hizzie!   hussy
I mow as I mow the lave,   rest
  And night and day I'm bisy.   busy

'I've bairn'd the servant gypsies baith,   both
  Forbye your titty Leah;   sister
Ye barren jad, ye put me mad,   jade
  What mair can I do wi you.

'There's ne'er a mow I've gi'en the lave,   rest
  But ye ha'e got a dizzen;   dozen
And dam a ane ye 'se get again,
  Altho your cunt should gizzen.   shrivel

Then Rachel calm, as ony lamb,   any
  She claps him on the waulies,   genitals
Quo she, 'ne'er fash a woman's clash,   heed, tongue
  In trowth, ye mow me braulies.   splendidly

'My dear 'tis true, for mony a mow,
    I'm your ungratefu debtor;
don't know   But ance again, I dinna ken,
    We'll aiblens happen better.'

Then honest man! wi little wark,
    He soon forgat his ire;
cast off, shirt   The patriarch, he coost the sark,
    And up and till 't like fire!!!

THE TROGGER

TUNE: *Gillicrankie*

Probably traditional to some extent, it was largely
inspired by John Lewars who wagered that Burns
'could not get a word to clink with' Ecclefechan,
which they were visiting at the time. Burns uses
'troggin' (trucking) as a metaphor for coitus.

As I cam down by Annan side,
    Intending for the border,
scrubby   Amang the scroggie banks and braes,
pedlar   Wha met I but a trogger.
He laid me down upon my back,
    I thought he was but jokin,
Till he was in me to the hilts,
pack-ware   O the deevil tak sic troggin!

What could I say, what could I do,
cursed, sore   I bann'd and sair misca'd him,
up and down   But whiltie-whaltie gae'd his arse
    The mair that I forbade him:
braced, stone   He stell'd his foot against a stane,
every   And doubl'd ilka stroke in,
went crazy   Till I gaed daft amang his hands,
    O the deevil tak sic troggin!

Then up we raise, and took the road,
    And in by Ecclefechan,
made   Where brandy-stoup we gart it clink,
froth, cup (quaich)   And the strang-beer ream the quech in.
below, bent-grass, slopes   Bedown the bents o Bonshaw braes,
    We took the partin yokin;
scratched, sorry, since then   But I've claw'd a sairy cunt synsine,
    O the deevil tak sic troggin!

THE JOLLY GAUGER

TUNE: *We'll gang nae mair a rovin*

A fellow-exciseman is said to have composed the
original, but it incorporates an anecdote picked up by
Burns, concerning a beggar woman in the Merse, and
may have been reworked by him.

There was a jolly gauger, a gauging he did ride,
And he has met a beggar down by yon river side.
    An we'll gang nae mair a rovin wi ladies to the wine,
    When a beggar wi her meal-pocks can fidge her tail sae fine.   -bags, shake

Amang the broom he laid her, amang the broom sae green,
And he 's fa'n to the beggar, as she had been a queen.
    An we'll gang, &c.

My blessings on thee, laddie, thou 's done my turn sae weel,
Wilt thou accept, dear laddie, my pock and pickle meal?   little
    An we'll, &c.

Sae blyth the beggar took the bent, like ony bird in spring,
Sae blyth the beggar took the bent, and merrily did sing.
    An we'll, &c.

My blessings on the gauger, o gaugers he 's the chief.
Sic kail ne'er crost my kettle, nor sic a joint o beef.
    An we'll, &c.

WHA'LL MOW ME NOW?

TUNE: *Comin thro the rye*

Attributed to Burns by Scott Douglas and J. de L.
Ferguson on stylistic grounds. In this case military
terms (bandoliers, pistol) are used as sexual metaphors.

O wha'll mow me now, my jo,   darling
    An wha'll mow me now:
A sodger wi his bandileers   bandoliers (testicles)
    Has bang'd my belly fu.

O, I hae tint my rosy cheek,   lost
    Likewise my waste sae sma',   waist
O wae gae by the sodger lown,   woe befall, fool
    The sodger did it a'.
    An wha'll, &c.

Now I maun thole the scornfu sneer   must, tolerate
    O mony a saucy quine;   girl
When, curse upon her godly face!
    Her cunt 's as merry 's mine.
    An wha'll, &c.

holds, vulva

miscalls

leave own husband

salty

brat

Our dame hauds up her wanton tail,
    As due as she gaes lie;
An yet misca's a young thing,
    The trade if she but try.
      An wha'll, &c.

Our dame can lae her ain gudeman,
    An mow for glutton greed;
An yet misca's a poor thing
    That 's mowin for its bread.
      An wha'll, &c.

Alake! sae sweet a tree as love,
    Sic bitter fruit should bear!
Alake, that e'er a merry arse,
    Should draw a sa'tty tear.
      An wha'll, &c.

But deevil damn the lousy loun,
    Denies the bairn he got!
Or lea's the merry arse he lo'ed
    To wear a ragged coat!
      An wha'll, &c.

O SAW YE MY MAGGIE

Burns's burlesque parody of 'Saw ye nae my Peggy' was
probably based on a bawdy original. The Abbotsford MS
has a mock-testament from Burns bequeathing these verses
to his friend Alexander Findlater.

Saw ye my Maggie?
    Saw ye my Maggie?
Saw ye my Maggie?
    Comin oer the lea?

What mark has your Maggie,
What mark has your Maggie,
What mark has your Maggie,
    That ane may ken her be?

one, know

My Maggie has a mark,
Ye'll find it in the dark,
It 's in below her sark,
    A little aboon her knee.

chemise

What wealth has your Maggie,
What wealth has your Maggie,
What wealth has your Maggie,
    In tocher, gear, or fee?

dowry, possessions

606

O Saw Ye My Maggie

My Maggie has a treasure,
A hidden mine o pleasure,
I'll howk it at my leisure,   dig
    It 's alane for me.

How loe ye your Maggy,
How loe ye your Maggy,
How loe ye your Maggy,
    An loe nane but she?

Ein that tell our wishes,
Eager glowing kisses,
Then diviner blisses,
    In holy ecstacy!

How meet you your Maggie,
How meet you your Maggie,
How meet you your Maggie,
    When nane 's to hear or see?

Heavenly joys before me,
Rapture trembling o'er me,
Maggie I adore thee,
    On my bended knee!!!

GIE THE LASS HER FAIRIN

TUNE: *Cauld kail in Aberdeen*

**This song was set to one of the poet's favourite melodies.
A fairing was a present from a fairground, a favour given
as a love-token, and hence used as a metaphor for sexual
favours.**

O gie the lass her fairin, lad,
    O gie the lass her fairin,
An something else she'll gie to you,
    That 's waly worth the wearin;   choice
Syne coup her o'er amang the creels,   then knock her over baskets
    When ye hae taen your brandy,
The mair she bangs the less she squeels,
    An hey for houghmagandie.   fornication

Then gie the lass a fairin, lad,
    O gie the lass her fairin,
An she'll gie you a hairy thing,
    An of it be na sparin;
But coup her o'er amang the creels,
    An bar the door wi baith your heels,
The mair she gets the less she squeels;
    An hey for houghmagandie.

THE BOOK-WORMS

Said by Cunningham to have been inscribed in a volume of Shakespeare in a nobleman's library. A variant copied by John Syme was written in a Bible which a friend offered Burns for his inscription.

Through and through th' inspir'd leaves,
　　Ye maggots, make your windings;
But O, respect his lordship's taste,
　　And spare the golden bindings!

ON MARRIAGE

Published in the Henley-Henderson edition, from an undated holograph.

King Solomon

That hackney'd judge of human life,
　　The Preacher and the King,
Observes: 'The man that gets a wife
　　He gets a noble thing.'

But how capricious are mankind,
　　Now loathing, now desirous!
We married men, how oft we find
　　The best of things will tire us!

HERE'S A BOTTLE

'There's nane that's blest of human kind,
But the cheerful and the gay, man.'

In this drinking toast Burns combines two of the things
in life he valued: good wine and good companionship.

would, more
knows

Here's a bottle and an honest man!
　　What wad ye wish for mair, man?
Wha kens, before his life may end,
　　What his share may be o care, man?

Then catch the moments as they fly,
　　And use them as ye ought, man!
Believe me, Happiness is shy,
　　And comes not ay when sought, man!

HER FLOWING LOCKS

An undated fragment which Burns no doubt intended to set to some popular tune.

Her flowing locks, the raven's wing,
Adown her neck and bosom hing.
How sweet unto that breast to cling,
　　And round that neck entwine her!

BURNS STATUE SQUARE, AYR

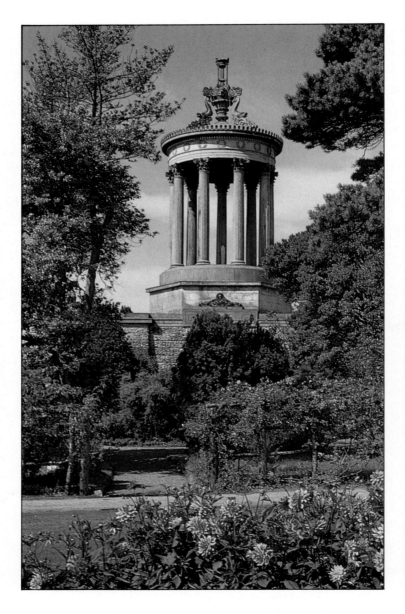

BURNS MONUMENT, ALLOWAY

Her Flowing Locks

Her lips are roses wat wi dew—
O, what a feast, her bonie mou!   mouth
Her cheeks a mair celestial hue,
A crimson still diviner!

A TALE

The origin of this poem has long been disputed, in
spite of the existence of a revised holograph. Dewar
suggested that Burns may have copied out a poem sent
to him and corrected it for the author, but Kinsley
quite rightly points out that it would not have been
necessary to make a fair copy before making a few
minor corrections.

'Twas where the birch and sounding thong are plyed,
The noisy domicile of Pedant-pride;
Where Ignorance her darkening vapour throws,
And cruelty directs the thickening blows;
Upon a time, Sir Abece the great,
In all his pedagogic powers elate,
His awful Chair of state resolves to mount,
And call the trembling Vowels to account.

First enter'd A; a grave, broad, solemn Wight,
But ah! deform'd, dishonest to the sight!
His twisted head look'd backward on his way,
And flagrant from the scourge he grunted, AI!

Reluctant, E stalk'd in; with piteous race
The jostling tears ran down his honest face!
That name, that well-worn name, and all his own,
Pale he surrenders at the tyrant's throne!
The Pedant stifles keen the Roman sound
Not all his mongrel diphthongs can compound;
And next the title following close behind,
He to the nameless, ghastly wretch assign'd.

The cob-webb'd, Gothic dome resounded, Y!
In sullen vengeance, I, disdain'd reply;
The Pedant swung his felon cudgel round,
And knock'd the groaning Vowel to the ground!

In rueful apprehension enter'd O,
The wailing minstrel of despairing woe;
Th' Inquisitor of Spain the most expert
Might there have learnt new mysteries of his art:
So grim, deform'd, with horrors, entering U,
His dearest friend and brother scarcely knew!

As trembling U stood staring all aghast,
The Pedant in his left hand clutch'd him fast;
In helpless infant's tears he dipp'd his right,
Baptiz'd him EU, and kick'd him from his sight.

609

v

THE HENPECKED HUSBAND

Burns's robust commentary on nagging wives and the way to cure them of the habit.

Curs'd be the man, the poorest wretch in life,
The crouching vassal to the tyrant wife!
Who has no will but by her high permission;
Who has not sixpence but in her possession;
Who must to her his dear friend's secret tell,
Who dreads a curtain lecture worse than hell!
Were such the wife had fallen to my part,
I'd break her spirit, or I'd break her heart.
I'd charm her with the magic of a switch,
I'd kiss her maids, and kick the perverse bitch.

ON A DOG OF LORD EGLINTON'S

One of a number of short pieces and fragments collected by James Grierson of Dalgoner, an early collector of Burnsiana (c.1805).

I never barked when out of season,
    I never bit without a reason;
I ne'er insulted weaker brother,
    Nor wronged by force or fraud another.
We brutes are placed a rank below;
    Happy for man could he say so.

EPITAPH

A stark little couplet, collected by James Grierson.

Lo worms enjoy the seat of bliss
Where Lords and Lairds afore did kiss.

BROOM BESOMS

These traditional couplets are redolent of phallic symbolism: 'buying brooms' was a popular Scottish euphemism for female sexual adventures.

CHORUS

Buy broom besoms! wha will buy them now;
Fine heather ringers, better never grew.

I maun hae a wife, whatsoe'er she be;
An she be a woman, that 's eneugh for me.

If that she be bony, I shall think her right:
If that she be ugly, where's the odds at night?

O, an she be young, how happy shall I be!
If that she be auld, the sooner she will die.

Broom Besoms

If that she be fruitfu, O! what joy is there!
If she should be barren, less will be my care.

If she like a drappie, she and I'll agree;   drink
If she dinna like it, there's the mair for me.   does not, more

Be she green or gray; be she black or fair;
Let her be a woman, I shall seek nae mair.   no more

Alternative Verses

Young and souple was I, when I lap the dyke;   pliant, leaped fence
Now I'm auld and frail, I douna step a syke.   cannot, stream

Young and souple was I, when at Lautherslack,
Now I'm auld and frail, and lie at Nansie's back.

Had she gien me butter, when she gae me bread,
I wad looked baulder, wi my beld head.   bolder, bald

NOW HEALTH FORSAKES THAT ANGEL FACE

Burns's authorship has been questioned, despite the existence of a holograph in the Alloway MS.

Now health forsakes that angel face,
    Nae mair my Dearie smiles;   no more
Pale sickness withers ilka grace,   every
    And a' my hopes beguiles:
The cruel Powers reject the prayer
    I hourly mak for thee;
Ye heavens how great is my despair,
    How can I see him die!

PRETTY PEG

Burns's revision of a song which may have been traditional, first published from his holograph in 1808.

As I gaed up by yon gate-end,
    When day was waxin weary,
Wha did I meet come down the street,
    But pretty Peg, my dearie?

Her air sae sweet, an shape complete,
    Wi nae proportion wanting
The Queen of Love did never move
    Wi motion mair enchanting!

Wi linked hands we took the sands
    Down by yon winding river;
And O! that hour and shady bower,
    Can I forget it? Never!

611

WHEN FIRST I SAW

TUNE: *Maggie Lauder*

Published in all major editions except Kinsley who
rejected it as spurious. Perhaps the references to 'fair
Jeanie' were too obvious. Henry Dundas (1742-1811),
Treasurer of the Navy (1782), Home Secretary (1791),
created Viscount Melville (1802) was the most
powerful man in Scotland in his time. The 4th Earl of
Hopetoun was one of Scotland's wealthiest landowners
in the 1790s.

CHORUS

She's aye, aye sae blythe, sae gay,
She's aye sae blythe and cheerie,
She's aye sae bonie, blythe and gay,
O, gin I were her dearie!

if

When first I saw fair Jeanie's face,
I couldna tell what ail'd me:
My heart went fluttering pit-a-pat,
My een they almost fail'd me.
She's aye sae neat, sae trim, sae tight,
All grace does round her hover!
Ae look deprived me o my heart,
And I became her lover.

eyes

Had I Dundas's whole estate,
Or Hopetoun's wealth to shine in;
Did warlike laurels crown my brow,
Or humbler bays entwining;
I'd lay them a' at Jeanie's feet,
Could I but hope to move her,
And, prouder than a belted knight
I'd be my Jeanie's lover.

But sair I fear some happier swain
Has gained my Jeanie's favour.
If so, may every bliss be hers,
Though I maun never have her!
But gang she east, or gang she west,
'Twixt Forth and Tweed all over,
While men have eyes, or ears, or taste,
She'll always find a lover.

must
go

SWEET ARE THE BANKS

TUNE: *Cambdelmore*

Sweet are the banks — the banks o Doon,
The spreading flowers are fair,
And everything is blythe and glad,
But I am fu o care.
Thou'll break my heart, thou bonie bird,
That sings upon the bough!

Sweet Are The Banks

Thou minds me o the happy days
    When my fause Luve was true.
Thou'll break my heart, thou bonie bird,
    That sings beside thy mate;
For sae I sat, and sae I sang,
    And wist na o my fate!

Aft hae I rov'd by bonie Doon,
    To see the woodbine twine,
And ilka bird sang o its luve,
    And sae did I o mine.
Wi lightsome heart I pu'd a rose,
    Upon its thorny tree,
But my fause luver staw my rose,
    And left the thorn wi me.
Wi lightsome heart I pu'd a rose,
    Upon a morn in June,
And sae I flourished on the morn,
    And sae was pu'd or noon.

OPEN THE DOOR TO ME

TUNE: *Open the door softly*

Included in all major editions except Kinsley.

O, open the door some pity to shew,
    If love it may na be, O!
Tho thou hast been false, I'll ever prove true—
    O, open the door to me, O!

Cauld is the blast upon my pale cheek,
    But caulder thy love for me, O:
The frost, that freezes the life at my heart,
    Is nought to my pains frae thee, O!

The wan moon sets behind the white wave,
    And Time is setting with me, O:
False friends, false love, farewell! for mair
    I'll ne'er trouble them nor thee, O!

She has open'd the door, she has open'd it wide,
    She sees the pale corse on the plain, O,
'My true love!' she cried, and sank down by his side
    Never to rise again, O!

ALTHO HE HAS LEFT ME

Published in many editions up to 1959, but omitted by
Barke (1955) and Kinsley (1968) as spurious.

Altho he has left me for greed o the siller,
   I dinna envy him the gains he can win:
I rather wad bear a' the lade o my sorrow
   Than ever hae acted sae faithless to him.

NO COLD APPROACH

TUNE: *Ianthy the lovely*

No cold approach, no alter'd mein,
   Just what would make suspicion start,
No pause the dire extremes between:
   He made me blest—and broke my heart.

DELUDED SWAIN, THE PLEASURE

TUNE: *The Collier's Dochter*

Deluded swain, the pleasure
   The fickle Fair can give thee,
Is but a fairy treasure—
   Thy hopes will soon deceive thee:
The billows on the ocean,
   The breezes idly roaming,
The cloud's uncertain motion,
   They are but types of Woman.

O, art thou not ashamed
   To doat upon a feature?
If Man thou wouldst be named
   Despise the silly creature!
Go, find an honest fellow,
   Good claret set before thee,
Hold on till thou are mellow,
   And then to bed in glory!

YOUNG JAMIE, PRIDE OF A'
THE PLAIN

TUNE: *The carlin o the glen*

Young Jamie, pride of a' the plain,
Sae gallant and sae gay a swain,
Thro a' our lasses he did rove,
And reign resistless King of Love.

But now, wi sighs and starting tears,
He strays amang the woods and breers;
Or in the glens and rocky caves
gloomy   His sad complaining dowie raves:—

'I, wha sae late did range and rove,
And chang'd with every moon my love—
I little thought the time was near,
Repentance I should buy sae dear.

'The slighted maids my torments see,
endure   And laugh at a' the pangs I dree;
While she, my cruel, scornful Fair,
Forbids me e'er to see her mair.'

THE WITCH OF DUNDRUM

This fragment, probably collected by Burns from a traditional ballad, is known in holograph, complete with the poet's signature, and was sold for £675 at an auction in London in 1982.

Hae ye heard o the Witch o Dundrum
When she tae Scotland did come,
   'Twas Ireland's lament
   And Scotland's content
Hurrah for the Witch o Dundrum.

Ye ken what she's done for us a'
What enchantments she's used and a'
How she's simply lo'ed us and a'
   God bless the Witch o Dundrum.
And her at the tale o the Year
Well of this let us have little fear
All of us can truthfully cheer
   Hurroo! for the Witch o Dundrum.

GLOSSARY

A, he, she, it
A, have
A', all
ABACK, away, aloof, in the rear
ABEIGH, aside, at a distance
ABOON, ABUNE, above, overhead
ABOUT, here and there
ABREAD, ABREED, in breadth, abroad
ACQUENT, acquainted
ADLE, slurry
ADO, to do
ADVICES, counsel
ADVISEMENT, thought, deliberation
AE, one
AFF, off
AFF-HAN', on the spur of the moment
AFF-LOOF, extempore, off the cuff
A-FIEL, outside, in the field
AFORE, before
AFT, AFTEN, often
AGLEY, askew
AHINT, behind
AIBLINS, perhaps
AIK, AIKEN, oak, oaken
AIN, own
AIR, early
AIRLE-PENNY, contract money
AIRN, iron
AIRT, quarter, direction
AITH, oath
AITS, oats
AIVER, old horse
AIX, axe
AIZLE, ember, cinder
A-JEE, ajar
ALAKE, alas
ALANE, alone
AMAIST, almost
AMANG, among
AN, if, and
ANATHEM, curse
ANCE, once
ANE, one
ANEUCH, enough
ANITHER, another
AQUA-FONTIS, spring water
AQUA VITAE, spirits (whisky)
ARCH, rise in a curve
ASE, ashes
ASK, lizard
ASKLENT, slanting, askance
ASPAR, legs apart
ASTEER, stirring
ATHORT, across
ATWEEL, indeed
AUGHT, eight, anything
AUGHT, possessed of
AULD, old
AULD-FAC'D, ancient looking
AULDFARRAN, old fashioned
AUMOUS, alms dish
AVA, at all
AWAUK, awake
AWE, owe
AWEE, for a moment
AWNIE, bearded
AYONT, beyond
BA', ball
BABIE-CLOUTS, baby linen, nappies
BACKLINS, backwards
BACK-STYLE, fence gate at rear of house
BAGGIE, belly
BAIGINETS, bayonets
BAIR, uncover
BAIRN, child
BAIRNTIME, offspring
BAITH, both
BAKES, biscuits

BAN, curse
BANDILEERS, bandoliers, testicles
BANE, bone
BANG, thrash, thump, copulate vigorously
BANIE, big-boned, stout
BANNOCK, round flat cake of oats or barley
BARDIE, minor poet
BAREFIT, barefoot
BARLEY-BREE, whisky
BARMIE, fermenting with ideas
BASTART, bastard
BATCH, crew, gang
BATTS, colic
BAUCKIE-BIRD, bat
BAUDRONS, cat
BAUK, cross-beam
BAULD, bold
BAUMY, balmy
BAWBEE, billon coin worth 6d Scots (½d sterling)
BAWK, strip of unploughed land
BAWS'NT, white-faced
BAWTIE, pet name for a dog
BEAR, barley
BEARERS, legs
BEASTIE, animal
BEAVER, kind of hat
BECK, curtsey
BEDEEN, early, quickly
BEESE, vermin
BEET, mend, kindle, stoke a fire
BEFA', befall
BELANG, belong to
BELD, bald
BELLUM, onslaught, force
BELLYS, bellows
BELYVE, by and bye
BEN, inside, indoors, inner room of house
BENMOST, innermost
BENORTH, to the north of
BENT, bent-grass, hillock thus covered
BESOUTH, to the south of
BESTEAD, placed
BEUK, book
BICKER, rush, scurry
BICKER, wooden drinking vessel
BID, ask
BIDE, remain, stay
BIELD, shelter
BIEN, cosy, snug
BIG, build
BIGGIN, building
BIKE, BYKE, hive, swarm, crowd
BILL, bull
BILLIE, friend, comrade, fellow
BIRDIE, BURDIE, girl
BIRDY, chicken
BIRK, birch tree
BIRKIE, lively lad
BIRRIN, noise of partridges in flight
BIRSE, bristle, hair
BIRTH, berth
BIT, nick of time
BITCH-FOU, beastly drunk
BIZZ, buzz
BIZZARD, buzzard
BLACKGUARDING, roistering
BLACK-NEBBIT, radical
BLAE, blue
BLAST, cursed, withered, blight
BLATE, bashful
BLATHER, bladder
BLATTER, work noisily
BLAUD, piece, example
BLAUD, slap, beat
BLAW, blow
BLAZE, brilliance
BLEAR, BLEERIT, bleary

617

BLEEZE, blaze
BLELLUM, babbler, blusterer
BLETHER, babble, talk nonsense
BLIN', blind
BLINK, glance, glimpse, an instant
BLINKERS, spies, cheats
BLITTER, snipe
BLOOSTER, bluster
BLUDE,BLUID, blood
BLUE-BORAM, syphilis
BLUE-CLUE, blue yarn used in divining
BLUE-GOWN, beggar
BLUNTIE, fool
BLYPE, shred
BOB, move up and down
BOCK, vomit, belch
BOD(D)LE, copper twopenny piece (one sixth of a penny sterling)
BODE, look for
BODIE, BODY, person, fellow
BOGGIE, marsh
BOGLE, demon, goblin
BOLE, wall recess, hole
BOLUS, large pill
BON TON, good breeding
BONE, BONY, fair, pretty, fine
BOON, see aboon
BOORD-EN', table-end
BOORTREE, shrub elder
BOOST, must, ought
BORE, crack, crevice
BOTCH, angry tumour
BOTHER, fuss
BOUK, body, carcase
BOW, bend, subdue
BOW'T, crooked, bent
BOW-HOUGH'D, bandy-legged
BOW-KAIL, cabbage
BOWSE, booze
BRA', fine
BRACHEN, BRECKAN, ferns, bracken
BRAE, slope, hills
BRAID, broad
BRAID MONEY, gold coins
BRAID-CLAITH, broad-cloth
BRAIK, harrow
BRAINGE, plunge
BRAK, broke
BRANKIE, finely dressed
BRANKS, halter, bridle
BRASH, sudden illness
BRAT, child
BRATS, rags
BRATTLE, clatter, rush, noise
BRAULIES, finely, admirably
BRAW, fine, handsome
BRAWDS, ruffians
BRAWNIT, brindled
BRAXIES, diseased sheep carcasses
BREASTET, pulled forward
BREASTIE, breast
BRECHAN, horse-collar lined with straw
BREE, brew
BREE, BRIE, brow
BREEKS, breeches
BREER, briar
BRENT, smooth
BRENT, branded, brand new
BRIEF, literary skill
BRIG, bridge
BRISKET, breast
BRITHER, brother
BROCK, badger
BRODED, braided
BROGUE, trick, hoax
BROO, water, soup
BROOSE, wedding race
BROSE, gruel
BROWST, brew, mischief

BROWSTER, brewer
BRUGH, borough
BRULZIE, brawl, affray
BRUNSTANE, brimstone
BRUNT, burnt
BRUSH, onset, attack
BUCKIE, buck
BUCKLE, curliness
BUCKSKIN, American
BUDGET, leather wallet
BUFF, thrash
BUGHT, fold sheep
BUIRDLY, stalwart
BULLER, loud road, whirlpool
BUM, hum
BUM-CLOCK, cockchafer, humming-beetle
BUMMLE, idle bungler
BUNTER, drab, whore
BURDIE, girl
BURE, won, carried
BURN, BURNIE, brook, stream
BURNEWIN, blacksmith
BUSK, dress, prepare
BUSS, bush
BUSSLE, bustle, fuss
BUT, without
BUTT OUT, outer room
BUTT AND BEN, two-roomed cottage
BUTCHING, butchering
BUTTOCK-HIRE, church penalty for fornication
BYE ATTOUR, in addition
BY-JOB, fornication
BYKE, BIKE, hive, swarm, crowd
BYRE, cowshed
BYRE-EN', gable-end of cowshed
CA', call, drive
CA' THE CRACK, gossip
CA' THRO, work away
CACKIT, soiled with excrement
CAD(D)IE, lackey, vassal, servant, rascal
CADGER, pedlar
CAFF, chaff
CAIRD, tinker, itinerant blacksmith
CAITION, surety
CALCES, chalk powder
CALF-WARD, enclosure for calves
CALLAN(T), stripling, youth
CALLER, cool, fresh
CALLET, wench, trollop
CAM, came
CANKER, become peevish
CANKERT, ill-natured
CANKRIE, peevish
CANNA, cannot
CAN(N)IE, careful, cautious, shrewd, frugal
CANT, chant, song, tale
CANTAN, whining
CANTIE,CANTY, cheerful, jolly, lively
CANTRAIP, magic
CAPE-STONE, coping stone
CAR, primitive wheelless cart
CARD, chart
CARE, sweetheart
CAREERIN, running this way and that
CARELESS, untroubled
CARITCH, catechism
CARL, CARLIE, old man
CARL-HEMP, seed-bearing hemp
CARLIN, old woman, beldam
CARMAGNOLE, rascal
CARTES, playing cards
CASE, enclose
CAST OUT, quarrel
CATCH-THE-PLACK, money-grubbing

618

CATTLE, horses, beasts
CAUDRON, cauldron
CAUF, calf
CAUF-LEATHER, calfskin
CAUK AND KEEL, (literally 'chalk and pencil') - drawing
CAULD, cold
CAUP, wooden bowl
CAUSE, legal case
CAUSEY-CLEANER, street sweeper
CAVIE, hencoop
CESS, land-tax
CHAFFT-BLADE, jaw-bone
CHAINET, fitted with chains
CHAMER, bedroom, chamber
CHANGE-HOUSE, ale-house
CHANLER-CHAFFIT, lantern-jawed
CHANTER, bagpipe
CHAP, blow, knock
CHAPPIN, CHOPIN, half a Scots pint
CHAPMAN, pedlar
CHEEK, side-piece
CHEEK FOR CHOW, cheek by jowl
CHIEL, CHIELD, lad, fellow
CHIMLA, CHIMLIE, fireplace, hearth
CHITTERING, shivering, trembling
CHOW, chew
CHUCK(IE), mother hen, sweetheart
CHUFFIE, fat-faced
CIT, city-dweller
CLACHAN, hamlet
CLAES, CLAISE, CLAITHING, clothes, dress
CLAG, burden on property
CLAMB, climbed
CLANKIE, knock, blow
CLAP, caress, fondle
CLARK, scholar
CLARKET, written up
CLARTY, dirty, sticky
CLASH, chatter, gossip
CLATTER, uproar, gossip
CLAUGHT, clutched
CLAUT(E) grip, handful
CLAVER, clover
CLAVERS, chatter, babble
CLAW, scratch, beat
CLAYMORE, Highland broadsword
CLEAN, comely, empty, quite
CLEAR, quite free
CLEARIN, beating
CLECKIN, brood
CLEED, clothe
CLEEK, clutch, pilfer, link arms in a dance
CLEEKS, cramps in horses
CLEG, horse-fly
CLEW, scratched
CLINK, cash, jingle, rhyme
CLINKER, roguish fellow
CLIPS, clippers, shears
CLISHMACLAVERS, tittle-tattle
CLOCKIN-TIME, hatching time, childbirth
CLOOT, cloven hoof
CLOOTS, CLOOTIE, the Devil
CLOSE, constant
CLOUR, bruise, swelling
CLOUT, cloth, patch
CLUD, cloud
CLUNK, gurgle
COATIE, petticoat
COAXIN, wheedling
COCK, good fellow
COCKIE, crony
COD, pillow
COFF, buy
COFT, bought
COG(GIE), staved wooden vessel, womb
COLLIESHANGIE, dispute, quarrel, brawl

COMMAND, commandment
COMMERCE-CHAUMER, chamber of commerce
COMPLEENIN, complaining
COOD, cud
COOF, CUIF, dolt, fool, lout
COOKET, appeared and disappeared by fits
COOR, cover, protect
COOSER, stallion, lecher
COOST, cast, thrown off, discarded
COOTIE, basin, tub
COOTIE, with feathered legs
CORBIE, raven
CORE, crew, crowd, band
CORN-MOU, corn stack
CORSS, cross
COT (-HOUSE), cottage
COTILLION, French dance
COTTER, cottager
COULDNA, could not
COUNTRA, countrified, rustic
COUP, COWP, capsize, upset
COUP THE CRAN, somersault, become ruined
COUPER, cooper
COUR, lower, fold crouch
COURT-DAY, rent day
COUTHIE, loving, kindly
COW(E), crop, trim, scold
COWE, demon, goblin, terror
COWT(E), colt
COZIE, snug, comfortable
CRABBET, crabbed, ill-natured
CRACK, chat, gossip
CRAFT, croft
CRAIG, crag
CRAIGIE, neck, windpipe, throat, gullet
CRAIK, corncake
CRAMBO-CLINK, doggerel verse
CRAN, crane, tripod for cooking pot
CRANKOUS, fretful
CRANK, harsh, grating
CRANREUCH, hoar-frost
CRAP, trim, crop
CRAW, crow
CREEL, wicker basket
CREEPIE-CHAIR, stool of repentance
CREESHIE, filthy, greasy
CRIB, barred manger
CROCK, old ewe
CROOD, coo
CROOKIT, crooked, deformed
CROOKS, disease of sheep resulting in neck curvature
CROON, moan, whine, bellow
CROOSE, CROUSE, cocksure
CROUCHIE, hunchbacked
CROWDIE, gruel, porridge
CROWDIE-TIME, breakfast
CROWLAN, crawling
CRUMMIE, crooked-horned cow
CRUMMOCK, crook, stick with curved head
CRUNT, blow from a cudgel
CRY, call, summon, protest
CUMMER, wench, hussy
CUMMOCK, short staff with crooked head
CURCH, kerchief
CURCHIE, curtsey
CURMURRING, slight, rumbling noise, flatulence
CURPAN, crupper, rump
CURPLE, buttocks
CURRY, dressing, beating
CUSHANT, wood-pigeon
CUSTOCK, cabbage stalk
CUTE, ankle
CUT-LUGGIT, crop-eared
CUTTY, short, brief
CUTTY-STOOL, stool of repentance

DADIE, father
DAEZ'T, dazed, stupefied
DAFFIN, fooling about, frolic, flirting
DAFT, mad, silly, foolish, wild
DAIL, dale
DAIL, deal, pinewood
DAIMEN-ICKER, occasional ear of corn
DAINTY, treat, worthy, pleasant, agreeable
DANDER, saunter, stroll
DANG, pushed, overcome
DARKLINS, in the dark
DASHING, cast down
DATE, season, time of life
DAUD, thrash, abuse, pelt
DAUNTON, subdue, discourage, put down
DAUR, dare
DAURK, day's labour
DAUT, DAWT, fondle, caress
DAWTIE, pet, darling
DAW, DAWIN, dawn
DAWD, hunk, piece
DEAD, death
DEAD—SWEER, quite disinclined
DEAL ABOUT, distribute, share out
DEARTHFU, costly
DEAVE, deafen
DECREET, judgement in a court of law
DEEP-LAIRING, sinking into snowdrifts
DEEVIL, DEIL, devil
DEIL A, not a
DEIL NA, DEIL NOR, strong negative
DEIL-MAK-MATTER, no matter
DEIL-HAET, devil take it
DELEERIT, delirious
DELVER, gardener
DELVIN, digging
DEN, dean, dingle
DERN, hide
DETACH, disengage
DEU(C)K, duck
DEVEL, violent blow
DIBBLE, pointed stick for planting seedlings, penis
DID(D)LE, jig, move jerkily
DIGHT, wipe, clean, prepare
DIN, dun, dark, dingy
DINE, dinnertime
DING, overcome, beat, vanquish, be worn out
DINK, trim, neat, finely dressed
DINNA, do not
DINSOME, noisy
DINT, chance, occasion, pierce with an arrow
DIRL, shake, rattle, reel off
DISCOVER, reveal pregnancy
DITTY, ground of indictment, reproof
DIZZEN, dozen
DO, put up with
DOCHT, DOGHT, dared
DOCHTER, daughter
DOCK(IE), backside
DOCKIN, dock-leaf
DOIT, to be crazed, enfeebled
DOITED, senile, stupefied, bemused
DONSIE, hapless, unlucky, ill-tempered
DOOL, misery, woe, sorrow
DOOLFU, doleful
DORY, haughty, arrogant
DOUBT, fear, think, suspect
DOUCE, douse, sedate, sober, prudent
DOUDLE, dandle

DOUK, dip duck
DOUNA, DOWNA, cannot
DOUP, buttocks
DOUP-SKELPER, lecher
DOUR, stubborn, harsh, severe
DOW, dove, pigeon
DOW, be able, dare
DOWF, listless, dull
DOWIE, gloomy, sad
DOWNA, cannot
DOWN-BRAE, downhill
DOWR, see DOUR
DOXY, beggar's wench
DOYLT, DAZED, muddled
DOYTAN, stumbling, blundering
DOZEN, DOZIN, impotent
DRAIGLE, bedraggle
DRANT, DRUNT, sulks
DRAP(PIE) drop, liquor
DRAUNT, drone, whine
DRAVE ON, passed
DREE, put up with
DREEPING, dripping
DREICH, DREIGH, tedious, dreary
DRESS YOUR DRODDUM, thrash your backside
DRID(D)LE, dawdle
DRIFT, flock, herd, windblown snow
DRODDUM, bottom
DRONE, supplementary pipe of bagpipe, monotonous humming
DROOP-RUMPL'T, with drooping haunches
DROOK, DROUK, soak, drench
DROUKIT, drenched
DROUTH, thirst
DROUTHY, thirsty
DRU(C)KEN, drunken
DRUMLIE, muddy
DRUMMOCK, oatmeal and water
DRY, thirsty
DRY-BOB, masturbation
DUAN, canto
DUB, puddle, stagnant pool
DUDDIE, ragged
DUD(D)IES, DUDS, clothes
DUNT, dull knock, thud
DURK, dirk
DUSHT, butted by a ram
DWALL, dwell
DYKE, low dry-stone fence
DYVOR, bankrupt

EASTLIN, easterly
E'E, eye
E'EN, eyes, evening, even, simply
EERIE, apprehensive, fearful, gloomy
EFTER, afterwards
EILD, ELD, old age
EITH, easy
ELBUCK, elbow
ELDRITCH, uncanny, unearthly, supernatural
ELECKIT, elected, chosen
ELL, unit of length (37.059 inches)
ELLER, church elder
ENEUCH, ENEUGH, enough
ENOW, sufficient
ERSE, Irish, Gaelic
ETHER-STANE, adder stone (used as a talisman)
ETTLE, aim, purpose
EVEN TILL, mathced with
EV'N DOWN, downright, sheer
EXPECKIT, expected
EYDENT, alert, diligent

FA', fall, befall, come by, win
FA', fortune, turn of events
FADDOM, fathon
FAE, foe

FAEM, foam, froth
FAIKIT, excused
FAIN, glad, content
FAIN O' ITHER, fond of each other
FAIR, easy
FAIR FA', good luck to
FAIRIN, present from a fair, reward
FAIRY, dwarfish
FAITH YE, damn you
FALLOW, fellow
FAMOUS, grand, fine
FAND, found
FANK, entangle
FARINA, flour, meal
FARL, quarter bannock
FASH, bother, trouble
FASHIOUS, tricky, awkward
FATT'RELS, ribbon ends
FAUGHT, fought
FAULD, enfold, enclose, gather
  (sheep) in a pen
FAULDING SLAP, fold gate
FAUSE, false
FAUSONT, FAWSONT, decent,
  seemly
FAUT(E), fault, transgression
FAUTEOR, defaulter, wrong-doer
FEAR, frighten, scare
FEAR'D, afraid
FEAT, trim, spruce, neat
FECHT, fight
FECHTIN, FECHTAN, fighting
FECKET, waistcoat
FEE, hire, wages
FEETIE, feet
FEG, fig
FEGS, indeed
FEIDE, enmity
FEIRRIE, sturdy
FELL, quick (cuticle)
FELL, pungent, harsh, dread
FELLY, bitter
FEND, support, effort
FERLIE, marvel, wonder
FETCH, gasp, pant
FEY, doomed
FIDGE, fidget, twitch, shrug
FIDGE FU' FAIN, twitch with
  excitement
FIDGIN FAIN, excited, eager
FIEL, softly, cosily
FIENT A, strong negative
FIER, hearty, sound
FIERE, comrade, friend
FIN', find
FISCAL, procurator fiscal, attorney
FISSLE, bustle
FIT, foot, foothold
FIT, poem, melody
FITTIE-LAN', rear left-hand horse in
  plough team
FLAE, flea
FLAFF, flap, flutter
FLANNEN, flannel
FLAIRING, gaudy, extravagant
FLEE, fly
FLEECH, wheedle, coax
FLEESH, fleece
FLEET-WING, fly swiftly
FLEG, blow, kick
FLETH'RAN, wheedling, flattering
FLEWIT, slap
FLEY, terrify
FLICHTER, flutter
FLIE, fly, something worthless
FLINDERS, fragments
FLINGIN-TREE, flail-swingle
FLISK, fret at the yoke
FLIT, move, shift, change abode
FLITTERING, fluttering
FLYTE, scold, rail
FOCK, folk

FODGEL, plump, good-humoured
FOGGAGE, coarse grass
FOOR, fared, went, travelled
FORBYE, besides, as well as
FORFAIRN, undone, worn out
FORGATHER, assemble
FORGIE, forgive
FORJESKET, vitiated, worn out
FORRIT, forward
FOTHER, fodder
FOU, FU, full, drunk, very
FOUGHTEN, harassed
FOUMART, pole-cat
FOUTH, abundance
FOW, firlot, full measure
FRAE, from
FRAETH, foam, froth
FRANK, lavish
FREAK, fancy, notion
FREE, leap over
FREMIT, strange, cold
FRIEN, FREEN, friend
FRIG, masturbation
FRIGHT, freak
FRYTHE, fry
FU, full, drunk
FU-HAN'T, having enough
FUD, backside, tail, scut
FUFF, puff of smoke
FUN', found
FURDER, progress
FURM, form, bench
FURR, furrow, ditch
FURR AHIN, right hand rear horse
  in plough team
FUSION, melting
FUSHIONLESS, weak, feeble, useless
FYKE, fidget, fuss
FYLE, foul, defile

GAB, noisy chatter, eloquence,
  mouth
GAE, go, walk
GAE, gave
GAETS, habits
GAILIES, well enough
GAIR, strip of cloth, gusset
GAIT, goat
GAMESOME, merry, sportive
GANG, go, depart
GAR, make, cause, compel
GARTEN, garter
GASH, prattle, smart, shrewd, witty
GAT, got
GATE, way, road, fashion
GAUD, goad
GAUDSMAN, boy who goads the
  team
GAUGER, exciseman
GAUN, going
GAUNT, gasp, gape
GAUSIE, GAWSY, jovial, plump,
  ample
GAWKIE, fool, booby
GAWKY, stupid, empty-headed
GEAR, wealth, possessions, money
GECK, scoff at
GED, pike (fish)
GENTLES, gentry
GENTY, dainty, graceful, genteel
GET, offspring
GHAIST, ghost
GIE, give
GIEN, have given
GIF, if
GIFTIE, talent, power
GIGA, jig, gigue
GILPEY, young girl
GIMMER, pet lamb
GIN, if, whether
GIRD, iron hoop
GIRDIN, girthing, copulation

GIRDLE, iron plate for baking, griddle
GIRN, snarl
GIRR, hoop of a barrel
GIRT, great
GIZ(Z), wig
GIZZEN, wither, shrivel
GLAIKIT, giddy, careless, stupid, irresponsible
GLAIVE, sword
GLAZIE, glittering, glassy
GLAUM, grab, snatch
GLAUR, mud
GLED, kite
GLEEDE, live coal
GLEESOME, cheerful
GLEG, smart
GLEIB, glebe, portion of land
GLIB-GABBET, smooth-tongued
GLIMPSE, take a look at
GLINT, go quickly
GLOAMIN, twilight
GLOWR, stare, gaze, scowl
GLUNCH, frown, scowl
GOAVE, stare vacantly at
GOOM, gum
GOR-COCK, grouse
GOS, goshawk
GOSSIP, neighbour woman
GOWAN, daisy, dandelion
GOWD, gold
GOWDSPINK, goldfinch
GOWFF, golf, hit with open palm
GOWK, cuckoo, dolt, fool
GOWLING, howling, yelling
GRACE-PROOD, sanctimonious
GRACIOUS, amiable
GRAFF, grave
GRAIN, bough of a tree
GRAIP, pitchfork
GRAITH, equipment, tools, dress
GRAITHING, vestments
GRAIZLE, scrape, grind
GRANE, groan
GRAPE, grope
GRAT, wept
GRAY-NECK, gambler
GREAT, intimate, friendly
GREE, social degree
GREE,CARRY THE, come off best
GREE, agree
GREEN, yearn for
GREET, weep
GREIVE, farm-manager
GRIP, grasp
GRIPET, apprehended, gripes
GRISSLE, gristle, stump of quill pen
GROAT, small silver coin
GROAZLE, grunt, breathe heavily
GROZET, gooseberry
GRUMPHIE, grumbler, sow
GRUN', ground
GRUNSTANE, grindstone
GRUNTLE, snout, nose, grunt
GRUNZIE, snout
GRUSHIE, lusty, strong
GRUTTEN, cried, wept
GUDE, GUID, good
GUIDEEN, good evening
GUID-FATHER, father-in-law
GUDEMAN, husband, head of household
GUDEWIFE, mistress of household
GUDE-WILLY, generous
GUDE-WILLIE-WAUGHT, cup of kindness
GULLIE, GULLY, large knife, dig, cut
GULRAVAGE, romp, roister, horseplay
GUMLIE, muddy
GUMPTION, commonsense

GUST, taste, relish, flavour
GUSTY, appetising
GUTCHER, grandfather
GUTSCRAPER, fiddler
GUTTY, pot-bellied
GYVEL, gable, vulva

HA', hall
HA' FOLK, servants
HA', have
HAE, have
HAERSE, hoarse
HAE'T, have it
HAFF, half
HAFFET, temple, sideburn
HAFFLINS, partly, half-measure
HAG(G), scar in moorland
HAGGIS, economic pudding boiled in a sheep's stomach
HAIL, small shot, pellets
HAIN, save, spare
HAINCH, haunch, hip
HAIR, whit, trifle
HAIRST, harvest
HAITH, a petty oath
HAIVERS, nonsence
HALD, hold, dwelling
HALE, whole, sound, healthy
HALF-LANG, half-length
HALLAN, porch, partition between house and byre
HALLION, idler, rascal
HALLOWEEN, All Hallows Eve
HALY, holy
HAME, home
HAMELY, homely, familiar
HAMEWARD, homewards
HAMMERS, clumsy fellows
HAN', HAUN, hand
HAN' DAURK, manual labour
HAN'-BREAD, hand's breadth
HAN' WALED, hand-picked
HANGIT, hung
HANGIE, hangman, the Devil
HANKER, hang about, loiter
HANSEL, new-year or good-luck gift
HANSEL IN, be a first gift of the new year
HAP, cover, protect
HAP, hop, drop in quick succession
HAPPEN, turn out, manage
HAPPER, mill hopper
HAP-STEP-AN-LOUP, hop, step and -jump
HARDY, bold, foolhardy
HARK, listen
HARN, coarse linen, sackcloth
HARPY, plundering
HASH, mangle, waste
HASLOCK, wool on sheep's neck
HAUD, hold
HAUD AFF, keep away
HAUD TAE, persist
HAUF, half
HAUF-MUTCHKIN, eighth of a Scots pint
HAUGH, river plain
HAUN, hand
HAURL, drag
HAUSE, embrace
HAUVER, oat
HAUVER-MEAL, oatmeal
HAVINS, behaviour, sense
HAV(E)REL, halfwit, simpleton
HAWKIE, pet cow
HAWKIT, spotted, streaked with white
HEAD, behead
HEADINMAN, executioner, headsman
HEAL, healthy, well
HEALSOME, wholesome

HEAPET, heaped, well-filled
HECH, ejaculation
HECHT, promise, offer, threat
HECKLE, flax comb
HEE-BALOU, hush
HEED, care
HEEZE, lift, elevate
HELD AWA, took way
HELLIM, helm, tiller
HEM-SHIN'D, haim-shinned
HEN, dear
HERD, shepherd, herd-boy
HERE AWA, hereabouts, hither
HERRY, harry, plunder, devastation
HERRYMENT, waste
HET, hot, burning, excited
HEUGH, ravine, steep bank
HEUK, hook, sickle
HICH, HIE, high
HIGH-GATE, highway
HILCH, lurch, limp
HILT AN HAIR, every bit
HILTIE-SKILTIE, helter-skelter,
   pell-mell
HINDMOST, last, final
HINEY, HINNIE, HINNY
   honey, sweetheart
HING, hang
HIRPLE, limp
HISSEL, flock of sheep
HISTIE, dry, stony
HIT, manage, achieve
HIZZIE, hussy, wench, silly girl,
   whore
HOAST, cough
HODDAN, jogging along
HODDEN, coarse grey homespun
   cloth
HOGGIE, hogget, young sheep
HOG-SCORE, distance-line in curling
HOG-SHOUTHER, shove with the
   shoulder
HOLLAN(D), fine linen
HOLLOW, halloo
HOODIE (craw), carrion crow
HOODOCK, carrion crow, rapacious
   person
HOOL, membrane
HOOLIE, gently, slowly
HOORD, hoard, drift
HORN, horn spoon or vessel
HORNIE, the Devil
HOTCH, hitch, jerk
HOUGH, disable by cutting tendons
HOUGHMAGANDIE, fornication
HOULET, owl
HOUPE, hope
HOVE, rise, distend
HOWK, dig up, exhume
HOWDIE, midwife
HOWE, hollow
HOWE-BACKET, sunk in the back
HOWKS, disease affecting animals'
   eyes
HOYSE, hoist, pull upwards
HOYTE, waddle, lope
HUFF SCOLD, berate
HUM, hoax, humbug
HUM, mumble
HUMPHIE, hunch-back
HUNDER, hundred
HUNG, eloquent
HUNKERS, haunches
HURCHEON, HURCHIN, hedgehog,
   urchin
HURDIES, buttocks
HURL, drive, trundle, move violently
HURLY, onrush, diarrhoea
HUSHIAN, footless stocking
HYTE, daft, crazy

I', in
IER-OE, great-grandchild

ILK, ILKA, each, every
ILL-TAEN, resented
ILL-THIEF, the Devil
ILL-WILLIE, malignant, ill-disposed
IN FOR'T, liable to punishment
INDENTIN, pledging
INGINE, talent, genius, wit
INGLE, fire burning on the hearth
INGLE-CHEEK, chimney corner
INGLE-LOWE, firelight
INGLE-NEUK, chimney corner
I'SE, I shall
ITHER, other

JAD, jade, mare, hussy
JAG THE FLAE, tailor
JAUK, daily, trifle with
JAUKIN, delay
JAUNER, idle chatter
JAUNTIE, jaunt, trip
JAUP, splash
JAW, dash, throw, pour
JAWPISH, urethritis
JEE, sideways
JEEG, jig, gigue
JILLET, jilt, silly girl
JIMP, jump
JIMP, gimp, tiny-waisted, slender
JIMPS, skirts
JINGS, mild expletive
JINK, dodge, dart
JINKER, high-spirited beast, a lively
   girl
JIRKINET, liberty bodice
JIRT, jerk
JO, sweetheart, darling
JOB, intrigue
JOBBIN, fornication
JOCTELEG, clasp-knife
JOG, trudge
JORUM, punch-bowl, drinking vessel
JOUK, dodge, duck
JOW, toll (bell)
JOWLER, heavy-jawed dog
JUNDIE, elbow, jostle, shove aside
JURR, skivvy, servant-maid

KAE, jackdaw, thief
KAIL, greens, broth, semen
KAIL-BLADE, cabbage leaf
KAILYARD, cabbage patch, kitchen
   garden
KAIM, comb
KALE-RUNT, stalk stripped of leaves
KANE, payment in kind
KEBAR, rafter
KEBBUCK, home-made cheese
KEBBUCK-HEEL, cheese-rind
KECKLE, cackle
KEEK, peer, peep
KEEKIN GLASS, mirror
KELPIE, water demon
KEN, know, be aware of, recognise,
   identify
KENNIN, trifle
KEP, keep, catch
KET, matted fleece
KETTLE, cauldron, pit, vulva
KIAUGH, anxiety
KILT, hitch up the skirt
KIMMER, CUMMER, gossip, woman,
   wench
KIN', kind nature, kindly, agreeable
KING'S HOOD, second stomach in a
   cow, paunch, scrotum
KINTRA, KOONTRIE, country,
   rustic
KIRK, church
KIRK-HAMMER, church-bell
KIRN, churn
KIRN, harvest home, merrymaking
KIRS'N, christen, dilute with water
KIRTLE, gown, skirts, petticoat

KIST, chest, coffer
KITCHEN, season, give relish to
KITH AND KIN, kinsfolk
KITTLE, tickle, excite, tune up, play,
  fickle, ticklish, skittish, tricky,
  dangerous
KITTLEN, kitten
KIUTLE WI, caress, fondle,
KNAG(G), knot, spur, stump
KNAGGIE, knobbly
KNAPPIN HAMMER, stonebreaking
  hammer
KNOIT, knock
KNOWE, knoll, hillock
KNURL, KNURLIN, dwarf
KYE, cows, cattle
KYLES, skittles
KYTCH, toss, jerk
KYTE, belly
KYTHE, discover, tell, inform
KYVEL, thump, bang vigorously

LADE, load
LAE, lay, lie down
LAFT, loft
LAG, laggard, backward
LAGGEN, angle between sides and
  bottom of a dish
LAID UPON, assailed
LAIGH, low
LAIK, LAKE, lack
LAIMPET, limpet
LAIR, grave, bed
LAIRD, squire, landowner
LAITH, loath, unwilling
LAITHRON, lazy, sluggish
LALLAN(D), lowland
LALLANS lowland Scots language
LAMMAS, 1st August
LAN', land, country
LAN' AFORE, front right-hand horse
  in plough team
LAN' AHIN, rear right-hand horse in
  plough team
LANE, alone
LANELY, lonely
LANG, long
LANG-KALE, borecole
LANG SYNE, long ago
LANG-TOCHER'D, well-dowered
LANK, languid
LAP, leapt
LAP, wrapped, enfolded
LAVE, rest, remainder
LAV(E)ROCK, lark
LAW, decree, determine
LAWIN, reckoning, bill
LAWLAND, lowland
LAY, attribute, allay
LAY, LEA, LEE, meadow, pasture
LEA-RIG, ridge of unploughed grass
  between arable fields
LEAD, cart, lead in
LEA'E, leave
LEAL, loyal, true
LEAR, learning, lore
LEARN, teach
LEAST, lest
LEATHER, hide, lining of throat,
  vagina
LEDDY, lady
LEE, leeward
LEE-LANG, live-long
LEFT-HAND, sinister
LEISTER, trident
LEN' give, grant
LET, allow
LET BE, cease
LEUGH, laughed
LEUK, look, watch, appearance
LEEZE . . . ON, blessing
LIBBET, castrated
LICK, measure, little bit, thrashing

LIEN, lain
LIEVE (AS), rather
LIFT, sky, horizon
LIFT, load, amount
LIFT ABOON, boost
LIGHT, alight
LIGHTLY, disparage
LILT, lift up the voice
LIMMER, scoundrel, jade, whore
LIMPAN, limping
LINK, trip, dance, skip
LIN(N), cascade, waterfall
LINNENS, shroud, winding-sheet
LINT, flax
LINTWHITE, flaxen-haired
LINTWHITE, linnet
LIPPEN, trust, depend on
LIST, enlist
LOAN, LOANING, lane, strip of
  grass between fields, used as a
  milking place
LOCKED, closely fastened
LO'E, love
LOGGER, thick, stupid
LOOF, palm, hand-shake
LOON, LOUN, LOWN, rascal, rogue,
  fellow, whore
LOOSOME, lovely, sweet
LOOT, allowed
LOOT ON, revealed, disclosed
LOOVE, love
LOOVES, palms
LOSH, mild expletive
LOUGH, loch, lake
LOUP, leap, jump
LOUPER, dancer
LOUR, look menacingly
LOUSE, LOWSE, loose
LOWE, flame, blaze
LUCKIE, LUCKY, ale-wife
LUG, drag, draw out
LUG, ear
LUGGET CAUP, drinking vessel with
  twin handles
LUGGIE, wooden dish with side
  projections
LUM, chimney
LUNARDI, balloon bonnet named
  after Vincenzo Lunardi
LUNT, smoke (pipe), puff of smoke
LUNZIE-BANES, haunch-bones
LYART, grizzled, withered

MAE, more
MAHOUN, the Devil
MAILEN, MAILIN, small-holding,
  farm
MAINGIE, scabby
MAIR, greater, more
MAIST, most, mostly
MAIST, almost
MAK, make
MAK O, fuss over
MAMIE, mummy, mother
'MANG, among
MANSWEAR, perjure
MANTEELE, mantle, cape
MANTIE, gown
MANTLING, foaming
MARK, two-thirds of a Scots pound
MARLED, marbled, parti-coloured
MASHLUM, mixed meal
MASKIN-PAT, teapot
MASON, Freemason
MAUD, shepherd's grey plaid
MAUKIN, hare
MAUN, must
MAUNA, must not
MAUT(E), malt, barley
MAVIS, thrush
MAW, mow, reap
MAWN, maund, two-handled wicker
  basket

MEARE, MEERE, mare
MEIKLE, MICKLE, MUCKLE, great, large
MELDER, meal ground at a session
MELL, consort with, meddle
MELVIE, soil with meal
MEN', MEND, cure, heal, repair, repent
MENSE, sense, tact, good manners
MENSELESS, boorish, ill-bred
MENZIE, retinue
MERCIES, liquor
MESS, Master of Arts
MESSAN, cur, lap-dog
METE, complete the full measure of
MIDDEN-CREEL, dung basket
MIDDEN-HOLE, dunghill drain
MILKIN-SHIEL, milking shed
MIM, demure, prim
MIM-MOU'D affectedly modest
MIN, mind, recollection
MIND, remind, remember, take care of
MIND'T, minded, disposed, inclined
MINNIE, mummy
MIRK, darkness
MIRKSOME, dark
MISCA', abuse, malign
MISHANTER, mishap
MISGUIDIN, mismanagement
MISLEAR'D, mischievous
MISS, mistress, whore
MIST, missed
MITE-HORN, horn on the harvest-bug
MITHER, mother
MIXTIE-MAXTIE, jumbled, confused
MIZL'D, mystified
MOCK, derision
MONIE, MONY, many
MOOL, earth, clod, grave
MOOP, nibble, copulate
MORN, tomorrow
MOSS, bog
MOTTIE, speckled, spotted, dusty
MOU, mouth
MOUDIEWORT, MOUDIEWARK, mole
MOW(E), copulate
MUCH ABOUT IT, about the same
MUIR, moor
MUSCLE, mussel
MUSLIN-KAIL, thin broth
MUTCHKIN, quarter Scots pint
MUVE, move

NA, NAE, not, no
NAIG, small horse
NAIL, clinch, prove
NANE, none
NAPPY, ale
NATCH, notch
NAUR, near
NEAR-HAND, almost
NEEBOR, neighbour
NEGLECKIT, neglected
NEIST, next
NEUK, corner
NEW-CA'D, newly calved
NICE, neat, fine, dainty
NICK, cut, slit, reap, seize
NICK, the Devil
NIDGE, nudge, push, thrust
NIEST, next
NIEVE, fist
NIFFER, exchange, comparison
NIGHTLY, appearing at night
NIT, nut
NOCHT, nothing, not
NODDLE, head, brain
NOR, than
NORLAND, northern

NOTION, fancy, desire
NOWT(E), cattle
NYVEL, navel

OCH, interjection of surprise
OCHON, alas
O'ER, over
OERGANG, overcome
O'ERLAY, cravat, necktie
OFFER, promise, seem likely to turn out
ONIE, ONY, any
OR, ere, before
ORRA, odd, spare
OSTLER HOUSE, hostelry
O'T, of it
OUGHT, anything
OUGHTLINS, at all
OURIE, poor, dreary
OUTCAST, quarrel
OUTLER QUEY, young cow out all night
OUT OWRE, over across, about, beyond
OUT THRO, right through
OWERWORD, burden, refrain
OWRE, OWER, over, too
OWREHIP, over the hip
OWSEN, oxen
OWTHER, author
OXTER, armpit
OXTER'D, armed

PACK AFF, depart
PACK, intimate, familiar
PAIDLE, wade, paddle
PAIDLE, hoe
PAINCH, paunch, belly
PAINCH-LIPPIT, pouting
PAITRICK, partridge
PALAVER, idle chatter
PANG, cram, stuff
PARLE, speech
PARLIAMENTIN, attending parliament
PARRITCH, porridge
PARTY-MATCH, card contest
PAT, pot
PATTLE, plough-scraper
PAUGHTY, proud, haughty
PAUKY, PAWKIE, cunning, sly, shrewd
PAY, flog, give deserts
PECH, PEGH, pant, gasp
PEEL, palisade, castle, keep
PEER, equal
PEGHAN, stomach
PEGO, penis
PELL MELL, in violent disarray
PENDLE, pendant
PENNY-FEE, cash wages
PENNY-WHEEP, small beer
PERISH, destroy
PET, sulk
PHILIBEG, little kilt
PHIZ, face, countenance, expression
PHRASE, flatter
PHRAISIN, exaggerating
PIBROCH, classical pipe music
PICKLE, small amount
PICTUR'D BEUK, playing card
PIKE, PYKE, pluck, pick at
PILLIE, penis
PIN, skewer, peg, penis
PINE, sorrow, pain
PINTLE, penis
PINT-STOWP, pint tankard
PISH, urinate
PIT, put
PLACAD, placard, proclamation
PLACK, coin worth 4d Scots (about a farthing)

PLAID(E), woollen cloak
PLAISTER, plaster
PLANTED, settled in
PLAY, joy, pleasure
PLEA, legal action
PLEUGH, PLEW, plough
PLISKIE, trick
PLIVER, peewit, plover
PLUMPET, plunged, sank
PLUMPIN, swelling
POACHER-COURT, kirk session
POCK, poke, bag
POIND, distrain
POORTITH, poverty
POOSIE, pussy, female genitalia, hence a pejorative name for a loose woman
POOSION, posion
POU, POW, PU, pull
POUK, poke, prod
POUSE, push
POUTHER, POWTHER, (gun)powder
POW, pate, head
POWNIE, pony
POWT, poult, chicken
PREE, try, sample, taste
PREEN, pin
PRENT, print
PRESES, president, chairman
PREST, oppressed
PRICK, penis
PRIDE, make proud
PRIDEFU, proud
PRIE, try, taste
PRIE . . . MOU, kiss
PRIEF, proof, quality
PRIGGIN, haggling
PRIMSIE, demure, precise, affected
PROPER, handsome, elegant
PROVES, provost
PU, pull
PUDDOCK-STOOL, toadstool
PUIR, poor
PUN, PUND, pound
PYET, magpie
PYKE, pluck
PYLE, spike, blade, ear of corn

QUARREL, dispute, challenge
QUAT, quit, left abandoned
QUAUKIN, quaking
QUEAN, QUINE, young girl, hussy
QUECH, quaich, shallow drinking vessel
QUEER, roguish, odd
QUEIR, choir
QUESTIONS, catechism
QUEY, heifer
QUITELINSWISE, quitely
QUO, said

RACKED, extortionate, excessive
RADE, rode, copulated with
RAEP, RAPE, rope
RAGGED, unkempt, shaggy
RAGWEED, ragwort
RAIBLE, rabble
RAIR, roar
RASE, rose
RAIZE, provoke, excite, rouse
RAMBLAN, rambling
RAMFEEZL'D, exhausted
RAMGUNSHOCH, ill-tempered
RAM-STAM, headstrong, reckless
RANDOM SPLORE, carousal, frolic
RANDY, rough, rude, riotous, roistering
RANT, make merry, spree, tirade
RANTER, roisterer
RAP, knock
RAPE, rope
RAPLOCH, coarse, homely

RARELY, finely
RASH, rush
RASH-BUSS, clump of rushes
RATTAN, RATTON, rat
RATTLIN, loquacious
RAUCLE, rough, coarse, robust
RAUGHT, reached
RAW, row, file
RAX, stretch, elastic
REAM, froth, cream
REAVE, rustle cattle, steal
REBUTE, reproach
RECK, heed, care, regard
REDE, counsel, advise, warn
RED-WAT-SHOD, shod with wet blood
RED-WUD, distraught, mad
REEK, smoke
REEKIN-RED, steaming with warm blood
REEST, stand restive
REESTET, cured, smoked
REMARKIN, observation
REMEAD, redress, remedy
RESPECKIT, respected
RIBBAN, riband
RICE, branch
RICKLE, pile of sheaves
RIEF, plunder
RIG, arable ridge, vulva
RIGGIN, ridge, roof
RIG-WOODIE, withered, coarse
RIN, run
RINGER, circlet
RIPP, handful of unthreshed corn
RIPPLE, draw flax through a comb, heckle
RIPPLIN-KAME, heckling-comb
RISK, grate, rasp
RIVE, break up, tear asunder
ROARING, riotous, noisy
ROCK, distaff
ROOD, quarter-acre
ROGER, penis, copulate with
ROOK, impudent cheat
ROON, circuit, round
ROOSE, stir up, agitate, praise, boast
ROOSTY, rusty
ROTTAN, rat
ROUND, confidently
ROUPET, husky, hoarse
ROUSE, stir up
ROUT, road, route, course
ROUTH, abundance, plenty
ROVE, ramble
ROWAN, mountain ash-tree
ROW(E), roll up, wrap up
ROWTE, bellow, roar
ROZET, resin
RUMMING, drinking
RUN-DEIL, thorough-going devil
RUNG, cudgel
RUNKL'D, wrinkled
RUNT, cabbage stalk, stunted
RUPIT, husky
RUTH, pity
RYKE, reach

SAB, sob
SAE, so
SAFT, soft, silly, lax
SAIR, serve, satisfy sexually
SAIR, sore, very
SAIRIE, SAIRY, sorry, mean
SALD, sold
SALL, shall
SANG, song
SAPPY, succulent
SARK, shirt, chemise
SAUGH, sallow, willow
SAUL, soul
SAUMONT, SAWMONT, salmon

626

SAUNT, saint, godly person
SAUT, salt
SAUT-BUCKET, salt-box
SAW, sow
SAX, six
SCANDAL-POTION, tea
SCAR, cliff, rocky outcrop
SCAUD, scald
SCAUR, see scar
SCAWL, scold
SCHO, she
SCHULIN, schooling
SCLATES, slates
SCONNER, feel sick, revulsion,
  disgust
SCORE, indentation
SCOW'R, roister
SCOWR'D, ran, ranged
SCRAICHAN, screaming
SCRIEGH, cry shrilly
SCREED, tear, rattle off
SCRIEVE, glide swiftly along
SCRIMP, be sparing
SCRIMPET, stunted
SCROGGIE, scrubby
SEE'D, saw
SEISIN, sasine
SELL'T, sold
SEMPLE-FOLK, common people
SEN', send
SET, start off, suit, become
SHACHL'T, shapeless
SHAIRD, shard, fragment
SHANGAN, cleft stick
SHANK, walk
SHANNA, shall not
SHAUL, shallow
SHAVER, barber, young wag
SHAVIE, trick
SHAW, copse, wood
SHAW, show, reveal
SHEAR, reap with sickle
SHEEPSHANK, person of no
  importance
SHEERLY, wholly, entirely
SHEUCH, SHEUGH, trench, ditch
SHEUK, shool
SHEIL, sheiling, hut, shanty
SHIFT, change abode
SHILL, shrill
SHOG, jog, shock
SHOOL, shovel
SHOON, shoes
SHORE, threaten, offer
SHOT, movement of weaver's
  shuttle
SHOUTHER, shoulder
SHURE, reaped
SIB, kin
SIC, such
SICCAN, such-like
SICKER, certain, sure
SIDELINS, sideways
SIE, see
SILLER, money, wealth, silver
SILLY, poor, hopeless
SIMMER, summer
SIN, SEN, since, from that time
SIN, son
SINGET, singed, shrunken
SINN, sun
SINSYNE, since then
SKAITH, harm, damage, hurt
SKEIGH, fierce, proud, disdainful
SKELLUM, rogue, scoundrel
SKELP, thrash, smack, hurry
SKELVY, ledged
SKINKING, watery
SKINKLIN, glittering
SKIRL, shriek, yell
SKLENT, slanting, aslant, squint
SKOUTH, scope, freedom

SKYRE, shine brightly
SKYTE, sudden blow
SLADE, slid, slipped
SLAE, sloe
SLAP, cut, drive down
SLAP, gap in fence
SLAW, slow
SLEE, sly, witty, clever
SLEEKIT, glossy, slick
SLIGHT, skill, dexterity
SLIP, quick-release leash
SLOKEN, slake, satisfy
SLYPE, fall over
SMA', small
SMEDDUM, dust, fine powder
SMEEK, smoke
SMIDDIE, smithy
SMIRKING, smiling
SMIT, smite
SMOOR, smother
SMOUTIE, smutty, obscene
SMYTRIE, numerous collection
SNAP, quick, smart
SNAPPER, stumble
SNASH, abuse
SNAW, snow
SNAW-BROO, slush
SNAW-DRAP, snowdrop
SNED, trim, lop off, prune
SNEESHIN MILL, snuff mull
SNELL, keen, bitter
SNICK, latch
SNICK-DRAWING, crafty
SNIRTLE, snigger
SNOOD, girl's head-band, bandeau
SNOOL, snub, sneak, submit tamely
SNOOVE, go steadily on
SNORE, snort
SNOWCK, snuffle
SNUFF, sniff
SO(D)GER, soldier
SONSIE, SONSY, good-natured,
  plump, buxom
SORT, meet together
S(O)UGH, deep breath, sigh
SOUK, suck, swig
SOUP(E), SOWP, sup, drink
SOUPLE, soften, soft, pliant
SOUR-MOU'D, peevish,
  sharp-tongued
SOUSE, beat, strike
S(O)UTER, SOWTER, shoemaker
SOWENS, sour pudding of oats and
  water
SOWTH, whistle a tune
SOWTHER, solder, patch up
SPAE, foretell
SPAIL, splinter
SPAIR, spare, reticent
SPAIRGE, sprinkle, bespatter
SPAK, spoke
SPAN-LANG, hand-length (22cm)
SPAVIE, spavin
SPAVET, spavined
SPEAN, wean
SPEAT, spate, flood
SPEEL, climb
SPEET, spit, transfix
SPELL, study, contemplate
SPENCE, parlour, inner room
SPEN'T, spend it
SPENT, ejaculated sexually
SPIER, ask, enquire
SPILL WASTE, destroy
SPIN'LE, spindle, axle
SPLATTER, bespatter, splash
SPLEUCHAN, tobacco-pouch, purse,
  scrotum, vagina
SPLORE, frolic, carousal
SPORT, gambol
SPORT, sexual adventure
SPORTIN LADY, harlot

627

SPOTTING, staining
SPOUT, dart, spurt
SPRACHLE, clamber
SPRATTLE, scramble
SPRAWL, struggle
SPRING, lively dance
SPRITTIE, rushy
SPUNK, spirit, spark
SPURTLE, wooden spoon
SPURTLE-BLADE, swordstick
SQUAD, company, party
SQUATTER, flutter in water
SQUATTLE, squat, nestle down
STACHER, stagger, toddle
STACK, stuck
STAIG, young horse
STAINCHER, STANCHEL,
   stanchion, iron bar
STAINCHER-FITTED, iron-footed
STAMMER, stumble
STAN', stand, stop, remain
STAN'IN, erect
STANE, stone, 14 pounds weight
STANG, stake, rail
STANG'D, ridden on a rail
STANG, sting, goad
STANK, pool of stagnant water
STAP, stop
STAPPLE, stopper
STARE, confront, express forcefully
STARK, strong
STARN, star
STARNIES, starlets
STARTLE, stampede, take fright,
   caper
STAUKIN, stalking, walking stealthily
STAUMREL, stammering, silly
STAW, stall, satiate
STAW, stole
STAY, hindrance
STEEK, stitch, shut, enclose
STEEL-WAMIT, steel-bellied
STEER, stir, agitate
STEEVE, firm, strong
STEGH, cram the stomach with food
STELL, (whisky) still
STELL, fix, post
STEN', leap, bound
STENT, turned, reared
STEY, steep
STIBBLE, stubble, pubic hair
STICK, club, cudgel, splinter
STILT, plough handle, prance
STIMPART, quarter peck (grain
   measure)
STIRK, young bullock
STOCK, stem, plant
STOITED, STOITER'D, staggered
STOOK, set of corn sheaves
STOOR, stern, massive, harsh
STOT, young bullock
STOUN(D), thrill of pleasure
STOUP, STOWP(E), tankard,
   measure
STOURE, STOOR, storm, adversity,
   dust
STOURIE, dusty
STOW'D, filled, crammed
STOWNLINS, stealthily
STOYTE, stagger, stumble
STRACK, struck
STRADE, strode
STRAE, straw
STRAE-DEATH, natural death
STRAIK, stroke
STRAK, struck
STRANG, strong, violent
STRAPPAN, sturdy, strapping
STRAUGHT, stretch, straight
STREEK, stretch
STRIDDLE, straddle, stride
STROAN'T, urinated

STRUNT, liquor
STRUNT, move with assurance
STUDE, stood
STUDDIE, anvil
STUFF, store of corn
STUMP, walk clumsily
STUMPIE, worn quill pen
STURT, fret, trouble
STYME, glimmer of light
SUCKER, sugar
SUD, should
SUMPH, simpleton
SUNE, soon
SUTHRON, southern, Englishman
SUTOR, shoemaker
SWAIRD, sward
SWANK, agile
SWANKIE, strapping lad
SWARF, swoon
SWAT, sweated
SWATCH, sample
SWATS, new small beer
SWINGE, flog
SWIRL, knot in wood, whirlpool
   eddy
SWITH, away!, quickly!
SWITHER, flurry
SWOOR, swore
SYBOW, spring onion
SYKE, ditch, brooklet
SYNE, then, now, since

TACK, lease, tenure
TACKET, hobnail
TAE, toe, to
TAED, toad
TA'EN, taken
TAET, taste, tuft, handful, morsel
TAIL, vagina
TAIRGE, constrain
TAK, take, seize
TAK AFF, drink up
TAK THE GATE, take to the road,
   go home
TALD, told
TANE . . .TITHER, the one. . . the
   other
TANGLE, seaweed
TANGS, tongs
TAP, top, head
TAPMAIST, topmost
TAPER, slender
TAPETLESS, headless, foolish
TAPPIT-HEN, lidded drinking vessel
TARGE, small shield
TARROW, hestitate, show reluctance
TARROW'T, murmured
TARRY-BREEKS, tarpaulin trousers
   (i.e. a sailor, 'jack tar')
TASSIE, goblet
TAULD, told
TAUTED, TAWTED, matted, shaggy
TAWIE, docile (of a horse)
TAWPIE, silly girl
TEEN, chagrin, vexation
TEETHIN, putting fresh teeth into
TELL, enumerate, count
TELL DOWN, count out, pay
TELL THE TALE TO, defeat, defy
TEMPER-PIN, tuning screw,
   regulator screw
TENT, heed, care, tend
TENTIE, watchful, careful
TESTER, testoon, shilling
TETHER, rope, noose
TEUGH, tough, hardy
THACK, thatch
THAE, those
THAIRM, guts, fiddle strings
THAIRM-INSPIRIN, gifted on the
   fiddle
THANKIT, thanked

THEEK, thatch
THEEKIT, thatched
THEGITHER, together, continuously
THICK, intimate, familiar
THIE, thigh
THIEVELESS, cold, devoid of
  warmth
THIG, take, accept, beg
THIR, these
THIRL, pierce, penetrate
THOLE, tolerate, endure, suffer
THOWE, thaw
THOWLESS, spiritless
THRANG, crowd, crowded, busy,
  jostle
THRAPPLE, throat
THRAVE, two stooks of corn
THRAW, turn, twist, frustrate
THRAWS, throes, pangs
THREAP, argue, obstinately
THRESH, thrash, flail, copulate
  violently
THRETTEN, thirteen
THRETTY, thirty
THRIPPLIN, rippled
THRISSLE, thistle
THRIST, thirst
THRUM, end of warp-thread
THRUM, hum, drone
THRUMMART, polecat
THUMP, strike
THUMPIN, exceptionally large
THYSEL, yourself
TICHED, touched, affected
TICKLE, rouse, amuse
TIEND, tythe, tax, due
TIGHT, neat, shapely, tidy, snug,
  capable
TILL, to
TIMMER, timber, trees, wood
TINE, TYNE, lose, get lost
TINT, lost
TINKLER, tinker, itinerant pot-
  mender
TIP, young ram
TIPPENCE, twopence
TIPPENNY, small beer sold for 2d
  Scots
TIRL, strip, lay bare
TIRL, rattle at door by turning the
  latch
TIRLIE-WHIRLIE, vulva
TITTIE, TITTY, sister
TITTLAN, tattling, whispering
TOCHER, dowry
TOCHER BAND, marriage settle-
  ment
TOD, fox
TODDLAN, TODLIN, toddling,
  hurrying
TON, fashion, mode
TOOFA, falling to, beginning (of
  night)
TOOLZIE, quarrel, contest
TOOM, empty
TOOP, TIP, tup, young ram
TOSS, toast, belle
TOUN, TOWN, hamlet, farm
TOUR, turf, sod
TOUT, trumpet blast
TOUZLE, towsle, ruffle
TOWZIE, shaggy, unkempt
TOW, bell-rope, gallows-rope
TOW, flax fibre prepared for spinning
TOWMOND, twelvemonth
TOY, close-fitting cap worn by old
  ladies
TRAC'D, fitted in traces, harnessed
TRAM, shaft of cart
TRASHTRIE, trash, rubbish
TREE, timber, wood
TREPAN, ensnare, beguile

TREWS, trousers
TRICK, habit, turn
TRICKIE, crafty, deceitful
TRIG, smart, trim
TRINKLE, trickle, flow
TRIN'LE, wheel of barrow
TROGGER, pedlar
TROGGIN, packware
TROKE, truck, barter
TROT, run
TROW, trust, believe
TROUTH, TROWTH, truly, indeed
TRYSTE, meeting, assembly, cattle-
  market
TUG, rawhide
TULZIE, quarrel, contest
TUN, cask
TWA(Y), two
TWA-THREE, two or three
'TWAD, it would
TWAL, twelve
TWALPENNIE, shilling
TWALT, twelfth
TWIN, separate, deprive
TWISSLE, wrench, twist
TYKE, mongrel, cur
TYNE, lose
TYTA, daddy, father

ULZIE, oil
UNCHANCY, dangerous
UNCO, odd, uncommon, very,
  mighty
UNCOS, strange tales, news
UNKENN'D, UNKEND, unkown
UNSICKER, uncertain, fickle
UNSKAITH'D, unscathed
UPO', upon
UP WI', here's to
USQUABAE, whisky

VAPOUR, caprice, whim
VAP'RIN, blustering, fuming
VAUNTIE, vain, proud
VEND, sell, advance, utter
VERA, very, real, true
VIEWIN, view, sight
VIRL, ivory or metal band
VITTEL, VITTLE, grain, fodder
VOGIE, vain
WA', wall
WAB, web, woven fabric
WABSTER, weaver
WAD, wed, wager, contract, pledge
WAD, would
WADNA, would not
WADSET, conveyance of land
  pledged for a debt
WAE, woe
WAESUCKS, alas
WAFF, WAFT, carry by water,
  voyage
WAFT, weft in a web
WAG-WITS, jokers, scandal-mongers
WAIL, bewail
WAIR, spend, bestow
WALE, choice, chose, select
WALIE, WAULIE, handsome, fine
WALIES, genitals
WALLOW, wither, fade, grow pale
WAME, belly, womb
WAMEFOU, meal, bellyful
WAN, won
WANCHANCIE, hazardous,
  dangerous, unlucky
WANRESTFU, restless
WAP, wrap
WAPONSCHAW, muster, review of
  men at arms
WARE, worn
WARK, work, labour
WARKLUM, tool, penis

629

WARL(D), world
WARLOCK, wizard
WARLOCK-BREEF, charm
WARLY, worldly
WARP, weave
WARRAN, guarantee, warrant
WARSLE, wrestle, struggle
WASTRIE, extravagance, wasteful-
ness
WASTE, waist
WAT, wet
WAT, know, be aware, wot
WATNA, don't know
WATTLE, wand, stick
WAUBLE, swing, wobble
WAUGHT, heavy drink
WAUK, WAUKEN, awake, wake up,
arouse
WAUKRIFE, wakeful, vigilant
WAUKET, calloused, horny
WAUR, worse, get the better of
WAVERING, wandering, fluttering
WEAN, child, infant
WEARING, passing (time)
WEARY FA', a curse upon
WEASON, gullet
WECHT, sieve
WEE, small, a little bit
WEE-THING, infant
WEEL, well, fine, satisfied, welfare,
well-being
WEEL-GAUN, active, good-going
WEEL-HOORDET, closely hoarded
WEEL-KNOOZ'D, well-beaten
WEEL-SWALL'D, fully stretched
WEEL-TOCHER'D, well-dowered
WEEPERS, cuffs
WEET, wet, dew, rain
WENCHING, whoring
WRESTLIN, westering, westerly
WETHER, castrated ram
WHA, who
WHAM, whom
WHASE, whose, who is
WHAIZLE, wheeze
WHALP, whelp
WHAN, when
WHANG, thick slice of cheese
WHANG, beat, flog
WHATFOR NO, why not?
WHATRECK, nevertheless, what
does it matter, fornication
WHATT, whetted
WHAUP, curlew
WHEEP, jig, jerk
WHID, thieving cant, lie
WHID, move nimbly and noiselessly
WHIG, puritan, hypocrite
WHIGGISH, rigid, precise
WHIGMALEERIE, whimsical orna-
ment, trifle
WHILES, WYLES, sometimes, then,
at times
WHIN, gorse, furze
WHINGE, whine, complain
WHIN-ROCK, whinstone
WHIRL, rush
WHIRLYGIGUMS, bizarre orna-
ments
WHIRRY, hurry, drive
WHIST, silence
WHITTER, draught of liquor
WHITTLE, knife
WHUNSTANE, whinstone
WHYLES, sometimes, then
WI, with
WICKER, branch
WIDDEFU, rascally, deserving to be
hanged
WIDDLE, trouble, strife
WIEL, eddy
WIERD, fate, fortune

WIGHT, fellow, chap, creature
WIGHT, strong, stout
WILLIE, willow
WILLYART, shy, awkward
WIMBLE, gimlet, penis
WIMPLE, meander, wind, twist
WIN, reach, get, gain, earn
WIN', wind
WIN'T, wound
WINKERS, eye-lashes, eyes
WINN, winnow
WINNA, will not
WINNOCK, window
WINNOCK-BUNKER, window seat
WINTER-HAP, winter protection
WINTLE, sway, swing from side to
side
WINZE, curse
WISS, wish
WIT, know
WITCHING, fascintating
WITHOUTTEN, without
WON(E), dwell
WONNER, wonder, marvel
WONTED, accustomed
WOO, wool
WOODIE, WOODY, withy, rope,
noose
WOOER-BAB, garter worn by a
suitor
WOOR, worn out
WORDIE, little word
WORM, spiral condensor tube in
whisky still
WORSET, worsted, coarse woollen
fabric
WRACK, wreckage, waste, flotsam
WRACK, rubbish, possessions
WRACK, torment, punish
WRAITH, spirit ghost
WRANG, wrong
WREETH, snowdrift
WUD, angry, enraged
WUMBLE, gimlet, penis
WYLE, lure, beguiled
WYLECOAT, flannel vest
WYTE, blame, reproach

YAD, jade, old mare
YARD, garden
YEALING, co-eval
YEARN, eagle
YELL, barren, dry (of milk)
YERD, yard
YERK, lash, stir up
YE'SE, you shall
YESTREEN, last night
YET(T), gate
YEUK, itch
YILL, ale
YIRD, earth
YIRR, bark
YISK, hiccup, belch
YOKIN, contest, copulation
'YONT, beyond, on far side of
YOUNKERS, youngsters
YOWE, ewe
YOWIE, ewe-lamb
YULE, Christmas

LIST OF SUBSCRIBERS

Alexander Abercrombie, 6 Denfield Avenue, Cardenden
Archibald D Abercrombie, Shawsmill Farm, Cardenden
Aberdeen Burns Club (2 copies)
Aberdeen City Libraries, Rosemount Viaduct, Aberdeen (2 copies)
William Adair, 36 Woodlands Avenue, Gartcosh, Glasgow
James Adam, 21 Titchfield Road, Troon
Pauline Adam, 87 Bank Street, Irvine
Ronald Charles Kerr Adam, 87 Bank Street, Irvine
Ruth Adam, 87 Bank Street, Irvine
William D Adam, Peterhead Burns Club
K H Adams, 99 Abbots View, Haddington
James Adamson, 1031 Parkwood Way, SE, Calgary, Canada
James Adamson. Rossieden, Gifford
William Addison, Peterhead Burns Club
Gillian Adie, 75 Derran Drive, Cardenden
Mr William Adie, 75 Derran Drive, Cardenden
Sheila Aird, Carindon, 8 Roberts Crescent, Dumfries
Andrew Aitken, 10 Lochview Road, Bearsden
J Aitken, 4 Dunollie Gardens, Haddington
Mr James Aitken, 73rd Avenue, Bayside, New York, USA
Mr & Mrs R D Aitken, 5 Foss Avenue, Wetherby
Dr Thomas Alcorn, Sunnyside, Carmanhill, Renton
David E Alexander, Marchbank, Fenwick
George Alexander, 3 Blaven Head, Irvine
Hugh Alexander, 98 Hunters Avenue, Ayr
Martin G Alexander, Marchbank, Fenwick
Miss Morven J Alexander, Marchbank, Fenwick
Robert S Alexander, Dunshaughlin, Ireland
Robert W Alexander, Dunshaughlin, Ireland
Ronald Alexander, MA, 16 Kerr Drive, Irvine
Sam G B Alexander, Marchbank, Fenwick
Thomas Alexander, Mayfield, Union Road, Fort William
Alexandria Burns Club
David John Allan, 56 Maryport Road, Dearham, Maryport
Glen Allan, RR2, Westdown Road, Ladysmith, Canada
Ian Alexander Allan, 69 Wards Road, Elgin
Jack H Allan, 22 Mill Road, Irvine
Ross M Allan, Cedar Avenue, Broad Acres. South Africa

Thomas Allan, 37 Croftfoot Road, Glasgow
Allanton Jolly Beggars Burns Club
Sidney Allcock, 24 Love Street, Kilwinning
H V Allen, Hame, Kingswood Road, Gunnislake
Alexander Walker Allison, 46 King Street, Newton Stewart
James Allison, 46 King Street, Newton Stewart
James Allison, Shaldar, 9 Redmoss Terrace, Aberdeen
George Anderson, 49C Upper Bourtree Drive, Rutherglen
Gordon S Anderson, 24 Blair Drive, Milton of Campsie
Mrs Helen Anderson, 3 Jubilee Place, Stewarton
Jean Anderson, 36 Linfern Avenue East, Kilmarnock
Peter Anderson, Uphouse, Haroldswick, Unst
William A Anderson, 3 Jubilee Place, Stewarton
J B R Arbuckle, BVM&S, PhD, FRCVS, 17 Aldersey Rd, Guildford
Alex Archibald, 37 Gray Park, Perth Road, Cowdenbeath
Leslie G Archibald, 912 Ingersoll Street, Winnipeg, Canada
P Ariell-Wright, 9 Briar Court, Burnham-on-Sea
Edward C Armstrong, MBE, FSAScot, Kumasi, Langholm
R Armstrong 44 Tollerton Drive, Irvine
Mr William Arnott, 64 Cardenden Road, Cardenden
Tom & Betty Arrol, 15 Elmcroft Crescent, Harrow
Marion Morrison Ash, 307 Charter Ave, St Johns, Nfld, Canada
Mrs Ellen P Astridge, 4 Eastfield Drive, Hanslope
David W L Auld, The Dales, Springs, Stair, by Mauchline
Jean Auld, 10 Brown Walk, Irvine
Mary Auld, 27 Baidland Avenue, Dalry
Ayr Burns Club, Tam o' Shanter Museum
Ayrshire Association of Burns Clubs (10 copies)
Kenneth Babington, 4 Mansfield Road, Prestwick
Rodney Babington, 4 Mansfield Road, Prestwick
Dr Louis S Baer, Burlingame, California, USA
David Baillie, 16 Bentinck Street, Galston
Dr T Baird, 43 St Pauls Road, Coventry
Graham J Balmer, 23 Hawkhill Avenue, Ayr
John R Banks, 31 St Mary's Road, Little Haywood, Stafford
Mrs Agnes Barbour, 16 Bruce Street, Lincluden, Dumfries
Mrs E Barlow, 9 West Road, Willington, Crook
Dr Thomas Barlow, 41 Dumbuck Crescent, Dumbarton
George Barn, 8 Dorking Walk, Corby
Robert J Barnes, 6 Glamis Gardens, Bishopbriggs, Glasgow
J W Barnett, 3 Oxbury Road, Trough Lane, Watnall, Nottingham
Donald McLeod Barr, 73 Winnington Road, Enfield
Janet McKay Barr, 172 Erskine Faulds Road, Linwood
Cllr Tom Barrie, JP, Barmyle, Belmont Street, Kilsyth
Mr T H Bartlett, 17 Ewart Drive, New Abbey Road, Dumfries

Albert Bateman, 88 Patrick Road, Corby
Victor E Bates, 91 Bank Street, Irvine
William Mearns Bates, Glenhead, Uplawmoor
David W Baynham, CA, 72 Loirston Avenue, Cove Bay, Aberdeen
W D Beaton, 79 Meadowlands Dr W, Ottawa, Canada (2 copies)
John Beattie, 59 Newmains Road, Renfrew
Robert Beattie, 34 East Park Crescent, Kilmaurs
Frank Beaumont, Easdale Drive, Sandyhills, Glasgow
Graham Shearer Begg, Durham
Dr James A Begg, 19a Ewenfield Road, Ayr
James S Begg, Busbiehill Burns Club
Wallace Begg, 15 Braid Hills Avenue, Edinburgh
A V & M B Bell, 24 Prospect Vale, Wallasey
Grace Hamilton Bell, 114 Meadow Road, Coventry
Rebecca Grace Waddle Bell, 114 Meadow Road, Coventry
Ruth Agnes McConnell Bell, 114 Meadow Road, Coventry
Tom Bell, 49 Drum Brae South, Edinburgh
William McConnell Bell, 114 Meadow Road, Coventry
Ian Alastair Bennett, 9 Lowca Lane, Seaton, Workington
Robert & Phyllis Bennett, 61 Braehead, Irvine
David Bennie, 18 John Street, Catrine
Anna S Bett, 40 Gardner Avenue, Anstruther
George Russell Beveridge, Star Inn, Newton Stewart
Thomas & Pamela Beveridge, 21A Dogwood Acres, Chapel Hill, USA
James Bicker, 14 Ardmory Road, Rothesay
John Biggart, 33 Mains Road, Beith
Mary Biggart, 72 Beech Avenue, Beith
Michael Birkenshaw, 32 Greenlea Road, Muirhead, Chryston
Harry Birkhead, 27 Weaver Court, Gateacre, Liverpool
Jean E W Birkhead, MBE, Box 261, Millboro, USA
Margaret J Birkhead, 27 Weaver Court, Gateacre, Liverpool
Thomas L Birkmyre, 14/5 Maxwell Tower, Falkirk
Birnbeck Burns Club, Weston-Super-Mare
Norman Bissett, 3-4 Bruntsfield Crescent, Edinburgh
David Black, 897 Cumbernauld Road, Riddrie, Glasgow
Gordon Black, 6 Queens Drive, Surbiton
Nina Black, 19 Mastrick Road, Aberdeen
W G Black, 1 Isla Road, Luncarty, by Perth
William Gordon Black, 5 Kidsneuk, Irvine
Hendry Dougal Blackie, Fortview, Eyemouth
Alex Blackwood, 90 Ayr Road, Cumnock
P W Blackwood, 68 Marmion Avenue, Colgrain, Helensburgh
James Blaik, 12 The Elms, Stoke Road, Linslade
John Blain, Torwood, Gartocharn
Richard M Blain, 62 Mosspark Avenue, Dumfries

Miss Catriona Anne Blair, Bughtlin Park, Corstorphine, Edinburgh
Miss Iris S Blair, 48 Bellevue Crescent, Ayr
Kay & Alistair Blair, 9 Douglas Drive, Ashgill, Larkhall
Murray S Blair, TD, 29 Glenpark Avenue, Glasgow
Robert Blakley, Hillview, 14 Abbey Gardens, Coupar Angus
Donald H M Blamey, 39 Rupert Street, Glasgow
John Blamey, 2 Hugh Avenue, Lochgelly
Thomas Blamey, 12 Page Street, Lochgelly
Andrew L T Blance, President 1984/5, Dollar Burns Club
Blane Valley Burns Club, Blanefield, Glasgow
K Blyth, 11 Hillside Road, Cardross
Mrs Isobel Boller, 336 Moore Avenue, Kenmore, New York, USA
E R Bonnar, 29 Gagie Bank, Wellbank, Dundee
Rick Bookham, Edmonton Dundonald Burns Club, Canada
Alan R Booth & Sondra D Stigen, Annapolis, USA
Miss Madge Borland, Port Glasgow
Mrs Cecilia Bottomley, LRAM, 23 Kingswood Gardens, Leeds
Vincent Bovo, 4D Wesley Street, Airdrie
Bowhill Peoples Burns Club (3 copies)
Mr William Bowie, 48 Lowana Street, Sydney, Australia
Charles Bowman, Esq, JP, 13 Ancrum Gardens, Dundee
John J Boyd, 12023 Aspen Dr W, Edmonton, Alberta, Canada
Andrew Boyle, 14 Arran Gardens, Troon
Andrew H Boyle, 12 Astley Road, Harwood, Bolton
Mr Robert M Boyle, 13 Lapwing Close, South Beach, Blyth
William Boyle, 50 Hillcrest Drive, Stevenston
John Brabender, 45 Duns Crescent, Wishaw
Mr L M Braby, Firman & Sons, 14 Soho Square, London
Lilias Jarvie Bradley, Queens Park Hotel, Glasgow
J S Brady, 11 Woodside, Bedlington
Edmiston M M Breingan, 4 Walton Crescent, Dollar
James Brew, 15 Friendly Drive, Islington, Canada
British Council, 3-4 Bruntsfield Crescent, Edinburgh
E C T Bromfield, Viewfield, 44 Annick Road, Irvine
Jessie Brooks, 19 Fraser Avenue, Hamilton, Canada
Mrs Agnes Brooks, 52 Garstang Avenue, Breightmet, Bolton
David Broom
John L Broom, 21A Franklin Road, Stromness
Mrs Margaret Brotherston, 8 Braehead, Girdle Toll, Irvine
C Murray & Ancel Brown, Lexington, Kentucky, USA
Eric O Brown, 33 Bramblewood Road, Worle, Weston-Super-Mare
Mr Henry Brown, 14 Penzance Ave, Christie's Beach, Australia
Mr J Brown, 48 Bradda Avenue, Burnside, Glasgow
J L Brown, 5 Overton Crescent, Redding, Falkirk
Jack Brown, Piersland House Hotel, Troon

James A Brown, Ardenlea, 109 Ardlochan Road, Maidens
John M P Brown, Airlie Cottage, Broadlie Road, Neilston
Lilian A Brown, 5 Springfield Lane, Morley, Leeds
Loftus W Brown, 4 Airds Avenue, Dumfries
M J Brown, 7 Overton Crescent, Redding, Falkirk
Martin Brown, 2 Fairfield Crescent, Georgetown, Dumfries
Matt Brown, Eglinton Street, Irvine
Norman R Brown, 9 Northfield Avenue, Ayr
Peter Campbell Brown, Sunnyside, 70 Townfoot, Dreghorn
Robert Brown, 11 Quality Street, Edinburgh
Robert Brown, 190 Lutterworth Road, Nuneaton
Cllr Robert Brown, SNP, KLDC, Steward, Irvine Burns Club
Sam Brown, 3 Ballmacormick Gardens, Bangor
William Brown, 26 Drew Avenue, Newton Stewart
William Brown, Hillhead House, Coylton
Richard F Bruce, 24 Greenock Avenue, Cathcart, Glasgow
Charles M Bryan III, Roswell, Georgia, USA A
J Bryan, 9 Rozelle Terrace, Ayr
Samuel Bryson, 53 Braehead, Girdle Toll, Irvine
Margaret W Buchanan, 143 Dundonald Road, Troon
John H Bull, 49 Annanhill Avenue, Kilmarnock
Harry Burford, 28 Stewart Avenue, Currie
C Douglas Burgess, 1 Wolfe Avenue, Newton Mearns, Glasgow
J C Burn, 22 Dalbeattie Road, Dumfries
Gerrard Burnett, The Hermitage, 9 London Road, Slough
Dr Robin Ross Burnett, 79 Bank Street, Irvine
Burns Committee of Rhode Island
Burns House Museum, Mauchline
Alexander Burns, JP, 88 Livingstone Terrace, Irvine
Conway Burns, Millboro, Virginia, USA
Mr Daniel Burns, 7 George Street, Wigton
John J Burns, 39 Alford Lane, Stockton-on-Tees
Thomas & Elspeth Burns, Niagara Falls Burns Club
William Burns, 75 Plean Street, Flat 125, Glasgow
E Burstow, Latimer, Deacons Lane, Hermitage, Newbury
Bury St Edmunds & District Caledonian Society
Busbiehill Burns Club, Crosshouse, Kilmarnock
Henry Bush, 16 West Burn Park, Edinburgh
Mr James E Butler, Limekilns Road, Dunfermline
Mr Patraic Butler, 4 Eston Grove Fulwell Mill, Sunderland
John Cairney, 44 St Vincent Crescent, Glasgow
T Anderson Cairns, Giffen House, Dalry
Thomas & Mrs Ann Cairns, 69 Boydfield Avenue, Prestwick
Mrs Anne Caldwell, 30 Samson Avenue, Kilmarnock
Mr & Mrs J J Caldwell, 51 Kirkgate, Irvine

James Caldwell, 90 East Road, Irvine
Miss Leigh Caldwell, Craig Isla, Cairston Road, Stromness
Caledonian Society of Colchester & District
Caledonian Society of Sheffield
Calgary Burns Club, Calgary, Canada (5 copies)
Robert A Callander, Milnfaulds, Boghead Road, Dumbarton
Alistair C Cameron, 5E Cedar Place, Barrhead
Colin Cameron, 7 Kidsneuk Cottage, Irvine
Mrs Constance Cameron, 64 Ironcliff Road, Penguin, Australia
D Rankin Cameron, FISM, LVCM, ALCM, Croftend Ave, Glasgow
Donald Cameron, 17 Castlecroft Gardens, Uddingston
Hugh B Cameron, 24 Woodside Gardens, Brightons, Falkirk
Provost Ken Cameron, JP, 59 Wallamhill Road, Dumfries
Sheona M Cameron, 59 West Portland Street, Troon
Mrs J Campain-Burns, 52 Darley Road, Paradise, Australia
Dr Alan Campbell, 15 Greenlaw Drive, Paisley
Alastair J Campbell, 2502 Rosefield Drive, Houston, USA
Mrs Helen Campbell, 1 Bridge Street, Kirkcudbright
James Campbell, 23 Burnside Place, Irvine
James Blair Campbell, Leicester
Joe Campbell, 30 Racecourse Road, Ayr
John R Campbell, 3 North Crescent Avenue, Ardrossan
Lionel Campbell, BA, MEd, 2 Maple Leaf Court, Cottingham
Mr R & Mrs A Campbell, 27 Austin Street, Fairlight, Australia
R D Campbell, 7 Burns Street, Irvine
Cllr Robert Campbell, 28 Thornwood Avenue, Ayr
Robert Campbell, 3 Gulliland Place, Irvine
Robert M Campbell, 21 Garden Street, Tarbolton
Robert R Campbell, 9 Selkirk Avenue, Cowdenbeath
William G Campbell, 45 St Peter Street, Peterhead
William McKay Hunter Campbell, 903 Lawrence Rd, Hamilton, Canada
James Cannell, 77 Marchburn Avenue, Prestwick
George Brown Cant, 30 Millhill Avenue, Kilmaurs
Canterbury Burns Club, Barrington, New Zealand
Robert F Carey, 18 Aldergreen, Middleton Park, Irvine
Eileen Carnegie, Hale, Manchester
R H Carnie, Dept of English, University of Calgary, Canada
Milton Stover Carothers, 706 Waverly Road, Tallahassee, USA
Mr & Mrs Carr, 3 Solsgirth House, Kirkintilloch
Mr & Mrs Frank Carroll, Colorado Springs, USA
Alexander Carson, 14 Remilton Street, Whyalla, South Australia
Janis Carson, 17 Berry Drive, Irvine
William Carson, 17 Berry Drive, Irvine
Ruth Carswell, 95 Clark Street, Airdrie
Elizabeth Cassels, 51 Main Street, Dunlop

Evans J Casso, 108 North Gatehouse Drive, Metairie, USA
C Stuart Chalmers, 2860 Lionel Cr, Calgary, Canada
James L Chalmers, 39 Cardowan Drive, Stepps, Glasgow
Thomas Chalmers, Peterhead Burns Club
William Chambers, 47 Leslie Crescent , Ayr
William Cheyne, 16 Mackerel Hall, Royston
Mrs J A Chisholm, 35 Gannochy Road, Perth
John Chisholm
Choppington Burns Club
"Clarinda" Edinburgh Ladies Burns Club
Edward Clark, 14826 Delbarton Drive, Houston, USA
Elizabeth Clark, 6 Hill Street, Irvine
Gordon A Clark, Cladach, Ainslie Road, Girvan
Mrs Mary M Clark, 52 Cloan Crescent, Bishopbriggs
Mrs Sally Clark, Niaroo, Nethergribton, Dumfries
Annette H Clarke, 34 Canmore Gardens, Kirkcaldy
James M Clarke, 362 Broughty Ferry Road, Dundee
R B Cleland, 20 Oakfield Tower, Motherwell
Mrs Mary Clements, 56 Linden Lea, Hamilton
Mrs Sandra Clifton, 55 Bentinck Drive, Troon
J B Clow, 111 Ainsdale Road, Leicester
Kirsten & Lynsey Clubb, 42 Rockall Drive, Glasgow
Coalsnaughton Burns Club
Eric G R Cochrane, 14 Boghead Road, Dumbarton
Joseph A W Cochrane, 48 Manor Avenue, Kilmarnock
Mr R A Coghill, 37 Norton Park View, Sheffield
Mrs Brenda Colburn, Box 324, Endsburgh Falls, Vermont, USA
Sylvia Colclough, 18 Monkwood Place, Alloway
George Cole, 19 Donaldson Drive, Irvine
P J Coleman, 23 Doon Place, Saltcoats
Henry Wilson Collin, Paxton Terrace, Eyemouth
Peter P Collin, Peterhead Burns Club
David Anderson Conn, MA, Laloki, Papua New Guinea
James B Conn, Bellfield, Kilmarnock
John Conn, BEM, 16 Houlton Road, Poole
Allan E Connor, Mississauga, Canada
Mrs Bunty Connor, London, Canada
Dr Jim Connor, Vice-President, Burns Federation (2 copies)
Jim T H Connor, London, Canada
Moira Ramage Conroy, 4917 South Miro Street, New Orleans, USA
John W Conway, 39 Watters Crescent, Lochgelly (2 copies)
Daniel Cook, Dumfries Burns Howff Club (2 copies)
Alex M Cooper, 47 Raemoir Avenue, Banchory
Mrs J Cooper, 27 Braehead, Irvine
J Copeland, 16 Taylor Street, Whyalla, South Australia

James Corbett, 11 Towerhill Avenue, Kilmaurs
Robert Y Corbett, Enterkin, 36 Riccartsbar Avenue, Paisley
Colonel E W Cormack, 52061 Range Road, Sherwood Park, Canada
Mrs Stella A Cormie, 4 Craiglea Road, Perth
Cotgrave Burns Club
Martin Coulter, 50 Hillmoss, Kilmaurs, Kilmarnock
George Couper, Greenock Burns Club
Robert Couper, Cruachan, 22 Oxgangs Road, Edinburgh
Derek G Cowan, 4 Cluny Gardens, Edinburgh
Joseph R Cowan, 24 Herbertson Crescent, Irvine
Ralph Cowan, Dunira, Uplawmoor
William Cowan, 3 East Lorimer Place, Cockenzie
William Cowan, Norwood, 75 Bank Street, Irvine
James M Cowie, 43 Pitfour Court, Peterhead
Michael J Cowie, 18 George Road, Peterhead
John N Cowper, 67 Balgillo Road, Broughty Ferry, Dundee
Edward Coyle, 10 Ingram Place, Kilmarnock
Ian W Coyle, Manderley, 6 Applegarth Road, Strathaven
Robert Crabbe, 129 Portland Street, Troon
Henry A Craddock, 70 Wallace Avenue, Elderslie
Alison Shiona Craig, 48A Beach Road, Troon
Charles I Craig, 490 Dick Road, Depew, NY, USA
Mr George Craig, 6 Finlay Rise, Milngavie
Ian Woodrow Craig, 48A Beach Road, Troon
James F. Craig, 9 Parkhill Avenue, Crosshouse, Kilmarnock
Peter Crammond, 1 Teesdale Road, Barnard Castle
Cramond Brig Burns Club
Alexander Crawford, Ash Villa, Main Street, Straiton
Flora Blair Crawford, 55 Oakmount Road, Toronto, Canada
Hugh W J Crawford, 24 Minto Street, Edinburgh
James Crawford, 7 Sidehead Road, Stonehouse, Lanarkshire
James Crawford, 74 Argyll Street, Corby
John McNiven Crawford, Camlarg, 28 Findhorn Place, Troon
S W Crawford, PO Box 150, Tweespruit, South Africa
May & Alex Crawley, 5 Castlemere Ct, St Catharines, Canada
Oliver S Creelman, 47 Bute Crescent, Dykehead, Shotts
Mrs Joan Creighton, 36 Windmill Heights, Enniskillen
D R H Crichton, 3 Hillview Avenue, Dumfries
John Crilley, 386 Maryhill Road, Glasgow
John K Crockett, 35 Drumellan Road, Alloway
Mrs Jean M Crombie, 80 Standalane, Annan
Margaret Crotch, 7 Central Avenue, Shortlees, Kilmarnock
Ken Crozier, New Cottage, 21 Campbell Street, Dollar
E G Cruikshank, 3 Clochrie Court, Locharbriggs, Dumfries
Cumbernauld & District Burns Club

Leonard D Cumming, 3 Royal Terrace, Craigmore
Robert Cumming, 32 Templeton Crescent, Prestwick
Cumnock & Doon Valley District Library, Bank Glen, Cumnock
Corbert Cunningham, 75 Clarkwell Road, Hillhouse, Hamilton
G M Cunningham, 2463 Stonecroft Drive, Horseheads, USA
H B Cunningham, 10 Southfield Close, Wrenthorpe
Hugh Cunningham, Carrick Lea, 99 Edinburgh Road, Dumfries
Ian Cunningham, 9 Overton Crescent, Redding, Falkirk
James M Cunningham, 23 Carlyle Drive, Kitchener, Canada
Robert Cunningham, 6 Tarryholme Drive, Irvine
Robert Cunningham, BSc, MSc, 3 Merrick Place, Symington
William M Cunningham, 27 Fern Drive, Barrhead
Abigail Curdy
John Curdy
Richard Curlewis, Finlayson St, Bayswater Nth, Australia
Frank Curran, 12 Barnton Drive, Dumfries
Alison Margaret Currie, Calgary, Alberta, Canada
Barbara Hamilton Currie, 75 Fairby Road, Lee Green, London
Charles C M Currie, Drumadoon Farm, Blackwaterfoot, Arran
Mr & Mrs I Q Currie, 4 Cotswold Avenue, Duston, Northampton
Iain H M Currie, Penpont, Thornhill, Dumfries
Irene Campbell Currie, Drumadoon, Isle of Arran
James Currie, Jnr, Calgary, Alberta, Canada
Rev. James Currie, MA, BD, JP, The Manse, Dunlop
Dr James Currie, MB, ChB, Calgary, Canada
Robert P Currie, 4 Overton Road, Strathaven
Stephen James Harvie Currie, Drumadoon, Isle of Arran
Suzanne Maclean Currie, Tigh-Na-Crioch, Penpont, Dumfries
William Anderson Currie, Calgary, Alberta, Canada
William Angus Currie, 70 Bryant Road, Kettering
Robert Cuthbertson, Bywell, 100 Ayr Road, Prestwick
William Cuthill, 11 Mina Crescent, Kinglassie
Mrs J M Cutting, 56 Dean Road West, Hinckley
Lawrence & Caron Dalgleish, The Garth, Troon
Mrs M S Dalgleish, 13A Climie Place, Kilmarnock (2 copies)
Margaret S Dalgleish, 11A Climie Place, Kilmarnock
Ronald Dalgleish, 17 Briants Close, Pinner
Tom & Ella Dalgleish, 50 Rowallan Drive, Kilmarnock
Margaret Davey, 36 Thornhouse Avenue, Irvine
Elizabeth C Davidson, 22 Wellington Crescent, Kirkton
James Richard Davidson, Beechgrove Farm, Annan
Robert M Davidson, 12 Awliscombe Road, Welling
Jimmy Davie, Hon President, Burns Federation (3 copies)
Robert Davie, 3 Tontine Place, Springhall, Rutherglen
Eric Davies, 6 Cottage Farm Road, Keresley, Coventry

Robert Davies, Conifers, 32 Naseby Close, Coventry
Ronald S Davies, 84 Lammermoor Avenue, Glasgow
John Davis, 28 Springhall Road, Garrowhill, Ballieston
E A M Dawes, Plenty River Drive, Greensborough, Australia
G S Dawes, 5 Laurieston Court, Dundonald
Christopher Dawson, 55 Wardlaw Street, Coalsnaughton
James Alexander Dawson, Beannie Farm, Braco
James Deans, 25 John Brown Place, Muirhead, Chryston
Miss Fiona Delaney, 21 Station Road, Lochgelly
Alfred Delorey, Melville Bank, Balcurvie, Windygates
John Dempster, 11 Wellpark Avenue, Kilmarnock
Mrs M Dempster, 16 Hoylake Square, Ashgrove, Kilwinning
Brian Des Champs, 211 Cardiff Drive, Calgary, Canada
Carol Des Champs, 116 Silvercrest Dr NW, Calgary, Canada
Janis Des Champs, 211 Cardiff Drive, Calgary, Canada
Marion & Allan Des Champs, 211 Cardiff Drive, Calgary, Canada
Sandra Des Champs, 1718-14th Ave SW, Calgary, Canada
Bobby Devine, Edmonton Dundonald Burns Club, Canada
Edward Devine, 25 Byres Road, Elderslie
Alexander McKenzie Dewar, 22 Harling Drive, Troon
Matthew B Dewar, Glendale, California, USA
Annette Dewson, 8 Flavel Street, Whyalla, South Australia
Alastair W Dick, Glencree, 13 Bank Glen, New Cumnock
Edward Dick, Victoria Dairy, Victoria Street, Ayr
Ian Grant Dick, 3/2 Springfield, Edinburgh
Iain F Y Dick
Lucy Dick, Glencree, 13 Bank Glen, New Cumnock
John Dickie, County Hotel, Wigtown
Mrs A A Dickson, 47 Fullarton Street, Kilmarnock
James Dickson, 17 Cecil Road, Weston-Super-Mare
Mrs Minnie Dickson, 62 Lochlea Drive, Ayr
Robert J Dickson, 12 Brockley Close, Weston-Super-Mare
Mrs Wilhelmina G Diggle, 18 Gorses Mount, Darcy Lever, Bolton
Robert Dobson, 1 Park Place, Dollar
William J Dobson, 122 James Campbell Road, Ayr
Hugh Docherty, 11 Kirkshotts Terrace, Cardenden
John Dodds, Severn Road, Epping Forest, Annapolis, USA
Norman Robert Dodds, 3 Eglinton Drive, Troon
Alistair J M Donaldson, DA, 14 Forehill Road, Ayr
Duncan N Donaldson, 28 Gunsgreen Crescent, Eyemouth
George M Donaldson, JP, 6 McGibney Drive, Irvine
Robin G Doncaster, 27 Ladywell Road, Maybole
Elizabeth Doughty, 35 Colenso Road, Leeds
Joseph Douglas, 230 Calder Street, Coatbridge
Captain R B Douglas, Berneray, Whyte Avenue, Irvine

Robin B Dow, Box 478, Bragg Creek, Alberta, Canada
Dr Arthur L Down, 13319 Myrtlea, Houston, Texas, USA
D H Downie, 50 Jean Armour's Avenue, Edinburgh
D W Downie, 14 Kenfin Avenue, Agincourt, Canada
Ian Downs, Woodneuk Cottage, Benslie, Kilwinning
Horst W Drescher, Scottish Studies Centre, Mainz, Germany
Miss Katherine Drever, 20 Seafield Drive, Ayr
Alexander C Duff, 15 Crambeth Place, Kelty
William Duffy, 98 Leander Crescent, Deanpark, Renfrew
Dr W P Duguid, 209 Calais Drive, Baie d'Urfe, Canada
Dumbarton Burns Club
Dumfries & District Round Table
Dumfries & Galloway College of Technology donated by Howff Club
Dumfries & Galloway Regional Council Library Service
Dumfries Academy donated by Howff Club
Dumfries Burns Club
Dumfries Burns Howff Club
Dumfries High School donated by Howff Club
Dumfries Ladies Burns Club No 1
W Dunbar, 22 Braehead, Alloa
Mrs C G Duncan, Leprechaun, Belmont, Durham
Douglas Ogilvie Duncan, Manderston, Nr Duns
Mr & Mrs George Duncan
Gordon Rhoderick Duncan, 19 Berry St., Vincentia, Australia
Jean Duncan, 5 Henderson Street, Toowoomba, Australia
William Duncan, 50 Kilbagie Street, Kincardine-on-Forth
Dr Charles F Dundas, Linwood, 16 Kirk Road, Bathgate
Dundee Burns Club
Mary B Dunklee, Fresno, California
Ms Elva Dunlop, 10 Learmouth Avenue, Birkenhead, New Zealand
Elza Dunlop, 16 Half Edge Lane, Eccles
Hunter Gilfillan Dunlop, 5 Dalhanna Drive, New Cumnock
Mrs Christian R H Dunn, Nesacrag, The Tors, Kingskerswell
G H Dunn, 9 Ferndale Road, Knighton, Leicester
Mr D M Dustan, 26 Thornsett Road, Sheffield
I M Duthie, 7 South Headlands Crescent, Newtonhill
John Duthie, Peterhead Burns Club
David Dyer, 4 Seafield Court, Aberdeen
Donald Graham Dyer, 7913 Westgate Drive, Lenexa, KS, USA
East Antrim Burns Association
George Eastcroft, 5 Kirkburn Drive, Strathblane
Mrs Muriel M Easton, 55 Rosehill Drive, Aberdeen
Eastwood District Libraries, Rouken Glen Road, Giffnock
Fiona MacDonald Edelstein, 850 Oregon Av, Schenectady, USA
Helen Edgar, 41 Larchfield Road, Dumfries

Hugh Edgar, 5 Southpark Avenue, Prestwick
Mrs Rose Edgar, Dalmalinn, Terregles, Dumfries
Edinburgh Ayrshire Association
Roy Edmundson, 93 Broomfield Road, Glasgow
John C Eliseo, 4639 Royal Oak, Santa Maria, CA, USA
Mr & Mrs A N Elliot, 5 Academy Place, Langholm
Alison Mae Elliott, 1 Garden Place, Troon
John Urquhart Elliott, 1 Garden Place, Troon
Lynne Frances Elliott, 1 Garden Place, Troon
The Ellisland Trust
J D Emmerson, 21 Colmore Avenue, Bebington
Scott Anthony Erdmann, 4610 Cave Road, Billings, USA
Joseph & Magdalene Erdos, 2 Great Oak Court, London, Canada
R S Erskine, Esq, FBOA, Inverlochy, Dunblane
Dr David Evans, Chatham, Canada
Mrs Isabel J G Everingham, 9 Sunningdale Avenue, Ayr
Mr Humphrey Evry, 24 Bilsland Road, Glenrothes
Mr James Ewan, 39 Kirkburn Drive, Cardenden
Ewart Public Library, Dumfries
Richard A C Ewart, Adderley Coach House, Monifeith
William Pirie Ewen, 12 Lapland Walk, Corby
Morton Ewing, 1 Macara Drive, Irvine
Robert Fairbairn, 10 Woodhall Close, Stanningley
Ian Falconer, 17 Bridge Road, Balerno
Kenneth John Falconer, 28 Crosswood Crescent, Balerno
Dr Ralph Fallows, St Andrews, Dundonald (2 copies)
Jean & James Farquhar, 4 Henry Ross Place, South Queensferry
G Farquharson, Geomar, 95 Thorniecroft Drive, Cumbernauld
Hugh C Farrell, 42 Willow Park, Ayr
W M Farrell, 7 Craigvale Court, Dumfries
Ian Faulds, Eriska, 15 Holmlands Place, Kilmarnock
John Fearns, 25 Albion Tower, Motherwell
A D Ferguson, 16 Lower Mains, Dollar
Douglas Ferguson, 104 McKinlay Crescent, Irvine
J M & Mrs C L Ferguson, 15 Maxwell Green, Irvine
Mrs Roma Ferguson, 55 Bellesleyhill Avenue, Ayr
Thomas Hanson Ferguson, 12 Lynmouth Place, Corby
William E Ferguson, 29 Leechmere Crescent, Seaham
W V Fernie, 19 York Road, Nunthorpe, Middlesbrough
Mr Steven Ferns, 4 Flagholme, Cotgrave, Nottingham
Mr William Ferns, 6 Flagholme, Cotgrave, Nottingham
R G Ferrari, Peterhead Burns Club
Bob Ferrier, 443 Cedar Park Drive SW, Calgary, Canada
D M Ferrier
Mr M Findlay, 5 Solway Rise, Dronfield Woodhouse

Brenda Finlay, 29 Snowden Street, Eston, Middlesbrough
The Rev. Harry Warren Firth
Albert Fisher, 72 Welwyn Drive, Salford
Jack Fisher, 17 Moss Road, Ilkeston
Dr Brian Fitzpatrick, Cape Town, South Africa
Charles R Fleetham, 127 Lumphinnans Road, Lochgelly
Henry Fleetham, 315 Tarland Knowe, Glenrothes
J T Fleming, 10 Abertay Crescent, Barnhill, Dundee
John Fleming, 33 Milne Avenue, Auchinleck
William R Fleming, 26 Ochil Court, Irvine
Sheila & Duncan Foggon, Glenvue, 4 Braepark Road, Edinburgh
James Forsyth, 9 Fairneylaw Place, Stirches, Hawick
Christina Foster, 84 Edinbeg Avenue, Toryglen, Glasgow
Frank C Foster, Jr, Marietta, Georgia, USA
James Taylor Foulds, 3 Thornwood Drive, Irvine
W Iain Foulds, 3 Allanvale Road, Prestwick
George Frame, 27 Eckford Street, Glasgow
Duncan W Francis, 9 Redmire Crescent, Allanton, Shotts
Mr William Francis, 9 Redmire Crescent, Allanton, Shotts
Alexander Fraser, 7 Hawthorn Avenue, Prestwick
Christopher Fraser, President, Hartlepool Caledonian Society
Donald Fraser, 26 Foxhall Road, Timperley
Douglas K Fraser, 3 Hunt Street, Corby
Elisabeth Fraser, Wellington Cottage, Marlborough St, Edinburgh
George Greig Fraser, 120 Clark Drive, Irvine
Hector Craig Fraser, Tayvallich, Molls Lane, Brampton, Beccles
Cllr Hugh D G Fraser, 181 Braid Road, Edinburgh
John Fraser, 4 Ramsay Crescent, Aberdeen
John A D Fraser, 181 Braid Road, Edinburgh
Mr & Mrs R Fraser, 58 Fullarton Avenue, Dundonald
James Freeman, Strathview, Croftamie, Glasgow
Joseph & Elizabeth Freeman, Niagara Falls Burns Club
Andrew Stewart Frew, Kirkland Cottage, Springside, Irvine
Mr & Mrs Thomas Frew, 3 Cockersand Avenue, Hutton, Preston
Elizabeth Alison Frontczak, 45 Smiths Avenue, Huddersfield
John Fulton, Glencairn, 12 Annick Road, Irvine
Mr & Mrs N P Gaffney, 55 Springfield, Thringstone
John Gallagher, 89 Edmiston Drive, Linwood
John P & Elizabeth Gallagher, Rochester, New York, USA
William J & Elenor L Gallagher, Cheetawaga, New York, USA
Stuart Ingram Galley, Sa Goba, Wickham Way, East Brent
Victoria Ann Galt
Cameron B Gamble, 6031 Garfield Street, New Orleans, USA
A J B Gardiner, 18 Stonefield Avenue, Paisley
Robert Garmory, 44 Church Street, Lochgelly

Oliver George Baring Garrod, 24 Polnoon Street, Eaglesham
Gartmorn Ladies Burns Club, Sauchie
Ronald Garvie, 5 West Albert Road, Kirkcaldy
Dr W A Gatherer, 44 Liberton Drive, Edinburgh
Alasdair J Gaw, 7 Highfield Place, Girdle Toll, Irvine
Anne Gaw, 7 Highfield Place, Girdle Toll, Irvine
Samuel K Gaw, Director, Irvine Burns Club
Ian Geddes, 345 Billing Road East, Northampton
Richard Gee, 6 Jellicoe Court, Worle, Weston-Super-Mare
Mary B Gemmel, 1 Old Doune Road, Dunblane
John Gemmill, 115 Constable Road, Corby
David S Gibb, 29 Beechgrove, Craigie, Ayr
Sir Alexander Gibson, 15 Cleveden Gardens, Glasgow
Mr Gordon Gibson, 82 Bonnyton Road, Kilmarnock
James Gibson, Craigowan, Cottage, Brewlands Road, Symington
John Gibson, 24 Blairderry Road, Streatham Hill, London
Mrs M D Gibson, 60 Glasgow Road, Kilmarnock
Nan Gibson, 205 Yoakum Parkway, Alexandria, USA
Peter Gibson, 205 Yoakum Parkway, Alexandria, USA
Robert S Gibson, 47 Napsbury Lane, St Albans
Douglas George Gillespie, 1 Jubilee Terrace, Johnstone
Elizabeth Gilliland, 9 Sillars Meadow, Irvine
John & Cath Gillon, Balloch
Vince & Helen Gillon, Bramalea, Canada
Mrs Isabel D Gilmour, 10 Chalmers Crescent , East Kilbride
Ian A Gilmour, Corbiere, 57 Round Riding Road, Dumbarton
Paul S Gionfriddo, 1281 Atwater Street, San Diego, USA
Mrs A M Giovannone, 2 Ladypark Farm, Ladypark, Gateshead
Ron S Girardau, 119-37th Street NW, Calgary, Canada
Glasgow Masonic Burns Club
Glasgow & District Burns Association
James Glass, 31 Glenconner Road, Ayr
Pauline Glen, 21 Lochlibo Terrace, Barrhead
Robert Glen, 77 Roseland Drive, Wahna Pitae, Canada
Capt G P StC Glendinning, BA, FSAScot, Dumfries
James E A Glendinning, West Gray, Houston, USA (3 copies)
Brian R Gloag, 24 Bryanston Road, Solihull
The Globe Inn, 56 High Street, Dumfries
Mrs Catherine Glover, 9 Borebraes Crescent, Newmilns
J E Godden, 181 Northridge, Bedlington
Dr James Goldie, 7 Graham Crescent, Dumbarton
Mrs Agnes McVittie Good, 26 Hillhead, Coylton
Robert J D Goodall, 71 Kingswood Road, Bishopton
Mr & Mrs W J Goodall, 1 Officials Terrace, Malton, Lanchester
D S Goodbrand, 10 Birch Polygon, Manchester

George Linscott Goode, 1 Meadow Grove, Cockermouth
David L Goodloe, Midway, Kentucky, USA
Bruce C Gordon, 3404 Underwood Place NW, Calgary, Canada
Charles B Gordon, 30 Back Street, Tarbolton
Heath F Gordon, 3404 Underwood Place NW, Calgary, Canada
Kenneth A Gordon, 59 Cedar Road, Ayr
Ross C Gordon, 3404 Underwood Place NW, Calgary, Canada
James Norman Gorrie, 65 Boylestone Road, Barrhead
Lydia M D Goshgarian, Hamilton, Canada
Martin Kevin Goudie, 30 Craigrownie Gardens, Kilcreggan
Ian M Gow, 42 Easter Drylaw View, Edinburgh
Ally Gowans, Lochee Burns Club, Dundee
Dr Maureen Gowans, 19 Old Kirk Road, Dunfermline
R M Gowans, 1 Cardy Road, Hemel Hempstead
John W Graham, 112 Crosswood Crescent, Balerno
Malise John Graham, 8719 Lee Blvd, Leawood, Kansas, USA
Mrs Mary E Graham, The Rufflets, 115 Gartree Road, Oadby
Grampian (Corby) Association "Burns Club", Patrick Rd, Corby
C B Grant, Field House, Wickenby
Gordon Grant, 1 Newmills Court, Balerno
Irene Grant, The Cottage, Newlands Rise, Annan
Thomas G Grant, 64 Beckwith Road, Harrogate
Mrs Allison Gray, The Pine, Blacktop, Kingswells, Aberdeen
Mrs Ann Gray, 116 Lochside Road, Dumfries
David F Gray, 92 High Street, Newmilns
James M Gray, 43 Carmel Place, Kilmaurs
Jessie M Gray, 10 Murchland Way, Irvine
Robert Gray, 7 Plateau Drive, Barassie
William Gray, 5 Craigskeen Place, Prestwick
William Gray, 51 East Park Drive, Kilmaurs
William Allan Gray, 1327 Peachtree, Atlanta, USA
Greenock Burns Club
Gordon Craise Greig, 67 Fairfield Road, Elizabeth, Australia
Group Captain James Greig, OBE, RAF Hospital, Ely
James Grubb, Peterhead Burns Club
Robert H Haddow, 6 Geirston Road, Kilbirnie
Samuel Emerson Hagen, 17 Herford Close, Corby
Richard John Hainey, 10 Melville Road, Coundon, Coventry
Mr Archibald Haining, 10 Wood Avenue, Annan
Mrs Elizabeth Haining, 74 Laghall Court, Dumfries
Arthur Hale, 24 Mount Blow House, Clydebank
Mrs Catherine MacKinnon Hall, 15 Studland Road, Byfleet
James B Hall, 142 Hamilton Road, Rutherglen, Glasgow
John Hall, 60 Caroline Crescent, Alva
Robert Daly Jack Hall, Parcell's Road, Harrisville, Australia

Sandy Hall, 188 Ames Street, Brockton, Mass, USA
T K Hall, Tighgarry, Inchmarlo Road, Banchory
Walter Hallyburton, 2 Cherry Tree Crescent, Balerno
Lt Cdr J Hamilton, RN, Monkwood, Alloway
Mr J F Hamilton, 17 Calderbraes Avenue, Uddingston
Dr John M Hamilton, 120 Adel Lane, Leeds
Dr Sheila C C Hamilton, 120 Adel Lane, Leeds
Stanley P Hamilton, Dumfries Burns Howff Club
R Hands, Millearn Apts, 42 Racecourse Road, Ayr
Mr James Hanley, 448 Waterloo Street, Cambridge, Canada
David A Hannah, Hillside, Church Lane, Brighouse
James B Hannah, 24 Kilmaurs Road, Knockentiber
Sam Hannah, 55 Ayr Road, Kilmarnock
William Hannah, 166 Wilson Avenue, Toronto, Canada
David Hannakin, 34 Heyes Drive, Wallasey
Mrs E Hannested, 272 Annan Road, Dumfries
Mrs Mary Harbottle, RR1 Millet, Alberta, Canada
Mr William Harcus, 4 Miller Avenue, Abbey Village, Chorley
Denise Hardie, 42 Arden Grove, Kilsyth
J Miller Hardie, Gatehead View, by Riccarton, Kilmarnock
Albert Donald Hardy, 110 Orkney Walk, Corby
Keith Fraser Hardy, 28 Eastbourne Avenue, Corby
Ronald Hardy, 14 Humbie Holdings, Kirknewton
Mrs J C Hare, 17 Wentworth Close, Hinckley
John M Harkins, Top Flat, The Kennels, Yaxham Road, Dereham
T E Harkness 114 Deyes Lane, Maghull
W S Harland, Greenbank, The Shore, Bolton-le-Sands, Carnforth
Graham Harley, Humberside Burns Society
Alastair N Harman, 8 Pine Road, Kilmarnock
Robert L Harper, BA, 87 Dundonald Road, Kilmarnock
Sqn Ldr E H Harris, BA RAF (Retd), Hillside Road, Bleadon
Alex M Harrison, 95 Carlogie Road, Carnoustie
Edyth E Harrison, 28 Nant-Y-Felin, Pentraeth
Peter Roy Harrison, Kenilworth Court, Hagley Road, Edgbaston
Mrs Ruth Harrison, 75 Bradley Road, Bradley, Huddersfield
Robert Harrower, South Queensferry (2 copies)
J H Hartill, 32 Leadervale Road, Edinburgh
Amelia Millar Harvey, 7 Wallace Street, Kilmarnock
Miss Andrea M R Harvey, Murchland Way, Irvine
Henry Harvey, 61 Alderminster Road, Mount Nod, Coventry
James B Harvey, Schedar, Berstane Road, Kirkwall
Raymond Henderson Harvey, Clifton, 6 Argyll Place, Rothesay
Donald M Hastie, 7 Lovedale Avenue, Balerno
Ian Hatton, Viewfield, Shilford, by Neilston
Richard Haugh, Screel, St Abbs Road, Coldingham

Alistair I Haughan, ARIBA, 7 Barns Terrace, Ayr
Kenneth M Haughan, 30 Cumnock Road, Mauchline
Hawick Burns Club
James Irving Hawkins, Achill, Back of the Hill, Annan
Colin William Hay, 18 Dunvegan Place, Irvine
John McClure Hay, 7 Newark Crescent, Doonfoot, Ayr
Margaret Hay, 18 Dunvegan Place, Irvine
Martin T Hay, Roddin, 11 Courtfield Close, Sudbrooke
Thomas & Flora Hay, 825 Charles Street, Aurora, Ill, USA
Catherine Hayball, 42 Humberston Ave, Humberston, Grimsby
E H R Head, Lauriston, 7 Cambridge Road, Wigmore, Gillingham
Albert Heasman, Whitemoss House, East Kilbride
Diana & Peter Hemphill, Knoweside, Failford
James L Hempstead, 10 Chapelton Gardens, Dumbarton
Alexander Henderson, 32 Clayflat Lane, Rossington
James W Henderson, 698 Kenton Lane, Harrow
Stuart L Henderson, 10 Delray Avenue, Wahroonga, Australia
William Hendry, 54 Townend Road, Dumbarton
James & Catherine Henry, 16 South Dean Road, Kilmarnock
David M Herbertson, 4 Burnside Place, Irvine
E S D Herbertson, 45 James Crescent, Irvine
Ian L Herd, 1 Shalloch Park, Ayr
James Heron, 2 Harland Park, Belfast
Thomas Heron, 20 Killoch Way, Stanecastle, Irvine
Beverley M Herron, 18 Aspen Avenue, Putnoe, Bedford
Hertfordshire Guild of Sommeliers
R Campbell Hewson, 6 West Albert Road, Kirkcaldy
Ian Highet, Sydney, Australia
Frances A D Highway, 36 Eaves Green, Meriden, Coventry
Grizelle M Hill, 76 Summerfield Drive, Annapolis, USA
T Hill, 8 Quadrant, North Berwick
J Hobkirk, 47 Craiglockhart Terrace, Edinburgh
Mrs Nosca Pluim Hoenderdos, 24 Leistrella Rd, Christchurch, NZ
Douglas McNeil Hogge, 2 Mentmore Close, Harrow
Mr Gavin Hollas, 41 Gort Avenue, Toronto, Canada
Alexander Holliman, 9 East Abercromby Street, Helensburgh
David L Holmes, 715 Cindy Blair Way, Lexington, USA
Alexander J Hood, 13 Cairns Drive, Balerno
Andrew J G Hood, 13 Cairns Drive, Balerno
Mrs David Hood, 11 Craigneil Drive, Prestwick
James A Hood, 8 Marchbank Drive, Balerno
Robin Hood, 177 Nithsdale Road, Glasgow
Miss Margaret Hopkin, 5 Climie Place, Kilmarnock
John W N Hopton, 5 Torphin Place, Kirkcaldy
Thomas Hopton, 15 Parliament Place, Kinglassie

Henry J Horrell, MBE, ED, 96 Cavell Street, Tainui, New Zealand
Fred Horton, Barweil, 25 Monkton Road, Prestwick
Colin J Hosie, 7 Bainfield Road, Cardross
M Fay Howard, 60A Chorley Road, Westhoughton, Bolton
Robert Howatson, 13 Portland Road, Dalrymple
Dr Douglas P K Howie, 8A Seafield Drive, Ayr
Peter Howie, 39 Donald Crescent, Troon
Thomas Howie, Dalshian, Shaw Road, Prestwick
Alexander Howitt, Burnside of Culbeuchly, by Banff
Mr Basil H J Hoyle, Ferris Street, Christie's Beach, Australia
Keith Hudston, Silver Birches, Newbold Road, Kirby Mallory
Mr Edward Hughes, 45 Percival Street, Darwen
Norman Hughes, 27 Earnock Street, Glasgow
Mrs D J E Hulbert, 8 Albany Crescent, Claygate
John Hume, Heather & Thistle Society, Houston, USA
Mrs Margaret W Hume, 101 Lammermuir Road, Kilmarnock
Robert Wyllie Hume, 59 Irvine Road, Kilmarnock
Kenneth Humphreys, Bournemouth
David Proudfoot Hunter, 123 Overslade Cres, Keresley, Coventry
Ellen Hunter, Glenartney, 102 Bank Street, Irvine
Colin Hush, 35 Long Craigs Terrace, Kinghorn
Janet Margaret Hutchinson, 11 Lochlea Avenue, Muirhead, Troon
Kirsty Joanne Hutchinson, 11 Lochlea Avenue, Muirhead, Troon
Harry Hutchison, 50 Archers Court Road, Whitfield, Dover
Zoe Lorn Hutchison, 23 Churchdown Road, Malvern
James Hutton, 10 Barloan Crescent, Dumbarton
Lewis James McLean Hynd, OBE, 2 Victoria Place, Stirling
Peter Hynd, Corrie, 50 Ayr Road, Prestwick
Robert Graham Hynd, 12 Princes Terrace, Glasgow
Mrs H M Hyslop, 4 Seaforth Avenue, Annan
Robert Hyslop, 26 Smallwood Terrace, Cheektowaga, USA
Jim & Chris Imlah, 10 Caistor Drive, Hartlepool
Agnes Inglis, 11 Afton Brigend, New Cumnock
Elaine K Inglis, 16 Berry Drive, Irvine
Iain M Inglis, 9 Dalry Road, Kilwinning
Mr & Mrs John M M Inglis, 16 Berry Drive, Irvine (5 copies)
Margaret L Inglis, 7 Jessfield Terrace, Edinburgh
Mrs M B Ingram, 10 Mortain Road, Rotherham
Dr David Innes, 10 Mead Haze, Maidenhead
E Innes, 20 Berry Drive, Irvine
Inverclyde District Libraries, Clyde Square, Greenock (2 copies)
Irvine Burns Club, Wellwood, Irvine
Irvine Lasses Burns Club
Angus D Irvine, 4 Romford Road, Sale
Alex J Irving, 74 Moyness Park Drive, Blairgowrie

James Irving, Dumfries Burns Howff Club
R Gilmour Ivey, Northbrae, Courthill Street, Dalry
Robert Hendry Jack, 78 Thornton Road, Morecambe
W Jack, Ford Cottage, Ford Drive, Mirfield
David Edward James, 30 Prestwick Road, Ayr
Ann Jamieson, 14 Granville Close, Wallasey
Mrs Mary Jamieson, 2 Elm Park Gardens, London
May W Jamieson, 19 Leslie Terrace, Prestwick
Arthur H G Jardine, Spedlins, Terregles Street, Dumfries
Leslie Jeavons, 36 Brunswick Road, Rotherham
Marion E Jeffery, 453 Belvedere Avenue, London, Canada
Andrew Sloan Jess, 1 Forehill Road, Ayr
David N Johnson, 5011 Lamar Avenue, Mission, Kansas, USA
F R Johnson, 38 Tunstall Road, Stockton (2 copies)
Brian A Johnston, 52 Hill Street, Dysart
R Dickson Johnston, 48 East Clyde Street, Helensburgh
Wilson D Johnston
Albert Bath Johnstone, 6 Kirkhouse Road, Blanefield, Glasgow
Brian Johnstone, Picton Street, Niagara-on-the-Lake, Canada
James Johnstone, 2 Horsburgh Gardens, Pilmuir, Balerno
Jim & Vena Johnstone, Picton Street, Niagara-on-the-Lake, Canada
John Johnstone, 20 Montague Street, Dumfries
Lawrence Johnstone, 22 John Wilson Drive, Kilsyth, Glasgow
Mrs Mary P Johnstone, 2075 Tryon Road, Sidney, BC, Canada
Thomas Johnstone, 7 Hermitage Crescent, Dumfries
William Johnstone, 15 Pitlochie Terrace, Kinglassie
Mr L F Jolly, Causey, 1 Keswick Road, Liverpool
Derek John Jones, 23 Aynho Close, Mount Nod, Coventry
Katriona A Jones, Kates Cottage, Frilford, nr Abingdon
Pearl Jones, 122 Graham Avenue South, Hamilton, Canada
William Jones, Mossgiel, 7 Kenilworth Avenue, Helensburgh
William Jones, Sheriff Clerk, Dumfries
Mr & Mrs William Jones, 31 Lockhart Place, Wishaw
William B Jones, 2 De Walden Terrace, Kilmarnock
Millicent G Jordan, 56 Oakfield Avenue, Markfield
Mr A & Mrs M Joyce, 33 McClure Crescent, Scarborough, Canada
Martin F Joyce, 74 Rue De Grunewald, Luxembourg (2 copies)
Andrew Kay & Co (Curling Stones) Ltd, Mauchline
Joseph M Keegan, 48 Ainslie Road, Cumbernauld
Alaister R Keir, 34 Abbey Road, Scone, Perth
James R Keir, 38 Graham Street, Holytown
Thomas Kellock, 68 Herriot Crescent, Methil
Christopher Robert Ramsay Kelly, 7 Spearshill Road, Tayport
Jim Kelly, 7 Knowes Loan, Barry, Carnoustie
Lewis Kelly, 20 Royal Avenue, Stranraer

Mary C Kelly, 117 Blairbeth Road, Burnside, Glasgow
Moira Kelly, Marylea, 3 Stewarthall Gardens, Dumfries
Mr Rankin Kelly, Greenock Burns Club
Robert Pitt Kelly, 398 Prospecthill Road, Glasgow (2 copies)
William L Kelly, 48 St Phillans Avenue, Ayr
Charles Baird Kelman, Jnr, Member of Peterhead Burns Club
Charles Baird Kelman, President, Peterhead Burns Club 1980
Mr & Mrs Kelso, Burns House Museum, Mauchline
John Kemp, Wester Rottearns, Greenloaning, Dunblane, Perthshire
Klaus D Kemp, Blautannen, Wickham Way, East Brent
Charles Kennedy, 101 Dundonald Park, Cardenden (3 copies)
Ian Bruce Kennedy, 110 Henderson Street, Bridge of Allan
Dr J Kennedy, 1 Westminster Close, High Wycombe
Robert Bruce Kennedy, 7905 Mission-Bonita Dr, San Diego, USA
Stewart M Kennedy, 29 Murchland Way, Irvine
Miss Agness Kerr, 19 Zetland Place, Lochgelly
Duncan MacIntyre Kerr, 56 Stewart Drive, Whitburn
Mrs Hazel Kerr, Brockwood, 21 Airds Avenue, Dumfries
Iain Kenneth Kerr, 3 Vauxhall Gardens, Tonbridge
James Kerr, 3 Shanter Place, Kilmarnock
Mr James Warden Kerr, 32 Taits Lane, Dundee
John Joseph Kerr, 24 Milgarholm Avenue, Irvine
Thomas MacIntosh Kerr, 3 Vauxhall Gardens, Tonbridge
Mrs Vivian Kerr, 21 Glencaple Avenue, Dumfries
H G J Kerrison, 57 Kennedy Avenue, Halesworth
Thomas Kettle, Ardmore, Walker Street, Kincardine
Kilmarnock & Loudoun District Council
Kilmarnock & Loudoun District Council Libraries (14 copies)
Robert Kincaid, Butterstone Village, Dunkeld
J S King, 14 Hyslop Street, Kirkconnel
Dr T A King, 16 Branch Road, Larne
W J King-Gillies, 36 Queen's Crescent, Edinburgh
George Kinnear, 57A Belsize Park Gardens, London
James Neilson Kinniburh, Owlcroft, Knockbuckle Rd, Kilmacolm
Thomas Kirby, Friars' Carse, Auldgirth, Dumfries
John A W Kirk, 8 Lugar Street, Coatbridge
Mrs Elizabeth Kirkland, 15 Parkhead Drive, Dumfries
Alexander Kirkwood, 71 Draffen Tower, Motherwell
Gordon Kirkwood, 11 Greville Road, Rosanna, Australia
John Kirkwood, 80 Ridout Street, London, Canada
Alan C Knight, Flattichstrasse 10, Muenchingen, Germany
Mr R Knox, 12 Sunningdale Square, Whitehirst Park, Kilwinning
Maureen Kolosky, 20 Holmston Drive, Ayr
Sheila Kurczynski, Picton Street, Niagara-on-the-Lake, Canada

Mrs Jean Kvarfordt, Husebybakken 7a, Oslo 3, Norway
Kyle & Carrick District Council, Burns House, Ayr
Mr Alastair C Laing, 1 West Campbell Street, Newmilns
G Henderson Laing, 50 Marionville Drive, Edinburgh
M J Laird
Alexander Lamb, 7 Dunkeld Road, Perth
Kenneth Lamb, 9 Oxford Road, Corby
J Thomas Lambie, 5 Deacons Court, Linlithgow
Callum Lamont, Irvine Burns Club
Raymond Lamont-Brown, MA, Author & Broadcaster, St Andrews
Lanarkshire Association of Burns Clubs
Margaret Lane, 47 Lanyard Road, Weston, Toronto, Canada
Hugh Lang, 20 Ravenscroft, Irvine
Mr & Mrs T Lapsley, 2 Goukscroft Park, Doonfoot, Ayr
Alex Lauchlan, 471 Rooney Crescent, Edmonton, Canada
Alex G Lauchlan, 471 Rooney Crescent, Edmonton, Canada
Gary Lauchlan, 471 Rooney Crescent, Edmonton, Canada
Jessie Ross Lauchlan, 471 Rooney Crescent, Edmonton, Canada
Mark B Lauchlan, 471 Rooney Crescent, Edmonton, Canada
Thomas B Lauchlan, 1 Frew Terrace, Irvine
Mr Forbes B Lauder, 11 South Hamilton Street, Kilmarnock
John Lauder, 3 Georgetown Crescent, Dumfries
Vida L Lauder, 5 Whyte Avenue, Irvine
Hugh C Law, 5 Seagate, Prestwick
John Law, 74 Caerlaverock Road, Prestwick
Rev. William James Lawler, 45 Broughton Road, Wallasey
Mr Albert Lawrie, 39 Bankfield Street, Deane, Bolton
Mrs Janet M G Lawrie (2 copies)
Robert Lawrie, 40 Langley Crescent, St Albans
C M Lawson, 13 Findhorn Place, Troon
Mrs Margaret Lawson, 30 Sutherland Crescent, Dundee
James Leask, 18 Kerr Drive, Irvine
William Charles Le Breton, 7 Mendip Edge, Weston-Super-Mare
James Lees, 44 Oakfield Road, Motherwell
James Lees, Glencoe, 2 Breck Avenue, Paisley
John R Lees, 12 Barrhill Road, Cumnock
Leicestershire Libraries & Information Service (2 copies)
Andrew Leitch, 1 Doncaster Close, Wyken, Coventry
George Leitch, The Crown Inn, Welton, Midsomer Norton
Maureen B Leitch, 4 Warrix Gardens, Troon
Mrs Alice Lennon, 63 Fergushill Road, Kilwinning
Mr & Mrs Hugh Lennon, Route 2, Box 130R, Warsaw, USA
Katherine Lennon, 22 Brewland Street, Galston
Henry Lennox, 50 Yarrow Crescent, Wishaw
Lawrie I Lennox, 50 Auchendoon Crescent, Ayr

John Leonhardt, 3900 Pacific Avenue, Marina Del Rey, USA
C T Lewis, Vice-President, Canterbury Burns Club, N.Z.
John Lewis, 39 Freesia Court, Motherwell
Fiona Lindop, 174 Cambridge Road, Hitchin
Charles McC K Lindsay, 72 Lothian Road, Stewarton
David Lindsay, P.P. Caledonia Burns Club
William & Mary Lindsay, 138 Bond Street, Hamilton, Canada
Bessie Little, 82 Sherman Avenue North, Hamilton, Canada
J Kerr Little, Redbank, New Abbey Road, Dumfries
John Little, 82 Sherman Avenue North, Hamilton, Canada
Johnny, Jamie & Tommy Little, 82 Sherman Ave N, Hamilton, Can
Thomas Little, 10 Avocado Lane, Rochester, NY, USA
Walter Little, Bankhouse, Rotchell Park, Dumfries
Liverpool Burns Club
Mr James Livingstone, Ashbank, Gorebridge
William B Livingstone, 11 Linburn Road, Dunfermline
William Llewellyn, 288 High Street, Kirkcaldy
Lochee Burns Club, Old Muirton Road, Lochee
Desmond Lock, 8 Anchor Buildings, Paisley
Mrs Rosemary Lockerbie, 14 Loganbarns Road, Dumfries
A Christian S Lockhart, Nether Auchendrane, Alloway
G W Lockhart, 59 Oatlands Park, Linlithgow
William Lockhart, 32 Kilwinning Road, Irvine
Lodge Camperdown Burns Club, 7 Dura Street, Dundee
H Joe Loe, 4800 Rowan Drive, Fort Worth, Texas, USA
Alexander Logan, 36 Beresford Terrace, Ayr
Enez Logan, 6 Hugh Watt Place, Kilmaurs
Gordon Gerrie Logan, 9 Spynie Place, Bishopmill, Elgin
James Templeton Logan, 40 Park Grove, Parkmains, Erskine
Rev. Tom Logan, 206 Bank Street, Irvine
W G Logan, Golden Meadows Cr, Nanaimo, Canada (2 copies)
London (Ont) Burns Club, Canada
Denis Gordon Thomas Lothian
David Loudon, 9 Ailsa Street, Prestwick
Jean Loudon, 9 Ailsa Street, Prestwick
Mr Albert Loughran, 84A Brooms Road, Dumfries
D Love, 80 Holland Crescent, Drumbrochan, Cumnock
John C Lovie, 7 Milgarholm Avenue, Irvine
James Scott Lowson, Lesley Souter House, Whitehall Rd, Rugby
Dr & Mrs C P Lowther, 15 Lennox Street, Edinburgh
Elizabeth M Loye
Luath Press Ltd, Publishers, Forest Bank, Barr
Robert M Luke, Ashlea, 2 Macara Drive, Irvine
Douglas Lumsden, 8000 Falmouth, Prairie Village, USA
Geoffrey Lund, 47 Howick Park Drive, Penwortham, Preston

Mrs Annie Lundie, 2 Wood Road, Troon
Luseland School Library, Luseland, Saskatchewan, Canada
Ian Lyle, 5 McQueen Avenue, Cumnock
Mr William Dougall Lyle, 1 Midton Avenue, Prestwick
John Michael Lynch, P.P. Caledonia Burns Club
Mr Neil Lynch, 43 Gallowhill Avenue, Tarbolton
T Mabon, Snr, 2E Richardland Place, Kilmarnock
Alan J McAdam, 3 Tinto Square, Renfrew
Elizabeth McAdam, 1 Callendar Place, Hunters Ave, Irvine
James H McAlister, Dumfries Burns Howff Club
Derrick MacAllister, 59 Beach Road, Barassie, Troon
Mr William McAllister, 48 Tandridge Gardens, Sanderstead
J E McAlpine
Hector McAndrew, 3 Boyd Orr Crescent, Kilmaurs
Archie McArthur, 33 Inchmead Drive, Kelso
Duncan McArthur, 164 Hillend Crescent, Clarkston, Glasgow
Russell Stuart McArthur, 26 Cameron Place, Carronshore
Helen & Frank McAvoy, 6 Shalloch Park, Doonfoot, Ayr
J D McBain, 33 Humbledon Park, Sunderland
R McBride, Hayfield, Darvel
Alexa McCaffery, 31 Ardrossan Road, Saltcoats
John McCaig, 9 Glenbrook, Balerno
James H McCall, Solana Beach, CA, USA (2 copies)
Joan McCall, 6 Knockinlaw Road, Kilmarnock
Alistair McCallum, 45 Neuk Crescent, Houston
Ken McCallum, Westwood, Glenpatrick Road, Elderslie
Norma A McCallum, 10440 Wornall Road, Kansas City, USA
R McCallum, 34 Oswald Road, Ayr
William McCallum, 2 Redwood Crescent, Bishopton
George McCance, North Street, Hadfield, Melbourne, Australia
Grant McCance, Alexandra Avenue, Torquay, Australia
William Grant McCance, 66 Paisley Road, Renfrew
Carol McCann, 9 Clochranhill Road, Alloway
David Scott McCartney, 13 Adams Walk, Irvine
Elizabeth McCartney, 53 Main Street, East Kilbride
Frederick William McCartney, 59 Dunlop Crescent, Dreghorn
James McCaw, Tam o' Shanter Club, Hertford Place, Coventry
Andrew McClure, Ballochmyle, Inverlael Avenue, Bolton
Arthur McClune, 39 Thomson Crescent, Port Seton
Cameron McClurg, Westwood, 27 Irvine Road, Kilmaurs
Isabella Watson McClurg, 18 Fenwick Road, Kilmaurs
Morag Gillies McClurg, 18 Fenwick Road, Kilmaurs
Barbara Frances McColl, 21 Lemon Grove, Nunawading, Australia
James McColl, 48 Darley Park Road, Darley Abbey, Derby
Ronald Vernon McColl, 21 Lemon Grove, Nunawading, Australia

Mr William Strachen McColm, 2 Smithfield Crescent, Tarbolton
William Burns McConnell, 22 Indale Avenue, Prestwick
Mr & Mrs James McConville, 83 Ettrick Street, Wishaw
Cllr John McCorkindale, Macharioch Lodge, Campbeltown
Jessie M MacCorquodale, 24 Manor Road, Regina, Canada
Dr John S McCrae, CBE, The Retreat, Clevedon
John McCraw, Edina, 22 Carseloch Road, Alloway
Margaret L McCreath, 4 Kennedy Drive, Dunure, by Ayr
Peter Wallace McCrorie, 11 Mabbutt Cl, Bricket Wood
Donald C McCuaig, 70 Pleasance Avenue, Dumfries
Bill McCue, OBE, Bothwell, Lanarkshire
Edward McCue, 5 Deanburn Park, Linlithgow
A McL McCulloch, 39 Mill Road, Irvine
John P McCulloch, 4 Morrison Drive, Lennoxtown, Glasgow
Jeanie McCutcheon, Townfoot of Glengaber, Dumfries
Cameron McDiarmid, 5 Muircot Place, Coalsnaughton
D McDonald, 37 West Road, Irvine
David McDonald, 8B Morison House, Burns Road, Kildrum
David Taylor McDonald, 7 Bury Close, Cottingham
Emerson L MacDonald, 1380 Weston Road, Toronto, Canada
Mr Ian McDonald, 1 Birnam Road, Kirkcaldy
Ian Handley Macdonald, MA, 17 Grange Terrace, Kilmarnock
Rev. Ian U & Mrs Macdonald, The Manse, Tarbolton
John Macdonald, 12 Hollow Park, Alloway
Neil Macdonald, 58 Stockiemuir Avenue, Bearsden
Mr Norman S & Mrs Isabelle McDonald, West Lindfield, Australia
Robert McDonald, 13 Albert Drive, Burnside, Glasgow
Colin Roy Macdougall, 58 Hillbury Avenue, Kenton
James A McDougall, TD, FCII, 2 Woodside Close, Ferndown
John David Macdougall, 58 Hillbury Avenue, Kenton
John Murray Macdougall, 58 Hillbury Avenue, Kenton
Lesley Anne Macdougall, 58 Hillbury Avenue, Kenton
Lorna Joyce Macdougall, 58 Hillbury Avenue, Kenton
A M McDowall, 5 Fairways Close, Allesley, Coventry
Carol Anne McEwan, 18 Auchinbaird, Sauchie, Alloa
Douglas F McEwan, 18 Auchinbaird, Sauchie, Alloa
Dr JW Grant MacEwan, Calgary (Hon President, Burns Federation)
Susan Jane McEwan, 18 Auchinbaird, Sauchie, Alloa
Sydney McEwan, 17 McTaggart Road, Cumbernauld, Glasgow
Mr William F McEwan, 18 Hamilton Avenue, Mauchline
John A C McFadden, 54 Moffat Road, Dumfries (4 copies)
Andrew McFarlane, Beinn Dorain, Kirkton Road, Fenwick
John McFarlane, 14 Edina Place, Edinburgh
Mary McFarlane, 14 Edina Place, Edinburgh
David K McFayden, 8 Park Crescent, Torrance, Glasgow
John A McGee, Real Colegio de Escoceses, Valladolid, Spain

H McGeechan, 36 Christophers Road, Sunderland
D & V C McGhee, 18 Courtney Road, Liskeard
Hugh McGhee, 3 High Street, Newmilns
Hugh H McGhee, 23 Braeface, Alness
Archibald McGilp, 5 Craigston Avenue, Ayr
James McGinn, 72 Forth Street, Glasgow (2 copies)
Rev. J Walter McGinty, The Manse, Alloway
Robert McGlasson, 10 Ravenswood Drive, Auckley, Doncaster
Archie MacGregor, 9 Seville Drive, Clearwater, USA
Donald S MacGregor, Ayrshire & European Community (2 copies)
Major W R McGregor, TD, 9 Thomson Drive, Bearsden
Harold McGuffog, 30 South Edge, Shipley
John M McGuire, 19 Girdle Toll, Irvine
T McGuire, 39 Flynt Avenue, Allesley, Coventry
Morag McHarg, 11 Cappers Court, Kelso
Daniel J McIldowie, Invermay, Doune Road, Dunblane
Dr E A McIlroy, 17 Oaktree Way, Strensall, York
Helen H McIlwraith, 8 Silverknowes Bank, Edinburgh
Thomas D McIlwraith, 8 Silverknowes Bank, Edinburgh
George McInnes, 100 Camnethan Street, Stonehouse
Hugh McInnes, The Spinney, Loudwater, Rickmansworth
R McInnes, 101 Forest Road, Loughborough
Robert McInnes, 42 Burnside Cottages, Stewarton
Dr R A McInroy, 112 Allerton Road, Bradford (2 copies)
Ian G McIntosh, Cruachan, Tomintoul (2 copies)
Keith W MacIntosh, 106A Sinclair Street, Helensburgh
Anne McIntyre, 21 Wallace Street, Kilmarnock
George McIntyre, Lexington, Kentucky, USA
Dr S G MacIsaac, 1650 Cedar Avenue, Montreal, Canada
Alexander B McIver, Harviestoun Lodge, Dollar
Alastair A Mackay, Amersham
Alastair L Mackay, 8 Blaven Head, Irvine
Andrew H & Margaret Mackay, Rochester, New York, USA
David McKay, Rozelle Gardens, Alloway
Mr David & Mrs Marjorie S Mackay, 14 Holmston Drive, Ayr
Ian M Mackay, FRICS, 38 The Paddock, Perceton, Irvine
Iain McKay, Rozelle Gardens, Alloway
James A Mackay, Newall Terrace, Dumfries
John McKay, 15 Milncroft Place, Glasgow
Joyce M Mackay, Newall Terrace, Dumfries
Mrs M S Mackay, St John Street, Creetown
Paraig Currie McKay, Northwest Fire Station, Glasgow
Roderick U Mackay, 11 Maxwell Drive, East Kilbride
Jean Y S McKee, 46 Keir Hardie Crescent, Kilwinning
Louis W McKee, 2 Bannockburn Place, Kilmarnock

Mrs Margaret M McKee, 132 Lancaster Terrace, Edmonton, Canada
T R McKee, 123 Cairnhill Road, Airdrie
Gordon McKellar, 72 St Quivox Road, Prestwick
Martha McKellar, 125 Hillfoot Road, Ayr
John D McKendrick, 62 High Park Avenue, Toronto, Canada
Alastair W A MacKenzie, Tullich House, Delny
Alexander & Doreen MacKenzie, 5 Burnbank Road, Ayr
Archibald M MacKenzie, Millerston, Boghead Road, Dumbarton
Miss Ardil MacKenzie, Woodend, 134 Culduthel Road, Inverness
Miss Ismay McKenzie, Stewarton
Mr Kenneth C McKenzie, 28 Grougar Drive, Kilmarnock
Mrs Lisa I P McKenzie, 2 Lower Langley, Gt Tey, Colchester
Mrs M J C MacKenzie, 2 Brookfield Court, Ramsey
Captain TM Mackenzie, 22 Westbourne House, Wheatlands, Heston
Mr William McKenzie, Cabar Feidh, 2 Fir Lane, Larbert
S McKenzie-McHarg
Alisdair Alexander E McKerrell, 37 Springfield, Balfour St, Leith
H George McKerrow, Whiterne, Dumfries
James Lamb McKiddie, 16 Deanburn Park, Linlithgow
Mrs Annie S Mackie, OBE, JP, 30 Samson Avenue, Kilmarnock
Mr James G Mackie, 10 Bridge Street, Prestwick
Mr Peter McKillop, 5 Elizabeth Street, Stirling
Mr Richard McKinlay, 9 Crawford Grove, Corby
Angus McKinnon, 2-5 Maidencraig Court, Edinburgh
Angus McKinnon, 9 Esplanade Terrace, Edinburgh
A G Mackintosh, 3708 Howden Drive, Nanaimo, Canada
Alan James Mackintosh, Ontario, Canada
T Bryan McKirgan, CA, 4 Balmoral Drive, Cambuslang
Gordon M Mackley
Hamish D McLaren, Dalriada, 23 Mavisbank Gardens, Perth
James H L McLaren, 26 Netherthird Road, Cumnock
R A B McLaren, 11 South Lauder Road, Edinburgh, P. Pres.1976/7
William McLaren, Netherton Farm, Blackford
Samuel McLarty, 38 Corserine Tce, Dalmellington, Ayr
James H McLatchie, 37 Wester Broom Place, Edinburgh
E McLauchlan, Clovelly House, Main Street, Beal
Alasdair C W MacLean, 131 Muirdrum Avenue, Glasgow
Capt A J MacLean, MA, BA(Cantab), FRSA(Lond), Lossiemouth
Rose MacLean, 280 West Princes Street, Woodside, Glasgow
Ronald A McLean, 1 Logie Lodge, Crimond, Fraserburgh
W D & B S McLean, 297 Blue Forest Drive, London, Canada
Mary McLellan, 23 Brown Walk, Irvine
Mr P W McLellan, 26 Murdoch Crescent, Stevenston
Mrs I MacLennan, 9 Birnie Terrace, Inverness
Mr Donald MacLeod, 11 Harvey Street, Woodville, Australia
Frank Macleod, OBE, 6 Anson Way, Buckie

George McLeod, Maryslea, Annathill, by Coatbridge
Ronald E McLeod, 54 Pleasance Avenue, Dumfries
William McLeod, 93 Bridgeburn Drive, Chryston, Glasgow
Ronald W McLucas, 86 Mary Street, Toowoomba, Australia
Richard J McMahon, 103 Bank Street, Irvine
Samuel F McMaster, 7 Woodlands Avenue, Irvine
J McMenamin, 67 Medway Parade, Greenford
Blanche McMillan, 5364 Salem Road, Burlington, Canada
Sir Graham Macmillan, 46 Crown Street, Bury St Edmunds
Mrs J B MacMillan, 2 Earl Grey Street, Mauchline
John B McMillan, 5364 Salem Road, Burlington, Canada
Robert Burns McMillan, 57 Small Street, Lochgelly
Mr M McMullen, Hunter Valley Burns Club, Newcastle, Australia
Michael McMullen, 5 Nooroo Close, Windale, Australia
David McMurray, 100 Albert Road, Glasgow
R G McNab, 54 Montgomery Street, Grangemouth
Dr R N McNamee, 77 Bonhill Road, Dumbarton
Norman T McNaughton, 6 Willow Road, Kilmarnock
John William McNay, 68 Makbrar Road, Calside, Dumfries
Robert McNay, 19 Hardthorn Crescent, Dumfries
David Thomas Irving McNeil
Dr D W Macnish, 6 Hill Street, Dumfries
Charles McNulty, 30 Humbie Terrace, Aberdour
Rennie McOwan, 7 Williamfield Avenue, Stirling
John McPhee, 6 Meadow Street, Coventry
Alexander Macpherson, 15 Burnton Road, Dalrymple
Alistair G MacPherson, 84 Newmains Road, Renfrew
Ian Macpherson, Lakeshore Road East, Oakville, Canada
Ian A Macpherson, MBE, CStJ, JP, Garnock Park, East Kilbride
Mrs S McQuade, 4 Melville Street, Kilmarnock
Kenneth Ian MacRae, Humberside Burns Society
George Lorimer McRobb, 26 Miller Ave, Ashburton, New Zealand
Anna Leigh McSherry, 28 Bibby Terrace, Irvine
Charles Lockhart McWhirter, 40F Fenwickland Avenue, Ayr
William Maguire, Esq, 1 Colvend Drive, Fernhill, Rutherglen
Mrs Moira Mailer, 46 Rowan Drive, Bearsden, Glasgow
Malcolm Main, 10 Glenfield Gardens, Cowdenbeath
G Douglas Mair, 1 Victoria Road, Dumfries
Malcolm Maclean Mair, 108 Tunstall Road, Sunderland
Mr Peter Mallan, Newlands, Glasgow
Thomas Swanton Maltman, Paxton Terrace, Eyemouth
James H A Manderson, 46 Bathurst Drive, Alloway
John A Mann, 12 Goodman Drive, London, Canada
Mr & Mrs W Manson, Glassmakers, 13 Athole Drive, Stanley, Perth
John Marriott, 14 Bognor Road, Corby

James Marsh, 1 Rosepark, West Belfast
Albert E R Marshall, 372 Kedleston Road, Allestree, Derby
Charles McCartney Marshall, 177 Farne Drive, Glasgow
Dr George Marshall, 1820 Bay Shore Road, SW, Calgary, Canada
Ivor Marshall, 17 Millar Crescent, Edinburgh
Peter R Marshall, 3 Derwent Close, Royal Leamington Spa
Robertson Marshall, 36 Carnegie Place, Perth
T K Marshall, 46 Beech Avenue, Nairn
Alan & Norma Martin, Niagara Falls Burns Club
Daniel Martin, 27 The Gardens, Doddinghurst, Brentwood
Edward Martin, 10 Phipps Avenue, Rugby
Mrs Margaret Martin, 16 Glebe Road, Arbroath
Michael Martin, 97 Woodlands Avenue, Irvine
Nicholas Martin, 27 The Gardens, Doddinghurst, Brentwood
S Douglas Martin, 4203-14A Street, SW, Calgary, Canada
Thomas B Martin, 5 Bathurst Drive, Alloway
Warren Martin, 27 The Gardens, Doddinghurst, Brentwood
Mr William Martin, 114 Ringleas, Cotgrave, Nottingham
R W Marwick, Ardvohr, 9 Dunbeth Avenue, Coatbridge
Gilbert Masiye, 4178 Nanwenga Road, Lusaka, Zambia
James Mason, 83 Dorchester Way, Kenton, Harrow
Masonic Arms Pub, Redding Road, Redding, Falkirk
Miss Jean C Massey, 97 Park Grange Croft, Sheffield
Mrs Agnes Lapraik Masterton, 20 Old Road, Elderslie
Derek L G Masterton, 40 Kilwinning Road, Irvine
John Mathers, 64 Johnsburn Road, Balerno, Edinburgh
Mr & Mrs David Matheson, 60 Spynie Street, Bishopmill, Elgin
Andrew Mathieson, Ettrick Bank, 33 Ayr Road, Prestwick
Mrs Evelyn Mathieson, Ashkirk Drive, Mosspark, Glasgow
James D Matthew, 82 Uist Road, Glenrothes
Maxwelltown High School, Dumfries, donated by Howff Club
David Medlen, 34 Thorpe Lane, Almondbury, Huddersfield
Thos C Meiklejohn, 96 Webster Street, Nedlands, Australia
Douglas Meldrum, The Heritage, Mill Wynd, Falkland
Jas Meldrum, 36 Maclean Place, Gorebridge
John J Melrose, 1A Victoria Terrace, Dumfries
Colin H Menzies, 49 Kilwinning Road, Irvine
Robert T Mercer, 194 Foulford Road, Cowdenbeath
Claude Edward Meslage, Ericson Street, Fermont, Canada
Stephanie Burns Meslage, Chicoutimi, Quebec, Canada
Colin Metclaf, 54 Marine Parade, Shoreham, Australia
William H Miles, 27 Crichton Avenue, Pathhead
Andrew Millar, 29 Lucy Lane, Stanway, Colchester
Miss Joan N Millar, 13 Spruce Drive, Lenzie, Glasgow
Robert B Millar, 7 Broomlands Drive, Irvine

Andrew Miller, 3 Gladstone Terrace, Lerwick
Hugh & Florence N Miller, Saltwell, Aiket Road, Dunlop
Scott Miller, 39 Thorndene Avenue, Carfin, Motherwell
Tom Miller, 2300 Dakmoor Drive SW, Calgary, Canada
William Miller, 16 Hillcrest, Cowdenbeath
William J Miller, The Avenue, Eyemouth
Alexander Muir Milloy, 2 Sunnyfield Close, Evington, Leicester
Gavin Taylor Milne, Peterhead Burns Club
James N Milne, 57 Glencaple Avenue, Dumfries
Kenneth M Milne, 22 Lomond Drive, Dumbarton
Mr & Mrs Peter M Milne, 2 Woodside, West Kilbride
Thomas Milne, 303-204A Hespeler Road, Cambridge, Canada
Mr Robert Wallace Milton, 11A Auldlea Road, Beith
James Edward Minns, 84 Cambusnethan Street, Wishaw
The Mitchell Library, Glasgow
Glenne Mitchell, Bowbridge Lane, Prestbury, Cheltenham
Hugh Mitchell, 55 Barshare Road, Cumnock
James Mitchell, 62A Rosetta Road, Peebles
John G Mitchell, Overdale, 32 Ridgewood Drive, Cromford
Keith S S Mitchell, 16 Rue Du Buat, Maule, France
Patrick D Mitchell, Lofthillock, Inverurie
Peter R Mitchell, 25 Maybury Avenue, Flamstead End
Robert Mitchell, 76 Cleland Place, East Kilbride
Una B Mitchell, 12 Hunter Crescent, Troon
George Mochan, The Cottage, Canal Crescent, Stevenston
Iain S Moffat, 11 Westbourne Gardens, Prestwick
Mrs M E Moffat, 9 Cornal Court, Beattock, Moffat
James Strang Mollison, 25 Lanchester Road, Coventry
William & Margaret Molloy, Niagara Falls Burns Club
Mr J S Monach, 36 Bole Hill Lane, Sheffield
Peter Monaghan, 7 Thornly Park Drive, Paisley
Andrew Montgomery, 79 Cumbernauld Road, Cumbernauld
Dr James Montgomery, 229 Bank Street, Irvine
James M Montgomery, Green Oak Ct NW, Atlanta, USA
Percy Montgomery, 89 Kelvin Drive, Moodiesburn, Chryston
Montreal General Hospital Burns Society, Canada
Gordon Fraser Moore, 7 St Ives Road, Moodiesburn, Chryston
James M Moore, Marchmont, 11 Bellevue Road, Ayr
Robert L Morris, 175 Saxmundham Road, Aldeburgh
Mrs Christina J Morrison, 95 Main Street, Callander
Gerald B Morrison, 5617 N Adrian Avenue, Kansas City, USA
Mr James Hill Morrison, 10 Milne Avenue, Auchinleck
Mr John Morrison, 85 Broom Crescent, Ochiltree
John A Morrison, 90 Curwendale, Stainburn, Workington
John Anderson Morrison, 6 Lovedale Crescent, Balerno

John Sutherland Morrison, 16 Erica Avenue, Bedworth
R D Morrison, 84 Newton Crescent, Dunblane
William Morrison, 37 Paidmyre Road, Newton Mearns
Mr William Morrison, 71 Gallowhill Quadrant, Coylton
William & Jessie Morrison, 12 Brook Lane, Ainthorpe, Danby
Wm G Morrison, 19 Campbell Street, Newmilns
William L Morrison, 32 Longbraes Gardens, Kirkcaldy
Henrietta Craig Morrow, 7A Ranald Gdns, Rutherglen, Glasgow
Ewan J H Mowat, Seton Lodge Southpark Road, Ayr
Gregor W Mowat, Seton Lodge, Southpark Road, Ayr
Rev. John Mowat, 15 Airds Drive, Dumfries
Lyndsay A Mowat, Seton Lodge, Southpark Road, Ayr
Margaret A Mowat, Seton Lodge, Southpark Road, Ayr
Andrew D Mowatt, 3 Bent Road, Hamilton
Mr George R Moyes, 434 Hough Fold Way, Harwood, Bolton
P M Moyes, 2 Pennine Close, Lupset Park, Wakefield
Audrey Mudd, 5 Charles Avenue, Oakes, Huddersfield
Andrew Muir, 44 Kelsey Dr West, Seneca, NY, USA
Douglas Muir, 4415 107 Avenue, Edmonton, Alberta, Canada
Jacquelyne Muir, 44 Bellrock Avenue, Prestwick
Mr James Alistair Robertson Muir, Old Schoolhouse, Gt Smeaton
John Muir, 44 Bellrock Avenue, Prestwick
Dr John Robertson Muir, 60 Hillpark Avenue, Edinburgh
Robert S Muir, 6 Taylor's Road, Larbert
Robert P Muirhead, 17 Hendry Street, Bainsford, Falkirk
Thomas F Muirhead, 34 Coronation Place, Skinflats, Bothkennar
William Muirhead, 236 Haugh Street, Bainsford, Falkirk
Peter J Mulholland, 12 Cramond Avenue, Deanpark, Renfrew
Mr J G D Munro, Brackenhill, Alness
Jim Murdoch, Home & Gardens, 84 George Street, Stranraer
Anne M Murray, 91 Broomlands Drive, Irvine
David Robert Murray, Woodcot, Dollar
E B K Murray, 187 Craigcrook Road, Edinburgh
Mrs Gerda Murray, 20 Emery St West, London, Canada
Mr H Murray, 15 Braeside, Catrine
James Murray, 35 Brandenburg Road, Danesholme, Corby
Mrs Janette Dunlop Murray, Conheath, Glencaple, Dumfries
Jim Murray, 1167 Heritage Blvd, North Vancouver, Canada
John Murray, 23 Craigie Road, Hurlford, Kilmarnock
Mr John S Murray, 56 Frederick Road, Rainham
Robert JR Murray, 28 Dalbeath Cres, Hill of Beath, Cowdenbeath
William Murray, 33 Riverside Close, Whitley, Coventry
William R Murray, 114 Jamieson Gardens, Tillicoultry
Cyril M Mutch, Croupier, Peterhead Burns Club
Thomas Mutch, Hon Piper, Greenock Burns Club

Thomas B Myles, 7B Wallace House, Berryhill Rd, Cumbernauld
Stevenson Naismith, 11 Boyd Drive, Motherwell
Prof Toshio Namba (Tam o' Shanter Museum, Ayr)
Toshio Namba, 1-70-24 Tenjin-Cho, Kodaira-Shi, Tokyo
Nanaimo Burns Club, Canada
The National Guest Flat, Culzean Castle, Ayrshire
National Library of Scotland, George IV Bridge, Edinburgh
Thomas Neil, 9 Berrima Road, Roleystone, Australia
Daniel Stevenson Neilson, 412 Bellshill Road, Motherwell
William A D Neish, 36/3 Woodlands Street, Milngavie
David M Nelson, Netherley, 2 McNabb Street, Dollar
J Moir Nelson, Croit Mhor, 44 Ledrish Avenue, Balloch
John Nelson, 46 Roundriding Road, Dumbarton
John Paterson Newlands, 54 Garrowhill Drive, Baillieston
Fred Newton, 12 Elmbank Drive, Dumfries
John Newton, 8 Burns Terrace, Bathgate
Robert J Newton, 169 E 35th Street, Hamilton, Canada
William Newton, 108 West Main Street, Broxburn
John & Moira Nicholson, 29 Reigate Avenue, Brampton, Canada
E Nicholson-Pegg, 43 Hurstbourne House, Tangley Grove, London
Archibald Nicol, Seaview, Largiebeg, Whiting Bay
Mr Ian Nicol, Balerno High School, Balerno, Edinburgh
James Nicol, Jnr, Past Croupier, Peterhead Burns Club
James CW Nicol, Esq., OBE, BL, 14 Landsborough Dr, Kilmarnock
James G Nicol, 10 Wednesbury Road, Harold Hill, Romford
James Walker Nicol, 52 The Avenue, Girvan
Mr Alan E Nisbet, 15 Berry Drive, Irvine
Mr Donald J Nisbet, Slepe House, Organford, Nr Poole
Nithsdale District Council (2 copies)
Alexander R Niven, Perceton Paddock, Irvine
Mr W A Niven, Ballochmyle Cott, Mauchline
North Berwick Burns Club
David J North, BA, 15 Finsbury Road, Leagrave, Luton
Maxwell Norton, 35 Dixon Road, Glasgow
William Denis O'Connell, 9 Feregait, Kincardine-on-Forth
David S Ogilvie, Lingerwood, Nelson Street, Dumfries
Wilson & Irene Ogilvie, Lingerwood, 2 Nelson Street, Dumfries
Yvonne E Ogilvie, Lingerwood, Nelson Street, Dumfries
R D Ogston, 5381 Lost Lake Road, Nanaimo, Canada
Arnold O'Hara, 6 Hillfoot Crescent, Ayr
David Oliphant, 40 West Woodside, Bexley
Mrs Mary Oliver, 147 Parker Street, Sarnia, Canada
James O'Lone, 9 Windsor Road, East Fremantle, Australia
George Murray Olsen, 15 Peveril Close, Ashley Heath, Ringwood
Linda M Ormiston, 39 Colinhill Road, Strathaven

David C M Orr, PO Box 287, Whyalla, South Australia
Mr & Mrs James Orr, 23 Charles Street, Kilmarnock
John Orr, Kilnholm, 16 Bowes Rigg, Stewarton
Jim Osborne, Calgary, Alberta, Canada
Marie Otley, 1 Silbury Close, Kingsride, Westbury
Rev. John Pagan, FRSA, St Michael's Manse, Dumfries
Mrs Janis Page, RSD, 189 Sisters Creek, Australia
Ian Park, 26 Ramsay Lane, Kincardine
Andrew S Parker, 4 Milton Drive, Kilmarnock
Mrs Mary Parker, 8 Kirkland Road, Terregles, Dumfries
James Parnham, North Lane Gardens, Roundhay, Leeds
C F Parr
James Paterson, 133 Wellhall Road, Hamilton
James Paterson, 49 Ford Crescent, Thornton
Margaret Elizabeth Paterson, Craiglea, Craig Road, Dingwall
Robert Paterson, 67 Stevenston Road, Kilwinning
Mrs Ruth Paterson, 84 Stirling Drive, Bishopbriggs, Glasgow
Thomas Naismith Paterson, 84 Branchalfield Drive, Wishaw
Colin Campbell Paton, 23 Sleigh Street, Figtree, Australia
Donald N M Paton, 75 Needless Road, Perth
Mr George H Paton, 7 Whitesneuk, Lanark
Gordon Paton, Lodge 236
Harry Anderson Paton, 6 Heys Street, Barrhead, Glasgow
John Bryce Paton, Dapto, NSW, Australia
William Bruce Paton, 37 Cranford Lane, Figtree, Australia
Rev. Dr Johnstone G Patrick, 8 North Street, Braunton
Thomas Patrick, 51 Well Road, Auchinleck
Mr A G Patterson, 34 Hill Rise, Birstall, Leicester
Mrs Maureen Pavey, 110 Nappers Wood, Fernhurst, Haslemere
Mr James Pearson, 29 Castle Street, Dumfries
George Peebles, 22 Simpson Drive, Coalsnaughton
Alan Pemberton, 17 Comely Bank Grove, Edinburgh
Miss Vera Pennington, 29 Perry Oaks, Bracknell
Mr T A Peoples, MBE, JP, Riverside, Ballyclare
Mr George Currie Perry, 52 The Grove, Edinburgh Rd, Dumfries
George Sim Peterkin, 24 Pansport Road, Elgin
Marion Alice Peterkin, 22 Newburgh Street, Bridge of Don
Alexander Esplin Petrie, 9A Macaulay Street, Dundee
Mrs Elizabeth Petrie, 23 Slug Road, Stonehaven
Mr Adam Pettigrew, 16 West Park Avenue, Mauchline
John M Philliben, 6327 Calhoun, Dearborn, Mich, USA
Elaine M J Phillips, Ivybank, Elgin
Gareth William Phillips, Ivybank, Elgin
John & Margaret Phillips, Niagara Falls Burns Club
Kimberly Margaret Phillips, Grand Island, New York, USA

Neil Thomas Phillips, Grand Island, New York, USA
James Picken, 19 Grange Terrace, Kilmarnock
James Ronald Picken, 69 Monach Gardens, Dreghorn, Ayrshire
Mrs Ann C Pickering, 95 Dyfrig Street, Shotts
John Pickles, 6 The Craigs, Devonside, Tillicoultry
Robert J Pine, Springside, Tarbert
John Pinkerton, 29C Braeface Road, Cumbernauld
Walter Pinnington, 18 Roehampton Drive, Liverpool
John Piper, 24 Belmont Crescent, Ayr
Brian Lumsden Pirie, 54 Shakespeare Way, Corby
Ian Nay Pirie, St Annes Mount, Belmont Road, Juniper Green
McKenzie G Pirret, 38 Rosemar Circ, Viewbank, Australia
W Richard Platt, 18 Silverknowes Drive, Edinburgh
Miss Ellen Pollock, Neilston
Euan A Pollock, Barnaigh, 12 Dewar Street, Dollar
John Pollock, 178 Landemer Drive, Rutherglen, Glasgow
John R Pollock, Shian, 9 Sunnyside Avenue, Bathgate
Neil R Pollock, Banaigh, 12 Dewar Street, Dollar
William J Pollock, Barnaigh, 12 Dewar Street, Dollar
William Wilson Pollock, 18 Main Street, Dundonald
Sheila Polson, Aberdeen
O Poolman, 19 Princess Crescent, Freuchie
John Clingan Porteous, 18 Norman Crescent, Irvine (9 copies)
Robert William Porter, 62 Elm Avenue, Blythswood
Harry Powell, 37A Bentinck Drive, Troon
Mrs Dorothy Ruth Prakke-Sclater, 18 Rutland Road, Harrogate
Tom Prentice, 5612-151 Street, Edmonton, Canada
William Prentice, 12 Elvan Tower, Motherwell
Prestwick Burns Club (2 copies)
Steven J Pritchard, 8 Mossview, Dumfries
Mrs Mary Proctor, 609 Griffith Street, London, Canada
John M Prosser, 4B Boydfield Avenue, Prestwick
Mr J Prott, 21 Simmonds Blvrd, Brampton, Canada
John Prott, 8 Hannahston Avenue, Drongan
Dr David Purdie, University of Leeds
Alexander H S Quinn, 80 Etherington Road, Hull
David Quinn, 19 Beauly Crescent, Bellfield, Kilmarnock
Ernst Radau, 255-40 Tannery East, Cambridge, Canada
Elizanne Rafferty, Littleover, 30 Burnham Avenue, Bognor Regis
Michael M Raguin, 280 Boston Avenue, Medford, MA, USA
Roy Ramage, 15 Glenwinnel Road, Alva
Jack P Ramsay, 15 East Park Avenue, Mauchline
William Ramsay, 109 St Andrew's Drive, Glasgow
William Ramsay, BSc (Hon), MB, FRCS, Mauchline Mains
Luciano Rebecchi, 1 Old Inverkip Road, Greenock

Michael A Reddy, 39 Bank Street, Greenock
Edward G Redmond, The Old Vicarage, Crakehall
David Reed, 2 Friendship Way, Renfrew
Donald Lees Reid, 20 Inchmurrin Drive, Kilmarnock
Ernest Reid, 37 Grattan Place, Fraserburgh
Fraser Reid, 20 Inchmurrin Drive, Kilmarnock
James Lees Reid, 6 Park Crescent, Dalmellington
Mrs Jenny Reid, 134 Caledonia Road, Ayr
Renfrew District Libraries, Central Library, High Street, Paisley
Mrs Molly Rennie, Past President, Burns Federation
William J Rennie, Adenaich, High Street, New Pitsligo
Robert A Reoch, 2317 Robinhood Place, Orange, CA, USA
Mr & Mrs Richardson, Nundah, Brisbane, Australia
G D Richardson, OBE, 16 Eriskay Road, Inverness
Mr Jack A Richardson, 8 Montrose Way, Dunblane
Hugh Richmond, 20 Knockinlaw Road, Kilmarnock
Mr Andrew Richmond, 26 Frew Terrace, Irvine
Andrew Richmond, Thornhill, Ontario, Canada
John Richmond, Elim, 84 Caledonian Road, Stevenston
Mary S Riddell, 8 Meadow View, Cumbernauld
T & A Rielly, 18 Belgrave Road, Edinburgh
Andrew Duncan Rigg, 28 Main Street, Dundonald
Albert Soutar Ritchie, 6 Ivy Lane, Dysart
Catherine Ritchie, Hamilton, Ontario
Jim Robb, 5 Dunedin Road, Corby
John Robb, 12 Churchill Crescent, Fergus, Canada
Robert Burns Society of the Midlands, Columbia, USA
Ian F Roberts, Treasurer, Peterhead Burns Club
John Baird Roberts, 89 Manor Road, Barton Le Clay
Mr Donald Robertson, 26 King Street, New Elgin, Elgin
Eric Robertson, Strathden, 104 Russell Street, Wishaw
Hugh P Robertson, Oakdene, 81 Bonhill Road, Dumbarton
Mr I Robertson, 38 Almondhill Road, Kirkliston
I Robertson, 8 Reid Street, Whyalla, Australia (2 copies)
J Robertson, TEng, FIED, REngDes, 20 Gray Crescent, Irvine
J P Robertson, 27 Abden Avenue, Kinghorn
Jack G D Robertson, P.P. Caledonia Burns Club
Joe B Robertson, Tucker, Georgia, USA
Kenneth McIntyre Robertson, Hastings Terr, Newcastle on Tyne
Mr Peter Robertson, 21 Reid Street, Bishopmill, Elgin
Mr S E Robertson, Falcon Court, Edinburgh
Brian Robinson, 5 Maple Close, Newcastle on Tyne
Mr John Robson, 12 Baberton Mains Grove, Edinburgh
K W Robson, New Milton
Anna A Rodger, 2 Auchenbeg Crescent, Ayr
David Rodger, RSF (ex Stalag 383), Dryfesdale Court, Lockerbie

Mary Rodger, 27 Hanover Close, Lochside, Dumfries
Peter Rodger, 10 Durham Crescent, Lower Largo
Robert Rodger, 5 Joanne Court, Sefton, Australia
William Rodger, 17 Westview Walk, Westfield, Workington
Dr Louis D Rodgers, 715 53rd Street, Des Moines, Iowa, USA
C Kenneth Rogerson, 306, 2425-90 Ave SW, Calgary, Canada
Derek D Rogerson, 49 Gillbrae Crescent, Dumfries
Margaret W Rogerson, 38 Barnsley Road, Wakefield
James G Rollo, 383 Windermere Road, Beaconsfield, Canada
Jospeh Roney, 70 Calder Tower, St Leonards, East Kilbride
Alexander Ross, 10 Abbotsburn Way, Jockston, Paisley
Alistair C Ross, 45 Stratford Pl SW, Calgary, Canada
Mr & Mrs Donald Ross, 112 Patetown Road, Goldsboro, Australia
Evelyn Jean Ross, 49 O'Quinn Street, Toowoomba, Australia
Mr H Ross, 150 Westwick Crescent, Sheffield
John D Ross, 7 Centennial Court, Fredericton, Canada
Steven Ross, Belltrees, 29 Harling Drive, Troon
Tracey Ross, Belltrees, 29 Harling Drive, Troon
Wendy Ross, Belltrees, 29 Harling Drive, Troon
Mrs E Roxburgh, Lilymount, 5 Kilmarnock Road, Kilmaurs
G Ross Roy, University of South Carolina, USA
Royal Scots College, Valladolid, Spain
Alex A Rubie, 251 Bank Street, Irvine
Andrew John Russell, 2 Tolmount Crescent, Montrose
William Russell, 16 Moray Place, Muirhead, Chryston
Mr Martin Sadler, 4 Hugh Avenue, Lochgelly
Mrs Peter St Germain, 125 East 72nd St, New York City, USA
St Joseph's College, Dumfries donated by Howff Club
William Bryant Salmon, Taunton
Mrs Jean Samson, King Street East, Hamilton, Canada (2 copies)
A Saunders, 12 Burns Street, Kirkconnel
Ian Saunders, 12 Burns Street, Kirkconnel
John David Saville, Barrels Park, Ullenhall
Jack & Betty Scarlett, 72 Monterey, Kenner, USA
James M Scarlett, 1 Southesk Gardens, Bishopbriggs, Glasgow
Mrs Mary B Schlag, 68 Margaret Walk, Lincluden, Dumfries
Rev. Melville & Christine Schofield, Laigh Kirk Manse, Kilmarnock
David James Scobie, 23 Barleyknowe Terrace, Gorebridge
Mrs Jane Scolley, Debonnair, 6 Meadowpark, Coylton
Alex Scott, 1 Brora Place, Crossford, Dunfermline
Alexander G Scott, 77 Earls Road, Nuneaton
Christine D Scott, 1 Brora Place, Crossford
Evelyn J Scott, 75 Sinclair Drive, Cowdenbeath
Harold F Scott, 60 Station Road, Lochgelly
James Scott, Dumfries Burns Howff Club

James Jarvis Scott, 34 Dawson Road, Broughty Ferry
John Scott, Inverlochy, 49 King Street, Coatbridge
John Scott, 88 Colston Road, Bishopbriggs, Glasgow
Rev. John M Scott, MA, FSAScot, St Andrews Church, Jerusalem
Robert Scott, 13 Caledonian Road, Stevenston
Robert Scott, Garrion, 27 Forest View, Cumbernauld
Robert J Scott, 15 Young Terrace, Cowdenbeath
S Scott, 93 Farndale Drive, Loughborough
Tom Scott, Rowanlea, Braco
W M Scott, Kilmarnock
William Scott, Oakfield, Ayr Road, Larkhall
Wm C Scott, 3 Moore Street, Gwynneville, Australia
William James Scott, Coylton Arms, Low Coylton, by Ayr
Scottish Society and Burns Club of Australia
John W Scoular, 731 Dunboyne Crescent, London, Canada
Graham Lester Settles, 8 Gearholm Road, Doonfoot, Ayr
Wm R Shanks, 15 Deanpark Grove, Balerno
William Sharkey, 10 Wellesley Road, Methil, Fife
Sir George Sharp, OBE, DL, JP, Strath Lea, Station Rd, Thornton
David B Shaw, 33 Dalrymple Drive, Irvine
Mrs Mary Shearer, 211 Lochside Road, Dumfries
Lorna Shearne, 424 Broadwater Crescent, Stevenage
Mr Norman B Shedden, 23 Denholm Drive, Wishaw
G W Shepherd, The Old Rectory, Market Overton, Oakham
Isabella A Shepherd, 238 Duddingston Drive, Kirkcaldy
Robert Shepherd, 238 Duddingston Drive, Kirkcaldy
Robert T Shepherd, 66 Keirs Brae, Cardenden
Fiona & Paul Shutler, Chesham
David D Sibbald, 6 Brentham Crescent, Stirling
E B B McD Simpson, Woodend House, Dalcross
Harold Simpson, 12 Albert Terrace, Musselburgh
J I Simpson, 5 Coastguard Cottages, Cove, Cockburnspath
James P Simpson, 39 Ripon Drive, Glasgow
Jasmine A Simpson, 17 Wilmington Ct, Tankerville Road, London
John M Simpson, 17 Glenview, Cumbernauld
Frederick Sinden, Hon Member Bolton Burns Club
Ann Sinforiani, 13 Moorefield Avenue, Kilmarnock
Dario Sinforiani, 13 Moorefield Avenue, Kilmarnock
C Siseman, 5 Godfrey Crescent, Larbert
Robert N H Skilling, 9 Dick Road, Kilmarnock
Robert Skinner, 10 Glebe Gardens, Bonhill, by Alexandria
David Scott Skipper, 8198 Wenonga Ct, Tallahassee, USA
Hugh D Sloan, 34 Gilbert Circle, Dumfries
Stanislaus C Sloan, Invergarry Drive, Deaconsbank, Glasgow
W M Sloan, Cairnpat, 12 Holmes Road, Kilmarnock

D Gordon Smaill, 11 Marchbank Drive, Balerno
Keith D W Smaill, 110 Burghmuir Court, Linlithgow
John Lyall Smart, 29 Valley Road, Clevedon
Mr Alexander K Smith, 15 Faskally Ave, Bishopbriggs, Glasgow
Alison Smith, Chamberhouses, Mill Road, Irvine
Andrew Smith, 85 Montrose Road, Foxbar, Paisley
Charles W Smith, 29 Lochty Avenue, Kinglassie
David Smith, Dumfries Burns Howff Club
David M Smith, Wellwood, 28 Eglinton Street, Irvine
Elizabeth Smith, 8 Kay Park Terrace, Kilmarnock
Hugh Smith, 20 Sheardale Drive, Coalsnaughton
Ian R Smith, 9 Holmes Road, Kilmarnock
J M M Smith, Secretary, Peterhead Burns Club
James R Smith, Auchenlay Cottage, Dunblane
Jim Smith, 22 Glencairn, Cumnock
John Smith, 3 Muircot Place, Coalsnaughton
John L Smith, 3 Redmoss Avenue, Nigg, Aberdeen
Mrs Mary J Smith, 49 McNeish Avenue, Annan
Robert L Smith, 37 Victoria Terrace, Markinch
Royal A Smith, 81 Bank Street, Irvine
T J J Smith, 24 Totley Lane, Bradway, Sheffield
W R Smith, 17 Miller Street, Millport
Yvonne Smith, 15 Hillside Drive, Bishopbriggs, Glasgow
Mr Richard Hamilton Sneddon, 631 Eramosa Rd, Guelph, Canada
Anthony Guy Snook, 2 Verlands, Congresbury, Bristol
Roy Solomon, 34 Waun-y-Groes Road, Rhiwbina, Cardiff
Robert George Somerville, 12 Lowther Bank, Irvine
James Sommerville, 42 Cumbernauld Road, Chryston
John Fleming Sorbie, 16 Chapelton Gardens, Dumbarton
H H Souter, 9 Coverdale Place, Chaucer Way, Plymouth
Dr W P & Mrs W C Soutter, 45 Crimicar Lane, Sheffield
James M & Karen J Spaith, 12307 West 79th Terrace, Lenexa, USA
D Graham Speirs, 25 Pearson Drive, Renfrew
Ernest Speirs, 14 Glendee Road, Renfrew
Mrs N Speirs, 5 Vancouver Road, Glasgow
W S C Speirs, LlB (Hons), 24 Gorse Drive, Barrhead
William Speirs, 8 Berry Drive, Irvine (3 copies)
J M Spittal, Les Bourgs, St Andrews, Guernsey
William M Sprowl, Eastlands Farm, Rothesay
E S Stainthorpe, 14 Hoylake Square, Ashgrove, Kilwinning
Alan Robertson Stalker, 70 Harborne Road, Warley
John Stark, 58 Hinkar Way, Eyemouth
H J Stearn, 58 Hartley Old Road, Purley
Mr Robert Malcolm Steele, 136 Prestwick Road, Ayr
Mrs Sheena M Stein, 33 Cardoness Street, Dumfries

Mr Angus Stephen, 9 Northleach Cl, Walshaw Park, Bury
M Stevens, 34 Elmete Walk, Leeds
Allan Stevenson, 43 Monument Road, Ayr
Anne Clelland Stevenson, 2E Elizabethan Way, Renfrew
George Stevenson, Tanzieknowe, Bentinck Drive, Troon
James Stevenson, 20 Crofthead Street, Strathaven
John Stevenson, 19 Silverburn Road, Bridge of Don, Aberdeen
Marion M Stevenson, Tanzieknowe, Bentinck Drive, Troon
Robert David Guy Stevenson, 22 Crofthead Street, Strathaven
Robert Louis Stevenson, 55 Haining Road, Renfrew
W Stevenson, Whyalla, South Australia (2 copies)
Archibald H Stewart, 53 Milgarholm Avenue, Irvine
Gordon Stewart, Dundonald Burns Club
Henry Stalker Stewart, 118 Caledonia Road, Ayr
Neil J Stewart, 828 Madison Ave SW, Calgary, Canada
Robert Stewart, 15 Kelvin Drive, Bishopbriggs, Glasgow
Samuel Stewart, 41 McKinlay Crescent, Irvine
Mr William Stewart, 12 McGavin Avenue, Kilwinning
Wm Gordon Stewart, Hidcote, 66 Leadhall Lane, Harrogate
Mr & Mrs A M Stirling, 11B Gleniffer Court, Paisley
R Stirling, 14 Mincher Crescent, Motherwell ML1 2RZ
Malcolm Howard Stockdale, 11A Corpach Drive, Dunfermline
Allan Stoddart, 35 Morton Avenue, Ayr
Mrs G Storrar, 76A Dundonald Road, Kilmarnock
John Strachan, 35 Waterloo Road, Prestwick
James T Strain, 13720 101 Ave, Edmonton, Alberta, Canada
Strathclyde "Bonnie Jean" Burns Club
Strathkelvin District Libraries, Kirkintilloch Road, Bishopbriggs
Charles Street, 9 Bensley Avenue, Girdle Toll, Irvine
Mr R Strickland, 2 Ladypark Farm, Ladypark, Gateshead
David Low Struthers, 8 Knoweholm, Doonfoot, Ayr
J Stuart, 67 Grange Close, Hoveton, Norwich
J Stuart, 9 St Mathias Court, Leeds
James Sturgeon, 6 Birch Road, Ayr
W B Sullivan, 24 Park Gate Road, Cannock Wood
William P Summers, 71 Reigate Walk, Corby
Mrs Jean Sutcliffe, Dunbrock, Common Lane, Beal
Rev. Alex Sutherland, The Manse, Symington
Betsy Sutherland, Spragatup, Haroldswick, Unst
Donald F Sutherland, 32 Martinton Road, Heathhall, Dumfries
Peter Sutherland, The Ord, 31A Milgarholm Avenue, Irvine
William A Sutherland, 36 Glencaple Avenue, Dumfries
William John Sutherland, Coillebhar, Main Street, Urquhart, Elgin
Mrs Mary Ross Sutton, 205 Linwood Avenue, Goldsboro, USA
Christopher J Swindells, 52 Bathurst Drive, Alloway

Graham C Swindells, 52 Bathurst Drive, Alloway
John W Swinton, 123 Superior Avenue, SW, Calgary, Canada
David Michael Tait, Melbourne Cottage, Dollar
Donald F Tait, 40 Carabol Court, Scarborough, Canada
J Stewart Tait, 98 Grange Road, Belmont, Durham
James M Tait, 701 Don Mills Road, Don Mills, Canada
William A Tait, Southerwud, Paxton
Tam o' Shanter Club, Hertford Place, Coventry
Carol B H Taylor, 11 Fullarton Crescent, Troon
Mrs Heather Taylor, 23 Heath Moor Drive, Fulford, York
James Taylor, Keithmore, St Catherines Place, Elgin
Rev. John Taylor, MA, BD, DipEd, Rector, Auchenharvie Academy
Robert Taylor, 34 Graffham Avenue, Giffnock, Glasgow
William Taylor, 73 Gallowhill Quadrant, Coylton
James Cameron Telfer, 8 Eglinton Terrace, Ayr
Ian McDonald Terris, Carey, Promenade, Limekilns
Clare J Terry, 11 Walden Road, Hornchurch
Paul A Terry, 11 Walden Road, Hornchurch
Robin Paul Terry, 4 Parkview Gardens, Barking
Mr Cliff Thomas, 5 Flagholme, Cotgrave, Nottingham
Mr Harold Thomas, 24 Cessnock Place, Holmston, Ayr
Mrs D S Thompson, 13 Oliver Road, Wooler
David D P Thompson, 41 Stead Lane, Bedlington
Mr Henry Thompson, 31 Green Avenue, Irvine
James G Thompson, Dunwoody, Georgia, USA
Thomas H Thompson, Nethermuir, Troon
A Stewart Thomson, 23 Salisbury Avenue, North Shields
Albert Thomson, 50 Irvine Road, Largs
David M Thomson, 41 Gilloch Crescent, Dumfries
George Thomson, 20 Dalbeattie Road, Dumfries
Graham Douglas Thomson, 1 Burnside Road, Balbeggie, Perth
Ian Campbell Thomson, Rathan, New Abbey Road, Dumfries
Ian R Thomson, 105 Main Street, Dreghorn, Irvine
James B Thomson, Greenock Burns Club
John Thomson, 5 Braeside Way, Larkhall
M H Thomson, 4 Treebank Crescent, Masonhill, Ayr
Mr M S Thomson, 27 Glenalla Crescent, Doonbank, Ayr
Peggy Thomson, 52A Dundonald Road, Kilmarnock
Peter J Thomson, Sonderend Street, Helderkruin Roodepoort, SA
T Alex Thomson, MC, TD, CA, Bovingdon
Sandra W Thomson, 11A King Street, Stonehaven
Wm D Thomson, 32 Tarfside Gardens, Glasgow
William M Thomson, 39 Adamton Road North, Prestwick
Angus H Thow, 9 Baxter Park Terrace, Dundee
Henry B Thow, The Wicket, 8 Carleton Gardens, Prestwick

Mrs Margaret Thow, The Old Castle, Skeldon, Dalrymple
Mr Victor Thow, The Old Castle, Skeldon, Dalrymple
Alfred E Thurgood, 13 Kidston Drive, Helensburgh
David Tindall, 1 Briar Grove, Ayr
George Hay Tinning, 235 Ayr Road, Newton Mearns
Felix Todd, 5 Springhill Terrace, Springside
Jim Todd, 1 The Knowe, Sauchie, Alloa
Toowoomba Caledonian Society and Burns Club, Australia
Alex Torrance, Esq, 124 Linne Crescent, Wishaw
Elizabeth & Joseph Totten, 29 Eastwood Dv, Newmains, Wishaw
John Traill, MA, FEIS, 25 Crichton Avenue, Pathhead
Abe & Elizabeth Train, 71 Woodside Crescent, Newmains, Wishaw
Helen Tripp, 16 Olivers Mill, New Ashgreen, Dartford
Evelyn Trombala, St Leonards, The Crescent, Dunblane
Troon Burns Club
Trusteees of Burns Monument, Burns Cottage, Alloway
Mrs E Tulloch, 30 Kingholm Drive, Dumfries
David McInnes Turnbull, 68 Dunalastair Drive, Stepps
Cllr George Turnbull, Kilmarnock
James J & Ishbel M Turnbull, 2600 Portage Ave, Winnipeg, Canada
Dick & Rita Turner, 50 West Crescent, Muirhead, Troon
Ian Turner, 3 Earn Road, Troon
Joseph B P Turner, 21 Gillies Street, Troon
Raymond M Turpie, 11 Ash Place, Kilmarnock
Mrs E D Tweedie, Woodside Farm, New Abbey
Graham Underwood, 760 Cedarille Way SW, Calgary, Canada
Norman Ure, Secretary, Greenloaning Burns Club
Donald R Urquhart, Glebe House, 39 Glebe Street, Dumfries
Robert J Utterson, Oak Cottages, Kirknewton
Robert Climie Vallanee, 14 Arthurlie Drive, Uplawmoor, Glasgow
Mrs H Vincent, 20 Norrie Street, Christchurch, New Zealand
A G Wake, 3 Smiddy Row, East Fortune, North Berwick
A J C Waldie, Newlands, Westminster, South Africa
James S Wales, 14 Whyte Avenue, Irvine
A Walker, 6 Lothian Crescent, Glenburn, Paisley
Mr A S Walker, 57 Lochinver Drive, Glasgow
Brian E Walker, 35 Longmeanygate, Leyland
G I G Walker, 6 Dalmailing Avenue, Dreghorn
J A Walker, 97 Hilton Road, Bishopbriggs
James Walker, Derbrook, Kilwinning Road, Irvine
W Walker
Dr A Bruce Wallace, Cheltenham
Mary Walsh, 5 Simpson Court, Muirhead, Troon
Michael A Wanko, Castle Rock, St Abbs
Mary Waring, 13A Hollin Terrace, Marsh, Huddersfield

George Dennis Warman, 10 Connaught Place, Weston-Super-Mare
Barbara Elizabeth Warren, 73 Turnage Road, Dagenham
Beth Warren, 12 Lyall Crescent, Polmont, Falkirk
Thomas Charles Warren, 73 Turnage Road, Dagenham
Alexander H Watson, 102 Crowhill Road, Bishopbriggs, Glasgow
Calum Anderson Watson, 5 North Neuk, Barassie, Troon
Mr David Watson, 17 North Street, Bainsford
David Watson, 2 Ochil Road, Bishopbriggs, Glasgow
Gail Jane Watson, 5 North Neuk, Barassie, Troon
George W Watson, Hamilfield, Kilwinning Road, Irvine
James H Watson, Meadow Cottage, 23 Quarry Road, Irvine
James U Watson, 102 Crowhill Road, Bishopbriggs, Glasgow
Lisa Helen Watson, 5 North Neuk, Barassie, Troon
Robert D Watson, 318-38 Ave SW, Calgary, Alberta, Canada
Walter N Watson, 75 Peartree Close, South Ockendon
Mr & Mrs Alexander Watt, Toll-Luchag, Montgomery St, Edinburgh
Mrs Elizabeth Watt, 50 James Crescent, Irvine
George R Watt, Cherry Valley, Canada
Graeme B Watt, 26 Reid Street, Elgin
Graham Watt, Smithy Place, Brockholes
John Kerr Watt, 1 Baron Path, Bargeddie, Baillieston
Kenneth M Watt, 26 Reid Street, Elgin
A N Watters, 17 Townsend Crescent, Kirkcaldy
David A K Watters, Dept of Surgery, Lusaka, Zambia
W W Watters, 203 Hillfoot Road, Ayr
Miss W R Webster, 23 Glenshee Drive, Rattray, Blairgowrie
Mrs Hazel Weierter, 5 William Street, Kirkcaldy
Alexander N Weir, 30 Corslet Road, Currie, Edinburgh
Christopher N Weir, 63 Kenneth Street, Stornoway
John Weir, 6 Brownshill Avenue, Coatbridge
John Weir, DSO, OBE, JP, MA, FEIS, PGM, Ayrshire
John A Weir, Lawrence, Kansas, USA
Margaret Glen Weir, 40 Gateside Road, Galston
Mr Thomas Weir, 46 Bantaskine Drive, Falkirk
Andrew T Wells, 21 Waugh Drive, Sanquhar
Mrs A W Welsh, Dunaverty, Kirkhill Drive, Lhanbryde, Elgin
Mr Martin Welsh, 63 High Road, Stevenston
William Gordon Wemyss, 2 Roosevelt Avenue, Chatham
Peter J Westwood, 28 Stranka Avenue, Paisley
Mrs A C White, Dungannon, Edzell
David Laird White, 23 Mosspark Square, Glasgow
Hugh White, 430 St Patrick St East, Fergus, Canada
Dr Ian R White, BSc, PhD, FBCS, FRAS, Daymer Gdns, Pinner
Wylie G C White, Swithland, Wyatts Road, Chorleywood
Ian A Whitehead, 9 Rowanbank Road, Dumfries

James McGowan Whitelaw, Carradale, 5A McKay Road, Macduff
John Tait Whitelock, 363 Glamorgan Cres SW, Calgary, Canada
Jack Whyte, 1726-8 Ave NW, Calgary, Canada
Jordan D Whyte, The Bungalow, Wyllie Place, Stewarton
Michelle Hay Whyte, The Bungalow, Wyllie Place, Stewarton
Johanna Wigdor, 43 Teg Close, Portslade by Sea
J R Wignall, 67 Aylestone Lane, Wigston, Leicester
Dr Lindsay Wilkie, Braeside, Willunga, South Australia
Mrs D Williams, 40 Hillbury Avenue, Kenton, Harrow
Ian & Susan Williams, 12 Barony Court, Irvine
Mr & Mrs L J C Williams, 50 Porterfield, Comrie
R Arthur Williams, 23 Whitehill Avenue, Musselburgh
Mrs Janet Williamson, 202 Grangemoor, Runcorn
Robert W Williamson, 8 Wheatlands Road, Harrogate
Mr & Mrs Thomas Ritchie Williamson, 10 Earlswood Ave, Leeds
William Williamson, 30 Ivanhoe Road, Foxbar, Paisley
Robert A Willson, 1304-15 Ave SW, Calgary, Canada
A F Wilson, 14 Wellpark, Alloway
A J & Geoffrey R Wilson
Alex Wilson, 27 Pinegrove, Westquarter, Falkirk
Mr Alexander Wilson, 24 Bedlay Street, Springburn, Glasgow
Mr David Wilson, 18 Waverley Gardens, Shawlands, Glasgow
David F Wilson, 29 Main Street, Kinglassie
Mrs Ellen Kay Wilson, 38 Keir Street, Pollokshields, Glasgow
Gavin Wilson, Mid Feddal House, Braco
George B Wilson, 66 Dukes Ride, Crowthorne
Hugh C Wilson, St Helens, Houndlaw Park, Eyemouth
J Wilson, 16 Alexander Avenue, Eaglesham
James Wilson, 6 Oswald Place, Ayr (4 copies)
Mr James A Wilson, 82 Muir Drive, Irvine
James W Wilson, Skelmorlie Castle
Mrs M O H Wilson, 91 Ashby Road, Burton-on-Trent
Miss M R Wilson, BSc, 19B Gillsburn Gardens, Kilmarnock
Moira D Wilson, 88 Mauchline Road, Annbank Station, Ayr
Peter Wilson, 1 St James Avenue, Paisley
Dr R B Wilson, Mile Ash, Dumfries
Robert Blane Wilson, Burns Howff Club, Dumfries
Robert Hardie Wilson, 15 Castle Avenue, Edinburgh
William Wilson, 47 Carbarns West, Wishaw
William Wilson, Rosebery 377, 9 Balfour Avenue, Beith
William J Wilson, Montalto, Newtowncrommelin
Winnipeg Burns Club
Andrew S Winton, 12 Ventnor Terrace, Edinburgh
Richard Wismach, Stenmuir Cott, Kirkton, Dumfries
Susan E Withers, 52 Dundonald Road, Kilmarnock

Hazel Wood, 5 Clint Terrace, Yeskett, Lockerbie
Dr I H Y Wood, Kincraig, Kilwinning Road, Irvine
Gerry Wood, Woodridge Sales Ltd, Calgary, Canada
Mr & Mrs Christoper Woods, 13 Keir Crescent, Coltness, Wishaw
Douglas Woolven, 1419 Commissioner W, London, Canada
A B Wright, Mountfair, 41 Manor Avenue, Kilmarnock
Herbert Halliday Wright, 7212 Masonville Drive, Annandale, USA
Miss I R Wright, 68 Ashgrove Street, Ayr
James Wyllie, Willowbank, Mauchline
Mary Jane Wyllie, Thornthwaite, Mauchline
John (Sandy) Wyness, 2181 Avenue Road, Toronto, Canada
Mr & Mrs Brian J Wynne, 52 Smith Drive, Bishopmill, Elgin
James Wyper, 2 Watson Terrace, Irvine
James D Wyper, 139 Bank Street, Irvine
Emma Jane Yates, Airlie House, Carronvale Road, Larbert
James Bennett Yates, Jnr, Airlie House, Carronvale Rd, Larbert
James Bennett Yates, Snr, Airlie House, Carronvale Rd, Larbert
Katie Ann Yates, Airlie House, Carronvale Road, Larbert
Mr Robert Yates, 36 Glencairn Road, Ayr
David Gardner Young, 33 Paterson Avenue, Irvine
David S Young, Roedt/Trintange, Luxembourg (2 copies)
Mrs E Young, 76 Silcoates Lane, Wrenthorpe, Wakefield
Edwin I Young, Sanquhar, President New Cumnock Burns Club
Eric Young, ARICS, Exeter
Francis B Young, 65 Glenconner Road, Ayr
Gordon Andrew Young, 45 Ravenscroft, Irvine
Hugh Young, 432 Manora Rise NE, Calgary, Canada
Iain David Young, 52 Mowbray, Calderwood, East Kilbride
John Dalziel Young, 74 Titchfield Road, Troon
Lt Col M H G Young, RCT, 22 Oaklands, Haslemere
Margaret Young, 4 High Road, Stevenston
Norman Scott Young, RIBA, Edinburgh Road, Dumfries
Robert Young, 10816 Maplecrest Rise, Calgary, Canada
Thelma Young, 32 Sequoia Crescent, Sunnydale, Owhato, NZ

INDEX OF TITLES AND FIRST LINES

Titles are given in capitals, alternative names are given in capitals followed by an asterisk, and first lines in lower-case lettering.

INDEX OF TITLES AND FIRST LINES

Titles are given in capitals, alternative names are given in capitals followed by an asterisk, and first lines in lower-case lettering.

INDEX OF TITLES AND FIRST LINES

Titles are given in capitals, alternative names are given in capitals followed by an asterisk, and first lines in lower-case lettering.

INDEX OF TITLES AND FIRST LINES
Titles are given in capitals, alternative names are given in capitals followed by an
asterisk, and first lines in lower-case lettering.

INDEX OF TITLES AND FIRST LINES

Titles are given in capitals, alternative names are given in capitals followed by an asterisk, and first lines in lower-case lettering.

INDEX OF TITLES AND FIRST LINES

Titles are given in capitals, alternative names are given in capitals followed by an asterisk, and first lines in lower-case lettering.

Titles are given in capitals, alternative names are given in capitals followed by an asterisk, and first lines in lower-case lettering.

INDEX OF TITLES AND FIRST LINES

Titles are given in capitals, alternative names are given in capitals followed by an asterisk, and first lines in lower-case lettering.

INDEX OF TITLES AND FIRST LINES

Titles are given in capitals, alternative names are given in capitals followed by an asterisk, and first lines in lower-case lettering.

INDEX OF TITLES AND FIRST LINES
Titles are given in capitals, alternative names are given in capitals followed by an
asterisk, and first lines in lower-case lettering.

INDEX OF TITLES AND FIRST LINES

Titles are given in capitals, alternative names are given in capitals followed by an asterisk, and first lines in lower-case lettering.

INDEX OF TITLES AND FIRST LINES

Titles are given in capitals, alternative names are given in capitals followed by an asterisk, and first lines in lower-case lettering.

INDEX OF TITLES AND FIRST LINES

Titles are given in capitals, alternative names are given in capitals followed by an asterisk, and first lines in lower-case lettering.

Titles are given in capitals, alternative names are given in capitals followed by an asterisk, and first lines in lower-case lettering.

INDEX OF TITLES AND FIRST LINES

Titles are given in capitals, alternative names are given in capitals followed by an asterisk, and first lines in lower-case lettering.